Microsoft® SQL Server™ 2012

A BEGINNER'S GUIDE

Fifth Edition

D1411815

Dušan Petković

New York Chicago San Francisco Lisbon
London Madrid Mexico City Milan
New Delhi San Juan Seoul Singapore
Sydney Toronto

The McGraw·Hill Companies

Library of Congress Cataloging-in-Publication Data

Petkovic, Dusan.
   Microsoft SQL Server 2012 : a beginners guide / Dusan Petkovic.
     p.   cm.
   "Fifth edition."
   ISBN 978-0-07-176160-4 (pbk.)
   1. Client/server computing.   2. SQL server.   3. Relational databases.
I. Title.
   QA76.9.C55P479   2012
   005.75'6—dc23

                 2012007034

McGraw-Hill books are available at special quantity discounts to use as premiums and sales promotions, or for use in corporate training programs. To contact a representative, please e-mail us at bulksales@mcgraw-hill.com.

Microsoft® SQL Server® 2012: A Beginner's Guide, Fifth Edition

1234567890   QFR QFR   1 0 9 8 7 6 5 4 3 2

ISBN   978-0-07-176160-4
MHID   0-07-176160-8

Sponsoring Editor Wendy Rinaldi	**Indexer** Claire Splan
Editorial Supervisor Janet Walden	**Production Supervisor** Jean Bodeaux
Project Manager Nidhi Chopra, Cenveo Publisher Services	**Composition** Cenveo Publisher Services
Acquisitions Coordinator Joya Anthony	**Illustration** Cenveo Publisher Services
Technical Editor Todd Meister	**Art Director, Cover** Jeff Weeks
Copy Editor Bill McManus	**Cover Designer** Jeff Weeks
Proofreader Claire Splan	

Dedicated to my sons, Ilja and Igor.

About the Author

Dušan Petković is a professor in the Department of Computer Science at the University of Applied Sciences in Rosenheim, Germany. He is the bestselling author of four editions of *SQL Server: A Beginner's Guide* and has authored numerous articles for *SQL Server Magazine* and technical papers for *Embarcadero*.

About the Technical Editor

Todd Meister has been working in the IT industry for over 15 years. He's been a technical editor on over 75 titles ranging from SQL Server to the .NET Framework. Besides technical editing books, he is the Senior IT Architect at Ball State University in Muncie, Indiana. He lives in central Indiana with his wife, Kimberly, and their four clever children.

Contents at a Glance

Contents

Acknowledgments

First, I would like to thank my sponsoring editor, Wendy Rinaldi. Since 1998, Wendy has been in charge of all five books that I have published with McGraw-Hill. I appreciate very much her extraordinary support over all these years. Also, I would like to acknowledge the important contributions of my technical editor, Todd Meister, and my copy editor, Bill McManus.

Introduction

There are a couple of reasons why SQL Server, the system that comprises the Database Engine, Analysis Services, Reporting Services, Integration Services, and SQLXML, is the best choice for a broad spectrum of end users and database programmers building business applications:

▶ SQL Server is certainly the best system for Windows operating systems, because of its tight integration (and low pricing). Because the number of installed Windows systems is enormous and still increasing rapidly, SQL Server is a widely used database system.

▶ The Database Engine, as the relational database system component, is the easiest database system to use. In addition to the well-known user interface, Microsoft offers several different tools to help you create database objects, tune your database applications, and manage system administration tasks.

Generally, SQL Server isn't only a relational database system. It is a platform that not only manages structured, semistructured, and unstructured data but also offers comprehensive, integrated operational and analysis software that enables organizations to reliably manage mission-critical information.

Goals of the Book

Microsoft SQL Server 2012: A Beginner's Guide follows four previous editions that covered SQL Server 7, 2000, 2005, and 2008.

Generally, all SQL Server users who want to get a good understanding of this database system and to work successfully with it will find this book very helpful. If you are a new SQL Server user but understand SQL, read the section "Differences Between SQL and Transact-SQL Syntax" later in this introduction.

This book addresses users of all components of the SQL Server system. For this reason, it is divided into several parts: The first three parts are most useful to users who want to learn more about Microsoft's relational database component called the Database Engine. The fourth part of the book is dedicated to business intelligence (BI) users who use either Analysis Services or relational extensions concerning BI. The last part of the book provides insight for users who want to learn features beyond the relational data, such as XML technologies, spatial data, and how to search data in documents.

SQL Server 2012 New Features Described in the Book

SQL Server 2012 has a lot of new features, and almost all of them are discussed in this book. For each feature, at least one running example is provided to enable you to understand that feature better. The following table lists the chapters that describe new features and provides a brief summary of the new features introduced in each chapter. (The table also contains features from SQL Server 2008 Release 2.)

Chapter 2	The installation process of SQL Server 2012 in general and the use of Upgrade Advisor in particular are described in this chapter. (Upgrade Advisor analyzes all components of previous releases that are installed and identifies issues to fix before you upgrade to SQL Server 2012.)
Chapter 3	Management Studio Debugger has been enhanced in SQL Server 2012. The new debugger features described in this chapter are the specification of a breakpoint condition, breakpoint hit count, breakpoint filter, and breakpoint action, as well as the use of the QuickWatch window.
Chapter 5	This chapter describes contained databases in general and partially contained databases, a new feature of SQL Server 2012, in particular. (For an example of how to create such databases, see Example 5.20.)
Chapter 6	This chapter introduces two new clauses of the SELECT statement: OFFSET and FETCH. It also introduces sequences and their creation in the section "CREATE SEQUENCE Statement."
Chapter 8	Exception handling of the Database Engine in SQL Server 2012 is enhanced with the new statement called THROW (see Example 8.4). The use of the OFFSET and FETCH clauses for server-side paging is shown in Example 8.5. The extension of the EXECUTE statement with the RESULT SETS option is shown in Example 8.11.
Chapter 9	The section "Dynamic Management Views and Functions" describes two new views: **sys.dm_exec_describe_first_result_set** and **sys.dm_db_uncontained_entites** (see Example 9.4).
Chapter 12	This chapter introduces the CREATE SERVER ROLE statement, which is used to create user-defined server roles. Also, the management of authorization and authentication of contained databases (see Chapter 5) is described.
Chapter 16	This chapter describes one of the most important new features in SQL Server 2012: high availability and disaster recovery (HADR). HADR overcomes the drawbacks of database mirroring and allows you to maximize availability for your databases.

Chapter 22	This chapter introduces the new and powerful tool for querying analytical data: PowerPivot for Excel. This tool allows you to analyze data using the most popular Microsoft tool for such purpose, Microsoft Excel. PowerPivot for Excel was introduced for the first time in SQL Server 2008 R2.
Chapter 23	This chapter describes new window functions. First, the window frame with its clauses (CURRENT ROW, UNBOUNDED PRECEDING and UNBOUNDED FOLLOWING) is explained using an example. After that, the differences between the ROWS and RANGE clauses are listed. The new functions, LEAD and LAG are explained, too.
Chapter 24	Shared datasets, which were introduced for the first time in SQL Server 2008 R2, are discussed in this chapter.
Chapter 25	The final part of this chapter, which is entirely new material, describes columnstore indices.
Chapter 27	The last section of this chapter, "New Spatial Data Features in SQL Server 2012," describes three new subtypes of circular arcs (compound strings, compound curves, and curve polygons), a new spatial index, and two new system stored procedures concerning spatial data.
Chapter 28	The last section of this chapter, "New Features in SQL Server 2012 FTS," introduces two enhancements to full-text search: customizing a proximity search and searching extended properties.

Organization of the Book

The book has 28 chapters and is divided into five parts.

Part I, "Basic Concepts and Installation," describes the notion of database systems and explains how to install SQL Server 2012 and its components. It includes the following chapters:

▶ Chapter 1, "Relational Database Systems: An Introduction," discusses databases in general and the Database Engine in particular. The notion of normal forms and the **sample** database are presented here. The chapter also introduces the syntax conventions that are used in the rest of the book.

▶ Chapter 2, "Planning the Installation and Installing SQL Server," describes the first system administration task: the installation of the overall system. Although the installation of SQL Server is a straightforward task, there are certain steps that warrant explanation.

▶ Chapter 3, "SQL Server Management Studio," describes the component called SQL Server Management Studio. This component is presented early in the book in case you want to create database objects and query data without knowledge of SQL.

Part II, "Transact-SQL Language," is intended for end users and application programmers of the Database Engine. It comprises the following chapters:

▶ Chapter 4, "SQL Components," describes the fundamentals of the most important part of a relational database system: a database language. For all such systems, there is only one language that counts: SQL. In this chapter, all components of SQL Server's own database language, called Transact-SQL, are described. You can also find the basic language concepts and data types in this chapter. Finally, system functions and operators of Transact-SQL are described.

▶ Chapter 5, "Data Definition Language," describes all data definition language (DDL) statements of Transact-SQL. The DDL statements are presented in three groups, depending on their purpose. The first group contains all forms of the CREATE statement, which is used to create database objects. The second group contains all forms of the ALTER statement, which is used to modify the structure of some database objects. The third group contains all forms of the DROP statement, which is used to remove different database objects.

▶ Chapter 6, "Queries," discusses the most important Transact-SQL statement: SELECT. This chapter introduces you to database data retrieval and describes the use of simple and complex queries. Each SELECT clause is separately defined and explained with reference to the **sample** database.

▶ Chapter 7, "Modification of a Table's Contents," discusses the four Transact-SQL statements used for updating data: INSERT, UPDATE, DELETE, and MERGE. Each of these statements is explained through numerous examples.

▶ Chapter 8, "Stored Procedures and User-Defined Functions," describes procedural extensions, which can be used to create powerful programs called stored procedures and user-defined functions (UDFs), programs that are stored on the server and can be reused. Because Transact-SQL is a complete computational language, all procedural extensions are inseparable parts of the language. Some stored procedures are written by users; others are provided by Microsoft and are referred to as system stored procedures. The implementation of stored procedures and UDFs using the Common Language Runtime (CLR) is also discussed in this chapter.

▶ Chapter 9, "System Catalog," describes one of the most important parts of a database system: system tables and views. The system catalog contains tables that are used to store the information concerning database objects and their relationships. The main characteristic of system tables of the Database Engine is that they cannot be accessed directly. The Database Engine supports several interfaces that you can use to query the system catalog.

▶ Chapter 10, "Indices," covers the first and most powerful method that database application programmers can use to tune their applications to get better system response and therefore better performance. This chapter describes the role of indices and gives you guidelines for how to create and use them. The end of the chapter introduces the special types of indices supported by the Database Engine.

▶ Chapter 11, "Views," explains how you create views, discusses the practical use of views (using numerous examples), and explains a special form of views called indexed views.

▶ Chapter 12, "Security System of the Database Engine," provides answers to all your questions concerning security of data in the database. It addresses questions about authorization (which user has been granted legitimate access to the database system) and authentication (which access privileges are valid for a particular user). Three Transact-SQL statements are discussed in this chapter, GRANT, DENY, and REVOKE, which provide the access privileges of database objects against unauthorized access. The end of the chapter explains how data changes can be tracked using the Database Engine.

▶ Chapter 13, "Concurrency Control," describes concurrency control in depth. The beginning of the chapter discusses the two different concurrency models supported by the Database Engine. All Transact-SQL statements related to transactions are also explained. Locking as a method to solve concurrency control problems is discussed further. At the end of the chapter, you will learn what isolation levels and row versions are.

▶ Chapter 14, "Triggers," describes the implementation of business logic using triggers. Each example in this chapter concerns a problem that you may face in your everyday life as a database application programmer. The implementation of managed code for triggers using CLR is also shown in the chapter.

Part III, "SQL Server: System Administration," describes all objectives of Database Engine system administration. It comprises the following chapters:

▶ Chapter 15, "System Environment of the Database Engine," discusses some internal issues concerning the Database Engine. It provides a detailed description of the Database Engine disk storage elements, system databases, and utilities.

▶ Chapter 16, "Backup, Recovery, and System Availability," provides an overview of the fault-tolerance methods used to implement a backup strategy using either SQL Server Management Studio or corresponding Transact-SQL statements. The first part of the chapter specifies the different methods used to implement a backup strategy. The second part of the chapter discusses the restoration of databases. The final part of the chapter describes in detail the following options available for system availability: failover clustering, database mirroring, log shipping, and high availability and disaster recovery (HADR).

▶ Chapter 17, "Automating System Administration Tasks," describes the Database Engine component called SQL Server Agent that enables you to automate certain system administration jobs, such as backing up data and using the scheduling and alert features to notify operators. This chapter also explains how to create jobs, operators, and alerts.

▶ Chapter 18, "Data Replication," provides an introduction to data replication, including concepts such as the publisher and subscriber. It introduces the different models of replication, and serves as a tutorial for how to configure publications and subscriptions using the existing wizards.

▶ Chapter 19, "Query Optimizer," describes the role and the work of the query optimizer. It explains in detail all the Database Engine tools (the SET statement, SQL Server Management Studio, and various dynamic management views) that can be used to edit the optimizer strategy. The end of the chapter provides optimization hints.

▶ Chapter 20, "Performance Tuning," discusses performance issues and the tools for tuning the Database Engine that are relevant to daily administration of the system. After introductory notes concerning the measurements of performance, this chapter describes the factors that affect performance and presents tools for monitoring SQL Server.

Part IV, "SQL Server and Business Intelligence," discusses business intelligence (BI) and all related topics. The chapters in this part of the book introduce Microsoft Analysis Services and Microsoft Reporting Services. SQL/OLAP and existing optimization techniques concerning relational data storage are described in detail, too. This part includes the following chapters:

▶ Chapter 21, "Business Intelligence: An Introduction," introduces the notion of data warehousing. The first part of the chapter explains the differences between online transaction processing and data warehousing. The data store for a data warehousing process can be either a data warehouse or a data mart. Both types of data stores are discussed, and their differences are listed in the second part of the chapter. The data warehouse design is explained at the end of the chapter.

▶ Chapter 22, "SQL Server Analysis Services," discusses the architecture of Analysis Services and the main component of Analysis Services, Business Intelligence Development Studio (BIDS). The development of a cube using BIDS is shown using two examples. At the end of the chapter, several ways to retrieve and deliver data to users are shown.

▶ Chapter 23, "Business Intelligence and Transact-SQL," explains how you can use Transact-SQL to solve business intelligence problems. This chapter discusses the window construct, with its partitioning, ordering and framing, CUBE and ROLLUP operators, rank functions, the TOP n clause, and the PIVOT relational operator.

▶ Chapter 24, "SQL Server Reporting Services," describes the Microsoft enterprise reporting solution. This component is used to design and deploy reports. The chapter discusses the development environment that you use to design and create reports, and shows you different ways to deliver a deployed report.

▶ Chapter 25, "Optimizing Techniques for Relational Online Analytical Processing," describes three of the several specific optimization techniques that can be used especially in the area of business intelligence: data partitioning, star join optimization, and columnstore indices. The data partitioning technique called range partitioning is described. In relation to star join optimization, the role of bitmap filters in the optimization of joins is explained. The final part of the chapter explains the use of columnstore indices. You will see how to create such an index and use it to increase the performance of a specific group of analytical queries.

Part V, "Beyond Relational Data," is dedicated to three "nonrelational" topics, XML, spatial data, and full-text search, because SQL Server, as a data platform, doesn't have to handle only relational data. The following chapters are included in this part:

▶ Chapter 26, "SQL Server and XML," discusses SQLXML, Microsoft's set of data types and functions that supports XML in SQL Server, bridging the gap between XML and relational data. The beginning of the chapter introduces the standardized data type called XML and explains how stored XML documents can be retrieved. After that, the presentation of relational data as XML documents is discussed in detail. At the end of the chapter you will find a description of the methods that can be used to query XML data.

▶ Chapter 27, "Spatial Data," discusses spatial data and two different data types (GEOMETRY and GEOGRAPHY) that can be used to create such data. Several different standardized functions in relation to spatial data are also shown.

▶ Chapter 28, "SQL Server Full-Text Search," first discusses general concepts related to full-text search. The second part describes the general steps that are required to create a full-text index and then demonstrates how to apply those steps first using Transact-SQL and then using SQL Server Management Studio. The rest of the chapter is dedicated to full-text queries. It describes two predicates and two row functions that can be used for full-text search. For these predicates and functions, several examples are provided to show how you can solve specific problems in relation to extended operations on documents.

Almost all chapters include at their end numerous exercises that you can use to improve your knowledge concerning the chapter's content. All solutions to the given exercises can be found both at McGraw-Hill Professional's web site (www.mhprofessional.com/computingdownload) and at my own home page (www.fh-rosenheim.de/~petkovic).

Changes from the Previous Edition

If you are familiar with the previous edition of this book, *Microsoft SQL Server 2008: A Beginner's Guide,* you should be aware that I have made significant changes in this edition. To make the book easier to use, I separated some topics and described them in totally new chapters. (For instance, Chapter 28 is an entirely new chapter and describes full-text search in depth.) The following table gives you an outline of *significant* structural changes in the book (minor changes aren't listed).

Chapter 4	An entirely new section, "Storage Options," describes two different storage options available as of SQL Server 2008: FILESTREAM and sparse columns. The FILESTREAM storage option supports the management of large objects, which are stored in the NTFS file system, while sparse columns help to minimize data storage space. (These columns provide an optimized way to store column values that are predominantly NULL.)
Chapter 7	The Transact-SQL data modification statements TRUNCATE TABLE and MERGE are now described together, in the final section of the chapter, "Other T-SQL Modification Statements and Clauses."
Chapter 10	All existing special types of indices are listed in the final section of the chapter, "Special Types of Indices." Some types are described in this chapter, while for the other types a cross reference is provided to the chapter in which their description can be found.
Chapter 15	The Declarative Management Framework, which was covered in Chapter 16 of the previous edition of the book, has been renamed Policy-Based Management and its coverage has been moved to this chapter. (Note: Chapter 16, "Managing Instances and Maintaining Databases," from the prior edition has been eliminated from this edition and its material that is relevant to SQL Server 2012 has been redistributed to other chapters. Consequently, Chapters 17 through 26 of the prior edition are now numbered Chapters 16 through 25, respectively, in this edition. The new chapter numbers are reflected in the left column of this table.)

Chapter 16	Coverage of the Maintenance Plan Wizard has been moved from Chapter 16 of the previous edition and placed in this chapter (which was Chapter 17 in the prior edition).
Chapter 18	The structure of the chapter has been significantly changed. Methods for distributing data are now streamlined and discussed at the beginning of the chapter.
Chapter 19	This chapter includes a new section called "Plan Caching." The section has been enhanced with a new example that shows how you can influence the execution of queries.
Chapter 20	For each section concerning monitoring system resources (CPU, I/O, and network), several examples concerning dynamic management views have been added.
Chapter 22	This chapter has been significantly revised from the previous edition (in which it was Chapter 23). A new main section has been added, "Retrieving and Delivering Data," which introduces PowerPivot for Excel and describes the Multidimensional Expressions (MDX) language. Also, there is a new section concerning security of SQL Server Analysis Services.
Chapter 23	A new section called "Ordering and Framing" replaces the old one ("Ordering").
Chapter 24	A new main section called "Managing Reports" describes how reports can be delivered.
Chapter 25	In addition to the new topic "Columnstore Index," the section "Star Join Optimization" has been enhanced with several examples.
Chapter 26	Chapter 27, "Overview of XML," and Chapter 28, "SQL Server and XML," from the prior edition were streamlined and merged into this single chapter, retaining the title "SQL Server and XML." Two new main sections have been added, which describe all features concerning presentation and retrieval of data.
Chapter 27	This chapter, which was Chapter 29 in the previous edition, has been rewritten from scratch to provide more extensive coverage of spatial data.
Chapter 28	This is a new chapter in this edition, addressing an entirely new topic: SQL Server Full-Text search.

Differences Between SQL and Transact-SQL Syntax

Transact-SQL, SQL Server's relational database language, has several nonstandardized properties that generally are not known to people who are familiar with SQL only:

▶ Whereas the semicolon (;) is used in SQL to separate two SQL statements in a statement group (and you will generally get an error message if you do not include the semicolon), in Transact-SQL, use of semicolons is optional.

▶ Transact-SQL uses the GO statement. This nonstandardized statement is generally used to separate statement groups from each other, whereas some Transact-SQL statements (such as CREATE TABLE, CREATE INDEX, and so on) must be the only statement in the group.

▶ The USE statement, which is used very often in this book, changes the database context to the specified database. For example, the statement USE **sample** means that the statements that follow will be executed in the context of the **sample** database.

Working with the Sample Databases

This edition of the book uses three sample databases:

▶ This book's own **sample** database

▶ Microsoft's **AdventureWorks** database

▶ Microsoft's **AdventureWorksDW** database

An introductory book like this requires a sample database that can be easily understood by each reader. For this reason, I used a very simple concept for my own **sample** database: it has only four tables with several rows each. On the other hand, its logic is complex enough to demonstrate the hundreds of examples included in the text of the book. The **sample** database that you will use in this book represents a company with departments and employees. Each employee belongs to exactly one department, which itself has one or more employees. Jobs of employees center on projects: each employee works at the same time for one or more projects, and each project engages one or more employees.

The tables of the **sample** database are shown next.

The **department** table:

dept_no	dept_name	location
d1	Research	Dallas
d2	Accounting	Seattle
d3	Marketing	Dallas

The **employee** table:

emp_no	emp_fname	emp_lname	dept_no
25348	Matthew	Smith	d3
10102	Ann	Jones	d3
18316	John	Barrimore	d1
29346	James	James	d2
9031	Elsa	Bertoni	d2
2581	Elke	Hansel	d2
28559	Sybill	Moser	d1

The **project** table:

project_no	project_name	budget
p1	Apollo	120000
p2	Gemini	95000
p3	Mercury	185600

The **works_on** table:

emp_no	project_no	Job	enter_date
10102	p1	Analyst	2006.10.1
10102	p3	Manager	2008.1.1
25348	p2	Clerk	2007.2.15
18316	p2	NULL	2007.6.1
29346	p2	NULL	2006.12.15
2581	p3	Analyst	2007.10.15
9031	p1	Manager	2007.4.15
28559	p1	NULL	2007.8.1
28559	p2	Clerk	2008.2.1
9031	p3	Clerk	2006.11.15
29346	p1	Clerk	2007.1.4

You can download the **sample** database from McGraw-Hill Professional's web site (www.mhprofessional.com/computingdownload) or my own home page (www .fh-rosenheim.de/~petkovic). Also, you can download all the examples in the book as well as solutions for exercises from my home page.

Although the **sample** database can be used for many of the examples in this book, for some examples, tables with a lot of rows are necessary (to show optimization features, for instance). For this reason, two Microsoft sample databases—**AdventureWorks** and **AdventureWorksDW**—are also used. Both of them can be found at the Microsoft CodePlex web site www.codeplex.com/MSFTDBProdSamples.

Part I

Basic Concepts and Installation

Chapter 1

Relational Database Systems: An Introduction

In This Chapter

- ▶ **Database Systems: An Overview**
- ▶ **Relational Database Systems**
- ▶ **Database Design**
- ▶ **Syntax Conventions**

This chapter describes database systems in general. First, it discusses what a database system is, and which components it contains. Each component is described briefly, with a reference to the chapter in which it is described in detail. The second major section of the chapter is dedicated to relational database systems. It discusses the properties of relational database systems and the corresponding language used in such systems—Structured Query Language (SQL).

Generally, before you implement a database, you have to design it, with all its objects. The third major section of the chapter explains how you can use normal forms to enhance the design of your database, and also introduces the entity-relationship model, which you can use to conceptualize all entities and their relationships. The final section presents the syntax conventions used throughout the book.

Database Systems: An Overview

A database system is an overall collection of different database software components and databases containing the following parts:

- ▶ Database application programs
- ▶ Client components
- ▶ Database server(s)
- ▶ Databases

A database application program is special-purpose software that is designed and implemented by users or by third-party software companies. In contrast, client components are general-purpose database software designed and implemented by a database company. By using client components, users can access data stored on the same or a remote computer.

The task of a database server is to manage data stored in a database. Each client communicates with a database server by sending user queries to it. The server processes each query and sends the result back to the client.

In general, a database can be viewed from two perspectives, the users' and the database system's. Users view a database as a collection of data that logically belong together. For a database system, a database is simply a series of bytes, usually stored on a disk. Although these two views of a database are totally different, they do have something in common: the database system needs to provide not only interfaces that enable users to create databases and retrieve or modify data, but also system components to manage the stored data. Hence, a database system must provide the following features:

- ▶ Variety of user interfaces
- ▶ Physical data independence
- ▶ Logical data independence
- ▶ Query optimization
- ▶ Data integrity
- ▶ Concurrency control
- ▶ Backup and recovery
- ▶ Database security

The following sections briefly describe these features.

Variety of User Interfaces

Most databases are designed and implemented for use by many different types of users with varied levels of knowledge. For this reason, a database system should offer many distinct user interfaces. A user interface can be either graphical or textual. Graphical user interfaces (GUIs) accept user's input via the keyboard or mouse and create graphical output on the monitor. A form of textual interface, which is often used by database systems, is the command-line interface (CLI), where the user provides the input by typing a command with the keyboard and the system provides output by printing text on the computer monitor.

Physical Data Independence

Physical data independence means that the database application programs do not depend on the physical structure of the stored data in a database. This important feature enables you to make changes to the stored data without having to make any changes to database application programs. For example, if the stored data is previously ordered using one criterion, and this order is changed using another criterion, the modification of the physical data should not affect the existing database applications or the existing database *schema* (a description of a database generated by the data definition language of the database system).

Logical Data Independence

In file processing (using traditional programming languages), the declaration of a file is done in application programs, so any change to the structure of that file usually requires the modification of all programs using it. Database systems provide logical data independence—in other words, it is possible to make changes to the logical structure of the database without having to make any changes to the database application programs. For example, if the structure of an object named PERSON exists in the database system and you want to add an attribute to PERSON (say the address), you have to modify only the logical structure of the database, and not the existing application programs. (The application would have to be modified to utilize the newly added column.)

Query Optimization

Most database systems contain a subcomponent called *optimizer* that considers a variety of possible execution strategies for querying the data and then selects the most efficient one. The selected strategy is called the *execution plan* of the query. The optimizer makes its decisions using considerations such as how big the tables are that are involved in the query, what indices exist, and what Boolean operator (AND, OR, or NOT) is used in the WHERE clause. (This topic is discussed in detail in Chapter 19.)

Data Integrity

One of the tasks of a database system is to identify logically inconsistent data and reject its storage in a database. (The date February 30 and the time 5:77:00 P.M. are two examples of such data.) Additionally, most real-life problems that are implemented using database systems have *integrity constraints* that must hold true for the data. (One example of an integrity constraint might be the company's employee number, which must be a five-digit integer.) The task of maintaining integrity can be handled by the user in application programs or by the DBMS. As much as possible, this task should be handled by the DBMS. (Data integrity is discussed in two chapters of this book: declarative integrity in Chapter 5 and procedural integrity in Chapter 14.)

Concurrency Control

A database system is a multiuser software system, meaning that many user applications access a database at the same time. Therefore, each database system must have some kind of control mechanism to ensure that several applications that are trying to update the same data do so in some controlled way. The following is an example of a problem that can arise if a database system does not contain such control mechanisms:

1. The owners of bank account 4711 at bank X have an account balance of $2000.
2. The two joint owners of this bank account, Mrs. A and Mr. B, go to two different bank tellers, and each withdraws $1000 *at the same time*.
3. After these transactions, the amount of money in bank account 4711 should be $0 and not $1000.

All database systems have the necessary mechanisms to handle cases like this example. Concurrency control is discussed in detail in Chapter 13.

Backup and Recovery

A database system must have a subsystem that is responsible for recovery from hardware or software errors. For example, if a failure occurs while a database application updates 100 rows of a table, the recovery subsystem must roll back all previously executed updates to ensure that the corresponding data is consistent after the error occurs. (See Chapter 16 for further discussion on backup and recovery.)

Database Security

The most important database security concepts are authentication and authorization. *Authentication* is the process of validating user credentials to prevent unauthorized users from using a system. Authentication is most commonly enforced by requiring the user to enter a (user) name and a password. This information is evaluated by the system to determine whether the user is allowed to access the system. This process can be strengthened by using encryption.

Authorization is the process that is applied after the identity of a user is authenticated. During this process, the system determines what resources the particular user can use. In other words, structural and system catalog information about a particular entity is now available only to principals that have permission to access that entity. (Chapter 12 discusses these concepts in detail.)

Relational Database Systems

The component of Microsoft SQL Server called the Database Engine is a relational database system. The notion of relational database systems was first introduced by E. F. Codd in his article "A Relational Model of Data for Large Shared Data Banks" in 1970. In contrast to earlier database systems (network and hierarchical), *relational database systems* are based upon the relational data model, which has a strong mathematical background.

NOTE

A data model is a collection of concepts, their relationships, and their constraints that are used to represent data of a real-world problem.

The central concept of the relational data model is a relation—that is, a table. Therefore, from the user's point of view, a relational database contains tables and nothing but tables. In a table, there are one or more columns and zero or more rows. At every row and column position in a table there is always exactly one data value.

Working with the Book's Sample Database

The sample database used in this book represents a company with departments and employees. Each employee in the example belongs to exactly one department, which itself has one or more employees. Jobs of employees center on projects: each employee works at the same time on one or more projects, and each project engages one or more employees.

The data of the **sample** database can be represented using four tables:

- ▶ department
- ▶ employee
- ▶ project
- ▶ works_on

Tables 1-1 through 1-4 show all the tables of the **sample** database.

The **department** table represents all departments of the company. Each department has the following attributes:

department (dept_no, dept_name, location)

dept_no represents the unique number of each department. **dept_name** is its name, and **location** is the location of the corresponding department.

The **employee** table represents all employees working for a company. Each employee has the following attributes:

employee (emp_no, emp_fname, emp_lname, dept_no)

dept_no	dept_name	location
d1	Research	Dallas
d2	Accounting	Seattle
d3	Marketing	Dallas

Table 1-1   *The Department Table*

emp_no	emp_fname	emp_lname	dept_no
25348	Matthew	Smith	d3
10102	Ann	Jones	d3
18316	John	Barrimore	d1
29346	James	James	d2
9031	Elke	Hansel	d2
2581	Elsa	Bertoni	d2
28559	Sybill	Moser	d1

Table 1-2   *The Employee Table*

project_no	project_name	budget
p1	Apollo	120000
p2	Gemini	95000
p3	Mercury	186500

Table 1-3   *The Project Table*

emp_no	project_no	job	enter_date
10102	p1	Analyst	2006.10.1
10102	p3	Manager	2008.1.1
25348	p2	Clerk	2007.2.15
18316	p2	NULL	2007.6.1
29346	p2	NULL	2006.12.15
2581	p3	Analyst	2007.10.15
9031	p1	Manager	2007.4.15
28559	p1	NULL	2007.8.1
28559	p2	Clerk	2008.2.1
9031	p3	Clerk	2006.11.15
29346	p1	Clerk	2007.1.4

Table 1-4   *The works_on Table*

emp_no represents the unique number of each employee. **emp_fname** and **emp_lname** are the first and last name of each employee, respectively. Finally, **dept_no** is the number of the department to which the employee belongs.

Each project of a company is represented in the **project** table. This table has the following columns:

project (project_no, project_name, budget)

project_no represents the unique number of each project. **project_name** and **budget** specify the name and the budget of each project, respectively.

The **works_on** table specifies the relationship between employees and projects. It has the following columns:

works_on (emp_no, project_no, job, enter_date)

emp_no specifies the employee number and **project_no** specifies the number of the project on which the employee works. The combination of data values belonging to these two columns is always unique. **job** and **enter_date** specify the task and the starting date of an employee in the corresponding project, respectively.

Using the **sample** database, it is possible to describe some general properties of relational database systems:

▶ Rows in a table do not have any particular order.

▶ Columns in a table do not have any particular order.

▶ Every column must have a unique name within a table. On the other hand, columns from different tables may have the same name. (For example, the **sample** database has a **dept_no** column in the **department** table and a column with the same name in the **employee** table.)

▶ Every single data item in the table must be single valued. This means that in every row and column position of a table there is never a set of multiple data values.

▶ For every table, there is at least one column with the property that no two rows have the same combination of data values for all table columns. In the relational data model, such an identifier is called a *candidate key*. If there is more than one candidate key within a table, the database designer designates one of them as the *primary key* of the table. For example, the column **dept_no** is the primary key of the **department** table; the columns **emp_no** and **project_no** are the primary keys of the tables **employee** and **project**, respectively. Finally, the primary key for the **works_on** table is the combination of the columns **emp_no, project_no**.

▶ In a table, there are never two identical rows. (This property is only theoretical; the Database Engine and all other relational database systems generally allow the existence of identical rows within a table.)

SQL: A Relational Database Language

The SQL Server relational database language is called Transact-SQL. It is a dialect of the most important database language today: Structured Query Language (SQL). The origin of SQL is closely connected with the project called System R, which was designed and implemented by IBM in the early 1980s. This project showed that it is possible, using the theoretical foundations of the work of E. F. Codd, to build a relational database system.

In contrast to traditional languages like C, C++, and Java, SQL is a set-oriented language. (The former are also called record-oriented languages.) This means that SQL can query many rows from one or more tables using just one statement. This feature is one of the most important advantages of SQL, allowing the use of this language at a logically higher level than the level at which traditional languages can be used.

Another important property of SQL is its nonprocedurality. Every program written in a procedural language (C, C++, Java) describes *how* a task is accomplished, step by step. In contrast to this, SQL, as any other nonprocedural language, describes *what* it is that the user wants. Thus, the system is responsible for finding the appropriate way to solve users' requests.

SQL contains two sublanguages: a data definition language (DDL) and a data manipulation language (DML). DDL statements are used to describe the schema of database tables. The DDL contains three generic SQL statements: CREATE object, ALTER object, and DROP object. These statements create, alter, and remove database objects, such as databases, tables, columns, and indexes. (These statements are discussed in detail in Chapter 5.)

In contrast to the DDL, the DML encompasses all operations that manipulate the data. There are always four generic operations for manipulating the database: retrieval, insertion, deletion, and modification. The retrieval statement SELECT is described in Chapter 6, while the INSERT, DELETE, and UPDATE statements are discussed in detail in Chapter 7.

Database Design

Designing a database is a very important phase in the database life cycle, which precedes all other phases except the requirements collection and the analysis. If the database design is created merely intuitively and without any plan, the resulting database will most likely not meet the user requirements concerning performance.

Another consequence of a bad database design is superfluous data redundancy, which in itself has two disadvantages: the existence of data anomalies and the use of an unnecessary amount of disk space.

Normalization of data is a process during which the existing tables of a database are tested to find certain dependencies between the columns of a table. If such dependencies exist, the table is restructured into multiple (usually two) tables, which eliminates any column dependencies. If one of these generated tables still contains data dependencies, the process of normalization must be repeated until all dependencies are resolved.

The process of eliminating data redundancy in a table is based upon the theory of functional dependencies. A *functional dependency* means that by using the known value of one column, the corresponding value of another column can always be uniquely determined. (The same is true for column groups.) The functional dependencies between columns A and B is denoted by $A \Rightarrow B$, specifying that a value of column A can always be used to determine the corresponding value of column B. ("B is functionally dependent on A.")

Example 1.1 shows the functional dependency between two attributes of the table **employee** in the **sample** database.

EXAMPLE 1.1

emp_no $\Rightarrow$ emp_lname

By having a unique value for the employee number, the corresponding last name of the employee (and all other corresponding attributes) can be determined. This kind of functional dependency, where a column is dependent upon the primary key of a table, is called *trivial* functional dependency.

Another kind of functional dependency is called *multivalued dependency*. In contrast to the functional dependency just described, the multivalued dependency is specified for multivalued attributes. This means that by using the known value of one attribute (column), the corresponding *set of values* of another multivalued attribute can be uniquely determined. The multivalued dependency is denoted by $\Rightarrow \Rightarrow$.

Example 1.2 shows the multivalued dependency that holds for two attributes of the object BOOK.

EXAMPLE 1.2

ISBN $\Rightarrow \Rightarrow$ Authors

The ISBN of a book always determines all of its authors. Therefore, the **Authors** attribute is multivalued dependent on the **ISBN** attribute.

Normal Forms

Normal forms are used for the process of normalization of data and therefore for the database design. In theory, there are at least five different normal forms, of which the first three are the most important for practical use. The third normal form for a table can be achieved by testing the first and second normal forms at the intermediate states, and as such, the goal of good database design can usually be fulfilled if all tables of a database are in the third normal form.

NOTE

The multivalued dependency is used to test the fourth normal form of a table. Therefore, this kind of dependency will not be used further in this book.

First Normal Form

First normal form (1NF) means that a table has no multivalued attributes or composite attributes. (A composite attribute contains other attributes and can therefore be divided into smaller parts.) All relational tables are by definition in 1NF, because the value of any column in a row must be *atomic*—that is, single valued.

Table 1-5 demonstrates 1NF using part of the **works_on** table from the **sample** database. The rows of the **works_on** table could be grouped together, using the employee number. The resulting Table 1-6 is not in 1NF because the column **project_no** contains a set of values (p1, p3).

Second Normal Form

A table is in second normal form (2NF) if it is in 1NF and there is no nonkey column dependent on a partial primary key of that table. This means if (A,B) is a combination

emp_no	project_no	....
10102	p1	....
10102	p3	....
....	....	. . ..

Table 1-5   *Part of the works_on Table*

emp_no	project_no	....
10102	(p1, p3)	....
....	....	....

Table 1-6   *This "Table" Is Not in 1NF*

of two table columns building the key, then there is no column of the table depending either on only A or only B.

For example, Table 1-7 shows the **works_on1** table, which is identical to the **works_on** table except for the additional column, **dept_no**. The primary key of this table is the combination of columns **emp_no** and **project_no**. The column **dept_no** is dependent on the partial key **emp_no** (and is independent of **project_no**), so this table is not in 2NF. (The original table, **works_on**, is in 2NF.)

NOTE

Every table with a one-column primary key is always in 2NF.

Third Normal Form

A table is in third normal form (3NF) if it is in 2NF and there are no functional dependencies between nonkey columns. For example, the **employee1** table (see Table 1-8), which is identical to the **employee** table except for the additional column, **dept_name**, is not in 3NF, because for every known value of the column **dept_no** the corresponding value of the column **dept_name** can be uniquely determined. (The original table, **employee**, as well as all other tables of the **sample** database are in 3NF.)

emp_no	project_no	job	enter_date	dept_no
10102	p1	Analyst	2006.10.1	d3
10102	p3	Manager	2008.1.1	d3
25348	p2	Clerk	2007.2.15	d3
18316	p2	NULL	2007.6.1	d1
....	....	....		....

Table 1-7   *The works_on1 Table*

emp_no	emp_fname	emp_lname	dept_no	dept_name
25348	Matthew	Smith	d3	Marketing
10102	Ann	Jones	d3	Marketing
18316	John	Barrimore	d1	Research
29346	James	James	d2	Accounting
....	....	....	....	....

Table 1-8   *The employee1 Table*

Entity-Relationship Model

The data in a database could easily be designed using only one table that contains all data. The main disadvantage of such a database design is its high redundancy of data. For example, if your database contains data concerning employees and their projects (assuming each employee works at the same time on one or more projects, and each project engages one or more employees), the data stored in a single table contains many columns and rows. The main disadvantage of such a table is that data is difficult to keep consistent because of its redundancy.

The *entity-relationship (ER) model* is used to design relational databases by removing all existing redundancy in the data. The basic object of the ER model is an *entity*—that is, a real-world object. Each entity has several *attributes*, which are properties of the entity and therefore describe it. Based on its type, an attribute can be

▶ **Atomic (or single valued)**   An atomic attribute is always represented by a single value for a particular entity. For example, a person's marital status is always an atomic attribute. Most attributes are atomic attributes.

▶ **Multivalued**   A multivalued attribute may have one or more values for a particular entity. For example, **Location** as the attribute of an entity called ENTERPRISE is multivalued, because each enterprise can have one or more locations.

▶ **Composite**   Composite attributes are not atomic because they are assembled using some other atomic attributes. A typical example of a composite attribute is a person's address, which is composed of atomic attributes, such as **City, Zip,** and **Street.**

The entity PERSON in Example 1.3 has several atomic attributes, one composite attribute, **Address,** and a multivalued attribute, **College_degree.**

EXAMPLE 1.3

PERSON (Personal_no, F_name, L_name, Address(City,Zip,Street),{College_degree})

Each entity has one or more key attributes that are attributes (or a combination of two or more attributes) whose values are unique for each particular entity. In Example 1.3, the attribute **Personal_no** is the key attribute of the entity PERSON.

Besides entity and attribute, *relationship* is another basic concept of the ER model. A relationship exists when an entity refers to one (or more) other entities. The number of participating entities defines the degree of a relationship. For example, the relationship **works_on** between entities EMPLOYEE and PROJECT has degree two.

Every existing relationship between two entities must be one of the following three types: 1:1, 1:N, or M:N. (This property of a relationship is also called *cardinality ratio*.) For example, the relationship between the entities DEPARTMENT and EMPLOYEE is 1:N, because each employee belongs to exactly one department, which itself has one or more employees. Also, the relationship between the entities PROJECT and EMPLOYEE is M:N, because each project engages one or more employees and each employee works at the same time on one or more projects.

A relationship can also have its own attributes. Figure 1-1 shows an example of an ER diagram. (The ER diagram is the graphical notation used to describe the ER model.)

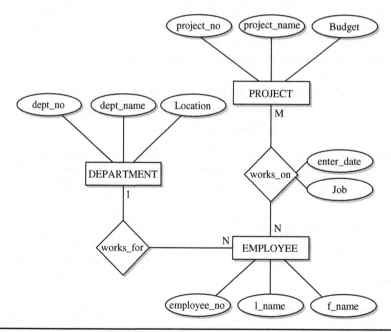

Figure 1-1   *Example of an ER diagram*

Using this notation, entities are modeled using rectangular boxes, with the entity name written inside the box. Attributes are shown in ovals, and each attribute is attached to a particular entity (or relationship) using a straight line. Finally, relationships are modeled using diamonds, and entities participating in the relationship are attached to it using straight lines. The cardinality ratio of each entity is written on the corresponding line.

Syntax Conventions

This book uses the conventions shown in Table 1-9 for the syntax of the Transact-SQL statements and for the indication of the text.

> **NOTE**
> *In contrast to brackets and braces, which belong to syntax conventions, parentheses, **( )**, belong to the syntax of a statement and must always be typed!*

Convention	Indication
Italics	New terms or items of emphasis.
UPPERCASE	Transact-SQL keywords—for example, CREATE TABLE. Additional information about the keywords of the Transact-SQL language can be found in Chapter 5.
lowercase	Variables in Transact-SQL statements—for example, CREATE TABLE tablename. (The user must replace "tablename" with the actual name of the table.)
var1 | var2	Alternative use of the items var1 and var2. (You may choose only one of the items separated by the vertical bar.)
{ }	Alternative use of more items. Example: { expression | USER | NULL }
[ ]	Optional item(s). Example: [FOR LOAD]
{ }...	Item(s) that can be repeated any number of times. Example: {, @param1 typ1} ...
bold	Name of database object (database itself, tables, columns) in the text.
<u>Default</u>	The default value is always underlined. Example: <u>ALL</u> | DISTINCT

Table 1-9   *Syntax Conventions*

Summary

All database systems provide the following features:

- ▶ Variety of user interfaces
- ▶ Physical data independence
- ▶ Logical data independence
- ▶ Query optimization
- ▶ Data integrity
- ▶ Concurrency control
- ▶ Backup and recovery
- ▶ Database security

The next chapter shows you how to install SQL Server 2012.

Exercises

E.1.1

What does "data independence" mean and which two forms of data independence exist?

E.1.2

Which is the main concept of the relational model?

E.1.3

What does the **employee** table represent in the real world? And what does the row in this table with the data for Ann Jones represent?

E.1.4

What does the **works_on** table represent in the real world (and in relation to the other tables of the **sample** database)?

E.1.5

Let **book** be a table with two columns: **isbn** and **title**. Assuming that **isbn** is unique and there are no identical titles, answer the following questions:

a. Is **title** a key of the table?
b. Does **isbn** functionally depend on **title**?
c. Is the **book** table in 3NF?

E.1.6

Let **order** be a table with the following columns: **order_no, customer_no, discount.** If the column **customer_no** is functionally dependent on **order_no** and the column **discount** is functionally dependent on **customer_no**, answer the following questions and explain in detail your answers:

a. Is **order_no** a key of the table?
b. Is **customer_no** a key of the table?

E.1.7

Let **company** be a table with the following columns: **company_no, location.** Each company has one or more locations. In which normal form is the **company** table?

E.1.8

Let **supplier** be a table with the following columns: **supplier_no, article, city.** The key of the table is the combination of the first two columns. Each supplier delivers several articles, and each article is delivered by several suppliers. There is only one supplier in each city. Answer the following questions:

a. In which normal form is the **supplier** table?
b. How can you resolve the existing functional dependencies?

E.1.9

Let R(A, B, C) be a relation with the functional dependency B $\Rightarrow$ C. (The underlined attributes A and B build the composite key, and the attribute C is functionally dependent on B.) In which normal form is the relation R?

E.1.10

Let R(A, B, C) be a relation with the functional dependency C $\Rightarrow$ B. (The underlined attributes A and B build the composite key, and the attribute B is functionally dependent on C.) In which normal form is the relation R?

Chapter 2

Planning the Installation and Installing SQL Server

In This Chapter

- ▶ SQL Server Editions
- ▶ Planning Phase
- ▶ Installing SQL Server

his chapter begins by introducing the various SQL Server editions, so that you can identify which edition is appropriate for your environment. Before you proceed to the actual installation of this database system, you need to develop an installation plan. Therefore, the second part of this chapter is dedicated to the planning phase. It first provides some general recommendations, and then leads you through the planning steps provided by SQL Server Installation Center, a component of the SQL Server software. The final part of the chapter describes the actual installation of the SQL Server database server. Again, the same component, SQL Server Installation Center, is used to install the system on your computer.

NOTE

This chapter covers the basic installation of SQL Server.

SQL Server Editions

As you plan your installation, you need to know which SQL Server editions exist so that you can choose the most appropriate edition. Microsoft supports the following editions of SQL Server 2012:

▶ **Express Edition** The lightweight version of SQL Server, designed for use by application developers. For this reason, the product includes the basic Express Manager (XM) program and supports Common Language Runtime (CLR) integration and native XML. Also, you can download SQL Server Management Express for SQL Server Express to easily manage a database. SQL Server Express is available as a free download at http://msdn.microsoft.com/express.

▶ **Workgroup Edition** Designed for small businesses and for use at the department level. This edition provides relational database support without the business intelligence (BI) and high-availability capabilities. It supports up to two processors and a maximum of 2GB of RAM.

▶ **Standard Edition** Designed for small and medium-sized businesses. It supports up to four processors as well as 2TB of RAM and includes the full range of BI functionality, including Analysis Services, Reporting Services, and Integration Services. This edition does not include many enterprise-based features from Enterprise Edition (such as failover clustering, for instance).

▶ **Web Edition** Designed for web-hosting providers. In addition to the Database Engine, this edition includes Reporting Services. It provides support for up to four processors and 2TB of RAM.

▶ **Enterprise Edition**   The special form of the SQL Server system that is intended for time-critical applications with a huge number of users. In contrast to Standard Edition, this edition contains additional features that can be useful for very high-end installations with symmetrical multiprocessors or clusters. The most important additional features of Enterprise Edition are data partitioning, database snapshots, and online database maintenance.

▶ **Developer Edition**   Allows developers to build and test any type of application with SQL Server on 32- and 64-bit platforms. It includes all the functionality of Enterprise Edition, but is licensed only for use in development, testing, and demonstration. Each license of Developer Edition entitles one developer to use the software on as many systems as necessary; additional developers can use the software by purchasing additional licenses. For rapid deployment into production, the database system of Developer Edition can easily be upgraded to Enterprise Edition.

▶ **Datacenter Edition**   A new edition as of SQL Server 2008 R2 that is designed to support the highest level of scalability. It doesn't have any memory limitations, and you can create up to 25 instances. It also supports a maximum of 256 logical processors.

▶ **Parallel Data Warehouse Edition**   Dedicated to data warehousing and supports data warehouse databases from 10TB to 1PB (petabyte). To manage such huge databases, it uses MPP (massively parallel processing) architecture, introduced by Microsoft with its High Performance Computing (HPC) Windows operating systems.

Planning Phase

The description of the planning phase is divided into two parts. The first part gives some general recommendations, while the second part discusses how to use SQL Server Installation Center to plan the system installation.

General Recommendations

During the installation process, you have to make many choices. As a general guideline, it is best to familiarize yourself with their effects before installing your system. At the beginning, you should answer the following questions:

▶ Which SQL Server components should be installed?

▶ Where will the root directory be stored?

▶ Should multiple instances of the Database Engine be used?

▶ Which authentication mode for the Database Engine should be used?

The following subsections discuss these topics.

Which SQL Server Components Should Be Installed?

Before you start the installation process, you should know exactly which SQL Server components you want to install. Figure 2-1 shows a partial list of all the components. You will see this Feature Selection page again when you install SQL Server later in this chapter, but knowing ahead of time which components you want to select means you don't have to interrupt the installation process to do research. There are two groups of components on the Feature Selection page: main features and shared features.

Figure 2-1   *A preview of the Feature Selection page*

This section introduces only the main components. For a description of the shared components, refer to SQL Server Books Online.

The first item in the list of the main features is Database Engine Services. The Database Engine is the relational database system of SQL Server. Parts II and III of this book describe different aspects of the Database Engine. The first of the two features under Database Engine Services, SQL Server Replication, allows you to replicate data from one system to another. In other words, using data replication, you can achieve a distributed data environment. Detailed information on data replication can be found in Chapter 18.

The second feature under Database Engine Services is Full-Text Search. The Database Engine allows you to store structured data in columns of relational tables. By contrast, the unstructured data is primarily stored as text in file systems. For this reason, you will need different methods to retrieve information from unstructured data. Full-Text Search is a component of SQL Server that allows you to store and query unstructured data. Chapter 28 is dedicated to Full-Text Search.

Besides the Database Engine, SQL Server comprises Analysis Services and Reporting Services, which are components related to business intelligence (BI). Analysis Services is a group of services that is used to manage and query data that is stored in a data warehouse. (A data warehouse is a database that includes all corporate data that can be uniformly accessed by users.) Part IV of this book describes SQL Server and business intelligence in general, while Chapter 22 discusses Analysis Services in particular.

Reporting Services allows you to create and manage reports. This component of SQL Server is described in detail in Chapter 24.

Where Will the Root Directory Be Stored?

The root directory is where the Setup program stores all program files and those files that do not change as you use the SQL Server system. By default, the installation process stores all program files in the subdirectory Microsoft SQL Server, although you can change this setting during the installation process. Using the default name is recommended because it uniquely determines the version of the system.

Should Multiple Instances of the Database Engine Be Used?

With the Database Engine, you can install and use several different instances. An *instance* is a database server that does not share its system and user databases with other instances (servers) running on the same computer.

There are two instance types:

▶ Default

▶ Named

The *default instance* operates the same way as the database servers in earlier versions of SQL Server, where only one database server without instance support existed. The computer name on which the instance is running specifies solely the name of the default instance. Any instance of the database server other than the default instance is called a *named instance*. To identify a named instance, you have to specify its name as well as the name of the computer on which the instance is running: for example, NTB11901\ INSTANCE1. On one computer, there can be several named instances (in addition to the default instance). Additionally, you can configure named instances on a computer that does not have the default instance.

Although all instances running on a computer do not share most system resources (SQL Server and SQL Server Agent services, system and user databases, and registry keys), there are some components that are shared among them:

▶ SQL Server program group

▶ Analysis Services server

▶ Development libraries

The existence of only one SQL Server program group on a computer also means that only one copy of each utility exists, which is represented by an icon in the program group. (This includes SQL Server Books Online, too.) Therefore, each utility works with all instances configured on a computer.

You should consider using multiple instances if both of the following are true:

▶ You have different types of databases on your computer.

▶ Your computer is powerful enough to manage multiple instances.

The main purpose of multiple instances is to divide databases that exist in your organization into different groups. For instance, if the system manages databases that are used by different users (production databases, test databases, and sample databases), you should divide them to run under different instances. That way you can encapsulate your production databases from databases that are used by casual or inexperienced users. A single-processor machine will not be the right hardware platform to run multiple instances of the Database Engine, because of limited resources. For this reason, you should consider the use of multiple instances only with multiprocessor computers.

Which Authentication Mode for the Database Engine Should Be Used?

In relation to the Database Engine, there are two different authentication modes:

▶ **Windows mode**   Specifies security exclusively at the operating system level—that is, it specifies the way in which users connect to the Windows operating system using their user accounts and group memberships.

▶ **Mixed mode**   Allows users to connect to the Database Engine using Windows authentication or SQL Server authentication. This means that some user accounts can be set up to use the Windows security subsystem, while others can use the SQL Server security subsystem in addition to the Windows security subsystem.

Microsoft recommends the use of Windows mode. (For details, see Chapter 12.)

Planning the Installation

SQL Server contains a tool called Installation Center (see Figure 2-2), which appears when you start the installation of the software. This tool supports you during the planning, installation, and maintenance phases of your database system.

To begin the planning phase, insert the SQL Server DVD into your DVD drive. (This software product can also be distributed as an ISO image file.) The Install Shield wizard opens and prompts you to specify the location in which to save the extracted files. When you click Next, the Install Shield wizard extracts all necessary files from the DVD and completes its task.

The first phase of Installation Center leads you through the process of planning the installation. As shown in Figure 2-2, when you click Planning, the following tasks, among others, can be executed:

▶   Hardware and Software Requirements

▶   Security Documentation

▶   Online Release Notes

▶   Setup Documentation

▶   System Configuration Checker

▶   Install Upgrade Advisor

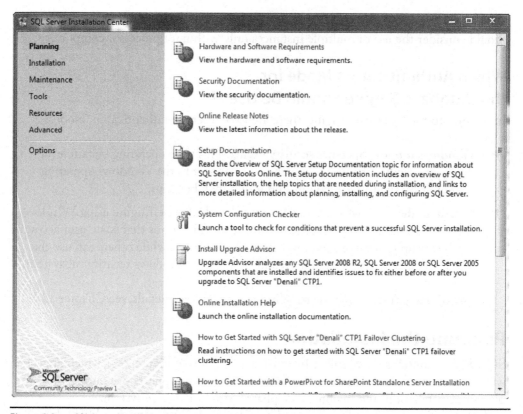

Figure 2-2 *SQL Server Installation Center*

Upgrade Advisor analyzes all components of previous releases that are installed and identifies issues to fix before you upgrade to SQL Server 2012. The supported previous releases are SQL Server 2005 and 2008 (together with Release 2).

The following subsections describe the first five tasks.

Hardware and Software Requirements

The fact that the SQL Server system runs only on Microsoft operating systems simplifies decisions concerning hardware and software requirements. The system administrator has to be concerned only about the hardware and network requirements.

Hardware Requirements   Windows operating systems are supported on the Intel and AMD (Opteron and Athlon 64) hardware platforms. Processor speed should be 1.4 GHz at a minimum.

> **NOTE**
>
> *Generally, two SQL Server edition groups exist: 32-bit and 64-bit. The requirements for these two groups differ. Therefore, the values listed in this section are general values.*

Officially, the minimum requirement for main memory is 512MB. However, almost everybody recognizes that such a minimal configuration will not perform very well, and as a general guideline, main memory of your computer should be at least 2GB or more.

Hard disk space requirements depend on your system configuration and the applications you choose to install. The more SQL Server components you want to install, the more disk space you will need.

Network Requirements   To connect to any SQL Server components, you must have a network protocol enabled. The SQL Server system can serve requests on several protocols at once. Clients connect to the system using a single protocol. If the client program does not know which protocol the system is listening on, configure the client to sequentially attempt multiple protocols.

As a client/server system, SQL Server allows clients to use different network protocols to communicate with the server, and vice versa. During connectivity installation, the system administrator must decide which network protocols (as libraries) should be available to give clients access to the system. The following network protocols can be selected on the server side:

▶ **Shared memory**   Used by connections to the system from a client running on the same computer. Shared memory has no configurable properties, and this protocol is always tried first.

▶ **Named Pipes**   An alternative network protocol on the Windows platforms. After the installation process, you can drop the support for Named Pipes and use another network protocol for communication between the server and clients.

▶ **Transmission Control Protocol/Internet Protocol (TCP/IP)**   Allows the system to communicate using standard Windows Sockets as the Internet protocol communication (IPC) method across the TCP/IP protocol.

▶ **Virtual Interface Adapter (VIA) protocol**   Works with VIA hardware. For information about how to use VIA, contact your hardware vendor. (The VIA protocol is deprecated and will be removed in a future version of SQL Server.)

> **NOTE**
>
> *Shared memory is not supported on failover clusters (see Chapter 16).*

Security Documentation

When you click Security Documentation, the system takes you to the Microsoft page that discusses general considerations concerning security. One of the most important security measures is to isolate services from each other. To isolate services, run separate SQL Server services under separate Windows accounts. (Chapter 12 discusses Windows accounts and other security aspects.) Information about all other security aspects can be found in Books Online.

Online Release Notes

There are two main sources to get information concerning all the features of the SQL Server system: Books Online and Online Release Notes. Books Online is the online documentation that is delivered with all SQL Server components, whereas Online Release Notes contain only the newest information, which is not necessarily provided in the Books Online documentation. (The reason is that bugs and specific behavior issues affecting the system sometimes are detected after Books Online is written and published.) It is strongly recommended that you read the Online Release Notes carefully to get a picture of features that were modified shortly before the delivery of the final release.

Setup Documentation

The Setup documentation includes an overview of SQL Server installation; all help topics that are relevant during installation; and links to information about planning, installing, and configuring SQL Server. During the installation process, if you encounter an issue that isn't addressed in this chapter, look for coverage of the issue in the help topics.

System Configuration Checker

One of the most important planning tasks is to check whether all conditions are fulfilled for a successful installation of the database system. When you click System Configuration Checker, the component called Setup Support Rules is automatically started. (The same tool is launched at the beginning of the installation phase, described next.) Setup Support Rules identifies problems that might occur when you install SQL Server support files. After finishing this task, the system shows you how many operations were checked and how many of them failed. All failures have to be corrected before the installation can continue.

Installing SQL Server

If you have done an installation of a complex software product before, you probably recognize that feeling of uncertainty that accompanies starting the installation for the first time. This feeling comes from the complexity of the product to be installed and the diversity of questions to be answered during the installation process. Because you may not completely understand the product, you (or the person who installs the software) may be less than confident that you can give accurate answers for all the questions that the Setup program asks to complete its tasks. This section will help you to find your way through the installation by giving you answers to most of the questions that you are likely to encounter.

As its name suggests, besides planning, Installation Center supports the installation of the software, too. Installation Center shows you several options related to the installation of the database system and its components. After clicking Installation, choose New SQL Server Stand-Alone Installation or Add Features To An Existing Installation, which launches a wizard to install SQL Server 2012.

The first page of the wizard, Setup Support Rules (see Figure 2-3), identifies problems that might occur when you install SQL Server Setup support files. (Again, it is the same tool that is launched when you click System Configuration Checker during the planning phase.) Failures must be corrected before Setup can continue. If no problems are reported, click Next.

On the Installation Type page, choose one of the two radio buttons:

► Perform a new installation of SQL Server

► Add features to an existing instance of SQL Server

If you select the latter option, use the drop-down list to select the instance of SQL Server to update. After you have chosen an option, click Next.

On the next page of the wizard, Product Key, enter the 25-character key from the product packaging. (The alternative is to specify a free edition of the software, SQL Server Express, for instance.) Click Next to continue. On the License Terms page, click I Accept the License Terms.

The next page, Setup Role, allows you to choose between installing only the main components of SQL Server 2012 (Database Engine Services, Analysis Services, and Reporting Services) and installing additional auxiliary components, such as Power Pivot for SharePoint. Choose SQL Server Feature Installation and click Next.

Setup Support Rules

Setup Support Rules identify problems that might occur when you install SQL Server Setup support files. Failures must be corrected before Setup can continue.

Setup Support Rules

Installation Type

Product Key

License Terms

Setup Role

Feature Selection

Installation Rules

Disk Space Requirements

Error Reporting

Installation Configuration Rules

Ready to Install

Installation Progress

Complete

Operation completed. Passed: 9. Failed 0. Warning 1. Skipped 0.

Hide details <<   Re-run

View detailed report

Ru	Rule	Status
✅	Fusion Active Template Library (ATL)	Passed
✅	Performance counter registry hive consistency	Passed
✅	Previous releases of SQL Server 2008 Business Intelligence Devel...	Passed
✅	No SxS install with SQL Server "Denali" CTP0	Passed
✅	Consistency validation for SQL Server registry keys	Passed
✅	Computer domain controller	Passed
✅	Microsoft .NET Application Security	Passed
✅	Edition WOW64 platform	Passed
⚠	Windows Firewall	Warning
✅	Windows PowerShell	Passed

< Back   Next >   Cancel   Help

Figure 2-3 *Summary of Setup Support Rules page*

On the Feature Selection page (see Figure 2-4), select the components to install by checking the corresponding check boxes. Also, toward the bottom of the page, you can specify the directory in which to store the shared components. After that, click Next to continue.

NOTE

All the shared features in Figure 2-4 are grayed out, which means that these features are not selected. For your own installation, you should decide which of these features should be installed and check their corresponding check boxes.

Feature Selection

Select the Evaluation features to install.

Setup Support Rules
Installation Type
Product Key
License Terms
Setup Role
Feature Selection
Installation Rules
Instance Configuration
Disk Space Requirements
Server Configuration
Database Engine Configuration
Analysis Services Configuration
Reporting Services Configuration
Error Reporting
Installation Configuration Rules
Ready to Install
Installation Progress
Complete

Features:

- ☑ Database Engine Services
  - ☑ SQL Server Replication
  - ☑ Full-Text Search
- ☑ Analysis Services
- ☑ Reporting Services

Shared Features
- ☑ Business Intelligence Development Studio
- ☑ Client Tools Connectivity
- ☑ Integration Services
- ☑ Client Tools Backwards Compatibility
- ☑ Client Tools SDK
- ☑ SQL Server Books Online
- ☑ Management Tools - Basic
  - ☑ Management Tools - Complete
- ☑ SQL Client Connectivity SDK
- ☑ Microsoft Sync Framework

[Select All] [Unselect All]

Shared feature directory: C:\Program Files\Microsoft SQL Server\ [...]

Shared feature directory (x86): C:\Program Files (x86)\Microsoft SQL Server\ [...]

Feature description:

Includes the Database Engine, the core service for storing, processing and securing data. The Database Engine provides controlled access and rapid transaction processing and also provides rich support for sustaining high availability. The Database Engine also

Prerequisites for selected features:

Already installed:
- Microsoft .NET Framework 4.0
- Windows PowerShell 2.0

[< Back] [Next >] [Cancel] [Help]

Figure 2-4   *Feature Selection page*

NOTE

Components of SQL Server that are selected will be installed one after the other in the order in which they are listed on the Feature Selection page. The installation process starts with the installation of the Database Engine, followed by the installation of Analysis Services, and so on. Only the selected components will be installed.

On the next page, Installation Rules, the setup runs rules to determine if the installation process will be blocked. If all checks are passed (or marked "Not applicable"), click Next to continue.

On the Instance Configuration page (see Figure 2-5), you can choose between the installation of a default or named instance. (A detailed discussion of these type of instances can be found in the section "Should Multiple Instances of the Database Engine Be Used?" earlier in this chapter.) To install the default instance, click Default Instance. If a default instance is already installed and you select Default Instance, the Setup program upgrades it and gives you the option to install additional components. Therefore, you have another opportunity to install components that you skipped in the previous installation processes.

To install a new named instance, click Named Instance and type a new name in the given text box. In the lower part of the page, you can see the list of instances already installed on your system. As you can see from Figure 2-5, the computer on which I installed the instance already contains an installed instance. (MSSQLSERVER is the name of the default instance for the Database Engine.) Click Next to continue.

Instance Configuration

Specify the name and instance ID for the instance of SQL Server. Instance ID becomes part of the installation path.

Setup Support Rules	○ Default instance
Setup Role	◉ Named instance: MSSQLSERVER
Feature Selection	
Installation Rules	
Instance Configuration	
Disk Space Requirements	Instance ID: MSSQLSERVER
Server Configuration	Instance root directory: C:\Program Files (x86)\Microsoft SQL Server\
Database Engine Configuration	
Analysis Services Configuration	SQL Server directory: C:\Program Files (x86)\Microsoft SQL Server\MSSQL11.MSSQLSERVER
Reporting Services Configuration	Analysis Services directory: C:\Program Files (x86)\Microsoft SQL Server\MSAS11.MSSQLSERVER
Error Reporting	Reporting Services directory: C:\Program Files (x86)\Microsoft SQL Server\MSRS11.MSSQLSERVER
Installation Configuration Rules	
Ready to Install	Installed instances:
Installation Progress	
Complete	

Instance Name	Instance ID	Features	Edition	Version
SQLEXPRESS	MSSQL10.SQLEXP...	SQLEngine,SQLEn...	Express	10.1.2531.0

[< Back] [Next >] [Cancel] [Help]

Figure 2-5 *Instance Configuration page*

The Disk Space Requirements page shows whether the space available on your disk is sufficient for the installation of the database system. If so, click Next to continue.

The next page, Server Configuration (see Figure 2-6), allows you to specify usernames and corresponding passwords for services of all components that will be installed during the installation process. (You can apply one account for all services, but this is not recommended, for security reasons.)

To choose the collation of your instance, click the Collation tab of the same page. (Collation defines the sorting behavior for your instance.) You can either choose the default collations for the components that will be installed, or click Customize to select some other collations that are supported by the system. Click Next to continue.

On the Database Engine Configuration page (see Figure 2-7), you choose the authentication mode for your Database Engine system. As you already know, the

Server Configuration

Specify the service accounts and collation configuration.

Setup Support Rules
Setup Role
Feature Selection
Installation Rules
Instance Configuration
Disk Space Requirements
Server Configuration
Database Engine Configuration
Analysis Services Configuration
Reporting Services Configuration
Error Reporting
Installation Configuration Rules
Ready to Install
Installation Progress
Complete

Service Accounts | Collation

Microsoft recommends that you use a separate account for each SQL Server service.

Service	Account Name	Password	Startup Type
SQL Server Agent	Administrator		Automatic ▾
SQL Server Database Engine	Administrator		Automatic ▾
SQL Server Analysis Services	Administrator		Automatic ▾
SQL Server Reporting Services	Administrator		Automatic ▾
SQL Server Integration Services 1...	Administrator		Automatic ▾
SQL Full-text Filter Daemon Laun...	NT AUTHORITY\LOCA...		Manual
SQL Server Browser	NT-AUTORITÄT\LOKA...		Manual ▾

Use the same account for all SQL Server services

< Back | Next > | Cancel | Help

Figure 2-6   *Server Configuration (Service Accounts tab)*

Figure 2-7 *Database Engine Configuration (Account Provisioning tab)*

Database Engine supports Windows authentication mode and Mixed mode. If you select the Windows Authentication Mode radio button, the Setup process creates the **sa** (system administrator) login, which is disabled by default. (For the discussion of logins, see Chapter 12.) If you choose the Mixed Mode radio button, you must enter and confirm the system administrator login. Click Add Current User if you want to add one or more users that will have unrestricted access to the instance of the Database Engine.

NOTE

You can change the information concerning account provisioning after installation. In that case, you have to restart the Database Engine service called MSSQLSERVER.

The other tab of the Database Engine Configuration page, Data Directories (see Figure 2-8), allows you to specify the locations for all the directories in which Database Engine–related files are stored. After that, click Next to continue.

What appears for the next step depends on whether or not you chose to install Analysis Services. (A Configuration page appears for each SQL Server component that you chose to install.) If you did choose to install it, a page similar to Figure 2-7 will appear for Analysis Services. Specify users that will have access to Analysis Services and click Next to continue.

Similarly, what appears for the next step depends on whether or not you decided to install Reporting Services. If you indicated that Reporting Services should be installed, the Reporting Services Configuration page (see Figure 2-9) appears. On this page, you

Figure 2-8   *Database Engine Configuration (Data Directories tab)*

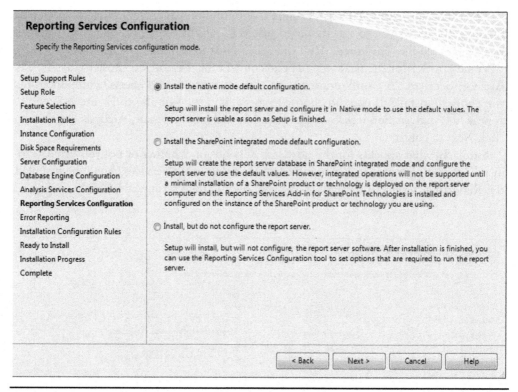

Figure 2-9 *Reporting Services Configuration page*

can decide just to install the report server (without its configuration) or to install and configure it. The third alternative is to integrate the report server with Microsoft Office SharePoint Server (a server program that can be used to facilitate collaboration, provide content management features, and implement business processes). After that, click Next to continue.

On the Error Reporting page, specify the information, if any, that you would like to send to Microsoft automatically. Clear the check box if you do not want to take part in this automatic reporting. Click Next.

The next page, Installation Configuration Rules, is similar to the earlier page called Installation Rules. At the end of this step, the summary of all configuration rules will be displayed.

The last page, before the installation process actually starts, is the Ready to Install page. This page allows you to review the summary of all SQL Server components that will be installed. To start the installation process, click Install. Setup shows you the progress of your installation process. If the installation process succeeds, click Next.

At the end, the Complete page (see Figure 2-10) appears, with the location of the file in which the summary log is stored. Click Close to complete the installation process. After that, you can use all components that you installed during the installation process.

Figure 2-10 *Complete page*

Summary

The SQL Server Installation Center component can be used both to plan the installation and to accomplish it. The most important step in the planning phase is the invocation of System Configuration Checker. This component identifies problems that might occur when you install SQL Server files.

The installation of SQL Server is straightforward. The most important decision that you have to make during this phase is which components to install, a decision you prepared for during the planning phase.

The next chapter describes SQL Server Management Studio. This component of SQL Server is used by database administrators as well as users to interact with the system.

Chapter 3

SQL Server Management Studio

In This Chapter

- ▶ **Introduction to SQL Server Management Studio**
- ▶ **Using SQL Server Management Studio with the Database Engine**
- ▶ **Authoring Activities Using SQL Server Management Studio**

This chapter first introduces SQL Server Management Studio, including how to connect it to a server, its Registered Servers and Object Explorer components, and its various user interface panes. After that, the chapter explains in detail the SQL Server Management Studio functions related to the Database Engine, including administering and managing databases, which you need to understand to be able to create and execute any Transact-SQL statements. Finally, the chapter covers using Query Editor, Solution Explorer, and the debugging tool to perform authoring activities in SQL Server Management Studio.

Introduction to SQL Server Management Studio

SQL Server 2012 provides various tools that are used for different purposes, such as system installation, configuration, auditing, and performance tuning. (All these tools will be discussed in different chapters of this book.) The administrator's primary tool for interacting with the system is SQL Server Management Studio. Both administrators and end users can use this tool to administer multiple servers, develop databases, and replicate data, among other things.

NOTE

This chapter is dedicated to the activities of the end user. Therefore, only the functionality of SQL Server Management Studio with respect to the creation of database objects using the Database Engine is described in detail. All administrative tasks and all tasks related to Analysis Services and other components that this tool supports are discussed beginning in Part III.

To open SQL Server Management Studio, choose Start | All Programs | Microsoft SQL Server 2012 | SQL Server Management Studio.

SQL Server Management Studio comprises several different components that are used for the authoring, administration, and management of the overall system. The following are the main components used for these tasks:

► Registered Servers

► Object Explorer

► Query Editor

► Solution Explorer

The first two components in the list are discussed in this section. Query Editor, and Solution Explorer are explained later in this chapter, in the section "Authoring Activities Using SQL Server Management Studio."

To get to the main SQL Server Management Studio interface, you first must connect to a server, as described next.

Connecting to a Server

When you open SQL Server Management Studio, it displays the Connect to Server dialog box (see Figure 3-1), which allows you to specify the necessary parameters to connect to a server:

▶ **Server Type**   For purposes of this chapter, choose Database Engine.

NOTE

With SQL Server Management Studio, you can manage objects of the Database Engine and Analysis Server, among others. This chapter demonstrates the use of SQL Server Management Studio only with the Database Engine.

▶ **Server Name**   Select or type the name of the server that you want to use. (Generally, you can connect SQL Server Management Studio to any of the installed products on a particular server.)

Figure 3-1   *The Connect to Server dialog box*

▶ **Authentication**   Choose between the two authentication types:

    ▶ **Windows Authentication**   Connect to SQL Server using your Windows account. This option is much simpler and is recommended by Microsoft.

    ▶ **SQL Server Authentication**   The Database Engine uses its own authentication.

NOTE

For more information concerning SQL Server Authentication, see Chapter 12.

When you click Connect, the Database Engine connects to the specified server. After connecting to the database server, the default SQL Server Management Studio window appears. The default appearance is similar to Visual Studio, so users can leverage their experience of developing in Visual Studio to use SQL Server Management Studio more easily. Figure 3-2 shows the SQL Server Management Window with several panes.

NOTE

SQL Server Management Studio gives you a unique interface to manage servers and create queries across all SQL Server components. This means that SQL Server Management Studio offers one interface for the Database Engine, Analysis Services, Integration Services, and Reporting Services.

Registered Servers

Registered Servers is represented as a pane that allows you to maintain connections to already used servers (see Figure 3-2). (If the Registered Servers pane isn't visible, select its name from the View menu.) You can use these connections to check a server's status or to manage its objects. Each user has a separate list of registered servers, which is stored locally.

You can add new servers to the list of all servers, or remove one or more existing servers from the list. You also can group existing servers into server groups. Each group should contain the servers that belong together logically. You can also group servers by server type, such as Database Engine, Analysis Services, Reporting Services, and Integration Services.

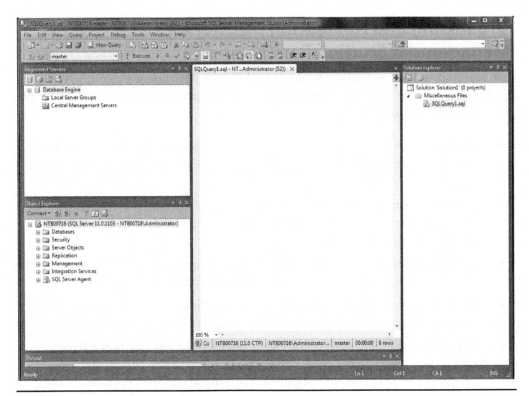

Figure 3-2   *SQL Server Management Studio*

Object Explorer

The Object Explorer pane contains a tree view of all the database objects in a server. (If the Object Explorer pane isn't visible, select View | Object Explorer.) The tree view shows you a hierarchy of the objects on a server. Hence, if you expand a tree, the logical structure of a corresponding server will be shown.

Object Explorer allows you to connect to multiple servers in the same pane. The server can be any of the existing servers for Database Engine, Analysis Services, Reporting Services, or Integration Services. This feature is user-friendly, because it allows you to manage all servers of the same or different types from one place.

NOTE

Object Explorer has several other features, explained later in this chapter.

Organizing and Navigating SQL Server Management Studio's Panes

You can dock or hide each of the panes of SQL Server Management Studio. By right-clicking the title bar at the top of the corresponding pane, you can choose between the following presentation possibilities:

▶ **Floating** The pane becomes a separate floating pane on top of the rest of SQL Server Management Studio panes. Such a pane can be moved anywhere around the screen.

▶ **Dockable** Enables you to move and dock the pane in different positions. To move the pane to a different docking position, click and drag its title bar and drop it in the new position.

▶ **Tabbed Document** You can create a tabbed grouping using the Designer window. When this is done, the pane's state changes from dockable to tabbed document.

▶ **Hide** Closes the pane. (Alternatively, you can click the × in the upper-right corner of the pane.) To display a closed pane, select its name from the View menu.

▶ **Auto Hide** Minimizes the pane and stores it on the left side of the screen. To reopen (maximize) such a pane, move your mouse over the tabs on the left side of the screen and click the push pin to pin the pane in the open position.

NOTE

The difference between the Hide and Auto Hide options is that the former option removes the pane from view in SQL Server Management Studio, while the latter collapses the pane to the side panel.

To restore the default configuration, choose Window | Reset Window Layout. The Object Explorer pane appears on the left, while the Object Explorer Details tab appears on the right side of SQL Server Management Studio. (The Object Explorer Details tab displays information about the currently selected node of Object Explorer.)

NOTE

You will find that often there are several ways of accomplishing the same task within SQL Server Management Studio. This chapter will indicate more than one way to do things, whereas only a single method will be given in subsequent chapters. Different people prefer different methods (some like to double-click, some like to click the +/− signs, some like to right-click, others like to use the pull-down menus, and others like to use the keyboard shortcuts as much as possible). Experiment with the different ways to navigate, and use the methods that feel most natural to you.

Within the Object Explorer and Registered Servers panes, a subobject appears only if you click the plus (+) sign of its direct predecessor in the tree hierarchy. To see the properties of an object, right-click the object and choose Properties. A minus (–) sign to the left of an object's name indicates that the object is currently expanded. To compress all subobjects of an object, click its minus sign. (Another possibility would be to double-click the folder, or press the LEFT ARROW key while the folder is selected.)

Using SQL Server Management Studio with the Database Engine

SQL Server Management Studio has two main purposes:

▶ Administration of the database servers

▶ Management of database objects

The following sections describe these functions of SQL Server Management Studio.

Administering Database Servers

The administrative tasks that you can perform by using SQL Server Management Studio are, among others, the following:

▶ Register servers

▶ Connect to a server

▶ Create new server groups

▶ Manage multiple servers

▶ Start and stop servers

The following subsections describe these administrative tasks.

Registering Servers

SQL Server Management Studio separates the activities of registering servers and exploring databases and their objects. (Both of these activities can be done using Object Explorer.) Every server (local or remote) must be registered before you can use its databases and objects. A server can be registered during the first execution of SQL Server Management Studio or later. To register a database server, right-click the folder of your database server in Object Explorer and choose Register. (If the Object Explorer pane doesn't appear on your screen, select View | Object Explorer.) The New Server

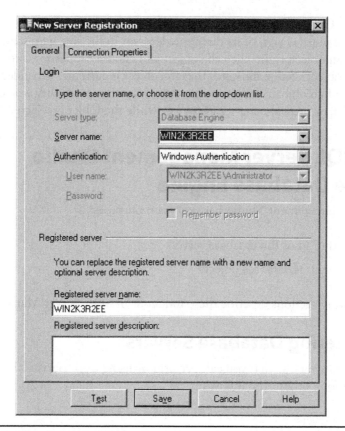

Figure 3-3 *The New Server Registration dialog box*

Registration dialog box appears, as shown in Figure 3-3. Choose the name of the server that you want to register and the authentication mode (Windows Authentication or SQL Server Authentication). Click Save.

Connecting to a Server

SQL Server Management Studio also separates the tasks of registering a server and connecting to a server. This means that registering a server does not automatically connect you to the server. To connect to a server from the Object Explorer window, right-click the server name and choose Connect.

Creating a New Server Group

To create a new server group in the Registered Servers pane, right-click Local Server Groups and choose New Server Group. In the New Server Group properties dialog box, enter a (unique) group name and optionally describe the new group.

Managing Multiple Servers

SQL Server Management Studio allows you to administer multiple database servers (called instances) on one computer by using Object Explorer. Each instance of the Database Engine has its own set of database objects (system and user databases) that are not shared between different instances.

To manage a server and its configuration, right-click the server name in Object Explorer and choose Properties. The Server Properties dialog box that opens contains several different pages, such as General, Security, and Permissions.

The General page (see Figure 3-4) shows general properties of the server. The Security page contains the information concerning the authentication mode of the

Figure 3-4   *The Server Properties dialog box: the General page*

server and the login auditing mode. The Permissions page shows all logins and roles that can access the server. The lower part of the page shows all permissions that can be granted to the logins and roles.

You can replace the existing server name with a new name. Right-click the server in the Object Explorer window and choose Register. Now you can rename the server and modify the existing server description in the Registered Server frame.

NOTE

Do not rename servers, because changing names can affect other servers that reference them.

Starting and Stopping Servers

A Database Engine server starts automatically by default each time the Windows operating system starts. To start the server using SQL Server Management Studio, right-click the selected server in the Object Explorer pane and click Start in the context menu. The menu also contains Stop and Pause functions that you can use to stop or pause the activated server, respectively.

Managing Databases Using Object Explorer

The following are the management tasks that you can perform by using SQL Server Management Studio:

▶ Create databases without using Transact-SQL

▶ Modify databases without using Transact-SQL

▶ Manage tables without using Transact-SQL

▶ Generate and execute SQL statements (will be described later, in the section "Query Editor")

Creating Databases Without Using Transact-SQL

You can create a new database by using Object Explorer or the Transact-SQL language. (Database creation using Transact-SQL is discussed in Chapter 5.) As the name suggests, you also use Object Explorer to explore the objects within a server. From the Object Explorer pane, you can inspect all the objects within a server and manage your server and databases. The existing tree contains, among other folders, the Databases folder. This folder has several subfolders, including one for the system databases and one for each new database that is created by a user. (System and user databases are discussed in detail in Chapter 15.)

To create a database using Object Explorer, right-click Databases and select New Database. In the New Database dialog box (see Figure 3-5), type the name of the new database in the Database Name field and then click OK. Each database has several different properties, such as file type, initial size, and so on. Database properties can be selected from the left pane of the New Database dialog box. There are several different pages (property groups):

▶ General

▶ Files

Figure 3-5 *The New Database dialog box*

- ► Filegroups
- ► Options
- ► Change Tracking
- ► Permissions
- ► Extended Properties
- ► Mirroring
- ► Transaction Log Shipping

NOTE

For an existing database, the system displays all property groups in the preceding list. For a new database, as shown in Figure 3-5, there are only three groups: General, Options, and Filegroups.

The General page of the Database Properties dialog box (see Figure 3-6) displays, among other things, the database name, the owner of the database and its collation. The properties of the data files that belong to a particular database are listed in the Files page and comprise the name and initial size of the file, where the database will be stored, and the type of the file (PRIMARY, for instance). A database can be stored in multiple files.

NOTE

*SQL Server has dynamic disk space management. This means that databases can be set up to automatically expand and shrink as needed. If you want to change the **Autogrowth** property in the Files page, click the ellipses (...) in the Autogrowth column and make your changes in the Change Autogrowth dialog box. The Enable Autogrowth check box should be checked to allow the database to autogrow. Each time there is insufficient space within the file when data is added to the database, the server will request the additional space from the operating system. The amount (in megabytes) of the additional space is set by the number in the File Growth frame of the same dialog box. You can also decide whether the file can grow without any restrictions (the default value) or not. If you restrict the file growth, you have to specify the maximum file size.*

The Filegroups page of the Database Properties dialog box displays the name(s) of the filegroup(s) to which the database file belongs, the art of the filegroup (default or nondefault), and the allowed operation on the filegroup (read/write or read-only).

The Options page of the Database Properties dialog box enables you to display and modify all database-level options. There are several groups of options: Automatic, Containment, Cursor, Miscellaneous, Recovery, Service Broker, and State. For instance, the following four options exist for State:

Figure 3-6   *Database Properties dialog box: General page*

▶ **Database Read-Only**   Allows read-only access to the database. This prohibits users from modifying any data. (The default value is False.)

▶ **Database State**   Describes the state of the database. (The default value is Normal.)

▶ **Restrict Access**   Restricts the use of the database to one user at a time. (The default value is MULTI_USER.)

▶ **Encryption Enabled**   Controls the database encryption state. (The default value is False.)

The Extended Properties page displays additional properties of the current database. Existing properties can be deleted and new properties can be added from this dialog box.

If you choose the Permissions page, the system opens the corresponding dialog box and displays all users and roles along with their permissions. (For the discussion of permissions, see Chapter 12.)

The rest of the pages (Change Tracking, Mirroring, and Transaction Log Shipping) describe the features which are related to data availability and are therefore explained in detail in Chapter 16.

Modifying Databases Without Using Transact-SQL

Object Explorer can also be used to modify an existing database. Using this component, you can modify files and filegroups that belong to the database. To add new data files, right-click the database name and choose Properties. In the Database Properties dialog box, select Files, click Add, and type the name of the new file. You can also add a (secondary) filegroup for the database by selecting Filegroups and clicking Add.

NOTE

Only the system administrator or the database owner can modify the database properties just mentioned.

To delete a database using Object Explorer, right-click the database name and choose Delete.

Managing Tables Without Using Transact-SQL

After you create a database, your next task is to create all tables belonging to it. As with database creation, you can create tables by using either Object Explorer or Transact-SQL. Again, only Object Explorer is discussed here. (The creation of a table and all other database objects using the Transact-SQL language is discussed in detail in Chapter 5.)

To create a table using Object Explorer, expand the Databases folder, expand the database, right-click the Tables subfolder, and then click New Table.

To demonstrate the creation of a table using Object Explorer, the **department** table of the **sample** database will be used as an example. Enter the names of all columns with their properties. Enter the column names, their data types, and the NULL property of each column in the two-dimensional matrix, as shown in the top-right pane of Figure 3-7.

Figure 3-7   *Creating the department table using Object Explorer*

All data types supported by the system can be displayed (and one of them selected) by clicking the arrow sign in the Data Type column (the arrow appears after the cell has been selected). Subsequently, you can type entries in the **Length, Precision**, and **Scale** rows for the chosen data type on the Column Properties tab (see the bottom-right pane of Figure 3-7). Some data types, such as CHAR, require a value for the **Length** row, and some, such as DECIMAL, require a value in the **Precision** and **Scale** rows. On the other hand, data types such as INTEGER do not need any of these entries to be specified. (The valid entries for a specified data type are highlighted in the list of all possible column properties.)

The check box in the Allow Nulls column must be checked if you want a table column to permit NULL values to be inserted into that column. Similarly, if there is a default value, it should be entered in the **Default Value or Binding** row of the Column Properties tab. (A default value is a value that will be inserted in a table column when there is no explicit value entered for it.)

The column **dept_no** is the primary key of the **department** table. (For the discussion of primary keys of the **sample** database, see Chapter 1.) To specify a column as the primary key of a table, you must right-click the column and choose Set Primary Key. Finally, click the × in the right pane with the information concerning the new table. After that, the system will display the Choose Name dialog box, where you can type the table name.

To view the properties of an existing table, double-click the folder of the database to which the table belongs, double-click Tables, and then right-click the name of the table and choose Properties. Figure 3-8 shows the Table Properties dialog box for the **employee** table.

Figure 3-8   *Table Properties dialog box for the employee table*

To rename a table, right-click the name of the table in the Tables folder and choose Rename. To remove a table, right-click the name of the table in the Tables folder in the database to which the table belongs and select Delete.

NOTE

*You should now create the other three tables of the **sample** database.*

After you have created all four tables of the **sample** database (**employee, department, project**, and **works_on**), you can use another feature of SQL Server Management Studio to display the corresponding entity-relationship (ER) diagram of the **sample** database. (The process of converting the existing tables of a database into the corresponding ER diagram is called *reverse engineering*.)

To see the ER diagram of the **sample** database, right-click the Database Diagrams subfolder of the **sample** database and select New Database Diagram.

NOTE

If a dialog box opens asking you whether the support objects should be created, click Yes.

The first (and only) step is to select tables that will be added to the diagram. After adding all four tables of the **sample** database, the wizard completes the work and creates the diagram (see Figure 3-9).

The diagram shown in Figure 3-9 is not the final diagram of the **sample** database because, although it shows all four tables with their columns (and the corresponding primary keys), it does not show any relationship between the tables. A relationship between two tables is based on the primary key of one table and the (possible) corresponding column(s) of the other table. (For a detailed discussion of these relationships and referential integrity, see Chapter 5.)

There are exactly three relationships between the existing tables of the **sample** database: first, the tables **department** and **employee** have a 1:N relationship, because for each value in the primary key column of the **department** table (**dept_no**), there is one or more corresponding values in the column **dept_no** of the **employee** table. Analogously, there is a relationship between the tables **employee** and **works_on**, because only those values that exist in the primary key of the **employee** table (**emp_no**) appear also in the column **emp_no** of the **works_on** table. The third relationship is between the tables **project** and **works_on**, because only values that

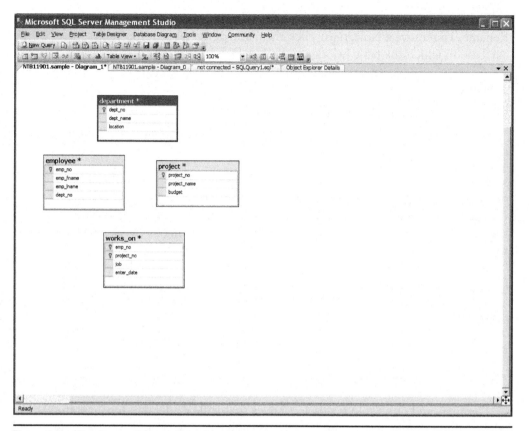

Figure 3-9 *First diagram of the sample database*

exist in the primary key of the **project** table (**pr_no**) appear also in the **pr_no** column of the **works_on** table.

To create each of the three relationships described, you have to redesign the diagram with the column that corresponds to the primary key column of the other table. (Such a column is called a *foreign key*.) To see how to do this, use the **employee** table and define its column **dept_no** as the foreign key of the **department** table:

1. Click the created diagram, right-click the graphical form of the **employee** table in the detail pane, and select Relationships. In the Foreign Key Relationships dialog box, click Add.

2. In the dialog box, expand the Tables and Columns Specification column and click the ... button.

3. Select the table with the corresponding primary key (the **department** table).

4. Choose the **dept_no** column of this table as the primary key and the column with the same name in the **employee** table as the foreign key and click OK. Click Close.

Figure 3-10 shows the modified diagram after all three relationships in the **sample** database have been created.

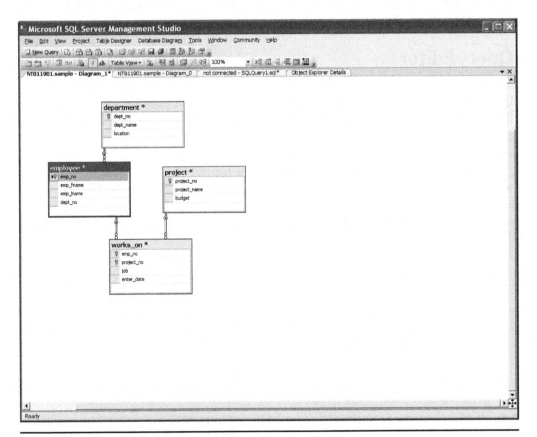

Figure 3-10   *The final diagram of the sample database*

Authoring Activities Using SQL Server Management Studio

SQL Server Management Studio gives you a complete authoring environment for all types of queries. You can create, save, load, and edit queries. SQL Server Management Studio allows you to work on queries without being connected to a particular server. This tool also gives you the option of developing your queries with different projects.

The authoring capabilities are associated with Query Editor as well as Solution Explorer, both of which are described in this section. Besides these two components of SQL Server Management Studio we will describe how you can debug SQL code using the existing debugger.

Query Editor

To launch the Query Editor pane, click the New Query button in the toolbar of SQL Server Management Studio. If you expand it to show all the possible queries, it shows more than just a Database Engine query. By default, you get a new Database Engine query, but other queries are possible, such as MDX queries, XMLA queries, and other queries.

Once you open Query Editor, the status bar at the bottom of the pane tells you whether your query is in a connected or disconnected state. If you are not connected automatically to the server, the Connect to SQL Server dialog box appears, where you can type the name of the database server to which you want to connect and select the authentication mode.

NOTE

Disconnected editing has more flexibility than connected editing. You can edit queries without having to choose a server, and you can disconnect a given Query Editor window from one server and connect it to another without having to open another window. (You can use disconnected editing by clicking the Cancel button in the Connect to SQL Server dialog box.)

Query Editor can be used by end users for the following tasks:

- ▶ Generating and executing Transact-SQL statements
- ▶ Storing the generated Transact-SQL statements in a file
- ▶ Generating and analyzing execution plans for generated queries
- ▶ Graphically illustrating the execution plan for a selected query

Query Editor contains an internal text editor and a selection of buttons in its toolbar. The main window is divided into a query pane (upper) and a results pane (lower). Users enter the Transact-SQL statements (queries) that they want to execute into the query pane, and after the system has processed the queries, the output is displayed in the results pane.

The example shown in Figure 3-11 demonstrates a query entered into Query Editor and the output returned. The first statement in the query pane, USE, specifies the **sample** database as the current database. The second statement, SELECT, retrieves all the rows of the **works_on** table. Clicking the Query button in the Query Editor toolbar and then selecting Execute or pressing F5 returns the results of these statements in the results pane of Query Editor.

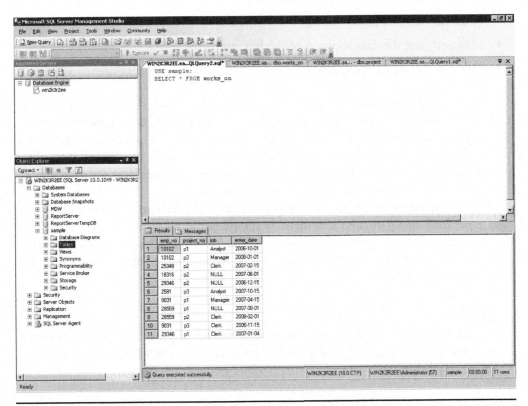

Figure 3-11 *Query Editor with a query and its results*

NOTE

You can open several different windows—that is, several different connections to one or more Database Engine instances. You create new connections by clicking the New Query button in the toolbar.

The following additional information concerning the execution of the statement(s) is displayed in the status bar at the bottom of the Query Editor window:

▶ The status of the current operation (for example, "Query executed successfully")

▶ Database server name

▶ Current username and server process ID

▶ Current database name

▶ Elapsed time for the execution of the last query

▶ The number of retrieved rows

One of the main features of SQL Server Management Studio is that it's easy to use, and that also applies to the Query Editor component. Query Editor supports a lot of features that make coding of Transact-SQL statements easier. First, Query Editor uses syntax highlighting to improve the readability of Transact-SQL statements. It displays all reserved words in blue, all variables in black, strings in red, and comments in green. (For a discussion of reserved words, see the next chapter.)

There is also the context-sensitive help function called Dynamic Help that enables you to get help on a particular statement. If you do not know the syntax of a statement, just highlight that statement in the editor and select Help | Dynamic Help. You can also highlight options of different Transact-SQL statements to get the corresponding text from Books Online.

NOTE

SQL Server 2012 supports the SQL Intellisense tool. Intellisense is a form of automated autocompletion. In other words, this add-in allows you to access descriptions of frequently used elements of Transact-SQL statements without using the keyboard.

Object Explorer can also help you edit queries. For instance, if you want to see the corresponding CREATE TABLE statement for the **employee** table, drill down to this database object, right-click the table name, select Script Table As, and choose CREATE to New Query Editor Window. Figure 3-12 shows the Query Editor

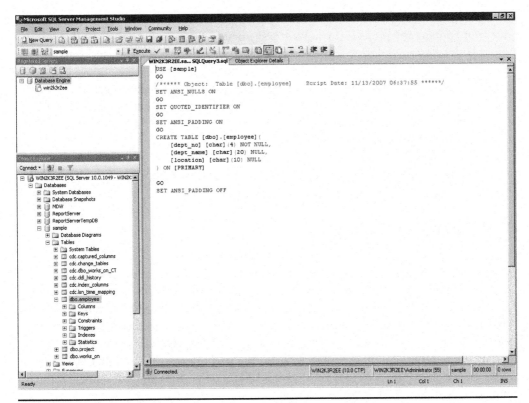

Figure 3-12   *The Query Editor windows with the CREATE TABLE statement*

window with the CREATE TABLE statement. (This capability extends also to other objects, such as stored procedures and functions.)

Object Explorer is very useful if you want to display the graphical execution plan for a particular query. (The *execution plan* is the plan selected by the optimizer to execute a given query.) If you select Query | Display Estimated Execution Plan, the system will display the graphical plan instead of the result set for the given query. This topic is discussed in detail in Chapter 19.

Solution Explorer

Query editing in SQL Server Management Studio is solution-based. If you start a blank query using the New Query button, it will still be based on a blank solution. You can see this by choosing View | Solution Explorer right after you open your blank query.

A solution can have zero, one, or more projects associated with it. A blank solution does not contain any project. If you want to associate a project with the solution, close your blank solution, Solution Explorer, and the Query Editor window, and start a new project by choosing File | New | Project. In the New Project window, choose SQL Server Scripts. A project is a method of organizing files in a selected location. You can choose a name for the project and select its location on disk. When you create a new project, by default you start a new solution. You can add a project to an existing solution using Solution Explorer.

Once the new project and solution are created, Solution Explorer shows nodes in each project for Connections, Queries, and Miscellaneous. To open a new Query Editor window, right-click the Queries node and choose New Query.

SQL Server Debugging

Since SQL Server 2008, you can debug SQL code using the existing debugger. To start debugging, choose Debug | Start Debugging in the main menu of SQL Server Management Studio. A batch from Chapter 8 (see Example 8.1) will be used here to demonstrate how the debugger works. (A *batch* is a sequence of SQL statements and procedural extensions that comprises a logical unit and is sent to the Database Engine for execution of all statements included in the batch.) Figure 3-13 shows a batch that counts the number of employees working for the p1 project. If the number is 4 or more, the corresponding message is displayed. Otherwise, first and last names of the employees will be printed.

You can set the breakpoints shown in Figure 3-13 just by clicking in front of the line where the execution process should stop. At the beginning, the editor shows a yellow arrow to the left of the first line of code. You can move the arrow by choosing Debug | Continue. In that case, all statements up to the first breakpoint are executed, and the yellow arrow moves to that breakpoint.

In debugger mode, SQL Server Management Studio opens two panes, which are placed at the bottom of the editor. All the information concerning the debugging process is displayed in these two panes. Both panes have tabs that you can select to control which set of information is displayed in the pane. The left pane contains Autos, Locals and up to four Watch tabs. The right pane contains Call Stack, Threads, Breakpoints, Command Window, Immediate Window, and Output tabs. For instance, you can use the Locals tab to view values of variables, the Call Stack tab to review the call stack, and the Watch tabs to type (or drag) a part of the code of an SQL expression and to evaluate it. (In Figure 3-13, for instance, the Watch1 tab is activated in the left pane, and the Breakpoints tab is activated in the right pane.)

To end the debugging process, select the blue square icon in the debugging toolbar or choose Debug | Stop Debugging.

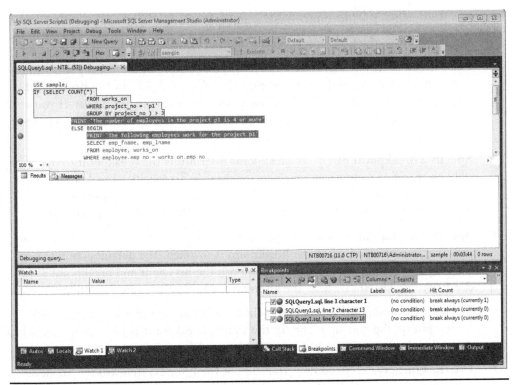

Figure 3-13   *Debugging SQL code*

SQL Server 2012 enhances the functionality of the SQL Server Management Studio
Debugger with several new features. You can now do the following:

▶ **Specify a breakpoint condition**   A breakpoint condition is an SQL expression
whose evaluation determines whether the breakpoint is invoked. To specify a
breakpoint condition, right-click the breakpoint glyph and click Condition on the
pop-up menu. In the Breakpoint Condition dialog box, enter a Boolean expression
and choose either Is True, if you want to break when the expression evaluates to
true, or Has Changed, if you want to break, when the value has changed.

▶ **Specify a breakpoint hit count**   A hit count is a counter that specifies the
number of times a breakpoint is reached. If the specified hit count is reached, and
any specified breakpoint condition is satisfied, the debugger performs the action
specified for the breakpoint. The action could be any of the following:

  ▶ Break always (the default action)

  ▶ Break when the hit count equals a specified value

▶ Break when the hit count equals a multiple of a specified value

▶ Break when the hit count is greater than or equal to a specified value

To specify a hit count, right-click the breakpoint glyph on the Breakpoint window and click Hit Count on the pop-up menu (see Figure 3-13). In the Breakpoint Hit Count dialog box, select one of the actions from the preceding list. If you need to set the hit count to a value, enter an integer in the text box that appears. Click OK to make the modifications.

▶ **Specify a breakpoint filter** A breakpoint filter limits the breakpoint to operating only on specified computers, processes, or threads. To specify a breakpoint filter, choose Breakpoint | Filter. You can then specify the resource that you want to limit in the Breakpoint Filters dialog box. Click OK to make the modifications.

▶ **Specify a breakpoint action** A breakpoint When Hit action specifies a custom task that is performed when the breakpoint is invoked. The default action for a breakpoint is to break execution when both the hit count and breakpoint condition have been satisfied. The alternative could be to print a specified message.

To specify a breakpoint action, right-click the breakpoint glyph and then click When Hit on the pop-up menu. In the When Breakpoint Is Hit dialog box, select the action you want. Click OK to make the modifications.

▶ **Use the QuickWatch window** You can use the QuickWatch window to view the value of a Transact-SQL expression, and then save that expression to a Watch window. (To select the Quick Watch window, choose Debug | Quick Watch.) To select an expression in QuickWatch, either select or enter the name of the expression in the Expression field of the Quick Watch window.

▶ **Use the Quick Info pop-up** When you move the cursor over an SQL identifier, the Quick Info pop-up displays the name of the expression and its current value.

Summary

This chapter covered the most important SQL Server tool: SQL Server Management Studio. SQL Server Management Studio is very useful for end users and administrators alike. It allows many administrative functions to be performed. These are touched on here but are covered in more detail later in the book. This chapter discussed most of the important functions of SQL Server Management Studio concerning end users, such as database and table creation.

SQL Server Management Studio contains, among others, the following components:

▶ **Registered Servers**   Allows you to register SQL Server instances and connect to them.

▶ **Object Explorer**   Contains a tree view of all the database objects in a server.

▶ **Query Editor**   Allows end users to generate, execute, and store Transact-SQL statements. Additionally, it provides the ability to analyze queries by displaying the execution plan.

▶ **Solution Explorer**   Allows you to create solutions. A solution can have zero or more projects associated with it.

▶ **Debugger**   Allows you to debug code.

The next chapter introduces the Transact-SQL language and describes its main components. After introducing the basic concepts and existing data types, the chapter also describes system functions that Transact-SQL supports.

Exercises

E.3.1
Using SQL Server Management Studio, create a database called **test**. Store the database in a file named **testdate_a** in the directory C:\tmp and allocate 10MB of space to it. Configure the file in which the database is located to grow in increments of 2MB, not to exceed a total of 20MB.

E.3.2
Using SQL Server Management Studio, change the transaction log for the **test** database. Give the file an initial size of 3MB, with growth of 20 percent. Allow the file for the transaction log to autogrow.

E.3.3
Using SQL Server Management Studio, allow only the database owner and system administrator to use the **test** database. Is it possible that both users could use the database at the same time?

E.3.4

Using SQL Server Management Studio, create all four tables of the **sample** database (see Chapter 1) with all their columns.

E.3.5

Using SQL Server Management Studio, view which tables the **AdventureWorks** database contains. After that, choose the **Person.Address** table and view its properties.

E.3.6

Using Query Editor, type the following Transact-SQL statement:

```
CREATE DATABASE test
```

Explain the error message shown in the result pane.

E.3.7

Store the Transact-SQL statement in E.3.6 in the file C:\tmp\createdb.sql.

E.3.8

Using Query Editor, how can you make the **test** database the current database?

E.3.9

Using Query Editor, make the **AdventureWorks** database the current database and execute the following Transact-SQL statement:

```
SELECT * FROM Sales.Customer
```

How can you stop the execution of the statement?

E.3.10

Using Query Editor, change the output of the SELECT statement (E.3.9) so that the results appear as the text (and not as the grid).

Part II

Transact-SQL Language

Chapter 4

SQL Components

In This Chapter

- ▶ SQL's Basic Objects
- ▶ Data Types
- ▶ Transact-SQL Functions
- ▶ Scalar Operators
- ▶ NULL Values

his chapter introduces the elementary objects and basic operators supported by the Transact-SQL language. First, the basic language elements, including constants, identifiers, and delimiters, are described. Then, because every elementary object has a corresponding data type, data types are discussed in detail. Additionally, all existing operators and functions are explained. At the end of the chapter, NULL values are introduced.

SQL's Basic Objects

The language of the Database Engine, Transact-SQL, has the same basic features as other common programming languages:

▶ Literal values (also called constants)

▶ Delimiters

▶ Comments

▶ Identifiers

▶ Reserved keywords

The following sections describe these features.

Literal Values

A *literal* value is an alphanumerical, hexadecimal, or numeric constant. A string constant contains one or more characters of the character set enclosed in two single straight quotation marks (' ') or double straight quotation marks (" "). (Single quotation marks are preferred due to the multiple uses of double quotation marks, as discussed in a moment.) If you want to include a single quotation mark within a string delimited by single quotation marks, use two consecutive single quotation marks within the string. Hexadecimal constants are used to represent nonprintable characters and other binary data. Each hexadecimal constant begins with the characters '0x' followed by an even number of characters or numbers. Examples 4.1 and 4.2 illustrate some valid and invalid string constants and hexadecimal constants.

EXAMPLE 4.1

Some valid string constants and hexadecimal constants follow:

'Philadelphia'
"Berkeley, CA 94710"
'9876'
'Apostrophe is displayed like this: can''t' (note the two consecutive single quotation marks)
0x53514C0D

EXAMPLE 4.2

The following are *not* string constants:

'AB'C' (odd number of single quotation marks)
'New York" (same type of quotation mark—single or double—must be used at each
end of the string)

The numeric constants include all integer, fixed-point, and floating-point values with
and without signs (see Example 4.3).

EXAMPLE 4.3

The following are numeric constants:

130
−130.00
−0.357E5 (scientific notation—nEm means n multiplied by 10^m)
22.3E-3

A constant always has a data type and a length, and both depend on the format of
the constant. Additionally, every numeric constant has a precision and a scale factor.
(The data types of the different kinds of literal values are explained later in this
chapter.)

Delimiters

In Transact-SQL, double quotation marks have two meanings. In addition to enclosing
strings, double quotation marks can also be used as delimiters for so-called *delimited
identifiers*. Delimited identifiers are a special kind of identifier usually used to allow the
use of reserved keywords as identifiers and also to allow spaces in the names of database
objects.

NOTE

*Differentiation between single and double quotation marks was first introduced in the SQL92 standard. In the
case of identifiers, this standard differentiates between regular and delimited identifiers. Two key differences
are that delimited identifiers are enclosed in double quotation marks and are case sensitive. (Transact-SQL also
supports the use of square brackets instead of double quotation marks.) Double quotation marks are used only
for delimiting strings. Generally, delimited identifiers were introduced to allow the specification of identifiers,
which are otherwise identical to reserved keywords. Specifically, delimited identifiers protect you from using
names (identifiers and variable names) that could be introduced as reserved keywords in one of the future SQL
standards. Also, delimited identifiers may contain characters that are normally illegal within identifier names,
such as blanks.*

In Transact-SQL, the use of double quotation marks is defined using the QUOTED_IDENTIFIER option of the SET statement. If this option is set to ON, which is the default value, an identifier in double quotation marks will be defined as a delimited identifier. In this case, double quotation marks cannot be used for delimiting strings.

Comments

There are two different ways to specify a comment in a Transact-SQL statement. Using the pair of characters /* and */ marks the enclosed text as a comment. In this case, the comment may extend over several lines. Furthermore, the characters -- (two hyphens) indicate that the remainder of the current line is a comment. (The two -- comply with the ANSI SQL standard, while /* and */ are the extensions of Transact-SQL.)

Identifiers

In Transact-SQL, identifiers are used to identify database objects such as databases, tables, and indices. They are represented by character strings that may include up to 128 characters and may contain letters, numerals, or the following characters: _, @, #, and $. Each name must begin with a letter or one of the following characters: _, @, or #. The character # at the beginning of a table or stored procedure name denotes a temporary object, while @ at the beginning of a name denotes a variable. As indicated earlier, these rules don't apply to delimited identifiers (also known as quoted identifiers), which can contain, or begin with, any character (other than the delimiters themselves).

Reserved Keywords

Each programming language has a set of names with reserved meanings, which must be written and used in the defined format. Names of this kind are called *reserved keywords*. Transact-SQL uses a variety of such names, which, as in many other programming languages, cannot be used as object names, unless the objects are specified as delimited or quoted identifiers.

NOTE

In Transact-SQL, the names of all data types and system functions, such as CHARACTER and INTEGER, are not reserved keywords. Therefore, they can be used to denote objects. (Do not use data types and system functions as object names! Such use makes Transact-SQL statements difficult to read and understand.)

Data Types

All the data values of a column must be of the same data type. (The only exception specifies the values of the SQL_VARIANT data type.) Transact-SQL uses different data types, which can be categorized as follows:

- ▶ Numeric data types
- ▶ Character data types
- ▶ Temporal (date and/or time) data types
- ▶ Miscellaneous data types

The following sections describe all these categories.

Numeric Data Types

Numeric data types are used to represent numbers. The following table shows the list of all numeric data types:

Data Type	Explanation
INTEGER	Represents integer values that can be stored in 4 bytes. The range of values is −2,147,483,648 to 2,147,483,647. INT is the short form for INTEGER.
SMALLINT	Represents integer values that can be stored in 2 bytes. The range of values is −32768 to 32767.
TINYINT	Represents nonnegative integer values that can be stored in 1 byte. The range of values is 0 to 255.
BIGINT	Represents integer values that can be stored in 8 bytes. The range of values is -2^{63} to $2^{63} - 1$.
DECIMAL(p,[s])	Describes fixed-point values. The argument **p** (precision) specifies the total number of digits with assumed decimal point **s** (scale) digits from the right. DECIMAL values are stored, depending on the value of **p**, in 5 to 17 bytes. DEC is the short form for DECIMAL.
NUMERIC(p,[s])	Synonym for DECIMAL.
REAL	Used for floating-point values. The range of positive values is approximately 2.23E − 308 to 1.79E + 308, and the range of negative values is approximately −1.18E − 38 to −1.18E + 38 (the value zero can also be stored).
FLOAT[(p)]	Represents floating point values, like REAL. **p** defines the precision, with **p** < 25 as single precision (stored in 4 bytes) and **p** >= 25 as double precision (stored in 8 bytes).
MONEY	Used for representing monetary values. MONEY values correspond to 8-byte DECIMAL values and are rounded to four digits after the decimal point.
SMALLMONEY	Corresponds to the data type MONEY but is stored in 4 bytes.

Character Data Types

There are two general forms of character data types. They can be strings of single-byte characters or strings of Unicode characters. (Unicode uses several bytes to specify one character.) Further, strings can have fixed or variable length. The following character data types are used:

Data Type	Explanation
CHAR[(n)]	Represents a fixed-length string of single-byte characters, where **n** is the number of characters inside the string. The maximum value of **n** is 8000. CHARACTER(n) is an additional equivalent form for CHAR(n). If **n** is omitted, the length of the string is assumed to be 1.
VARCHAR[(n)]	Describes a variable-length string of single-byte characters (0 < **n** ≤ 8000). In contrast to the CHAR data type, the values for the VARCHAR data type are stored in their actual length. This data type has two synonyms: CHAR VARYING and CHARACTER VARYING.
NCHAR[(n)]	Stores fixed-length strings of Unicode characters. The main difference between the CHAR and NCHAR data types is that each character of the NCHAR data type is stored in 2 bytes, while each character of the CHAR data type uses 1 byte of storage space. Therefore, the maximum number of characters in a column of the NCHAR data type is 4000.
NVARCHAR[(n)]	Stores variable-length strings of Unicode characters. The main difference between the VARCHAR and the NVARCHAR data types is that each NVARCHAR character is stored in 2 bytes, while each VARCHAR character uses 1 byte of storage space. The maximum number of characters in a column of the NVARCHAR data type is 4000.

NOTE

*The VARCHAR data type is identical to the CHAR data type except for one difference: if the content of a CHAR(n) string is shorter than **n** characters, the rest of the string is padded with blanks. (A value of the VARCHAR data type is always stored in its actual length.)*

Temporal Data Types

Transact-SQL supports the following temporal data types:

- ▶ DATETIME
- ▶ SMALLDATETIME
- ▶ DATE
- ▶ TIME
- ▶ DATETIME2
- ▶ DATETIMEOFFSET

The DATETIME and SMALLDATETIME data types specify a date and time, with each value being stored as an integer value in 4 bytes or 2 bytes, respectively. Values of DATETIME and SMALLDATETIME are stored internally as two separate numeric values. The date value of DATETIME is stored in the range 01/01/1753 to 12/31/9999. The analog value of SMALLDATETIME is stored in the range 01/01/1900 to 06/06/2079. The time component is stored in the second 4-byte (or 2-byte for SMALLDATETIME) field as the number of three-hundredths of a second (DATETIME) or minutes (SMALLDATETIME) that have passed since midnight.

The use of DATETIME and SMALLDATETIME is rather inconvenient if you want to store only the date part or time part. For this reason, SQL Server introduced the data types DATE and TIME, which store just the DATE or TIME component of a DATETIME, respectively. The DATE data type is stored in 3 bytes and has the range 01/01/0001 to 12/31/9999. The TIME data type is stored in 3–5 bytes and has an accuracy of 100 nanoseconds (ns).

The DATETIME2 data type stores high-precision date and time data. The data type can be defined for variable lengths depending on the requirement. (The storage size is 6–8 bytes). The accuracy of the time part is 100 ns. This data type isn't aware of Daylight Saving Time.

All the temporal data types described thus far don't have support for the time zone. The data type called DATETIMEOFFSET has the time zone offset portion. For this reason, it is stored in 6–8 bytes. (All other properties of this data type are analogous to the corresponding properties of DATETIME2.)

The date value in Transact-SQL is by default specified as a string in a format like 'mmm dd yyyy' (e.g., 'Jan 10 1993') inside two single quotation marks or double quotation marks. (Note that the relative order of month, day, and year can be controlled by the SET DATEFORMAT statement. Additionally, the system recognizes numeric month values with delimiters of / or –.) Similarly, the time value is specified in the format 'hh:mm' and the Database Engine uses 24-hour time (23:24, for instance).

NOTE

Transact-SQL supports a variety of input formats for DATETIME values. As you already know, both objects are identified separately; thus, date and time values can be specified in any order or alone. If one of the values is omitted, the system uses the default values. (The default value for time is 12:00 AM.)

Examples 4.4 and 4.5 show the different ways date and time values can be written using the different formats.

EXAMPLE 4.4

The following date descriptions can be used:

'28/5/1959' (with SET DATEFORMAT dmy)
'May 28, 1959'
'1959 MAY 28'

EXAMPLE 4.5

The following time expressions can be used:

'8:45 AM'
'4 pm'

Miscellaneous Data Types

Transact-SQL supports several data types that do not belong to any of the data type groups described previously:

▶ Binary data types

▶ BIT

▶ Large object data types

▶ CURSOR (discussed in Chapter 8)

▶ UNIQUEIDENTIFIER

▶ SQL_VARIANT

▶ TABLE (discussed in Chapters 5 and 8)

▶ XML (discussed in Chapter 26)

▶ Spatial (e.g., GEOGRAPHY and GEOMETRY) data types (discussed in Chapter 27)

▶ HIERARCHYID

▶ TIMESTAMP

▶ User-defined data types (discussed in Chapter 5)

The following sections describe each of these data types (other than those designated as being discussed in another chapter).

Binary and BIT Data Types

BINARY and VARBINARY are the two binary data types. They describe data objects being represented in the internal format of the system. They are used to store bit strings. For this reason, the values are entered using hexadecimal numbers.

The values of the BIT data type are stored in a single bit. Therefore, up to 8 bit columns are stored in 1 byte. The following table summarizes the properties of these data types:

Data Type	Explanation
BINARY[(n)]	Specifies a bit string of fixed length with exactly **n** bytes (0 < **n** ≤ 8000).
VARBINARY[(n)]	Specifies a bit string of variable length with up to **n** bytes (0 < **n** ≤ 8000).
BIT	Used for specifying the Boolean data type with three possible values: FALSE, TRUE, and NULL.

Large Object Data Types

Large objects (LOBs) are data objects with the maximum length of 2GB. These objects are generally used to store large text data and to load modules and audio/video files. Transact-SQL supports the following LOB data types:

▶ VARCHAR(max)

▶ NVARCHAR(max)

▶ VARBINARY(max)

Starting with SQL Server 2005, you can use the same programming model to access values of standard data types and LOBs. In other words, you can use convenient system functions and string operators to work with LOBs.

The Database Engine uses the max parameter with the data types VARCHAR, NVARCHAR, and VARBINARY to define variable-length columns. When you use max by default (instead of an explicit value), the system analyzes the length of the particular string and decides whether to store the string as a convenient value or as a LOB. The max parameter indicates that the size of column values can reach the maximum LOB size of the current system.

Although the database system decides how a LOB will be stored, you can override this default specification using the **sp_tableoption** system procedure with the LARGE_VALUE_TYPES_OUT_OF_ROW option. If the option's value is set to 1, the data in columns declared using the max parameter will be stored separately from all other data. If this option is set to 0, the Database Engine stores all values for the row size < 8060 bytes as regular row data.

Since SQL Server 2008, you can apply the new FILESTREAM attribute to a VARBINARY(max) column to store large binary data directly in the NTFS file system. The main advantage of this attribute is that the size of the corresponding LOB is limited only by the file system volume size. (This storage attribute will be described in the upcoming "Storage Options" section.)

UNIQUEIDENTIFIER Data Type

As its name implies, a value of the UNIQUEIDENTIFIER data type is a unique identification number stored as a 16-byte binary string. This data type is closely related to the globally unique identifier (GUID), which guarantees uniqueness worldwide. Hence, using this data type, you can uniquely identify data and objects in distributed systems.

The initialization of a column or a variable of the UNIQUEIDENTIFIER type can be provided using the functions NEWID and NEWSEQUENTIALID, as well as with a string constant written in a special form using hexadecimal digits and hyphens. (The functions NEWID and NEWSEQUENTIALID are described in the section "System Functions" later in this chapter.)

A column of the UNIQUEIDENTIFIER data type can be referenced using the keyword ROWGUIDCOL in a query to specify that the column contains ID values. (This keyword does not generate any values.) A table can have several columns of the UNIQUEIDENTIFIER type, but only one of them can have the ROWGUIDCOL keyword.

SQL_VARIANT Data Type

The SQL_VARIANT data type can be used to store values of various data types at the same time, such as numeric values, strings, and date values. (The only types of values that cannot be stored are TIMESTAMP values.) Each value of an SQL_VARIANT column has two parts: the data value and the information that describes the value. (This information contains all properties of the actual data type of the value, such as length, scale, and precision.)

Transact-SQL supports the SQL_VARIANT_PROPERTY function, which displays the attached information for each value of an SQL_VARIANT column. For the use of the SQL_VARIANT data type, see Example 5.5 in Chapter 5.

NOTE

Declare a column of a table using the SQL_VARIANT data type only if it is really necessary. A column should have this data type if its values may be of different types or if determining the type of a column during the database design process is not possible.

HIERARCHYID Data Type

The HIERARCHYID data type is used to store an entire hierarchy. (For instance, you can use this data type to store a hierarchy of all employees or a hierarchy of all folder lists.) It is implemented as a Common Language Runtime (CLR) user-defined type that comprises several system functions for creating and operating on hierarchy nodes. The following functions, among others, belong to the methods of this data type: GetLevel(), GetAncestor(), GetDescendant(), Read(), and Write(). (The detailed description of this data type is outside the scope of this book.)

TIMESTAMP Data Type

The TIMESTAMP data type specifies a column being defined as VARBINARY(8) or BINARY(8), depending on nullability of the column. The system maintains a current value (not a date or time) for each database, which it increments whenever any row with a TIMESTAMP column is inserted or updated and sets the TIMESTAMP column to that value. Thus, TIMESTAMP columns can be used to determine the relative time at which rows were last changed. (ROWVERSION is a synonym for TIMESTAMP.)

NOTE

The value stored in a TIMESTAMP column isn't important by itself. This column is usually used to detect whether a specific row has been changed since the last time it was accessed.

Storage Options

Since SQL Server 2008, there are two different storage options, each of which allows you to store LOBs and to save storage space:

- ▶ FILESTREAM
- ▶ Sparse columns

The following subsections describe these options.

FILESTREAM Storage

As you already know, SQL Server supports the storage of LOBs using the VARBINARY(max) data type. The property of this data type is that binary large objects (BLOBs) are stored inside the database. This solution can cause performance problems if the stored files are very large, as in the case of video or audio files. In that case, it is common to store such files outside the database, in external files.

The FILESTREAM storage option supports the management of LOBs, which are stored in the NTFS file system. The main advantage of this type of storage is that the database system manages data, although the data is stored outside the database. Therefore, this storage type has the following properties:

▶ You use the CREATE TABLE statement to store FILESTREAM data and use the data modification statements (SELECT, INSERT, UPDATE, and DELETE) to query and update such data.

▶ The database system assures the same level of security for FILESTREAM data as for relational data stored inside the database.

The creation of FILESTREAM data will be described in detail in Chapter 5.

Sparse Columns

The aim of sparse columns as a storage option is quite different from the FILESTREAM storage support. Whereas FILESTREAM is Microsoft's solution for the storage of LOBs outside the database, sparse columns help to minimize data storage space. These columns provide an optimized way to store column values, which are predominantly NULL. (NULL values are described at the end of this chapter.) If you use sparse columns, NULL values require no disk space, but on the other side, non-NULL data needs an additional 2 to 4 bytes, depending on the data type of the non-NULL values. For this reason, Microsoft recommends using sparse columns only when the overall storage space savings will be at least 20 percent.

You specify and access sparse columns in the same way as you specify and access all other columns of a table. This means that the statements SELECT, INSERT, UPDATE, and DELETE can be used to access sparse columns in the same way as you use them for usual columns. (These four SQL statements are described in detail in Chapters 6 and 7.) The only difference is in relation to creation of a sparse column: you use the SPARSE option (after the column name) to specify that a particular column is a sparse column: col_name data_type SPARSE.

If a table has several sparse columns, you can group them in a column set. Therefore, a column set is an alternative way to store and access all sparse columns in a table. For more information concerning column sets, see Books Online.

Transact-SQL Functions

Transact-SQL functions can be either aggregate functions or scalar functions. The following sections describe these function types.

Aggregate Functions

Aggregate functions are applied to a group of data values from a column. Aggregate functions always return a single value. Transact-SQL supports several groups of aggregate functions:

- ▶ Convenient aggregate functions
- ▶ Statistical aggregate functions
- ▶ User-defined aggregate functions
- ▶ Analytic aggregate functions

Statistical and analytic aggregate functions are discussed in Chapter 23. User-defined aggregates are beyond the scope of this book. That leaves the convenient aggregate functions, described next:

- ▶ **AVG** Calculates the arithmetic mean (average) of the data values contained within a column. The column must contain numeric values.

- ▶ **MAX** and **MIN** Calculate the maximum and minimum data value of the column, respectively. The column can contain numeric, string, and date/time values.

- ▶ **SUM** Calculates the total of all data values in a column. The column must contain numeric values.

- ▶ **COUNT** Calculates the number of (non-null) data values in a column. The only aggregate function that is not applied to columns is COUNT(*). This function returns the number of rows (whether or not particular columns have NULL values).

- ▶ **COUNT_BIG** Analogous to COUNT, the only difference being that COUNT_BIG returns a value of the BIGINT data type.

The use of convenient aggregate functions with the SELECT statement can be found in Chapter 6.

Scalar Functions

In addition to aggregate functions, Transact-SQL provides several scalar functions that are used in the construction of scalar expressions. (A scalar function operates on a single value or list of values, whereas an aggregate function operates on the data from multiple rows.) Scalar functions can be categorized as follows:

▶ Numeric functions

▶ Date functions

▶ String functions

▶ System functions

▶ Metadata functions

The following sections describe these function types.

Numeric Functions

Numeric functions within Transact-SQL are mathematical functions for modifying numeric values. The following numeric functions are available:

Function	Explanation
ABS(n)	Returns the absolute value (i.e., negative values are returned as positive) of the numeric expression **n**. Example: SELECT ABS(−5.767) = 5.767, SELECT ABS(6.384) = 6.384
ACOS(n)	Calculates arc cosine of **n**. **n** and the resulting value belong to the FLOAT data type.
ASIN(n)	Calculates the arc sine of **n**. **n** and the resulting value belong to the FLOAT data type.
ATAN(n)	Calculates the arc tangent of **n**. **n** and the resulting value belong to the FLOAT data type.
ATN2(n,m)	Calculates the arc tangent of **n/m**. **n**, **m**, and the resulting value belong to the FLOAT data type.
CEILING(n)	Returns the smallest integer value greater than or equal to the specified parameter. Examples: SELECT CEILING(4.88) = 5 SELECT CEILING(−4.88) = −4
COS(n)	Calculates the cosine of **n**. **n** and the resulting value belong to the FLOAT data type.
COT(n)	Calculates the cotangent of **n**. **n** and the resulting value belong to the FLOAT data type.
DEGREES(n)	Converts radians to degrees. Examples: SELECT DEGREES(PI()/2) = 90 SELECT DEGREES(0.75) = 42
EXP(n)	Calculates the value e^n. Example: SELECT EXP(1) = 2.7183

Function	Explanation
FLOOR(n)	Calculates the largest integer value less than or equal to the specified value **n**. Example: SELECT FLOOR(4.88) = 4
LOG(n)	Calculates the natural (i.e., base e) logarithm of **n**. Examples: SELECT LOG(4.67) = 1.54 SELECT LOG(0.12) = −2.12
LOG10(n)	Calculates the logarithm (base 10) for **n**. Examples: SELECT LOG10(4.67) = 0.67 SELECT LOG10(0.12) = −0.92
PI()	Returns the value of the number pi (3.14).
POWER(x,y)	Calculates the value **x^y**. Examples: SELECT POWER(3.12,5) = 295.65 SELECT POWER(81,0.5) = 9
RADIANS(n)	Converts degrees to radians. Examples: SELECT RADIANS(90.0) = 1.57 SELECT RADIANS(42.97) = 0.75
RAND()	Returns a random number between 0 and 1 with a FLOAT data type.
ROUND(n, p,[t])	Rounds the value of the number **n** by using the precision **p**. Use positive values of **p** to round on the right side of the decimal point and use negative values to round on the left side. An optional parameter **t** causes **n** to be truncated. Examples: SELECT ROUND(5.4567,3) = 5.4570 SELECT ROUND(345.4567,−1) = 350.0000 SELECT ROUND(345.4567,−1,1) = 340.0000
ROWCOUNT_BIG	Returns the number of rows that have been affected by the last Transact-SQL statement executed by the system. The return value of this function has the BIGINT data type.
SIGN(n)	Returns the sign of the value **n** as a number (+1 for positive, −1 for negative, and 0 for zero). Example: SELECT SIGN(0.88) = 1.00
SIN(n)	Calculates the sine of **n**. **n** and the resulting value belong to the FLOAT data type.
SQRT(n)	Calculates the square root of **n**. Example: SELECT SQRT(9) = 3
SQUARE(n)	Returns the square of the given expression. Example: SELECT SQUARE(9) = 81
TAN(n)	Calculates the tangent of **n**. **n** and the resulting value belong to the FLOAT data type.

Date Functions

Date functions calculate the respective date or time portion of an expression or return the value from a time interval. Transact-SQL supports the following date functions:

Function	Explanation
GETDATE()	Returns the current system date and time. Example: SELECT GETDATE() = 2011-01-01 13:03:31.390
DATEPART(item,date)	Returns the specified part **item** of a date **date** as an integer. Examples: SELECT DATEPART(month, '01.01.2005') = 1 (1 = January) SELECT DATEPART(weekday, '01.01.2005') = 7 (7 = Sunday)
DATENAME(item,date)	Returns the specified part **item** of the date **date** as a character string. Example: SELECT DATENAME(weekday, '01.01.2005') = Saturday
DATEDIFF(item,dat1,dat2)	Calculates the difference between the two date parts **dat1** and **dat2** and returns the result as an integer in units specified by the value **item**. Example (returns the age of each employee): SELECT DATEDIFF(year, BirthDate, GETDATE()) AS age FROM employee
DATEADD(i,n,d)	Adds the number **n** of units specified by the value **i** to the given date **d**. (**n** could be negative, too.) Example (adds three days to the start date of employment of every employee; see the **sample** database): SELECT DATEADD(DAY,3,HireDate) AS age FROM employee

String Functions

String functions are used to manipulate data values in a column, usually of a character data type. Transact-SQL supports the following string functions:

Function	Explanation
ASCII(character)	Converts the specified character to the equivalent integer (ASCII) code. Returns an integer. Example: SELECT ASCII('A') = 65
CHAR(integer)	Converts the ASCII code to the equivalent character. Example: SELECT CHAR(65) = 'A'
CHARINDEX(z1,z2)	Returns the starting position where the partial string **z1** first occurs in the string **z2**. Returns 0 if **z1** does not occur in **z2**. Example: SELECT CHARINDEX('bl', 'table') = 3
DIFFERENCE(z1,z2)	Returns an integer, 0 through 4, that is the difference of SOUNDEX values of two strings **z1** and **z2**. (SOUNDEX returns a number that specifies the sound of a string. With this method, strings with similar sounds can be determined.) Example: SELECT DIFFERENCE('spelling', 'telling') = 2 (sounds a little bit similar, 0 = doesn't sound similar)

Function	Explanation
LEFT(z, length)	Returns the first **length** characters from the string **z**.
LEN(z)	Returns the number of characters, instead of the number of bytes, of the specified string expression, excluding trailing blanks.
LOWER(z1)	Converts all uppercase letters of the string **z1** to lowercase letters. Lowercase letters and numbers, and other characters, do not change. Example: SELECT LOWER('BiG') = 'big'
LTRIM(z)	Removes leading blanks in the string **z**. Example: SELECT LTRIM(' String') = 'String'
NCHAR(i)	Returns the Unicode character with the specified integer code, as defined by the Unicode standard.
QUOTENAME(char_string)	Returns a Unicode string with the delimiters added to make the input string a valid delimited identifier.
PATINDEX(%p%,expr)	Returns the starting position of the first occurrence of a pattern **p** in a specified expression **expr**, or zeros if the pattern is not found. Examples (the second query returns all first names from the **customers** column): SELECT PATINDEX('%gs%', 'longstring') = 4 SELECT RIGHT(ContactName, LEN(ContactName)-PATINDEX('% %',ContactName)) AS First_ name FROM Customers
REPLACE(str1,str2,str3)	Replaces all occurrences of the **str2** in the **str1** with the **str3**. Example: SELECT REPLACE('shave' , 's' , 'be') = behave
REPLICATE(z,i)	Repeats string **z i** times. Example: SELECT REPLICATE('a',10) = 'aaaaaaaaaa'
REVERSE(z)	Displays the string **z** in the reverse order. Example: SELECT REVERSE('calculate') = 'etaluclac'
RIGHT(z,length)	Returns the last **length** characters from the string **z**. Example: SELECT RIGHT('Notebook',4) = 'book'
RTRIM(z)	Removes trailing blanks of the string **z**. Example: SELECT RTRIM('Notebook ') = 'Notebook'
SOUNDEX(a)	Returns a four-character SOUNDEX code to determine the similarity between two strings. Example: SELECT SOUNDEX('spelling') = S145
SPACE(length)	Returns a string with spaces of length specified by **length**. Example: SELECT SPACE(4) = ' '
STR(f,[len [,d]])	Converts the specified float expression **f** into a string. **len** is the length of the string including decimal point, sign, digits, and spaces (10 by default), and **d** is the number of digits to the right of the decimal point to be returned. Example: SELECT STR(3.45678,4,2) = '3.46'

Function	Explanation
STUFF(z1,a,length,z2)	Replaces the partial string **z1** with the partial string **z2** starting at position **a**, replacing **length** characters of **z1**. Examples: SELECT STUFF('Notebook',5,0, ' in a ') = 'Note in a book' SELECT STUFF('Notebook',1,4, 'Hand') = 'Handbook'
SUBSTRING(z,a,length)	Creates a partial string from string **z** starting at the position **a** with a length of **length**. Example: SELECT SUBSTRING('wardrobe',1,4) = 'ward'
UNICODE	Returns the integer value, as defined by the Unicode standard, for the first character of the input expression.
UPPER(z)	Converts all lowercase letters of string **z** to uppercase letters. Uppercase letters and numbers do not change. Example: SELECT UPPER('loWer') = 'LOWER'

System Functions

System functions of Transact-SQL provide extensive information about database objects. Most system functions use an internal numeric identifier (ID), which is assigned to each database object by the system at its creation. Using this identifier, the system can uniquely identify each database object. System functions provide information about the database system. The following table describes several system functions. (For the complete list of all system functions, please see Books Online.)

Function	Explanation
CAST(a AS type [(length)])	Converts an expression **a** into the specified data type **type** (if possible). **a** could be any valid expression. Example: SELECT CAST(3000000000 AS BIGINT) = 3000000000
COALESCE($a_1, a_2, \ldots$)	Returns for a given list of expressions a_1, a_2,... the value of the first expression that is not NULL.
COL_LENGTH(obj,col)	Returns the length of the column **col** belonging to the database object (table or view) **obj**. Example: SELECT COL_LENGTH('customers', 'cust_ID') = 10
CONVERT(type[(length)],a)	Equivalent to CAST, but the arguments are specified differently. CONVERT can be used with any data type.

Function	Explanation
CURRENT_TIMESTAMP	Returns the current date and time. Example: SELECT CURRENT_TIMESTAMP = '2011-01-01 17:22:55.670'
CURRENT_USER	Returns the name of the current user.
DATALENGTH(z)	Calculates the length (in bytes) of the result of the expression **z**. Example (returns the length of each field): SELECT DATALENGTH(ProductName) FROM products
GETANSINULL('dbname')	Returns 1 if the use of NULL values in the database **dbname** complies with the ANSI SQL standard. (See also the explanation of NULL values at the end of this chapter.) Example: SELECT GETANSINULL('AdventureWorks') = 1
ISNULL(expr, value)	Returns the value of **expr** if that value is not null; otherwise, it returns **value**.
ISNUMERIC(expression)	Determines whether an expression is a valid numeric type.
NEWID()	Creates a unique ID number that consists of a 16-byte binary string intended to store values of the UNIQUEIDENTIFIER data type.
NEWSEQUENTIALID()	Creates a GUID that is greater than any GUID previously generated by this function on a specified computer. (This function can be used only as a default value for a column.)
NULLIF(expr$_1$,expr$_2$)	Returns the NULL value if the expressions **expr$_1$** and **expr$_2$** are equal. Example (returns NULL for the project with the project_no = 'p1'): SELECT NULLIF(project_no, 'p1') FROM projects
SERVERPROPERTY(propertyname)	Returns the property information about the database server.
SYSTEM_USER	Returns the login ID of the current user. Example: SELECT SYSTEM_USER = LTB13942\dusan
USER_ID([user_name])	Returns the identifier of the user **user_name**. If no name is specified, the identifier of the current user is retrieved. Example: SELECT USER_ID('guest') = 2
USER_NAME([id])	Returns the name of the user with the identifier **id**. If no name is specified, the name of the current user is retrieved. Example: SELECT USER_NAME(1) = 'dbo'

All string functions can be nested in any order; for example, REVERSE(CURRENT_USER).

Metadata Functions

Generally, metadata functions return information about the specified database and database objects. The following table describes several metadata functions. (For the complete list of all metadata functions, please see Books Online.)

Function	Explanation
COL_NAME(tab_id, col_id)	Returns the name of a column belonging to the table with the ID **tab_id** and column ID **col_id**. Example: SELECT COL_NAME(OBJECT_ID('employee') , 3) = 'emp_lname'
COLUMNPROPERTY(id, col, property)	Returns the information about the specified column. Example: SELECT COLUMNPROPERTY(object_id('project'), 'project_no', 'PRECISION') = 4
DATABASEPROPERTYEX(database, property)	Returns the named database property value for the specified database and property. Example (specifies whether the database follows SQL-92 rules for allowing NULL values): SELECT DATABASEPROPERTYEX('sample', 'IsAnsiNullDefault') = 0
DB_ID([db_name])	Returns the identifier of the database **db_name**. If no name is specified, the identifier of the current database is returned. Example: SELECT DB_ID('AdventureWorks') = 6
DB_NAME([db_id])	Returns the name of the database with the identifier **db_id**. If no identifier is specified, the name of the current database is displayed. Example: SELECT DB_NAME(6) = 'AdventureWorks'
INDEX_COL(table, i, no)	Returns the name of the indexed column in the table **table**, defined by the index identifier **i** and the position **no** of the column in the index.
INDEXPROPERTY(obj_id, index_name, property)	Returns the named index or statistics property value of a specified table identification number, index or statistics name, and property name.
OBJECT_NAME(obj_id)	Returns the name of the database object with the identifier **obj_id**. Example: SELECT OBJECT_NAME(453576654) = 'products'
OBJECT_ID(obj_name)	Returns the identifier of the database object **obj_name**. Example: SELECT OBJECT_ID('products') = 453576654
OBJECTPROPERTY(obj_id,property)	Returns the information about the objects from the current database.

Scalar Operators

Scalar operators are used for operations with scalar values. Transact-SQL supports numeric and Boolean operators as well as concatenation.

There are unary and binary arithmetic operators. Unary operators are + and − (as signs). Binary arithmetic operators are +, −, *, /, and %. (The first four binary operators have their respective mathematical meanings, whereas % is the modulo operator.)

Boolean operators have two different notations depending on whether they are applied to bit strings or to other data types. The operators NOT, AND, and OR are applied to all data types (except BIT). They are described in detail in Chapter 6.

The bitwise operators for manipulating bit strings are listed here, and Example 4.6 shows how they are used:

► ~ Complement (i.e., NOT)

► & Conjunction of bit strings (i.e., AND)

► | Disjunction of bit strings (i.e., OR)

► ∧ Exclusive disjunction (i.e., XOR or Exclusive OR)

EXAMPLE 4.6

~(1001001) = (0110110)
(11001001) | (10101101) = (11101101)
(11001001) & (10101101) = (10001001)
(11001001) ∧ (10101101) = (01100100)

The concatenation operator + can be used to concatenate two character strings or bit strings.

Global Variables

Global variables are special system variables that can be used as if they were scalar constants. Transact-SQL supports many global variables, which have to be preceded by the prefix @@. The following table describes several global variables. (For the complete list of all global variables, see Books Online.)

Variable	Explanation
@@CONNECTIONS	Returns the number of login attempts since starting the system.
@@CPU_BUSY	Returns the total CPU time (in units of milliseconds) used since starting the system.
@@ERROR	Returns the information about the return value of the last executed Transact-SQL statement.
@@IDENTITY	Returns the last inserted value for the column with the IDENTITY property (see Chapter 6).
@@LANGID	Returns the identifier of the language that is currently used by the database system.
@@LANGUAGE	Returns the name of the language that is currently used by the database system.
@@MAX_CONNECTIONS	Returns the maximum number of actual connections to the system.

Variable	Explanation
@@PROCID	Returns the identifier for the stored procedure currently being executed.
@@ROWCOUNT	Returns the number of rows that have been affected by the last Transact-SQL statement executed by the system.
@@SERVERNAME	Retrieves information about the local database server. This information contains, among other things, the name of the server and the name of the instance.
@@SPID	Returns the identifier of the server process.
@@VERSION	Returns the current version of the database system software.

NULL Values

A NULL value is a special value that may be assigned to a column. This value normally is used when information in a column is unknown or not applicable. For example, in the case of an unknown home telephone number for a company's employee, it is recommended that the NULL value be assigned to the **home_telephone** column.

Any arithmetic expression results in a NULL if any operand of that expression is itself a NULL value. Therefore, in unary arithmetic expressions (if A is an expression with a NULL value), both +A and −A return NULL. In binary expressions, if one (or both) of the operands A or B has the NULL value, A + B, A − B, A * B, A / B, and A % B also result in a NULL. (The operands A and B have to be numerical expressions.)

If an expression contains a relational operation and one (or both) of the operands has (have) the NULL value, the result of this operation will be NULL. Hence, each of the expressions A = B, A <> B, A < B, and A > B also returns NULL.

In the Boolean AND, OR, and NOT, the behavior of the NULL values is specified by the following truth tables, where T stands for true, U for unknown (NULL), and F for false. In these tables, follow the row and column represented by the values of the Boolean expressions that the operator works on, and the value where they intersect represents the resulting value.

AND	T	U	F		OR	T	U	F		NOT	
T	T	U	F		T	T	T	T		T	F
U	U	U	F		U	T	U	U		U	U
F	F	F	F		F	T	U	F		F	T

Any NULL value in the argument of aggregate functions AVG, SUM, MAX, MIN, and COUNT is eliminated before the respective function is calculated (except for the function COUNT(*)). If a column contains only NULL values, the function returns NULL. The aggregate function COUNT(*) handles all NULL values the same as non-NULL values. If the column contains only NULL values, the result of the function COUNT(DISTINCT column_name) is 0.

A NULL value has to be different from all other values. For numeric data types, there is a distinction between the value zero and NULL. The same is true for the empty string and NULL for character data types.

A column of a table allows NULL values if its definition explicitly contains NULL. On the other hand, NULL values are not permitted if the definition of a column explicitly contains NOT NULL. If the user does not specify NULL or NOT NULL for a column with a data type (except TIMESTAMP), the following values are assigned:

▶ **NULL**   If the ANSI_NULL_DFLT_ON option of the SET statement is set to ON

▶ **NOT NULL**   If the ANSI_NULL_DFLT_OFF option of the SET statement is set to ON

If the SET statement isn't activated, a column will contain the value NOT NULL by default. (The columns of TIMESTAMP data type can be declared only as NOT NULL.)

Summary

The basic features of Transact-SQL consist of data types, predicates, and functions. Data types comply with data types of the ANSI SQL92 standard. Transact-SQL supports a variety of useful system functions.

The next chapter introduces you to Transact-SQL statements in relation to SQL's data definition language. This part of Transact-SQL comprises all the statements needed for creating, altering, and removing database objects.

Exercises

E.4.1

What is the difference between the numeric data types INT, SMALLINT, and TINYINT?

E.4.2

What is the difference between the data types CHAR and VARCHAR? When should you use the latter (instead of the former) and vice versa?

E.4.3

How can you set the format of a column with the DATE data type so that its values can be entered in the form 'yyyy/mm/dd'?

In the following two exercises, use the SELECT statement in the Query Editor component window of SQL Server Management Studio to display the result of all system functions and global variables. (For instance, SELECT host_id() displays the ID number of the current host.)

E.4.4

Using system functions, find the ID number of the **test** database (Exercise 2.1).

E.4.5

Using the system variables, display the current version of the database system software and the language that is used by this software.

E.4.6

Using the bitwise operators &, |, and ^, calculate the following operations with the bit strings:

(11100101) & (01010111)
(10011011) | (11001001)
(10110111) ^ (10110001)

E.4.7

What is the result of the following expressions? (A is a numerical expression and B is a logical expression.)

A + NULL
NULL = NULL
B OR NULL
B AND NULL

E.4.8

When can you use both single and double quotation marks to define string and temporal constants?

E.4.9

What is a delimited identifier and when do you need it?

Chapter 5

Data Definition Language

In This Chapter

- ► **Creating Database Objects**
- ► **Modifying Database Objects**
- ► **Removing Database Objects**

This chapter describes all the Transact-SQL statements concerning data definition language (DDL). The DDL statements are divided into three groups, which are discussed in turn. The first group includes statements that create objects, the second group includes statements that modify the structure of objects, and the third group includes statements that remove objects.

Creating Database Objects

The organization of a database involves many different objects. All objects of a database are either physical or logical. The physical objects are related to the organization of the data on the physical device (disk). The Database Engine's physical objects are files and filegroups. Logical objects represent a user's view of a database. Databases, tables, columns, and views (virtual tables) are examples of logical objects.

The first database object that has to be created is a database itself. The Database Engine manages both system and user databases. An authorized user can create user databases, while system databases are generated during the installation of the database system.

This chapter describes the creation, alteration, and removal of user databases, while Chapter 15 covers all system databases in detail.

Creation of a Database

Two basic methods are used to create a database. The first method involves using Object Explorer in SQL Server Management Studio (see Chapter 3). The second method involves using the Transact-SQL statement CREATE DATABASE. This statement has the following general form, the details of which are discussed next:

```
CREATE DATABASE db_name
     [ON [PRIMARY] { file_spec1} ,...]
     [LOG ON {file_spec2} ,...]
       [COLLATE collation_name]
  [FOR {ATTACH | ATTACH_REBUILD_LOG } ]
```

NOTE

For the syntax of the Transact-SQL statements, the conventions used are those described in the section "Syntax Conventions" in Chapter 1. According to the conventions, optional items appear in brackets, [ ]. Items written in braces, { }, and followed by "..." are items that can be repeated any number of times.

db_name is the name of the database. The maximum size of a database name is 128 characters. (The rules for identifiers described in Chapter 4 apply to database names.) The maximum number of databases managed by a single system is 32,767.

All databases are stored in files. These files can be explicitly specified by the system administrator or implicitly provided by the system. If the ON option exists in the CREATE DATABASE statement, all files containing the data of a database are explicitly specified.

NOTE

The Database Engine uses disk files to store data. Each disk file contains data of a single database. Files themselves can be organized into filegroups. Filegroups provide the ability to distribute data over different disk drives and to back up and restore subsets of the database (useful for very large databases).

file_spec1 represents a file specification, which includes further options such as the logical name of the file, the physical name, and the size. The PRIMARY option specifies the first (and most important) file that contains system tables and other important internal information concerning the database. If the PRIMARY option is omitted, the first file listed in the specification is used as the primary file.

A login account of the Database Engine that is used to create a database is called a database owner. A database can have one owner, who always corresponds to a login account name. The login account, which is the database owner, has the special name **dbo**. This name is always used in relation to a database it owns.

dbo uses the LOG ON option to define one or more files as the physical destination of the transaction log of the database. If the LOG ON option is not specified, the transaction log of the database will still be created because every database must have at least one transaction log file. (The Database Engine keeps a record of each change it makes to the database. The system keeps all those records, in particular before and after values, in one or more files called the transaction log. Each database of the system has its own transaction log. Transaction logs are discussed in detail in Chapter 13.)

With the COLLATE option, you can specify the default collation for the database. If the COLLATE option is not specified, the database is assigned the default collation of the **model** database, which is the same as the default collation of the database system.

The FOR ATTACH option specifies that the database is created by attaching an existing set of files. If this option is used, you have to explicitly specify the first primary file. The FOR ATTACH_REBUILD_LOG option specifies that the database is created by attaching an existing set of operating system files. (Attaching and detaching a database is described later in this chapter.)

During the creation of a new database, the Database Engine uses the **model** database as a template. The properties of the **model** database can be changed to suit the personal conception of the system administrator.

NOTE

*If you have a database object that should exist in each user database, you should create that object in the **model** database first.*

Example 5.1 creates a simple database without any further specifications. To execute this statement, type it in the Query Editor window of SQL Server Management Studio and press F5.

EXAMPLE 5.1

```
USE master;
CREATE DATABASE sample;
```

Example 5.1 creates a database named **sample**. This concise form of the CREATE DATABASE statement is possible because almost all options of that statement have default values. The system creates, by default, two files. The logical name of the data file is **sample** and its original size is 2MB. Similarly, the logical name of the transaction log is **sample_log** and its original size is 1MB. (Both size values, as well as other properties of the new database, depend on corresponding specifications in the **model** database.)

Example 5.2 creates a database with explicit specifications for database and transaction log files.

EXAMPLE 5.2

```
USE master;
CREATE DATABASE projects
   ON (NAME=projects_dat,
       FILENAME = 'C:\projects.mdf',
       SIZE = 10,
       MAXSIZE = 100,
       FILEGROWTH = 5)
LOG ON
   (NAME=projects_log,
       FILENAME = 'C:\projects.ldf',
       SIZE = 40,
       MAXSIZE = 100,
       FILEGROWTH = 10);
```

Example 5.2 creates a database called **projects**. Because the PRIMARY option is omitted, the first file is assumed to be the primary file. This file has the logical name **projects_dat** and is stored in the file **projects.mdf**. The original size of this file is 10MB. Additional portions of 5MB of disk storage are allocated by the system, if needed. If the MAXSIZE option is not specified or is set to UNLIMITED, the file will grow until the disk is full. (The KB, TB, and MB suffixes can be used to specify kilobytes, terabytes, or megabytes, respectively—the default is MB.)

There is also a single transaction log file with the logical name **projects_log** and the physical name **projects.ldf**. All options of the file specification for the transaction log have the same name and meaning as the corresponding options of the file specification for the data file.

Using the Transact-SQL language, you can apply the USE statement to change the database context to the specified database. (The alternative way is to select the database name in the Database pull-down menu in the toolbar of SQL Server Management Studio.)

The system administrator can assign a default database to a user by using the CREATE LOGIN statement or the ALTER LOGIN statement (see also Chapter 12). In this case, the users do not need to execute the USE statement if they want to use their default database.

Creation of a Database Snapshot

The CREATE DATABASE statement can also be used to create a database snapshot of an existing database (source database). A database snapshot is transactionally consistent with the source database as it existed at the time of the snapshot's creation.

The syntax for the creation of a snapshot is

```
CREATE DATABASE database_snapshot_name
    ON  (NAME = logical_file_name,
            FILENAME = 'os_file_name') [ ,...n ]
            AS SNAPSHOT OF source_database_name
```

As you can see, if you want to create a database snapshot, you have to add the AS SNAPSHOT OF clause in the CREATE DATABASE statement. Example 5.3 creates a snapshot of the **AdventureWorks** database and stores it in the C:\temp data directory. (You must create this directory before you start the following example. Also, you have to download and create the **AdventureWorks** database, if this database does not exist on your system.) The **AdventureWorks** database is a sample database of SQL Server and can be downloaded from Microsoft's Codeplex page.

EXAMPLE 5.3

```
USE master;
CREATE DATABASE AdventurWorks_snapshot
    ON (NAME = 'AdventureWorks_Data' ,
            FILENAME = 'C:\temp\snapshot_DB.mdf')
        AS SNAPSHOT OF AdventureWorks;
```

An existing database snapshot is a read-only copy of the corresponding database that reflects the point in time when the database is copied. (For this reason, you can have multiple snapshots for an existing database.) The snapshot file (in Example 5.3, 'C:\temp\snapshot_DB.mdf') contains only the modified data that has changed from the source database. Therefore, the process of creating a database snapshot must include the logical name of each data file from the source database as well as new corresponding physical names (see Example 5.3).

While the snapshot contains only modified data, the disk space needed for each snapshot is just a small part of the overall space required for the corresponding source database.

NOTE

To create snapshots of a database, you need NTFS disk volumes, because only such volumes support the sparse file technology that is used for storing snapshots.

Database snapshots are usually used as a mechanism to protect data against user errors.

Attaching and Detaching Databases

All data of a database can be detached and then attached to the same or another database server. Detaching and attaching a database should be done if you want to move the database.

You can detach a database from a database server by using the **sp_detach_db** system procedure. (The detached database must be in the single-user mode.)

To attach a database, use the CREATE DATABASE statement with the FOR ATTACH clause. When you attach a database, all data files must be available. If any data file has a different path from when the database was first created, you must specify the file's current path.

CREATE TABLE: A Basic Form

The CREATE TABLE statement creates a new base table with all corresponding columns and their data types. The basic form of the CREATE TABLE statement is

```
CREATE TABLE table_name
    (col_name1 type1 [NOT NULL| NULL]
    [{, col_name2 type2 [NOT NULL| NULL]} ...])
```

> **NOTE**
>
> _Besides base tables, there are also some special kinds of tables, such as temporary tables and views (see Chapters 6 and 11, respectively)._

table_name is the name of the created base table. The maximum number of tables per database is limited by the number of objects in the database (there can be more than 2 billion objects in a database, including tables, views, stored procedures, triggers, and constraints). **col_name1**, **col_name2**,... are the names of the table columns. **type1**, **type2**,... are data types of corresponding columns (see Chapter 4).

> **NOTE**
>
> _The name of a database object can generally contain four parts, in the form:_
> `[server_name. [db_name. [schema_name. ]]]object_name`
> **object_name** _is the name of the database object._ **schema_name** _is the name of the schema to which the object belongs._ **server_name** _and_ **db_name** _are the names of the server and database to which the database object belongs. Table names, combined with the schema name, must be unique within the database. Similarly, column names must be unique within the table._

The first constraint that will be discussed in this book is the existence and nonexistence of NULL values within a column. If NOT NULL is specified, the assignment of NULL values for the column is not allowed. (In that case, the column may not contain NULLs, and if there is a NULL value to be inserted, the system returns an error message.)

As already stated, a database object (in this case, a table) is always created within a schema of a database. A user can create a table only in a schema for which she has ALTER permissions. Any user in the **sysadmin**, **db_ddladmin**, or **db_owner** role can create a table in any schema. (The ALTER permissions, as well as database and server roles, are discussed in detail in Chapter 12.)

The creator of a table must not be its owner. This means that you can create a table that belongs to someone else. Similarly, a table created with the CREATE TABLE statement must not belong to the current database if some other (existing) database name, together with the schema name, is specified as the prefix of the table name.

The schema to which a table belongs has two possible default names. If a table is specified without the explicit schema name, the system checks for a table name in the corresponding default schema. If the object name cannot be found in the default schema, the system searches in the **dbo** schema.

NOTE

You should always specify the table name together with the corresponding schema name. That way you can eliminate possible ambiguities.

Temporary tables are a special kind of base table. They are stored in the **tempdb** database and are automatically dropped at the end of the session. The properties of temporary tables and examples concerning them are given in Chapter 6.

Example 5.4 shows the creation of all tables of the **sample** database. (The **sample** database should be the current database.)

EXAMPLE 5.4

```
USE sample;
CREATE TABLE employee   (emp_no INTEGER NOT NULL,
                         emp_fname CHAR(20) NOT NULL,
                         emp_lname CHAR(20) NOT NULL,
                         dept_no CHAR(4) NULL);
CREATE TABLE department (dept_no CHAR(4) NOT NULL,
                         dept_name CHAR(25) NOT NULL,
                         location CHAR(30) NULL);
CREATE TABLE project    (project_no CHAR(4) NOT NULL,
                         project_name CHAR(15) NOT NULL,
                         budget FLOAT NULL);
CREATE TABLE works_on   (emp_no INTEGER NOT NULL,
                         project_no CHAR(4) NOT NULL,
                         job CHAR (15) NULL,
                         enter_date DATE NULL);
```

Besides the data type and the nullability, the column specification can contain the following options:

▶ DEFAULT clause

▶ IDENTITY property

The DEFAULT clause in the column definition specifies the default value of the column—that is, whenever a new row is inserted into the table, the default value for the particular column will be used if there is no value specified for it. A constant value, such as the system functions USER, CURRENT_USER, SESSION_USER, SYSTEM_USER, CURRENT_TIMESTAMP, and NULL, among others, can be used as the default values.

A column with the IDENTITY property allows only integer values, which are usually implicitly assigned by the system. Each value, which should be inserted in the column, is calculated by incrementing the last inserted value of the column. Therefore, the definition of a column with the IDENTITY property contains (implicitly or explicitly) an initial value and an increment. This property will be discussed in detail in the next chapter (see Example 6.42).

To close this section, Example 5.5 shows the creation of a table with a column of the SQL_VARIANT type.

EXAMPLE 5.5

```
USE sample;
CREATE TABLE Item_Attributes  (
        item_id INT NOT NULL,
        attribute NVARCHAR(30) NOT NULL,
        value SQL_VARIANT NOT NULL,
        PRIMARY KEY (item_id, attribute) )
```

In Example 5.5, the table contains the **value** column, which is of type SQL_VARIANT. As you already know from Chapter 4, the SQL_VARIANT data type can be used to store values of various data types at the same time, such as numeric values, strings, and date values. Note that in Example 5.5 the SQL_VARIANT data type is used for the column values, because different attribute values may be of different data types. For example, the size attribute stores an integer attribute value, and the name attribute stores a character string attribute value.

CREATE TABLE and Declarative Integrity Constraints

One of the most important features that a DBMS must provide is a way of maintaining the integrity of data. The constraints, which are used to check the modification or insertion of data, are called *integrity constraints*. The task of maintaining integrity constraints can be handled by the user in application programs or by the DBMS. The most important benefits of handling integrity constraints by the DBMS are the following:

▶ Increased reliability of data

▶ Reduced programming time

▶ Simple maintenance

Using the DBMS to define integrity constraints increases the reliability of data because there is no possibility that the integrity constraints can be forgotten by a programmer. (If an integrity constraint is handled by application programs, *all* programs concerning the constraint must include the corresponding code. If the code is omitted in one application program, the consistency of data is compromised.)

An integrity constraint not handled by the DBMS must be defined in every application program that uses the data involved in the constraint. In contrast, the same integrity constraint must be defined only once if it is to be handled by the DBMS. Additionally, application-enforced constraints are usually more complex to code than are database-enforced constraints.

If an integrity constraint is handled by the DBMS, the modification of the structure of the constraint must be handled only once, in the DBMS. The modification of a structure in application programs requires the modification of every program that involves the corresponding code.

There are two groups of integrity constraints handled by a DBMS:

▶ Declarative integrity constraints

▶ Procedural integrity constraints that are handled by triggers (for the definition of triggers, see Chapter 13)

The declarative constraints are defined using the DDL statements CREATE TABLE and ALTER TABLE. They can be column-level constraints or table-level constraints. Column-level constraints, together with the data type and other column properties, are placed within the declaration of the column, while table-level constraints are always defined at the end of the CREATE TABLE or ALTER TABLE statement, after the definition of all columns.

NOTE

There is only one difference between column-level constraints and table-level constraints: a column-level constraint can be applied only upon one column, while a table-level constraint can cover one or more columns of a table.

Each declarative constraint has a name. The name of the constraint can be explicitly assigned using the CONSTRAINT option in the CREATE TABLE statement or the ALTER TABLE statement. If the CONSTRAINT option is omitted, the Database Engine assigns an implicit name for the constraint.

NOTE

Using explicit constraint names is strongly recommended. The search for an integrity constraint can be greatly enhanced if an explicit name for a constraint is used.

All declarative constraints can be categorized into several groups:

▶ DEFAULT clause
▶ UNIQUE clause
▶ PRIMARY KEY clause
▶ CHECK clause
▶ FOREIGN KEY clause and referential integrity

The definition of the default value using the DEFAULT clause was shown earlier in this chapter (see also Example 5.6). All other constraints are described in detail in the following sections.

The UNIQUE Clause

Sometimes more than one column or group of columns of the table have unique values and therefore can be used as the primary key. All columns or groups of columns that qualify to be primary keys are called *candidate keys*. Each candidate key is defined using the UNIQUE clause in the CREATE TABLE or the ALTER TABLE statement.

The UNIQUE clause has the following form:

```
[CONSTRAINT c_name]
    UNIQUE [CLUSTERED | NONCLUSTERED] ({ col_name1} ,...)
```

The CONSTRAINT option in the UNIQUE clause assigns an explicit name to the candidate key. The option CLUSTERED or NONCLUSTERED relates to the fact that the Database Engine always generates an index for each candidate key of a table. The index can be clustered—that is, the physical order of rows is specified using the indexed order of the column values. If the order is not specified, the index is nonclustered (see also Chapter 10). The default value is NONCLUSTERED. **col_name1** is a column name that builds the candidate key. (The maximum number of columns per candidate key is 16.)

Example 5.6 shows the use of the UNIQUE clause. (You have to drop the **projects** table, via DROP TABLE **projects**, before you execute the following example.)

EXAMPLE 5.6

```
USE sample;
CREATE TABLE projects   (project_no CHAR(4)  DEFAULT 'p1',
                         project_name CHAR(15) NOT NULL,
                         budget FLOAT NULL
                         CONSTRAINT unique_no UNIQUE (project_no));
```

Each value of the **project_no** column of the **projects** table is unique, including the NULL value. (Just as with any other value with a UNIQUE constraint, if NULL values are allowed on a corresponding column, there can be at most one row with the NULL value for that particular column.) If an existing value should be inserted into the column **project_no**, the system rejects it. The explicit name of the constraint that is defined in Example 5.6 is **unique_no**.

The PRIMARY KEY Clause

The *primary key* of a table is a column or group of columns whose value is different in every row. Each primary key is defined using the PRIMARY KEY clause in the CREATE TABLE or the ALTER TABLE statement.

The PRIMARY KEY clause has the following form:

```
[CONSTRAINT c_name]
 PRIMARY KEY [CLUSTERED | NONCLUSTERED] ({col_name1} ,...)
```

All options of the PRIMARY KEY clause have the same meaning as the corresponding options with the same name in the UNIQUE clause. In contrast to UNIQUE, the PRIMARY KEY column must be NOT NULL, and its default value is CLUSTERED.

Example 5.7 shows the specification of the primary key for the **employee** table of the **sample** database.

NOTE

*You have to drop the **employee** table (DROP TABLE **employee**) before you execute the following example.*

EXAMPLE 5.7

```
USE sample;
CREATE TABLE employee  (emp_no INTEGER NOT NULL,
                emp_fname CHAR(20) NOT NULL,
                emp_lname CHAR(20) NOT NULL,
                dept_no CHAR(4) NULL,
                CONSTRAINT prim_empl PRIMARY KEY (emp_no));
```

The **employee** table is re-created and its primary key is defined in Example 5.7. The primary key of the table is specified using the declarative integrity constraint named **prim_empl**. This integrity constraint is a table-level constraint, because it is specified after the definition of all columns of the **employee** table.

Example 5.8 is equivalent to Example 5.7, except for the specification of the primary key of the **employee** table as a column-level constraint.

NOTE

*Again, you have to drop the **employee** table (DROP TABLE **employee**) before you execute the following example.*

EXAMPLE 5.8

```
USE sample;
CREATE TABLE employee
       (emp_no INTEGER NOT NULL CONSTRAINT prim_empl PRIMARY KEY,
        emp_fname CHAR(20) NOT NULL,
        emp_lname CHAR(20) NOT NULL,
        dept_no CHAR(4) NULL);
```

In Example 5.8, the PRIMARY KEY clause belongs to the declaration of the corresponding column, together with its data type and nullability. For this reason, it is called a column-level constraint.

The CHECK Clause

The *check constraint* specifies conditions for the data inserted into a column. Each row inserted into a table or each value updating the value of the column must meet these conditions. The CHECK clause is used to specify check constraints. This clause can be defined in the CREATE TABLE or ALTER TABLE statement. The syntax of the CHECK clause is

```
[CONSTRAINT c_name]
    CHECK [NOT FOR REPLICATION] expression
```

expression must evaluate to a Boolean value (*true* or *false*) and can reference any columns in the current table (or just the current column if specified as a column-level constraint), but no other tables. The CHECK clause is not enforced during a replication of the data if the option NOT FOR REPLICATION exists. (A database, or a part of it, is said to be replicated if it is stored at more than one site. Replication can be used to enhance the availability of data. Chapter 19 describes data replication.)

Example 5.9 shows how the CHECK clause can be used.

EXAMPLE 5.9

```
USE sample;
CREATE TABLE customer
    (cust_no INTEGER NOT NULL,
    cust_group CHAR(3) NULL,
    CHECK (cust_group IN ('c1', 'c2', 'c10')));
```

The **customer** table that is created in Example 5.9 contains the **cust_group** column with the corresponding check constraint. The database system returns an error if the **cust_group** column, after a modification of its existing values or after the insertion of a new row, would contain a value different from the values in the set ('c1', 'c2', 'c10').

The FOREIGN KEY Clause

A *foreign key* is a column or group of columns in one table that contains values that match the primary key values in the same or another table. Each foreign key is defined using the FOREIGN KEY clause combined with the REFERENCES clause.

The FOREIGN KEY clause has the following form:

```
[CONSTRAINT c_name]
        [[FOREIGN KEY] ({col_name1} ,...)]
        REFERENCES table_name ({col_name2},...)
            [ON DELETE {NO ACTION| CASCADE | SET NULL | SET DEFAULT}]
            [ON UPDATE {NO ACTION | CASCADE | SET NULL | SET DEFAULT}]
```

The FOREIGN KEY clause defines all columns explicitly that belong to the foreign key. The REFERENCES clause specifies the table name with all columns that build the corresponding primary key. The number and the data types of the columns in the FOREIGN KEY clause must match the number and the corresponding data types of columns in the REFERENCES clause (and, of course, both of these must match the number and data types of the columns in the primary key of the referenced table).

The table that contains the foreign key is called the *referencing table*, and the table that contains the corresponding primary key is called the *parent table* or *referenced table*. Example 5.10 shows the specification of the foreign key in the **works_on** table of the **sample** database.

NOTE

*You have to drop the **works_on** table before you execute the following example.*

EXAMPLE 5.10

```
USE sample;
CREATE TABLE works_on  (emp_no INTEGER NOT NULL,
            project_no CHAR(4) NOT NULL,
              job CHAR (15) NULL,
              enter_date DATE NULL,
              CONSTRAINT prim_works PRIMARY KEY(emp_no, project_no),
              CONSTRAINT foreign_works FOREIGN KEY(emp_no)
                    REFERENCES employee (emp_no));
```

The **works_on** table in Example 5.10 is specified with two declarative integrity constraints: **prim_works** and **foreign_works**. Both constraints are table-level constraints, where the former specifies the primary key and the latter the foreign key of the **works_on** table. Further, the constraint **foreign_works** specifies the **employee** table as the parent table and its **emp_no** column as the corresponding primary key of the column with the same name in the **works_on** table.

The FOREIGN KEY clause can be omitted if the foreign key is defined as a column-level constraint, because the column being constrained is the implicit column "list" of the foreign key, and the keyword REFERENCES is sufficient to indicate what kind of constraint this is. The maximum number of FOREIGN KEY constraints in a table is 63.

A definition of the foreign keys in tables of a database imposes the specification of another important integrity constraint: the referential integrity, described next.

Referential Integrity

A *referential integrity* enforces insert and update rules for the tables with the foreign key and the corresponding primary key constraint. Examples 5.7 and 5.10 specify two such constraints: **prim_empl** and **foreign_works**. The REFERENCES clause in Example 5.10 determines the **employee** table as the parent table.

If the referential integrity for two tables is specified, the modification of values in the primary and the corresponding foreign key are not always possible. The following subsection discusses when it is possible and when not.

Possible Problems with Referential Integrity

There are four cases in which the modification of the values in the foreign key or in the primary key can cause problems. All of these cases will be shown using the **sample** database. The first two cases affect modifications of the referencing table, while the last two concern modifications of the parent table.

Case 1   Insert a new row into the **works_on** table with the employee number 11111.

The insertion of the new row in the referencing table **works_on** introduces a new employee number for which there is no matching employee in the parent table (**employee**). If the referential integrity for both tables is specified as is done in Examples 5.7 and 5.10, the Database Engine rejects the insertion of a new row. For readers who are familiar with the SQL language, the corresponding Transact-SQL statement is

```
USE sample;
INSERT INTO works_on (emp_no, ...)
    VALUES (11111, ...);
```

Case 2   Modify the employee number 10102 in all rows of the **works_on** table. The new number is 11111.

In Case 2, the existing value of the foreign key in the **works_on** table should be replaced using the new value, for which there is no matching value in the parent table **employee**. If the referential integrity for both tables is specified as is done in Examples 5.7 and 5.10, the database system rejects the modification of the rows in the **works_on** table. The corresponding Transact-SQL statement is

```
USE sample;
UPDATE works_on
    SET emp_no = 11111 WHERE emp_no = 10102;
```

Case 3   Modify the employee number 10102 in the corresponding row of the **employee** table. The new number is 22222.

In Case 3, the existing value of the primary key in the parent table and the foreign key of the referencing table is modified only in the parent table. The values in the referencing table are unchanged. Therefore, the system rejects the modification of the row with the employee number 10102 in the **employee** table. Referential integrity requires that no rows in the referencing table (the one with the FOREIGN KEY clause) can exist unless a corresponding row in the parent table (the one with the PRIMARY KEY clause) also exists. Otherwise, the rows in the parent table would be "orphaned." If the modification described above were permitted, then rows in the **works_on** table having the employee number 10102 would be orphaned, and the system would reject it. The corresponding Transact-SQL statement is

```
USE sample;
UPDATE employee
    SET emp_no = 22222 WHERE emp_no = 10102;
```

Case 4   Delete the row of the **employee** table with the employee number 10102.

Case 4 is similar to Case 3. The deletion would remove the employee for which matching rows exist in the referencing table. Example 5.11 shows the definition of tables of the **sample** database with all existing primary key and foreign key constraints. (If the **employee, department, project,** and **works_on** tables already exist, drop them first using the DROP TABLE **table_name** statement.)

EXAMPLE 5.11

```
USE sample;
CREATE TABLE department(dept_no CHAR(4) NOT NULL,
                        dept_name CHAR(25) NOT NULL,
                        location CHAR(30) NULL,
                        CONSTRAINT prim_dept PRIMARY KEY (dept_no));
CREATE TABLE employee  (emp_no INTEGER NOT NULL,
          emp_fname CHAR(20) NOT NULL,
          emp_lname CHAR(20) NOT NULL,
        dept_no CHAR(4) NULL,
        CONSTRAINT prim_emp PRIMARY KEY (emp_no),
        CONSTRAINT foreign_emp FOREIGN KEY(dept_no) REFERENCES department(dept_no));
CREATE TABLE project   (project_no CHAR(4) NOT NULL,
          project_name CHAR(15) NOT NULL,
          budget FLOAT NULL,
        CONSTRAINT prim_proj PRIMARY KEY (project_no));
CREATE TABLE works_on  (emp_no INTEGER NOT NULL,
  project_no CHAR(4) NOT NULL,
  job CHAR (15) NULL,
```

```
enter_date DATE NULL,
CONSTRAINT prim_works PRIMARY KEY(emp_no, project_no),
CONSTRAINT foreign1_works FOREIGN KEY(emp_no) REFERENCES employee(emp_no),
CONSTRAINT foreign2_works FOREIGN KEY(project_no) REFERENCES project(project_no));
```

The ON DELETE and ON UPDATE Options

The Database Engine can react differently if the values of the primary key of a table should be modified or deleted. If you try to update values of a foreign key, and those modifications result in inconsistencies in the corresponding primary key (see Case 1 and Case 2 in the previous section), the database system will always reject the modification and will display a message similar to the following:

Server: Msg 547, Level 16, State 1, Line 1 UPDATE statement conflicted with COLUMN FOREIGN KEY constraint 'FKemployee'. The conflict occurred in database 'sample', table 'employee', column 'dept_no'. The statement has been terminated.

But if you try to modify the values of a primary key, and these modifications result in inconsistencies in the corresponding foreign key (see Case 3 and Case 4 in the previous section), a database system could react very flexibly. Generally, there are four options for how a database system can react:

▶ **NO ACTION**   Allows you to modify (update or delete) only those values of the parent table that do not have any corresponding values in the foreign key of the referencing table.

▶ **CASCADE**   Allows you to modify (update or delete) all values of the parent table. If this option is specified, a row is updated (i.e., deleted) from the referencing table (i.e., the one with the foreign key) if the corresponding value in the primary key has been updated, or the whole row with that value has been deleted from the parent table (i.e., the one with the primary key).

▶ **SET NULL**   Allows you to modify (update or delete) all values of the parent table. If you want to update a value of the parent table and this modification would lead to data inconsistencies in the referencing table, the database system sets all corresponding values in the foreign key of the referencing table to NULL. Similarly, if you want to delete the row in the parent table and the deletion of the value in the primary key would lead to data inconsistencies, the database system sets all corresponding values in the foreign key to NULL. That way, all data inconsistencies are omitted.

▶ **SET DEFAULT**   Analogous to the SET NULL option, with one exception: all corresponding values in the foreign key are set to a default value. (Obviously, the default value must still exist in the primary key of the parent table after modification.)

NOTE

The Transact-SQL language supports the first two directives.

Example 5.12 shows the use of the ON DELETE and ON UPDATE options.

EXAMPLE 5.12

```
USE sample;
CREATE TABLE works_on1
(emp_no INTEGER NOT NULL,
  project_no CHAR(4) NOT NULL,
  job CHAR (15) NULL,
  enter_date DATE NULL,
  CONSTRAINT prim_works1 PRIMARY KEY(emp_no, project_no),
  CONSTRAINT foreign1_works1 FOREIGN KEY(emp_no)
      REFERENCES employee(emp_no) ON DELETE CASCADE,
  CONSTRAINT foreign2_works1 FOREIGN KEY(project_no)
      REFERENCES project(project_no) ON UPDATE CASCADE);
```

Example 5.12 creates the **works_on1** table that uses the ON DELETE CASCADE and ON UPDATE CASCADE options. If you load the **works_on1** table with the content shown in Table 1-4, each deletion of a row in the **employee** table will cause the additional deletion of all rows in the **works_on1** table that have the corresponding value in the **emp_no** column. Similarly, each update of a value in the **project_no** column of the project table will cause the same modification on all corresponding values in the **project_no** column of the **works_on1** table.

Creating Other Database Objects

A relational database contains not only base tables that exist in their own right but also *views*, which are virtual tables. The data of a base table exists physically—that is, it is stored on a disk—while a view is derived from one or more base tables. The CREATE VIEW statement creates a new view from one or more existing tables (or views) using a SELECT statement, which is an inseparable part of the CREATE VIEW statement. Since the creation of a view always contains a query, the CREATE VIEW statement belongs to the data manipulation language (DML) rather than to the data definition language (DDL). For this reason, the creation and removal of views is discussed in Chapter 11, after the presentation of all Transact-SQL statements for data modification.

The CREATE INDEX statement creates a new *index* on a specified table. The indices are primarily used to allow efficient access to the data stored on a disk. The existence of an index can greatly improve the access to data. Indices, together with the CREATE INDEX statement, are discussed in detail in Chapter 10.

A *stored procedure* is an additional database object that can be created using the corresponding CREATE PROCEDURE statement. (A stored procedure is a special kind of sequence of statements written in Transact-SQL, using the SQL language and procedural extensions. Chapter 8 describes stored procedures in detail.)

A *trigger* is a database object that specifies an action as a result of an operation. This means that when a particular data-modifying action (modification, insertion, or deletion) occurs on a particular table, the Database Engine automatically invokes one or more additional actions. The CREATE TRIGGER statement creates a new trigger. Triggers are described in detail in Chapter 14.

A *synonym* is a local database object that provides a link between itself and another object managed by the same or a linked database server. Using the CREATE SYNONYM statement, you can create a new synonym for the given object.

Example 5. 13 shows the use of this statement.

EXAMPLE 5.13

```
USE AdventureWorks;
CREATE SYNONYM  prod
          FOR AdventureWorks.Production.Product;
```

Example 5.13 creates a synonym for the **Product** table in the **Production** schema of the **AdventureWorks** database. This synonym can be used in DML statements, such as SELECT, INSERT, UPDATE, and DELETE.

NOTE

The main reason to use synonyms is to omit the use of lengthy names in DML statements. As you already know, the name of a database object can generally contain four parts. Introducing a (single-part) synonym for an object that has three or four parts can save you time when typing its name.

A *schema* is a database object that includes statements for creation of tables, views, and user privileges. (You can think of a schema as a construct that collects together several tables, corresponding views, and user privileges.)

NOTE

The Database Engine treats the notion of schema the same way it is treated in the ANSI SQL standard. In the SQL standard, a schema is defined as a collection of database objects that is owned by a single principal and forms a single namespace. A namespace is a set of objects that cannot have duplicate names. For example, two tables can have the same name only if they are in separate schemas. (Schema is a very important concept in the security model of the Database Engine. For this reason, you can find a detailed description of schema in Chapter 12.)

Integrity Constraints and Domains

A *domain* is the set of all possible legitimate values that columns of a table may contain. Almost all DBMSs use base data types such as INT, CHAR, and DATE to define the set of possible values for a column. This method of enforcing "domain integrity" is incomplete, as can be seen from the following example.

The **person** table has a column, **zip**, that specifies the ZIP code of the city in which the person lives. This column can be defined using the SMALLINT or CHAR(5) data type. The definition with the SMALLINT data type is inaccurate, because the SMALLINT data type contains all positive and negative values between $-2^{15}-1$ and 2^{15}. The definition using CHAR(5) is even more inaccurate, because all characters and special signs can also be used in such a case. Therefore, an accurate definition of ZIP codes requires defining an interval of positive integers between 00601 and 99950 and assigning it to the **zip** column.

CHECK constraints (defined in the CREATE TABLE or ALTER TABLE statement) can enforce more precise domain integrity because their expressions are flexible, and they are always enforced when the column is inserted or modified.

The Transact-SQL language provides support for domains by creating alias data types using the CREATE TYPE statement. The following two sections describe alias and Common Language Runtime (CLR) data types.

Alias Data Types

An alias data type is a special kind of data type that is defined by users using the existing base data types. Such a data type can be used with the CREATE TABLE statement to define one or more columns in a database.

The CREATE TYPE statement is generally used to create an alias data type. The syntax of this statement to specify an alias data type is as follows:

```
CREATE TYPE [ type_schema_name. ] type_name
{ [ FROM base_type [ ( precision [ , scale ] ) ] [ NULL | NOT NULL ] ]
  | [ EXTERNAL NAME assembly_name [ .class_name ] ]}
```

Example 5.14 shows the creation of an alias data type using the CREATE TYPE statement.

EXAMPLE 5.14

```
USE sample;
CREATE TYPE zip
   FROM SMALLINT NOT NULL;
```

Example 5.14 creates an alias type **zip** based on the standard data type CHAR(5). This user-defined data type can now be used as a data type of a table column, as shown in Example 5.15.

NOTE

*You have to drop the **customer** table (DROP TABLE **customer**) before you execute the following example.*

EXAMPLE 5.15

```
USE sample;
CREATE TABLE customer
    (cust_no INT NOT NULL,
     cust_name CHAR(20) NOT NULL,
     city CHAR(20),
     zip_code ZIP,
   CHECK (zip_code BETWEEN 601 AND 99950));
```

Example 5.15 uses the new **zip** data type to specify a column of the **customer** table. The values of this column have to be constrained to the region between 601 and 99950. As can be seen from Example 5.15, this can be done using the CHECK clause.

NOTE

Generally, the Database Engine implicitly converts between compatible columns of different data types. This is valid for the alias data types, too.

Since version 2008, SQL Server supports the creation of user-defined table types. Example 5.16 shows how you can use the CREATE TYPE statement to create such a table type.

EXAMPLE 5.16

```
USE sample;
CREATE TYPE person_table_t AS TABLE
    ( name VARCHAR(30), salary DECIMAL(8,2));
```

The user-defined table type called **person_table_t** has two columns: **name** and **salary**. The main syntactical difference in relation to alias data types is the existence of the AS TABLE clause, as can be seen in Example 5.16. User-defined table types are usually used in relation to table-valued parameters (see Chapter 8).

CLR Data Types

The CREATE TYPE statement can also be applied to create a user-defined data type using .NET. In this case, the implementation of a user-defined data type is defined in a class of an assembly in the Common Language Runtime (CLR). This means that you can use one of the .NET languages like C# or Visual Basic to implement the new data type. Further description of the user-defined data types is outside the scope of this book.

Modifying Database Objects

The Transact-SQL language supports changing the structure of the following database objects, among others:

▶ Database

▶ Table

▶ Stored procedure

▶ View

▶ Schema

▶ Trigger

The following two sections describe, in turn, how you can alter a database and a table. The modification of the structure of each of the last four database objects is described in Chapters 8, 11, 12, and 14, respectively.

Altering a Database

The ALTER DATABASE statement changes the physical structure of a database. The Transact-SQL language allows you to change the following properties of a database:

▶ Add or remove one or more database files

▶ Add or remove one or more log files

▶ Add or remove filegroups

▶ Modify file or filegroup properties

▶ Set database options

▶ Change the name of the database using the **sp_rename** stored procedure (discussed a bit later, in the section, "Altering a Table")

The following subsections describe these different types of database alterations. In this section, we will also use the ALTER DATABASE statement to show how FILESTREAM data can be stored in files and filegroups and to explain the notion of contained databases.

Adding or Removing Database Files, Log Files, or Filegroups

The ALTER DATABASE statement allows the addition and removal of database files. The clauses ADD FILE and REMOVE FILE specify the addition of a new file and the deletion of an existing file, respectively. (Additionally, a new file can be assigned to an existing filegroup using the TO FILEGROUP option.)

Example 5.17 shows how a new database file can be added to the **projects** database.

EXAMPLE 5.17

```
USE master;
GO
ALTER DATABASE projects
ADD FILE (NAME=projects_dat1,
     FILENAME = 'C:\projects1.mdf',   SIZE = 10,
     MAXSIZE = 100,   FILEGROWTH = 5);
```

The ALTER DATABASE statement in Example 5.17 adds a new file with the logical name **projects_dat1**. Its initial size is 10MB, and this file will grow using units of 5MB until it reaches the upper limit of 100MB. (Log files are added in the same way as database files. The only difference is that you use the ADD LOG FILE clause instead of ADD FILE.)

The REMOVE FILE clause removes one or more files that belong to an existing database. The file can be a data file or a log file. The file cannot be removed unless it is empty.

The CREATE FILEGROUP clause creates a new filegroup, while DELETE FILEGROUP removes an existing filegroup from the system. Again, you cannot remove a filegroup unless it is empty.

Modifying File or Filegroup Properties

You can use the MODIFY FILE clause to change the following file properties:

▶ Change the logical name of a file using the NEWNAME option of the MODIFY FILE clause

▶ Increase the value of the SIZE property

▶ Change the FILENAME, MAXSIZE, or FILEGROWTH property

▶ Mark the file as OFFLINE

Similarly, you can use the MODIFY FILEGROUP clause to change the following filegroup properties:

▶ Change the name of a filegroup using the NAME option of the MODIFY FILEGROUP clause

▶ Mark the filegroup as the default filegroup using the DEFAULT option

▶ Mark the filegroup as read-only or read-write using the READ_ONLY or READ_WRITE option, respectively

Setting Database Options

The SET clause of the ALTER DATABASE statement is used to set different database options. Some options must be set to ON or OFF, but most of them have a list of possible values. Each database option has a default value, which is set in the **model** database. Therefore, you can alter the **model** database to change the default values of specific options.

All options that you can set are divided into several groups. The most important groups are

▶ State options

▶ Auto options

▶ SQL options

The state options control the following:

▶ User access to the database (options are SINGLE_USER, RESTRICTED_USER, and MULTI_USER)

▶ The status of the database (options are ONLINE, OFFLINE, and EMERGENCY)

▶ The read/write modus (options are READ_ONLY and READ_WRITE)

The auto options control, among other things, the art of the database shutdown (the option AUTO_CLOSE) and how index statistics are built (the options AUTO_CREATE_STATISTICS and AUTO_UPDATE_STATISTICS).

The SQL options control the ANSI compliance of the database and its objects. All SQL options can be edited using the DATABASEPROPERTYEX function and modified using the ALTER DATABASE statement. The recovery options FULL, BULK-LOGGED, and SIMPLE influence the art of database recovery.

Storing FILESTREAM Data

The previous chapter explained what FILESTREAM data is and the reason for using it. This section discusses how FILESTREAM data can be stored as a part of a database. Before you can store FILESTREAM data, you have to enable the system for this task. The following subsection explains how to enable the operating system and the instance of your database system.

Enabling FILESTREAM Storage FILESTREAM storage has to be enabled at two levels:

▶ For the Windows operating system

▶ For the particular server instance

You use SQL Server Configuration Manager to enable FILESTREAM storage at the OS level. Choose Start | All Programs | SQL Server 2012 | Configuration Tools | SQL Server Configuration Manager. In the list of services, right-click SQL Server Services and click Open. After that, right-click the instance on which you want to enable the FILESTREAM storage and click Properties. In the SQL Server Properties dialog box, click the FILESTREAM tab (see Figure 5-1). If you want just to read FILESTREAM data, check the Enable FILESTREAM for Transact-SQL Access check box. If you want to be able to read as well as write data, also check the

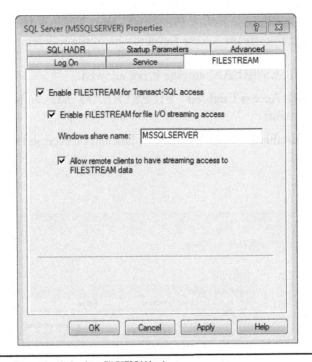

Figure 5-1   *SQL Server Properties dialog box, FILESTREAM tab*

Enable FILESTREAM for File I/O Streaming Access check box. Enter the name of the Windows share in the Windows Share Name box. (The Windows share is used for reading and writing FILESTREAM data using Win32 API. If you use a name to return the path of a FILESTREAM BLOB, it will use the name of the Windows share to display the path.)

SQL Server Configuration Manager creates a new share with the specified name on the host system. Click OK to apply the changes.

NOTE

*You need to be Windows Administrator on a local system and have administrator (**sysadmin**) rights to enable FILESTREAM storage. You need also to restart the instance for the changes to take effect.*

The next step is to enable FILESTREAM storage for a particular instance. SQL Server Management Studio will be used to show this task. (You can also use the **sp_configure** system procedure with the **filestream access level** option.) Right-click the instance in Object Explorer, click Properties, select Advanced in the left pane (see Figure 5-2), and set Filestream Access Level to one of the following levels:

- ▶ **Disabled**   FILESTREAM storage is not allowed.
- ▶ **Transact-SQL Access Enabled**   FILESTREAM data can be accessed using T-SQL statements.
- ▶ **Full Access Enabled**   FILESTREAM data can be accessed using T-SQL as well as Win32.

Figure 5-2   *Server Properties window with Filestream Access Level set to Full Access Enabled*

Adding a File to the Filegroup   After you enable FILESTREAM storage for your instance, you can use the ALTER DATABASE statement first to create a filegroup for FILESTREAM data and then to add a file to that filegroup, as shown in Example 5.18. (Of course, you can also use the CREATE DATABASE statement to accomplish this task.)

NOTE

Before you execute the statement in Example 5.18, change the name of the file in the FILENAME clause.

EXAMPLE 5.18

```
USE sample;
ALTER DATABASE sample
    ADD FILEGROUP Employee_FSGroup CONTAINS FILESTREAM;
GO
ALTER DATABASE sample
    ADD FILE (NAME= employee_FS,
    FILENAME = 'C:\DUSAN\emp_FS')
    TO FILEGROUP Employee_FSGroup
```

The first ALTER DATABASE statement in Example 5.18 adds a new filegroup called **Employee_FSGroup** to the **sample** database. The CONTAINS FILESTREAM option tells the system that this filegroup will contain only FILESTREAM data. The second ALTER DATABASE statement adds a new file to the existing filegroup.

Now you can create a table with one or more FILESTREAM columns. Example 5.19 shows the creation of a table with a FILESTREAM column.

EXAMPLE 5.19

```
CREATE TABLE employee_info
    (id UNIQUEIDENTIFIER ROWGUIDCOL NOT NULL UNIQUE,
    filestream_data VARBINARY(MAX) FILESTREAM NULL)
```

The **employee_info** table in Example 5.19 contains the **filestream_data** columns, which must be of the VARBINARY(max) data type. Such a column includes the FILESTREAM attribute, indicating that a column should store data in the FILESTREAM filegroup. All tables that store FILESTREAM data require the existence of a UNIQUE ROWGUILDCOL. For this reason, the **employee_info** table has the **id** column, defined using these two attributes.

To insert data into a FILESTREAM column, you use the standard INSERT statement, which is described in Chapter 7. Also, to read data from a FILESTREAM column, you can use the standard SELECT statement, which is described in the next chapter. The detailed description of read and write operations on FILESTREAM data are outside the scope of this book.

Contained Databases

One of the significant problems with SQL Server databases is that they cannot be exported (or imported) easily. As you already know from this chapter, you can attach and detach a database, but many important parts and properties of the attached database will be missing. (The main problem in such a case is database security in general and existing logins in particular, which are usually incomplete or wrong after the move.)

Microsoft intends to solve such problems by introducing contained databases. A contained database comprises all database settings and data required to specify the database and is isolated from the instance of the Database Engine on which it is installed. In other words, this form of databases has no configuration dependencies on the instance and can easily be moved from one instance of SQL Server to another.

Generally, there are three forms of databases in relation to containment:

▶ Fully contained databases
▶ Partially contained databases
▶ Noncontained databases

Fully contained databases are those where database objects cannot cross the application boundary. (An application boundary defines the scope of an application. For instance, user-defined functions are within the application boundary, while functions related to server instances are outside it.)

Partially contained databases allow database objects to cross the application boundary, while noncontained databases do not support the notion of an application boundary at all.

NOTE

SQL Server 2012 supports partially contained databases. A future version of SQL Server will support full containment, too. (All databases in previous versions of SQL Server are noncontained databases.)

Let's take a look at how you can create a partially contained database in SQL Server 2012. If a database called **my_sample** already exists, and it is created as a noncontained database (using the CREATE DATABASE statement, for instance), you can use the ALTER DATABASE statement to alter it to partial containment, as shown in Example 5.20.

EXAMPLE 5.20

```
EXEC sp_configure 'show advanced options' , 1;
RECONFIGURE WITH OVERRIDE;
EXEC sp_configure 'contained database authentication' , 1;
RECONFIGURE WITH OVERRIDE;
ALTER DATABASE my_sample SET CONTAINMENT = PARTIAL;
EXEC sp_configure 'show advanced options' , 0;
RECONFIGURE WITH OVERRIDE;
```

The ALTER DATABASE statement modifies the containment of the **my_sample** database from noncontained to partially contained. This means that the database system allows you to create both contained and noncontained database objects for the **my_sample** database. (All other statements in Example 5.20 just set the scene for the ALTER DATABASE statement.)

> **NOTE**
>
> *sp_configure is a system procedure that can be used to, among other things, change advanced configuration options, such as 'contained database authentication'. To make changes to advanced configuration options, you first have to set the value of the 'show advanced options' to 1 and reconfigure the system. At the end of Example 5.20, this option has been set again to its default value (0). The sp_configure system procedure is discussed in detail in the section "System Procedures" in Chapter 9.*

For the **my_sample** database, you can now create a user that is not tied to a login. This will be described in detail in the "Managing Authorization and Authentication of Contained Databases" section of Chapter 12.

Altering a Table

The ALTER TABLE statement modifies the schema of a table. The Transact-SQL language allows the following types of alteration:

▶ Add or drop one or more new columns

▶ Modify column properties

▶ Add or remove integrity constraints

▶ Enable or disable constraints

▶ Rename tables and other database objects

The following sections describe these types of changes.

Adding or Dropping a New Column

You can use the ADD clause of the ALTER TABLE statement to add a new column to the existing table. Only one column can be added for each ALTER TABLE statement. Example 5.21 shows the use of the ADD clause.

EXAMPLE 5.21

```
USE sample;
ALTER TABLE employee
    ADD telephone_no CHAR(12) NULL;
```

The ALTER TABLE statement in Example 5.21 adds the column **telephone_no** to the **employee** table. The Database Engine populates the new column either with NULL or IDENTITY values or with the specified default. For this reason, the new column must either be nullable or have a default constraint.

NOTE

There is no way to insert a new column in a particular position in the table. The column, which is added using the ADD clause, is always inserted at the end of the table.

The DROP COLUMN clause provides the ability to drop an existing column of the table, as shown in Example 5.22.

EXAMPLE 5.22

```
USE sample;
ALTER TABLE employee
    DROP COLUMN telephone_no;
```

The ALTER TABLE statement in Example 5.22 removes the **telephone_no** column, which was added to the **employee** table with the ALTER TABLE statement in Example 5.21.

Modifying Column Properties

The Transact-SQL language supports the ALTER COLUMN clause of ALTER TABLE to modify properties of an existing column. The following column properties can be modified:

▶ Data type

▶ Nullability

Example 5.23 shows the use of the ALTER COLUMN clause.

EXAMPLE 5.23

```
USE sample;
ALTER TABLE department
    ALTER COLUMN location CHAR(25) NOT NULL;
```

The ALTER TABLE statement in Example 5.23 changes the previous properties (CHAR(30), nullable) of the **location** column of the **department** table to new properties (CHAR(25), not nullable).

Adding or Removing Integrity Constraints

A new integrity constraint can be added to a table using the ALTER TABLE statement and its option called ADD CONSTRAINT. Example 5.24 shows how you can use the ADD CONSTRAINT clause in relation to a check constraint.

EXAMPLE 5.24

```
USE sample;
CREATE TABLE sales
    (order_no INTEGER NOT NULL,
    order_date DATE NOT NULL,
    ship_date DATE NOT NULL);
ALTER TABLE sales
    ADD CONSTRAINT order_check CHECK(order_date <= ship_date);
```

The CREATE TABLE statement in Example 5.24 creates the **sales** table with two columns of the DATE data type: **order_date** and **ship_date**. The subsequent ALTER TABLE statement defines an integrity constraint named **order_check**, which compares both of the values and displays an error message if the shipping date is earlier than the order date.

Example 5.25 shows how you can use the ALTER TABLE statement to additionally define the primary key of a table.

EXAMPLE 5.25

```
USE sample;
ALTER TABLE sales
    ADD CONSTRAINT primaryk_sales PRIMARY KEY(order_no);
```

The ALTER TABLE statement in Example 5.25 declares the primary key for the **sales** table.

Each integrity constraint can be removed using the DROP CONSTRAINT clause of the ALTER TABLE statement, as shown in Example 5.26.

EXAMPLE 5.26

```
USE sample;
ALTER TABLE sales
DROP CONSTRAINT order_check;
```

The ALTER TABLE statement in Example 5.26 removes the CHECK constraint called **order_check**, specified in Example 5.24.

NOTE

You cannot use the ALTER TABLE statement to modify a definition of an integrity constraint. In this case, the constraint must be re-created—that is, dropped and then added with the new definition.

Enabling or Disabling Constraints

As previously stated, an integrity constraint always has a name that can be explicitly declared using the CONSTRAINT option or implicitly declared by the system. The name of all (implicitly or explicitly) declared constraints for a table can be viewed using the system procedure **sp_helpconstraint**.

A constraint is enforced by default during future insert and update operations. Additionally, the existing values in the column(s) are checked against the constraint. Otherwise, a constraint that is created with the WITH NOCHECK option is disabled in the second case. In other words, if you use the WITH NOCHECK option, the constraint will be applied only to future insert and update operations. (Both options, WITH CHECK and WITH NOCHECK, can be applied only with the CHECK and FOREIGN KEY constraints.)

Example 5.27 shows how you can disable all existing constraints for a table.

EXAMPLE 5.27

```
USE sample;
ALTER TABLE sales
    NOCHECK CONSTRAINT ALL;
```

In Example 5.27, the keyword ALL is used to disable all the constraints on the **sales** table.

NOTE

Use of the NOCHECK option is not recommended. Any constraint violations that are suppressed may cause future updates to fail.

Renaming Tables and Other Database Objects

The **sp_rename** system procedure modifies the name of an existing table (and any other existing database objects, such as databases, views, or stored procedures). Examples 5.28 and 5.29 show the use of this system procedure.

EXAMPLE 5.28

```
USE sample;
EXEC sp_rename @objname = department, @newname = subdivision
```

Example 5.28 renames the **department** table to **subdivision**.

EXAMPLE 5.29

```
USE sample;
EXEC sp_rename @objname = 'sales.order_no' , @newname = ordernumber
```

Example 5.29 renames the **order_no** column in the **sales** table. If the object to be renamed is a column in a table, the specification must be in the form **table_name. column_name**.

NOTE

*Do not use the **sp_rename** system procedure, because changing object names can influence other database objects that reference them. Drop the object and re-create it with the new name.*

Removing Database Objects

All Transact-SQL statements that are used to remove a database object have the following general form:

```
DROP object_type object_name
```

Each CREATE **object** statement has the corresponding DROP **object** statement. The statement

```
DROP DATABASE database1 {, ...}
```

removes one or more databases. This means that all traces of the database are removed from your database system.

One or more tables can be removed from a database with the following statement:

```
DROP TABLE table_name1 {, ...}
```

All data, indices, and triggers belonging to the removed table are also dropped. (In contrast, all views that are defined using the dropped table are not removed.) Only the user with the corresponding privileges can remove a table.

In addition to DATABASE and TABLE, **objects** in the DROP statement can be, among others, the following:

► TYPE

► SYNONYM

► PROCEDURE

► INDEX

► VIEW

► TRIGGER

► SCHEMA

The statements DROP TYPE and DROP SYNONYM drop a type and a synonym, respectively. The rest of the statements are described in different chapters: DROP PROCEDURE in Chapter 8, DROP INDEX in Chapter 10, DROP VIEW in Chapter 11, DROP SCHEMA in Chapter 12, and DROP TRIGGER in Chapter 14.

Summary

The Transact-SQL language supports many data definition statements that create, alter, and remove database objects. The following database objects, among others, can be created and removed using the CREATE **object** and the DROP **object** statement, respectively:

- ▶ Database
- ▶ Table
- ▶ Schema
- ▶ View
- ▶ Trigger
- ▶ Stored procedure
- ▶ Index

A structure of all database objects in the preceding list can be altered using the ALTER **object** statement. Note that the ALTER TABLE statement is the only standardized statement from this list. All other ALTER **object** statements are Transact-SQL extensions to the SQL standard.

The next chapter addresses the data manipulation statement called SELECT.

Exercises

E.5.1

Using the CREATE DATABASE statement, create a new database named **test_db** with explicit specifications for database and transaction log files. The database file with the logical name **test_db_dat** is stored in the file C:\tmp\test_db.mdf and the initial size is 5MB, the maximum size is unlimited, and the file growth is 8 percent. The log file called **test_db_log** is stored in the file C:\tmp\test_db_log.ldf and the initial size is 2MB, the maximum size is 10MB, and the file growth is 500KB.

E.5.2

Using the ALTER DATABASE statement, add a new log file to the **test_db** database. The log file is stored in the file C:\tmp\emp_log.ldf and the initial size of the file is 2MB, with growth of 2MB and an unlimited maximum size.

E.5.3

Using the ALTER DATABASE statement, change the file size of the **test_db** database to 10MB.

E.5.4

In Example 5.4, there are some columns of the four created tables defined with the NOT NULL specification. For which column is this specification required and for which is it not required?

E.5.5

Why are the columns **dept_no** and **project_no** in Example 5.4 defined as CHAR values (and not as numerical values)?

E.5.6

Create the tables **customers** and **orders** with the following columns. (Do not declare the corresponding primary and foreign keys.)

customers	orders
customerid char(5) not null	orderid integer not null
companyname varchar(40) not null	customerid char(5) not null
contactname char(30) null	orderdate date null
address varchar(60) null	shippeddate date null
city char(15) null	freight money null
phone char(24) null	shipname varchar(40) null
fax char(24) null	shipaddress varchar(60) null
	quantity integer null

E.5.7

Using the ALTER TABLE statement, add a new column named **shipregion** to the **orders** table. The fields should be nullable and contain integers.

E.5.8

Using the ALTER TABLE statement, change the data type of the column **shipregion** from INTEGER to CHARACTER with length 8. The fields may contain NULL values.

E.5.9

Delete the formerly created column **shipregion**.

E.5.10

Describe exactly what happens if a table is deleted with the DROP TABLE statement.

E.5.11

Re-create the tables **customers** and **orders**, enhancing their definition with all primary and foreign keys constraints.

E.5.12

Using SQL Server Management Studio, try to insert a new row into the **orders** table with the following values:

(10, 'ord01', getdate(), getdate(), 100.0, 'Windstar', 'Ocean', 1).

Why isn't that working?

E.5.13

Using the ALTER TABLE statement, add the current system date and time as the default value to the **orderdate** column of the **orders** table.

E.5.14

Using the ALTER TABLE statement, create an integrity constraint that limits the possible values of the **quantity** column in the **orders** table to values between 1 and 30.

E.5.15

Display all integrity constraints for the **orders** table.

E.5.16

Delete the primary key of the **customers** table. Why isn't that working?

E.5.17

Delete the integrity constraint called **prim_empl** defined in Example 5.7.

E.5.18

Rename the **city** column of the **customers** table. The new name is **town**.

Chapter 6

Queries

In This Chapter

- ► SELECT Statement:
  Its Clauses and Functions
- ► Subqueries
- ► Temporary Tables
- ► Join Operator
- ► Correlated Subqueries
- ► Table Expressions

I n this chapter you will learn how to use the SELECT statement to perform retrievals. This chapter describes every clause in this statement and gives numerous examples using the **sample** database to demonstrate the practical use of each clause. After that, the chapter introduces aggregate functions and the set operators, as well as computed columns and temporary tables. The second part of the chapter tells you more about complex queries. It introduces the join operator, which is the most important operator for relational database systems, and looks at all its forms. Correlated subqueries and the EXISTS function are then introduced. The end of the chapter describes common table expressions, together with the APPLY operator.

SELECT Statement: Its Clauses and Functions

The Transact-SQL language has one basic statement for retrieving information from a database: the SELECT statement. With this statement, it is possible to query information from one or more tables of a database (or even from multiple databases). The result of a SELECT statement is another table, also known as a *result set*.

The simplest form of the SELECT statement contains a SELECT list with the FROM clause. (All other clauses are optional.) This form of the SELECT statement has the following syntax:

```
SELECT [ ALL |DISTINCT] column_list
    FROM {table1 [tab_alias1] } ,...
```

table1 is the name of the table from which information is retrieved. **tab_alias1** provides an alias for the name of the corresponding table. An *alias* is another name for the corresponding table and can be used as a shorthand way to refer to the table or as a way to refer to two logical instances of the same physical table. Don't worry; this will become clearer as examples are presented.

column_list contains one or more of the following specifications:

▶ The asterisk symbol (*), which specifies all columns of the named tables in the FROM clause (or from a single table when qualified, as in **table2.***)

▶ The explicit specification of column names to be retrieved

▶ The specification **column_name** [AS] **column_heading**, which is a way to replace the name of a column or to assign a new name to an expression

▶ An expression

▶ A system or an aggregate function

NOTE

In addition to the preceding specifications, there are other options that will be presented later in this chapter.

A SELECT statement can retrieve either columns or rows from a table. The first operation is called *SELECT list* (or *projection*), and the second one is called *selection*. The combination of both operations is also possible in a SELECT statement.

NOTE

*Before you start to execute queries in this chapter, re-create the entire **sample** database.*

Example 6.1 shows the simplest retrieval form with the SELECT statement.

EXAMPLE 6.1

Get full details of all departments:

```
USE sample;
SELECT dept_no, dept_name, location
 FROM department;
```

The result is

dept_no	dept_name	location
d1	Research	Dallas
d2	Accounting	Seattle
d3	Marketing	Dallas

The SELECT statement in Example 6.1 retrieves all rows and all columns from the **department** table. If you include all columns of a table in a SELECT list (as in Example 6.1), you can use * as shorthand, but this notation is not recommended. The column names serve as column headings of the resulting output.

The simplest form of the SELECT statement just described is not very useful for queries. In practice, there are always several more clauses in a SELECT statement than in the statement shown in Example 6.1. The following is the syntax of a SELECT statement that references a table, with (almost) all possible clauses included:

```
SELECT select_list
    [INTO new_table_]
    FROM table
    [WHERE search_condition]
    [GROUP BY group_by_expression]
    [HAVING search_condition]
    [ORDER BY order_expression [ASC | DESC] ];
```

NOTE

The clauses in the SELECT statement must be written in the syntactical order given in the preceding syntax—for example, the GROUP BY clause must come after the WHERE clause and before the HAVING clause. However, because the INTO clause is not as significant as the other clauses, it will be discussed later in the chapter, after the other clauses have been discussed.

The following subsections describe the clauses that can be used in a query, WHERE, GROUP BY, HAVING, and ORDER BY, as well as aggregate functions, the IDENTITY property, the new sequences feature, set operators, and the CASE expression.

WHERE Clause

Often, it is necessary to define one or more conditions that limit the selected rows. The WHERE clause specifies a Boolean expression (an expression that returns a value of TRUE or FALSE) that is tested for each row to be returned (potentially). If the expression is true, then the row is returned; if it is false, it is discarded.

Example 6.2 shows the use of the WHERE clause.

EXAMPLE 6.2

Get the names and numbers of all departments located in Dallas:

```
USE sample;
SELECT dept_name, dept_no
   FROM department
   WHERE location = 'Dallas';
```

The result is

dept_name	dept_no
Research	d1
Marketing	d3

In addition to the equal sign, the WHERE clause can contain other comparison operators, including the following:

<> (or !=)	not equal
<	less than
>	greater than
>=	greater than or equal
<=	less than or equal
!>	not greater than
!<	not less than

Example 6.3 shows the use of a comparison operator in the WHERE clause.

EXAMPLE 6.3

Get the last and first names of all employees with employee numbers greater than or equal to 15000:

```
USE sample;
SELECT emp_lname, emp_fname
   FROM employee
   WHERE emp_no >= 15000;
```

The result is

emp_lname	emp_fname
Smith	Matthew
Barrimore	John
James	James
Moser	Sybill

An expression can also be a part of the condition in the WHERE clause, as Example 6.4 shows.

EXAMPLE 6.4

Get the project names for all projects with a budget > 60000 £. The current rate of exchange is 0.51 £ per $1.

```
USE sample;
SELECT project_name
   FROM project
   WHERE budget*0.51 > 60000;
```

The result is

project_name
Apollo
Mercury

Comparisons of strings (that is, values of data types CHAR, VARCHAR, NCHAR, or NVARCHAR) are executed in accordance with the collating sequence in effect (the "sort order" specified when the Database Engine was installed). If two strings are compared using ASCII code (or any other code), each of the corresponding (first, second, third, and so on) characters will be compared. One character is lower in priority than the other if it appears in the code table before the other one. Two strings of different lengths are compared after the shorter one is padded at the right with blanks, so that the length of both strings is equal. Numbers compare algebraically. Values of temporal data types (such as DATE, TIME, and DATETIME) compare in chronological order.

Boolean Operators

WHERE clause conditions can either be simple or contain multiple conditions. Multiple conditions can be built using the Boolean operators AND, OR, and NOT. The behavior of these operators was described in Chapter 4 using truth tables.

If two conditions are connected by the AND operator, rows are retrieved for which both conditions are true. If two conditions are connected by the OR operator, all rows of a table are retrieved in which either the first or the second condition (or both) is true, as shown in Example 6.5.

EXAMPLE 6.5

Get the employee numbers for all employees who work for either project p1 or project p2 (or both):

```
USE sample;
SELECT project_no, emp_no
   FROM works_on
   WHERE project_no = 'p1'
   OR project_no = 'p2';
```

The result is

project_no	emp_no
p1	10102
p2	25348
p2	18316
p2	29346
p1	9031
p1	28559
p2	28559
p1	29346

The result of Example 6.5 contains some duplicate values of the **emp_no** column. To eliminate this redundant information, use the DISTINCT option, as shown here:

```
USE sample;
SELECT DISTINCT emp_no
    FROM works_on
    WHERE project_no = 'p1'
    OR project_no = 'p2';
```

In this case, the result is

emp_no
9031
10102
18316
25348
28559
29346

Note that the DISTINCT option can be used only once in a SELECT list, and it must precede all column names in that list. Therefore, Example 6.6 is *wrong*.

EXAMPLE 6.6 (EXAMPLE OF AN ILLEGAL STATEMENT)

```
USE sample;
SELECT emp_fname, DISTINCT emp_no
```

```
        FROM employee
        WHERE emp_lname = 'Moser';
```

The result is

```
Server: Msg 156, Level 15, State 1, Line 1
Incorrect syntax near the keyword 'DISTINCT'.
```

NOTE

When there is more than one column in the SELECT list, the DISTINCT clause displays all rows where the combination of columns is distinct.

The WHERE clause may include any number of the same or different Boolean operations. You should be aware that the three Boolean operations have different priorities for evaluation: the NOT operation has the highest priority, AND is evaluated next, and the OR operation has the lowest priority. If you do not pay attention to these different priorities for Boolean operations, you will get unexpected results, as Example 6.7 shows.

EXAMPLE 6.7

```
USE sample;
SELECT emp_no, emp_fname, emp_lname
   FROM employee
   WHERE emp_no = 25348 AND emp_lname = 'Smith'
   OR emp_fname = 'Matthew' AND dept_no = 'd1';
SELECT emp_no, emp_fname, emp_lname
   FROM employee
   WHERE ((emp_no = 25348 AND emp_lname = 'Smith')
   OR emp_fname ='Matthew') AND dept_no = 'd1';
```

The result is

emp_no	emp_fname	emp_lname
25348	Matthew	Smith

emp_no	emp_fname	emp_lname

As the results of Example 6.7 show, the two SELECT statements display two different result sets. In the first SELECT statement, the system evaluates both AND operators first (from the left to the right), and then evaluates the OR operator. In the second SELECT statement, the use of parentheses changes the operation execution, with all expressions within parentheses being executed first, in sequence from left to right. As you can see, the first statement returned one row, while the second statement returned zero rows.

The existence of several Boolean operations in a WHERE clause complicates the corresponding SELECT statement and makes it error prone. In such cases, the use of parentheses is highly recommended, even if they are not necessary. The readability of such SELECT statements will be greatly improved, and possible errors can be avoided. Here is the first SELECT statement from Example 6.7, modified using the recommended form:

```
USE sample;
SELECT emp_no, emp_fname, emp_lname
    FROM employee
    WHERE (emp_no = 25348 AND emp_lname = 'Smith')
    OR (emp_fname = 'Matthew' AND dept_no = 'd1');
```

The third Boolean operator, NOT, changes the logical value of the corresponding condition. The truth table for NOT in Chapter 4 shows that the negation of the TRUE value is FALSE and vice versa; the negation of the NULL value is also NULL.

Example 6.8 shows the use of the NOT operator.

EXAMPLE 6.8

Get the employee numbers and first names of all employees who do not belong to the department d2:

```
USE sample
SELECT emp_no, emp_lname
    FROM employee
    WHERE NOT dept_no = 'd2';
```

The result is

emp_no	emp_lname
25348	Smith
10102	Jones
18316	Barrimore
28559	Moser

In this case, the NOT operator can be replaced by the comparison operator <> (not equal).

NOTE

This book uses the operator <> (instead of !=) to remain consistent with the ANSI SQL standard.

IN and BETWEEN Operators

An IN operator allows the specification of two or more expressions to be used for a query search. The result of the condition returns TRUE if the value of the corresponding column equals one of the expressions specified by the IN predicate.

Example 6.9 shows the use of the IN operator.

EXAMPLE 6.9

Get all the columns for every employee whose employee number equals 29346, 28559, or 25348:

```
USE sample;
SELECT emp_no, emp_fname, emp_lname
   FROM employee
   WHERE emp_no IN (29346, 28559, 25348);
```

The result is

emp_no	emp_fname	emp_lname
25348	Matthew	Smith
29346	James	James
28559	Sybill	Moser

An IN operator is equivalent to a series of conditions, connected with one or more OR operators. (The number of OR operators is equal to the number of expressions following the IN operator minus one.)

The IN operator can be used together with the Boolean operator NOT, as shown in Example 6.10. In this case, the query retrieves rows that do not include any of the listed values in the corresponding columns.

EXAMPLE 6.10

Get all columns for every employee whose employee number is neither 10102 nor 9031:

```
USE sample;
SELECT emp_no, emp_fname, emp_lname, dept_no
```

```
FROM employee
WHERE emp_no NOT IN (10102, 9031);
```

The result is

emp_no	emp_fname	emp_lname	dept_no
25348	Matthew	Smith	d3
18316	John	Barrimore	d1
29346	James	James	d2
2581	Elke	Hansel	d2
28559	Sybill	Moser	d1

In contrast to the IN operator, which specifies each individual value, the BETWEEN operator specifies a range, which determines the lower and upper bounds of qualifying values. Example 6.11 provides an example.

EXAMPLE 6.11

Get the names and budgets for all projects with a budget between $95,000 and $120,000, inclusive:

```
USE sample;
SELECT project_name, budget
   FROM project
   WHERE budget BETWEEN 95000 AND 120000;
```

The result is

project_name	budget
Apollo	120000
Gemini	95000

The BETWEEN operator searches for all values in the range inclusively; that is, qualifying values can be between *or equal to* the lower and upper boundary values.

The BETWEEN operator is logically equal to two individual comparisons, which are connected with the Boolean operator AND. Example 6.11 is equivalent to Example 6.12.

EXAMPLE 6.12

```
USE sample;
SELECT project_name, budget
```

```
FROM project
WHERE budget >= 95000 AND budget <= 120000;
```

Like the BETWEEN operator, the NOT BETWEEN operator can be used to search for column values that do not fall within the specified range. The BETWEEN operator can also be applied to columns with character and date values.

The two SELECT statements in Example 6.13 show a query that can be written in two different, but equivalent, ways.

EXAMPLE 6.13

Get the names of all projects with a budget less than $100,000 and greater than $150,000:

```
USE sample;
SELECT project_name
  FROM project
   WHERE budget NOT BETWEEN 100000 AND 150000;
```

The result is

project_name
Gemini
Mercury

Using comparison operators, the query looks different:

```
USE sample;
SELECT project_name
  FROM project
   WHERE budget < 100000 OR budget > 150000;
```

NOTE

Although the English phrasing of the requirements, "Get the names of all projects with budgets that are less than $100,000 and greater than $150,000," suggests the use of the AND operator in the second SELECT statement presented in Example 6.13, the logical meaning of the query demands the use of the OR operator, because if you use AND instead of OR, you will get no results at all. (The reason is that there cannot be a budget that is at the same time less than $100,000 and greater than $150,000.) Therefore, the second query in the example shows a possible problem that can appear between English phrasing of an exercise and its logical meaning.

Queries Involving NULL Values

A NULL in the CREATE TABLE statement specifies that a special value called NULL (which usually represents unknown or not applicable values) is allowed in the column. These values differ from all other values in a database. The WHERE clause of a SELECT statement generally returns rows for which the comparison evaluates to TRUE. The concern, then, regarding queries is, how will comparisons involving NULL values be evaluated in the WHERE clause?

All comparisons with NULL values will return FALSE (even when preceded by NOT). To retrieve the rows with NULL values in the column, Transact-SQL includes the operator feature IS NULL. This specification in a WHERE clause of a SELECT statement has the following general form:

```
column IS [NOT] NULL
```

Example 6.14 shows the use of the IS NULL operator.

EXAMPLE 6.14

Get employee numbers and corresponding project numbers for employees with unknown jobs who work on project p2:

```
USE sample;
SELECT emp_no, project_no
   FROM works_on
   WHERE project_no = 'p2'
   AND job IS NULL;
```

The result is

emp_no	project_no
18316	p2
29346	p2

Because all comparisons with NULL values return FALSE, Example 6.15 shows syntactically correct, but logically incorrect, usage of NULL.

EXAMPLE 6.15

```
USE sample;
SELECT project_no, job
   FROM works_on
   WHERE  job <> NULL;
```

The result is

project_no	job

The condition "column IS NOT NULL" is equivalent to the condition "NOT (column IS NULL)."

The system function ISNULL allows a display of the specified value as substitution for NULL (see Example 6.16).

EXAMPLE 6.16

```
USE sample;
SELECT emp_no, ISNULL(job, 'Job unknown') AS task
   FROM works_on
   WHERE project_no = 'p1';
```

The result is

emp_no	task
10102	Analyst
9031	Manager
28559	Job unknown
29346	Clerk

Example 6.16 uses a column heading called **task** for the **job** column.

LIKE Operator

LIKE is an operator that is used for pattern matching; that is, it compares column values with a specified pattern. The data type of the column can be any character or date. The general form of the LIKE operator is

```
column [NOT] LIKE 'pattern'
```

pattern may be a string or date constant or expression (including columns of tables) and must be compatible with the data type of the corresponding column. For the specified column, the comparison between the value in a row and the pattern evaluates to TRUE if the column value matches the pattern expression.

Certain characters within the pattern—called wildcard characters—have a specific interpretation. Two of them are

- ▶ **% (percent sign)**   Specifies any sequence of zero or more characters
- ▶ **_ (underscore)**   Specifies any single character

Example 6.17 shows the use of the wildcard characters % and _.

EXAMPLE 6.17

Get the first and last names and numbers of all employees whose first name contains the letter *a* as the second character:

```
USE sample;
SELECT emp_fname, emp_lname, emp_no
   FROM employee
   WHERE emp_fname LIKE '_a%';
```

The result is

emp_fname	emp_lname	emp_no
Matthew	Smith	25348
James	James	29346

In addition to the percent sign and the underscore, Transact-SQL supports other characters that have a special meaning when used with the LIKE operator. These characters ([,], and ^) are demonstrated in Examples 6.18 and 6.19.

EXAMPLE 6.18

Get full details of all departments whose location begins with a character in the range *C* through *F*:

```
USE sample;
SELECT  dept_nt, dept_name, location
   FROM department
   WHERE location LIKE '[C-F]%';
```

The result is

dept_no	dept_name	location
d1	Research	Dallas
d3	Marketing	Dallas

As shown in Example 6.18, the square brackets, [ ], delimit a range or list of characters. The order in which characters appear in a range is defined by the collating sequence, which is determined during the system installation.

The character ^ specifies the negation of a range or a list of characters. This character has this meaning only within a pair of square brackets, as shown in Example 6.19.

EXAMPLE 6.19

Get the numbers and first and last names of all employees whose last name does not begin with the letter *J, K, L, M, N,* or *O* and whose first name does not begin with the letter *E* or *Z*:

```
USE sample;
SELECT emp_no, emp_fname, emp_lname
   FROM employee
   WHERE emp_lname LIKE '[^J-O]%'
   AND emp_fname LIKE '[^EZ]%';
```

The result is

emp_no	emp_fname	emp_lname
25348	Matthew	Smith
18316	John	Barrimore

The condition "column NOT LIKE 'pattern'" is equivalent to the condition "NOT (column LIKE 'pattern')."

Example 6.20 shows the use of the LIKE operator (together with NOT).

EXAMPLE 6.20

Get full details of all employees whose first name does not end with the character *n*:

```
USE sample;
SELECT emp_no, emp_fname, emp_lname
   FROM employee
   WHERE emp_fname NOT LIKE '%n';
```

The result is

emp_no	emp_fname	emp_lname
25348	Matthew	Smith
29346	James	James
2581	Elke	Hansel
9031	Elsa	Bertoni
28559	Sybill	Moser

Any of the wildcard characters (%, _, [,], or ^) enclosed in square brackets stands for itself. An equivalent feature is available through the ESCAPE option. Therefore, both SELECT statements in Example 6.21 have the same meaning.

EXAMPLE 6.21

```
USE sample;
SELECT project_no, project_name
   FROM project
   WHERE project_name LIKE '%[_]%';
SELECT project_no, project_name
          FROM project
          WHERE project_name LIKE '%!_%' ESCAPE '!';
```

The result is

project_no	project_name

project_no	project_name

Both SELECT statements search for the underscore as an actual character in the column **project_name**. In the first SELECT statement, this search is established by enclosing the sign _ in square brackets. The second SELECT statement uses a character (in Example 6.21, the character !) as an escape character. The escape character overrides the meaning of the underscore as the wildcard character and leaves it to be interpreted as an ordinary character. (The result contains no rows because there are no project names that include the underscore character.)

NOTE

The SQL standard supports the use of only %, _, and the ESCAPE operator. For this reason, if any wildcard character must stand for itself, using the ESCAPE operator instead of a pair of square brackets is recommended.

GROUP BY Clause

The GROUP BY clause defines one or more columns as a group such that all rows within any group have the same values for those columns. Example 6.22 shows the simple use of the GROUP BY clause.

EXAMPLE 6.22

Get all jobs of the employees:

```
USE sample;
SELECT job
   FROM works_on
   GROUP BY job;
```

The result is

job
NULL
Analyst
Clerk
Manager

In Example 6.22, the GROUP BY clause builds different groups for all possible values (NULL, too) appearing in the **job** column.

NOTE

There is a restriction regarding the use of columns in the GROUP BY clause. Each column appearing in the SELECT list of the query must also appear in the GROUP BY clause. This restriction does not apply to constants and to columns that are part of an aggregate function. (Aggregate functions are explained in the next subsection.) This makes sense, because only columns in the GROUP BY clause are guaranteed to have a single value for each group.

A table can be grouped by any combination of its columns. Example 6.23 shows the grouping of rows of the **works_on** table using two columns.

EXAMPLE 6.23

Group all employees using their project numbers and jobs:

```
USE sample;
SELECT project_no, job
   FROM works_on
   GROUP BY project_no, job;
```

The result is

project_no	job
p1	Analyst
p1	Clerk
p1	Manager
p1	NULL
p2	NULL
p2	Clerk
p3	Analyst
p3	Clerk
p3	Manager

The result of Example 6.23 shows that there are nine groups with different combinations of project numbers and jobs. The only two groups that contain more than one row are

p2	Clerk	25348, 28559
p2	NULL	18316, 29346

The sequence of the column names in the GROUP BY clause does not need to correspond to the sequence of the names in the SELECT list.

Aggregate Functions

Aggregate functions are functions that are used to get summary values. All aggregate functions can be divided into several groups:

▶ Convenient aggregate functions

▶ Statistical aggregate functions

▶ User-defined aggregate functions

▶ Analytic aggregate functions

The first three types are described in the following sections, while analytic aggregate functions are explained in detail in Chapter 23.

Convenient Aggregate Functions

The Transact-SQL language supports six aggregate functions:

▶ MIN

▶ MAX

▶ SUM

▶ AVG

▶ COUNT

▶ COUNT_BIG

All aggregate functions operate on a single argument, which can be either a column or an expression. (The only exception is the second form of the COUNT and COUNT_BIG functions, COUNT(*) and COUNT_BIG(*).) The result of each aggregate function is a constant value, which is displayed in a separate column of the result.

The aggregate functions appear in the SELECT list, which can include a GROUP BY clause. If there is no GROUP BY clause in the SELECT statement, and the SELECT list includes at least one aggregate function, then no simple columns can be included in the SELECT list (other than as arguments of an aggregate function). Therefore, Example 6.24 is *wrong*.

EXAMPLE 6.24 (EXAMPLE OF AN ILLEGAL STATEMENT)

```
USE sample;
SELECT emp_lname, MIN(emp_no)
   FROM employee;
```

The **emp_lname** column of the **employee** table must not appear in the SELECT list of Example 6.24 because it is not the argument of an aggregate function. On the other hand, all column names that are not arguments of an aggregate function may appear in the SELECT list if they are used for grouping.

The argument of an aggregate function can be preceded by one of two keywords:

▶ **ALL**   Indicates that all values of a column are to be considered (ALL is the default value)

▶ **DISTINCT**   Eliminates duplicate values of a column before the aggregate function is applied

MIN and MAX Aggregate Functions   The aggregate functions MIN and MAX compute the lowest and highest values in the column, respectively. If there is a WHERE clause, the MIN and MAX functions return the lowest or highest of values from selected rows. Example 6.25 shows the use of the aggregate function MIN.

EXAMPLE 6.25

Get the lowest employee number:

```
USE sample;
SELECT MIN(emp_no)  AS min_employee_no
   FROM employee;
```

The result is

min_employee_no
2581

The result of Example 6.25 is not user friendly. For instance, the name of the employee with the lowest number is not known. As already shown, the explicit specification of the **emp_name** column in the SELECT list is not allowed. To retrieve the name of the employee with the lowest employee number, use a subquery, as shown in Example 6.26, where the inner query contains the SELECT statement of the previous example.

EXAMPLE 6.26

Get the number and the last name of the employee with the lowest employee number:

```
USE sample;
SELECT emp_no, emp_lname
   FROM employee
   WHERE emp_no =
   (SELECT MIN(emp_no)
        FROM employee);
```

The result is

emp_no	emp_lname
2581	Hansel

Example 6.27 shows the use of the aggregate function MAX.

EXAMPLE 6.27

Get the employee number of the manager who was entered last in the **works_on** table:

```
USE sample;
SELECT emp_no
   FROM works_on
   WHERE enter_date =
   (SELECT MAX(enter_date)
        FROM works_on
        WHERE job = 'Manager');
```

The result is

emp_no
10102

The argument of the functions MIN and MAX can also be a string value or a date. If the argument has a string value, the comparison between all values will be provided using the actual collating sequence. For all arguments of temporal data types, the earliest date specifies the lowest value in the column and the latest date specifies the highest value in the column.

The DISTINCT option cannot be used with the aggregate functions MIN and MAX. All NULL values in the column that are the argument of the aggregate function MIN or MAX are always eliminated before MIN or MAX is applied.

SUM Aggregate Function   The aggregate function SUM calculates the sum of the values in the column. The argument of the function SUM must be numeric. Example 6.28 shows the use of the SUM function.

EXAMPLE 6.28

Calculate the sum of all budgets of all projects:

```
USE sample;
SELECT SUM(budget) sum_of_budgets
   FROM project;
```

The result is

sum_of_budgets
401500

The aggregate function in Example 6.28 groups all values of the projects' budgets and determines their total sum. For this reason, the query in Example 6.28 (as does each analog query) implicitly contains the grouping function. The grouping function from Example 6.28 can be written explicitly in the query, as shown in Example 6.29.

EXAMPLE 6.29

```
SELECT SUM(budget) sum_of_budgets
     FROM project
     GROUP BY();
```

The use of this syntax for the GROUP BY clause is recommended because it defines a grouping explicitly. (Chapter 23 describes several other GROUP BY features.)

The use of the DISTINCT option eliminates all duplicate values in the column before the function SUM is applied. Similarly, all NULL values are always eliminated before SUM is applied.

AVG Aggregate Function   The aggregate function AVG calculates the average of the values in the column. The argument of the function AVG must be numeric. All NULL values are eliminated before the function AVG is applied. Example 6.30 shows the use of the AVG aggregate function.

EXAMPLE 6.30

Calculate the average of all budgets with an amount greater than $100,000:

```
USE sample;
SELECT AVG(budget) avg_budget
   FROM project
   WHERE budget > 100000;
```

The result is

avg_budget
153250

COUNT and COUNT_BIG Aggregate Functions The aggregate function COUNT has two different forms:

```
COUNT([DISTINCT] col_name)
COUNT(*)
```

The first form calculates the number of values in the **col_name** column. When the DISTINCT keyword is used, all duplicate values are eliminated before COUNT is applied. This form of COUNT does not count NULL values for the column.

Example 6.31 shows the use of the first form of the aggregate function COUNT.

EXAMPLE 6.31

Count all different jobs in each project:

```
USE sample;
SELECT project_no, COUNT(DISTINCT job) job_count
   FROM works_on
   GROUP BY project_no;
```

The result is

project_no	job_count
p1	3
p2	1
p3	3

As can be seen from the result of Example 6.31, all NULL values are eliminated before the function COUNT(DISTINCT job) is applied. (The sum of all values in the column is 8 instead of 11.)

The second form of the function COUNT, COUNT(*), counts the number of rows in the table. Or, if there is a WHERE clause in the SELECT statement, COUNT(*) returns the number of rows for which the WHERE condition is true. In contrast to the first form of the function COUNT, the second form does not eliminate NULL values, because this function operates on rows and not on columns. Example 6.32 shows the use of COUNT(*).

EXAMPLE 6.32

Get the number of each job in all projects:

```
USE sample;
SELECT job, COUNT(*) job_count
   FROM works_on
   GROUP BY job;
```

The result is

job	job_count
NULL	3
Analyst	2
Clerk	4
Manager	2

The COUNT_BIG function is analogous to the COUNT function. The only difference between them is in relation to their return values: COUNT_BIG always returns a value of the BIGINT data type, while the COUNT function always returns a value of the INTEGER data type.

Statistical Aggregate Functions

The following aggregate functions belong to the group of statistical aggregate functions:

▶ **VAR**   Computes the variance of all the values listed in a column or expression

▶ **VARP**   Computes the variance for the population of all the values listed in a column or expression

▶ **STDEV** Computes the standard deviation (which is computed as the square root of the corresponding variance) of all the values listed in a column or expression

▶ **STDEVP** Computes the standard deviation for the population of all the values listed in a column or expression

Examples showing statistical aggregate functions will be provided in Chapter 23.

User-Defined Aggregate Functions

The Database Engine also supports the implementation of user-defined aggregate functions. Using these functions, you can implement and deploy aggregate functions that do not belong to aggregate functions supported by the system. These functions are a special case of user-defined functions, which will be described in detail in Chapter 8.

HAVING Clause

The HAVING clause defines the condition that is then applied to groups of rows. Hence, this clause has the same meaning to groups of rows that the WHERE clause has to the content of the corresponding table. The syntax of the HAVING clause is

```
HAVING condition
```

where **condition** contains aggregate functions or constants.

Example 6.33 shows the use of the HAVING clause with the aggregate function COUNT(*).

EXAMPLE 6.33

Get project numbers for all projects employing fewer than four persons:

```
USE sample;
SELECT project_no
   FROM works_on
   GROUP BY project_no
   HAVING COUNT(*) < 4;
```

The result is

project_no
p3

In Example 6.33, the system uses the GROUP BY clause to group all rows according to existing values in the **project_no** column. After that, it counts the number of rows in each group and selects those groups with three or fewer rows.

The HAVING clause can also be used without aggregate functions, as shown in Example 6.34.

EXAMPLE 6.34

Group rows of the **works_on** table by job and eliminate those jobs that do not begin with the letter *M*:

```
USE sample;
SELECT job
   FROM works_on
   GROUP BY job
      HAVING job LIKE 'M%';
```

The result is

job
Manager

The HAVING clause can also be used without the GROUP BY clause, although doing so is uncommon in practice. In such a case, all rows of the entire table belong to a single group.

ORDER BY Clause

The ORDER BY clause defines the particular order of the rows in the result of a query. This clause has the following syntax:

```
ORDER BY {[col_name | col_number [ASC | DESC]]} , ...
```

The **col_name** column defines the order. **col_number** is an alternative specification that identifies the column by its ordinal position in the sequence of all columns in the SELECT list (1 for the first column, 2 for the second one, and so on). ASC indicates ascending order and DESC indicates descending order, with ASC as the default value.

NOTE

The columns in the ORDER BY clause need not appear in the SELECT list. However, the ORDER BY columns must appear in the SELECT list if SELECT DISTINCT is specified. Also, this clause cannot reference columns from tables that are not listed in the FROM clause.

As the syntax of the ORDER BY clause shows, the order criterion may contain more than one column, as shown in Example 6.35.

EXAMPLE 6.35

Get department numbers and employee names for employees with employee numbers < 20000, in ascending order of last and first names:

```
USE sample;
SELECT emp_fname, emp_lname, dept_no
   FROM employee
   WHERE emp_no < 20000
   ORDER BY emp_lname, emp_fname;
```

The result is

emp_fname	emp_lname	dept_no
John	Barrimore	d1
Elsa	Bertoni	d2
Elke	Hansel	d2
Ann	Jones	d3

It is also possible to identify the columns in the ORDER BY clause by the ordinal position of the column in the SELECT list. The ORDER BY clause in Example 6.35 could be written in the following form:

```
ORDER BY 2,1
```

The use of column numbers instead of column names is an alternative solution if the order criterion contains any aggregate function. (The other way is to use column headings, which then appear in the ORDER BY clause.) However, using column names rather than numbers in the ORDER BY clause is recommended, to reduce the difficulty of maintaining the query if any columns need to be added or deleted from the SELECT list. Example 6.36 shows the use of column numbers.

EXAMPLE 6.36

For each project number, get the project number and the number of all employees, in descending order of the employee number:

```
USE sample;
SELECT project_no, COUNT(*) emp_quantity
```

```
FROM works_on
GROUP BY project_no
ORDER BY 2 DESC
```

The result is

project_no	emp_quantity
p1	4
p2	4
p3	3

The Transact-SQL language orders NULL values at the beginning of all values if the order is ascending and orders them at the end of all values if the order is descending.

Using ORDER BY to Support Paging

If you want to display rows on the current page, you can either implement that in your application or instruct the database server to do it. In the former case, all rows from the database are sent to the application, and the application's task is to retrieve the rows needed for printing and to display them. In the latter case, only those rows needed for the current page are selected from the server side and displayed. As you might guess, server-side paging generally provides better performance, because only the rows needed for printing are sent to the client.

SQL Server 2012 introduces two new clauses of the SELECT statement, OFFSET and FETCH, to support server-side paging. Example 6.37 shows the use of these two clauses.

EXAMPLE 6.37

Get the business entity ID, job title, and birthday for all female employees from the **AdventureWorks** database in ascending order of job title. Display the third page. (Ten rows are displayed per page.)

```
USE AdventureWorks;
SELECT BusinessEntityID, JobTitle, BirthDate
   FROM HumanResources.Employee
   WHERE Gender = 'F'
   ORDER BY JobTitle
   OFFSET 20 ROWS
   FETCH NEXT 10 ROWS ONLY;
```

NOTE

You can find further examples concerning the OFFSET clause in Chapter 23 (see Examples 23.24 and 23.25).

The OFFSET clause specifies the number of rows to skip before starting to return the rows. This is evaluated after the ORDER BY clause is evaluated and the rows are sorted. The FETCH NEXT clause specifies the number of rows to retrieve. The parameter of this clause can be a constant, an expression, or a result of a query. FETCH NEXT is analogous to FETCH FIRST.

The main purpose of server-side paging is to implement generic page forms, using variables. This can be done using a SQL Server batch. The corresponding example can be found in Chapter 8 (see Example 8.5).

SELECT Statement and IDENTITY Property

The IDENTITY property allows you to specify a counter of values for a specific column of a table. Columns with numeric data types, such as TINYINT, SMALLINT, INT, and BIGINT, can have this property. The Database Engine generates values for such columns sequentially, starting with an initial value. Therefore, you can use the IDENTITY property to let the system generate unique numeric values for the table column of your choice.

Each table can have only one column with the IDENTITY property. The table owner can specify the starting number and the increment value, as shown in Example 6.38.

EXAMPLE 6.38

```
USE sample;
CREATE TABLE product
   (product_no INTEGER IDENTITY(10000,1) NOT NULL,
     product_name CHAR(30) NOT NULL,
     price MONEY);
SELECT $identity
        FROM product
        WHERE product_name = 'Soap';
```

The result could be

product_no
10005

The **product** table is created first in Example 6.38. This table has the **product_no** column with the IDENTITY property. The values of the **product_no** column are automatically generated by the system, beginning with 10000 and incrementing by 1 for every subsequent value: 10000, 10001, 10002, and so on.

Some system functions and variables are related to the IDENTITY property. Example 6.38 uses the **$identity** variable. As the result set of Example 6.38 shows, this variable automatically refers to the column with the IDENTITY property.

To find out the starting value and the increment of the column with the IDENTITY property, you can use the IDENT_SEED and IDENT_INCR functions, respectively, in the following way:

```
SELECT IDENT_SEED('product'), IDENT_INCR('product)'
```

As you already know, the system automatically sets identity values. If you want to supply your own values for particular rows, you must set the IDENTITY_INSERT option to ON before the explicit value will be inserted:

```
SET IDENTITY_INSERT table_name ON
```

NOTE

Because the IDENTITY_INSERT option can be used to specify any values for a column with the IDENTITY property, IDENTITY does not generally enforce uniqueness. Use the UNIQUE or PRIMARY KEY constraint for this task.

If you insert values after the IDENTITY_INSERT option is set to ON, the system presumes that the next value is the incremented value of the highest value that exists in the table at that moment.

CREATE SEQUENCE Statement

Using the IDENTITY property has several significant disadvantages, the most important of which are the following:

▶   You can use it only with the specified table.

▶   You cannot obtain the new value before using it.

▶   You can specify the IDENTITY property only when the column is created.

For these reasons, SQL Server 2012 introduces sequences, which has the same semantics as the IDENTITY property but don't have the limitations from the preceding list. Therefore, a sequence is an independent database feature that enables you to specify a counter of values for different database objects, such as columns and variables.

Sequences are created using the CREATE SEQUENCE statement. The CREATE SEQUENCE statement is specified in the SQL standard and is implemented in other relational database systems, such as IBM DB2 and Oracle.

Example 6.39 shows how sequences can be specified in SQL Server.

EXAMPLE 6.39

```
USE sample;
CREATE SEQUENCE dbo.Sequence1
  AS INT
  START WITH 1 INCREMENT BY 5
  MINVALUE 1 MAXVALUE 256
  CYCLE;
```

The values of the sequence called **Sequence1** in Example 6.39 are automatically generated by the system, beginning with 1 and incrementing by 5 for every subsequent value. Therefore, the START clause specifies the initial value, while the INCREMENT clause defines the incremental value. (The incremental value can be positive or negative.)

The following two optional clauses, MINVALUE and MAXVALUE, are directives, which specify a minimal and maximum value for a sequence object. (Note that MINVALUE must be less than or equal to the start value, while MAXVALUE cannot be greater than the upper boundary for the values of the data type used for the specification of the sequence.) The CYCLE clause specifies that the object should restart from the minimum value (or maximum value, for descending sequence objects) when its minimum (or maximum) value is exceeded. The default value for this clause is NO CYCLE, which means that an exception will be thrown if its minimum or maximum value is exceeded.

The main property of a sequence is that it is table-independent; that is, it can be used with any database object, such as a table's column or variable. (This property positively affects storage and, therefore, performance. You do not need storage for a specified sequence; only the last-used value is stored.)

To generate new sequence values, you can use the NEXT VALUE FOR expression. Example 6.40 shows the use of this expression.

EXAMPLE 6.40

```
USE sample;
SELECT NEXT VALUE FOR dbo.sequence1;
SELECT NEXT VALUE FOR dbo.sequence1;
```

The result is

1
6

You can use the NEXT VALUE FOR expression to assign the results of a sequence to a variable or to a column. Example 6.41 shows how you can use this expression to assign the results to a table's column.

EXAMPLE 6.41

```
USE sample;
CREATE TABLE dbo.table1
        (column1 INT NOT NULL PRIMARY KEY,
         column2 CHAR(10));
        INSERT INTO dbo.table1 VALUES (NEXT VALUE FOR dbo.sequence1, 'A');
        INSERT INTO dbo.table1 VALUES (NEXT VALUE FOR dbo.sequence1, 'B');
```

Example 6.41 first creates a table called **table1** with two columns. The following two INSERT statements insert two rows in this table. (For the syntax of the INSERT statement, see Chapter 7.) The first column has values 11 and 16, respectively. (These two values are subsequent values, following the generated values in Example 6.40.)

Example 6.42 shows how you can use the catalog view called **sys.sequences** to check the current value of the sequence, without using it. (Catalog views are described in detail in Chapter 9.)

EXAMPLE 6.42

```
USE sample;
SELECT current_value
    FROM sys.sequences
    WHERE name = 'Sequence1';
```

NOTE

Generally, you use the NEXT VALUE FOR expression in the INSERT statement (see the following chapter) to let the system insert generated values. You can also use the NEXT VALUE FOR expression as part of a multirow query by using the OVER clause (see Example 23.8 in Chapter 23).

The ALTER SEQUENCE statement modifies the properties of an existing sequence. One of the most important uses of this statement is in relation to the RESTART WITH clause, which "reseeds" a given sequence. Example 6.43 shows the use of the ALTER SEQUENCE statement to reinitialize (almost) all properties of the existing sequence called **Sequence1**.

EXAMPLE 6.43

```
USE sample;
ALTER SEQUENCE dbo.sequence1
    RESTART WITH 100
    INCREMENT BY 50
    MINVALUE 50
    MAXVALUE 200
    NO CYCLE;
```

To drop a sequence, use the DROP SEQUENCE statement.

Set Operators

In addition to the operators described earlier in the chapter, three set operators are supported in the Transact-SQL language:

▶ UNION

▶ INTERSECT

▶ EXCEPT

UNION Set Operator

The result of the union of two sets is the set of all elements appearing in either or both of the sets. Accordingly, the union of two tables is a new table consisting of all rows appearing in either or both of the tables.

The general form of the UNION operator is

```
select_1 UNION [ALL] select_2 {[UNION [ALL] select_3]}...
```

select_1, **select_2**,... are SELECT statements that build the union. If the ALL option is used, all resulting rows, including duplicates, are displayed. The ALL option has the same meaning with the UNION operator as it has in the SELECT list, with one difference: the ALL option is the default in the SELECT list, but it must be specified with the UNION operator to display all resulting rows, including duplicates.

The **sample** database in its original form is not suitable for a demonstration of the UNION operator. For this reason, this section introduces a new table, **employee_enh**, which is identical to the existing **employee** table, up to the additional **domicile** column. The **domicile** column contains the place of residence of every employee.

The new **employee_enh** table has the following form:

emp_no	emp_fname	emp_lname	dept_no	domicile
25348	Matthew	Smith	d3	San Antonio
10102	Ann	Jones	d3	Houston
18316	John	Barrimore	d1	San Antonio
29346	James	James	d2	Seattle
9031	Elke	Hansel	d2	Portland
2581	Elsa	Bertoni	d2	Tacoma
28559	Sybill	Moser	d1	Houston

Creation of the **employee_enh** table provides an opportunity to show the use of the INTO clause of the SELECT statement. SELECT INTO has two different parts. First, it creates the new table with the columns corresponding to the columns listed in the SELECT list. Second, it inserts the existing rows of the original table into the new table. (The name of the new table appears with the INTO clause, and the name of the source table appears in the FROM clause of the SELECT statement.)

Example 6.44 shows the creation of the **employee_enh** table.

EXAMPLE 6.44

```
USE sample;
SELECT  emp_no, emp_fname, emp_lname, dept_no
   INTO employee_enh
   FROM employee;
ALTER TABLE employee_enh
        ADD domicile CHAR(25) NULL;
```

In Example 6.44, SELECT INTO generates the **employee_enh** table and inserts all rows from the initial table (**employee**) into the new one. Finally, the ALTER TABLE statement appends the **domicile** column to the **employee_enh** table.

After the execution of Example 6.44, the **domicile** column contains no values. The values can be added using SQL Server Management Studio (see Chapter 3) or the following UPDATE statements:

```
USE sample;
UPDATE employee_enh SET domicile = 'San Antonio'
    WHERE emp_no = 25348;
UPDATE employee_enh SET domicile = 'Houston'
    WHERE emp_no = 10102;
```

```
UPDATE employee_enh SET domicile = 'San Antonio'
            WHERE emp_no = 18316;
UPDATE employee_enh SET domicile = 'Seattle'
            WHERE emp_no = 29346;
        UPDATE employee_enh SET domicile = 'Portland'
            WHERE emp_no = 9031;
        UPDATE employee_enh SET domicile = 'Tacoma'
            WHERE emp_no = 2581;
        UPDATE employee_enh SET domicile = 'Houston'
            WHERE emp_no = 28559;
```

Example 6.45 shows the union of the tables **employee_enh** and **department**.

EXAMPLE 6.45

```
USE sample;
SELECT domicile
    FROM employee_enh
UNION
SELECT location
    FROM department;
```

The result is

domicile
San Antonio
Houston
Portland
Tacoma
Seattle
Dallas

Two tables can be connected with the UNION operator if they are compatible with each other. This means that both the SELECT lists must have the same number of columns, and the corresponding columns must have compatible data types. (For example, INT and SMALLINT are compatible data types.)

The ordering of the result of the union can be done only if the ORDER BY clause is used with the last SELECT statement, as shown in Example 6.46. The GROUP BY and HAVING clauses can be used with the particular SELECT statements, but not with the union itself.

EXAMPLE 6.46

Get the employee number for employees who either belong to department d1 or entered their project before 1/1/2007, in ascending order of employee number:

```
USE sample;
SELECT emp_no
    FROM employee
    WHERE dept_no = 'd1'
UNION
SELECT emp_no
    FROM works_on
    WHERE enter_date < '01.01.2007'
ORDER BY 1;
```

The result is

emp_no
9031
10102
18316
28559
29346

NOTE

The UNION operator supports the ALL option. When UNION is used with ALL, duplicates are not removed from the result set.

The OR operator can be used instead of the UNION operator if all SELECT statements connected by one or more UNION operators reference the same table. In this case, the set of the SELECT statements is replaced through one SELECT statement with the set of OR operators.

INTERSECT and EXCEPT Set Operators

The two other set operators are INTERSECT, which specifies the intersection, and EXCEPT, which defines the difference operator. The intersection of two tables is the set of rows belonging to both tables. The difference of two tables is the set of all rows, where the resulting rows belong to the first table but not to the second one. Example 6.47 shows the use of the INTERSECT operator.

EXAMPLE 6.47

```
USE sample;
SELECT emp_no
   FROM employee
   WHERE dept_no = 'd1'
INTERSECT
SELECT emp_no
   FROM works_on
   WHERE enter_date < '01.01.2008';
```

The result is

emp_no
18316
28559

NOTE

Transact-SQL does not support the INTERSECT operator with the ALL option. (The same is true for the EXCEPT operator.)

Example 6.48 shows the use of the EXCEPT set operator.

EXAMPLE 6.48

```
USE sample;
SELECT emp_no
   FROM employee
   WHERE dept_no = 'd3'
EXCEPT
SELECT emp_no
   FROM works_on
   WHERE enter_date > '01.01.2008';
```

The result is

emp_no
10102
25348

NOTE

You should be aware that the three set operators have different priorities for evaluation: the INTERSECT operator has the highest priority, EXCEPT is evaluated next, and the UNION operator has the lowest priority. If you do not pay attention to these different priorities, you will get unexpected results when you use several set operators together.

CASE Expressions

In database application programming, it is sometimes necessary to modify the representation of data. For instance, a person's gender can be coded using the values 1, 2, and 3 (for female, male, and child, respectively). Such a programming technique can reduce the time for the implementation of a program. The CASE expression in the Transact-SQL language makes this type of encoding easy to implement.

NOTE

CASE does not represent a statement (as in most programming languages) but an expression. Therefore, the CASE expression can be used (almost) everywhere where the Transact-SQL language allows the use of an expression.

The CASE expression has two different forms:

▶ Simple CASE expression
▶ Searched CASE expression

The syntax of the simple CASE expression is

```
CASE expression_1
   {WHEN expression_2 THEN result_1} ...
   [ELSE result_n]
END
```

A Transact-SQL statement with the simple CASE expression looks for the first expression in the list of all WHEN clauses that match **expression_1** and evaluates the corresponding THEN clause. If there is no match, the ELSE clause is evaluated.

The syntax of the searched CASE expression is

```
CASE
   {WHEN condition_1 THEN result_1} ...
      [ELSE result_n]
END
```

A Transact-SQL statement with the searched CASE expression looks for the first expression that evaluates to TRUE. If none of the WHEN conditions evaluates to TRUE, the value of the ELSE expression is returned. Example 6.49 shows the use of the searched CASE expression.

EXAMPLE 6.49

```
USE sample;
SELECT project_name,
    CASE
       WHEN budget > 0 AND budget < 100000   THEN 1
       WHEN budget >= 100000 AND budget < 200000   THEN 2
       WHEN budget >= 200000 AND budget < 300000   THEN 3
       ELSE 4
    END budget_weight
  FROM project;
```

The result is

project_name	budget_weight
Apollo	2
Gemini	1
Mercury	2

In Example 6.49, budgets of all projects are weighted, and the calculated weights (together with the name of the corresponding project) are displayed.

Example 6.50 shows another example with the CASE expression, where the WHEN clause contains inner queries as part of the expression.

EXAMPLE 6.50

```
USE sample;
SELECT project_name,
      CASE
          WHEN p1.budget < (SELECT AVG(p2.budget) FROM project p2)
               THEN 'below average'
          WHEN p1.budget = (SELECT AVG(p2.budget) FROM project p2)
               THEN 'on average'
          WHEN p1.budget > (SELECT AVG(p2.budget) FROM project p2)
               THEN 'above average'
      END budget_category
    FROM project p1;
```

The result is

project_name	budget_category
Apollo	below average
Gemini	below average
Mercury	above average

Subqueries

All previous examples in this chapter contain comparisons of column values with an expression, constant, or set of constants. Additionally, the Transact-SQL language offers the ability to compare column values with the result of another SELECT statement. Such a construct, where one or more SELECT statements are nested in the WHERE clause of another SELECT statement, is called a *subquery*. The first SELECT statement of a subquery is called the *outer query*—in contrast to the *inner query*, which denotes the SELECT statement(s) used in a comparison. The inner query will be evaluated first, and the outer query receives the values of the inner query.

NOTE

An inner query can also be nested in an INSERT, UPDATE, or DELETE statement, which will be discussed later in this book.

There are two types of subqueries:

▶ Self-contained

▶ Correlated

In a self-contained subquery, the inner query is logically evaluated exactly once. A correlated subquery differs from a self-contained one in that its value depends upon a variable from the outer query. Therefore, the inner query of a correlated subquery is logically evaluated each time the system retrieves a new row from the outer query. This section shows examples of self-contained subqueries. The correlated subquery will be discussed later in the chapter, together with the join operation.

A self-contained subquery can be used with the following operators:

▶ Comparison operators

▶ IN operator

▶ ANY or ALL operator

Subqueries and Comparison Operators

Example 6.51 shows the self-contained subquery that is used with the operator =.

EXAMPLE 6.51

Get the first and last names of employees who work in the Research department:

```
USE sample;
SELECT emp_fname, emp_lname
   FROM employee
   WHERE dept_no =
    (SELECT dept_no
       FROM department
     WHERE dept_name = 'Research');
```

The result is

emp_fname	emp_lname
John	Barrimore
Sybill	Moser

The inner query of Example 6.51 is logically evaluated first. That query returns the number of the research department (d1). Thus, after the evaluation of the inner query, the subquery in Example 6.51 can be represented with the following equivalent query:

```
USE sample
SELECT emp_fname, emp_lname
   FROM employee
   WHERE dept_no = 'd1';
```

A subquery can be used with other comparison operators, too. Any comparison operator can be used, provided that the inner query returns exactly one row. This is obvious because comparison between particular column values of the outer query and a set of values (as a result of the inner query) is not possible. The following section shows how you can handle the case in which the result of an inner query contains a set of values.

Subqueries and the IN Operator

The IN operator allows the specification of a set of expressions (or constants) that are subsequently used for the query search. This operator can be applied to a subquery for the same reason—that is, when the result of an inner query contains a set of values.

Example 6.52 shows the use of the IN operator in a subquery.

EXAMPLE 6.52

Get full details of all employees whose department is located in Dallas:

```
USE sample;
SELECT *
    FROM employee
    WHERE dept_no IN
    (SELECT dept_no
        FROM department
        WHERE location = 'Dallas');
```

The result is

emp_no	emp_fname	emp_lname	dept_no
25348	Matthew	Smith	d3
10102	Ann	Jones	d3
18316	John	Barrimore	d1
28559	Sybill	Moser	d1

Each inner query may contain further queries. This type of subquery is called a subquery with multiple levels of nesting. The maximum number of inner queries in a subquery depends on the amount of memory the Database Engine has for each SELECT statement. In the case of subqueries with multiple levels of nesting, the system first evaluates the innermost query and returns the result to the query on the next nesting level, and so on. Finally, the outermost query evaluates the final outcome.

Example 6.53 shows the query with multiple levels of nesting.

EXAMPLE 6.53

Get the last names of all employees who work on the project Apollo:

```
USE sample;
SELECT emp_lname
   FROM employee
   WHERE emp_no IN
   (SELECT emp_no
      FROM works_on
      WHERE project_no IN
      (SELECT project_no
            FROM project
            WHERE project_name = 'Apollo'));
```

The result is

emp_lname
Jones
James
Bertoni
Moser

The innermost query in Example 6.53 evaluates to the **project_no** value p1. The middle inner query compares this value with all values of the **project_no** column in the **works_on** table. The result of this query is the set of employee numbers: (10102, 29346, 9031, 28559). Finally, the outermost query displays the corresponding last names for the selected employee numbers.

Subqueries and ANY and ALL Operators

The operators ANY and ALL are always used in combination with one of the comparison operators. The general syntax of both operators is

```
column_name operator [ANY | ALL] query
```

where **operator** stands for a comparison operator and **query** is an inner query.

The ANY operator evaluates to TRUE if the result of the corresponding inner query contains at least one row that satisfies the comparison. The keyword SOME is the synonym for ANY. Example 6.54 shows the use of the ANY operator.

EXAMPLE 6.54

Get the employee numbers, project numbers, and job names for employees who have not spent the most time on one of the projects:

```
USE sample;
SELECT DISTINCT emp_no, project_no, job
   FROM works_on
   WHERE enter_date > ANY
   (SELECT  enter_date
      FROM works_on);
```

The result is

emp_no	project_no	job
2581	p3	Analyst
9031	p1	Manager
9031	p3	Clerk
10102	p3	Manager
18316	p2	NULL
25348	p2	Clerk
28559	p1	NULL
28559	p2	Clerk
29346	p1	Clerk
29346	p2	NULL

Each value of the **enter_date** column in Example 6.54 is compared with all values of this column. For all dates of the column, except the oldest one, the comparison is evaluated to TRUE at least once. The row with the oldest date does not belong to the result because the comparison does not evaluate to TRUE in any case. In other words, the expression "enter_date > ANY (SELECT enter_date FROM works_on)" is true if there are *any* (one or more) rows in the **works_on** table with a value of the **enter_date** column less than the value of **enter_date** for the current row. This will be true for all but the earliest value of the **enter_date** column.

The ALL operator evaluates to TRUE if the evaluation of the table column in the inner query returns all values of that column.

NOTE

Do not use ANY and ALL operators! Every query using ANY or ALL can be better formulated with the EXISTS function, which is explained later in this chapter (see the section "Subqueries and the EXISTS Function"). Additionally, the semantic meaning of the ANY operator can be easily confused with the semantic meaning of the ALL operator, and vice versa.

Temporary Tables

A temporary table is a database object that is temporarily stored and managed by the database system. Temporary tables can be local or global. Local temporary tables have physical representation—that is, they are stored in the **tempdb** system database. They are specified with the prefix **#** (for example, **#table_name**).

A local temporary table is owned by the session that created it and is visible only to that session. Such a table is thus automatically dropped when the creating session terminates. (If you define a local temporary table inside a stored procedure, it will be destroyed when the corresponding procedure terminates.)

Global temporary tables are visible to any user and any connection after they are created, and are deleted when all users that are referencing the table disconnect from the database server. In contrast to local temporary tables, global ones are specified with the prefix **##**.

Examples 6.55 and 6.56 show how the temporary table **project_temp** can be created using two different Transact-SQL statements.

EXAMPLE 6.55

```
USE sample;
CREATE TABLE #project_temp
   (project_no CHAR(4) NOT NULL,
    project_name CHAR(25) NOT NULL);
```

EXAMPLE 6.56

```
USE sample;
SELECT project_no, project_name
   INTO #project_temp1
   FROM project;
```

Examples 6.55 and 6.56 are similar. They use two different Transact-SQL statements to create the local temporary table, **#project_temp** and **#project_temp1**, respectively. However, Example 6.55 leaves it empty, while Example 6.56 populates the temporary table with the data from the **project** table.

Join Operator

The previous sections of this chapter demonstrated the use of the SELECT statement to query rows from one table of a database. If the Transact-SQL language supported only such simple SELECT statements, the attachment of two or more tables to retrieve data would not be possible. Consequently, all data of a database would have to be stored in one table. Although the storage of all the data of a database inside one table is possible, it has one main disadvantage—the stored data are highly redundant.

Transact-SQL provides the join operator, which retrieves data from more than one table. This operator is probably the most important operator for relational database systems, because it allows data to be spread over many tables and thus achieves a vital property of database systems—nonredundant data.

NOTE

The UNION operator also attaches two or more tables. However, the UNION operator always attaches two or more SELECT statements, while the join operator "joins" two or more tables using just one SELECT. Further, the UNION operator attaches rows of tables, while, as you will see later in this section, the join operator "joins" columns of tables.

The join operator is applied to base tables and views. In this chapter, joins between base tables are discussed, while joins concerning views will be discussed in Chapter 11.

There are several different forms of the join operator. This section discusses the following fundamental types:

- ▶ Natural join
- ▶ Cartesian product (cross join)
- ▶ Outer join
- ▶ Theta join, self-join, and semi-join

Before explaining different join forms, this section describes the different syntax forms of the join operator.

Two Syntax Forms to Implement Joins

To join tables, you can use two different forms:

- ▶ Explicit join syntax (ANSI SQL:1992 join syntax)
- ▶ Implicit join syntax (old-style join syntax)

The ANSI SQL:1992 join syntax was introduced in the SQL92 standard and defines join operations explicitly—that is, using the corresponding name for each type of join operation. The keywords concerning the explicit definition of join are

- ► CROSS JOIN
- ► [INNER] JOIN
- ► LEFT [OUTER] JOIN
- ► RIGHT [OUTER] JOIN
- ► FULL [OUTER] JOIN

CROSS JOIN specifies the Cartesian product of two tables. INNER JOIN defines the natural join of two tables, while LEFT OUTER JOIN and RIGHT OUTER JOIN characterize the join operations of the same names, respectively. Finally, FULL OUTER JOIN specifies the union of the right and left outer joins. (All these different join operations are explained in the following sections.)

The implicit join syntax is "old-style" syntax, where each join operation is defined implicitly via the WHERE clause, using the so-called join columns (see the second statement in Example 6.57).

NOTE

Use of the explicit join syntax is recommended. This syntax enhances the readability of queries. For this reason, all examples in this chapter concerning the join operation are solved using the explicit syntax forms. In a few introductory examples, you will see the old-style syntax, too.

Natural Join

Natural join is best explained through the use of an example, so check out Example 6.57.

NOTE

The phrases "natural join" and "equi-join" are often used as synonyms, but there is a slight difference between them. The equi-join operation always has one or more pairs of columns that have identical values in every row. The operation that eliminates such columns from the equi-join is called a natural join.

EXAMPLE 6.57

Get full details of each employee; that is, besides the employee's number, first and last names, and corresponding department number, also get the name of his or her department and its location, with duplicate columns displayed.

The following is the explicit join syntax:

```
USE sample;
SELECT employee.*, department.*
    FROM employee INNER JOIN department
    ON employee.dept_no = department.dept_no;
```

The SELECT list in Example 6.57 includes all columns of the **employee** and **department** tables. The FROM clause in the SELECT statement specifies the tables that are joined as well as the explicit name of the join form (INNER JOIN). The ON clause is also part of the FROM clause; it specifies the join columns from both tables. The condition employee.dept_no = department.dept_no specifies a *join condition*, and both columns are said to be *join columns*.

The equivalent solution with the old-style, implicit join syntax is as follows:

```
USE sample;
SELECT employee.*, department.*
   FROM employee, department
   WHERE employee.dept_no = department.dept_no;
```

This syntax has two significant differences from the explicit join syntax: the FROM clause of the query contains the list of tables that are joined, and the corresponding join condition is specified in the WHERE clause using join columns.

The result is

emp_no	emp_fname	emp_lname	dept_no	dept_no	dept_name	location
25348	Matthew	Smith	d3	d3	Marketing	Dallas
10102	Ann	Jones	d3	d3	Marketing	Dallas
18316	John	Barrimore	d1	d1	Research	Dallas
29346	James	James	d2	d2	Accounting	Seattle
9031	Elsa	Bertoni	d2	d2	Accounting	Seattle
2581	Elke	Hansel	d2	d2	Accounting	Seattle
28559	Sybill	Moser	d1	d1	Research	Dallas

NOTE

*It is strongly recommended that you use * in a SELECT list only when you are using interactive SQL, and avoid its use in an application program.*

Example 6.57 can be used to show how a join operation works. Note that this is just an illustration of how you can think about the join process; the Database Engine actually has several strategies from which it chooses to implement the join operator. Imagine each row of the **employee** table combined with each row of the **department** table. The result of this combination is a table with 7 columns (4 from the table **employee** and 3 from the table **department**) and 21 rows (see Table 6-1).

In the second step, all rows from Table 6-1 that do not satisfy the join condition employee.dept_no = department.dept_no are removed. These rows are prefixed in Table 6-1 with the * sign. The rest of the rows represent the result of Example 6.57.

emp_no	emp_fname	emp_lname	dept_no	dept_no	dept_name	location
*25348	Matthew	Smith	d3	d1	Research	Dallas
*10102	Ann	Jones	d3	d1	Research	Dallas
18316	John	Barrimore	d1	d1	Research	Dallas
*29346	James	James	d2	d1	Research	Dallas
*9031	Elsa	Bertoni	d2	d1	Research	Dallas
*2581	Elke	Hansel	d2	d1	Research	Dallas
28559	Sybill	Moser	d1	d1	Research	Dallas
*25348	Matthew	Smith	d3	d2	Accounting	Seattle
*10102	Ann	Jones	d3	d2	Accounting	Seattle
*18316	John	Barrimore	d1	d2	Accounting	Seattle
29346	James	James	d2	d2	Accounting	Seattle
9031	Elsa	Bertoni	d2	d2	Accounting	Seattle
2581	Elke	Hansel	d2	d2	Accounting	Seattle
*28559	Sybill	Moser	d1	d2	Accounting	Seattle
25348	Matthew	Smith	d3	d3	Marketing	Dallas
10102	Ann	Jones	d3	d3	Marketing	Dallas
*18316	John	Barrimore	d1	d3	Marketing	Dallas
*29346	James	James	d2	d3	Marketing	Dallas
*9031	Elsa	Bertoni	d2	d3	Marketing	Dallas
*2581	Elke	Hansel	d2	d3	Marketing	Dallas
*28559	Sybill	Moser	d1	d3	Marketing	Dallas

Table 6-1 *Result of the Cartesian Product Between the Tables employee and department*

The semantics of the corresponding join columns must be identical. This means both columns must have the same logical meaning. It is not required that the corresponding join columns have the same name (or even an identical type), although this will often be the case.

NOTE

It is not possible for a database system to check the logical meaning of a column. (For instance, project number and employee number have nothing in common, although both columns are defined as integers.) Therefore, database systems can check only the data type and the length of string data types. The Database Engine requires that the corresponding join columns have compatible data types, such as INT and SMALLINT.

The **sample** database contains three pairs of columns in which each column of the pair has the same logical meaning (and they have the same names as well). The **employee** and **department** tables can be joined using the columns **employee.dept_no** and **department.dept_no**. The join columns of the **employee** and **works_on** tables are the columns **employee.emp_no** and **works_on.emp_no**. Finally, the **project** and **works_on** tables can be joined using the join columns **project.project_no** and **works_on.project_no**.

The names of columns in a SELECT statement can be qualified. "Qualifying" a column name means that, to avoid any possible ambiguity about which table the column belongs to, the column name is preceded by its table name (or the alias of the table), separated by a period: **table_name.column_name**.

In most SELECT statements a column name does not need any qualification, although the use of qualified names is generally recommended for readability. If column names within a SELECT statement are ambiguous (like the columns **employee.dept_no** and **department.dept_no** in Example 6.57), the qualified names for the columns *must* be used.

In a SELECT statement with a join, the WHERE clause can include other conditions in addition to the join condition, as shown in Example 6.58.

EXAMPLE 6.58

Get full details of all employees who work on the project Gemini.

Explicit join syntax:

```
USE sample;
SELECT  emp_no, project.project_no, job, enter_date, project_name, budget
    FROM works_on JOIN project
    ON project.project_no = works_on.project_no
    WHERE project_name = 'Gemini';
```

Old-style join syntax:

```
USE sample;
SELECT  emp_no, project.project_no, job, enter_date, project_name, budget
   FROM works_on, project
   WHERE project.project_no = works_on.project_no
   AND project_name = 'Gemini';
```

NOTE

*The qualification of the columns **emp_no**, **project_name**, **job**, and **budget** in Example 6.58 is not necessary, because there is no ambiguity regarding these names.*

The result is

emp_no	project_no	job	enter_date	project_name	budget
25348	p2	Clerk	2007-02-15	Gemini	95000.0
18316	p2	NULL	2007-06-01	Gemini	95000.0
29346	p2	NULL	2006-12-15	Gemini	95000.0
28559	p2	Clerk	2008-02-01	Gemini	95000.0

From this point forward, all examples will be implemented using the explicit join syntax only.

Example 6.59 shows another use of the inner join.

EXAMPLE 6.59

Get the department number for all employees who entered their projects on October 15, 2007:

```
USE sample;
SELECT dept_no
     FROM employee JOIN works_on
     ON employee.emp_no = works_on.emp_no
     WHERE enter_date = '10.15.2007';
```

The result is

dept_no
d2

Joining More Than Two Tables

Theoretically, there is no upper limit on the number of tables that can be joined using a SELECT statement. (One join condition always combines two tables!) However, the Database Engine has an implementation restriction: the maximum number of tables that can be joined in a SELECT statement is 64.

Example 6.60 joins three tables of the **sample** database.

EXAMPLE 6.60

Get the first and last names of all analysts whose department is located in Seattle:

```
USE sample;
SELECT emp_fname, emp_lname
      FROM works_on JOIN employee ON works_on.emp_no=employee.emp_no
                    JOIN department ON employee.dept_no=department.dept_no
   AND location = 'Seattle'
   AND job = 'analyst';
```

The result is

emp_fname	emp_lname
Elke	Hansel

The result in Example 6.60 can be obtained only if you join at least three tables: **works_on, employee,** and **department.** These tables can be joined using two pairs of join columns:

```
(works_on.emp_no, employee.emp_no)
(employee.dept_no, department.dept_no)
```

Example 6.61 uses all four tables from the **sample** database to obtain the result set.

EXAMPLE 6.61

Get the names of projects (with redundant duplicates eliminated) being worked on by employees in the Accounting department:

```
USE sample;
SELECT DISTINCT project_name
      FROM project JOIN works_on
      ON project.project_no = works_on.project_no
                 JOIN employee ON works_on.emp_no = employee.emp_no
```

```
          JOIN department ON employee.dept_no = department.dept_no
    WHERE dept_name = 'Accounting';
```

The result is

project_name
Apollo
Gemini
Mercury

Notice that when joining three tables, you use two join conditions (linking two tables each) to achieve a natural join. When you join four tables, you use three such join conditions. In general, if you join n tables, you need $n - 1$ join conditions to avoid a Cartesian product. Of course, using more than $n - 1$ join conditions, as well as other conditions, is certainly permissible to further reduce the result set.

Cartesian Product

The previous section illustrated a possible method of producing a natural join. In the first step of this process, each row of the **employee** table is combined with each row of the **department** table. This intermediate result was made by the operation called *Cartesian product*. Example 6.62 shows the Cartesian product of the tables **employee** and **department**.

EXAMPLE 6.62

```
USE sample;
SELECT employee.*, department.*
    FROM employee CROSS JOIN department;
```

The result of Example 6.62 is shown in Table 6-1. A Cartesian product combines each row of the first table with each row of the second table. In general, the Cartesian product of two tables such that the first table has n rows and the second table has m rows will produce a result with n times m rows (or $n*m$). Thus, the result set in Example 6.62 contains 7*3 = 21 rows.

In practice, the use of a Cartesian product is highly unusual. Sometimes users generate the Cartesian product of two tables when they forget to include the join condition in the WHERE clause of the old-style join syntax. In this case, the output does not correspond to the expected result because it contains too many rows. (The existence of many and unexpected rows in the result is a hint that a Cartesian product of two tables, rather than the intended natural join, has been produced.)

Outer Join

In the previous examples of natural join, the result set included only rows from one table that have corresponding rows in the other table. Sometimes it is necessary to retrieve, in addition to the matching rows, the unmatched rows from one or both of the tables. Such an operation is called an *outer join*.

Examples 6.63 and 6.64 show the difference between a natural join and the corresponding outer join. (All examples in this section use the **employee_enh** table.)

EXAMPLE 6.63

Get full details of all employees, including the location of their department, who live and work in the same city:

```
USE sample;
SELECT employee_enh.*, department.location
    FROM employee_enh JOIN department
        ON domicile = location;
```

The result is

emp_no	emp_fname	emp_lname	dept_no	domicile	location
29346	James	James	d2	Seattle	Seattle

Example 6.63 uses a natural join to display the result set of rows. If you would like to know all other existing living places of employees, you have to use the (left) outer join. This is called a *left* outer join because all rows from the table on the *left* side of the operator are returned, whether or not they have a matching row in the table on the right. In other words, if there are no matching rows in the table on the right side, the outer join will still return a row from the table on the left side, with NULL in each column of the other table (see Example 6.64). The Database Engine uses the operator LEFT OUTER JOIN to specify the left outer join.

A *right* outer join is similar, but it returns all rows of the table on the *right* of the symbol. The Database Engine uses the operator RIGHT OUTER JOIN to specify the right outer join.

EXAMPLE 6.64

Get full details of all employees, including the location of their department, for all cities that are either the living place only or both the living and working place of employees:

```
USE sample;
SELECT employee_enh.*, department.location
    FROM employee_enh LEFT OUTER JOIN department
        ON domicile = location;
```

The result is

emp_no	emp_fname	emp_lname	dept_no	domicile	location
25348	Matthew	Smith	d3	San Antonio	NULL
10102	Ann	Jones	d3	Houston	NULL
18316	John	Barrimore	d1	San Antonio	NULL
29346	James	James	d2	Seattle	Seattle
9031	Elsa	Bertoni	d2	Portland	NULL
2581	Elke	Hansel	d2	Tacoma	NULL
28559	Sybill	Moser	d1	Houston	NULL

As you can see, when there is no matching row in the table on the right side (**department**, in this case), the left outer join still returns the rows from the table on the left side (**employee_enh**), and the columns of the other table are populated by NULL values. Example 6.65 shows the use of the right outer join operation.

EXAMPLE 6.65

Get full details of all departments, as well as all living places of their employees, for all cities that are either the location of a department or the living and working place of an employee:

```
USE sample;
SELECT employee_enh.domicile, department.*
    FROM employee_enh RIGHT OUTER JOIN department
        ON domicile =location;
```

The result is

domicile	dept_no	dept_name	location
Seattle	d2	Accounting	Seattle
NULL	d1	Research	Dallas
NULL	d3	Marketing	Dallas

In addition to the left and right outer joins, there is also the full outer join, which is defined as the union of the left and right outer joins. In other words, all rows from both tables are represented in the result set. If there is no corresponding row in one of the tables, its columns are returned with NULL values. This operation is specified using the FULL OUTER JOIN operator.

Every outer join operation can be simulated using the UNION operator plus the NOT EXISTS function. Example 6.66 is equivalent to the example with the left outer join (Example 6.64).

EXAMPLE 6.66

Get full details of all employees, including the location of their department, for all cities that are either the living place only or both the living and working place of employees:

```
USE sample;
SELECT employee_enh.*, department.location
   FROM employee_enh JOIN department
   ON domicile = location
UNION
SELECT employee_enh.*, 'NULL'
   FROM employee_enh
   WHERE NOT EXISTS
   (SELECT *
       FROM department
      WHERE location = domicile);
```

The first SELECT statement in the union specifies the natural join of the tables **employee_enh** and **department** with the join columns **domicile** and **location**. This SELECT statement retrieves all cities that are at the same time the living places and working places of each employee. The second SELECT statement in the union retrieves, additionally, all rows from the **employee_enh** table that do not match the condition in the natural join.

Further Forms of Join Operations

The preceding sections discussed the most important join forms. This section shows you three other forms:

- ▶ Theta join
- ▶ Self-join
- ▶ Semi-join

The following subsections describe these forms.

Theta Join

Join columns need not be compared using the equality sign. A join operation using a general join condition is called a theta join. Example 6.67, which uses the **employee_enh** table, shows the theta join operation.

EXAMPLE 6.67

Get all the combinations of employee information and department information where the domicile of an employee alphabetically precedes any location of departments.

```
USE sample;
SELECT emp_fname, emp_lname, domicile, location
    FROM employee_enh JOIN department
    ON domicile < location;
```

The result is

emp_fname	emp_lname	domicile	location
Matthew	Smith	San Antonio	Seattle
Ann	Jones	Houston	Seattle
John	Barrimore	San Antonio	Seattle
Elsa	Bertoni	Portland	Seattle
Sybill	Moser	Houston	Seattle

In Example 6.67, the corresponding values of columns **domicile** and **location** are compared. In every resulting row, the value of the **domicile** column is ordered alphabetically before the corresponding value of the **location** column.

Self-Join, or Joining a Table with Itself

In addition to joining two or more different tables, a natural join operation can also be applied to a single table. In this case, the table is joined with itself, whereby a single column of the table is compared with itself. The comparison of a column with itself means that the table name appears twice in the FROM clause of a SELECT statement. Therefore, you need to be able to reference the name of the same table twice. This can be accomplished using at least one alias name. The same is true for the column names in the join condition of a SELECT statement. In order to distinguish both column names, you use the qualified names. Example 6.68 joins the **department** table with itself.

EXAMPLE 6.68

Get full details of all departments located at the same location as at least one other department:

```
USE sample;
SELECT t1.dept_no, t1.dept_name, t1.location
    FROM department t1 JOIN department t2
```

```
      ON  t1.location = t2.location
  WHERE t1.dept_no <> t2.dept_no;
```

The result is

dept_no	dept_name	location
d3	Marketing	Dallas
d1	Research	Dallas

The FROM clause in Example 6.68 contains two aliases for the **department** table: **t1** and **t2**. The first condition in the WHERE clause specifies the join columns, while the second condition eliminates unnecessary duplicates by making certain that each department is compared with *different* departments.

Semi-Join

The semi-join is similar to the natural join, but the result of the semi-join is only the set of all rows from one table where one or more matches are found in the second table. Example 6.69 shows the semi-join operation.

EXAMPLE 6.69

```
USE sample;
SELECT emp_no, emp_lname, e.dept_no
  FROM employee e JOIN department d
  ON e.dept_no = d.dept_no
   WHERE location = 'Dallas';
```

The result is

emp_no	emp_lname	dept_no
25348	Smith	d3
10102	Jones	d3
18316	Barrimore	d1
28559	Moser	d1

As can be seen from Example 6.69, the SELECT list of the semi-join contains only columns from the **employee** table. This is exactly what characterizes the semi-join operation. This operation is usually used in distributed query processing to minimize data transfer. The Database Engine uses the semi-join operation to implement the feature called star join (see Chapter 25).

Correlated Subqueries

A subquery is said to be a *correlated subquery* if the inner query depends on the outer query for any of its values. Example 6.70 shows a correlated subquery.

EXAMPLE 6.70

Get the last names of all employees who work on project p3:

```
USE sample;
SELECT emp_lname
   FROM employee
   WHERE 'p3' IN
   (SELECT project_no
       FROM works_on
       WHERE works_on.emp_no = employee.emp_no);
```

The result is

emp_lname
Jones
Bertoni
Hansel

The inner query in Example 6.70 must be logically evaluated many times because it contains the **emp_no** column, which belongs to the **employee** table in the outer query, and the value of the **emp_no** column changes every time the Database Engine examines a different row of the **employee** table in the outer query.

Let's walk through how the system might process the query in Example 6.70. First, the system retrieves the first row of the **employee** table (for the outer query) and compares the employee number of that column (25348) with values of the **works_on.emp_no** column in the inner query. Since the only **project_no** for this employee is p2, the inner query returns the value p2. The single value in the set is not equal to the constant value p3 in the outer query, so the outer query's condition (WHERE 'p3' IN …) is not met and no rows are returned by the outer query for this employee. Then, the system retrieves the next row of the **employee** table and repeats the comparison of employee numbers in both tables. The second employee has two rows in the **works_on** table with **project_no** values of p1 and p3, so the result set of the inner query is (p1,p3). One of the elements in the result set is equal to the constant value p3, so the condition is evaluated to TRUE and the corresponding value of the **emp_lname** column in the second row (Jones) is displayed. The same process is applied to all rows of the **employee** table, and the final result set with three rows is retrieved.

More examples of correlated subqueries are shown in the next section.

Subqueries and the EXISTS Function

The EXISTS function takes an inner query as an argument and returns TRUE if the inner query returns one or more rows, and returns FALSE if it returns zero rows. This function will be explained using examples, starting with Example 6.71.

EXAMPLE 6.71

Get the last names of all employees who work on project p1:

```
USE sample;
SELECT emp_lname
   FROM employee
   WHERE EXISTS
   (SELECT *
      FROM works_on
     WHERE employee.emp_no = works_on.emp_no
    AND project_no = 'p1');
```

The result is

emp_lname
Jones
James
Bertoni
Moser

The inner query of the EXISTS function almost always depends on a variable from an outer query. Therefore, the EXISTS function usually specifies a correlated subquery.

Let's walk through how the Database Engine might process the query in Example 6.71. First, the outer query considers the first row of the **employee** table (Smith). Next, the EXISTS function is evaluated to determine whether there are any rows in the **works_on** table whose employee number matches the one from the current row in the outer query, and whose **project_no** is p1. Because Mr. Smith does not work on the project p1, the result of the inner query is an empty set and the EXISTS function is evaluated to FALSE. Therefore, the employee named Smith does not belong to the final result set. Using this process, all rows of the **employee** table are tested, and the result set is displayed.

Example 6.72 shows the use of the NOT EXISTS function.

EXAMPLE 6.72

Get the last names of all employees who work for departments not located in Seattle:

```
USE sample;
SELECT emp_lname
   FROM employee
   WHERE NOT EXISTS
   (SELECT *
       FROM department
       WHERE employee.dept_no = department.dept_no
       AND location = 'Seattle');
```

The result is

emp_lname
Smith
Jones
Barrimore
Moser

The SELECT list of an outer query involving the EXISTS function is not required to be of the form SELECT * as in the previous examples. The form SELECT column_list, where **column_list** is one or more columns of the table, is an alternate form. Both forms are equivalent, because the EXISTS function tests only the existence (i.e., nonexistence) of rows in the result set. For this reason, the use of SELECT * in this case is safe.

Should You Use Joins or Subqueries?

Almost all SELECT statements that join tables and use the join operator can be rewritten as subqueries, and vice versa. Writing the SELECT statement using the join operator is often easier to read and understand and can also help the Database Engine to find a more efficient strategy for retrieving the appropriate data. However, there are a few problems that can be easier solved using subqueries, and there are others that can be easier solved using joins.

Subquery Advantages

Subqueries are advantageous over joins when you have to calculate an aggregate value on-the-fly and use it in the outer query for comparison. Example 6.73 shows this.

EXAMPLE 6.73

Get the employee numbers and enter dates of all employees with enter dates equal to the earliest date:

```
USE sample;
SELECT emp_no, enter_date
    FROM works_on
    WHERE enter_date = (SELECT min(enter_date)
                          FROM works_on);
```

This problem cannot be solved easily with a join, because you would have to write the aggregate function in the WHERE clause, which is not allowed. (You can solve the problem using two separate queries in relation to the **works_on** table.)

Join Advantages

Joins are advantageous over subqueries if the SELECT list in a query contains columns from more than one table. Example 6.74 shows this.

EXAMPLE 6.74

Get the employee numbers, last names, and jobs for all employees who entered their projects on October 15, 2007:

```
USE sample;
SELECT employee.emp_no, emp_lname, job
    FROM employee, works_on
    WHERE employee.emp_no = works_on.emp_no
    AND enter_date = '10.15.2007';
```

The SELECT list of the query in Example 6.74 contains columns **emp_no** and **emp_lname** from the **employee** table and the **job** column from the **works_on** table. For this reason, the equivalent solution with the subquery would display an error, because subqueries can display information only from the outer table.

Table Expressions

Table expressions are subqueries that are used where a table is expected. There are two types of table expressions:

▶ Derived tables

▶ Common table expressions

The following subsections describe these two forms of table expressions.

Derived Tables

A derived table is a table expression that appears in the FROM clause of a query. You can apply derived tables when the use of column aliases is not possible because another clause is processed by the SQL translator before the alias name is known. Example 6.75 shows an attempt to use a column alias where another clause is processed before the alias name is known.

EXAMPLE 6.75 (EXAMPLE OF AN ILLEGAL STATEMENT)

Get all existing groups of months from the **enter_date** column of the **works_on** table:

```
USE sample;
SELECT MONTH(enter_date) as enter_month
FROM works_on
GROUP BY enter_month;
```

The result is

```
Message 207: Level 16, State 1, Line 4
          The invalid column 'enter_month'
```

The reason for the error message is that the GROUP BY clause is processed before the corresponding SELECT list, and the alias name **enter_month** is not known at the time the grouping is processed.

By using a derived table that contains the preceding query (without the GROUP BY clause), you can solve this problem, because the FROM clause is executed before the GROUP BY clause, as shown in Example 6.76.

EXAMPLE 6.76

```
USE sample;
SELECT enter_month
   FROM (SELECT MONTH(enter_date) as enter_month
            FROM works_on) AS m
GROUP BY enter_month;
```

The result is

enter_month
1
2
4
6
8
10
11
12

Generally, it is possible to write a table expression any place in a SELECT statement where a table can appear. (The result of a table expression is always a table or, in a special case, an expression.) Example 6.77 shows the use of a table expression in a SELECT list.

EXAMPLE 6.77

```
USE sample;
SELECT w.job, (SELECT e.emp_lname
               FROM employee e WHERE e.emp_no = w.emp_no) AS name
    FROM works_on w
    WHERE w.job IN('Manager', 'Analyst');
```

The result is

job	name
Analyst	Jones
Manager	Jones
Analyst	Hansel
Manager	Bertoni

Common Table Expressions

A common table expression (CTE) is a named table expression that is supported by Transact-SQL. There are two types of queries that use CTE:

► Nonrecursive queries

► Recursive queries

The following sections describe both query types.

NOTE

Common table expressions are also used by the APPLY operator, which allows you to invoke a table-valued function for each row returned by an outer table expression of a query. This operator is discussed in Chapter 8.

CTEs and Nonrecursive Queries

The nonrecursive form of a CTE can be used as an alternative to derived tables and views. Generally, a CTE is defined using the WITH statement and an additional query that refers to the name used in WITH (see Example 6.79).

NOTE

The WITH keyword is ambiguous in the Transact-SQL language. To avoid ambiguity, you have to use a semicolon (;) to terminate the statement preceding the WITH statement.

Examples 6.78 and 6.79 use the **AdventureWorks** database to show how CTEs can be used in nonrecursive queries. Example 6.78 uses the "convenient" features, while Example 6.79 solves the same problem using a nonrecursive query.

EXAMPLE 6.78

```
USE AdventureWorks;
SELECT SalesOrderID
 FROM Sales.SalesOrderHeader
  WHERE TotalDue > (SELECT AVG(TotalDue)
                     FROM Sales.SalesOrderHeader
                     WHERE YEAR(OrderDate) = '2002')
    AND Freight > (SELECT AVG(TotalDue)
                     FROM Sales.SalesOrderHeader
                     WHERE YEAR(OrderDate) = '2002')/2.5;
```

The query in Example 6.78 finds total dues whose values are greater than the average of all dues and whose freights are greater than 40 percent of the average of all dues. The main property of this query is that it is space-consuming, because an inner query has to be written twice. One way to shorten the syntax of the query is to create a view containing the inner query, but that is rather complicated because you would have to create the view and then drop it when you are done with the query. A better way is to write a CTE. Example 6.79 shows the use of the nonrecursive CTE, which shortens the definition of the query in Example 6.78.

EXAMPLE 6.79

```
USE AdventureWorks;
WITH price_calc(year_2002) AS
        (SELECT AVG(TotalDue)
              FROM Sales.SalesOrderHeader
            WHERE YEAR(OrderDate) = '2002')
SELECT SalesOrderID
      FROM Sales.SalesOrderHeader
     WHERE TotalDue > (SELECT year_2002  FROM price_calc)
AND Freight > (SELECT year_2002  FROM price_calc)/2.5;
```

The syntax for the WITH clause in nonrecursive queries is

```
WITH cte_name (column_list) AS
     ( inner_query)
outer_query
```

cte_name is the name of the CTE that specifies a resulting table. The list of columns that belong to the table expression is written in brackets. (The CTE in Example 6.79 is called **price_calc** and has one column, **year_2002**.) **inner_query** in the CTE syntax defines the SELECT statement, which specifies the result set of the corresponding table expression. After that, you can use the defined table expression in an outer query. (The outer query in Example 6.79 uses the CTE called **price_calc** and its column **year_2002** to simplify the inner query, which appears twice.)

CTEs and Recursive Queries

NOTE

The material in this subsection is complex. Therefore, you might want to skip it on the first reading of the book and make a note to yourself to return to it.

You can use CTEs to implement recursion because CTEs can contain references to themselves. The basic syntax for a CTE for recursive queries is

```
WITH cte_name (column_list) AS
    (anchor_member
     UNION ALL
     recursive_member)
outer_query
```

cte_name and **column_list** have the same meaning as in CTEs for nonrecursive queries. The body of the WITH clause comprises two queries that are connected with the UNION ALL operator. The first query will be invoked only once, and it starts to accumulate the result of the recursion. The first operand of UNION ALL does not reference the CTE (see Example 6.80). This query is called the *anchor query* or *seed*.

The second query contains a reference to the CTE and represents the recursive portion of it. For this reason it is called the *recursive member*. In the first invocation of the recursive part, the reference to the CTE represents the result of the anchor query. The recursive member uses the query result of the first invocation. After that, the system repeatedly invokes the recursive part. The invocation of the recursive member ends when the result of the previous invocation is an empty set.

The UNION ALL operator joins the rows accumulated so far, as well as the additional rows that are added in the current invocation. (Inclusion of UNION ALL means that no duplicate rows will be eliminated from the result.)

Finally, **outer query** defines a query specification that uses the CTE to retrieve all invocations of the union of both members.

The table definition in Example 6.80 will be used to demonstrate the recursive form of CTEs.

EXAMPLE 6.80

```
USE sample;
CREATE TABLE airplane
    (containing_assembly VARCHAR(10),
     contained_assembly VARCHAR(10),
     quantity_contained INT,
     unit_cost DECIMAL (6,2));
insert into airplane values ( 'Airplane', 'Fuselage',1, 10);
insert into airplane values ( 'Airplane', 'Wings', 1, 11);
insert into airplane values ( 'Airplane', 'Tail',1, 12);
insert into airplane values ( 'Fuselage', 'Cockpit', 1, 13);
insert into airplane values ( 'Fuselage', 'Cabin', 1, 14);
insert into airplane values ( 'Fuselage', 'Nose',1, 15);
insert into airplane values ( 'Cockpit', NULL, 1,13);
insert into airplane values ( 'Cabin', NULL, 1, 14);
insert into airplane values ( 'Nose', NULL, 1, 15);
insert into airplane values ( 'Wings', NULL,2, 11);
insert into airplane values ( 'Tail', NULL,  1, 12);
```

The **airplane** table contains four columns. The column **containing_assembly** specifies an assembly, while **contained_assembly** comprises the parts (one by one) that build the corresponding assembly. (Figure 6-1 shows graphically how an airplane with its parts could look.)

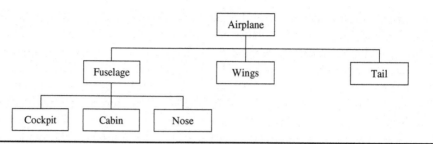

Figure 6-1 *Presentation of an airplane and its parts*

Suppose that the **airplane** table contains 11 rows, which are shown in Table 6-2. (The INSERT statements in Example 6.80 insert these rows in the **airplane** table.)

Example 6.81 shows the use of the WITH clause to define a query that calculates the total costs of each assembly.

EXAMPLE 6.81

```
USE sample;
WITH list_of_parts(assembly1, quantity, cost) AS
   (SELECT containing_assembly, quantity_contained, unit_cost
     FROM airplane
     WHERE contained_assembly IS NULL
   UNION ALL
   SELECT a.containing_assembly, a.quantity_contained,
```

Airplane	Fuselage	1	10
Airplane	Wings	1	11
Airplane	Tail	1	12
Fuselage	Cockpit	1	13
Fuselage	Cabin	1	14
Fuselage	Nose	1	15
Cockpit	NULL	1	13
Cabin	NULL	1	14
Nose	NULL	1	15
Wings	NULL	2	11
Tail	NULL	1	12

Table 6-2 *Content of the airplane Table*

```
        CAST(l.quantity*l.cost AS DECIMAL(6,2))
         FROM list_of_parts l,airplane a
        WHERE l.assembly1 = a.contained_assembly)
SELECT * FROM list_of_parts;
```

The WITH clause defines the CTE called **list_of_parts,** which contains three columns: **assembly, quantity,** and **cost.** The first SELECT statement in Example 6.81 will be invoked only once, to accumulate the results of the first step in the recursion process.

The SELECT statement in the last row of Example 6.81 displays the following result:

assembly	quantity	costs
Cockpit	1	13.00
Cabin	1	14.00
Nose	1	16.500
Wings	2	11.00
Tail	1	12.00
Airplane	1	12.00
Airplane	1	22.00
Fuselage	1	16.500
Airplane	1	16.500
Fuselage	1	14.00
Airplane	1	14.00
Fuselage	1	13.00
Airplane	1	13.00

The first five rows in the preceding output show the result set of the first invocation of the anchor member of the query in Example 6.81. All other rows are the result of the recursive member (second part) of the query in the same example. The recursive member of the query will be invoked twice: the first time for the fuselage assembly and the second time for the airplane itself.

The query in Example 6.82 will be used to get the costs for each assembly with all its subparts.

EXAMPLE 6.82

```
USE sample;
WITH list_of_parts(assembly, quantity, cost) AS
  (SELECT containing_assembly, quantity_contained, unit_cost
```

```
      FROM airplane
      WHERE contained_assembly IS NULL
   UNION ALL
   SELECT a.containing_assembly, a.quantity_contained,
         CAST(l.quantity*l.cost AS DECIMAL(6,2))
          FROM list_of_parts l,airplane a
          WHERE l.assembly = a.contained_assembly )
SELECT assembly, SUM(quantity) parts, SUM(cost) sum_cost
    FROM  list_of_parts
    GROUP BY assembly;
```

The output of the query in Example 6.82 is as follows:

assembly	parts	sum_cost
Airplane	5	76.00
Cabin	1	14.00
Cockpit	1	13.00
Fuselage	3	42.00
Nose	1	16.500
Tail	1	12.00
Wings	2	11.00

There are several restrictions for a CTE in a recursive query:

▶ The CTE definition must contain at least two SELECT statements (an anchor member and one recursive member) combined by the UNION ALL operator.

▶ The number of columns in the anchor and recursive members must be the same. (This is the direct consequence of using the UNION ALL operator.)

▶ The data type of a column in the recursive member must be the same as the data type of the corresponding column in the anchor member.

▶ The FROM clause of the recursive member must refer only once to the name of the CTE.

▶ The following options are not allowed in the definition part of a recursive member: SELECT DISTINCT, GROUP BY, HAVING, aggregation functions, TOP, and subqueries. (Also, the only join operation that is allowed in the query definition is an inner join.)

Summary

This chapter covered all the features of the SELECT statement regarding data retrieval from one or more tables. Every SELECT statement that retrieves data from a table must contain at least a SELECT list and the FROM clause. The FROM clause specifies the table(s) from which the data is retrieved. The most important optional clause is the WHERE clause, containing one or more conditions that can be combined using the Boolean operators AND, OR, and NOT. Hence, the conditions in the WHERE clause place the restriction on the selected row.

Exercises

E.6.1

Get all rows of the **works_on** table.

E.6.2

Get the employee numbers for all clerks.

E.6.3

Get the employee numbers for employees working on project p2 and having employee numbers lower than 10000. Solve this problem with two different but equivalent SELECT statements.

E.6.4

Get the employee numbers for employees who didn't enter their project in 2007.

E.6.5

Get the employee numbers for all employees who have a leading job (i.e., Analyst or Manager) in project p1.

E.6.6

Get the enter dates for all employees in project p2 whose jobs have not been determined yet.

E.6.7

Get the employee numbers and last names of all employees whose first names contain two letter *t*'s.

E.6.8

Get the employee numbers and first names of all employees whose last names have a letter *o* or *a* as the second character and end with the letters *es*.

E.6.9

Find the employee numbers of all employees whose departments are located in Seattle.

E.6.10

Find the last and first names of all employees who entered their projects on 04.01.2007.

E.6.11

Group all departments using their locations.

E.6.12

What is a difference between the DISTINCT and GROUP BY clauses?

E.6.13

How does the GROUP BY clause manage the NULL values? Does it correspond to the general treatment of these values?

E.6.14

What is the difference between COUNT(*) and COUNT(column)?

E.6.15

Find the highest employee number.

E.6.16

Get the jobs that are done by more than two employees.

E.6.17

Find the employee numbers of all employees who are clerks or work for department d3.

E.6.18

Why is the following statement wrong?

```
SELECT project_name
    FROM project
    WHERE project_no =
        (SELECT project_no FROM works_on WHERE Job = 'Clerk')
```

Write the correct syntax form for the statement.

E.6.19

What is a practical use of temporary tables?

E.6.20

What is a difference between global and local temporary tables?

> **NOTE**
> *Write all solutions for the following exercises that use a join operation using the explicit join syntax.*

E.6.21

For the **project** and **works_on** tables, create the following:
   a. Natural join
   b. Cartesian product

E.6.22

If you intend to join several tables in a query (say n tables), how many join conditions are needed?

E.6.23

Get the employee numbers and job titles of all employees working on project Gemini.

E.6.24

Get the first and last names of all employees who work for department Research or Accounting.

E.6.25

Get the enter dates of all clerks who belong to the department d1.

E.6.26

Get the names of projects on which two or more clerks are working.

E.6.27

Get the first and last names of the employees who are managers and work on project Mercury.

E.6.28

Get the first and last names of all employees who entered the project at the same time as at least one other employee.

E.6.29

Get the employee numbers of the employees living in the same location and belonging to the same department as one another. (Hint: Use the extended **sample** database.)

E.6.30

Get the employee numbers of all employees belonging to the Marketing department. Find two equivalent solutions using

▶ The join operator

▶ The correlated subquery

Chapter 7

Modification of a Table's Contents

In This Chapter

- ▶ INSERT Statement
- ▶ UPDATE Statement
- ▶ DELETE Statement
- ▶ Other T-SQL Modification Statements and Clauses

I n addition to the SELECT statement, which was introduced in Chapter 6, there are three other DML statements: INSERT, UPDATE, and DELETE. Like the SELECT statement, these three modification statements operate either on tables or on views. This chapter discusses these statements in relation to tables and gives examples of their use. Additionally, it explains two other statements: TRUNCATE TABLE and MERGE, as well as the OUTPUT clause. Whereas the TRUNCATE TABLE statement is a Transact-SQL extension to the SQL standard, MERGE is a standardized feature in SQL Server. The OUTPUT clause allows you to display explicitly the inserted (or updated) rows.

INSERT Statement

The INSERT statement inserts rows (or parts of them) into a table. It has two different forms:

```
INSERT [INTO] tab_name  [(col_list)]
   DEFAULT VALUES | VALUES ({ DEFAULT | NULL | expression } [ ,...n] )

INSERT INTO tab_name | view_name [(col_list)]
     {select_statement | execute_statement}
```

Using the first form, exactly one row (or part of it) is inserted into the corresponding table. The second form of the INSERT statement inserts the result set from the SELECT statement or from the stored procedure, which is executed using the EXECUTE statement. (The stored procedure must return data, which is then inserted into the table. The SELECT statement can select values from a different table or from the same table as the target of the INSERT statement, as long as the types of the columns are compatible.)

With both forms, every inserted value must have a data type that is compatible with the data type of the corresponding column of the table. To ensure compatibility, all character-based values and temporal data must be enclosed in apostrophes, while all numeric values need no such enclosing.

Inserting a Single Row

In both forms of the INSERT statement, the explicit specification of the column list is optional. This means that omitting the list of columns is equivalent to specifying a list of all columns in the table.

The option DEFAULT VALUES inserts default values for all the columns. If a column is of the data type TIMESTAMP or has the IDENTITY property, the value, which is automatically created by the system, will be inserted. For other data types, the column is set to the appropriate non-null default value if a default exists, or NULL, if it doesn't. If the column is not nullable and has no DEFAULT value, then the INSERT statement fails and an error will be indicated.

Examples 7.1 through 7.4 insert rows into the four tables of the **sample** database. This action shows the use of the INSERT statement to load a small amount of data into a database.

EXAMPLE 7.1

Load data into the **employee** table:

```
USE sample;
INSERT INTO employee VALUES (25348, 'Matthew', 'Smith','d3');
INSERT INTO employee VALUES (10102, 'Ann', 'Jones','d3');
INSERT INTO employee VALUES (18316, 'John', 'Barrimore', 'd1');
INSERT INTO employee VALUES (29346, 'James', 'James', 'd2');
INSERT INTO employee VALUES (9031, 'Elsa', 'Bertoni', 'd2');
INSERT INTO employee VALUES (2581, 'Elke', 'Hansel', 'd2');
INSERT INTO employee VALUES (28559, 'Sybill', 'Moser', 'd1');
```

EXAMPLE 7.2

Load data into the **department** table:

```
USE sample;
INSERT INTO department VALUES ('d1', 'Research', 'Dallas');
INSERT INTO department VALUES ('d2', 'Accounting', 'Seattle');
INSERT INTO department VALUES ('d3', 'Marketing', 'Dallas');
```

EXAMPLE 7.3

Load data into the **project** table:

```
USE sample;
INSERT INTO project VALUES ('p1', 'Apollo', 120000.00);
INSERT INTO project VALUES ('p2', 'Gemini', 95000.00);
INSERT INTO project VALUES ('p3', 'Mercury', 186500.00);
```

EXAMPLE 7.4

Load data into the **works_on** table:

```
USE sample;
INSERT INTO works_on VALUES (10102,'p1', 'Analyst', '2006.10.1');
INSERT INTO works_on VALUES (10102, 'p3', 'Manager', '2008.1.1');
INSERT INTO works_on VALUES (25348, 'p2', 'Clerk', '2007.2.15');
INSERT INTO works_on VALUES (18316, 'p2', NULL, '2007.6.1');
INSERT INTO works_on VALUES (29346, 'p2', NULL, '2006.12.15');
```

```
INSERT INTO works_on VALUES (2581, 'p3', 'Analyst', '2007.10.15');
INSERT INTO works_on VALUES (9031, 'p1', 'Manager', '2007.4.15');
INSERT INTO works_on VALUES (28559, 'p1', 'NULL', '2007.8.1');
INSERT INTO works_on VALUES (28559, 'p2', 'Clerk', '2008.2.1');
INSERT INTO works_on VALUES (9031, 'p3', 'Clerk', '2006.11.15');
INSERT INTO works_on VALUES (29346, 'p1','Clerk', '2007.1.4');
```

There are a few different ways to insert values into a new row. Examples 7.5 through 7.7 show these possibilities.

EXAMPLE 7.5

```
USE sample;
INSERT INTO employee VALUES (15201, 'Dave', 'Davis', NULL);
```

The INSERT statement in Example 7.5 corresponds to the INSERT statements in Examples 7.1 through 7.4. The explicit use of the keyword NULL inserts the null value into the corresponding column.

The insertion of values into some (but not all) of a table's columns usually requires the explicit specification of the corresponding columns. The omitted columns must either be nullable or have a DEFAULT value.

EXAMPLE 7.6

```
USE sample;
INSERT INTO employee (emp_no, emp_fname, emp_lname)
            VALUES (15201, 'Dave', 'Davis');
```

Examples 7.5 and 7.6 are equivalent. The **dept_no** column is the only nullable column in the **employee** table because all other columns in the **employee** table were declared with the NOT NULL clause in the CREATE TABLE statement.

The order of column names in the VALUE clause of the INSERT statement can be different from the original order of those columns, which is determined in the CREATE TABLE statement. In this case, it is absolutely necessary to list the columns in the new order.

EXAMPLE 7.7

```
USE sample;
INSERT INTO employee (emp_lname, emp_fname, dept_no, emp_no)
            VALUES ('Davis', 'Dave', 'd1', 15201);
```

Inserting Multiple Rows

The second form of the INSERT statement inserts one or more rows selected with a subquery. Example 7.8 shows how a set of rows can be inserted using the second form of the INSERT statement.

EXAMPLE 7.8

Get all the numbers and names for departments located in Dallas, and load the selected data into a new table:

```
USE sample;
CREATE TABLE dallas_dept
        (dept_no CHAR(4) NOT NULL,
         dept_name CHAR(20) NOT NULL);

INSERT INTO dallas_dept (dept_no, dept_name)
    SELECT dept_no, dept_name
        FROM department
        WHERE location = 'Dallas';
```

The new table created in Example 7.8, **dallas_dept,** has the same columns as the **department** table except for the **location** column. The subquery in the INSERT statement selects all rows with the value 'Dallas' in the **location** column. The selected rows will be subsequently inserted in the new table.

The content of the **dallas_dept** table can be selected with the following SELECT statement:

```
SELECT * FROM dallas_dept;
```

The result is

dept_no	dept_name
d1	Research
d3	Marketing

Example 7.9 is another example that shows how multiple rows can be inserted using the second form of the INSERT statement.

EXAMPLE 7.9

Get all employee numbers, project numbers, and project enter dates for all clerks who work in project p2, and load the selected data into a new table:

```
USE sample;
CREATE TABLE clerk_t
     (emp_no INT NOT NULL,
      project_no CHAR(4),
      enter_date DATE);

INSERT INTO clerk_t (emp_no, project_no, enter_date)
    SELECT emp_no, project_no, enter_date
       FROM works_on
       WHERE job = 'Clerk'
       AND project_no = 'p2';
```

The new table, **clerk_t**, contains the following rows:

emp_no	project_no	enter_date
25348	p2	2007-02-15
28559	p2	2008-02-01

The tables **dallas_dept** and **clerk_t** (Examples 7.8 and 7.9) were empty before the INSERT statement inserted the rows. If, however, the table already exists and there are rows in it, the new rows will be appended.

NOTE

You can replace both statements (CREATE TABLE and INSERT) in Example 7.9 with the SELECT statement with the INTO clause (see Example 6.48 in Chapter 6).

Table Value Constructors and INSERT

A *table* (or *row*) *value constructor* allows you to assign several tuples (rows) with a DML statement such as INSERT or UPDATE. Example 7.10 shows how you can assign several rows using such a constructor with an INSERT statement.

EXAMPLE 7.10

```
USE sample;
 INSERT INTO department VALUES
          ('d4', 'Human Resources', 'Chicago'),
```

```
('d5', 'Distribution', 'New Orleans'),
('d6', 'Sales', 'Chicago');
```

The INSERT statement in Example 7.10 inserts three rows at the same time in the **department** table using the table value constructor. As you can see from the example, the syntax of the constructor is rather simple. To use a table value constructor, list the values of each row inside the pair of parentheses and separate each list from the others by using a comma.

UPDATE Statement

The UPDATE statement modifies values of table rows. This statement has the following general form:

```
UPDATE tab_name
    { SET column_1 = {expression | DEFAULT | NULL} [,...n]
    [FROM tab_name1 [,...n]]
    [WHERE condition]
```

Rows in the **tab_name** table are modified in accordance with the WHERE clause. For each row to be modified, the UPDATE statement changes the values of the columns in the SET clause, assigning a constant (or generally an expression) to the associated column. If the WHERE clause is omitted, the UPDATE statement modifies all rows of the table. (The FROM clause will be discussed later in this section.)

NOTE

An UPDATE statement can modify data of a single table only.

The UPDATE statement in Example 7.11 modifies exactly one row of the **works_ on** table, because the combination of the columns **emp_no** and **project_no** builds the primary key of that table and is therefore unique. This example modifies the task of the employee, which was previously unknown or set to NULL.

EXAMPLE 7.11

Set the task of employee number 18316, who works on project p2, to be 'Manager':

```
USE sample;
UPDATE works_on
   SET job = 'Manager'
```

```
WHERE emp_no = 18316
AND project_no = 'p2';
```

Example 7.12 modifies rows of a table with an expression.

EXAMPLE 7.12

Change the budgets of all projects to be represented in English pounds. The current rate of exchange is 0.51£ for $1.

```
USE sample;
UPDATE project
   SET budget = budget*0.51;
```

In the example, all rows of the **project** table will be modified because of the omitted WHERE clause. The modified rows of the **project** table can be displayed with the following Transact-SQL statement:

```
SELECT * FROM project;
```

The result is

project_no	project_name	budget
p1	Apollo	61200
p2	Gemini	48450
p3	Mercury	95115

Example 7.13 uses an inner query in the WHERE clause of the UPDATE statement. Because of the use of the IN operator, more than one row can result from this query.

EXAMPLE 7.13

Due to her illness, set all tasks on all projects for Mrs. Jones to NULL:

```
USE sample;
UPDATE works_on
     SET job = NULL
     WHERE emp_no IN
     (SELECT emp_no
         FROM employee
         WHERE emp_lname = 'Jones');
```

Example 7.13 can also be solved using the FROM clause of the UPDATE statement. The FROM clause contains the names of tables that are involved in the

UPDATE statement. All these tables must be subsequently joined. Example 7.14 shows the use of the FROM clause. This example is identical to the previous one.

NOTE

The FROM clause is a Transact-SQL extension to the ANSI SQL standard.

EXAMPLE 7.14

```
USE sample;
UPDATE works_on
   SET job = NULL
    FROM works_on, employee
    WHERE emp_lname = 'Jones'
    AND works_on.emp_no = employee.emp_no;
```

Example 7.15 illustrates the use of the CASE expression in the UPDATE statement. (For a detailed discussion of this expression, refer to Chapter 6.)

EXAMPLE 7.15

The budget of each project should be increased by a percentage (20, 10, or 5) depending on its previous amount of money. Those projects with a lower budget will be increased by the higher percentages.

```
USE sample;
UPDATE project
   SET budget = CASE
            WHEN budget >0 and budget < 100000   THEN budget*1.2
            WHEN budget >= 100000 and budget < 200000   THEN budget*1.1
            ELSE budget*1.05
            END
```

DELETE Statement

The DELETE statement deletes rows from a table. This statement has two different forms:

```
DELETE FROM table_name
   [WHERE predicate];


DELETE table_name
        FROM table_name [,...n]
        [WHERE condition];
```

All rows that satisfy the condition in the WHERE clause will be deleted. Explicitly naming columns within the DELETE statement is not necessary (or allowed), because the DELETE statement operates on rows and not on columns.

Example 7.16 shows an example of the first form of the DELETE statement.

EXAMPLE 7.16

Delete all managers in the **works_on** table:

```
USE sample;
DELETE FROM works_on
    WHERE job = 'Manager';
```

The WHERE clause in the DELETE statement can contain an inner query, as shown in Example 7.17.

EXAMPLE 7.17

Mrs. Moser is on leave. Delete all rows in the database concerning her:

```
USE sample;
DELETE FROM works_on
    WHERE emp_no IN
    (SELECT emp_no
        FROM employee
        WHERE emp_lname = 'Moser');

DELETE FROM employee
    WHERE emp_lname = 'Moser';
```

Example 7.17 can also be performed using the FROM clause, as Example 7.18 shows. This clause has the same semantics as the FROM clause in the UPDATE statement.

EXAMPLE 7.18

```
USE sample;
DELETE works_on
    FROM works_on, employee
    WHERE works_on.emp_no = employee.emp_no
    AND emp_lname = 'Moser';

DELETE FROM employee
    WHERE emp_lname = 'Moser';
```

The use of the WHERE clause in the DELETE statement is optional. If the WHERE clause is omitted, all rows of a table will be deleted, as shown in Example 7.19.

EXAMPLE 7.19

```
USE sample;
DELETE FROM works_on;
```

NOTE

There is a significant difference between the DELETE and the DROP TABLE statements. The DELETE statement deletes (partially or totally) the contents of a table, whereas the DROP TABLE statement deletes both the contents and the schema of a table. Thus, after a DELETE statement, the table still exists in the database (although possibly with zero rows), but after a DROP TABLE statement, the table no longer exists.

Other T-SQL Modification Statements and Clauses

SQL Server supports two additional modification statements:

▶ TRUNCATE TABLE

▶ MERGE

and the OUTPUT clause.

Both statements, together with the OUTPUT clause, will be explained in turn in the following subsections.

TRUNCATE TABLE Statement

The Transact-SQL language also supports the TRUNCATE TABLE statement. This statement normally provides a "faster executing" version of the DELETE statement without the WHERE clause. The TRUNCATE TABLE statement deletes all rows from a table more quickly than does the DELETE statement because it drops the contents of the table page by page, while DELETE drops the contents row by row.

NOTE

The TRUNCATE TABLE statement is a Transact-SQL extension to the SQL standard.

The TRUNCATE TABLE statement has the following form:

```
TRUNCATE TABLE table_name
```

TIP

If you want to delete all rows from a table, use the TRUNCATE TABLE statement. This statement is significantly faster than DELETE because it is minimally logged and there are just a few entries in the log during its execution. (Logging is discussed in detail in Chapter 13.)

MERGE Statement

The MERGE statement combines the sequence of conditional INSERT, UPDATE, and DELETE statements in a single atomic statement, depending on the existence of a record. In other words, you can sync two different tables so that the content of the target table is modified based on differences found in the source table.

The main application area for MERGE is a data warehouse environment (see Chapter 23), where tables need to be refreshed periodically with new data arriving from online transaction processing (OLTP) systems. This new data may contain changes to existing rows in tables and/or new rows that need to be inserted. If a row in the new data corresponds to an item that already exists in the table, an UPDATE or a DELETE statement is performed. Otherwise, an INSERT statement is performed.

The alternative way, which you can use instead of applying the MERGE statement, is to write a sequence of INSERT, UPDATE, and DELETE statements, where, for each row, the decision is made whether to insert, delete, or update the data. This old approach has significant performance disadvantages: it requires multiple data scans and operates on a record-by-record basis.

Examples 7.20 and 7.21 show the use of the MERGE statement.

EXAMPLE 7.20

```
USE sample;
CREATE TABLE bonus
         (pr_no CHAR(4),
            bonus SMALLINT DEFAULT 100);
INSERT INTO bonus (pr_no) VALUES ('p1');
```

Example 7.20 creates the **bonus** table, which contains one row, (p1, 100). This table will be used for merging.

EXAMPLE 7.21

```
USE sample;
MERGE INTO bonus B
   USING (SELECT project_no, budget
                    FROM project) E
        ON (B.pr_no = E.project_no)
      WHEN MATCHED THEN
               UPDATE SET B.bonus = E.budget * 0.1
      WHEN NOT MATCHED THEN
               INSERT (pr_no, bonus)
                    VALUES (E.project_no, E.budget * 0.05);
```

The MERGE statement in Example 7.21 modifies the data in the **bonus** table depending on the existing values in the **pr_no** column. If a value from the **project_no** column of the **project** table appears in the **pr_no** column of the **bonus** table, the MATCHED branch will be executed and the existing value will be updated. Otherwise, the NON MATCHED branch will be executed and the corresponding INSERT statement will insert new rows in the **bonus** table.

The content of the **bonus** table after the execution of the MERGE statement is as follows:

pr_no	bonus
p1	12000
p2	4750
p3	9325

From the result set, you can see that a value of the **bonus** column represents 10 percent of the original value in the case of the UPDATE statement, and 5 percent in the case of the INSERT statement.

The OUTPUT Clause

The result of the execution of an INSERT, UPDATE, or DELETE statement contains by default only the text concerning the number of modified rows ("3 rows deleted," for instance). If the content of such a result doesn't fit your needs, you can use the OUTPUT clause, which displays explicitly the rows that are inserted or updated in the table or deleted from it.

NOTE

The OUTPUT clause is also part of the MERGE statement. It returns an output for each modified row in the target table (see Examples 7.25 and 7.26).

The OUTPUT clause uses the **inserted** and **deleted** tables (explained in Chapter 14) to display the corresponding result. Also, the OUTPUT clause must be used with an INTO expression to fill a table. For this reason, you use a table variable to store the result.

Example 7.22 shows how the OUTPUT statement works with a DELETE statement.

EXAMPLE 7.22

```
USE sample;
DECLARE @del_table TABLE (emp_no INT, emp_lname CHAR(20));
DELETE employee
OUTPUT DELETED.emp_no, DELETED.emp_lname INTO @del_table
WHERE emp_no > 15000;
SELECT * FROM @del_table
```

If the content of the **employee** table is in the initial state, the execution of the statements in Example 7.22 produces the following result:

emp_no	emp_lname
25348	Smith
18316	Barrimore
29346	James
28559	Moser

First, Example 7.22 declares the table variable **@del_table** with two columns: **emp_no** and **emp_lname**. (Variables are explained in detail in the following chapter.) This table will be used to store the deleted rows. The syntax of the DELETE statement is enhanced with the OUTPUT option:

```
OUTPUT DELETED.emp_no, DELETED.emp_lname INTO @del_table
```

Using this option, the system stores the deleted rows in the **deleted** table, which is then copied in the **@del** table variable.

Example 7.23 shows the use of the OUTPUT option in an UPDATE statement.

EXAMPLE 7.23

```
USE sample;
DECLARE @update_table TABLE
  (emp_no INT, project_no CHAR(20),old_job CHAR(20),new_job CHAR(20));
UPDATE works_on
SET job = NULL
OUTPUT DELETED.emp_no, DELETED.project_no,
      DELETED.job, INSERTED.job INTO @update_table
WHERE job = 'Clerk';
SELECT * FROM @update_table
```

The result is

emp_no	project_no	old_job	new_job
25348	p2	Clerk	NULL
28559	p2	Clerk	NULL
9031	p3	Clerk	NULL
29346	p1	Clerk	NULL

The following examples show the use of the OUTPUT clause within the MERGE statement.

Suppose that your marketing department decides to give customers a price reduction of 20 percent for all bikes that cost more than $500. The SELECT statement in Example 7.24 selects all products that cost more than $500 and inserts them in the **temp_PriceList** temporary table. The consecutive UPDATE statement searches for all bikes and reduces their price.

EXAMPLE 7.24

```
USE AdventureWorks;

SELECT ProductID, Product.Name as ProductName, ListPrice
INTO temp_PriceList
FROM Production.Product
WHERE ListPrice > 500;

UPDATE temp_PriceList
    SET ListPrice = ListPrice * 0.8
      WHERE ProductID IN (SELECT ProductID
      FROM AdventureWorks.Production.Product
        WHERE ProductSubcategoryID IN ( SELECT ProductCategoryID
```

```
            FROM AdventureWorks.Production.ProductSubcategory
                WHERE ProductCategoryID IN ( SELECT ProductCategoryID
                FROM AdventureWorks.Production.ProductCategory
                    WHERE Name = 'Bikes')));
```

The CREATE TABLE statement in Example 7.25 creates a new table, **temp_Difference**, that will be used to store the result set of the MERGE statement. After that, the MERGE statement compares the complete list of the products with the new list (given in the **temp_priceList** table) and inserts the modified prices for all bicycles by using the UPDATE SET clause. (Besides the insertion of the new prices for all bicycles, the statement also changes the **ModifiedDate** column for all products and sets it to the current date.) The OUTPUT clause in Example 7.25 writes the old and new prices in the temporary table called **temp_Difference**. That way, you can later calculate the aggregate differences, if needed.

EXAMPLE 7.25

```
USE AdventureWorks;
CREATE TABLE temp_Difference
     (old DEC (10,2), new DEC(10,2));
GO
MERGE INTO Production. Product
USING temp_PriceList ON Product.ProductID = temp_PriceList.ProductID
WHEN MATCHED AND Product.ListPrice <> temp_PriceList.ListPrice THEN
UPDATE SET ListPrice = temp_PriceList.ListPrice, ModifiedDate = GETDATE()
WHEN NOT MATCHED BY SOURCE THEN
UPDATE SET ModifiedDate = GETDATE()
OUTPUT DELETED.ListPrice, INSERTED.ListPrice  INTO temp_Difference1;
```

Example 7.26 shows the computation of the overall difference, the result of the preceding modifications.

EXAMPLE 7.26

```
USE AdventureWorks;
SELECT SUM(old) -  SUM(new) AS diff
  FROM AdventureWorks.dbo.temp_Difference;
```

The result is

diff
10773.60

Summary

Generally, only three SQL statements can be used to modify a table: INSERT, UPDATE, and DELETE. These statements are generic insofar as for all types of row insertion, you use only INSERT, for all types of column modification, you use only UPDATE, and for all types of row deletion, you use only DELETE.

The nonstandard statement TRUNCATE TABLE is just another form of the DELETE statement, but the deletion of rows is executed faster with TRUNCATE TABLE than with DELETE. The MERGE statement is basically an "UPSERT" statement: it combines the UPDATE and the INSERT statements in one statement.

Chapters 5 through 7 have introduced all SQL statements that belong to DDL and DML. Most of these statements can be grouped together to build a sequence of Transact-SQL statements. Such a sequence is the basis for *stored procedures*, which will be covered in the next chapter.

Exercises

E.7.1

Insert the data of a new employee called Julia Long, whose employee number is 11111. Her department number is not known yet.

E.7.2

Create a new table called **emp_d1_d2** with all employees who work for department d1 or d2, and load the corresponding rows from the **employee** table. Find two different, but equivalent, solutions.

E.7.3

Create a new table of all employees who entered their projects in 2007 and load it with the corresponding rows from the **employee** table.

E.7.4

Modify the job of all employees in project p1 who are managers. They have to work as clerks from now on.

E.7.5

The budgets of all projects are no longer determined. Assign all budgets the NULL value.

E.7.6

Modify the jobs of the employee with the employee number 28559. From now on she will be the manager for all her projects.

E.7.7

Increase the budget of the project where the manager has the employee number 10102. The increase is 10 percent.

E.7.8

Change the name of the department for which the employee named James works. The new department name is Sales.

E.7.9

Change the enter date for the projects for those employees who work in project p1 and belong to department Sales. The new date is 12.12.2007.

E.7.10

Delete all departments that are located in Seattle.

E.7.11

The project p3 has been finished. Delete all information concerning this project in the **sample** database.

E.7.12

Delete the information in the **works_on** table for all employees who work for the departments located in Dallas.

Chapter 8

Stored Procedures and User-Defined Functions

In This Chapter

- ▶ Procedural Extensions
- ▶ Stored Procedures
- ▶ User-Defined Functions

This chapter introduces batches and routines. A batch is a sequence of Transact-SQL statements and procedural extensions. A routine can be either a stored procedure or a user-defined function (UDF). The beginning of the chapter introduces all procedural extensions supported by the Database Engine. After that, procedural extensions are used, together with Transact-SQL statements, to show how batches can be implemented. A batch can be stored as a database object, as either a stored procedure or a UDF. Some stored procedures are written by users, and others are provided by Microsoft and are referred to as *system stored procedures*. In contrast to user-defined stored procedures, UDFs return a value to a caller. All routines can be written either in Transact-SQL or in another programming language such as C# or Visual Basic. The end of the chapter introduces table-valued parameters.

Procedural Extensions

The preceding chapters introduced Transact-SQL statements that belong to the data definition language and the data manipulation language. Most of these statements can be grouped together to build a batch. As previously mentioned, a *batch* is a sequence of Transact-SQL statements and procedural extensions that are sent to the database system for execution together. The number of statements in a batch is limited by the size of the compiled batch object. The main advantage of a batch over a group of singleton statements is that executing all statements at once brings significant performance benefits.

There are a number of restrictions concerning the appearance of different Transact-SQL statements inside a batch. The most important is that the data definition statements CREATE VIEW, CREATE PROCEDURE, and CREATE TRIGGER must each be the only statement in a batch.

NOTE

To separate DDL statements from one another, use the GO statement.

The following sections describe each procedural extension of the Transact-SQL language separately.

Block of Statements

A block allows the building of units with one or more Transact-SQL statements. Every block begins with the BEGIN statement and terminates with the END statement, as shown in the following example:

```
BEGIN
statement_1
statement_2
...
END
```

A block can be used inside the IF statement to allow the execution of more than one statement, depending on a certain condition (see Example 8.1).

IF Statement

The Transact-SQL statement IF corresponds to the statement with the same name that is supported by almost all programming languages. IF executes one Transact-SQL statement (or more, enclosed in a block) *if* a Boolean expression, which follows the keyword IF, evaluates to TRUE. If the IF statement contains an ELSE statement, a second group of statements can be executed if the Boolean expression evaluates to FALSE.

NOTE

Before you start to execute batches, stored procedures, and UDFs in this chapter, please re-create the entire sample database.

EXAMPLE 8.1

```
USE sample;
IF (SELECT COUNT(*)
            FROM works_on
            WHERE project_no = 'p1'
            GROUP BY project_no ) > 3
        PRINT 'The number of employees in the project p1 is 4 or more'
        ELSE BEGIN
            PRINT 'The following employees work for the project p1'
            SELECT emp_fname, emp_lname
            FROM employee, works_on
            WHERE employee.emp_no = works_on.emp_no
            AND project_no = 'p1'
        END
```

Example 8.1 shows the use of a block inside the IF statement. The Boolean expression in the IF statement,

```
(SELECT COUNT(*)
              FROM works_on
              WHERE project_no = 'p1'
               GROUP BY project_no) > 3
```

is evaluated to TRUE for the **sample** database. Therefore, the single PRINT statement in the IF part is executed. Notice that this example uses a subquery to return the number of rows (using the COUNT aggregate function) that satisfy the WHERE condition (project_no='p1'). The result of Example 8.1 is

```
The number of employees in the project p1 is four or more
```

NOTE

The ELSE part of the IF statement in Example 8.1 contains two statements: PRINT and SELECT. Therefore, the block with the BEGIN and END statements is required to enclose the two statements. (The PRINT statement is another statement that belongs to procedural extensions; it returns a user-defined message.)

WHILE Statement

The WHILE statement repeatedly executes one Transact-SQL statement (or more, enclosed in a block) *while* the Boolean expression evaluates to TRUE. In other words, if the expression is true, the statement (or block) is executed, and then the expression is evaluated again to determine if the statement (or block) should be executed again. This process repeats until the expression evaluates to FALSE.

A block within the WHILE statement can optionally contain one of two statements used to control the execution of the statements within the block: BREAK or CONTINUE. The BREAK statement stops the execution of the statements inside the block and starts the execution of the statement immediately following this block. The CONTINUE statement stops only the current execution of the statements in the block and starts the execution of the block from its beginning.

Example 8.2 shows the use of the WHILE statement.

EXAMPLE 8.2

```
USE sample;
WHILE (SELECT SUM(budget)
                FROM project) < 500000
          BEGIN
            UPDATE project SET budget = budget*1.1
```

```
    IF (SELECT MAX(budget)
            FROM project) > 240000
        BREAK
    ELSE CONTINUE
END
```

In Example 8.2, the budget of all projects will be increased by 10 percent until the sum of budgets is greater than $500,000. However, the repeated execution will be stopped if the budget of one of the projects is greater than $240,000. The execution of Example 8.2 gives the following output:

```
(3 rows affected)
(3 rows affected)
(3 rows affected)
```

NOTE

If you want to suppress the output, such as that in Example 8.2 (indicating the number of affected rows in SQL statements), use the SET NOCOUNT ON statement.

Local Variables

Local variables are an important procedural extension to the Transact-SQL language. They are used to store values (of any type) within a batch or a routine. They are "local" because they can be referenced only within the same batch in which they were declared. (The Database Engine also supports global variables, which are described in Chapter 4.)

Every local variable in a batch must be defined using the DECLARE statement. (For the syntax of the DECLARE statement, see Example 8.3.) The definition of each variable contains its name and the corresponding data type. Variables are always referenced in a batch using the prefix @. The assignment of a value to a local variable is done

▶ Using the special form of the SELECT statement
▶ Using the SET statement
▶ Directly in the DECLARE statement using the = sign (for instance, @extra_budget MONEY = 1500)

The usage of the first two statements for a value assignment is demonstrated in Example 8.3.

EXAMPLE 8.3

```
USE sample;
DECLARE @avg_budget MONEY, @extra_budget MONEY
          SET @extra_budget = 15000
          SELECT @avg_budget = AVG(budget) FROM project
          IF (SELECT budget
                     FROM project
                     WHERE project_no='p1') < @avg_budget
          BEGIN
            UPDATE project
                  SET budget = budget + @extra_budget
                  WHERE project_no ='p1'
              PRINT 'Budget for p1 increased by @extra_budget'
          END
          ELSE PRINT 'Budget for p1 unchanged'
```

The result is

```
Budget for p1 increased by @extra_budget
```

The batch in Example 8.3 calculates the average of all project budgets and compares this value with the budget of project p1. If the latter value is smaller than the calculated value, the budget of project p1 will be increased by the value of the local variable **@extra_budget**.

Miscellaneous Procedural Statements

The procedural extensions of the Transact-SQL language also contain the following statements:

▶ RETURN

▶ GOTO

▶ RAISEERROR

▶ WAITFOR

The RETURN statement has the same functionality inside a batch as the BREAK statement inside WHILE. This means that the RETURN statement causes the execution of the batch to terminate and the first statement following the end of the batch to begin executing.

The GOTO statement branches to a label, which stands in front of a Transact-SQL statement within a batch. The RAISEERROR statement generates a user-defined error message and sets a system error flag. A user-defined error number must be greater than 50000. (All error numbers <= 50000 are system defined and are reserved by the Database Engine.) The error values are stored in the global variable @@error. (Example 17.3 shows the use of the RAISEERROR statement.)

The WAITFOR statement defines either the time interval (if the DELAY option is used) or a specified time (if the TIME option is used) that the system has to wait before executing the next statement in the batch. The syntax of this statement is

```
WAITFOR {DELAY 'time' | TIME 'time' | TIMEOUT 'timeout' }
```

The DELAY option tells the database system to wait until the specified amount of time has passed. TIME specifies a time in one of the acceptable formats for temporal data. TIMEOUT specifies the amount of time, in milliseconds, to wait for a message to arrive in the queue. (Example 13.5 shows the use of the WAITFOR statement.)

Exception Handling with TRY, CATCH, and THROW

Versions of SQL Server previous to SQL Server 2005 required error handling code after every Transact-SQL statement that might produce an error. (You can handle errors using the @@error global variable. Example 13.1 shows the use of this variable.) Starting with SQL Server 2005, you can capture and handle exceptions using two statements, TRY and CATCH. This section first explains what "exception" means and then discusses how these two statements work.

An exception is a problem (usually an error) that prevents the continuation of a program. With such a problem, you cannot continue processing because there is not enough information needed to handle the problem. For this reason, the existing problem will be relegated to another part of the program, which will handle the exception.

The role of the TRY statement is to capture the exception. (Because this process usually comprises several statements, the term "TRY block" typically is used instead of "TRY statement.") If an exception occurs within the TRY block, the part of the system called the exception handler delivers the exception to the other part of the program, which will handle the exception. This program part is denoted by the keyword CATCH and is therefore called the CATCH block.

NOTE

Exception handling using the TRY and CATCH statements is the common way that modern programming languages like C# and Java treat errors.

Exception handling with the TRY and CATCH blocks gives a programmer a lot of benefits, such as:

▶ Exceptions provide a clean way to check for errors without cluttering code

▶ Exceptions provide a mechanism to signal errors directly rather than using some side effects

▶ Exceptions can be seen by the programmer and checked during the compilation process

SQL Server 2012 introduces the third statement in relation to handling errors: THROW. This statement allows you to throw an exception caught in the exception handling block. Simply stated, the THROW statement is another return mechanism, which behaves similarly to the already described RAISEERROR statement.

Example 8.4 shows how exception handling with the TRY/CATCH/THROW works. It shows how you can use exception handling to insert all statements in a batch or to roll back the entire statement group if an error occurs. The example is based on the referential integrity between the **department** and **employee** tables. For this reason, you have to create both tables using the PRIMARY KEY and FOREIGN KEY constraints, as done in Example 5.11.

EXAMPLE 8.4

```
USE sample;
BEGIN TRY
   BEGIN TRANSACTION
   insert into employee values(11111, 'Ann', 'Smith','d2');
   insert into employee values(22222, 'Matthew', 'Jones','d4'); --
referential integrity error
   insert into employee values(33333, 'John', 'Barrimore', 'd2');
   COMMIT TRANSACTION
   PRINT 'Transaction committed'
END TRY
BEGIN CATCH
  ROLLBACK
  PRINT 'Transaction rolled back';
  THROW
END CATCH
```

After the execution of the batch in Example 8.4, all three statements in the batch won't be executed at all, and the output of this example is

```
Transaction rolled back

Msg 547, Level 16, State 0, Line 4
The INSERT statement conflicted with the FOREIGN KEY constraint
"foreign_emp". The conflict occurred in database "sample", table
"dbo.department", column 'dept_no'.
```

The execution of Example 8.4 works as follows. The first INSERT statement is executed successfully. Then, the second statement causes the referential integrity error. Because all three statements are written inside the TRY block, the exception is "thrown" and the exception handler starts the CATCH block. CATCH rolls back all statements and prints the corresponding message. After that the THROW statement returns the execution of the batch to the caller. For this reason, the content of the **employee** table won't change.

NOTE

The statements BEGIN TRANSACTION, COMMIT TRANSACTION, and ROLLBACK are Transact-SQL statements concerning transactions. These statements start, commit, and roll back transactions, respectively. See Chapter 13 for the discussion of these statements and transactions generally.

Example 8.5 shows the batch that supports server-side paging (for the description of server-side paging, see Chapter 6).

EXAMPLE 8.5

```
USE AdventureWorks;
DECLARE
    @PageSize    TINYINT = 20,
    @CurrentPage INT     = 4;
SELECT BusinessEntityID, JobTitle, BirthDate
   FROM HumanResources.Employee
   WHERE Gender = 'F'
ORDER BY JobTitle
OFFSET (@PageSize * (@CurrentPage - 1)) ROWS
    FETCH NEXT @PageSize ROWS ONLY;
```

The batch in Example 8.5 uses the **AdventureWorks** database and its **Employee** table to show how generic server-side paging can be implemented. The **@Pagesize** variable is used with the FETCH NEXT statement to specify the number of rows per page (20, in this case). The other variable, **@CurrentPage**, specifies which particular page should be displayed. In this example, the content of the third page will be displayed.

Stored Procedures

A *stored procedure* is a special kind of batch written in Transact-SQL, using the SQL language and its procedural extensions. The main difference between a batch and a stored procedure is that the latter is stored as a database object. In other words, stored procedures are saved on the server side to improve the performance and consistency of repetitive tasks.

The Database Engine supports stored procedures and system procedures. Stored procedures are created in the same way as all other database objects—that is, by using the DDL. System procedures are provided with the Database Engine and can be used to access and modify the information in the system catalog. This section describes (user-defined) stored procedures, while system procedures are explained in the next chapter.

When a stored procedure is created, an optional list of parameters can be defined. The procedure accepts the corresponding arguments each time it is invoked. Stored procedures can optionally return a value, which displays the user-defined information or, in the case of an error, the corresponding error message.

A stored procedure is precompiled before it is stored as an object in the database. The precompiled form is stored in the database and used whenever the stored procedure is executed. This property of stored procedures offers an important benefit: the repeated compilation of a procedure is (almost always) eliminated, and the execution performance is therefore increased. This property of stored procedures offers another benefit concerning the volume of data that must be sent to and from the database system. It might take less than 50 bytes to call a stored procedure containing several thousand bytes of statements. The accumulated effect of this savings when multiple users are performing repetitive tasks can be quite significant.

Stored procedures can also be used for the following purposes:

▶ To control access authorization

▶ To create an audit trail of activities in database tables

The use of stored procedures provides security control above and beyond the use of the GRANT and REVOKE statements (see Chapter 12), which define different access privileges for a user. This is because the authorization to execute a stored procedure is independent of the authorization to modify the objects that the stored procedure contains, as described in the next section.

Stored procedures that audit write and/or read operations concerning a table are an additional security feature of the database. With the use of such procedures, the database administrator can track modifications made by users or application programs.

Creation and Execution of Stored Procedures

Stored procedures are created with the CREATE PROCEDURE statement, which has the following syntax:

```
CREATE PROC[EDURE] [schema_name.]proc_name
[({@param1} type1 [ VARYING] [= default1] [OUTPUT])] {, ...}
[WITH {RECOMPILE | ENCRYPTION | EXECUTE AS 'user_name'}]
[FOR REPLICATION]
AS batch | EXTERNAL NAME method_name
```

schema_name is the name of the schema to which the ownership of the created stored procedure is assigned. **proc_name** is the name of the new stored procedure. **@param1** is a parameter, while **type1** specifies its data type. The parameter in a stored procedure has the same logical meaning as the local variable for a batch. Parameters are values passed from the caller of the stored procedure and are used within the stored procedure. **default1** specifies the optional default value of the corresponding parameter. (Default can also be NULL.)

The OUTPUT option indicates that the parameter is a return parameter and can be returned to the calling procedure or to the system (see Example 8.9 later in this section).

As you already know, the precompiled form of a procedure is stored in the database and used whenever the stored procedure is executed. If you want to generate the compiled form each time the procedure is executed, use the WITH RECOMPILE option.

NOTE

The use of the WITH RECOMPILE option destroys one of the most important benefits of the stored procedures: the performance advantage gained by a single precompilation. For this reason, the WITH RECOMPILE option should be used only when database objects used by the stored procedure are modified frequently or when the parameters used by the stored procedure are volatile.

The EXECUTE AS clause specifies the security context under which to execute the stored procedure after it is accessed. By specifying the context in which the procedure is executed, you can control which user account the Database Engine uses to validate permissions on objects referenced by the procedure.

By default, only the members of the **sysadmin** fixed server role, and the **db_owner** and **db_ddladmin** fixed database roles, can use the CREATE PROCEDURE statement. However, the members of these roles may assign this privilege to other users by using the GRANT CREATE PROCEDURE statement. (For the discussion of user permissions, fixed server roles, and fixed database roles, see Chapter 12.)

Example 8.6 shows the creation of the simple stored procedure for the **project** table.

EXAMPLE 8.6

```
USE sample;
GO
CREATE PROCEDURE increase_budget (@percent INT=5)
          AS UPDATE project
                    SET budget = budget + budget*@percent/100;
```

NOTE

The GO statement is used to separate two batches. (The CREATE PROCEDURE statement must be the first statement in the batch.)

The stored procedure **increase_budget** increases the budgets of all projects for a certain percentage value that is defined using the parameter **@percent**. The procedure also defines the default value (5), which is used if there is no argument at the execution time of the procedure.

NOTE

It is possible to create stored procedures that reference nonexistent tables. This feature allows you to debug procedure code without creating the underlying tables first, or even connecting to the target server.

In contrast to "base" stored procedures that are placed in the current database, it is possible to create temporary stored procedures that are always placed in the temporary system database called **tempdb**. You might create a temporary stored procedure to avoid executing a particular group of statements repeatedly within a connection. You can create *local* or *global* temporary procedures by preceding the procedure name with a single pound sign (**#proc_name**) for local temporary procedures and a double pound sign (**##proc_name**, for example) for global temporary procedures. A local temporary stored procedure can be executed only by the user who created it, and only during the same connection. A global temporary procedure can be executed by all users, but only until the last connection executing it (usually the creator's) ends.

The life cycle of a stored procedure has two phases: its creation and its execution. Each procedure is created once and executed many times. The EXECUTE statement executes an existing procedure. The execution of a stored procedure is allowed for each user who either is the owner of or has the EXECUTE privilege for the procedure (see Chapter 12). The EXECUTE statement has the following syntax:

```
[[EXEC[UTE]] [@return_status =] {proc_name
        | @proc_name_var}
        {[[@parameter1 =] value | [@parameter1=] @variable [OUTPUT]] | DEFAULT}..
        [WITH RECOMPILE]
```

All options in the EXECUTE statement, other than **return_status,** have the equivalent logical meaning as the options with the same names in the CREATE PROCEDURE statement. **return_status** is an optional integer variable that stores the return status of a procedure. The value of a parameter can be assigned using either a value (**value**) or a local variable (**@variable**). The order of parameter values is not relevant if they are named, but if they are not named, parameter values must be supplied in the order defined in the CREATE PROCEDURE statement.

The DEFAULT clause supplies the default value of the parameter as defined in the procedure. When the procedure expects a value for a parameter that does not have a defined default and either a parameter is missing or the DEFAULT keyword is specified, an error occurs.

NOTE

When the EXECUTE statement is the first statement in a batch, the word "EXECUTE" can be omitted from the statement. Despite this, it would be safer to include this word in every batch you write.

Example 8.7 shows the use of the EXECUTE statement.

EXAMPLE 8.7

```
USE sample;
EXECUTE increase_budget 10;
```

The EXECUTE statement in Example 8.7 executes the stored procedure **increase_ budget** (Example 8.6) and increases the budgets of all projects by 10 percent each.

Example 8.8 shows the creation of a procedure that references the tables **employee** and **works_on**.

EXAMPLE 8.8

```
USE sample;
GO
CREATE PROCEDURE modify_empno (@old_no INTEGER, @new_no INTEGER)
        AS UPDATE employee
                SET emp_no = @new_no
```

```
                    WHERE emp_no = @old_no
         UPDATE works_on
                    SET emp_no = @new_no
                    WHERE emp_no = @old_no
```

The procedure **modify_empno** in Example 8.8 demonstrates the use of stored procedures as part of the maintenance of the referential integrity (in this case, between the **employee** and **works_on** tables). Such a stored procedure can be used inside the definition of a trigger, which actually maintains the referential integrity (see Example 14.3).

Example 8.9 shows the use of the OUTPUT clause.

EXAMPLE 8.9

```
USE sample;
GO
CREATE PROCEDURE delete_emp @employee_no INT, @counter INT OUTPUT
          AS SELECT @counter = COUNT(*)
                  FROM works_on
                   WHERE emp_no = @employee_no
          DELETE FROM employee
                   WHERE emp_no = @employee_no
            DELETE FROM works_on
                   WHERE emp_no = @employee_no
```

This stored procedure can be executed using the following statements:

```
DECLARE @quantity INT
EXECUTE delete_emp @employee_no=28559, @counter=@quantity OUTPUT
```

The preceding example contains the creation of the **delete_emp** procedure as well as its execution. This procedure calculates the number of projects on which the employee (with the employee number **@employee_no**) works. The calculated value is then assigned to the **@counter** parameter. After the deletion of all rows with the assigned employee number from the **employee** and **works_on** tables, the calculated value will be assigned to the **@quantity** variable.

NOTE

*The value of the parameter will be returned to the calling procedure if the OUTPUT option is used. In Example 8.9, the **delete_emp** procedure passes the **@counter** parameter to the calling statement, so the procedure returns the value to the system. Therefore, the **@counter** parameter must be declared with the OUTPUT option in the procedure as well as in the EXECUTE statement.*

The EXECUTE Statement with RESULT SETS Clause

SQL Server 2012 introduces the WITH RESULT SETS clause for the EXECUTE statement. Using this clause, you can change conditionally the form of the result set of a stored procedure.

The following two examples help to explain this clause. Example 8.10 is an introductory example that shows how the output looks when the WITH RESULT SETS clause is omitted.

EXAMPLE 8.10

```
USE sample;
GO
CREATE PROCEDURE employees_in_dept (@dept CHAR(4))
 AS SELECT emp_no, emp_lname
    FROM employee
    WHERE dept_no IN (SELECT @dept FROM department
                        GROUP BY dept_no)
```

employees_in_dept is a simple stored procedure that displays the numbers and family names of all employees working for a particular department. (The department number is a parameter of the procedure and must be specified when the procedure is invoked.) The result of this procedure is a table with two columns, named according to the names of the corresponding columns (**emp_no** and **emp_lname**). To change these names (and their data types, too), SQL Server 2012 supports the new WITH RESULTS SETS clause. Example 8.11 shows the use of this clause.

EXAMPLE 8.11

```
USE sample;
EXEC employees_in_dept 'd1'
  WITH RESULT SETS
  ( ([EMPLOYEE NUMBER] INT NOT NULL,
    [NAME OF EMPLOYEE] CHAR(20) NOT NULL));
```

The output is

EMPLOYEE NUMBER	NAME OF EMPLOYEE
18316	Barrimore
28559	Moser

As you can see, the WITH RESULT SETS clause in Example 8.11 allows you to change the name and data types of columns displayed in the result set. Therefore, this new functionality gives you the flexibility to execute stored procedures and place the output result sets into a new table.

Changing the Structure of Stored Procedures

The Database Engine also supports the ALTER PROCEDURE statement, which modifies the structure of a stored procedure. The ALTER PROCEDURE statement is usually used to modify Transact-SQL statements inside a procedure. All options of the ALTER PROCEDURE statement correspond to the options with the same name in the CREATE PROCEDURE statement. The main purpose of this statement is to avoid reassignment of existing privileges for the stored procedure.

NOTE

The Database Engine supports the CURSOR data type. You use this data type to declare cursors inside a stored procedure. A cursor is a programming construct that is used to store the output of a query (usually a set of rows) and to allow end-user applications to display the rows record by record. A detailed discussion of cursors is outside of the scope of this book.

A stored procedure (or a group of stored procedures with the same name) is removed using the DROP PROCEDURE statement. Only the owner of the stored procedure and the members of the **db_owner** and **sysadmin** fixed roles can remove the procedure.

Stored Procedures and CLR

SQL Server supports the Common Language Runtime (CLR), which allows you to develop different database objects (stored procedures, user-defined functions, triggers, user-defined aggregates, and user-defined types) using C# and Visual Basic. CLR also allows you to execute these database objects using the common run-time system.

NOTE

*You enable and disable the use of CLR through the **clr_enabled** option of the **sp_configure** system procedure. Execute the RECONFIGURE statement to update the running configuration value.*

Example 8.12 shows how you can enable the use of CLR with the **sp_configure** system procedure.

EXAMPLE 8.12

```
USE sample;
EXEC sp_configure 'clr_enabled',1
RECONFIGURE
```

To implement, compile, and store procedures using CLR, you have to execute the following four steps in the given order:

1. Implement a stored procedure using C# (or Visual Basic) and compile the program, using the corresponding compiler.
2. Use the CREATE ASSEMBLY statement to create the corresponding executable file.
3. Store the procedure as a server object using the CREATE PROCEDURE statement.
4. Execute the procedure using the EXECUTE statement.

Figure 8-1 shows how CLR works. You use a development environment such as Visual Studio to implement your program. After the implementation, start the C# or

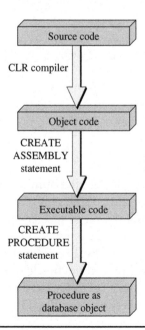

Figure 8-1   *The flow diagram for the execution of a CLR stored procedure*

Visual Basic compiler to generate the object code. This code will be stored in a .dll file, which is the source for the CREATE ASSEMBLY statement. After the execution of this statement, you get the intermediate code. In the next step you use the CREATE PROCEDURE statement to store the executable as a database object. Finally, the stored procedure can be executed using the already-introduced EXECUTE statement.

Examples 8.13 through 8.17 demonstrate the whole process just described. Example 8.13 shows the C# program that will be used to demonstrate how you apply CLR to implement and deploy stored procedures.

EXAMPLE 8.13

```
using System;
using System.Data;
using System.Data.Sql;
using System.Data.SqlClient;
using Microsoft.SqlServer.Server;
using System.Data.SqlTypes;
public partial class StoredProcedures
  { [SqlProcedure]
        public static int GetEmployeeCount()
    {
        int iRows;
        SqlConnection conn = new SqlConnection("Context Connection=true");
        conn.Open();
        SqlCommand sqlCmd = conn.CreateCommand();
        sqlCmd.CommandText = "select count(*) as 'Employee Count' " + "from
employee";
        iRows = (int)sqlCmd.ExecuteScalar();
        conn.Close();
        return iRows;
    }
};
```

This program uses a query to calculate the number of rows in the **employee** table. The **using** directives at the beginning of the program specify namespaces, such as **System.Data**. These directives allow you to specify class names in the source program without referencing the corresponding namespace. The **StoredProcedures** class is then defined, which is written with a **[SqlProcedure]** attribute. This attribute tells the compiler that the class is a stored procedure. Inside that class is defined a method called **GetEmployeeCount()**. The connection to the database system is established using the **conn** instance of the **SQLConnection** class. The **Open()** method is applied to that instance to open the connection. The **CreateCommand()** method, applied to **conn**, allows you to access the **SqlCommand** instance called **sqlCmd**.

The following lines of code

```
sqlCmd.CommandText =
"select count(*) as 'Employee Count' " + "from employee";
iRows = (int)sqlCmd.ExecuteScalar();
```

use the SELECT statement to find the number of rows in the **employee** table and to display the result. The command text is specified by setting the **CommandText** property of the **SqlCmd** instance returned by the call to the **CreateCommand()** method. Next, the **ExecuteScalar()** method of the **SqlCommand** instance is called. This returns a scalar value, which is finally converted to the **int** data type and assigned to the **iRows** variable.

Example 8.14 shows the first step in deploying stored procedures using CLR.

EXAMPLE 8.14

```
csc /target:library GetEmployeeCount.cs
    /reference:"C:\Program Files\Microsoft SQL Server\MSSQL11.MSSQLSERVER\
MSSQL\Binn\sqlaccess.dll"
```

Example 8.14 demonstrates how to compile the C# method called **GetEmployeeCount()** (Example 8.13). (Actually, this command can be used generally to compile any C# program, if you set the appropriate name for the source program.) **csc** is the command that is used to invoke the C# compiler. You invoke the **csc** command at the Windows command line. Before starting the command, you have to specify the location of the compiler using the PATH environment variable. At the time of writing this book, the C# compiler (the **csc.exe** file) can be found in the C:\WINDOWS\ Microsoft.NET\Framework directory. (You should select the appropriate version of the compiler.)

The **/target** option specifies the name of the C# program, while the **/reference** option defines the .dll file, which is necessary for the compilation process.

Example 8.15 shows the next step in creating the stored procedure. (Before you execute this example, copy the existing .dll file to the root of the C: drive.)

EXAMPLE 8.15

```
USE sample;
GO
CREATE ASSEMBLY GetEmployeeCount
     FROM 'C:\GetEmployeeCount.dll' WITH PERMISSION_SET = SAFE
```

The CREATE ASSEMBLY statement uses the managed code as the source to create the corresponding object, against which CLR stored procedures, UDFs, and triggers can be created. This statement has the following syntax:

```
CREATE ASSEMBLY assembly_name [ AUTHORIZATION owner_name ]
    FROM { dll_file}
    [WITH PERMISSION_SET = { SAFE | EXTERNAL_ACCESS | UNSAFE }]
```

assembly_name is the name of the assembly. The optional AUTHORIZATION clause specifies the name of a role as owner of the assembly. The FROM clause specifies the path where the assembly being uploaded is located. (Example 8.15 copies the .dll file generated from the source program from the **Framework** directory to the root of the C: drive.)

The WITH PERMISSION_SET clause is a very important clause of the CREATE ASSEMBLY statement and should always be set. It specifies a set of code access permissions granted to the assembly. SAFE is the most restrictive permission set. Code executed by an assembly with this permission cannot access external system resources, such as files. EXTERNAL_ACCESS allows assemblies to access certain external system resources, while UNSAFE allows unrestricted access to resources, both within and outside the database system.

NOTE

In order to store the information concerning assembly code, a user must have the ability to execute the CREATE ASSEMBLY statement. The user (or role) executing the statement is the owner of the assembly. It is possible to assign an assembly to another user by using the AUTHORIZATION clause of the CREATE SCHEMA statement.

The Database Engine also supports the ALTER ASSEMBLY and DROP ASSEMBLY statements. You can use the ALTER ASSEMBLY statement to refresh the system catalog to the latest copy of .NET modules holding its implementation. This statement also adds or removes files associated with the corresponding assembly. The DROP ASSEMBLY statement removes the specified assembly and all its associated files from the current database.

Example 8.16 creates the stored procedures based on the managed code implemented in Example 8.13.

EXAMPLE 8.16

```
USE sample;
GO
CREATE PROCEDURE GetEmployeeCount
AS EXTERNAL NAME GetEmployeeCount.StoredProcedures.GetEmployeeCount
```

The CREATE PROCEDURE statement in Example 8.16 is different from the same statement used in Examples 8.6 and 8.8, because it contains the EXTERNAL NAME option. This option specifies that the code is generated using CLR. The name in this clause is a three-part name:

```
assembly_name.class_name.method_name
```

- ▶ **assembly_name** is the name of the assembly (see Example 8.15).
- ▶ **class_name** is the name of the public class (see Example 8.13).
- ▶ **method_name**, which is optional, is the name of the method, which is specified inside the class.

Example 8.17 is used to execute the **GetEmployeeCount** procedure.

EXAMPLE 8.17

```
USE sample;
DECLARE @ret INT
EXECUTE @ret=GetEmployeeCount
PRINT @ret
```

The PRINT statement returns the current number of the rows in the **employee** table.

User-Defined Functions

In programming languages, there are generally two types of routines:

- ▶ Stored procedures
- ▶ User-defined functions (UDFs)

As discussed in the previous major section of this chapter, stored procedures are made up of several statements that have zero or more input parameters but usually do not return any output parameters. In contrast, functions always have one return value. This section describes the creation and use of UDFs.

Creation and Execution of User-Defined Functions

UDFs are created with the CREATE FUNCTION statement, which has the following syntax:

```
CREATE FUNCTION [schema_name.]function_name
        [({@param } type [= default])  {,...}
        RETURNS {scalar_type | [@variable] TABLE}
        [WITH {ENCRYPTION | SCHEMABINDING}
        [AS] {block | RETURN (select_statement)}
```

schema_name is the name of the schema to which the ownership of the created UDF is assigned. **function_name** is the name of the new function. **@param** is an input parameter, while **type** specifies its data type. Parameters are values passed from the caller of the UDF and are used within the function. **default** specifies the optional default value of the corresponding parameter. (Default can also be NULL.)

The RETURNS clause defines a data type of the value returned by the UDF. This data type can be any of the standard data types supported by the database system, including the TABLE data type. (The only standard data type that you cannot use is TIMESTAMP.)

UDFs are either scalar-valued or table-valued. A scalar-valued function returns an atomic (scalar) value. This means that in the RETURNS clause of a scalar-valued function, you specify one of the standard data types. Functions are table-valued if the RETURNS clause returns a set of rows (see the next subsection).

The WITH ENCRYPTION option encrypts the information in the system catalog that contains the text of the CREATE FUNCTION statement. In that case, you cannot view the text used to create the function. (Use this option to enhance the security of your database system.)

The alternative clause, WITH SCHEMABINDING, binds the UDF to the database objects that it references. Any attempt to modify the structure of the database object that the function references fails. (The binding of the function to the database objects it references is removed only when the function is altered, so the SCHEMABINDING option is no longer specified.)

Database objects that are referenced by a function must fulfill the following conditions if you want to use the SCHEMABINDING clause during the creation of that function:

▶   All views and UDFs referenced by the function must be schema-bound.

▶   All database objects (tables, views, or UDFs) must be in the same database as the function.

block is the BEGIN/END block that contains the implementation of the function. The final statement of the block must be a RETURN statement with an argument. (The value of the argument is the value returned by the function.) In the body of a BEGIN/END block, only the following statements are allowed:

- ▶ Assignment statements such as SET
- ▶ Control-of-flow statements such as WHILE and IF
- ▶ DECLARE statements defining local data variables
- ▶ SELECT statements containing SELECT lists with expressions that assign to variables that are local to the function
- ▶ INSERT, UPDATE, and DELETE statements modifying variables of the TABLE data type that are local to the function

By default, only the members of the **sysadmin** fixed server role and the **db_owner** and **db_ddladmin** fixed database roles can use the CREATE FUNCTION statement. However, the members of these roles may assign this privilege to other users by using the GRANT CREATE FUNCTION statement (see Chapter 12).

Example 8.18 shows the creation of the function called **compute_costs**.

EXAMPLE 8.18

```
-- This function computes additional total costs that arise
-- if budgets of projects increase
USE sample;
GO
CREATE FUNCTION compute_costs (@percent INT =10)
     RETURNS DECIMAL(16,2)
  BEGIN
   DECLARE @additional_costs DEC (14,2), @sum_budget dec(16,2)
   SELECT @sum_budget = SUM (budget) FROM project
   SET @additional_costs = @sum_budget * @percent/100
   RETURN @additional_costs
  END
```

The function **compute_costs** computes additional costs that arise when all budgets of projects increase. The single input variable, **@percent**, specifies the percentage of increase of budgets. The BEGIN/END block first declares two local variables: **@additional_costs** and **@sum_budget**. The function then assigns to **@sum_budget** the sum of all budgets, using the SELECT statement. After that, the function computes total additional costs and returns this value using the RETURN statement.

Invoking User-Defined Functions

Each UDF can be invoked in Transact-SQL statements, such as SELECT, INSERT, UPDATE, or DELETE. To invoke a function, specify the name of it, followed by parentheses. Within the parentheses, you can specify one or more arguments. *Arguments* are values or expressions that are passed to the input parameters that are defined immediately after the function name. When you invoke a function, and all parameters have no default values, you must supply argument values for all of the parameters and you must specify the argument values in the same sequence in which the parameters are defined in the CREATE FUNCTION statement.

Example 8.19 shows the use of the **compute_costs** function (Example 8.18) in a SELECT statement.

EXAMPLE 8.19

```
USE sample;
SELECT project_no, project_name
    FROM project
   WHERE budget < dbo.compute_costs(25)
```

The result is

project_no	project_name
p2	Gemini

The SELECT statement in Example 8.19 displays names and numbers of all projects where the budget is lower than the total additional costs of all projects for a given percentage.

NOTE

Each function used in a Transact-SQL statement must be specified using its two-part name—that is, schema_name.function_name.

Table-Valued Functions

As you already know, functions are table-valued if the RETURNS clause returns a set of rows. Depending on how the body of the function is defined, table-valued functions can be classified as inline or multistatement functions. If the RETURNS clause specifies TABLE with no accompanying list of columns, the function is an inline function. Inline functions return the result set of a SELECT statement as a variable of the TABLE data type (see Example 8.20). A multistatement table-valued function includes a name followed by TABLE. (The name defines an internal variable of the type TABLE.) You can use this variable to insert rows into it and then return the variable as the return value of the function.

Example 8.20 shows a function that returns a variable of the TABLE data type.

EXAMPLE 8.20

```
USE sample;
GO
CREATE FUNCTION employees_in_project (@pr_number CHAR(4))
    RETURNS TABLE
    AS RETURN (SELECT emp_fname, emp_lname
                     FROM works_on, employee
                  WHERE employee.emp_no = works_on.emp_no
               AND project_no = @pr_number)
```

The **employees_in_project** function is used to display names of all employees that belong to a particular project. The input parameter **@pr_number** specifies a project number. While the function generally returns a set of rows, the RETURNS clause contains the TABLE data type. (Note that the BEGIN/END block in Example 8.20 must be omitted, while the RETURN clause contains a SELECT statement.)

Example 8.21 shows the use of the **employees_in_project** function.

EXAMPLE 8.21

```
USE sample;
SELECT *
    FROM employees_in_project('p3')
```

The result is

emp_fname	emp_lname
Ann	Jones
Elsa	Bertoni
Elke	Hansel

Table-Valued Functions and APPLY

The APPLY operator is a relational operator that allows you to invoke a table-valued function for each row of a table expression. This operator is specified in the FROM clause of the corresponding SELECT statement in the same way as the JOIN operator is applied. There are two forms of the APPLY operator:

▶ CROSS APPLY
▶ OUTER APPLY

The CROSS APPLY operator returns those rows from the inner (left) table expression that match rows in the outer (right) table expression. Therefore, the CROSS APPLY operator is logically the same as the INNER JOIN operator.

The OUTER APPLY operator returns all the rows from the inner (left) table expression. (For the rows for which there are no corresponding matches in the outer table expression, it contains NULL values in columns of the outer table expression.) OUTER APPLY is logically equivalent to LEFT OUTER JOIN.

Examples 8.22 and 8.23 show how you can use APPLY.

EXAMPLE 8.22

```
-- generate function
CREATE FUNCTION dbo.fn_getjob(@empid AS INT)
      RETURNS TABLE AS
RETURN
      SELECT job
         FROM works_on
         WHERE emp_no = @empid
      AND job IS NOT NULL  AND project_no = 'p1';
```

The **fn_getjob()** function in Example 8.22 returns the set of rows from the **works_ on** table. This result set is "joined" in Example 8.23 with the content of the **employee** table.

EXAMPLE 8.23

```
-- use CROSS APPLY
SELECT E.emp_no, emp_fname, emp_lname, job
 FROM employee as E
    CROSS APPLY dbo.fn_getjob(E.emp_no) AS A
-- use OUTER APPLY
SELECT E.emp_no, emp_fname, emp_lname, job
 FROM employee as E
    OUTER APPLY dbo.fn_getjob(E.emp_no) AS A
```

The result is

emp_no	emp_fname	emp_lname	job
10102	Ann	Jones	Analyst
29346	James	James	Clerk
9031	Elsa	Bertoni	Manager
28559	Sybill	Moser	NULL

emp_no	emp_fname	emp_lname	job
25348	Matthew	Smith	NULL
10102	Ann	Jones	Analyst
18316	John	Barrimore	NULL
29346	James	James	Clerk
9031	Elsa	Bertoni	Manager
2581	Elke	Hansel	NULL
28559	Sybill	Moser	NULL

In the first query of Example 8.23, the result set of the table-valued function **fn_getjob()** is "joined" with the content of the **employee** table using the CROSS APPLY operator. **fn_getjob()** acts as the right input, and the **employee** table acts as the left input. The right input is evaluated for each row from the left input, and the rows produced are combined for the final output.

The second query is similar to the first one, but uses OUTER APPLY, which corresponds to the outer join operation of two tables.

Table-Valued Parameters

In all versions previous to SQL Server 2008, it was difficult to send many parameters to a routine. In that case you had to use a temporary table, insert the values into it, and then call the routine. Since SQL Server 2008, you can use table-valued parameters to simplify this task. These parameters are used to deliver a result set to the corresponding routine.

Example 8.24 shows the use of a table-valued parameter.

EXAMPLE 8.24

```
USE sample;
GO
CREATE TYPE departmentType AS TABLE
```

```
    (dept_no CHAR(4),dept_name CHAR(25),location CHAR(30));
GO
CREATE TABLE #dallasTable
    (dept_no CHAR(4),dept_name CHAR(25),location CHAR(30));
GO
CREATE PROCEDURE insertProc
    @Dallas departmentType READONLY
    AS SET NOCOUNT ON
    INSERT INTO #dallasTable (dept_no, dept_name, location)
     SELECT * FROM @Dallas
GO
DECLARE @Dallas AS departmentType;
INSERT INTO @Dallas( dept_no, dept_name, location)
SELECT * FROM department
WHERE location = 'Dallas'
EXEC insertProc @Dallas;
```

Example 8.24 first defines the type called **departmentType** as a table. This means that its type is the TABLE data type, so rows can be inserted in it. In the **insertProc** procedure, the @**Dallas** variable, which is of the **departmentType** type, is specified. (The READONLY clause specifies that the content of the table variable cannot be modified.) In the subsequent batch, data is added to the table variable, and after that the procedure is executed. The procedure, when executed, inserts rows from the table variable into the temporary table **#dallasTable**. The content of the temporary table is as follows:

dept_no	dept_name	location
d1	Research	Dallas
d3	Marketing	Dallas

The use of table-valued parameters gives you the following benefits:

▶ It simplifies the programming model in relation to routines.

▶ It reduces the round trips to the server.

▶ The resulting table can have different numbers of rows.

Changing the Structure of UDFs

The Transact-SQL language also supports the ALTER FUNCTION statement, which modifies the structure of a UDF. This statement is usually used to remove the schema binding. All options of the ALTER FUNCTION statement correspond to the options with the same name in the CREATE FUNCTION statement.

A UDF is removed using the DROP FUNCTION statement. Only the owner of the function (or the members of the **db_owner** and **sysadmin** fixed database roles) can remove the function.

User-Defined Functions and CLR

The discussion in "Stored Procedures and CLR" earlier in the chapter is also valid for UDFs. The only difference is that you use the CREATE FUNCTION statement (instead of CREATE PROCEDURE) to store a UDF as a database object. Also, UDFs are used in a different context from that of stored procedures, because UDFs always have a return value.

Example 8.25 shows the C# program used to demonstrate how UDFs are compiled and deployed.

EXAMPLE 8.25

```
using System;
using System.Data.Sql;
using System.Data.SqlTypes;
public class budgetPercent
{ private const float percent = 10;
    public static SqlDouble computeBudget(float budget)
    { float budgetNew;
        budgetNew = budget * percent;
        return budgetNew;
    }
};
```

The C# source program in Example 8.25 shows a UDF that calculates the new budget of a project using the old budget and the percentage increase. (The description of the C# program is omitted because this program is analog to the program in Example 8.13.) Example 8.26 shows the CREATE ASSEMBLY statement, which is necessary if you want to create a database object.

EXAMPLE 8.26

```
USE sample;
GO
CREATE ASSEMBLY computeBudget
FROM 'C:\computeBudget.dll'
WITH PERMISSION_SET = SAFE
```

The CREATE FUNCTION statement in Example 8.27 stores the **computeBudget** assembly as the database object, which can be used subsequently in data manipulation statements, such as SELECT, as shown in Example 8.28.

EXAMPLE 8.27

```
USE sample;
GO
CREATE FUNCTION ReturncomputeBudget (@budget Real)
RETURNS FLOAT
AS EXTERNAL NAME computeBudget.budgetPercent.computeBudget
```

EXAMPLE 8.28

```
USE sample;
SELECT dbo.ReturncomputeBudget (321.50)
```

The result is 3215.

NOTE

You can invoke an existing UDF at several places inside a SELECT statement. Example 8.19 shows its use with the WHERE clause, Example 8.21 in the FROM clause, and Example 8.28 in the SELECT list.

Summary

A stored procedure is a special kind of batch, written either in the Transact-SQL language or using the Common Language Runtime (CLR). Stored procedures are used for the following purposes:

► To control access authorization

► To create an audit trail of activities in database tables

▶ To enforce consistency and business rules with respect to data modification

▶ To improve the performance of repetitive tasks

User-defined functions have a lot in common with stored procedures. The main difference is that UDFs do not support parameters but return a single data value, which can also be a table.

Microsoft suggests using Transact-SQL as the default language for creating server-side objects. (CLR is recommended as an alternative only when your program contains a lot of computation.)

The next chapter discusses the system catalog of the Database Engine.

Exercises

E.8.1

Create a batch that inserts 3000 rows in the **employee** table. The values of the **emp_no** column should be unique and between 1 and 3000. All values of the columns **emp_lname**, **emp_fname**, and **dept_no** should be set to 'Jane', ' Smith', and ' d1', respectively.

E.8.2

Modify the batch from E.8.1 so that the values of the **emp_no** column should be generated randomly using the RAND function. (Hint: Use the temporal system functions DATEPART and GETDATE to generate the random values.)

Chapter 9

System Catalog

In This Chapter

- ▶ **Introduction to the System Catalog**
- ▶ **General Interfaces**
- ▶ **Proprietary Interfaces**

This chapter discusses the system catalog of the Database Engine. The introduction is followed by a description of the structure of several catalog views, each of which allows you to retrieve metadata. The use of dynamic management views and dynamic management functions is also covered in the first part of the chapter. Four alternative ways for retrieving metadata information are discussed in the second part: system stored procedures, system functions, property functions, and the information schema.

Introduction to the System Catalog

The system catalog consists of tables describing the structure of objects such as databases, base tables, views, and indices. (These tables are called *system base tables*.) The Database Engine frequently accesses the system catalog for information that is essential for the system to function properly.

The Database Engine distinguishes the system base tables of the **master** database from those of a particular user-defined database. System tables of the **master** database belong to the system catalog, while system tables of a particular database form the database catalog. Therefore, system base tables occur only once in the entire system (if they belong exclusively to the **master** database), while others occur once in each database, including the **master** database.

In all relational database systems, system base tables have the same logical structure as base tables. As a result, the same Transact-SQL statements used to retrieve information in the base tables can also be used to retrieve information in system base tables.

NOTE

The system base tables cannot be accessed directly: you have to use existing interfaces to query the information from the system catalog.

There are several different interfaces that you can use to access the information in the system base tables:

▶ **Catalog views**   Present the primary interface to the metadata stored in system base tables. (Metadata is data that describes the attributes of objects in a database system.)

▶ **Dynamic management views (DMVs) and functions (DMFs)**   Generally used to observe active processes and the contents of the memory.

▶ **Information schema**   A standardized solution for the access of metadata that gives you a general interface not only for the Database Engine, but for all existing relational database systems (assuming that the system supports the information schema).

▶ **System and property functions**   Allow you to retrieve system information. The difference between these two function types is mainly in their structure. Also, property functions can return more information than system functions.

▶ **System stored procedures**   Some system stored procedures can be used to access and modify the content of the system base tables.

Figure 9-1 shows a simplified form of the Database Engine's system information and different interfaces that you can use to access it.

NOTE

This chapter shows you just an overview of the system catalog and the ways in which you can access metadata. Particular catalog views, as well as all other interfaces, that are specific for different topics (such as indices, security, etc.) are discussed in the corresponding chapters.

These interfaces can be grouped in two groups: *general* interfaces (catalog views, DMVs and DMFs, and the information schema), and *proprietary* interfaces in relation to the Database Engine (system stored procedures and system and property functions).

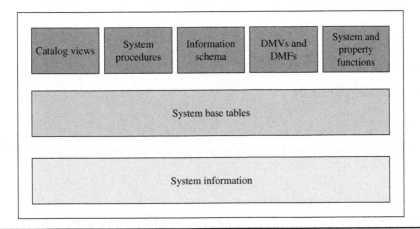

Figure 9-1   *Graphical presentation of different interfaces for the system catalog*

NOTE

"General" means that all relational database systems support such interfaces, but use different terminology. For instance, in Oracle's terminology, catalog views and DMVs are called "data dictionary views" and "V$ views," respectively.

The following section describes general interfaces. Proprietary interfaces are discussed later in the chapter.

General Interfaces

As already stated, the following interfaces are general interfaces:

► Catalog views

► DMVs and DMFs

► Information schema

Catalog Views

Catalog views are the most general interface to the metadata and provide the most efficient way to obtain customized forms of this information (see Examples 9.1 through 9.3).

Catalog views belong to the **sys** schema, so you have to use the schema name when you access one of the objects. This section describes the three most important catalog views:

► sys.objects

► sys.columns

► sys.database_principals

NOTE

You can find the description of other views either in different chapters of this book or in Books Online.

The **sys.objects** catalog view contains a row for each user-defined object in relation to the user's schema. There are two other catalog views that show similar information: **sys.system_objects** and **sys.all_objects**. The former contains a row for each system object, while the latter shows the union of all schema-scoped user-defined objects and

Column Name	Description
name	Object name
object_id	Object identification number, unique within a database
schema_id	ID of the schema in which the object is contained
type	Object type

Table 9-1   *Selected Columns of the sys.objects Catalog View*

system objects. (All three catalog views have the same structure.) Table 9-1 lists and describes the most important columns of the **sys.objects** catalog view.

The **sys.columns** catalog view contains a row for each column of an object that has columns, such as tables and views. Table 9-2 lists and describes the most important columns of the **sys.columns** catalog view.

The **sys.database_principals** catalog view contains a row for each security principal (that is, user, group, or role in a database). (For a detailed discussion of principals, see Chapter 12.) Table 9-3 lists and describes the most important columns of the **sys.objects** catalog view.

NOTE

SQL Server 2012 still supports so-called compatibility views for backward compatibility. Each compatibility view has the same name (and the same structure) as the corresponding system base table of the SQL Server 2000 system. Compatibility views do not expose any of the metadata related to features that are introduced in SQL Server 2005 and later. They are a deprecated feature and will be removed in a future version of SQL Server.

Querying Catalog Views

As already stated in this chapter, all system tables have the same structure as base tables. Because system tables cannot be referenced directly, you have to query catalog views,

Column Name	Description
object_id	ID of the object to which this column belongs
name	Column name
column_id	ID of the column (unique within the object)

Table 9-2   *Selected Columns of the sys.columns Catalog View*

Column Name	Description
name	Name of principal
principal_id	ID of principal (unique within the database)
type	Principal type

Table 9-3   *Selected Columns of the sys.database_principals Catalog View*

which correspond to particular system tables. Examples 9.1 through 9.3 use existing catalog views to demonstrate how information concerning database objects can be queried.

EXAMPLE 9.1

Get the table ID, user ID, and table type of the **employee** table:

```
USE sample;
SELECT object_id, principal_id, type
    FROM sys.objects
    WHERE name = 'employee';
```

The result is

object_id	principal_id	type
530100929	NULL	U

The **object_id** column of the **sys.objects** catalog view displays the unique ID number for the corresponding database object. The NULL value in the **principal_id** column indicates that the object's owner is the same as the owner of the schema. *U* in the **type** column stands for the user (table).

EXAMPLE 9.2

Get the names of all tables of the **sample** database that contain the **project_no** column:

```
USE sample;
SELECT sys.objects.name
  FROM sys.objects INNER JOIN sys.columns
  ON sys.objects.object_id = sys.columns.object_id
   WHERE sys.objects.type = 'U'
   AND sys.columns.name = 'project_no';
```

The result is

name
project
works_on

EXAMPLE 9.3

Who is the owner of the **employee** table?

```
SELECT sys.database_principals.name
FROM sys.database_principals INNER JOIN sys.objects
ON sys.database_principals.principal_id = sys.objects.schema_id
WHERE sys.objects.name = 'employee'
AND sys.objects.type = 'U';
```

The result is

name
dbo

Dynamic Management Views and Functions

Dynamic management views (DMVs) and functions (DMFs) return server state information that can be used to observe active processes and therefore to tune system performance or to monitor the actual system state. In contrast to catalog views, the DMVs and DMFs are based on internal structures of the system.

NOTE

The main difference between catalog views and DMVs is in their application: catalog views display the static information about metadata, while DMVs (and DMFs) are used to access dynamic properties of the system. In other words, you use DMVs to get insightful information about the database, individual queries, or an individual user.

DMVs and DMFs belong to the **sys** schema and their names start with the prefix **dm_**, followed by a text string that indicates the category to which the particular DMV or DMF belongs.

The following list identifies and describes some of these categories:

▸ **sys.dm_db_*** Contains information about databases and their objects

▸ **sys.dm_tran_*** Contains information in relation to transactions

▶ **sys.dm_io_***   Contains information about I/O activities

▶ **sys.dm_exec_***   Contains information related to the execution of user code

NOTE

Microsoft consecutively increases the number of supported DMVs in each new version of SQL Server. SQL Server 2012 contains 20 new DMVs, so the total number is now 155.

This section introduces two new DMVs:

▶ sys.dm_exec_describe_first_result_set

▶ sys.dm_db_uncontained_entities

The **sys.dm_exec_describe_first_result_set** view describes the first result set of a group of result sets. For this reason, you can apply this DMV when several subsequent queries are declared in a batch or a stored procedure (see Example 9.4). The **sys.dm_db_uncontained_entities** view shows any uncontained objects used in the database. (*Uncontained objects* are objects that cross the application boundary in a contained database. For the description of uncontained objects and the application boundary, see the section "Contained Databases" in Chapter 5.)

EXAMPLE 9.4

```
USE sample;
GO
CREATE PROC TwoSELECTS
AS
SELECT emp_no, job from works_on where emp_no BETWEEN 1000 and 9999;
SELECT emp_no, emp_lname FROM employee  where emp_fname LIKE 'S%';
GO
SELECT is_hidden hidden ,column_ordinal ord,
          name, is_nullable nul, system_type_id id
       FROM sys.dm_exec_describe_first_result_set ('TwoSELECTS', NULL, 0) ;
```

The result is

hidden	ord	name	nul	id
0	1	emp_no	0	56
0	2	job	1	175

The stored procedure in Example 9.4 contains two SELECT statements concerning the **sample** database. The subsequent query uses the **sys.dm_exec_describe_first_result_set** view to display several properties of the result set of the first query.

> **NOTE**
>
> *Many DMVs and DMFs are discussed in subsequent chapters of the book. For instance, index-related DMVs and DMFs are explained in the next chapter, while transaction-related DMVs and DMFs are discussed in Chapter 13.*

Information Schema

The information schema consists of read-only views that provide information about all tables, views, and columns of the Database Engine to which you have access. In contrast to the system catalog that manages the metadata applied to the system as a whole, the information schema primarily manages the environment of a database.

> **NOTE**
>
> *The information schema was originally introduced in the SQL92 standard. The Database Engine provides information schema views so that applications developed on other database systems can obtain its system catalog without having to use it directly. These standard views use different terminology, so when you interpret the column names, be aware that catalog is a synonym for database and domain is a synonym for user-defined data type.*

The following sections provide a description of the most important information schema views.

Information_schema.tables

The **Information_schema.tables** view contains one row for each table in the current database to which the user has access. The view retrieves the information from the system catalog using the **sys.objects** catalog view. Table 9-4 lists and describes the four columns of this view.

Column	Description
TABLE_CATALOG	The name of the catalog (database) to which the view belongs
TABLE_SCHEMA	The name of the schema to which the view belongs
TABLE_NAME	The table name
TABLE_TYPE	The type of the table (can be BASE TABLE or VIEW)

Table 9-4   *The Information_schema.tables View*

Column	Description
TABLE_CATALOG	The name of the catalog (database) to which the column belongs
TABLE_SCHEMA	The name of the schema to which the column belongs
TABLE_NAME	The name of the table to which the column belongs
COLUMN_NAME	The column name
ORDINAL_POSITION	The ordinal position of the column
DATA_TYPE	The data type of the column

Table 9-5   *The Information_schema.columns View*

Information_schema.columns

The **Information_schema.columns** view contains one row for each column in the current database accessible by the user. The view retrieves the information from the **sys.columns** and **sys.objects** catalog views. Table 9-5 lists and describes the six most important columns of this view.

Proprietary Interfaces

The previous section describes the use of the general interfaces for accessing system base tables. You can also retrieve system information using one of the following proprietary mechanisms of the Database Engine:

▶   System stored procedures

▶   System functions

▶   Property functions

The following sections describe these interfaces.

System Stored Procedures

System stored procedures are used to provide many administrative and end-user tasks, such as renaming database objects, identifying users, and monitoring authorization and resources. Almost all existing system stored procedures access system base tables to retrieve and modify system information.

NOTE

The most important property of system stored procedures is that they can be used for easy and reliable modification of system base tables.

This section describes two system stored procedures: **sp_help** and **sp_configure**. Depending on the subject matter of the chapters, certain system stored procedures were discussed in previous chapters, and additional procedures will be discussed in later chapters of the book.

The **sp_help** system stored procedure displays information about one or more database objects. The name of any database object or data type can be used as a parameter of this procedure. If **sp_help** is executed without any parameter, information on all database objects of the current database will be displayed.

The **sp_configure** system stored procedure displays or changes global configuration settings for the current server.

Example 9.5 shows the use of the **sp_configure** system stored procedure.

EXAMPLE 9.5

```
USE sample;
EXEC sp_configure 'show advanced options' , 1;
RECONFIGURE WITH OVERRIDE;
EXEC sp_configure 'fill factor', 100;
RECONFIGURE WITH OVERRIDE;
```

Generally, you do not have access to advanced configuration options of SQL Server. For this reason, the first EXECUTE statement in Example 9.5 tells the system to allow changes of advanced options. With the next statement, RECONFIGURE WITH OVERRIDE, these changes will be installed. Now it is possible to change any of the existing advanced options. Example 9.5 changes the fill factor to 100 and installs this change. (Fill factor specifies the storage percentage for index pages and will be described in detail in the next chapter.)

System Functions

System functions are described in Chapter 5. Some of them can be used to access system base tables. Example 9.6 shows two SELECT statements that retrieve the same information using different interfaces.

EXAMPLE 9.6

```
USE sample;
SELECT object_id
    FROM sys.objects
    WHERE name = 'employee';
SELECT object_id('employee');
```

The second SELECT statement in Example 9.6 uses the system function **object_id** to retrieve the ID of the **employee** table. (This information can be stored in a variable and used when calling a command, or a system stored procedure, with the object's ID as a parameter.)

The following system functions, among others, access system base tables. The names of these functions are self-explanatory.

- ▶ OBJECT_ID(object_name)
- ▶ OBJECT_NAME(object_id)
- ▶ USER_ID([user_name])
- ▶ USER_NAME([user_id])
- ▶ DB_ID([db_name])
- ▶ DB_NAME([db_id])

Property Functions

Property functions return properties of database objects, data types, or files. Generally, property functions can return more information than system functions can return, because property functions support dozens of properties (as parameters), which you can specify explicitly.

Almost all property functions return one of the following three values: 0, 1, or NULL. If the value is 0, the object does not have the specified property. If the value is 1, the object has the specified property. Similarly, the value NULL specifies that the existence of the specified property for the object is unknown to the system.

The Database Engine supports, among others, the following property functions:

- ▶ OBJECTPROPERTY(id, property)
- ▶ COLUMNPROPERTY(id, column, property)
- ▶ FILEPROPERTY(filename, property)
- ▶ TYPEPROPERTY(type, property)

The OBJECTPROPERTY function returns information about objects in the current database (see Exercise E.9.2). The COLUMNPROPERTY function returns information about a column or procedure parameter. The FILEPROPERTY function returns the specified filename and property value for a given filename and property name. The TYPEPROPERTY function returns information about a data type. (The description of existing properties for each property function can be found in Books Online.)

Summary

The system catalog is a collection of system base tables belonging to the **master** database and existing user databases. Generally, system base tables cannot be queried directly by a user. The Database Engine supports several different interfaces that you can use to access the information from the system catalog. Catalog views are the most general interface that you can apply to obtain system information. Dynamic management views (DMVs) and functions (DMFs) are similar to catalog views, but you use them to access dynamic properties of the system. System stored procedures provide easy and reliable read and write access to system base tables. It is strongly recommended to exclusively use system stored procedures for modification of system information.

The information schema is a collection of views defined on system base tables that provides unified access to the system catalog for all database applications developed on other database systems. The use of the information schema is recommended if you intend to port your system from one database system to another.

The next chapter introduces you to database indices.

Exercises

E.9.1

Using catalog views, find the operating system path and filename of the **sample** database.

E.9.2

Using catalog views, find how many integrity constraints are defined for the **employee** table of the **sample** database.

E.9.3

Using catalog views, find out if there is any integrity constraint defined for the **dept_no** column of the **employee** table.

E.9.4

Using the information schema, display all user tables that belong to the **AdventureWorks** database.

E.9.5

Using the information schema, find all columns of the **employee** table with their ordinal positions and the corresponding data types.

Chapter 10

Indices

In This Chapter

- ► Introduction
- ► Transact-SQL and Indices
- ► Guidelines for Creating and Using Indices
- ► Special Types of Indices

This chapter describes indices and their role in optimizing the response time of queries. The first part of the chapter discusses how indices are stored and the existing forms of them. The main part of the chapter explains three Transact-SQL statements pertaining to indices: CREATE INDEX, ALTER INDEX, and DROP INDEX. After that, index fragmentation and its impact on the performance of the system will be explained. The next part of the chapter gives you several general recommendations for how and when indices should be created. The final part of the chapter describes several special types of indices.

Introduction

Database systems generally use indices to provide fast access to relational data. An index is a separate physical data structure that enables queries to access one or more data rows fast. Proper tuning of indices is therefore a key for query performance.

An index is in many ways analogous to a book index. When you are looking for a topic in a book, you use its index to find the page(s) where that topic is described. Similarly, when you search for a row of a table, the Database Engine uses an index to find its physical location. However, there are two main differences between a book index and a database index:

▶ As a book reader, you can decide whether or not to use the book's index. This possibility generally does not exist if you use a database system: the system component called the query optimizer decides whether or not to use an existing index. (A user can manipulate the use of indices by using index hints, but their use is recommended only in a few special cases. Index hints are described in Chapter 19.)

▶ A particular book's index is edited together with the book and does not change at all. This means that you can find a topic exactly on the page where it is determined in the index. By contrast, a database index can change each time the corresponding data is changed.

If a table does not have an appropriate index, the database system uses the table scan method to retrieve rows. *Table scan* means that each row is retrieved and examined in sequence (from first to last) and returned in the result set if the search condition in the WHERE clause evaluates to TRUE. Therefore, all rows are fetched according to their physical memory location. This method is less efficient than an index access, as explained next.

Indices are stored in additional data structures called *index pages*. (The structure of index pages is very similar to the structure of data pages, as you will see in Chapter 15.)

For each indexed row there is an *index entry*, which is stored in an index page. Each index entry consists of the index key plus a pointer. For this reason, each index entry is significantly shorter than the corresponding row. Therefore, the number of index entries per (index) page is significantly higher than the number of rows per (data) page. This index property plays a very important role, because the number of I/O operations required to traverse the index pages is significantly lower than the number of I/O operations required to traverse the corresponding data pages. In other words, a table scan would probably result in many more I/O operations than a corresponding index access would.

The Database Engine's indices are constructed using the B⁺-tree data structure. As its name suggests, a B⁺-tree has a treelike structure in which all of the bottommost nodes (leaf nodes) are the same number of levels away from the top (root node) of the tree. This property is maintained even when new data is added or deleted from the indexed column.

Figure 10-1 illustrates the structure of the B⁺-tree and the direct access to the row of the **employee** table with the value 25348 in its **emp_no** column. (It is assumed that the **employee** table has an index on the **emp_no** column.) You can also see that each B⁺-tree consists of a root node, leaf nodes, and zero or more intermediate nodes.

Figure 10-1   *B⁺-tree for the emp_no column of the employee table*

Searching for the data value 25348 can be executed as follows: Starting from the root of the B+-tree, a search proceeds for a lowest key value greater than or equal to the value to be retrieved. Therefore, the value 29346 is retrieved from the root node; then the value 28559 is fetched from the intermediate level, and the searched value, 25348, is retrieved at the leaf level. With the help of the respective pointers, the appropriate row is retrieved. (An alternative, but equivalent, search method would be to search for smaller or equal values.)

Index access is generally the preferred and obviously advantageous method for accessing tables with many rows. With index access, it takes only a few I/O operations to find any row of a table in a very short time, whereas sequential access (i.e., table scan) requires much more time to find a row physically stored at the end of the table.

The two existing index types, clustered and nonclustered indices, are described next, after which you will find out how to create an index.

Clustered Indices

A clustered index determines the physical order of the data in a table. The Database Engine allows the creation of a single clustered index per table, because the rows of the table cannot be physically ordered more than one way. When using a clustered index, the system navigates down from the root of the B+-tree structure to the leaf nodes, which are linked together in a doubly linked list called a *page chain*. The important property of a clustered index is that its leaf pages contain data pages. (All other levels of a clustered index structure are composed of index pages.) If a clustered index is (implicitly or explicitly) defined for a table, the table is called a *clustered table*. Figure 10-2 shows the B+-tree structure of a clustered index.

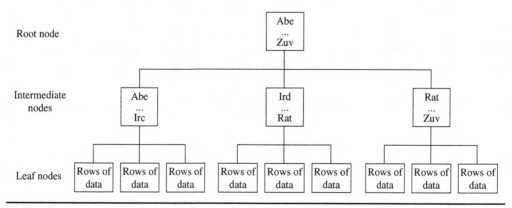

Figure 10-2   *Physical structure of a clustered index*

A clustered index is built by default for each table for which you define the primary key using the primary key constraint. Also, each clustered index is unique by default—that is, each data value can appear only once in a column for which the clustered index is defined. If a clustered index is built on a nonunique column, the database system will force uniqueness by adding a 4-byte identifier to the rows that have duplicate values.

NOTE

Clustered indices allow very fast access in cases where a query searches for a range of values (see Chapter 19).

Nonclustered Indices

A nonclustered index has the same index structure as a clustered index, with two important differences:

▶ A nonclustered index does not change the physical order of the rows in the table.

▶ The leaf pages of a nonclustered index consist of an index key plus a bookmark.

The physical order of rows in a table will not be changed if one or more nonclustered indices are defined for that table. For each nonclustered index, the Database Engine creates an additional index structure that is stored in index pages.

A bookmark of a nonclustered index shows where to find the row corresponding to the index key. The bookmark part of the index key can have two forms, depending on the form of the table—that is, the table can be a clustered table or a heap. (In SQL Server terminology, a *heap* is a table without a clustered index.) If a clustered index exists, the bookmark of the nonclustered index shows the B⁺-tree structure of the table's clustered index. If the table has no clustered index, the bookmark is identical to the row identifier (RID), which contains three parts: the address of the file to which the corresponding table belongs, the address of the physical block (page) in which the row is stored, and the offset, which is the position of the row inside the page.

As the preceding discussion indicates, searching for data using a nonclustered index could proceed in either of two different ways, depending on the form of the table:

▶ **Heap**   Traversal of the nonclustered index structure is followed by the retrieval of the row using the RID.

▶ **Clustered table**   Traversal of the nonclustured index structure is followed by traversal of the corresponding clustered index.

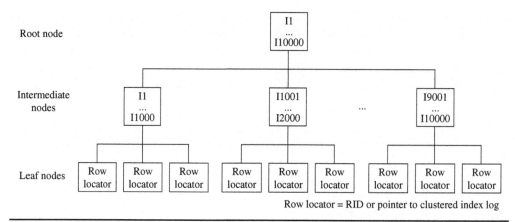

Figure 10-3   *Structure of a nonclustered index*

In both cases, the number of I/O operations is quite high, so you should design a nonclustered index with care and only when you are sure that there will be significant performance gains by using it. Figure 10-3 shows the B⁺-tree structure of a nonclustered index.

Transact-SQL and Indices

Now that you are familiar with the physical structure of indices, this section describes how you can create, alter, and drop indices; obtain index fragmentation information; and edit index information; all of which will prepare you for the subsequent discussion of how you can use indices to improve performance of the system.

Creating Indices

The CREATE INDEX statement creates an index for the particular table. The general form of this statement is

```
CREATE [UNIQUE] [CLUSTERED |NONCLUSTERED] INDEX index_name
    ON table_name (column1 [ASC | DESC] ,...)
          [ INCLUDE ( column_name [ ,... ] ) ]
   [WITH

             [FILLFACTOR=n]
             [[, ] PAD_INDEX = {ON | OFF}]
             [[, ] DROP_EXISTING = {ON | OFF}]
             [[, ] SORT_IN_TEMPDB = {ON | OFF}]
```

```
[[, ] IGNORE_DUP_KEY = {ON | OFF}]
 [[, ] ALLOW_ROW_LOCKS = {ON | OFF}]
 [[, ]ALLOW_PAGE_LOCKS = {ON | OFF}]
 [[, ] STATISTICS_NORECOMPUTE = {ON | OFF}]
 [[, ]ONLINE = {ON | OFF}]]
 [ON file_group | "default"]
```

index_name identifies the name of the created index. An index can be established for one or more columns of a single table (**table_name**). **column1** is the name of the column for which the index is created. (As you can see from the syntax of the CREATE INDEX statement, you can specify an index for several columns of a table.) The Database Engine supports indices on views too. Such views, called *indexed views*, are discussed in the next chapter.

NOTE

Each column of a table can be indexed. This means that columns with VARBINARY(max), BIGINT, and SQL_VARIANT data types can be indexed too.

An index can be either single or composite. A single index has one column, whereas a composite index is built on more than one column. Each composite index has certain restrictions concerning its length and number of columns. The maximum size of an index is 900 bytes, while the index can contain up to 16 columns.

The UNIQUE option specifies that each data value can appear only once in an indexed column. For a unique composite index, the combination of data values of all columns in each row must be unique. If UNIQUE is not specified, duplicate values in the indexed column(s) are allowed.

The CLUSTERED option specifies a clustered index. The NONCLUSTERED option (the default) specifies that the index does not change the order of the rows in the table. The Database Engine allows a maximum of 249 nonclustered indices per table.

The Database Engine has been enhanced to support indices with descending order on column values. The ASC option after the column name specifies that the index is created on the ascending order of the column's values, while DESC specifies the descending order. This gives you more flexibility for using an index. Descending indices should be used when you create a composite index on columns that have opposite sorting directions.

The INCLUDE option allows you to specify the nonkey columns, which are added to the leaf pages of the nonclustered index. Column names cannot be repeated in the INCLUDE list and cannot be used simultaneously as both key and nonkey columns. To understand the benefit of the INCLUDE option, you have to know what a *covering index* is. Significant performance gains can be achieved when *all* columns in a query are included in the index, because the query optimizer can locate all the column values within the index pages without having to access table data. This feature is called a covering index or covered query. So, if you include additional nonkey columns in the leaf pages of the nonclustered index, more queries will be covered and their performance will be significantly better. (Further discussion of this topic, as well as an example of how the query optimizer handles a covering index, can be found later in this chapter in the section "Covering Index.")

FILLFACTOR=n defines the storage percentage for each index page at the time the index is created. You can set the value of FILLFACTOR from 1 to 100. If the value of **n** is set to 100, each index page will be 100 percent filled—that is, the existing index leaf pages as well as nonleaf pages will have no space for the insertion of new rows. Therefore, this value is recommended only for static tables. (The default value, 0, also indicates that the leaf index pages are filled and the intermediate nonleaf pages contain one free entry each.)

If you set the FILLFACTOR option to a value between 1 and 99, the new index structure will be created with leaf pages that are not completely full. The bigger the value of FILLFACTOR, the smaller the space that is left free on an index page. For instance, setting FILLFACTOR to 60 means that 40 percent of each leaf index page is left free for future insertion of index rows. (Index rows will be inserted when you execute either the INSERT or the UPDATE statement.) For this reason, the value 60 could be a reasonable value for tables with rather frequent data modification. For all values of the FILLFACTOR option between 1 and 99, the intermediate nonleaf pages contain one free entry each.

NOTE

The FILLFACTOR value is not maintained—that is, it specifies only how much storage space is reserved with the existing data at the time the storage percentage is defined. If you want to reestablish the original value of the FILLFACTOR option, you need to use the ALTER INDEX statement, which is described later in this chapter.

The PAD_INDEX option is tightly connected to the FILLFACTOR option. The FILLFACTOR option mainly specifies the percentage of space that is left free on leaf index pages. On the other hand, the PAD_INDEX option specifies that the FILLFACTOR setting should be applied to the index pages as well as to the data pages in the index.

The DROP_EXISTING option allows you to enhance performance when re-creating a clustered index on a table that also has a nonclustered index. See the section "Rebuilding an Index" later in the chapter for more details.

The SORT_IN_TEMPDB option is used to place into the **tempdb** system database the data from intermediate sort operations used while creating the index. This can result in a performance benefit if the **tempdb** database is placed on another disk drive from the data itself.

The IGNORE_DUP_KEY option causes the system to ignore the attempt to insert duplicate values in the indexed column(s). This option should be used only to avoid the termination of a long transaction in cases where the INSERT statement inserts duplicate data in the indexed column(s). If this option is activated and an INSERT statement attempts to insert rows that would violate the uniqueness of the index, the database system returns a warning rather than causing the entire statement to fail. The Database Engine does *not* insert the rows that would add duplicate key values; it merely ignores those rows and adds the rest. (If this option is not set, the statement as a whole will be aborted.)

The ALLOW_ROW_LOCKS option specifies that the system uses row locks when this option is activated (set to ON). Similarly, the ALLOW_PAGE_LOCKS option specifies that the system uses page locks when this option is set to ON. (For the description of page and row locks, see Chapter 13.)

The STATISTICS_NORECOMPUTE option specifies that statistics of the specified index should not be automatically recomputed. (The statistics will be explained in Chapter 19.) The ON option creates either the specified index on the default file group ("default") or on the specified file group (**file_group**).

If you activate the ONLINE option, you can create, rebuild, or drop an index online. This option allows concurrent modifications to the underlying table or clustered index data and any associated indices during index execution. For example, while a clustered index is being rebuilt, you can continue to make updates to the underlying data and perform queries against the data.

NOTE

Before you start to execute queries in this chapter, re-create the entire sample database.

Example 10.1 shows the creation of a nonclustered index.

EXAMPLE 10.1

Create an index for the **emp_no** column of the **employee** table:

```
USE sample;
CREATE INDEX i_empno ON employee (emp_no);
```

Example 10.2 shows the creation of a unique composite index.

EXAMPLE 10.2

Create a composite index for the columns **emp_no** and **project_no** on the **works_on** table. The compound values in both columns must be unique. Eighty percent of each index leaf page should be filled.

```
USE sample;
CREATE UNIQUE INDEX i_empno_prno
        ON works_on (emp_no, project_no)
        WITH FILLFACTOR= 80;
```

The creation of a unique index for a column is not possible if the column already contains duplicate values. The creation of such an index is possible if each existing data value (including the NULL value) occurs only once. Also, any attempt to insert or modify an existing data value into a column with an existing unique index will be rejected by the system.

Obtaining Index Fragmentation Information

During the life cycle of an index, it can become *fragmented*, meaning the storage of data in its pages is done inefficiently. There are two forms of index fragmentation: internal and external. Internal fragmentation specifies the amount of data, which is stored within each page. External fragmentation occurs when the logical order of the pages is wrong.

To get information concerning internal index fragmentation, you use the dynamic management view (DMV) called **sys.dm_db_index_physical_stats**. This DMV returns size and fragmentation information for the data and indices of the specified table. For each index, one row is returned for each level of the B^+-tree. Using this DMV, you can obtain information about the degree of fragmentation of rows on data pages. You can use this information to decide whether reorganization of the data is necessary.

Example 10.3 shows how you can use the **sys.dm_db_index_physical_stats** view. (You need to drop all existing indices on the **works_on** table before you start the batch. Example 10.4 shows the use of the DROP INDEX statement.)

EXAMPLE 10.3

```
DECLARE @db_id INT;
DECLARE @tab_id INT;
DECLARE @ind_id INT;
SET @db_id = DB_ID('sample');
SET @tab_id = OBJECT_ID('employee');
SELECT avg_fragmentation_in_percent, avg_page_space_used_in_percent
 FROM sys.dm_db_index_physical_stats
(@db_id, @tab_id, NULL, NULL, NULL)
```

As you can see from Example 10.3, the **sys.dm_db_index_physical_stats** view has five parameters. The first three specify the IDs of the current database, table, and index, respectively. The fourth specifies the partition ID (see Chapter 25), and the last one specifies the scan level that is used to obtain statistics. (You can always use NULL to specify the default value of the particular parameter.)

This view has several columns, of which **avg_fragmentation_in_percent** and **avg_page_space_used_in_percent** are the most important. The former specifies the average fragmentation in percent, while the latter defines the percentage of the used space.

Editing Index Information

After you have viewed the index fragmentation information, as discussed in the previous section, you can use the following system features to edit that information and to edit other index information:

▶   **sys.indexes** catalog view

▶   **sys.index_columns** catalog view

▶   **sp_helpindex** system procedure

▶   OBJECTPROPERTY property function

▶   SQL Server Management Studio

▶   **sys.dm_db_index_usage_stats** DMV

▶   **sys.dm_db_missing_index_details** DMV

The **sys.indexes** catalog view contains a row for each index and a row for each table without a clustered index. The most important columns of this view are **object_id**, **name**, and **index_id**. **object_id** is the name of the database object to which the index belongs, while **name** and **index_id** are the name and the ID of that index, respectively.

The **sys.index_columns** catalog view contains a row per column that is part of an index or a heap. This information can be used together with the information from the **sys.indexes** catalog view to obtain further properties of a specific index.

sp_helpindex displays all indices on a table as well as column statistics. The syntax of this procedure is

```
sp_helpindex [@db_object = ] 'name',
```

where **db_object** is the name of a table.

The OBJECTPROPERTY property function has two properties in relation to indices: **IsIndexed** and **IsIndexable**. The former informs you whether a table or view has an index, while the latter specifies whether a table or view can be indexed.

To edit information about an existing index using SQL Server Management Studio, choose the database in the Databases folder and expand Tables. Expand the Indexes folder. The list of all existing indices for that table is shown. After you double-click one of the indices, the system shows you the Index Properties dialog box with all properties of that index. (You can also use Management Studio to create a new index or drop an existing one.)

The **sys.dm_db_index_usage_stats** view returns counts of different types of index operations and the time each type of operation was last performed. Every individual seek, lookup, or update on the specified index by one query execution is counted as a use of that index and increments the corresponding counter in this DMV. That way you can get general information about how often an index is used to determine which indices are used more heavily than the others.

The **sys.dm_db_missing_index_details** view returns detailed information about missing indices. The most important columns of this DMV are **index_handle** and **object_id**. The former identifies a particular missing index, while the latter specifies the table where the index is missing.

Altering Indices

The Database Engine is one of a few database systems that support the ALTER INDEX statement. This statement can be used for index maintenance activities. The syntax of the ALTER INDEX statement is very similar to the syntax of the CREATE INDEX statement. In other words, this statement allows you to change the settings for the options ALLOW_ROW_LOCKS, ALLOW_PAGE_LOCKS, IGNORE_DUP_KEY, and STATISTICS_NORECOMPUTE, previously described in relation to the CREATE INDEX statement.

In addition to the preceding options, the ALTER INDEX statement supports three other activities:

▶ Rebuilding an index using the REBUILD option

▶ Reorganizing leaf index pages using the REORGANIZE option

▶ Disabling an index using the DISABLE option

The following subsections discuss these options.

Rebuilding an Index

When you perform any data modifications using the INSERT, UPDATE, or DELETE statement, data fragmentation can occur. If these data are indexed, index fragmentation can occur as well, and the information in the index can get scattered on different physical pages. Fragmented index data can cause the Database Engine to perform additional data reads, which decreases the overall performance of the system. In such a case, you have to rebuild all fragmented indexes.

There are two ways in which you can rebuild an index:

▶ Use the REBUILD option of the ALTER INDEX statement

▶ Use the DROP_EXISTING option of the CREATE INDEX statement

With the REBUILD option, you can rebuild an index. If you specify ALL instead of an index name, all indices of the table will be rebuilt. (By allowing indices to be rebuilt dynamically, you don't have to drop and re-create them.)

The DROP_EXISTING option of the CREATE INDEX statement allows you to enhance performance when re-creating a clustered index on a table that also has nonclustered indices. It specifies that the existing clustered or nonclustered index should be dropped and the specified index rebuilt. As you already know, each nonclustered index in a clustered table contains in its leaf nodes the corresponding values of the table's clustered index. For this reason, all nonclustered indices must be rebuilt when a table's clustered index is dropped. Using the DROP_EXISTING option, you can prevent the nonclustered indices from being rebuilt twice.

NOTE
The DROP_EXISTING option is more powerful than REBUILD, because it is more flexible and offers several options, such as changing the columns that make up the index and changing a nonclustered index to a clustered one.

Reorganizing Leaf Index Pages

The REORGANIZE option of the ALTER INDEX statement specifies that the leaf pages of the corresponding index structure will be reorganized so that the physical order of the pages matches the left-to-right logical order of the leaf nodes. Therefore, this option removes some of the fragmentation from an index, thus improving performance.

Disabling an Index

The DISABLE option disables an existing index. Each disabled index is unavailable for use until you enable it again. Note that a disabled index won't be maintained as changes to the corresponding data are made. For this reason, indices must be completely rebuilt if you want to use them again. To enable a disabled index, use the REBUILD option of the ALTER TABLE statement.

NOTE

If you disable the clustered index of a table, the data won't be available, because all data pages are stored in the leaf level of the clustered index.

Removing and Renaming Indices

The DROP INDEX statement removes one or more existing indices from the current database. Note that removing the clustered index of a table can be a very resource-intensive operation, because all nonclustered indices will have to be rebuilt. (All the nonclustered indices use the index key of the clustered index as a pointer in their leaf index pages.) Example 10.4 shows how the **i_empno** index can be dropped.

EXAMPLE 10.4

Remove the index created in Example 10.1:

```
USE sample;
DROP INDEX i_empno ON employee;
```

The DROP INDEX statement has an additional option, MOVE TO, which is analogous to the ON option of CREATE INDEX. In other words, you can use this option to specify a location to which to move the data rows that are currently in the leaf pages of the clustered index. The data is moved to the new location in the form of a heap. You can specify either a default or named file group as the new location.

NOTE

The DROP INDEX statement cannot be used to remove indices that are implicitly generated by the system for integrity constraints, such as PRIMARY KEY or UNIQUE. To remove such indices, you must drop the constraint.

The **sp_rename** system procedure, which is discussed in Chapter 5, can be used to rename indices.

NOTE

You can create, alter, and drop indices using SQL Server Management Studio, too. To manage indices inside Management Studio, you can use either database diagrams or Object Explorer. The simplest way is to use the Indexes node of a particular table. The index management with Management Studio is analogous to the table management with the same tool. (For details, see Chapter 3.)

Guidelines for Creating and Using Indices

Although the Database Engine does not have any practical limitations concerning the number of indices, it is advisable to limit them, for a couple of reasons. First, each index uses a certain amount of disk space, so it is possible that the total number of index pages could exceed the number of data pages within a database. Second, in contrast to the benefits of using an index for retrievals, inserts and updates have a direct impact on the maintenance of the index. The more indices on the tables, the more index reorganizations that are necessary. The rule of thumb is to choose indices wisely for frequent queries and evaluate index usage afterwards.

This section gives some recommendations for creating and using indices.

NOTE

The following recommendations are general rules of thumb. They ultimately depend on how your database will be used in production and which queries are used most frequently. An index on a column that is never used will be counterproductive.

Indices and Conditions in the WHERE Clause

If the WHERE clause in a SELECT statement contains a search condition with a single column, you should create an index on this column. The use of an index is especially recommended if the selectivity of the condition is high. The *selectivity* of a condition is defined as the ratio of the number of rows satisfying the condition to the total number of rows in the table. (High selectivity corresponds to a small ratio.) The most successful processing of a retrieval with the indexed column will be achieved if the selectivity of a condition is 5 percent or less.

The column should not be indexed if the selectivity of the condition is constantly 80 percent or more. In such a case, additional I/O operations will be needed for the existing index pages, which would eliminate any time savings gained by index access. In this particular case, a table scan would be faster, and the query optimizer would usually choose to use a table scan, rendering the index useless.

If a search condition in a frequently used query contains one or more AND operators, it is best to create a composite index that includes all the columns of the table specified in the WHERE clause of the SELECT statement. Example 10.5 shows the creation of a composite index that includes all the columns specified in the WHERE clause of the SELECT statement.

EXAMPLE 10.5

```
USE sample;
CREATE INDEX i_works ON works_on(emp_no, enter_date);
SELECT emp_no, project_no, enter_date
```

```
FROM works_on
WHERE emp_no = 29346 AND enter_date='1.4.2006';
```

The AND operator in this query contains two conditions. As such, both of the columns appearing in each condition should be indexed using a composite nonclustered index.

Indices and the Join Operator

In the case of a join operation, it is recommended that you index each join column. Join columns often represent the primary key of one table and the corresponding foreign key of the other or the same table. If you specify the PRIMARY KEY and FOREIGN KEY integrity constraints for the corresponding join columns, only a nonclustered index for the column with the foreign key should be created, because the system will implicitly create the clustered index for the PRIMARY KEY column.

Example 10.6 shows the creation of indices, which should be used if you have a query with a join operation and an additional filter.

EXAMPLE 10.6

```
USE sample;
SELECT emp_lname, emp_fname
    FROM employee, works_on
    WHERE employee.emp_no = works_on.emp_no
    AND enter_date = '10.15.2007';
```

For Example 10.6, the creation of two separate indices for the **emp_no** column in both the **employee** and **works_on** tables is recommended. Also, an additional index should be created for the **enter_date** column.

Covering Index

As you already know, significant performance gains can be achieved when *all* columns in the query are included in the index. Example 10.7 shows a covering index.

EXAMPLE 10.7

```
USE AdventureWorks;
GO
DROP INDEX Person.Address.IX_Address_StateProvinceID;
GO
CREATE INDEX i_address_zip
  ON Person.Address (PostalCode)
  INCLUDE (City, StateProvinceID);
```

```
GO
SELECT City, StateProvinceID
      FROM Person.Address
      WHERE PostalCode = 84407;
```

Example 10.7 first drops the **IX_Address_StateProvinceID** index of the **Address** table. In the second step, it creates the new index, which additionally includes two other columns, on the **PostalCode** column. Finally, the SELECT statement at the end of the example shows a query covered by the index. For this query, the system does not have to search for data in data pages, because the optimizer can find all the column values in the leaf pages of the nonclustered index.

NOTE

The use of covering indices is recommended because index pages generally contain many more entries than the corresponding data pages contain. Also, to use this method, the filtered columns must be the first key columns in the index.

Special Types of Indices

The Database Engine allows you to create the following special types of indices:

▶ Indexed views

▶ Filtered indices

▶ Indices on computed columns

▶ Partitioned indices

▶ Column store indices

▶ XML indices

▶ Full-text indices

Indexed views are based on views and therefore will be discussed in the next chapter. Filtered indices are similar to indexed views. You can find their description in Books Online. Partitioned indices are used with partitioned tables and are described in Chapter 25. Column store indices are one of the most important new features in SQL Server 2012 and will also be explained in detail in Chapter 25. Indices in relation to XML are explained in detail in Chapter 26, while full-text indices are a topic of Chapter 28.

This section discusses computed columns and indices in relation to them.

A *computed column* is a column of a table that is used to store the result of a computation of the table's data. Such a column can be either virtual or persistent. The following subsections describe these two forms of computed columns.

Virtual Computed Columns

A computed column without a corresponding clustered index is logical—that is, it is not physically stored on the hard disk. Hence, it is recomputed each time a row is accessed.

Example 10.8 demonstrates the use of virtual computed columns.

EXAMPLE 10.8

```
USE sample;
CREATE TABLE orders
     (orderid INT NOT NULL,
      price MONEY NOT NULL,
      quantity INT NOT NULL,
      orderdate DATETIME NOT NULL,
       total AS price * quantity,
      shippeddate AS DATEADD (DAY, 7, orderdate));
```

The **orders** table in Example 10.8 has two virtual computed columns: **total** and **shippeddate**. The **total** column is computed using two other columns, **price** and **quantity**, while the **shippeddate** column is computed using the date function DATEADD and the column **orderdate**.

Persistent Computed Columns

The Database Engine allows you to build indices on deterministic computed columns, where the underlying columns have precise data types. (A computed column is called *deterministic* if the same values will always be returned for the same table data.)

An indexed computed column can be created only if the following options of the SET statement are set to ON. (These options guarantee the determinism of the column.)

▶ QUOTED_IDENTIFIER

▶ CONCAT_NULL_YIELDS_NULL

▶ ANSI_NULLS

▶ ANSI_PADDING

▶ ANSI_WARNINGS

Also, the NUMERIC_ROUNDABORT option must be set to OFF.

If you create a clustered index on a computed column, the values of the column will physically exist in the corresponding table rows, because leaf pages of the clustered index contain data rows (see the "Clustered Indices" section earlier in this chapter).

Example 10.9 shows the creation of a clustered index for the computed column **total** in Example 10.8.

EXAMPLE 10.9

```
CREATE CLUSTERED INDEX i1 ON orders (total);
```

After the execution of the CREATE INDEX statement in Example 10.9, the computed column **total** will physically exist. This means that all updates to the underlying columns that build the computed column will cause the modification of the computed column itself.

NOTE

There is an alternative way to specify a computed column as persistent, using the PERSISTED option. This option allows you to specify that the computed column will physically exist in the corresponding table rows, even if the corresponding clustered index isn't created. This feature is necessary for computed columns built upon approximate data types (FLOAT and REAL). (As you already know, you can create an index for a computed column only if the underlying columns have a precise data type.)

Summary

Indices are used to access data more efficiently. They can affect not only SELECT statements but also performance of INSERT, UPDATE, and DELETE statements. An index can be clustered or nonclustered, unique or nonunique, and single or composite. A clustered index physically sorts the rows of the table in the order of the specified column(s). A unique index specifies that each value can appear only once in that column of the table. A composite index is composed of more than one column.

A great feature in relation to indices is the Database Engine Tuning Advisor (DTA), which will, among other things, analyze a sample of your actual workload (supplied via either a script file from you or a captured trace file from SQL Server Profiler) and recommend indices for you to add or delete based on that workload. Use of DTA is highly recommended. For more information on SQL Server Profiler and DTA, see Chapter 20.

The next chapter discusses the notion of a view.

Exercises

E.10.1

Create a nonclustered index for the **enter_date** column of the **works_on** table. Sixty percent of each index leaf page should be filled.

E.10.2

Create a unique composite index for the **l_name** and **f_name** columns of the **employee** table. Is there any difference if you change the order of the columns in the composite index?

E.10.3

How can you drop the index that is implicitly created for the primary key of a table?

E.10.4

Discuss the benefits and disadvantages of an index.

In the following four exercises, create indices that will improve performance of the queries. (Assume that all tables of the **sample** database that are used in the following exercises have a very large number of rows.)

E.10.5

```
SELECT emp_no, emp_fname, emp_lname
        FROM employee
        WHERE emp_lname = 'Smith'
```

E.10.6

```
SELECT emp_no, emp_fname, emp_lname
        FROM employee
        WHERE emp_lname = 'Hansel'
        AND emp_fname = 'Elke'
```

E.10.7

```
SELECT job
    FROM works_on, employee
    WHERE employee.emp_no = works_on.emp_no
```

E.10.8

```
SELECT emp_lname, emp_fname
        FROM employee, department
        WHERE employee.dept_no = department.dept_no
        AND dept_name = 'Research'
```

Chapter 11

Views

In This Chapter

- ▶ DDL Statements and Views
- ▶ DML Statements and Views
- ▶ Indexed Views

his chapter is dedicated exclusively to the database object called a *view*. The structure of this chapter corresponds to the structure of Chapters 5 to 7, in which the DDL and DML statements for base tables were described. The first section of this chapter covers the DDL statements concerning views: CREATE VIEW, ALTER VIEW, and DROP VIEW. The second part of the chapter describes the DML statements SELECT, INSERT, UPDATE, and DELETE with views. The SELECT statement will be looked at separately from the other three statements. In contrast to base tables, views cannot be used for modification operations without certain limitations. These limitations are described at the end of each corresponding section.

The alternative form of a view, called an indexed view, is described in the last major section of this chapter. This type of index materializes the corresponding query and allows you to achieve significant performance gains in relation to queries with aggregated data.

DDL Statements and Views

In the previous chapters, base tables were used to describe DDL and DML statements. A base table contains data stored on the disk. By contrast, views, by default, do not exist physically—that is, their content is not stored on the disk. (This is not true for so-called indexed views, which are discussed later in this chapter.) Views are database objects that are always derived from one or more base tables (or views) using metadata information. This information (including the name of the view and the way the rows from the base tables are to be retrieved) is the only information concerning views that is physically stored. Thus, views are also called *virtual tables*.

Creating a View

A view is created using the CREATE VIEW statement. The general form of this statement is

```
CREATE VIEW view_name [(column_list)]
    [WITH {ENCRYPTION | SCHEMABINDING | VIEW_METADATA}]
    AS select_statement
    [WITH CHECK OPTION]
```

NOTE

The CREATE VIEW statement must be the only statement in a batch. (This means that you have to use the GO statement to separate this statement from other statements in a statement group.)

view_name is the name of the defined view. **column_list** is the list of names to be used for columns in a view. If this optional specification is omitted, column names of the underlying tables are used. **select_statement** specifies the SELECT statement that retrieves rows and columns from one or more tables (or views). The WITH ENCRYPTION option encrypts the SELECT statement, thus enhancing the security of the database system.

The SCHEMABINDING clause binds the view to the schema of the underlying table. When SCHEMABINDING is specified, database objects referenced in the SELECT statement must include the two-part names in the form **owner.db_object**, where **db_object** may be a table, a view, or a user-defined function.

Any attempt to modify the structure of views or tables that are referenced in a view created with this clause fails. You have to drop the view or change it so that it no longer has the SCHEMABINDING clause if you want to apply the ALTER or DROP statement to the referenced objects. (The WITH CHECK OPTION clause is discussed in detail later in this chapter in the section "INSERT Statement and a View.")

When a view is created with the VIEW_METADATA option, all of its columns (except columns with the TIMESTAMP data type) can be updated if the view has INSERT or UPDATE INSTEAD OF triggers. (Triggers are described in Chapter 14.)

NOTE

The SELECT statement in a view cannot include the ORDER BY clause or INTO option. Additionally, a temporary table cannot be referenced in the query.

Views can be used for different purposes:

▶ To restrict the use of particular columns and/or rows of tables. Therefore, views can be used for controlling access to a particular part of one or more tables (see Chapter 12).

▶ To hide the details of complicated queries. If database applications need queries that involve complicated join operations, the creation of corresponding views can simplify the use of such queries.

▶ To restrict inserted and updated values to certain ranges.

Example 11.1 shows the creation of a view.

EXAMPLE 11.1

```
USE sample;
GO
CREATE VIEW v_clerk
    AS SELECT emp_no, project_no, enter_date
        FROM works_on
        WHERE job = 'Clerk';
```

The query in Example 11.1 retrieves the rows of the **works_on** table for which the condition job = 'Clerk' evaluates to TRUE. The **v_clerk** view is defined as the rows and columns returned by this query. Table 11-1 shows the **works_on** table with the rows that belong to the **v_clerk** view bolded.

Example 11.1 specifies the selection of rows—that is, it creates a horizontal subset from the base table **works_on**. It is also possible to create a view that limits the columns as well as the rows to be included in the view. Example 11.2 shows the creation of such a view.

EXAMPLE 11.2

```
USE sample;
GO
CREATE VIEW v_without_budget
   AS SELECT project_no, project_name
          FROM project;
```

The **v_without_budget** view in Example 11.2 contains all columns of the **project** table except the **budget** column.

emp_no	project_no	job	enter_date
10102	p1	Analyst	2006.10.1 00:00:00
10102	p3	Manager	2008.1.1 00:00:00
25348	**p2**	**Clerk**	**2007.2.15 00:00:00**
18316	p2	NULL	2007.6.1 00:00:00
29346	p2	NULL	2006.12.15 00:00:00
2581	p3	Analyst	2007.10.15 00:00:00
9031	p1	Manager	2007.4.15 00:00:00
28559	p1	NULL	2007.8.1. 00:00:00
28559	**p2**	**Clerk**	**2008.2.1 00:00:00**
9031	**p3**	Clerk	2006.11.15 00:00:00
29346	p1	Clerk	2007.1.4 00:00:00

Table 11-1   *The Base Table works_on*

As already stated, specifying column names with a view in the general format of the CREATE VIEW statement is optional. On the other hand, there are also two cases in which the explicit specification of column names is required:

▶ If a column of the view is derived from an expression or an aggregate function

▶ If two or more columns of the view have the same name in the underlying tables

Example 11.3 shows the explicit specification of column names in relation to a view.

EXAMPLE 11.3

```
USE sample;
GO
CREATE VIEW v_count(project_no, count_project)
   AS SELECT project_no, COUNT(*)
            FROM works_on
            GROUP BY project_no;
```

The column names of the **v_count** view in Example 11.3 must be explicitly specified because the SELECT statement contains the aggregate function COUNT(*), and all columns in a view must be named.

You can avoid the explicit specification of the column list in the CREATE VIEW statement if you use column headers, as in Example 11.4.

EXAMPLE 11.4

```
USE sample;
GO
CREATE VIEW v_count1
   AS SELECT project_no, COUNT(*) count_project
           FROM works_on
           GROUP BY project_no;
```

A view can be derived from another existing view, as shown in Example 11.5.

EXAMPLE 11.5

```
USE sample;
GO
CREATE VIEW v_project_p2
  AS SELECT emp_no
           FROM v_clerk
           WHERE project_no ='p2';
```

The **v_project_p2** view in Example 11.5 is derived from the **v_clerk** view (see Example 11.1). Every query using the **v_project_p2** view is converted into the equivalent query on the underlying base table **works_on**.

You can also create a view using Object Explorer of SQL Server Management Studio. Select the database under which you want to create the view, right-click Views, and choose New View. The corresponding editor appears. Using the editor, you can do the following:

- ▶ Select underlying tables and columns from these tables for the view

- ▶ Name the view and define conditions in the WHERE clause of the corresponding query

Altering and Removing Views

The Transact-SQL language supports the nonstandard ALTER VIEW statement, which is used to modify the definition of the view query. The syntax of ALTER VIEW is analogous to that of the CREATE VIEW statement.

You can use the ALTER VIEW statement to avoid reassigning existing privileges for the view. Also, altering an existing view using this statement does not affect database objects that depend upon the view. Otherwise, if you use the DROP VIEW and CREATE VIEW statements to remove and re-create a view, any database object that uses the view will not work properly, at least in the time period between removing and re-creating the view.

Example 11.6 shows the use of the ALTER VIEW statement.

EXAMPLE 11.6

```
USE sample;
GO
ALTER VIEW v_without_budget
    AS SELECT project_no, project_name
            FROM project
            WHERE project_no >= 'p3';
```

The ALTER VIEW statement in Example 11.6 extends the SELECT statement of the **v_without_budget** view (see Example 11.2) with the new condition in the WHERE clause.

NOTE
The ALTER VIEW statement can also be applied to indexed views. This statement removes all indices that exist for such a view.

The DROP VIEW statement removes the definition of the specified view from the system tables. Example 11.7 shows the use of the DROP VIEW statement.

EXAMPLE 11.7

```
USE sample;
GO
DROP VIEW v_count;
```

If the DROP VIEW statement removes a view, all other views derived from it will be dropped, too, as demonstrated in Example 11.8.

EXAMPLE 11.8

```
USE sample;
GO
DROP VIEW v_clerk;
```

The DROP VIEW statement in Example 11.8 also implicitly removes the **v_project_ p2** view (see Example 11.5). For instance, if you query the **v_project_p2** view, you will get the error: "Invalid object name: 'v_clerk'."

NOTE

A view is not automatically dropped if the underlying table is removed. This means that any view from the removed table must be exclusively removed using the DROP VIEW statement. On the other hand, if a table with the same logical structure as the removed one is subsequently created, the view can be used again.

Editing Information Concerning Views

sys.objects is the most important catalog view concerning views. As you already know, this catalog view contains information in relation to all objects of the current database. All rows of this view that have the value **V** for the **type** column contain information concerning views.

Another catalog view called **sys.views** displays additional information about existing views. The most important column of this view is **with_check_option**, which instructs you whether or not WITH CHECK OPTION is specified.

Using the system procedure **sp_helptext**, you can display the query belonging to a particular view.

DML Statements and Views

Views are retrieved and modified with the same Transact-SQL statements that are used to retrieve and modify base tables. The following subsections discuss all four DML statements in relation to views.

View Retrieval

A view is used exactly like any base table of a database. You can think of selecting from a view as if the statement were transformed into an equivalent operation on the underlying base table(s). Example 11.9 shows this.

EXAMPLE 11.9

```
USE sample;
GO
CREATE VIEW v_d2
  AS SELECT emp_no, emp_lname
         FROM employee
         WHERE dept_no ='d2';
GO
SELECT emp_lname
     FROM v_d2
     WHERE emp_lname LIKE 'J%';
```

The result is

emp_lname
James

The SELECT statement in Example 11.9 is transformed into the following equivalent form, using the underlying table of the **v_d2** view:

```
SELECT emp_lname
    FROM employee
    WHERE emp_lname LIKE 'J%'
    AND dept_no ='d2';
```

The next three sections describe the use of views with the other three DML statements: INSERT, UPDATE, and DELETE. Data modification with these statements is treated in a manner similar to a retrieval. The only difference is that there are some restrictions on a view used for insertion, modification, and deletion of data from the table that it depends on.

INSERT Statement and a View

A view can be used with the INSERT statement as if it were a base table. When a view is used to insert rows, the rows are actually inserted into the underlying base table.

The **v_dept** view, which is created in Example 11.10, contains the first two columns of the **department** table. The subsequent INSERT statement inserts the row into the underlying table using the values 'd4' and 'Development'. The **location** column, which is not referenced by the **v_dept** view, is assigned a NULL value.

EXAMPLE 11.10

```
USE sample;
GO
CREATE VIEW v_dept
   AS SELECT dept_no, dept_name
          FROM department;
GO

INSERT INTO v_dept
    VALUES('d4', 'Development');
```

Using a view, it is generally possible to insert a row that does not satisfy the conditions of the view query's WHERE clause. The option WITH CHECK OPTION is used to restrict the insertion of only such rows that satisfy the conditions of the query. If this option is used, the Database Engine tests every inserted row to ensure that the conditions in the WHERE clause are evaluated to TRUE. If this option is omitted, there is no check of conditions in the WHERE clause, and therefore every row is inserted into the underlying table. This could lead to the confusing situation of a row being inserted using a view but subsequently not being returned by a SELECT statement against that view, because the WHERE clause is enforced for the SELECT. WITH CHECK OPTION is also applied to the UPDATE statement.

Examples 11.11 and 11.12 show the difference of applying and not applying WITH CHECK OPTION, respectively.

EXAMPLE 11.11

```
USE sample;
GO
CREATE VIEW v_2006_check
   AS SELECT emp_no, project_no, enter_date
          FROM works_on
          WHERE enter_date BETWEEN '01.01.2006' AND '12.31.2006'
          WITH CHECK OPTION;
GO

INSERT INTO v_2006_check
    VALUES (22334, 'p2', '1.15.2007');
```

In Example 11.11, the system tests whether the inserted value of the **enter_date** column evaluates to TRUE for the condition in the WHERE clause of the SELECT statement. The attempted insert fails because the condition is not met.

EXAMPLE 11.12

```
USE sample;
GO
CREATE VIEW v_2006_nocheck
    AS SELECT emp_no, project_no, enter_date
            FROM works_on
            WHERE enter_date BETWEEN '01.01.2006' AND '12.31.2006';
GO

INSERT INTO v_2006_nocheck
    VALUES (22334, 'p2', '1.15.2007');
SELECT *
    FROM v_2006_nocheck;
```

The result is

emp_no	project_no	enter_date
10102	p1	2006-10-01
29346	p2	2006-12-15
9031	p3	2006-11-15

Because Example 11.12 does not use WITH CHECK OPTION, the INSERT statement is executed and the row is inserted into the underlying **works_on** table. Notice that the subsequent SELECT statement does not display the inserted row because it cannot be retrieved using the **v_2006_nocheck** view.

The insertion of rows into the underlying tables is *not* possible if the corresponding view contains any of the following features:

▶ The FROM clause in the view definition involves two or more tables and the column list includes columns from more than one table

▶ A column of the view is derived from an aggregate function

▶ The SELECT statement in the view contains the GROUP BY clause or the DISTINCT option

▶ A column of the view is derived from a constant or an expression

Example 11.13 shows a view that cannot be used to insert rows in the underlying base table.

EXAMPLE 11.13

```
USE sample;
GO
CREATE VIEW v_sum(sum_of_budget)
   AS SELECT SUM(budget)
           FROM project;
GO

SELECT *
   FROM v_sum;
```

Example 11.13 creates the **v_sum** view, which contains an aggregate function in its SELECT statement. Because the view in the example represents the result of an aggregation of many rows (and not a single row of the **project** table), it does not make sense to try to insert a row into the underlying table using this view.

UPDATE Statement and a View

A view can be used with the UPDATE statement as if it were a base table. When a view is used to modify rows, the content of the underlying base table is actually modified.

Example 11.14 creates a view that is then used to modify the **works_on** table.

EXAMPLE 11.14

```
USE sample;
GO
CREATE VIEW v_p1
  AS SELECT emp_no, job
          FROM works_on
          WHERE project_no = 'p1';
GO

UPDATE v_p1
     SET job = NULL
     WHERE job = 'Manager';
```

You can think of updating the view in Example 11.14 as if the UPDATE statement were transformed into the following equivalent statement:

```
UPDATE works_on
    SET job = NULL
    WHERE job = 'Manager'
    AND project_no = 'p1'
```

WITH CHECK OPTION has the same logical meaning for the UPDATE statement as it has for the INSERT statement. Example 11.15 shows the use of WITH CHECK OPTION with the UPDATE statement.

EXAMPLE 11.15

```
USE sample;
GO
CREATE VIEW v_100000
    AS SELECT project_no, budget
            FROM project
            WHERE budget > 100000
            WITH CHECK OPTION;
GO

UPDATE v_100000
    SET budget = 93000
    WHERE project_no = 'p3';
```

In Example 11.15, the Database Engine tests whether the modified value of the **budget** column evaluates to TRUE for the condition in the WHERE clause of the SELECT statement. The attempted modification fails because the condition is not met—that is, the value 93000 is not greater than the value 100000.

The modification of columns in the underlying tables is *not* possible if the corresponding view contains any of the following features:

▶ The FROM clause in the view definition involves two or more tables and the column list includes columns from more than one table

▶ A column of the view is derived from an aggregate function

▶ The SELECT statement in the view contains the GROUP BY clause or the DISTINCT option

▶ A column of the view is derived from a constant or an expression

Example 11.16 shows a view that cannot be used to modify row values in the underlying base table.

EXAMPLE 11.16

```
USE sample;
GO
CREATE VIEW v_uk_pound (project_number, budget_in_pounds)
   AS SELECT project_no, budget*0.65
           FROM project
           WHERE budget > 100000;
GO

SELECT *
    FROM v_uk_pound;
```

The result is

project_number	budget_in_pounds
p1	78000
p3	121225

The **v_uk_pound** view in Example 11.16 cannot be used with an UPDATE statement (nor with an INSERT statement) because the **budget_in_pounds** column is calculated using an arithmetic expression, and therefore does not represent an original column of the underlying table.

DELETE Statement and a View

A view can be used to delete rows of a table that it depends on, as shown in Example 11.17.

EXAMPLE 11.17

```
USE sample;
GO
CREATE VIEW v_project_p1
   AS SELECT emp_no, job
           FROM works_on
           WHERE project_no = 'p1';
GO

DELETE FROM v_project_p1
   WHERE job = 'Clerk';
```

Example 11.17 creates a view that is then used to delete rows from the **works_on** table. The deletion of rows in the underlying tables is *not* possible if the corresponding view contains any of the following features:

▶ The FROM clause in the view definition involves two or more tables and the column list includes columns from more than one table

▶ A column of the view is derived from an aggregate function

▶ The SELECT statement in the view contains the GROUP BY clause or the DISTINCT option

In contrast to the INSERT and UPDATE statements, the DELETE statement allows the existence of a constant or an expression in a column of the view that is used to delete rows from the underlying table.

Example 11.18 shows a view that can be used to delete rows, but not to insert rows or modify column values.

EXAMPLE 11.18

```
USE sample;
GO
CREATE VIEW v_budget (budget_reduction)
   AS SELECT budget*0.9
            FROM project;
GO

DELETE FROM v_budget;
```

The DELETE statement in Example 11.18 deletes all rows of the **project** table, which is referenced by the **v_budget** view.

Indexed Views

As you already know from the previous chapter, there are several special index types. One of them is the indexed view, which will be described next.

A view always contains a query that acts as a filter. Without indices created for a particular view, the Database Engine builds dynamically the result set from each query that references a view. ("Dynamically" means that if you modify the content of a table, the corresponding view will always show the new information.) Also, if the view contains computations based on one or more columns of the table, the computations are performed each time you access the view.

Building dynamically the result set of a query can decrease performance, if the view with its SELECT statement processes many rows from one or more tables. If such a view is frequently used in queries, you could significantly increase performance by creating a clustered index on the view (see the next section). Creating a clustered index means that the system materializes the dynamic data into the leaf pages on an index structure.

The Database Engine allows you to create indices on views. Such views are called indexed or materialized views. When a unique clustered index is created on a view, the view is executed and the result set is stored in the database in the same way a table with a clustered index is stored. This means that the leaf nodes of the clustered index's B+-tree contain data pages (see also the description of the clustered table in Chapter 10).

NOTE

Indexed views are implemented through syntax extensions to the CREATE INDEX and CREATE VIEW statements. In the CREATE INDEX statement, you specify the name of a view instead of a table name. The syntax of the CREATE VIEW statement is extended with the SCHEMABINDING clause. For more information on extensions to this statement, see the description at the beginning of this chapter.

Creating an Indexed View

Creating an indexed view is a two-step process:

1. Create the view using the CREATE VIEW statement with the SCHEMABINDING clause.
2. Create the corresponding clustered index.

Example 11.19 shows the first step, the creation of a typical view that can be indexed to gain performance. (This example assumes that **works_on** is a very large table.)

EXAMPLE 11.19

```
USE sample;
GO
CREATE VIEW v_enter_month
  WITH SCHEMABINDING
  AS SELECT emp_no, DATEPART(MONTH, enter_date)  AS enter_month
      FROM dbo.works_on;
```

The **works_on** table in the **sample** database contains the **enter_date** column, which represents the starting date of an employee in the corresponding project. If you want to retrieve all employees that entered their projects in a specified month, you can use the view in Example 11.19. To retrieve such a result set using index access, the Database Engine cannot use a table index, because an index on the **enter_date** column would locate the values of that column by the date, and not by the month. In such a case, indexed views can help, as Example 11.20 shows.

EXAMPLE 11.20

```
USE sample;
GO
CREATE  UNIQUE CLUSTERED INDEX
      c_workson_deptno ON v_enter_month (enter_month, emp_no);
```

To make a view indexed, you have to create a unique clustered index on the column(s) of the view. (As previously stated, a clustered index is the only index type that contains the data values in its leaf pages.) After you create that index, the database system allocates storage for the view, and then you can create any number of nonclustered indices because the view is treated as a (base) table.

An indexed view can be created only if it is deterministic—that is, the view always displays the same result set. In that case, the following options of the SET statement must be set to ON:

▶ QUOTED_IDENTIFIER

▶ CONCAT_NULL_YIELDS_NULL

▶ ANSI_NULLS

▶ ANSI_PADDING

▶ ANSI_WARNINGS

Also, the NUMERIC_ROUNDABORT option must be set to OFF.

There are several ways to check whether the options in the preceding list are appropriately set, as discussed in the upcoming section "Editing Information Concerning Indexed Views."

To create an indexed view, the view definition has to meet the following requirements:

▶ All referenced (system and user-defined) functions used by the view have to be deterministic—that is, they must always return the same result for the same arguments.

▶ The view must reference only base tables.

▶ The view and the referenced base table(s) must have the same owner and belong to the same database.

▶ The view must be created with the SCHEMABINDING option. SCHEMABINDING binds the view to the schema of the underlying base tables.

▶ The referenced user-defined functions must be created with the SCHEMABINDING option.

▶ The SELECT statement in the view cannot contain the following clauses and options: DISTINCT, UNION, TOP, ORDER BY, MIN, MAX, COUNT, SUM (on a nullable expression), subqueries, derived tables, or OUTER.

The Transact-SQL language allows you to verify all of these requirements by using the **IsIndexable** parameter of the **objectproperty** property function, as shown in Example 11.21. If the value of the function is 1, all requirements are met and you can create the clustered index.

EXAMPLE 11.21

```
USE sample;
SELECT objectproperty(object_id('v_enter_month'), 'IsIndexable');
```

Modifying the Structure of an Indexed View

To drop the unique clustered index on an indexed view, you have to drop all nonclustered indices on the view, too. After you drop its clustered index, the view is treated by the system as a convenient view.

NOTE

If you drop an indexed view, all indices on that view are dropped.

If you want to change a standard view to an indexed one, you have to create a unique clustered index on it. To do so, you must first specify the SCHEMABINDING option for that view. You can drop the view and re-create it, specifying the SCHEMABINDING clause in the CREATE SCHEMA statement, or you can create another view that has the same text as the existing view but a different name.

NOTE

If you create a new view with a different name, you must ensure that the new view meets all the requirements for an indexed view that are described in the preceding section.

Editing Information Concerning Indexed Views

You can use the **sessionproperty** property function to test whether one of the options of the SET statement is activated (see the earlier section "Creating an Indexed View" for a list of the options). If the function returns 1, the setting is ON. Example 11.22 shows the use of the function to check how the QUOTED_IDENTIFIER option is set.

EXAMPLE 11.22

```
SELECT sessionproperty ('QUOTED_IDENTIFIER');
```

The easier way is to use the dynamic management view called **sys.dm_exec_sessions**, because you can retrieve values of all options discussed above using only one query. (Again, if the value of a column is 1, the corresponding option is set to ON.) Example 11.23 returns the values for the first four SET statement options from the list in "Creating an Indexed View." (The global variable **@@spid** is described in Chapter 4.)

EXAMPLE 11.23

```
USE sample;
SELECT quoted_identifier, concat_null_yields_null, ansi_nulls, ansi_padding
          FROM sys.dm_exec_sessions
          WHERE session_id = @@spid;
```

The **sp_spaceused** system procedure allows you to check whether the view is materialized—that is, whether or not it uses the storage space. The result of Example 11.24 shows that the **v_enter_month** view uses storage space for the data as well as for the defined index.

EXAMPLE 11.24

```
USE sample;
EXEC sp_spaceused 'v_enter_month';
```

The result is

name	rows	reserved	data	index_size	unused
v_enter_month	11	16KB	8KB	8KB	0KB

Benefits of Indexed Views

Besides possible performance gains for complex views that are frequently referenced in queries, the use of indexed views has two other advantages:

▶ The index of a view can be used even if the view is not explicitly referenced in the FROM clause.

▶ All modifications to data are reflected in the corresponding indexed view.

Probably the most important property of indexed views is that a query does not have to explicitly reference a view to use the index on that view. In other words, if the query contains references to columns in the base table(s) that also exist in the indexed views, and the optimizer estimates that using the indexed view is the best choice, it chooses the view indices in the same way it chooses table indices when they are not directly referenced in a query.

When you create an indexed view, the result set of the view (at the time the index is created) is stored on the disk. Therefore, all data that is modified in the base table(s) will also be modified in the corresponding result set of the indexed view.

Besides all the benefits that you can gain by using indexed views, there is also a (possible) disadvantage: indices on indexed views are usually more complex to maintain than indices on base tables, because the structure of a unique clustered index on an indexed view is more complex than a structure of the corresponding index on a base table.

The following types of queries can achieve significant performance benefits if a view that is referenced by the corresponding query is indexed:

▶ Queries that process many rows and contain join operations or aggregate functions

▶ Join operations and aggregate functions that are frequently performed by one or several queries

If a query references a standard view and the database system has to process many rows using the join operation, the optimizer will usually use a suboptimal join method. However, if you define a clustered index on that view, the performance of the query could be significantly enhanced, because the optimizer can use an appropriate method. (The same is true for aggregate functions.)

If a query that references a standard view does not process many rows, the use of an indexed view could still be beneficial if the query is used very frequently. (The same is true for groups of queries that join the same tables or use the same type of aggregates.)

NOTE

Since SQL Server 2008 R2, Microsoft offers an alternative solution to indexed views called filtered indices. Filtered indices are a special form of nonclustered indices, where the index is narrowed using a condition in the particular query. Using a filtered index has several advantages over using an indexed view.

Summary

Views can be used for different purposes:

▶ To restrict the use of particular columns and/or rows of tables—that is, to control access to a particular part of one or more tables

▶ To hide the details of complicated queries

▶ To restrict inserted and updated values to certain ranges

Views are created, retrieved, and modified with the same Transact-SQL statements that are used to create, retrieve, and modify base tables. The query on a view is always transformed into the equivalent query on an underlying base table. An update operation is treated in a manner similar to a retrieval. The only difference is that there are some restrictions on a view used for insertion, modification, and deletion of data from a table that it depends on. Even so, the way in which the Database Engine handles the modification of rows and columns is more systematic than the way in which other relational database systems handle such modification.

Indexed views are used to increase performance of certain queries. When a unique clustered index is created on a view, the view becomes indexed—that is, its result set is physically stored in the same way a base table is stored.

The following chapter explains in detail the security issues of the Database Engine.

Exercises

E.11.1

Create a view that comprises the data of all employees who work for the department d1.

E.11.2

For the **project** table, create a view that can be used by employees who are allowed to view all data of this table except the **budget** column.

E.11.3

Create a view that comprises the first and last names of all employees who entered their projects in the second half of the year 2007.

E.11.4

Solve Exercise E.11.3 so that the original columns **f_name** and **l_name** have new names in the view: **first** and **last**, respectively.

E.11.5

Use the view in E.11.1 to display full details of every employee whose last name begins with the letter *M*.

E.11.6

Create a view that comprises full details of all projects on which the employee named Smith works.

E.11.7

Using the ALTER VIEW statement, modify the condition in the view in E.11.1. The modified view should comprise the data of all employees who work for department d1, department d2, or both.

E.11.8

Delete the view created in E.11.3. What happens with the view created in E.11.4?

E.11.9

Using the view from E.11.2, insert the details of the new project with the project number p2 and the name Moon.

E.11.10

Create a view (with the WITH CHECK OPTION clause) that comprises the first and last names of all employees whose employee number is less than 10,000. After that, use the view to insert data for a new employee named Kohn with the employee number 22123, who works for the department d3.

E.11.11

Solve Exercise E.11.10 without the WITH CHECK OPTION clause and find the differences in relation to the insertion of the data.

E.11.12

Create a view (with the WITH CHECK OPTION clause) with full details from the **works_on** table for all employees who entered their projects during the years 2007 and 2008. After that, modify the entering date of the employee with the employee number 29346. The new date is 06/01/2006.

E.11.13

Solve Exercise E.11.12 without the WITH CHECK OPTION clause and find the differences in relation to the modification of the data.

Chapter 12

Security System of the Database Engine

Thisisisisisis chapter begins with a brief overview of the most important concepts of database security. It then discusses the specific features of the security system of the Database Engine.

The following are the most important database security concepts:

▶ Authentication

▶ Encryption

▶ Authorization

▶ Change tracking

Authentication requires evaluation of the following question: "Does this user have a legitimate right to access the system?" Therefore, this security concept specifies the process of validating user credentials to prevent unauthorized users from using a system. Authentication can be checked by requesting the user to provide, for example:

▶ Something the user is acquainted with (usually a password)

▶ Something the user owns, such as a magnetic card or badge

▶ Physical characteristics of the user, such as a signature or fingerprints

Authentication is most commonly confirmed using a name and a password. This information is evaluated by the system to determine whether you are the user who has a legitimate right to access the system. This process can be strengthened using encryption.

Data encryption is the process of scrambling information so that it is incomprehensible until it is decrypted by the intended recipient. Several methods can be used to encrypt data, as discussed in the section "Encryption" a bit later in this chapter.

Authorization is the process that is applied after the identity of a user is verified through authentication. During this process, the system determines which resources the particular user can use.

Change tracking means that actions of unauthorized users are followed and documented on your system. In other words, all insert, update, and delete operations that are applied to database objects are documented. After that, they can be viewed by the authorized users. (This process is useful to protect the system against users with elevated privileges.)

Before I describe these four concepts in the following sections, I will give you a concise definition of the security model that SQL Server uses. The security model comprises three different categories, which interact among themselves:

▶ **Principals**   Subjects that have permission to access a particular entity. Typical principals are Windows user accounts and SQL Server logins. In addition to these principals, there are also Windows groups and SQL Server roles. A Windows group is a collection of Windows user accounts and groups. Assigning a user account membership to a group gives the user all the permissions granted to the group. Similarly, a role is a collection of logins.

▶ **Securables** The resources to which the database authorization system regulates access. Most securables build a hierarchy, meaning that some of them can be contained within others. Most of them have a certain number of permissions that apply to them. (Securables will be discussed in detail later in this chapter.)

▶ **Permissions** Every securable has associated *permissions* that can be granted to a principal. Permissions are discussed in the section "Authorization" later in this chapter. (The list of all permissions with their corresponding securables can be found later in this chapter, in Table 12-3.)

Authentication

The Database Engine's security system includes two different security subsystems:

▶ Windows security

▶ SQL Server security

Windows security specifies security at the operating system level—that is, the method by which users connect to Windows using their Windows *user accounts*. (Authentication using this subsystem is also called Windows authentication.)

SQL Server security specifies the additional security necessary at the system level— that is, how users who have already logged on to the operating system can subsequently connect to the database server. SQL Server security defines a SQL Server login (also called "login") that is created within the system and is associated with a password. Some SQL Server logins are identical to the existing Windows user accounts. (Authentication using this subsystem is called SQL Server authentication.)

Based on these two security subsystems, the Database Engine can operate in one of the following authentication modes:

▶ Windows mode

▶ Mixed mode

Windows mode requires users to use Windows user accounts exclusively to log in to the system. The system accepts the user account, assuming it has already been validated at the operating system level. This kind of connection to a database system is called a *trusted connection*, because the system trusts that the operating system already validated the account and the corresponding password.

Mixed mode allows users to connect to the Database Engine using Windows authentication or SQL Server authentication. This means that some user accounts can be set up to use the Windows security subsystem, while others can be set up to use both the SQL Server security subsystem and the Windows security subsystem.

NOTE

SQL Server authentication is provided for backward compatibility only. For this reason, use Windows authentication instead.

Implementing an Authentication Mode

You use SQL Server Management Studio to choose one of the existing authentication modes. (Chapter 3 discusses the SQL Server Management Studio interface in depth.) To set up Windows mode, right-click the server and click Properties. In the Server Properties dialog box, choose the Security page and click Windows Authentication Mode. To choose Mixed mode, the only difference is that you have to click SQL Server and Windows Authentication Mode in the Server Properties dialog box.

After a user successfully connects to the Database Engine, the user's access to database objects is independent of whether Windows authentication or SQL Server authentication is used.

Before you learn how to set database server security, you need to understand encryption policies and mechanisms, discussed next.

Encrypting Data

Encryption is a process of obfuscating data, thereby enhancing the data security. Generally, the concrete encryption procedure is carried out using an algorithm. The most important algorithm for encryption is called RSA. (It is an acronym for Rivers, Shamir, and Adelman, the last names of the three men who invented it.)

The Database Engine secures data with hierarchical encryption layers and a key management infrastructure. Each layer secures the layer beneath it, using a combination of certificates, asymmetric keys, and symmetric keys (see Figure 12-1).

The service master key in Figure 12-1 specifies the key that rules all other keys and certificates. The service master key is created automatically when you install the Database Engine. This key is encrypted using the Windows Data Protection API (DPAPI).

The important property of the service master key is that it is managed by the system. Although the system administrator can perform several maintenance tasks, the only

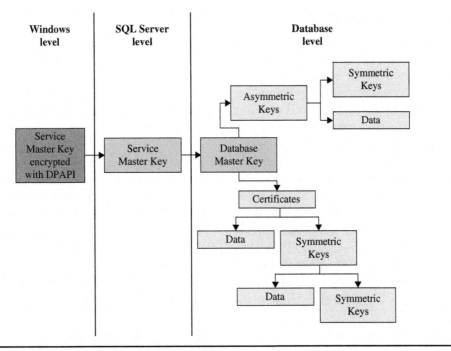

Figure 12-1   *The Database Engine hierarchical encryption layers*

task he or she should perform is to back up the service master key, so that it can be restored if it becomes corrupted.

As you can see in Figure 12-1, the database master key is the root encryption object for all keys, certificates, and data at the database level. Each database has a single database master key, which is created using the CREATE MASTER KEY statement (see Example 12.1). Because the database master key is protected by the service master key, it is possible for the system to automatically decrypt the database master key.

Once the database master key exists, users can use it to create keys. There are three forms of user keys:

▶ Symmetric keys

▶ Asymmetric keys

▶ Certificates

The following subsections describe the user keys.

Symmetric Keys

An encryption system that uses symmetric keys is one in which the sender and receiver of a message share a common key. Thus, this single key is used for both encryption and decryption.

Using symmetric keys has several benefits and one disadvantage. One advantage of using symmetric keys is that they can protect a significantly greater amount of data than can the other two types of user keys. Also, using this key type is significantly faster than using an asymmetric key.

On the other hand, in a distributed environment, using this type of key can make it almost impossible to keep encryption secure, because the same key is used to decrypt and encrypt data on both ends. So, the general recommendation is that symmetric keys should be used only with applications in which data is stored as encrypted text at one place.

The Transact-SQL language supports several statements and system functions related to symmetric keys. The CREATE SYMMETRIC KEY statement creates a new symmetric key, while the DROP SYMMETRIC KEY statement removes an existing symmetric key. Each symmetric key must be opened before you can use it to encrypt data or protect another new key. Therefore, you use the OPEN SYMMETRIC KEY statement to open a key.

After you open a symmetric key, you need to use the **EncryptByKey** system function for encryption. This function has two input parameters: the ID of the key and text, which has to be encrypted. For decryption, you use the **DecryptByKey** function.

NOTE

See Books Online for detailed descriptions of all Transact-SQL statements related to symmetric keys as well as the system functions EncryptByKey and DecryptByKey.

Asymmetric Keys

If you have a distributed environment or if a symmetric key does not keep your encryption secure, use asymmetric keys. An asymmetric key consists of two parts: a private key and the corresponding public key. Each key can decrypt data encrypted by the other key. Because of the existence of a private key, asymmetric encryption provides a higher level of security than does symmetric encryption.

The Transact-SQL language supports several statements and system functions related to asymmetric keys. The CREATE ASYMMETRIC KEY statement creates a new asymmetric key, while the ALTER ASYMMETRIC KEY statement changes the properties of an asymmetric key. The DROP ASYMMETRIC KEY statement drops an existing asymmetric key.

After you create an asymmetric key, use the **EncryptByAsymKey** system function to encrypt data. This function has two input parameters: the ID of the key and text, which has to be encrypted. For decryption, use the **DecryptByAsymKey** function.

NOTE

*See Books Online for detailed descriptions of all Transact-SQL statements related to asymmetric keys as well as the system functions **EncryptByAsymKey** and **DecryptByAsymKey**.*

Certificates

A public key certificate, usually simply called a certificate, is a digitally signed statement that binds the value of a public key to the identity of the person, device, or service that holds the corresponding private key. Certificates are issued and signed by a certification authority (CA). The entity that receives a certificate from a CA is the subject of that certificate.

NOTE

There is no significant functional difference between certificates and asymmetric keys. Both use the RSA algorithm. The main difference is that asymmetric keys are generated outside the server.

Certificates contain the following information:

- ▶ The subject's public key value
- ▶ The subject's identifier information
- ▶ Issuer identifier information
- ▶ The digital signature of the issuer

A primary benefit of certificates is that they relieve hosts of the need to maintain a set of passwords for individual subjects. When a host, such as a secure web server, designates an issuer as a trusted authority, the host implicitly trusts that the issuer has verified the identity of the certificate subject.

NOTE

Certificates provide the highest level of encryption in the Database Engine security model. The encryption algorithms for certificates are very processor-intensive. For this reason, use certificates sparingly.

The most important statement related to certificates is the CREATE CERTIFICATE statement. Example 12.1 shows the use of this statement.

EXAMPLE 12.1

```
USE sample;
CREATE MASTER KEY
ENCRYPTION BY PASSWORD = 'p1s4w9d16!'
GO
CREATE CERTIFICATE cert01
        WITH SUBJECT = 'Certificate for dbo';
```

If you want to create a certificate without the ENCRYPTION BY option, you first have to create the database master key. (Each CREATE CERTIFICATE statement that does not include this option is protected by the database master key.) For this reason, the first statement in Example 12.1 is the CREATE MASTER KEY statement. After that, the CREATE CERTIFICATE statement is used to create a new certificate, **cert01**, which is owned by **dbo** in the **sample** database, if the current user is **dbo**.

Editing User Keys

The most important catalog views in relation to encryption are the following:

► sys.symmetric_keys

► sys.asymmetric_keys

► sys.certificates

► sys.database_principals

The first three catalog views provide information about all symmetric keys, all asymmetric keys, and all the certificates installed in the current database, respectively. The **sys.database_principals** catalog view provides information about each of the principals in the current database. (You can join the last catalog view with any of the three others to see information about who owns a particular key.)

Example 12.2 shows how the existing certificates can be retrieved. (In a similar way, you can get information concerning symmetric and asymmetric keys.)

EXAMPLE 12.2

```
select p.name, c.name, certificate_id
    from sys.database_principals p, sys.certificates c
  where p.principal_id = p.principal_id
```

A part of the result is

public	cert01	256
dbo	cert01	256
guest	cert01	256
INFORMATION_SCHEMA	cert01	256
sys	cert01	256
db_owner	cert01	256
db_accessadmin	cert01	256
db_securityadmin	cert01	256

SQL Server Extensible Key Management

Another step in achieving greater key security is the use of Extensible Key Management (EKM). EKM has the following main goals:

▶ Enhanced key security through a choice of encryption provider

▶ General key management across your enterprise

EKM allows third-party vendors to register their devices in the Database Engine. Once the devices are registered, SQL Server logins can use the encryption keys stored on these modules as well as leverage advanced encryption features that these modules support. EKM also allows data protection from database administrators (except members of the **sysadmin** group). That way, you can protect the system against users with elevated privileges. Data can be encrypted and decrypted using Transact-SQL cryptographic statements, and SQL Server uses the external EKM device as the key store.

Methods of Data Encryption

SQL Server supports two methods of data encryption:

▶ Column-level encryption

▶ Transparent Data Encryption

Column-level encryption allows the encryption of particular data columns. Several pairs of complementary functions are used to implement column-level encryption. I will not discuss this encryption method further because its implementation is a complex manual process that requires the modification of your application.

Transparent Data Encryption (TDE) introduces a new database option that encrypts the database files automatically, without needing to alter any applications. That way, you can prevent the database access of unauthorized persons, even if they obtain the database files or database backup files.

Encryption of the database file is performed at the page level. The pages in an encrypted database are encrypted before they are written to disk and decrypted when they are read into memory.

TDE, like most other encryption methods, is based on an encryption key. It uses a symmetric key, which secures the encrypted database.

For a particular database, TDE can be implemented in four steps:

1. Create a database master key using the CREATE MASTER KEY statement. (Example 12.1 shows the use of the statement.)

2. Create a certificate using the CREATE CERTIFICATE statement (see Example 12.1).

3. Create an encryption key using the CREATE DATABASE ENCRYPTION KEY statement.

4. Configure the database to use encryption. (This step can be implemented by setting the SET ENCRPYTION clause of the ALTER DATABASE statement to ON.)

Setting Up the Database Engine Security

The security of the Database Engine can be set up using

▶ SQL Server Management Studio

▶ T-SQL statements

The following subsections discuss these two alternatives.

Managing Security Using Management Studio

To create a new login using SQL Server Management Studio, expand the server, expand Security, right-click Logins, and click New Login. The Login dialog box (see Figure 12-2) appears. First, you have to decide between Windows authentication and SQL Server authentication. If you choose Windows authentication, the login name must be a valid Windows name, which is written in the form **domain\user_name**. If you choose SQL Server authentication, you have to type the new login name and the corresponding password. Optionally, you may also specify the default database and language for the new login. (The default database is the database that the user is automatically connected to immediately after logging in to the Database Engine.) After that, the user can log in to the system under the new account.

Figure 12-2 *Login dialog box*

Managing Security Using Transact-SQL Statements

The three Transact-SQL statements that are used to manage security of the Database Engine are CREATE LOGIN, ALTER LOGIN, and DROP LOGIN.

The CREATE LOGIN statement creates a new SQL Server login. The syntax is as follows:

```
CREATE LOGIN login_name
{ WITH option_list1   |
FROM {WINDOWS [ WITH option_list2 [,...] ]
| CERTIFICATE certname   | ASYMMETRIC KEY key_name }}
```

login_name specifies the name of the login that is being created. As you can see from the syntax of the statement, you can use the WITH clause to specify one or more options for the login or use the FROM clause to define a certificate, asymmetric key, or Windows user account associated with the corresponding login.

option_list1 contains several options. The most important one is the PASSWORD option, which specifies the password of the login (see Example 12.3). (The other possible options are DEFAULT_DATABASE, DEFAULT_LANGUAGE, and CHECK_EXPIRATION.)

As you can see from the syntax of the CREATE LOGIN statement, the FROM clause contains one of the following options:

- ▶ **WINDOWS**   Specifies that the login will be mapped to an existing Windows user account (see Example 12.4). This clause can be specified with other suboptions, such as DEFAULT_DATABASE and DEFAULT_LANGUAGE.

- ▶ **CERTIFICATE**   Specifies the name of the certificate to be associated with this login.

- ▶ **ASYMMETRIC KEY**   Specifies the name of the asymmetric key to be associated with this login. (The certificate and the asymmetric key must already exist in the **master** database.)

The following examples show the creation of different login forms. Example 12.3 specifies the login called **mary**, with the password **you1know4it9**!

EXAMPLE 12.3

```
USE sample;
CREATE LOGIN mary WITH PASSWORD = 'you1know4it9!';
```

Example 12.4 creates the login called **pete**, which will be mapped to a Windows user account with the same name.

EXAMPLE 12.4

```
USE sample;
CREATE LOGIN [NTB11901\pete] FROM WINDOWS;
```

NOTE

You have to alter the username and the computer name (in the form domain\username) according to your environment.

The second security statement supported by Transact-SQL is ALTER LOGIN, which changes the properties of a particular login. Using the ALTER LOGIN statement, you can change the current password and its expiration properties, credentials, default database, and default language. You can also enable or disable the specified login.

Finally, the DROP LOGIN statement drops an existing login. A login cannot be dropped if it references (owns) other objects.

Schemas

The Database Engine uses schemas in its security model to simplify the relationship between users and objects, and thus schemas have a very big impact on how you interact with the Database Engine. This section describes the role of schemas in Database Engine security. The first subsection describes the relationship between schemas and users; the second subsection discusses all three Transact-SQL statements related to schema creation and modification.

User-Schema Separation

A schema is a collection of database objects that is owned by a single person and forms a single namespace. (Two tables in the same schema cannot have the same name.) The Database Engine supports named schemas using the notion of a *principal*. As you already know, a principal can be either of the following:

▶ An indivisible principal

▶ A group principal

An indivisible principal represents a single user, such as a login or Windows user account. A group principal can be a group of users, such as a role or Windows group. Principals are ownerships of schemas, but the ownership of a schema can be transferred easily to another principal and without changing the schema name.

The separation of database users from schemas provides significant benefits, such as:

▶ One principal can own several schemas.

▶ Several indivisible principals can own a single schema via membership in roles or Windows groups.

▶ Dropping a database user does not require the renaming of objects contained by that user's schema.

Each database has a default schema, which is used to resolve the names of objects that are referred to without their fully qualified names. The default schema specifies the first schema that will be searched by the database server when it resolves the names of objects. The default schema can be set and changed using the DEFAULT_SCHEMA option of the CREATE USER or ALTER USER statement. If DEFAULT_SCHEMA is left undefined, the database user will have **dbo** as its default schema. (All default schemas are described in detail in the section "Default Database Schemas" later in this chapter.)

DDL Schema-Related Statements

There are three Transact-SQL schema-related statements:

▶ CREATE SCHEMA

▶ ALTER SCHEMA

▶ DROP SCHEMA

The following subsections describe in detail these statements.

CREATE SCHEMA

Example 12.5 shows how schemas can be created and used to control database security.

NOTE

*Before you start Example 12.5, you have to create database users **peter** and **mary**. For this reason, first execute the Transact-SQL statements in Example 12.7, located in the section "Managing Database Security Using Transact-SQL Statements."*

EXAMPLE 12.5

```
USE sample;
GO
CREATE SCHEMA my_schema AUTHORIZATION peter
GO
CREATE TABLE product
     (product_no CHAR(10) NOT NULL UNIQUE,
     product_name CHAR(20) NULL,
      price MONEY NULL);
```

```
GO
CREATE VIEW product_info
    AS SELECT product_no, product_name
        FROM product;
GO
GRANT SELECT TO mary;
DENY UPDATE TO mary;
```

Example 12.5 creates the **my_schema** schema, which comprises the **product** table and the **product_info** view. The database user called **peter** is the database-level principal that owns the schema. (You use the AUTHORIZATION option to define the principal of a schema. The principal may own other schemas and may not use the current schema as his or her default schema.)

NOTE

The two other statements concerning permissions of database objects, GRANT and DENY, are discussed in detail later in this chapter. In Example 12.5, GRANT grants the SELECT permissions for all objects created in the schema, while DENY denies the UPDATE permissions for all objects of the schema.

The CREATE SCHEMA statement can create a schema, create the tables and views it contains, and grant, revoke, or deny permissions on a securable in a single statement. As you already know, securables are resources to which the SQL Server authorization system regulates access. There are three main securable scopes: server, database, and schema, which contain other securables, such as logins, database users, tables, and stored procedures.

The CREATE SCHEMA statement is atomic. In other words, if any error occurs during the execution of a CREATE SCHEMA statement, none of the Transact-SQL statements specified in the schema will be executed.

Database objects that are created in a CREATE SCHEMA statement can be specified in any order, with one exception: a view that references another view must be specified after the referenced view.

A database-level principal could be a database user, role, or application role. (Roles and application roles are discussed in the "Roles" section later in the chapter.) The principal that is specified in the AUTHORIZATION clause of the CREATE SCHEMA statement is the owner of all objects created within the schema. Ownership of schema-contained objects can be transferred to any other database-level principal using the ALTER AUTHORIZATION statement.

The user needs the CREATE SCHEMA permission on the database to execute the CREATE SCHEMA statement. Also, to create the objects specified within the CREATE SCHEMA statement, the user needs the corresponding CREATE permissions.

ALTER SCHEMA

The ALTER SCHEMA statement transfers an object between different schemas of the same database. The syntax of the ALTER SCHEMA statement is as follows:

```
ALTER SCHEMA schema_name TRANSFER object_name
```

Example 12.6 shows the use of the ALTER SCHEMA statement.

EXAMPLE 12.6

```
USE AdventureWorks;
ALTER SCHEMA HumanResources TRANSFER Person.Contact;
```

Example 12.6 alters the schema called **HumanResources** of the **AdventureWorks** database by transferring into it the **Contact** table from the **Person** schema of the same database.

The ALTER SCHEMA statement can only be used to transfer objects between different schemas in the same database. (Single objects within a schema can be altered using the ALTER TABLE statement or the ALTER VIEW statement.)

DROP SCHEMA

The DROP SCHEMA statement removes a schema from the database. You can successfully execute the DROP SCHEMA statement for a schema only if the schema does not contain any objects. If the schema contains any objects, the DROP SCHEMA statement will be rejected by the system.

As previously stated, the system allows you to change the ownership of a schema by using the ALTER AUTHORIZATION statement. This statement modifies the ownership of an entity.

NOTE

The Transact-SQL language does not support the CREATE AUTHORIZATION and DROP AUTHORIZATION statements. You specify the ownership of an entity by using the CREATE SCHEMA statement.

Database Security

A Windows user account or a SQL Server login allows a user to log in to the system. A user who subsequently wants to access a particular database of the system also needs a database user account to work with the database. Therefore, users must have a database user account for each database they want to use. The database user account can be mapped from the existing Windows user accounts, Windows groups (of which the user is a member), logins, or roles.

To manage database security, you can use

▶ SQL Server Management Studio

▶ Transact-SQL statements

The following subsections describes both ways to manage database security.

Managing Database Security Using Management Studio

To add users to a database using SQL Server Management Studio, expand the server, expand the Databases folder, expand the database, and expand Security. Right-click Users and click New User. In the Database User dialog box (see Figure 12-3), enter a

Figure 12-3   *Database User dialog box*

username and choose a corresponding login name. Optionally, you can choose a default schema for this user.

Managing Database Security Using Transact-SQL Statements

The CREATE USER statement adds a user to the current database. The syntax of this statement is

```
CREATE USER user_name
 [FOR {LOGIN login |CERTIFICATE cert_name |ASYMMETRIC KEY key_name}]
  [ WITH DEFAULT_SCHEMA = schema_name ]
```

user_name is the name that is used to identify the user inside the database. **login** specifies the login for which the user is being created. **cert_name** and **key_name** specify the corresponding certificate and asymmetric key, respectively. Finally, the WITH DEFAULT SCHEMA option specifies the first schema that will be searched by the server when it resolves the names of objects for this database user.

Example 12.7 demonstrates the use of the CREATE USER statement.

EXAMPLE 12.7

```
USE sample;
CREATE USER peter FOR LOGIN [NTB11901\pete];
CREATE USER mary FOR LOGIN mary WITH DEFAULT_SCHEMA =
my_schema;
```

NOTE

*To execute the first statement successfully, create the Windows account named **pete** and change the server (domain) name.*

The first CREATE USER statement creates the database user called **peter** for the Windows login called **pete**. **pete** will use **dbo** as its default schema because the DEFAULT SCHEMA option is omitted. (Default schemas will be described in the section "Default Database Schemas" later in this chapter.)

The second CREATE USER statement creates a new database user with the name **mary**. This user has **my_schema** as her default schema. (The DEFAULT_SCHEMA option can be set to a schema that does not currently exist in the database.)

NOTE

Each database has its own specific users. Therefore, the CREATE USER statement must be executed once for each database where a user account should exist. Also, a SQL Server login can have only a single corresponding database user for a given database.

The ALTER USER statement modifies a database username, changes its default schema, or remaps a user to another login. Similar to the CREATE USER statement, it is possible to assign a default schema to a user before the creation of the schema.

The DROP USER statement removes a user from the current database. Users that own securables (that is, database objects) cannot be dropped from the database.

Default Database Schemas

Each database within the system has the following default database schemas:

▶ guest

▶ dbo

▶ INFORMATION_SCHEMA

▶ sys

The Database Engine allows users without user accounts to access a database using the **guest** schema. (After creation, each database contains this schema.) You can apply permissions to the **guest** schema in the same way as you apply them to any other schema. Also, you can drop and add the **guest** schema from any database except the **master** and **tempdb** system databases.

Each database object belongs to one and only one schema, which is the default schema for that object. The default schema can be defined explicitly or implicitly. If the default schema isn't defined explicitly during the creation of an object, that object belongs to the **dbo** schema. Also, the login that is the owner of a database always has the special username **dbo** when using the database it owns.

The INFORMATION_SCHEMA schema contains all information schema views (see Chapter 11). The **sys** schema, as you may have already guessed, contains system objects, such as catalog views.

Roles

When several users need to perform similar activities in a particular database (and there is no corresponding Windows group), you can add a *database role*, which specifies a group of database users that can access the same objects of the database.

Members of a database role can be any of the following:

▶ Windows groups and user accounts
▶ SQL Server logins
▶ Other roles

The security architecture in the Database Engine includes several "system" roles that have special implicit permissions. There are two types of predefined roles (in addition to user-defined roles):

▶ Fixed server roles
▶ Fixed database roles

Beside these two, the following sections also describe the following types of roles:

▶ Application roles
▶ User-defined server roles
▶ User-defined database roles

The following sections describe in detail these role types.

Fixed Server Roles

Fixed server roles are defined at the server level and therefore exist outside of databases belonging to the database server. Table 12-1 lists all existing fixed server roles.

Fixed Server Role	Description
sysadmin	Performs any activity in the database system
serveradmin	Configures server settings
setupadmin	Installs replication and manages extended procedures
securityadmin	Manages logins and CREATE DATABASE permissions and reads audits
processadmin	Manages system processes
dbcreator	Creates and modifies databases
diskadmin	Manages disk files

Table 12-1 *Fixed Server Roles*

Managing Fixed Server Roles

You can add members to and delete members from a fixed server roles in two ways:

▶ Using Management Studio

▶ Using T-SQL statements

To add a login to a fixed server role using SQL Server Management Studio, expand the server, expand Security, and expand Server Roles. Right-click the role to which you want to add a login and then click Properties. On the Members page of the Server Role Properties dialog box (see Figure 12-4), click Add. Search for the login you want to add. Such a login is then a member of the role and inherits all credentials assigned to that role.

Figure 12-4 *Server Role Properties dialog box*

The Transact-SQL statements CREATE SERVER ROLE and DROP SERVER ROLE are used, respectively, to add members to and delete members from a fixed server role. There ALTER SERVER ROLE statement modifies the membership of a server role. Example 12.9, later in the chapter, shows the use of the CREATE SERVER ROLE and ALTER SERVER ROLE statements.

NOTE
You cannot add, remove, or rename fixed server roles. Additionally, only the members of fixed server roles can execute the system procedures to add or remove logins to or from the role.

The sa Login

The **sa** login is the login of the system administrator. In versions previous to SQL Server 2005, in which roles did not exist, the **sa** login was granted all possible permissions for system administration tasks. Now, the **sa** login is included just for backward compatibility. This login is always a member of the **sysadmin** fixed server role and cannot be removed from the role.

NOTE
Use the sa login only when there is not another way to log in to the database system.

Fixed Database Roles

Fixed database roles are defined at the database level and therefore exist in each database belonging to the database server. Table 12-2 lists all of the fixed database roles. Members

Fixed Database Role	Description
db_owner	Users who can perform almost all activities in the database
db_accessadmin	Users who can add or remove users
db_datareader	Users who can see data from all user tables in the database
db_datawriter	Users who can add, modify, or delete data in all user tables in the database
db_ddladmin	Users who can perform all DDL operations in the database
db_securityadmin	Users who can manage all activities concerning security permissions in the database
db_backupoperator	Users who can back up the database
db_denydatareader	Users who cannot see any data in the database
db_denydatawriter	Users who cannot change any data in the database

Table 12-2 *Fixed Database Roles*

of the fixed database role can perform different activities. Use Books Online to learn which activities are allowed for each of the fixed database roles.

Besides the fixed database roles listed in Table 12-2, there is a special fixed database role called **public**, which is explained next.

public Role

The **public** role is a special fixed database role to which every legitimate user of a database belongs. It captures all default permissions for users in a database. This provides a mechanism for giving all users without appropriate permissions a set of (usually limited) permissions. The **public** role maintains all default permissions for users in a database and cannot be dropped. This role cannot have users, groups, or roles assigned to it because they belong to the role by default. (Example 12.19, later in the chapter, shows the use of the **public** role.)

By default, the **public** role allows users to do the following:

▶ View system tables and display information from the **master** system database using certain system procedures

▶ Execute statements that do not require permissions—for example, PRINT

Assigning a User to a Fixed Database Role

To assign a user to a fixed database role using SQL Server Management Studio, expand the server, expand Databases, expand the database, expand Security, expand Roles, and then expand Database Roles. Right-click the role to which you want to add a user and then click Properties. In the Database Role Properties dialog box, click Add and browse for the user(s) you want to add. Such an account is then a member of the role and inherits all credentials assigned to that role.

Application Roles

Application roles allow you to enforce security for a particular application. In other words, application roles allow the application itself to accept the responsibility of user authentication, instead of relying on the database system. For instance, if clerks in your company may change an employee's data only using the existing application (and not Transact-SQL statements or any other tool), you can create an application role for the application.

Application roles differ significantly from all other role types. First, application roles have no members, because they use the application only and therefore do not need to grant permissions directly to users. Second, you need a password to activate an application role.

When an application role is activated for a session by the application, the session loses all permissions applied to the logins, user accounts and groups, or roles in all databases for the duration of the session. Because these roles are applicable only to the database in which they exist, the session can gain access to another database only by virtue of permissions granted to the **guest** user account in the other database. For this reason, if there is no **guest** user account in a database, the session cannot gain access to that database.

The next two subsections describe the management of application roles.

Managing Application Roles Using Management Studio

To create an application role using SQL Server Management Studio, expand the server, expand Databases, and then expand the database and its Security folder. Right-click Roles, click New, and then click New Application Role. In the Application Role dialog box, enter the name of the new role. Additionally, you must enter the password and may enter the default schema for the new role.

Managing Application Roles Using T-SQL

You can create, modify, and delete application roles using the Transact-SQL statements CREATE APPLICATION ROLE, ALTER APPLICATION ROLE, and DROP APPLICATION ROLE.

The CREATE APPLICATION ROLE statement creates an application role for the current database. This statement has two options: one to specify the password and one to define the default schema—that is, the first schema that will be searched by the server when it resolves the names of objects for this role.

Example 12.8 adds a new application role called **weekly_reports** to the **sample** database.

EXAMPLE 12.8

```
USE sample;
CREATE APPLICATION ROLE weekly_reports
WITH PASSWORD ='x1y2z3w4!',
                        DEFAULT_SCHEMA =my_schema;
```

The ALTER APPLICATION ROLE statement changes the name, password, or default schema of an existing application role. The syntax of this statement is similar to the syntax of the CREATE APPLICATION ROLE statement. To execute the ALTER APPLICATION ROLE statement, you need the ALTER permission on the role.

The DROP APPLICATION ROLE statement removes the application role from the current database. If the application role owns any objects (securables), it cannot be dropped.

Activating Application Roles

After a connection is started, it must execute the **sp_setapprole** system procedure to activate the permissions that are associated with an application role. This procedure has the following syntax:

```
sp_setapprole [@rolename =] 'role' ,
                        [@password =] 'password'
                        [, [@encrypt =] 'encrypt_style']
```

role is the name of the application role defined in the current database, **password** specifies the corresponding password, and **encrypt_style** defines the encryption style specified for the password.

When you activate an application role using **sp_setapprole**, you need to know the following:

▶ After the activation of an application role, you cannot deactivate it in the current database until the session is disconnected from the system.

▶ An application role is always database bound—that is, its scope is the current database. If you change the current database within a session, you are allowed to perform other activities based on the permissions in that database.

NOTE

The design of application roles in SQL Server 2012 is suboptimal, because it is not uniform. To create and delete application roles, you use Transact-SQL. After that, the activation of application roles is done by a system procedure.

User-Defined Server Roles

SQL Server 2012 introduces user-defined server roles. You can create and delete such roles using T-SQL statements CREATE SERVER ROLE and DROP SERVER ROLE, respectively. To add or delete members from a role, use the ALTER SERVER ROLE statement. Example 12.9 shows the use of the CREATE SERVER ROLE and ALTER SERVER ROLE statements. It creates a user-defined server role called **programadmin** and adds a new member to it.

EXAMPLE 12.9

```
USE master;
GO
CREATE SERVER ROLE programadmin;
ALTER SERVER ROLE programadmin ADD MEMBER mary;
```

User-Defined Database Roles

Generally, user-defined database roles are applied when a group of database users needs to perform a common set of activities within a database and no applicable Windows group exists. These roles are created and deleted using either SQL Server Management Studio or the Transact-SQL statements CREATE ROLE, ALTER ROLE, and DROP ROLE.

The following two subsections describe the management of user-defined database roles.

Managing User-Defined Database Roles Using Management Studio

To create a user-defined role using SQL Server Management Studio, expand the server, expand Databases, and then expand the database and its Security folder. Right-click Roles, click New, and then click New Database Role. In the Database Role dialog box (see Figure 12-5), enter the name of the new role. Click Add to add members to the new role. Choose the members (users and/or other roles) of the new role and click OK.

Figure 12-5   *Database Role dialog box*

Managing User-Defined Database Roles Using T-SQL

The CREATE ROLE statement creates a new user-defined database role in the current database. The syntax of this statement is

```
CREATE ROLE role_name [AUTHORIZATION owner_name]
```

role_name is the name of the user-defined role to be created. **owner_name** specifies the database user or role that will own the new role. (If no user is specified, the role will be owned by the user that executes the CREATE ROLE statement.)

The ALTER ROLE statement changes the name of a user-defined database role. Similarly, the DROP ROLE statement drops a role from the database. Roles that own database objects (securables) cannot be dropped from the database. To drop such a role, you must first transfer the ownership of those objects.

Example 12.10 shows how you can create and add members to a user-defined role.

EXAMPLE 12.10

```
USE sample;
CREATE ROLE marketing AUTHORIZATION peter;
GO
ALTER ROLE marketing ADD MEMBER 'peter';
ALTER ROLE marketing ADD MEMBER 'mary';
```

Example 12.10 first creates the user-defined role called **marketing**, and then, using the ADD MEMBER clause of the ALTER ROLE statement, adds two members, **peter** and **mary**, to the role.

Authorization

Only authorized users are able to execute statements or perform operations on an entity. If an unauthorized user attempts to do either task, the execution of the Transact-SQL statement or the operation on the database object will be rejected.

There are three Transact-SQL statements related to authorization:

► GRANT
► DENY
► REVOKE

Before you read about these three statements, I will repeat the most important facts concerning the security model of the Database Engine. The model separates the world into principals and securables. Every securable has associated permissions that can be granted to a principal. Principals, such as individuals, groups, or applications, can access securables. Securables are the resources to which the authorization subsystem regulates access. There are three securable classes: server, database, and schema, which contain other securables, such as login, database users, tables, and stored procedures.

GRANT Statement

The GRANT statement grants permissions to securables. The syntax of the GRANT statement is

```
GRANT {ALL [PRIVILEGES]} | permission_list
    [ON [class::] securable]  TO principal_list [WITH GRANT OPTION]
    [AS principal ]
```

The ALL clause indicates that all permissions applicable to the specified securable will be granted to the specified principal. (For the list of specific securables, see Books Online.) **permission_list** specifies either statements or objects (separated by commas) for which the permissions are granted. **class** specifies either a securable class or a securable name for which permission will be granted. ON **securable** specifies the securable for which permissions are granted (see Example 12.15 later in this section). **principal_list** lists all accounts (separated by commas) to which permissions are granted. **principal** and the components of **principal_list** can be a Windows user account, a login or user account mapped to a certificate, a login mapped to an asymmetric key, a database user, a database role, or an application role.

Table 12-3 lists and describes all the permissions and lists the corresponding securables to which they apply.

NOTE

Table 12-3 shows only the most important permissions. The security model of the Database Engine is hierarchical. Hence, there are many granular permissions that are not listed in the table. You can find the description of these permissions in Books Online.

The following examples demonstrate the use of the GRANT statement. To begin, Example 12.11 demonstrates the use of the CREATE permission.

EXAMPLE 12.11

```
USE sample;
GRANT CREATE TABLE, CREATE PROCEDURE
                TO peter, mary;
```

Permission	Applies To	Description
SELECT	Tables + columns, synonyms, views + columns, table-valued functions	Provides the ability to select (read) rows. You can restrict this permission to one or more columns by listing them. (If the list is omitted, all columns of the table can be selected.)
INSERT	Tables + columns, synonyms, views + columns	Provides the ability to insert rows.
UPDATE	Tables + columns, synonyms, views + columns	Provides the ability to modify column values. You can restrict this permission to one or more columns by listing them. (If the list is omitted, all columns of the table can be modified.)
DELETE	Tables + columns, synonyms, views + columns	Provides the ability to delete rows.
REFERENCES	User-defined functions (SQL and CLR), tables + columns, synonyms, views + columns	Provides the ability to reference columns of the foreign key in the referenced table when the user has no SELECT permission for the referenced table.
EXECUTE	Stored procedures (SQL and CLR), user-defined functions (SQL and CLR), synonyms	Provides the ability to execute the specified stored procedure or user-defined functions.
CONTROL	Stored procedures (SQL and CLR), user-defined functions (SQL and CLR), synonyms	Provides ownership-like capabilities; the grantee effectively has all defined permissions on the securable. A principal that has been granted CONTROL also has the ability to grant permissions on the securable. CONTROL at a particular scope implicitly includes CONTROL on all the securables under that scope (see Example 12.16).
ALTER	Stored procedures (SQL and CLR), user-defined functions (SQL and CLR), tables, views	Provides the ability to alter the properties (except ownership) of a particular securable. When granted on a scope, it also bestows the ability to ALTER, CREATE, or DROP any securable contained within that scope.
TAKE OWNERSHIP	Stored procedures (SQL and CLR), user-defined functions (SQL and CLR), tables, views, synonyms	Provides the ability to take ownership of the securable on which it is granted.
VIEW DEFINITION	Stored procedures (SQL and CLR), user-defined functions (SQL and CLR), tables, views, synonyms	Controls the ability of the grantee to see the metadata of the securable (see Example 12.15).
CREATE (Server securable)	n/a	Provides the ability to create the server securable.
CREATE (DB securable)	n/a	Provides the ability to create the database securable.

Table 12-3 *Permissions with Corresponding Securables*

In Example 12.11, the users **peter** and **mary** can execute the Transact-SQL statements CREATE TABLE and CREATE PROCEDURE. (As you can see from this example, the GRANT statement with the CREATE permission does not include the ON option.)

Example 12.12 allows the user **mary** to create user-defined functions in the **sample** database.

EXAMPLE 12.12

```
USE sample;
GRANT CREATE FUNCTION TO mary;
```

Example 12.13 shows the use of the SELECT permission within the GRANT statement.

EXAMPLE 12.13

```
USE sample;
GRANT SELECT ON employee
   TO peter, mary;
```

In Example 12.13, the users **peter** and **mary** can read rows from the **employee** table.

NOTE

When a permission is granted to a Windows user account or a login, this account (login) is the only one affected by the permission. On the other hand, if a permission is granted to a group or role, the permission affects all users belonging to the group (role).

Example 12.14 shows the use of the UPDATE permission within the GRANT statement.

EXAMPLE 12.14

```
USE sample;
GRANT UPDATE ON works_on (emp_no, enter_date) TO peter;
```

After the GRANT statement in Example 12.14 is executed, the user **peter** can modify values of two columns of the **works_on** table: **emp_no** and **enter_date**.

Example 12.15 shows the use of the VIEW DEFINITION permission, which controls the ability of users to read metadata.

EXAMPLE 12.15

```
USE sample;
GRANT VIEW DEFINITION ON OBJECT::employee TO peter;
GRANT VIEW DEFINITION ON SCHEMA::dbo TO peter;
```

Example 12.15 shows two GRANT statements for the VIEW DEFINITION permission. The first one allows the user **peter** to see metadata about the **employee** table of the **sample** database. (OBJECT is one of the base securables, and you can use this clause to give permissions for specific objects, such as tables, views, and stored procedures.) Because of the hierarchical structure of securables, you can use a "higher" securable to extend the VIEW DEFINITION (or any other base) permission. The second statement in Example 12.15 gives the user **peter** access to metadata of all the objects of the **dbo** schema of the **sample** database.

NOTE

In versions previous to SQL Server 2005, it is possible to query information on all database objects, even if these objects are owned by another user. The VIEW DEFINITION permission now allows you to grant or deny access to different pieces of your metadata and hence to decide which part of metadata is visible to other users.

Example 12.16 shows the use of the CONTROL permission.

EXAMPLE 12.16

```
USE sample;
GRANT CONTROL ON DATABASE::sample TO peter;
```

In Example 12.16, the user **peter** effectively has all defined permissions on the securable (in this case, the **sample** database). A principal that has been granted CONTROL also implicitly has the ability to grant permissions on the securable; in other words, the CONTROL permission includes the WITH GRANT OPTION clause (see Example 12.17). The CONTROL permission is the highest permission in relation to several base securables. For this reason, CONTROL at a particular scope implicitly includes CONTROL on all the securables under that scope. Therefore, the CONTROL permission of user **peter** on the **sample** database implies all permissions on this database, all permissions on all assemblies in the database, all permissions on all schemas in the **sample** database, and all permissions on objects within the **sample** database.

By default, if user A grants a permission to user B, then user B can use the permission only to execute the Transact-SQL statement listed in the GRANT statement. The WITH GRANT OPTION gives user B the additional capability of granting the privilege to other users, as shown in Example 12.17.

EXAMPLE 12.17

```
USE sample;
GRANT SELECT ON works_on  TO mary
   WITH GRANT OPTION;
```

In Example 12.17, the user **mary** can use the SELECT statement to retrieve rows from the **works_on** table and also may grant this privilege to other users of the **sample** database.

DENY Statement

The DENY statement prevents users from performing actions. This means that the statement removes existing permissions from user accounts or prevents users from gaining permissions through their group/role membership that might be granted in the future. This statement has the following syntax:

```
DENY {ALL [PRIVILEGES] } | permission_list
 [ON [class::] securable]  TO principal_list
[CASCADE]   [ AS principal ]
```

All options of the DENY statement have the same logical meaning as the options with the same name in the GRANT statement. DENY has an additional option, CASCADE, which specifies that permissions will be denied to user A and any other users to whom user A passed this permission. (If the CASCADE option is not specified in the DENY statement, and the corresponding object permission was granted with the WITH GRANT OPTION, an error is returned.)

The DENY statement prevents the user, group, or role from gaining access to the permission granted through their group or role membership. This means that if a user belongs to a group (or role) and the granted permission for the group is denied to the user, this user will be the only one of the group who cannot use this permission. On the other hand, if a permission is denied for a whole group, all members of the group will be denied the permission.

NOTE

You can think of the GRANT statement as a "positive" and the DENY statement as a "negative" user authorization. Usually, the DENY statement is used to deny already existing permissions for groups (roles) to a few members of the group.

Examples 12.18 and 12.19 show the use of the DENY statement.

EXAMPLE 12.18

```
USE sample;
DENY CREATE TABLE, CREATE PROCEDURE
   TO peter;
```

The DENY statement in Example 12.18 denies two previously granted statement permissions to the user **peter**.

EXAMPLE 12.19

```
USE sample;
GRANT SELECT ON project
    TO PUBLIC;
DENY SELECT ON project
        TO peter, mary;
```

Example 12.19 shows the negative authorization of some users of the **sample** database. First, the retrieval of all rows of the **project** table is granted to all users of the **sample** database. After that, this permission is denied to two users: **peter** and **mary**.

NOTE

Permissions denied at a higher scope of the Database Engine security model override granted permissions at a lower scope. For instance, if SELECT permission is denied on the level of the sample database, and SELECT is granted on the employee table, the result is that SELECT is denied to the employee table as well as all other tables.

REVOKE Statement

The REVOKE statement removes one or more previously granted or denied permissions. This statement has the following syntax:

```
REVOKE [GRANT OPTION FOR]
    { [ALL [PRIVILEGES] ]  | permission_list ]}
 [ON  [class:: ] securable ]
 FROM principal_list [CASCADE]  [ AS principal ]
```

The only new option in the REVOKE statement is GRANT OPTION FOR. (All other options have the same logical meaning as the options with the same names in the GRANT or DENY statement.) GRANT OPTION FOR is used to remove the effects of the WITH GRANT OPTION in the corresponding GRANT statement. This means that the user will still have the previously granted permissions but will no longer be able to grant the permission to other users.

NOTE

The REVOKE statement revokes "positive" permissions specified with the GRANT statement as well as "negative" permissions generated by the DENY statement. Therefore, its function is to neutralize the specified (positive or negative) permissions.

Example 12.20 shows the use of the REVOKE statement.

EXAMPLE 12.20

```
USE sample;
REVOKE SELECT ON project FROM public;
```

The REVOKE statement in Example 12.20 revokes the granted permission for the **public** role. At the same time, the existing "negative" permissions for the users **peter** and **mary** are not revoked (as in Example 12.19), because the explicitly granted or denied permissions are not affected by revoking roles or groups.

Managing Permissions Using Management Studio

Database users can perform activities that are granted to them. In this case, there is a corresponding entry in the **sys.database_permissions** catalog view (that is, the value of the **state** column is set to **G** for grant). A negative entry in the table prevents a user from performing activities. The entry **D** (deny) in the **state** column overrides a permission that was granted to a user explicitly or implicitly using a role to which the user belongs. Therefore, the user cannot perform this activity in any case. In the last case (value **R**), the user has no explicit privileges but can perform an activity if a role to which the user belongs has the appropriate permission.

To manage permissions for a user or role using Management Studio, expand the server and expand Databases. Right-click the database and click Properties. Choose the Permissions page and click the Search button. In the Database Properties dialog box, shown in Figure 12-6, you can select one or more object types (users and/or roles) to which you want to grant or deny permissions. To grant a permission, check the corresponding box in the Grant column and click OK. To deny a permission, check the corresponding box in the Deny column. (The With Grant column specifies that the user has the additional capability of granting the privilege to other users.) Blanks in these columns mean no permission.

To manage permissions for a single database object using SQL Server Management Studio, expand the server, expand Databases, expand the database, and then expand Tables, Views, or Synonyms, depending on the database object for which you want to manage permissions. Right-click the object, choose Properties, and select the Permissions page. (Figure 12-7 shows the Table Properties dialog box for the **department** table.) Click the Search button to open the Select Users or Roles dialog box. Click Object Types and select one or more object types (users, database roles, application roles). After that, click Browse and check all objects to which permissions should be granted. To grant a permission, check the corresponding box in the Grant column. To deny a permission, check the corresponding box in the Deny column.

Figure 12-6 *Managing statement permissions using SQL Server Management Studio*

Managing Authorization and Authentication of Contained Databases

As you already know from Chapter 5, contained databases have no configuration dependencies on the server instance where they are created and can therefore be easily moved from one instance of the Database Engine to another one. In this section you will learn how to authenticate users for contained databases. Each user that belongs to a contained database is not tied to a login, because such a user has no external dependencies and can be attached elsewhere.

Example 12.21 shows the creation of such a user.

Figure 12-7 *Managing object permissions for the department table*

EXAMPLE 12.21

```
USE my_sample;
CREATE USER my_login WITH PASSWORD = 'x1y2z3w4?';
```

Example 12.21 creates a user **my_login** that is not tied to a login. (The **my_sample** database is a contained database that was created in Example 5.20.) If you try to create such a user in a convenient database, you get the following error:

```
Msg 33233, Level 16, State 1, Line 1
You can only create a user with a password in a contained database.
```

The system stored procedure **sp_migrate_user_to_contained** converts a database user that is mapped to a SQL Server login to a contained database user with a password. **sp_migrate_user_to_contained** separates the user from the original SQL Server login, so that settings such as password and default language can be administered separately for the contained database. This system stored procedure removes dependencies on the instance of the Database Engine and can be used before moving the contained database to a different server instance.

Example 12.22 shows the use of this system stored procedure.

EXAMPLE 12.22

```
USE my_sample;
EXEC sp_migrate_user_to_contained
@username = 'mary_a',
@rename = N'keep_name',
@disablelogin = N'do_not_disable_login' ;
```

Example 12.22 migrates a SQL Server login named **mary_a** to a contained database user with a password. The example does not change the username and retains the login as enabled.

NOTE

*The SQL Server login **mary_a** must be created before the system procedure in Example 12.22 is executed. To create this login, use the CREATE LOGIN statement (see Example 12.3).*

Also, you can use the dynamic management view called **sys.dm_db_uncontained_entities** to learn which parts of your database cannot be moved to a different server instance.

Change Tracking

Change tracking refers to documenting all insert, update, and delete activities that are applied to tables of the database. These changes can then be viewed to find out who accessed the data and when they accessed it. There are two ways to do it:

▶ Using triggers

▶ Using change data capture (CDC)

You can use triggers to create an audit trail of activities in one or more tables of the database. The section "AFTER Triggers" in Chapter 14 and Example 14.1 show how triggers can be used to track such changes. Therefore, the focus of this section is CDC.

CDC is a tracking mechanism that you can use to see changes as they happen. The primary goal of CDC is to audit who changed what data and when, but it can also be used to support concurrency updates. (If an application wants to modify a row, CDC can check the change tracking information to make sure that the row hasn't been changed since the last time the application modified the row. This check is called a *concurrency update*.)

NOTE

CDC is available only in the Enterprise and Developer editions.

Before a capture instance can be created for individual tables, the database that contains the tables must be enabled for CDC, which you do with the system stored procedure **sys.sp_cdc_enable_db**, as shown in Example 12.23. (Only members of the **sysadmin** fixed server role can execute this procedure.)

EXAMPLE 12.23

```
USE sample;
EXECUTE sys.sp_cdc_enable_db
```

To determine whether the **sample** database is enabled for CDC, you can retrieve the value of the column **is_cdc_enabled** in the **sys.databases** catalog view. The value 1 indicates the activation of CDC for the particular database.

When a database is enabled for CDC, the **cdc** schema, **cdc** user, metadata tables, and other system objects are created for the database. The **cdc** schema contains the CDC metadata tables as well as the individual tracking tables that serve as a repository for CDC.

Once a database has been enabled for CDC, you can create a target table that will capture changes for a particular source table. You enable the table by using the stored procedure **sys.sp_cdc_enable_table**. Example 12.24 shows the use of this system stored procedure.

NOTE

The SQLServerAgent service must be running before you enable tables for CDC.

EXAMPLE 12.24

```
USE sample;
EXECUTE sys.sp_cdc_enable_table
    @source_schema = N'dbo', @source_name = N'works_on',
    @role_name = N'cdc_admin';
```

The **sys.sp_cdc_enable_table** system procedure in Example 12.24 enables CDC for the specified source table in the current database. When a table is enabled for CDC, all DML statements are read from the transaction log and captured in the associated change table. The **@source_schema** parameter specifies the name of the schema in which the source table belongs. **@source_name** is the name of the source table on which you enable CDC. The **@role_name** parameter specifies the name of the database role used to allow access to data.

Creating a capture instance also creates a tracking table that corresponds to the source table. You can specify up to two capture instances for a source table. Example 12.25 changes the content of the source table (**works_on**).

EXAMPLE 12.25

```
USE sample;
INSERT INTO works_on VALUES (10102, 'p2', 'Analyst', NULL);
INSERT INTO works_on VALUES (9031, 'p2', 'Analyst', NULL);
INSERT INTO works_on VALUES (29346, 'p3', 'Clerk', NULL);
```

By default, at least one table-valued function is created to access the data in the associated change table. This function allows you to query all changes that occur within a defined interval. The function name is the concatenation of **cdc.fn_cdc_get_all_ changes_** and the value assigned to the **@capture_instance** parameter. In this case, the suffix of the parameter is **dbo_works_on**, as Example 12.26 shows.

EXAMPLE 12.26

```
USE sample;
SELECT *
FROM cdc.fn_cdc_get_all_changes_dbo_works_on
     (sys.fn_cdc_get_min_lsn('dbo_works_on'), sys.fn_cdc_get_max_lsn(),
'all');
```

The following output shows part of the result of Example 12.26:

__$start_lsn	__$update_mask	emp_no	project_no	job	enter_date
0x0000001C000001EF0003	0x0F	10102	p2	Analyst	NULL
0x0000001D000000100003	0x0F	9031	p2	Analyst	NULL
0x0000001D000000110003	0x0F	29346	p3	Clerk	NULL

Example 12.26 shows all changes that happened after the execution of the three INSERT statements. If you want to track all changes in a certain time interval, you can use a batch similar to the one shown in Example 12.27.

EXAMPLE 12.27

```
USE sample;
  DECLARE @from_lsn binary(10), @to_lsn binary(10);
    SELECT @from_lsn =
        sys.fn_cdc_map_time_to_lsn('smallest greater than', GETDATE() - 1);
    SELECT @to_lsn =
        sys.fn_cdc_map_time_to_lsn('largest less than or equal', GETDATE());
    SELECT * FROM
        cdc.fn_cdc_get_all_changes_dbo_works_on (@from_lsn, @to_lsn, 'all');
```

The only difference between Example 12.27 and Example 12.26 is that Example 12.27 uses two parameters (**@from_lsn** and **@to_lsn**) to define the beginning and end of the time interval. (The assignment of time boundaries is done using the **sys.fn_cdc_map_time_to_lsn()** function.)

Data Security and Views

As already stated in Chapter 11, views can be used for the following purposes:

▶ To restrict the use of particular columns and/or rows of tables

▶ To hide the details of complicated queries

▶ To restrict inserted and updated values to certain ranges

Restricting the use of particular columns and/or rows means that the view mechanism provides itself with the control of data access. For example, if the **employee** table also contains the salaries of each employee, then access to these salaries can be restricted using a view that accesses all columns of the table except the **salary** column. Subsequently, retrieval of data from the table can be granted to all users of the database using the view, while only a small number of (privileged) users will have the same permission for all data of the table.

The following three examples show the use of views to restrict the access to data.

EXAMPLE 12.28

```
USE sample;
GO
CREATE VIEW v_without_budget
    AS SELECT project_no, project_name
              FROM project;
```

Using the **v_without_budget** view, as shown in Example 12.28, it is possible to divide users into two groups: the group of privileged users who can access the budget of all projects, and the group of common users who can access all rows from the **projects** table but not the data from the **budget** column.

EXAMPLE 12.29

```
USE sample;
GO
ALTER TABLE employee
   ADD user_name CHAR(60) DEFAULT SYSTEM_USER;
GO
CREATE VIEW v_my_rows
        AS SELECT emp_no, emp_fname, emp_lname, dept_no
            FROM employee
            WHERE user_name = SYSTEM_USER;
```

The schema of the **employee** table is modified in Example 12.29 by adding the new column **user_name**. Every time a new row is inserted into the **employee** table, the system login is inserted into the **user_name** column. After the creation of the corresponding views, every user, who uses this view, can retrieve only the rows that he or she inserted into the table.

EXAMPLE 12.30

```
USE sample;
GO
CREATE VIEW v_analyst
   AS SELECT employee.emp_no, emp_fname, emp_lname
            FROM employee, works_on
            WHERE employee.emp_no = works_on.emp_no
            AND job = 'Analyst';
```

The **v_analyst** view in Example 12.30 represents a horizontal and a vertical subset (in other words, it limits the rows and columns that can be accessed) of the **employee** table.

Summary

The following are the most important concepts of database system security:

▶ Authentication

▶ Encryption

► Authorization

► Change tracking

Authentication is the process of validating user credentials to prevent unauthorized users from using a system. It is most commonly enforced by requiring a username and password. Data encryption is the process of scrambling information so that it is incomprehensible until it is decrypted by the intended recipient. Several different methods can be used to encrypt data.

During the authorization process, the system determines which resources the particular user can use. The Database Engine supports authorization with the following Transact-SQL statements: GRANT, DENY, and REVOKE. Change tracking means that actions of unauthorized users are followed and documented on your system. This process is useful to protect the system against users with elevated privileges.

The next chapter discusses the features concerning the Database Engine as a multiuser software system and describes the notions of optimistic and pessimistic concurrency.

Exercises

E.12.1

What is a difference between Windows mode and Mixed mode?

E.12.2

What is a difference between a SQL Server login and a database user account?

E.12.3

Create three logins called **ann, burt,** and **chuck.** The corresponding passwords are **a1b2c3d4e5!, d4e3f2g1h0!,** and **f102gh285!,** respectively. The default database is the **sample** database. After creating the logins, check their existence using the system catalog.

E.12.4

Create three new database usernames for the logins in E.12.3. The new names are **s_ann, s_burt,** and **s_charles.**

E.12.5

Create a new user-defined database role called **managers** and add three members (see E.12.4) to the role. After that, display the information for this role and its members.

E.12.6

Using the GRANT statement, allow the user **s_burt** to create tables and the user **s_ann** to create stored procedures in the **sample** database.

E.12.7

Using the GRANT statement, allow the user **s_charles** to update the columns **lname** and **fname** of the **employee** table.

E.12.8

Using the GRANT statement, allow the users **s_burt** and **s_ann** to read the values from the columns **emp_lname** and **emp_fname** of the **employee** table. (Hint: Create the corresponding view first.)

E.12.9

Using the GRANT statement, allow the user-defined role **managers** to insert new rows in the **project** table.

E.12.10

Revoke the SELECT rights from the user **s_burt**.

E.12.11

Using Transact-SQL, do not allow the user **s_ann** to insert the new rows in the **project** table either directly or indirectly (using roles).

E.12.12

Discuss the difference between the use of views and Transact-SQL statements GRANT, DENY, and REVOKE in relation to security.

E.12.13

Display the existing information about the user **s_ann** in relation to the **sample** database. (Hint: Use the system procedure **sp_helpuser**.)

Chapter 13

Concurrency Control

In This Chapter

- ▶ Concurrency Models
- ▶ Transactions
- ▶ Locking
- ▶ Isolation Levels
- ▶ Row Versioning

As you already know, data in a database is generally shared between many user application programs. The situation in which several user application programs read and write the same data at the same time is called *concurrency*. Thus, each DBMS must have some kind of control mechanism to solve concurrency problems.

A high level of concurrency is possible in a database system that can manage many active user applications without them interfering with each other. Conversely, a database system in which different active applications interfere with each other supports a low level of concurrency.

This chapter begins by describing the two concurrency control models that the Database Engine supports. The next section explains how concurrency problems can be solved using transactions. This discussion includes an introduction to the four properties of transactions, known as ACID properties, an overview of the Transact-SQL statements related to transactions, and an introduction to transaction logs. The third major section addresses locking and the three general lock properties: lock modes, lock resources, and lock duration. Deadlock, an important problem that can arise as a consequence of locking, is also introduced.

The behavior of transactions depends on the selected isolation level. The five isolation levels are introduced, including whether each belongs to the pessimistic or the optimistic concurrency model. The differences between existing isolation levels and their practical meaning will be explained too.

The end of the chapter introduces row versioning, which is how the Database Engine implements the optimistic concurrency model. The two isolation levels related to this model—SNAPSHOT and READ COMMITTED SNAPSHOT—are discussed, as well as use of the **tempdb** system database as a version store.

Concurrency Models

The Database Engine supports two different concurrency models:

▶ Pessimistic concurrency

▶ Optimistic concurrency

Pessimistic concurrency uses locks to block access to data that is used by another process at the same time. In other words, a database system that uses pessimistic concurrency assumes that a conflict between two or more processes can occur at any time and therefore locks resources (row, page, table), as they are required, for the duration of a transaction. As you will see in the section "Locking," pessimistic concurrency issues shared locks on data being read so that no other process can modify that data. Also, pessimistic concurrency issues exclusive locks for data being modified so that no other processes can read or modify that data.

Optimistic concurrency works on the assumption that a transaction is unlikely to modify data that another transaction is modifying at the same time. The Database Engine supports optimistic concurrency so that older versions of data rows are saved, and any process that reads the same data uses the row version that was active when it started reading data. For that reason, a process that modifies the data can do so without any limitation, because all other processes that read the same data access the saved versions of the data. The only conflict scenario occurs when two or more write operations use the same data. In that case, the system displays an error so that the client application can handle it.

NOTE

The notion of optimistic concurrency is generally defined in a broader sense. Optimistic concurrency control works on the assumption that resource conflicts between multiple users are unlikely, and allows transactions to execute without using locks. Only when a user is attempting to change data are resources checked to determine if any conflicts have occurred. If a conflict occurs, the application must be restarted.

Transactions

A transaction specifies a sequence of Transact-SQL statements that is used by database programmers to package together read and write operations, so that the database system can guarantee the consistency of data. There are two forms of transactions:

▶ **Implicit** Specifies any single INSERT, UPDATE, or DELETE statement as a transaction unit

▶ **Explicit** Generally, a group of Transact-SQL statements, where the beginning and the end of the group are marked using statements such as BEGIN TRANSACTION, COMMIT, and ROLLBACK

The notion of a transaction is best explained through an example. In the **sample** database, the employee Ann Jones should be assigned a new employee number. The employee number must be modified in two different tables at the same time. The row in the **employee** table and all corresponding rows in the **works_on** table must be modified at the same time. (If only one of these tables is modified, data in the **sample** database would be inconsistent, because the values of the primary key in the **employee** table and the corresponding values of the foreign key in the **works_on** table for Ann Jones would not match.) Example 13.1 shows the implementation of this transaction using Transact-SQL statements.

EXAMPLE 13.1

```
USE sample;
BEGIN TRANSACTION /* The beginning of the transaction */
UPDATE employee
    SET emp_no = 39831
    WHERE emp_no = 10102
    IF (@@error <> 0)
        ROLLBACK /* Rollback of the transaction */
UPDATE works_on
    SET emp_no = 39831
    WHERE emp_no = 10102
    IF (@@error <> 0)
        ROLLBACK
COMMIT /*The end of the transaction */
```

The consistent state of data used in Example 13.1 can be obtained only if both UPDATE statements are executed or neither of them is executed. The global variable **@@error** is used to test the execution of each Transact-SQL statement. If an error occurs, **@@error** is set to a negative value and the execution of all statements is rolled back. (The Transact-SQL statements BEGIN TRANSACTION, COMMIT, and ROLLBACK are defined in the upcoming section "Transact-SQL Statements and Transactions.")

NOTE

The Transact-SQL language supports exception handling. Instead of using the global variable @@error, used in Example 13.1, you can use TRY and CATCH statements to implement exception handling in a transaction. The use of these statements is discussed in Chapter 8.

The next section explains the ACID properties of transactions. These properties guarantee that the data used by application programs will be consistent.

Properties of Transactions

Transactions have the following properties, which are known collectively by the acronym ACID:

► Atomicity

► Consistency

► Isolation

► Durability

The atomicity property guarantees the indivisibility of a set of statements that modifies data in a database and is part of a transaction. This means that either all data modifications in a transaction are executed or, in the case of any failure, all already executed changes are undone.

Consistency guarantees that a transaction will not allow the database to contain inconsistent data. In other words, the transactional transformations on data bring the database from one consistent state to another.

The isolation property separates concurrent transactions from each other. In other words, an active transaction can't see data modifications in a concurrent and incomplete transaction. This means that some transactions might be rolled back to guarantee isolation.

Durability guarantees one of the most important database concepts: persistence of data. This property ensures that the effects of the particular transaction persist even if a system error occurs. For this reason, if a system error occurs while a transaction is active, all statements of that transaction will be undone.

Transact-SQL Statements and Transactions

There are six Transact-SQL statements related to transactions:

- ▶ BEGIN TRANSACTION
- ▶ BEGIN DISTRIBUTED TRANSACTION
- ▶ COMMIT [WORK]
- ▶ ROLLBACK [WORK]
- ▶ SAVE TRANSACTION
- ▶ SET IMPLICIT_TRANSACTIONS

The BEGIN TRANSACTION statement starts the transaction. It has the following syntax:

```
BEGIN TRANSACTION [ {transaction_name | @trans_var }
    [WITH MARK ['description']]]
```

transaction_name is the name assigned to the transaction, which can be used only on the outermost pair of nested BEGIN TRANSACTION/COMMIT or BEGIN TRANSACTION/ROLLBACK statements. **@trans_var** is the name of a user-defined variable containing a valid transaction name. The WITH MARK option specifies that the transaction is to be marked in the log. **description** is a string that describes the mark. If WITH MARK is used, a transaction name must be specified. (For more information on transaction log marking for recovery, see Chapter 16.)

The BEGIN DISTRIBUTED TRANSACTION statement specifies the start of a distributed transaction managed by the Microsoft Distributed Transaction Coordinator (MS DTC). A *distributed* transaction is one that involves databases on more than one server. For this reason, there is a need for a coordinator that will coordinate execution of statements on all involved servers. The server executing the BEGIN DISTRIBUTED TRANSACTION statement is the transaction coordinator and therefore controls the completion of the distributed transaction. (See Chapter 18 for a discussion of distributed transactions.)

The COMMIT WORK statement successfully ends the transaction started with the BEGIN TRANSACTION statement. This means that all modifications made by the transaction are stored on the disk. The COMMIT WORK statement is a standardized SQL statement. (The WORK clause is optional.)

NOTE

The Transact-SQL language also supports the COMMIT TRANSACTION statement, which is functionally equivalent to COMMIT WORK, with the exception that the former accepts a user-defined transaction name. COMMIT TRANSACTION is an extension of Transact-SQL in relation to the SQL standard.

In contrast to the COMMIT statement, the ROLLBACK WORK statement reports an unsuccessful end of the transaction. Programmers use this statement if they assume that the database might be in an inconsistent state. In this case, all executed modification operations within the transaction are rolled back. The ROLLBACK WORK statement is a standardized SQL statement. (The WORK clause is optional.)

NOTE

Transact-SQL also supports the ROLLBACK TRANSACTION statement, which is functionally equivalent to ROLLBACK WORK, with the exception that ROLLBACK TRANSACTION accepts a user-defined transaction name.

The SAVE TRANSACTION statement sets a savepoint within a transaction. A *savepoint* marks a specified point within the transaction so that all updates that follow can be canceled without canceling the entire transaction. (To cancel an entire transaction, use the ROLLBACK statement.)

NOTE

The SAVE TRANSACTION statement actually does not commit any modification operation; it only creates a target for the subsequent ROLLBACK statement with the label with the same name as the SAVE TRANSACTION statement.

Example 13.2 shows the use of the SAVE TRANSACTION statement.

EXAMPLE 13.2

```
BEGIN TRANSACTION;
INSERT INTO department (dept_no, dept_name)
      VALUES ('d4', 'Sales');
SAVE TRANSACTION a;
INSERT INTO department (dept_no, dept_name)
       VALUES ('d5', 'Research');
SAVE TRANSACTION b;
INSERT INTO department (dept_no, dept_name)
     VALUES ('d6', 'Management');
ROLLBACK TRANSACTION b;
INSERT INTO department (dept_no, dept_name)
   VALUES ('d7', 'Support');
ROLLBACK TRANSACTION a;
COMMIT TRANSACTION;
```

The only statement in Example 13.2 that is executed is the first INSERT statement. The third INSERT statement is rolled back by the ROLLBACK **b** statement, while the other two INSERT statements are rolled back by the ROLLBACK **a** statement.

NOTE

The SAVE TRANSACTION statement, in combination with the IF or WHILE statement, is a useful transaction feature for the execution of parts of an entire transaction. On the other hand, the use of this statement is contrary to the principle of operational databases that a transaction should be as short as possible, because long transactions generally reduce data availability.

As you already know, each Transact-SQL statement always belongs either implicitly or explicitly to a transaction. The Database Engine provides implicit transactions for compliance with the SQL standard. When a session operates in the implicit transaction mode, selected statements implicitly issue the BEGIN TRANSACTION statement. This means that you do nothing to start an implicit transaction. However, the end of each implicit transaction must be explicitly committed or rolled back using the COMMIT or ROLLBACK statement. (If you do not explicitly commit the transaction, the transaction and all the data changes it contains are rolled back when the user disconnects.)

To enable an implicit transaction, you have to enable the IMPLICIT_ TRANSACTIONS clause of the SET statement. This statement sets the implicit transaction mode for the current session. When a connection is in the implicit transaction mode and the connection is not currently in a transaction, executing any of the following statements starts a transaction:

ALTER TABLE	FETCH	REVOKE
CREATE TABLE	GRANT	SELECT
DELETE	INSERT	TRUNCATE TABLE
DROP TABLE	OPEN	UPDATE

In other words, if you have a sequence of statements from the preceding list, each statement will represent a single transaction.

The beginning of an explicit transaction is marked with the BEGIN TRANSACTION statement. The end of an explicit transaction is marked with the COMMIT or ROLLBACK statement. Explicit transactions can be nested. In this case, each pair of statements BEGIN TRANSACTION/COMMIT or BEGIN TRANSACTION/ROLLBACK is used inside one or more such pairs. (The nested transactions are usually used in stored procedures, which themselves contain transactions and are invoked inside another transaction.) The global variable **@@trancount** contains the number of active transactions for the current user.

BEGIN TRANSACTION, COMMIT, and ROLLBACK can be specified using a name assigned to the transaction. (The named ROLLBACK statement corresponds either to a named transaction or to the SAVE TRANSACTION statement with the same name.) You can use a named transaction only in the outermost statement pair of nested BEGIN TRANSACTION/COMMIT or BEGIN TRANSACTION/ROLLBACK statements.

Transaction Log

Relational database systems keep a record of each change they make to the database during a transaction. This is necessary in case an error occurs during the execution of the transaction. In this situation, all previously executed statements within the transaction have to be rolled back. As soon as the system detects the error, it uses the stored records to return the database to the consistent state that existed before the transaction was started.

The Database Engine keeps all stored records, in particular the before and after values, in one or more files called the *transaction log*. Each database has its own transaction log. Thus, if it is necessary to roll back one or more modification operations executed on the tables of the current database, the Database Engine uses the entries in the transaction log to restore the values of columns that the database had before the transaction was started.

The transaction log is used to roll back or restore a transaction. If an error occurs and the transaction does not completely execute, the system uses all existing before values from the transaction log (called *before images*) to roll back all modifications since the start of the transaction. The process in which before images from the transaction log are used to roll back all modifications is called the *undo* activity.

Transaction logs also store after images. *After images* are modified values, which are used to roll forward all modifications since the start of the transaction. This process is called the *redo* activity and is applied during recovery of a database. (For further details concerning transaction logs and recovery, see Chapter 16.)

Every entry written into the log is uniquely identified using the log sequence number (LSN). All log entries that are part of the particular transaction are linked together, so that all parts of a transaction can be located for undo and redo activities.

Locking

Concurrency can lead to several negative effects, such as the reading of nonexistent data or loss of modified data. Consider this real-world example illustrating one of these negative effects, called *dirty read*: User U_1 in the personnel department gets notice of an address change for the employee Jim Smith. U_1 makes the address change, but when viewing the bank account information of Mr. Smith in the consecutive dialog step, he realizes that he modified the address of the wrong person. (The enterprise employs two persons with the name Jim Smith.) Fortunately, the application allows the user to cancel this change by clicking a button. U_1 clicks the button, knowing that he has committed no error.

At the same time, user U_2 in the technical department retrieves the data of the latter Mr. Smith to send the newest technical document to his home, because the employee seldom comes to the office. As the employee's address was wrongly changed just before U_2 retrieved the address, U_2 prints out the wrong address label and sends the document to the wrong person.

To prevent problems like these in the pessimistic concurrency model, every DBMS must have mechanisms that control the access of data by all users at the same time. The Database Engine, like all relational DBMSs, uses locks to guarantee the consistency of the database in case of multiuser access. Each application program locks the data it needs, guaranteeing that no other program can modify the same data. When another application program requests the modification of the locked data, the system either stops the program with an error or makes a program wait.

Locking has several different aspects:

▶ Lock duration

▶ Lock modes

▶ Lock granularity

Lock duration specifies a time period during which a resource holds the particular lock. Duration of a lock depends on, among other things, the mode of the lock and the choice of the isolation level.

The next two sections describe lock modes and lock granularity.

> **NOTE**
>
> *The following discussion concerns the pessimistic concurrency model. The optimistic concurrency model is handled using row versioning, and will be explained at the end of this chapter.*

Lock Modes

Lock modes specify different kinds of locks. The choice of which lock mode to apply depends on the resource that needs to be locked. The following three lock types are used for row- and page-level locking:

▶ Shared (S)

▶ Exclusive (X)

▶ Update (U)

A *shared lock* reserves a resource (page or row) for reading only. Other processes cannot modify the locked resource while the lock remains. On the other hand, several processes can hold a shared lock for a resource at the same time—that is, several processes can read the resource locked with the shared lock.

An *exclusive lock* reserves a page or row for the exclusive use of a single transaction. It is used for DML statements (INSERT, UPDATE, and DELETE) that modify the resource. An exclusive lock cannot be set if some other process holds a shared or exclusive lock on the resource—that is, there can be only one exclusive lock for a resource. Once an exclusive lock is set for the page (or row), no other lock can be placed on the same resource.

> **NOTE**
>
> *The database system automatically chooses the appropriate lock mode according to the operation type (read or write).*

An *update lock* can be placed only if no other update or exclusive lock exists. On the other hand, it can be placed on objects that already have shared locks. (In this case, the update lock acquires another shared lock on the same object.) If a transaction that modifies the object is committed, the update lock is changed to an exclusive lock if there are no other locks on the object. There can be only one update lock for an object.

NOTE

Update locks prevent certain common types of deadlocks. (Deadlocks are described at the end of this section.)

Table 13-1 shows the compatibility matrix for shared, exclusive, and update locks. The matrix is interpreted as follows: suppose transaction T_1 holds a lock as specified in the first column of the matrix, and suppose some other transaction, T_2, requests a lock as specified in the corresponding column heading. In this case, "yes" indicates that a lock of T_2 is possible, whereas "no" indicates a conflict with the existing lock.

NOTE

The Database Engine also supports other lock forms, such as latches and spinlocks. The description of these lock forms can be found in Books Online.

At the table level, there are five different types of locks:

▶ Shared (S)

▶ Exclusive (X)

▶ Intent shared (IS)

▶ Intent exclusive (IX)

▶ Shared with intent exclusive (SIX)

Shared and exclusive locks correspond to the row-level (or page-level) locks with the same names. Generally, an *intent* lock shows an intention to lock the next-lower resource in the hierarchy of the database objects. Therefore, intent locks are placed at

	Shared	Update	Exclusive
Shared	Yes	Yes	No
Update	Yes	No	No
Exclusive	No	No	No

Table 13-1 *Compatibility Matrix for Shared, Exclusive, and Update Locks*

	S	X	IS	SIX	IX
S	Yes	No	Yes	No	No
X	No	No	No	No	No
IS	Yes	No	Yes	Yes	Yes
SIX	No	No	Yes	No	No
IX	No	No	Yes	No	Yes

Table 13-2   *Compatibility Matrix for All Kinds of Table Locks*

a level in the object hierarchy above that which the process intends to lock. This is an efficient way to tell whether such locks will be possible, and it prevents other processes from locking the higher level before the desired locks can be attained.

Table 13-2 shows the compatibility matrix for all kinds of table locks. The matrix is interpreted exactly as the matrix in Table 13-1.

Lock Granularity

Lock granularity specifies which resource is locked by a single lock attempt. The Database Engine can lock the following resources:

▶ Row

▶ Page

▶ Index key or range of index keys

▶ Table

▶ Extent

▶ Database itself

NOTE

The system automatically chooses the appropriate lock granularity.

A row is the smallest resource that can be locked. The support of row-level locking includes both data rows and index entries. Row-level locking means that only the row that is accessed by an application will be locked. Hence, all other rows that belong to the same page are free and can be used by other applications. The Database Engine can also lock the page on which the row that has to be locked is stored.

> **NOTE**
>
> For clustered tables, the data pages are stored at the leaf level of the (clustered) index structure and are therefore locked with index key locks instead of row locks.

Locking is also done on disk units, called *extents*, that are 64K in size (see Chapter 15). Extent locks are set automatically when a table (or index) grows and the additional disk space is needed.

Lock granularity affects concurrency. In general, the more granular the lock, the more concurrency is reduced. This means that row-level locking maximizes concurrency because it leaves all but one row on the page unlocked. On the other hand, system overhead is increased because each locked row requires one lock. Page-level locking (and table-level locking) restricts the availability of data but decreases the system overhead.

Lock Escalation

If many locks of the same granularity are held during a transaction, the Database Engine automatically upgrades these locks into a table lock. This process of converting many page-, row-, or index-level locks into one table lock is called *lock escalation*. The escalation threshold is the boundary at which the database system applies the lock escalation. Escalation thresholds are determined dynamically by the system and require no configuration. (Currently, the threshold boundary is 5000 locks.)

The general problem with lock escalation is that the database server decides when to escalate a particular lock, and this decision might be suboptimal for applications with different requirements. You can use the ALTER TABLE statement to change the lock escalation mechanism. This statement supports the TABLE option with the following syntax:

```
SET ( LOCK_ESCALATION = { TABLE | AUTO | DISABLE } )
```

The TABLE option is the default value and specifies that lock escalation will be done at table-level granularity. The AUTO option allows the Database Engine to select the lock escalation granularity that is appropriate for the table schema. Finally, the DISABLE option allows you to disable lock escalation in most cases. (There are some cases in which the Database Engine must take a table lock to protect data integrity.)

Example 13.3 disables the lock escalation for the **employee** table.

EXAMPLE 13.3

```
USE sample;
ALTER TABLE employee SET (LOCK_ESCALATION = DISABLE);
```

Affecting Locks

You can use either locking hints or the LOCK_TIMEOUT option of the SET statement to affect locks. The following subsections describe these features.

Locking Hints

Locking hints specify the type of locking used by the Database Engine to lock table data. Table-level locking hints can be used when finer control of the types of locks acquired on a resource is required. (Locking hints override the current transaction isolation level for the session.)

All locking hints are written as a part of the FROM clause in the SELECT statement. You can use the following locking hints:

▶ **UPDLOCK**   Places update locks for each row of the table during the read operation. All update locks are held until the end of the transaction.

▶ **TABLOCK (TABLOCKX)**   Places a shared (or exclusive) table lock on the table. All locks are held until the end of the transaction.

▶ **ROWLOCK**   Replaces the existing shared table lock with shared row locks for each qualifying row of the table.

▶ **PAGLOCK**   Replaces a shared table lock with shared page locks for each page containing qualifying rows.

▶ **NOLOCK**   Synonym for READUNCOMMITTED (see the description of isolation-level hints later in this chapter).

▶ **HOLDLOCK**   Synonym for REPEATABLEREAD (see the description of isolation-level hints later in this chapter).

▶ **XLOCK**   Specifies that exclusive locks are to be taken and held until the transaction completes. If XLOCK is specified with ROWLOCK, PAGLOCK, or TABLOCK, the exclusive locks apply to the appropriate level of granularity.

▶ **READPAST**   Specifies that the Database Engine does not read rows that are locked by other transactions.

NOTE

All these options can be combined in any order if the combination makes sense. (For example, the combination of TABLOCK and PAGLOCK does not make sense, because both options are applied to different resources.)

LOCK_TIMEOUT Option

If you don't want your process to wait without any time limitations, you can use the LOCK_TIMEOUT option of the SET statement. This option specifies the number of milliseconds a transaction will wait for a lock to be released. For instance, if you want your processes to wait eight seconds, you write the following statement:

```
SET LOCK_TIMEOUT 8000
```

If the particular resource cannot be granted to your process within this time period, the statement will be aborted with the corresponding error message.

The value of −1 (the default value) indicates no time-out; in other words, the transaction won't wait at all. (The READPAST locking hint provides an alternative to the LOCK_TIMEOUT option.)

Displaying Lock Information

The most important utility to display lock information is a dynamic management view called **sys.dm_tran_locks**. This view returns information about currently active lock manager resources. Each row represents a currently active request for a lock that has been granted or is waiting to be granted. The columns of this view relate to two groups: resource and request. The resource group describes the resource on which the lock request is being made, and the request group describes the lock request. The most important columns of this view are as follows:

- ▶ **resource_type**   Represents the resource type
- ▶ **resource_database_id**   Specifies the ID of the database under which this resource is scoped
- ▶ **request_mode**   Specifies the mode of the request
- ▶ **request_status**   Specifies the current status of the request

Example 13.4 displays all the locks that are in a wait state.

EXAMPLE 13.4

```
USE AdventureWorks;
SELECT resource_type, DB_NAME(resource_database_id) as db_name,
    request_session_id, request_mode, request_status
    FROM sys.dm_tran_locks
    WHERE request_status = 'WAIT;'
```

Deadlock

A *deadlock* is a special concurrency problem in which two transactions block the progress of each other. The first transaction has a lock on some database object that the other transaction wants to access, and vice versa. (In general, several transactions can cause a deadlock by building a circle of dependencies.) Example 13.5 shows the deadlock situation between two transactions.

> **NOTE**
>
> *The parallelism of processes cannot be achieved naturally using the small **sample** database, because every transaction in it is executed very quickly. Therefore, Example 13.5 uses the WAITFOR statement to pause both transactions for ten seconds to simulate the deadlock.*

EXAMPLE 13.5

```
USE sample;
BEGIN TRANSACTION                 BEGIN TRANSACTION
UPDATE works_on                   UPDATE employee
    SET job = 'Manager'               SET dept_no = 'd2'
    WHERE emp_no = 18316              WHERE emp_no = 9031
    AND project_no = 'p2'         WAITFOR DELAY '00:00:10'
WAITFOR DELAY '00:00:10'          DELETE FROM works_on
UPDATE employee                       WHERE emp_no = 18316
    SET emp_lname = 'Green'            AND project_no = 'p2'
    WHERE emp_no = 9031           COMMIT
COMMIT
```

If both transactions in Example 13.5 are executed at the same time, the deadlock appears and the system returns the following output:

```
Server: Msg 1205, Level 13, State 45
Transaction (Process id 56) was deadlocked with another process and
has been chosen as deadlock victim. Rerun your command.
```

As the output of Example 13.5 shows, the database system handles a deadlock by choosing one of the transactions as a "victim" (actually, the one that closed the loop in lock requests) and rolling it back. (The other transaction is executed after that.) A programmer can handle a deadlock by implementing the conditional statement that tests for the returned error number (1205) and then executes the rolled-back transaction again.

You can affect which transaction the system chooses as the "victim" by using the DEADLOCK_PRIORITY option of the SET statement. There are 21 different priority levels, from −10 to 10. The value LOW corresponds to −5, NORMAL (the default value) corresponds to 0, and HIGH corresponds to 5. The "victim" session is chosen according to the session's deadlock priority.

Isolation Levels

In theory, each transaction should be fully isolated from other transactions. But, in such a case, data availability is significantly reduced, because read operations in a transaction block write operations in other transactions, and vice versa. If data availability is an important issue, this property can be loosened using isolation levels. *Isolation levels* specify the degree to which data being retrieved in a transaction is protected from changes to the same data by other transactions. Before you are introduced to the existing isolation levels, the following section takes a look at scenarios that can arise if locking isn't used and, hence, there is no isolation between transactions.

Concurrency Problems

If locking isn't used, and thus no isolation exists between transactions, the following four problems may appear:

- ▶ Lost update
- ▶ Dirty reads (discussed earlier, in the "Locking" section)
- ▶ Nonrepeatable reads
- ▶ Phantoms

The *lost update* concurrency problem occurs when no isolation is provided to a transaction from other transactions. This means that several transactions can read the same data and modify it. The changes to the data by all transactions, except those by the last transaction, are lost.

The *nonrepeatable read* concurrency problem occurs when one process reads data several times, and another process changes the same data between two read operations of the first process. Therefore, the values read by both read operations of the first process are different.

The *phantom* concurrency problem is similar to the nonrepeatable read concurrency problem, because two subsequent read operations can display different values, but in this case, the reason for this behavior lies in the different number of rows being read the first time and the second time. (Additional rows, called *phantoms*, are inserted by other transactions.)

The Database Engine and Isolation Levels

Using isolation levels, you can specify which of the concurrency problems discussed in the preceding section may occur and which you want to avoid. The Database Engine supports the following five isolation levels, which control how your read operations are executed:

▶ READ UNCOMMITTED

▶ READ COMMITTED

▶ REPEATABLE READ

▶ SERIALIZABLE

▶ SNAPSHOT

READ UNCOMMITTED, REPEATABLE READ, and SERIALIZABLE are available only in the pessimistic concurrency model, whereas SNAPSHOT is available only in the optimistic concurrency model. READ COMMITTED is available in both models. The four isolation levels available in the pessimistic concurrency model are described next. SNAPSHOT is described in the next section, "Row Versioning."

READ UNCOMMITTED

READ UNCOMMITTED provides the simplest form of isolation between transactions, because it does not isolate the read operations from other transactions at all. When a transaction retrieves a row at this isolation level, it acquires no locks and respects none of the existing locks. The data that is read by such a transaction may be inconsistent. In this case, a transaction reads data that is updated from some other active transaction. If the latter transaction rolls back later, the former transaction reads data that never really existed.

Of the four concurrency problems described in the preceding section, READ UNCOMMITTED allows dirty reads, nonrepeatable reads, and phantoms.

NOTE

The READ UNCOMMITTED isolation level is usually very undesirable and should be used only when the accuracy of the data read is not important or the data is seldom modified.

READ COMMITTED

As you already know, the READ COMMITTED isolation level has two forms. The first form applies to the pessimistic concurrency model, while the second form applies to the optimistic concurrency model. This section discusses the former. The second form, READ COMMITTED SNAPSHOT, is discussed in the following section, "Row Versioning."

A transaction that reads a row and uses the READ COMMITTED isolation level tests only whether an exclusive lock is placed on the row. If no such lock exists, the transaction fetches the row. (This is done using a shared lock.) This action prevents the transaction from reading data that is not committed and that can be subsequently rolled back. After reading the data values, the data can be changed by some other transaction.

Shared locks used by this isolation level are released immediately after the data is processed. (Generally, all locks are released at the end of the transaction.) For this reason, the access to the concurrent data is improved, but nonrepeatable reads and phantoms can still happen.

NOTE

The READ COMMITTED isolation level is the default isolation level of the Database Engine.

REPEATABLE READ

In contrast to the READ COMMITTED isolation level, REPEATABLE READ places shared locks on all data that is read and holds these locks until the transaction is committed or rolled back. Therefore, in this case, the execution of a query several times inside a transaction will always display the same result. The disadvantage of this isolation level is that concurrency is further reduced, because the time interval during which other transactions cannot update the same data is significantly longer than in the case of READ COMMITTED.

This isolation level does not prevent another transaction from inserting new rows, which are included in subsequent reads, so phantoms can appear.

SERIALIZABLE

SERIALIZABLE is the strongest isolation level, because it prevents all four concurrency problems already discussed. It acquires a range lock on all data that is read by the corresponding transaction. Therefore, this isolation level also prevents the insertion of new rows by another transaction until the former transaction is committed or rolled back.

NOTE

The SERIALIZABLE isolation level is implemented using a key-range locking method. This method locks individual rows and the ranges between them. A key-range lock acquires locks for index entries rather than locks for the particular pages or the entire table. In this case, any modification operation of another transaction cannot be executed, because the necessary changes of index entries are not possible.

As a conclusion to the discussion of all four isolation levels above, you have to know that each isolation level in the preceding description reduces the concurrency more than the previous one. Thus, the isolation level READ UNCOMMITTED reduces concurrency the least. On the other hand, it also has the smallest isolation from concurrent transactions. SERIALIZABLE reduces concurrency the most, but guarantees full isolation between concurrent transactions.

Setting and Editing Isolation Levels

You can set an isolation level by using the following:

▶   The TRANSACTION ISOLATION LEVEL clause of the SET statement

▶   Isolation-level hints

The TRANSACTION ISOLATION LEVEL option of the SET statement provides five constant values, which have the same names and meanings as the standard isolation levels just described. The FROM clause of the SELECT statement supports several hints for isolation levels:

▶   READUNCOMMITTED

▶   READCOMMITTED

▶   REPEATABLEREAD

▶   SERIALIZABLE

These hints correspond to the isolation levels with the same name (but with a space in the name). The specification of isolation levels in the FROM clause of the SELECT statement overrides the current value set by the SET TRANSACTION ISOLATION LEVEL statement.

The DBCC USEROPTIONS statement returns, among other things, information about the isolation level. Look at the value of the ISOLATION LEVEL option of this statement to find out the isolation level of your process.

Row Versioning

The Database Engine supports an optimistic concurrency control mechanism based on row versioning. When data is modified using row versioning, logical copies of the data are maintained for all data modifications performed in the database. Every time a row is modified, the database system stores a before image of the previously committed row in the **tempdb** system database. Each version is marked with the transaction sequence number (XSN) of the transaction that made the change. (The XSN is used to identify all operations to be managed under the corresponding transaction.) The newest version of a row is always stored in the database and chained in the linked list to the corresponding version stored in **tempdb**. An old row version in the **tempdb** database might contain pointers to other, even older versions. Each row version is kept in the **tempdb** database as long as there are operations that might require it.

Row versioning isolates transactions from the effects of modifications made by other transactions without the need for requesting shared locks on rows that have been read. This significant reduction in the total number of locks acquired by this isolation level significantly increases availability of data. However, exclusive locks are still needed: transactions using the optimistic isolation level called SNAPSHOT request exclusive locks when they modify rows.

Row versioning is used, among other things, to

▶ Support the READ COMMITTED SNAPSHOT isolation level

▶ Support the SNAPSHOT isolation level

▶ Build the **inserted** and **deleted** tables in triggers

The following subsections describe the SNAPSHOT and READ COMMITTED SNAPSHOT isolation levels, while Chapter 14 discusses in detail the **inserted** and **deleted** tables.

READ COMMITTED SNAPSHOT Isolation Level

READ COMMITTED SNAPSHOT is a slight variation of the READ COMMITTED isolation level discussed in the previous section. It is a statement-level isolation, which means that any other transaction will read the committed values as they exist at the beginning of the statement. In the case of updates, this isolation level reverts from row versions to actual data to select rows to update and uses update locks on the data rows selected. Actual data rows that have to be modified acquire exclusive locks.

The main advantage of READ COMMITTED SNAPSHOT is that read operations do not block updates, and updates do not block read operations. On the other hand, updates block other updates, because exclusive locks are set before an update operation is executed.

You use the SET clause of the ALTER DATABASE statement to enable the READ COMMITTED SNAPSHOT isolation level. After activation, no further changes are necessary. Any transaction specified with the READ COMMITTED isolation level will now run under READ COMMITTED SNAPSHOT.

SNAPSHOT Isolation Level

The SNAPSHOT isolation level is a transaction-level isolation, which means that any other transaction will read the committed values as they exist just before the snapshot transaction starts. Also, the snapshot transaction will return the initial value until it completes, even if another transaction changed it in the meantime. Therefore, only after the snapshot transaction ends will the other transaction read a modified value.

Transactions running under the SNAPSHOT isolation level acquire exclusive locks on data before performing the modification only to enforce constraints. Otherwise, locks are not acquired on data until the data is to be modified. When a data row meets the update criteria, the snapshot transaction verifies that the data row has not been modified by a concurrent transaction that committed after the transaction began. If the data row has been modified in a concurrent transaction, an update conflict occurs and the snapshot transaction is terminated. The update conflict is handled by the database system, and no way exists to disable the update conflict detection.

Enabling the SNAPSHOT isolation level is a two-step process. First, on the database level, enable the ALLOW_SNAPSHOT_ISOLATION database option (using SQL Server Management Studio, for instance). Second, for each session that will use this isolation level, set the SET TRANSACTION ISOLATION LEVEL statement to SNAPSHOT. When these options are set, versions are built for all rows that are modified in the database.

READ COMMITTED SNAPSHOT vs. SNAPSHOT

The most important difference between the two optimistic isolation levels is that SNAPSHOT can result in update conflicts when a process sees the same data for the duration of its transaction and is not blocked. By contrast, the READ COMMITTED SNAPSHOT isolation level does not use its own XSN when choosing row versions. Each time a statement is started, such a transaction reads the latest XSN issued for that instance of the database system and selects the row based on that number.

Another difference is that the READ COMMITTED SNAPSHOT isolation level allows other transactions to modify the data before the row versioning transaction completes. This can lead to a conflict if another transaction modified the data between the time the row versioning transaction performs a read and subsequently tries to execute the corresponding write operation. (For an application based on the SNAPSHOT isolation level, the system detects the possible conflicts and sends the corresponding error message.)

Summary

Concurrency in multiuser database systems can lead to several negative effects, such as the reading of nonexistent data or loss of modified data. The Database Engine, like all other DBMSs, solves this problem by using transactions. A transaction is a sequence of Transact-SQL statements that logically belong together. All statements inside a transaction build an atomic unit. This means that either all statements are executed or, in the case of failure, all statements are canceled.

The locking mechanism is used to implement transactions. The effect of the lock is to prevent other transactions from changing the locked object. Locking has the following aspects: lock modes, lock granularity, and lock duration. Lock mode specifies different kinds of locks, the choice of which depends on the resource that needs to be locked. Lock duration specifies a time period during which a resource holds the particular lock.

The Database Engine provides a mechanism called a trigger that enforces, among other things, general integrity constraints. This mechanism is discussed in detail in the next chapter.

Exercises

E.13.1

What is a purpose of transactions?

E.13.2

What is the difference between a local and a distributed transaction?

E.13.3

What is the difference between implicit and explicit transaction mode?

E.13.4

What kinds of locks are compatible with an exclusive lock?

E.13.5

How can you test the successful execution of each T-SQL statement?

E.13.6

When should you use the SAVE TRANSACTION statement?

E.13.7

Discuss the difference between row-level and page-level locking.

E.13.8

Can a user explicitly influence the locking behavior of the system?

E.13.9

What is a difference between basic lock types (shared and exclusive) and an intent lock?

E.13.10

What does lock escalation mean?

E.13.11

Discuss the difference between the READ UNCOMMITTED and SERIALIZABLE isolation levels.

E.13.12

What is deadlock?

E.13.13

Which process is used as a victim in a deadlock situation? Can a user influence the decision of the system?

Chapter 14

Triggers

In This Chapter

- ▶ Introduction
- ▶ Application Areas for DML Triggers
- ▶ DDL Triggers and Their Application Areas
- ▶ Triggers and CLR

This chapter is dedicated to a mechanism called a *trigger*. The beginning of the chapter describes Transact-SQL statements for creating, deleting, and modifying triggers. After that, examples of different application areas for DML triggers are given. Each example is created using one of three statements, INSERT, UPDATE, or DELETE. The second part of the chapter covers DDL triggers, which are based on DDL statements such as CREATE TABLE. Again, examples of different application areas related to DDL triggers are given. The end of the chapter discusses the implementation of triggers using CLR (Common Language Runtime).

Introduction

A trigger is a mechanism that is invoked when a particular action occurs on a particular table. Each trigger has three general parts:

▶ A name

▶ The action

▶ The execution

The maximum size of a trigger name is 128 characters. The action of a trigger can be either a DML statement (INSERT, UPDATE, or DELETE) or a DDL statement. Therefore, there are two trigger forms: DML triggers and DDL triggers. The execution part of a trigger usually contains a stored procedure or a batch.

NOTE

The Database Engine allows you to create triggers using either Transact-SQL or CLR programming languages such as C# and Visual Basic. This section describes the use of Transact-SQL to implement triggers. The implementation of triggers using CLR programming languages is shown at the end of the chapter.

Creating a DML Trigger

A trigger is created using the CREATE TRIGGER statement, which has the following form:

```
CREATE TRIGGER [schema_name.]trigger_name
   ON {table_name | view_name}
      [WITH dml_trigger_option [,...]]
   {FOR | AFTER | INSTEAD OF} { [INSERT] [,] [UPDATE] [,] [DELETE]}
   [WITH APPEND]
   {AS  sql_statement   | EXTERNAL NAME method_name}
```

NOTE

The preceding syntax covers only DML triggers. DDL triggers have a slightly different syntax, which will be shown later in this chapter.

schema_name is the name of the schema to which the trigger belongs. **trigger_name** is the name of the trigger. **table_name** is the name of the table for which the trigger is specified. (Triggers on views are also supported, as indicated by the inclusion of **view_name.**)

AFTER and INSTEAD OF are two additional options that you can define for a trigger. (The FOR clause is a synonym for AFTER.) AFTER triggers fire after the triggering action occurs. INSTEAD OF triggers are executed instead of the corresponding triggering action. AFTER triggers can be created only on tables, while INSTEAD OF triggers can be created on both tables and views. Examples showing the use of these two trigger types are provided later in this chapter.

The INSERT, UPDATE, and DELETE options specify the trigger action. (The trigger action is the type of Transact-SQL statement that activates the trigger.) These three statements can be written in any possible combination. The DELETE statement is not allowed if the IF UPDATE option is used.

As you can see from the syntax of the CREATE TRIGGER statement, the AS **sql_statement** specification is used to determine the action(s) of the trigger. (You can also use the EXTERNAL NAME option, which is explained later in this chapter.)

NOTE

The Database Engine allows you to create multiple triggers for each table and for each action (INSERT, UPDATE, and DELETE). By default, there is no defined order in which multiple triggers for a given modification action are executed. (You can define the order by using the first and last triggers, as described later in this chapter.)

Only the database owner, DDL administrators, and the owner of the table on which the trigger is defined have the authority to create a trigger for the current database. (In contrast to the permissions for other CREATE statements, this permission is not transferable.)

Modifying a Trigger's Structure

Transact-SQL also supports the ALTER TRIGGER statement, which modifies the structure of a trigger. The ALTER TRIGGER statement is generally used to modify the body of the trigger. All clauses and options of the ALTER TRIGGER statement correspond to the clauses and options with the same names in the CREATE TRIGGER statement.

The DROP TRIGGER statement removes one or more existing triggers from the current database.

The following section describes deleted and inserted tables, which play a significant role in a triggered action.

Using deleted and inserted Virtual Tables

When creating a triggered action, you usually must indicate whether you are referring to the value of a column before or after the triggering action changes it. For this reason, two virtual tables with special names are used to test the effect of the triggering statement:

▶ **deleted** Contains copies of rows that are deleted from the triggered table

▶ **inserted** Contains copies of rows that are inserted into the triggered table

The structure of these tables is equivalent to the structure of the table for which the trigger is specified.

The **deleted** table is used if the DELETE or UPDATE clause is specified in the CREATE TRIGGER statement. The **inserted** table is used if the INSERT or UPDATE clause is specified in the CREATE TRIGGER statement. This means that for each DELETE statement executed in the triggered action, the **deleted** table is created. Similarly, for each INSERT statement executed in the triggered action, the **inserted** table is created.

An UPDATE statement is treated as a DELETE, followed by an INSERT. Therefore, for each UPDATE statement executed in the triggered action, the **deleted** and **inserted** tables are created (in this sequence).

The materialization of **inserted** and **deleted** tables is done using row versioning, which is discussed in detail in Chapter 13. When DML statements such as INSERT, UPDATE, and DELETE are executed on a table with corresponding triggers, all changes to the table are always versioned. When the trigger needs the information from the **deleted** table, it accesses the data from the version store. In the case of the **inserted** table, the trigger accesses the most recent versions of the rows.

NOTE

*Row versioning uses the **tempdb** database as the version store. For this reason, you must expect significant growth of this system database if your database contains many triggers that are often used.*

Application Areas for DML Triggers

The first part of the chapter introduced how you can create a DML trigger and modify its structure. This trigger form can be used to solve different problems. This section describes several application areas for DML triggers (AFTER triggers and INSTEAD OF triggers).

AFTER Triggers

As you already know, AFTER triggers fire after the triggering action has been processed. You can specify an AFTER trigger by using either the AFTER or FOR reserved keyword. AFTER triggers can be created only on base tables.

AFTER triggers can be used to perform the following actions, among others:

▶ Create an audit trail of activities in one or more tables of the database (see Example 14.1)

▶ Implement business rules (see Example 14.2)

▶ Enforce referential integrity (see Examples 14.3 and 14.4)

Creating an Audit Trail

Chapter 12 discussed how you can capture data changes using the mechanism called CDC (change data capture). DML triggers can also be used to solve the same problem. Example 14.1 shows how triggers can create an audit trail of activities in one or more tables of the database.

EXAMPLE 14.1

```
/* The audit_budget table is used as an audit trail of activities in the
project table */
USE sample;
GO
CREATE TABLE audit_budget
   (project_no CHAR(4) NULL,
    user_name CHAR(16) NULL,
    date DATETIME NULL,
    budget_old FLOAT NULL,
    budget_new FLOAT NULL);
```

```
GO

CREATE TRIGGER modify_budget
   ON project AFTER UPDATE
   AS IF UPDATE(budget)
   BEGIN
   DECLARE @budget_old FLOAT
   DECLARE @budget_new FLOAT
   DECLARE @project_number CHAR(4)
   SELECT @budget_old = (SELECT budget FROM deleted)
   SELECT @budget_new = (SELECT budget FROM inserted)
   SELECT @project_number = (SELECT project_no FROM deleted)
   INSERT INTO audit_budget VALUES
   (@project_number,USER_NAME(),GETDATE(),@budget_old, @budget_new)
   END
```

Example 14.1 shows how triggers can be used to implement an audit trail of the activity within a table. This example creates the **audit_budget** table, which stores all modifications of the **budget** column of the **project** table. Recording all the modifications of this column will be executed using the **modify_budget** trigger.

Every modification of the **budget** column using the UPDATE statement activates the trigger. In doing so, the values of the rows of the **deleted** and **inserted** tables are assigned to the corresponding variables **@budget_old, @budget_new**, and **@project_ number**. The assigned values, together with the username and the current date, will be subsequently inserted into the **audit_budget** table.

NOTE

Example 14.1 assumes that only one row will be updated at a time. Therefore, it is a simplification of a general case in which a trigger handles multirow updates. The implementation of such a general (and complicated) trigger is beyond the introductory level of this book.

If the following Transact-SQL statement is executed,

```
UPDATE project
   SET budget = 200000
   WHERE project_no = 'p2';
```

the content of the **audit_budget** table is as follows:

project_no	user_name	date	budget_old	budget_new
p2	Dbo	2011-01-31 14:00:05	95000	200000

Implementing Business Rules

Triggers can be used to create business rules for an application. Example 14.2 shows the creation of such a trigger.

EXAMPLE 14.2

```
-- The trigger total_budget is an example of using a trigger to implement
-- a business rule
USE sample;
GO
CREATE TRIGGER total_budget
    ON project AFTER UPDATE
    AS IF UPDATE (budget)
    BEGIN
    DECLARE @sum_old1 FLOAT
    DECLARE @sum_old2 FLOAT
    DECLARE @sum_new FLOAT
    SELECT @sum_new = (SELECT SUM(budget) FROM inserted)
    SELECT @sum_old1 = (SELECT SUM(p.budget)
                           FROM project p WHERE p.project_no
        NOT IN (SELECT d.project_no FROM deleted d))
    SELECT @sum_old2 = (SELECT SUM(budget) FROM deleted)
    IF @sum_new > (@sum_old1 + @sum_old2)  *1.5
    BEGIN
        PRINT 'No modification of budgets'
        ROLLBACK TRANSACTION
         END
    ELSE
         PRINT 'The modification of budgets executed'
      END
```

Example 14.2 creates the rule controlling the modification of the budget for the projects. The **total_budget** trigger tests every modification of the budgets and executes only such UPDATE statements where the modification does not increase the sum of all budgets by more than 50 percent. Otherwise, the UPDATE statement is rolled back using the ROLLBACK TRANSACTION statement.

Enforcing Integrity Constraints

As previously stated in Chapter 5, a DBMS handles two types of integrity constraints:

▶ Declarative integrity constraints, defined by using the CREATE TABLE and ALTER TABLE statements

▶ Procedural integrity constraints (handled by triggers)

Generally, you should use declarative integrity constraints, because they are supported by the system and you do not have to implement them. The use of triggers is recommended only for cases where declarative integrity constraints do not exist.

Example 14.3 shows how you can enforce the referential integrity for the **employee** and **works_on** tables using triggers.

EXAMPLE 14.3

```
USE sample;
GO
CREATE TRIGGER workson_integrity
   ON works_on AFTER INSERT, UPDATE
   AS IF UPDATE(emp_no)
      BEGIN
      IF (SELECT employee.emp_no
          FROM employee, inserted
          WHERE employee.emp_no = inserted.emp_no) IS NULL
        BEGIN
        ROLLBACK TRANSACTION
        PRINT 'No insertion/modification of the row'
        END
      ELSE PRINT 'The row inserted/modified'
      END
```

The **workson_integrity** trigger in Example 14.3 checks the referential integrity for the **employee** and **works_on** tables. This means that every modification of the **emp_no** column in the referenced **works_on** table is checked, and any violation of the constraint is rejected. (The same is true for the insertion of new values into the **emp_no** column.) The ROLLBACK TRANSACTION statement in the second BEGIN block rolls back the INSERT or UPDATE statement after a violation of the referential constraint.

The trigger in Example 14.3 checks case 1 and case 2 for referential integrity between the **employee** and **works_on** tables (see the definition of referential integrity in Chapter 5). Example 14.4 introduces the trigger that checks for the violation of integrity constraints between the same tables in case 3 and case 4.

EXAMPLE 14.4

```
USE sample;
GO
CREATE TRIGGER refint_workson2
   ON employee AFTER DELETE, UPDATE
   AS IF UPDATE (emp_no)
```

```
BEGIN
  IF (SELECT COUNT(*)
    FROM WORKS_ON, deleted
    WHERE works_on.emp_no = deleted.emp_no) > 0
    BEGIN
    ROLLBACK TRANSACTION
    PRINT 'No modification/deletion of the row'
    END
  ELSE PRINT 'The row is deleted/modified'
END
```

INSTEAD OF Triggers

A trigger with the INSTEAD OF clause replaces the corresponding triggering action. It is executed after the corresponding **inserted** and **deleted** tables are created, but before any integrity constraint or any other action is performed.

INSTEAD OF triggers can be created on tables as well as on views. When a Transact-SQL statement references a view that has an INSTEAD OF trigger, the database system executes the trigger instead of taking any action against any table. The trigger always uses the information in the **inserted** and **deleted** tables built for the view to create any statements needed to build the requested event.

There are certain requirements on column values that are supplied by an INSTEAD OF trigger:

▶ Values cannot be specified for computed columns.

▶ Values cannot be specified for columns with the TIMESTAMP data type.

▶ Values cannot be specified for columns with an IDENTITY property, unless the IDENTITY_INSERT option is set to ON.

These requirements are valid only for INSERT and UPDATE statements that reference a base table. An INSERT statement that references a view that has an INSTEAD OF trigger must supply values for all non-nullable columns of that view. (The same is true for an UPDATE statement: an UPDATE statement that references a view that has an INSTEAD OF trigger must supply values for each view column that does not allow nulls and that is referenced in the SET clause.)

Example 14.5 shows the different behavior during insertion of values for computed columns using a table and its corresponding view.

EXAMPLE 14.5

```
CREATE VIEW all_orders
    AS SELECT orderid, price, quantity, orderdate, total, shippeddate
      FROM orders;
GO
CREATE TRIGGER tr_orders
    ON all_orders INSTEAD OF INSERT
    AS BEGIN
        INSERT INTO orders
          SELECT orderid, price, quantity, orderdate
            FROM inserted
        END
```

Example 14.5 uses the **orders** table from Chapter 10 with two computed columns (see Example 10.8). The **all_orders** view retrieves all rows from this table. This view is used to specify a value for a view column that maps to a computed column in a base table. That way, an INSTEAD OF trigger can be used, which, in the case of an INSERT statement, is replaced by a batch that inserts the values into the base table via the **all_orders** view. (An INSERT statement that refers directly to the base table cannot supply a value for a computed column.)

First and Last Triggers

The Database Engine allows multiple triggers to be created for each table or view and for each modification action (INSERT, UPDATE, and DELETE) on them. Additionally, you can specify the order of multiple triggers defined for a given action. Using the system stored procedure **sp_settriggerorder**, you can specify that one of the AFTER triggers associated with a table be either the first AFTER trigger or the last AFTER trigger executed for each triggering action. This system procedure has a parameter called **@order** that can contain three values:

▶ **first**   Specifies that the trigger is the first AFTER trigger fired for a modification action.

▶ **last**   Specifies that the trigger is the last AFTER trigger fired for a triggering action.

▶ **none**   Specifies that there is no specific order in which the trigger should be fired. (This value is generally used to reset a trigger from being either first or last.)

NOTE

If you use the ALTER TRIGGER statement to modify the structure of a trigger, the order of that trigger (first or last) will be dropped.

Example 14.6 shows the use of the system stored procedure **sp_settriggerorder**.

EXAMPLE 14.6

```
EXEC sp_settriggerorder @triggername = 'modify_budget',
                        @order = 'first', @stmttype='update'
```

NOTE

There can be only one first and one last AFTER trigger on a table. The sequence in which all other AFTER triggers fire is undefined.

To display the order of a trigger, you can use the following:

▶ sp_helptrigger
▶ OBJECTPROPERTY function

The system procedure **sp_helptrigger** contains the **order** column, which displays the order of the specified trigger. Using the OBJECTPROPERTY function, you can specify either **ExecIsFirstTrigger** or **ExecIsLastTrigger** as the value of the second parameter of this function. The first parameter is always the identification number of the database object. The OBJECTPROPERTY function displays 1 if the particular property is TRUE.

NOTE

Because an INSTEAD OF trigger is fired before data modifications are made to the underlying table, INSTEAD OF triggers cannot be specified as first or last triggers.

DDL Triggers and Their Application Areas

The first part of this chapter described DML triggers, which specify an action that is performed by the server when a modification of the table using an INSERT, UPDATE, or DELETE statement is executed. The Database Engine allows you to define triggers for DDL statements, such as CREATE DATABASE, DROP TABLE, and ALTER TABLE. The syntax for DDL triggers is

```
CREATE TRIGGER [schema_name.]trigger_name
   ON {ALL SERVER | DATABASE }
 [WITH {ENCRYPTION | EXECUTE AS clause_name]
   {FOR | AFTER } { event_group | event_type | LOGON}
 AS {batch  | EXTERNAL NAME method_name}
```

As you can see from the preceding syntax, DDL triggers are created the same way DML triggers are created. (The ALTER TRIGGER and DROP TRIGGER statements are used to modify and drop DDL triggers, too.) Therefore, this section describes only those options of CREATE TRIGGER that are new in the syntax for DDL triggers.

When you define a DDL trigger, you first must decide on the scope of your trigger. The DATABASE clause specifies that the scope of a DDL trigger is the current database. The ALL SERVER clause specifies that the scope of a DDL trigger is the current server.

After specifying the trigger's scope, you have to decide whether the trigger fires to a single DDL statement or a group of statements. **event_type** specifies a DDL statement that, after execution, causes a trigger to fire. **event_group** defines a name of a predefined group of Transact-SQL language events. The DDL trigger fires after execution of any Transact-SQL language event belonging to **event_group**. You can find the list of all event groups and types in Books Online. The LOGON keyword specifies a logon trigger (see Example 14.8, later in this section).

Besides the similarities that exist between DML and DDL triggers, there are several significant differences. The main difference between these two trigger forms is that a DDL trigger can be used to define as its scope an entire database or even an entire server, not just a single object. Also, DDL triggers do not support INSTEAD OF triggers. As you might have guessed, **inserted** and **deleted** tables are not necessary, because DDL triggers do not change a table's content.

The two different forms of DDL triggers, database-level and server-level, are described next.

Database-Level Triggers

Example 14.7 shows how you can implement a DDL trigger whose scope is the current database.

EXAMPLE 14.7

```
USE sample;
GO
```

```
CREATE TRIGGER prevent_drop_triggers
  ON DATABASE FOR DROP_TRIGGER
  AS PRINT 'You must disable "prevent_drop_triggers" to drop any trigger'
  ROLLBACK
```

The trigger in Example 14.7 prevents all users from deleting any trigger that belongs to the **sample** database. The DATABASE clause specifies that the **prevent_drop_triggers** trigger is a database-level trigger. The DROP_TRIGGER keyword is a predefined event type that prevents a deletion of any trigger.

Server-Level Triggers

Server-level triggers respond to changes on the server. You use the ALL SERVER clause to implement server-level triggers. Depending on the action, there are two different flavors of server-level triggers: conventional DDL triggers and logon triggers. The triggering action of conventional DDL triggers is based on DDL statements, while the triggering action of logon triggers is a logon event.

Example 14.8 shows a server-level trigger that is at the same time a logon trigger.

EXAMPLE 14.8

```
USE master;
GO
CREATE LOGIN login_test WITH PASSWORD = 'login_test§$!',
    CHECK_EXPIRATION = ON;
GO
GRANT VIEW SERVER STATE TO login_test;
GO
CREATE TRIGGER connection_limit_trigger
ON ALL SERVER WITH EXECUTE AS 'login_test'
FOR LOGON AS
BEGIN
IF ORIGINAL_LOGIN()= 'login_test' AND
    (SELECT COUNT(*) FROM sys.dm_exec_sessions
            WHERE is_user_process = 1 AND
                original_login_name = 'login_test') > 1
    ROLLBACK;
END;
```

Example 14.8 first creates the SQL Server login called **login_test**. This login is subsequently used in a server-level trigger. For this reason, it requires server permission VIEW SERVER STATE, which is given to it with the GRANT statement. After that, the **connection_limit_trigger** trigger is created. This trigger belongs to logon triggers, because of the LOGON keyword. The use of the **sys.dm_exec_sessions** view allows you to check if there is already a session established using the **login_test** login. In that case, the ROLLBACK statement is executed. That way, the **login_test** login can establish only one session at a time.

Triggers and CLR

Triggers, as well as stored procedures and user-defined functions, can be implemented using the Common Language Runtime (CLR). The following steps are necessary if you want to implement, compile, and store CLR triggers:

▶ Implement a trigger using C# or Visual Basic and compile the program using the corresponding compiler (see Examples 14.9 and 14.10).

▶ Use the CREATE ASSEMBLY statement to create the corresponding executable file (see Example 14.11).

▶ Create the trigger using the CREATE TRIGGER statement (see Example 14.12).

The following examples demonstrate these steps. Example 14.9 shows the C# source program that will be used to implement the trigger from Example 14.1.

NOTE

*Before you can create the CLR trigger in the following examples, you first have to drop the **prevent_drop_triggers** trigger (see Example 14.7) and then drop the **modify_budget** trigger (see Example 14.1) by using the DROP TRIGGER statement.*

EXAMPLE 14.9

```
using System;
using System.Data;
using System.Data.SqlClient;
using Microsoft.SqlServer.Server;
public class StoredProcedures
{
  public static void Modify_Budget()
   {
       SqlTriggerContext context = SqlContext.TriggerContext;
       if(context.IsUpdatedColumn(2)) //Budget
```

```
        {
            float budget_old;
            float budget_new;
            string project_number;
            SqlConnection conn = new SqlConnection("context connection=true");
            conn.Open();
            SqlCommand cmd = conn.CreateCommand();
            cmd.CommandText = "SELECT budget FROM DELETED";
            budget_old = (float)Convert.ToDouble(cmd.ExecuteScalar());
            cmd.CommandText = "SELECT budget FROM INSERTED";
            budget_new = (float)Convert.ToDouble(cmd.ExecuteScalar());
            cmd.CommandText = "SELECT project_no FROM DELETED";
            project_number = Convert.ToString(cmd.ExecuteScalar());
            cmd.CommandText = @"INSERT INTO audit_budget
                            VALUES(@project_number, USER_NAME(), GETDATE(),
                              @budget_old, @budget_new)";
            cmd.Parameters.AddWithValue("@project_number",project_number);
            cmd.Parameters.AddWithValue("@budget_old",budget_old);
            cmd.Parameters.AddWithValue("@budget_new",budget_new);
            cmd.ExecuteNonQuery();
        }
    }
}
```

The **Microsoft.SQLServer.Server** namespace comprises all client classes that a C# program needs. **SqlTriggerContext** and **SqlFunction** are examples of the classes that belong to this namespace. Also, the **System.Data.SqlClient** namespace contains classes such as **SQLConnection** und **SQLCommand**, which are used to establish the connection and communication between the client and a database server. The connection is established using the connection string "context connection = true":

```
SqlConnection conn = new SqlConnection("context connection=true");
```

After that, the **StoredProcedure** class is defined, which is used to implement triggers. The **Modify_Budget()** method implements the trigger with the same name.

The instance of the **SQLTriggerContext** class called **context** allows the program to access the virtual table that is created during the execution of the trigger. The table stores the data that caused the trigger to fire. The **IsUpdatedColumn()** method of the **SQLTriggerContext** class allows you to find out whether the specified column of the table is modified.

The C# program contains two other important classes: **SQLConnection** and **SQLCommand**. An instance of **SQLConnection** is generally used to establish the connection to a database, while an instance of **SQLCommand** allows you to execute an SQL statement.

The following statements use the **Parameters** property of the **SQLCommand** class to display parameters and the **AddWithValue()** method to insert the value in the specified parameter:

```
cmd.Parameters.AddWithValue("@project_number",project_number);
cmd.Parameters.AddWithValue("@budget_old",budget_old);
cmd.Parameters.AddWithValue("@budget_new",budget_new);
```

Example 14.10 shows the execution of the **csc** command. Using this command, you can compile the C# program in Example 14.9.

EXAMPLE 14.10

```
csc /target:library Example14_9.cs
/reference:"c:\Program Files\Microsoft
SQLServer\MSSQL11.MSSQLSERVER\MSSQL\Binn\sqlaccess.dll"
```

You can find the detailed description of the **csc** command in Chapter 8.

NOTE

*You enable and disable the use of CLR through the **clr_enabled** option of the **sp_configure** system procedure. Execute the RECONFIGURE statement to update the running configuration value (see Example 8.9).*

Example 14.11 shows the next step in creating the **modify_budget** trigger. (Use SQL Server Management Studio to execute this statement.)

EXAMPLE 14.11

```
CREATE ASSEMBLY Example14_9 FROM
            'C:\Programs\Microsoft SQL Server\assemblies\Example14_9.dll'
            WITH PERMISSION_SET=EXTERNAL_ACCESS
```

The CREATE ASSEMBLY statement uses the managed code as the source to create the corresponding object, against which the CLR trigger is created. The WITH PERMISSION SET clause in this example specifies that access permissions are set to the value EXTERNAL_ACCESS, which does not allow assemblies to access external system resources, except a few of them.

Example 14.12 creates the **modify_budget** trigger using the CREATE TRIGGER statement.

EXAMPLE 14.12

```
CREATE TRIGGER modify_budget ON project
    AFTER UPDATE AS
    EXTERNAL NAME Example14_9.StoredProcedures.Modify_Budget
```

The CREATE TRIGGER statement in Example 14.12 differs from the statement used in Examples 14.1 to 14.5 because it uses the EXTERNAL NAME option. This option specifies that the code is generated using CLR. The name in this clause is a three-part name. The first part is the name of the corresponding assembly (**Example14_9**), the second part (**StoredProcedures**) is the name of the public class defined in Example 14.9, and the third part (**Modify_Budget**) is the name of the method, which is specified inside the class.

Example 14.13 shows how the trigger in Example 14.3 can be implemented using the C# language.

NOTE

*You have to drop the trigger called **workson_integrity** (see Example 14.3) using the DROP TRIGGER statement before you can create the CLR trigger in Example 14.13.*

EXAMPLE 14.13

```
using System;
using System.Data;
using System.Data.SqlClient;
using Microsoft.SqlServer.Server;
public class StoredProcedures
{
    public static void WorksOn_Integrity()
    {
        SqlTriggerContext context = SqlContext.TriggerContext;
        if(context.IsUpdatedColumn(0)) //Emp_No
        {
            SqlConnection conn = new SqlConnection("context connection=true");
            conn.Open();
            SqlCommand cmd = conn.CreateCommand();
            cmd.CommandText = "SELECT employee.emp_no
                            FROM employee, inserted
                            WHERE employee.emp_no = inserted.emp_no";
            SqlPipe pipe = SqlContext.Pipe;
            if(cmd.ExecuteScalar() == null)
```

```
      {  System.Transactions.Transaction.Current.Rollback();
          pipe.Send("No insertion/modification of the row");
      }
      else
          pipe.Send("The row inserted/modified");
      }
   }
}
```

Only the two new features used in Example 14.13 require description. The **SqlPipe** class belongs to the **Microsoft.SQLServer.Server** namespace and allows you to send messages to the caller, such as:

```
pipe.Send("No insertion/modification of the row");
```

To set (or get) the current transaction inside a trigger, you use the **Current** property of the **Transaction** class. Example 14.13 uses the **Rollback()** method to roll back the whole transaction after violation of the integrity constraint.

Example 14.14 shows the creation of the assembly and the corresponding trigger based on the C# program in Example 14.13. (Compilation of the C# program using the **csc** command as the intermediate step is necessary, but it is omitted here because it is analog to the same command in Example 14.10.)

EXAMPLE 14.14

```
CREATE ASSEMBLY Example14_13 FROM
       'C:\Programs\Microsoft SQL Server\assemblies\Example14_13.dll'
WITH PERMISSION_SET=EXTERNAL_ACCESS
GO
CREATE TRIGGER workson_integrity ON works_on
AFTER INSERT, UPDATE AS
EXTERNAL NAME Example14_13.StoredProcedures.WorksOn_Integrity
```

Summary

A trigger is a mechanism that resides in the database server and comes in two flavors: DML triggers and DDL triggers. DML triggers specify one or more actions that are automatically performed by the database server when a modification of the table using an INSERT, UPDATE, or DELETE statement is executed. (A DML trigger cannot be used with the SELECT statement.) DDL triggers are based on DDL statements. They come in two different forms, depending on the scope of the trigger. The DATABASE clause specifies that the scope of a DDL trigger is the current database. The ALL SERVER clause specifies that the scope of a DDL trigger is the current server.

This chapter is the last chapter of the second part of the book. The next chapter starts the third part and discusses the system environment of the Database Engine.

Exercises

E.14.1

Using triggers, define the referential integrity for the primary key of the **department** table, the **dept_no** column, which is the foreign key of the **works_on** table.

E.14.2

With the help of triggers, define the referential integrity for the primary key of the **project** table, the **project_no** column, which is the foreign key of the **works_on** table.

E.14.3

Using CLR, implement the trigger from Example 14.4.

Part III

SQL Server: System Administration

Chapter 15

System Environment of the Database Engine

In This Chapter

- ► **System Databases**
- ► **Disk Storage**
- ► **Utilities and the DBCC Command**
- ► **Policy-Based Management**

This chapter describes several features of the Database Engine that belong to the system environment. First, the chapter provides a detailed description of the system databases that are created during the installation process. It then discusses data storage by examining several types of disk pages and describing how different data types are stored on the disk. Next, the chapter presents the **bcp**, **sqlcmd**, and **sqlservr** system utilities and the DBCC system command. The final major section of the chapter introduces Policy-Based Management, a new technology as of SQL Server 2008.

System Databases

During the installation of the Database Engine, the following system databases are generated:

- ▶   master
- ▶   model
- ▶   tempdb
- ▶   msdb

NOTE

*There is another, "hidden" system database, called the **resource** database, which is used to store system objects, such as system stored procedures and functions. The content of this database is generally used for system upgrades.*

The following sections describe each of the system databases in turn.

master Database

The **master** database is the most important system database of the Database Engine. It comprises all system tables that are necessary for your work. For example, the **master** database contains information about all other databases managed by the Database Engine, system connections to clients, and user authorizations.

Because of the importance of this system database, you should always keep a current backup copy of it. Also, the **master** database is modified each time you perform an operation such as creating user databases or user tables. For this reason, you should back it up after the execution of such operations. (The section "Backing Up the master Database" in Chapter 16 explains when it is necessary to back up the **master** database.)

model Database

The **model** database is used as a template when user-defined databases are created. It contains the subset of all system tables of the **master** database, which every user-defined database needs. The system administrator can change the properties of the **model** database to adapt it to the specific needs of their system.

NOTE

*Because the **model** database is used as a model each time you create a new database, you can extend it with certain database objects and/or permissions. After that, all new databases will inherit the new properties. Use the ALTER DATABASE statement to extend or modify the **model** database, the same way as you modify user databases.*

tempdb Database

The **tempdb** database provides the storage space for temporary tables and other temporary objects that are needed. For example, the system stores intermediate results of the calculation of each complex expression in the **tempdb** database. The **tempdb** database is used by all the databases belonging to the entire system. Its content is destroyed every time the system is restarted.

The system stores three different elements in the **tempdb** database:

▶ User objects

▶ Internal objects

▶ Version store

Private and global temporary tables, which are created by users, are stored in the **tempdb** database. The other objects stored in this system database are table variables and table-valued functions. All user objects stored in **tempdb** are treated by the system in the same way as any other database object. This means that entries concerning a temporary object are stored in the system catalog and you can retrieve information about it using the **sys.objects** catalog view.

Internal objects are similar to user objects, except that they are not visible using catalog views or other tools to retrieve metadata. There are three types of internal objects: work files, work tables, and sort units. Work files are created when the system retrieves information using particular operators. Work tables are created by the system when certain operations, such as spooling and recovering databases and tables by the DBCC command, are executed. Finally, sort units are created when a sort operation is executed.

Optimistic concurrency (see Chapter 13) uses the **tempdb** database as a place to store versions of rows. Hence, the **tempdb** database grows each time the system performs the following operations, among others:

▶ A trigger is executed

▶ An INSERT, UPDATE, or DELETE statement is executed in a database that allows snapshot isolation

NOTE

*Because of optimistic concurrency, the **tempdb** database is heavily used by the system. For this reason, make sure that **tempdb** is large enough and monitor its space regularly. (The use of the **tempdb** database for optimistic concurrency is described in Chapter 13.)*

msdb Database

The **msdb** database is used by the component called SQL Server Agent to schedule alerts and jobs. This system database contains task scheduling, exception handling, alert management, and system operator information; for example, the **msdb** database holds information for all the operators, such as e-mail addresses and pager numbers, and history information about all the backups and restore operations. For more information how this system database can be restored, see Chapter 16.

Disk Storage

The storage architecture of the Database Engine contains several units for storing database objects:

▶ Page

▶ Extent

▶ File

▶ Filegroup

NOTE

Files and filegroups will not be discussed in this chapter. They are described in Chapter 5.

The main unit of data storage is the *page*. The size of a page is always 8KB. Each page has a 96-byte header used to store the system information. Data rows are placed on the page immediately after the header.

The Database Engine supports different page types. The most important are

► Data pages

► Index pages

NOTE

Data and index pages are actually physical parts of a database where the corresponding tables and indices are stored. The content of a database is stored in one or more files, and each file is divided into page units. Therefore, each table or index page (as a database physical unit) can be uniquely identified using a database ID, database file ID, and a page number.

When you create a table or index, the system allocates a fixed amount of space to contain the data belonging to the table or index. When the space fills, the space for additional storage must be allocated. The physical unit of storage in which space is allocated to a table (index) is called an *extent*. An extent comprises eight contiguous pages, or 64KB. There are two types of extents:

► Uniform extents

► Mixed extents

Uniform extents are owned by a single table or index, while mixed extents are shared by up to eight tables or indices. The system always allocates pages from mixed extents first. After that, if the size of the table (index) is greater than eight pages, it switches to uniform extents.

Properties of Data Pages

All types of data pages have a fixed size (8KB) and consist of the following three parts:

► Page header

► Space reserved for data

► Row offset table

> **NOTE**
>
> *This chapter does not include a separate discussion of the properties of index pages because index pages are almost identical to data pages.*

The following sections describe these parts.

Page Header

Each page has a 96-byte page header used to store the system information, such as page ID, the ID of the database object to which the page belongs, and the previous and next page in a page chain. As you may have already guessed, the page header is stored at the beginning of each page. Table 15-1 shows the information stored in the page header.

Page Header Information	Description
pageId	Database file ID plus the page ID
level	For index pages, the level of the page (leaf level is level 0, first intermediate level is level 1, and so on)
flagBits	Additional information concerning the page
nextPage	Database file ID plus the page ID of the next page in the chain (if a table has a clustered index)
prevPage	Database file ID plus the page ID of the previous page in the chain (if a table has a clustered index)
objId	ID of the database object to which the page belongs
lsn	Log sequence number (see Chapter 13)
slotCnt	Total number of slots used on this page
indexId	Index ID of the page (0, if the page is a data page)
freeData	Byte offset of the first available free space on the page
pminlen	Number of bytes in fixed-length part of rows
freeCnt	Number of free bytes on page
reservedCnt	Number of bytes reserved by all transactions
xactReserved	Number of bytes reserved by the most recently started transaction
xactId	ID of the most recently started transaction
tornBits	One bit per sector for detecting torn page write

Table 15-1 *Information Contained in the Page Header*

Space Reserved for Data

The part of the page reserved for data has a variable length that depends on the number and length of rows stored on the page. For each row stored on the page, there is an entry in the space reserved for data and an entry in the row offset table at the end of the page. (A data row cannot span two or more pages, except for values of VARCHAR(max) and VARBINARY(max) data that are stored in their own specific pages.) Each row is stored subsequently after already-stored rows, until the page is filled. If there is not enough space for a new row of the same table, it is stored on the next page in the chain of pages.

For all tables that have only fixed-length columns, the same number of rows is stored at each page. If a table has at least one variable-length column (a VARCHAR column, for instance), the number of rows per page may differ and the system then stores as many rows per page as will fit on it.

Row Offset Table

The last part of a page is tightly connected to a space reserved for data, because each row stored on a page has a corresponding entry in the row offset table (see Figure 15-1). The row offset table contains 2-byte entries consisting of the row number and the offset byte address of the row on the page. (The entries in the row offset table are in reverse order from

Figure 15-1 *The structure of a data page*

the sequence of the rows on the page.) Suppose that each row of a table is fixed-length, 36 bytes in length. The first table row is stored at byte offset 96 of a page (because of the page header). The corresponding entry in the row offset table is written in the last 2 bytes of a page, indicating the row number (in the first byte) and the row offset (in the second byte). The next row is stored subsequently in the next 36 bytes of the page. Therefore, the corresponding entry in the row offset table is stored in the third- and fourth-to-last bytes of the page, indicating again the row number (1) and the row offset (132).

Types of Data Pages

Data pages are used to store data of a table. There are two types of data pages, each of which is used to store data in a different format:

▶ In-row data pages
▶ Row-overflow data pages

In-Row Data Pages

There is nothing special to say about in-row data pages: they are pages in which it is convenient to store data and index information. All data that doesn't belong to large objects is always stored in-row. Also, VARCHAR(max), NVARCHAR(max), VARBINARY(max), and XML values can be stored in-row, if the **large value types out of row** option of the **sp_tableoption** system procedure is set to 0. In this case, all such values are stored directly in the data row, up to a limit of 8000 bytes and as long as the value can fit in the record. If the value does not fit in the record, a pointer is stored in-row and the rest is stored out of row in the storage space for large objects.

Row-Overflow Data

Values of the VARCHAR(MAX), NVARCHAR(MAX), and VARBINARY(MAX) columns can be stored outside of the actual data page. As you already know, 8KB is the maximum size of a row on a data page, but you can exceed this size limit if you use columns of such large data types. In this case, the system stores the values of these columns in extra pages, which are called row-overflow pages.

The storage in row-overflow pages is done only under certain circumstances. The primary factor is the length of the row: if the row needs more than 8060 bytes, some of the column's values will be stored on overflow pages. (A value of a column cannot be split between the actual data page and a row-overflow page.)

As an example of how content of a table with large values is stored, Example 15.1 creates such a table and inserts a row into it.

EXAMPLE 15.1

```
USE sample;
CREATE TABLE mytable
        (col1 VARCHAR(1000),
         col2 VARCHAR(3000),
         col3 VARCHAR(3000),
          col4 VARCHAR(3000));
    INSERT INTO mytable
        SELECT REPLICATE('a', 1000), REPLICATE('b', 3000),
               REPLICATE('c', 3000), REPLICATE('d', 3000);
```

The CREATE TABLE statement in Example 15.1 creates the **mytable** table. The subsequent INSERT statement inserts a new row in the table. The length of the inserted row is 10,000 bytes. For this reason, the row doesn't fit in a page.

The query in Example 15.2 uses several catalog views to display information concerning page type description.

EXAMPLE 15.2

```
USE sample;
SELECT  rows, type_desc AS page_type, total_pages AS pages
       FROM sys.partitions p JOIN sys.allocation_units a ON
                       p.partition_id = a.container_id
       WHERE object_id = object_id('mytable');
```

The result is

rows	page_type	pages
1	IN_ROW_DATA	2
1	ROW_OVERFLOW_DATA	2

In Example 15.2, the **sys.partition** and **sys.allocation_units** catalog views are joined together to display the information in relation to the **mytable** table and the storage of its row(s). The **sys.partition** view contains one row for each partition of each table or index. (Nonpartitioned tables, such as **mytable**, have only one partition unit.)

A set of pages of one particular data page type is called an *allocation unit*. Different allocation units can be displayed using the **type_desc** column of the **sys.allocation_units** catalog view. As you can see from the result of Example 15.2, for the single row of the **mytable** table, two convenient pages plus two row-overflow pages are allocated (or reserved) by the system.

> **NOTE**
>
> *The performance of a system can significantly degrade if your queries access many row-overflow data pages.*

Parallel Processing of Tasks

The Database Engine can execute different database tasks in parallel. The following tasks can be parallelized:

- ▶ Bulk load
- ▶ Backup
- ▶ Query execution
- ▶ Indices

The Database Engine allows data to be loaded in parallel using the **bcp** utility. (For the description of the **bcp** utility, see the next section.) The table into which the data is loaded must not have any indices, and the load operation must not be logged. (Only applications using the ODBC or OLE DB–based APIs can perform parallel data loads into a single table.)

The Database Engine can back up databases or transaction logs to multiple devices (tape or disk) using parallel striped backup. In this case, database pages are read by multiple threads one extent at a time (see also Chapter 16).

The Database Engine provides parallel queries to enhance the query execution. With this feature, the independent parts of a SELECT statement can be executed using several native threads on a computer. Each query that is planned for the parallel execution contains an exchange operator in its query execution plan. (An *exchange operator* is an operator in a query execution plan that provides process management, data redistribution, and flow control.) For such a query, the database system generates a parallel query execution plan. Parallel queries significantly improve the performance of the SELECT statements that process very large amounts of data.

On computers with multiple processors, the Database Engine automatically uses more processors to perform index operations, such as creation and rebuilding of an index. The number of processors employed to execute a single index statement is determined by the configuration option **max degree of parallelism** as well as the current workload. If the database system detects that the system is busy, the degree of parallelism is automatically reduced before the statement is executed.

Utilities and the DBCC Command

Utilities are components that provide different features such as data reliability, data definition, and statistics maintenance functions. The following utilities are described next:

- bcp
- sqlcmd
- sqlservr

Following the description of these utilities, the DBCC command is described.

bcp Utility

bcp (Bulk Copy Program) is a useful utility that copies database data to/from a data file. Therefore, **bcp** is often used to transfer a large amount of data into a Database Engine database from another relational DBMS using a text file, or vice versa.

The syntax of the **bcp** utility is

```
bcp [[db_name.]schema_name.]table_name {IN | OUT | QUERYOUT | FORMAT}
                              file_name    [{-option parameter} ...]
```

db_name is the name of the database to which the table (**table_name**) belongs. IN or OUT specifies the direction of data transfer. The IN option copies data from the **file_name** file into the **table_name** table, and the OUT option copies rows from the **table_name** table into the **file_name** file. The FORMAT option creates a format file based on the options specified. If this option is used, the option **–f** must also be used.

NOTE

The IN option appends the content of the file to the content of the database table, whereas the OUT option overwrites the content of the file.

Data can be copied as either SQL Server–specific text or ASCII text. Copying data as SQL Server–specific text is referred to as working in native mode, whereas copying data as ASCII text is referred to as working in character mode. The parameter **–n** specifies native mode, and the parameter **–c** specifies character mode. Native mode is used to export and import data from one system managed by the Database Engine to another system managed by the Database Engine, and character mode is commonly used to transfer data between a Database Engine instance and other database systems.

Example 15.3 shows the use of the **bcp** utility. (You have to execute this statement from a command line of your Windows operating system.)

EXAMPLE 15.3

```
bcp AdventureWorks.Person.Address out "address.txt" -T -c
```

The **bcp** command in Example 15.3 exports the data from the **address** table of the **AdventureWorks** database in the output file **address.txt**. The option **–T** specifies that the trusted connection is used. (*Trusted connection* means that the system uses integrated security instead of the SQL Server authentication.) The option **–c** specifies character mode; thus, the data is stored in the ASCII file.

NOTE

*Be aware that the BULK INSERT statement is an alternative to **bcp**. It supports all of the **bcp** options (although the syntax is a bit different) and offers much greater performance. BULK INSERT is described in Chapter 7.*

To import data from a file to a database table, you must have INSERT and SELECT permissions on the table. To export data from a table to a file, you must have SELECT permission on the table.

sqlcmd Utility

sqlcmd allows you to enter Transact-SQL statements, system procedures, and script files at the command prompt. The general form of this utility is

```
sqlcmd {option [parameter]} ...
```

where **option** is the specific option of the utility, and **parameter** specifies the value of the defined option. The **sqlcmd** utility has many options, the most important of which are described in Table 15-2.

Example 15.4 shows the use of **sqlcmd**.

EXAMPLE 15.4

```
sqlcmd -S NTB11901 -i C:\ms0510.sql -o C:\ms0510.rpt
```

NOTE

Before you execute Example 15.4, you have to change the server name and make sure the input file is available.

Option	Description
−S server_name[\instance_name]	Specifies the name of the database server and the instance to which the connection is made. If this option is omitted, the connection is made to the database server set with the environment variable SQLSERVER. If this environment variable is not set, the connection is established to the local machine.
−U login_id	Specifies the SQL Server login. If this option is omitted, the value of the environment variable SQLCMDUSER is used.
−P password	Specifies a password corresponding to the login. If neither the **−U** option nor the **−P** option is specified, **sqlcmd** attempts to connect by using Windows authentication mode. Authentication is based on the account of the user who is running **sqlcmd**.
−c command_end	Specifies the batch terminator. (The default value is GO.) This option can be used to set the command terminator to a semicolon (;), which is the default terminator for almost all other database systems.
−i input_file	Specifies the name of the file that contains a batch or a stored procedure. The file must contain (at least one) command terminator. The sign **<** can be used instead of **−i**.
−o output_file	Specifies the name of the file that receives the result from the utility. The sign **>** can be used instead of **−o**.
−E	Uses a trusted connection (see Chapter 12) instead of requesting a password.
−A	Starts the dedicated administrator connection (DAC), which is described following this table.
−L	Shows a list of all database instances found on the network.
−t seconds	Specifies the number of seconds. The time interval defines how long the utility should wait before it considers the connection to the server to be a failure.
−?	Specifies a standard request for all options of the **sqlcmd** utility.
−d dbname	Specifies which database should be the current database when **sqlcmd** is started.

Table 15-2   *Most Important Options of the sqlcmd Utility*

In Example 15.4, a user of the database system named NTB11900 executes the batch stored in the file ms0510.sql and stores the result in the output file ms0510.rpt. Depending on the authentication mode, the system prompts for the username and password (SQL Server authentication) or just executes the statement (Windows authentication).

One of the most important options of the **sqlcmd** utility is the **−A** option. As you already know from Table 15-2, this option allows you to start a dedicated administration connection (DAC) to an instance of the Database Engine. Usually, you make the connection to an instance of the Database Engine with SQL Server Management Studio. But, there are certain extraordinary situations in which users cannot connect to the instance. In that case, the use of the DAC can help.

Command	Description
:ED	Starts the text editor. This editor can be used to edit the current batch or the last executed batch. The editor is defined by the SQLCMDEDITOR environment variable. For instance, if you want to set the text editor to Microsoft WordPad, type **SET SQLCMDEDITOR=wordpad**.
:!!	Executes operating system commands. For example, **:!! dir** lists all files and directories in the current directory.
:r filename	Parses additional Transact-SQL statements and **sqlcmd** commands from the file specified by **filename** into the statement cache. It is possible to issue multiple **:r** commands. Hence, you can use this command to chain scripts with the **sqlcmd** utility.
:List	Prints the content of the statement cache.
:QUIT	Ends the session started by **sqlcmd**.
:EXIT [(statement)]	Allows you to use the result of a SELECT statement as the return value from **sqlcmd**.

Table 15-3   *Most Important Commands of the sqlcmd Utility*

DAC is a special connection that can be used by DBAs in case of extreme server resource depletion. Even when there are not enough resources for other users to connect, the Database Engine will attempt to free resources for the DAC. That way, administrators can troubleshoot problems on an instance, without having to take down that instance.

The **sqlcmd** utility supports several specific commands that can be used within the utility, in addition to Transact-SQL statements. Table 15-3 describes the most important commands of the **sqlcmd** utility.

Example 15.5 shows the use of the **exit** command of the **sqlcmd** utility.

EXAMPLE 15.5

```
1>USE sample;
2>SELECT * FROM project
3>:EXIT(SELECT @@rowcount)
```

This example displays all rows from the **project** table and the number 3, if the **project** table contains three rows.

sqlservr Utility

The most convenient way to start an instance of the Database Engine is automatically with the boot process of the computer. However, certain circumstances might require different handling of the system. Therefore, the Database Engine offers, among others, the **sqlservr** utility for starting an instance.

NOTE

*You can also use SQL Server Management Studio or the **net** command to start or stop an instance of the Database Engine.*

The **sqlservr** utility is invoked using the following command:

```
sqlservr option_list
```

option_list contains all options that can be invoked using the application. Table 15-4 describes the most important options.

DBCC Command

The Transact-SQL language supports the DBCC (Database Console Commands) statement that act as a command for the Database Engine. Depending on the options used with DBCC, the DBCC commands can be divided into the following groups:

- ▶ Maintenance
- ▶ Informational
- ▶ Validation
- ▶ Miscellaneous

NOTE

This section discusses only the validation commands. Other commands will be discussed in relation to their application. For instance, DBCC SHOW_STATISTICS is discussed in detail in Chapter 19, while the description of DBCC USEROPTIONS can be found in Chapter 13.

Option	Description
−f	Indicates that the instance is started with the minimal configuration.
−m	Indicates that the instance is started in single-user mode. Use this option if you have problems with the system and want to perform maintenance on it (this option must be used to restore the **master** database).
−s *instance_name*	Specifies the instance of the Database Engine. If no named instance is specified, **sqlservr** starts the default instance of the Database Engine.

Table 15-4 *Most Important Options of the sqlservr Utility*

Validation Commands

The validation commands do consistency checking of the database. The following commands belong to this group:

▶ DBCC CHECKALLOC

▶ DBCC CHECKTABLE

▶ DBCC CHECKCATALOG

▶ DBCC CHECKDB

The DBCC CHECKALLOC command validates whether every extent indicated by the system has been allocated, as well as that there are no allocated extents that are not indicated by the system. Therefore, this command performs cross-referencing checks for extents.

The DBCC CHECKTABLE command checks the integrity of all the pages and structures that make up the table or indexed view. All performed checks are both physical and logical. The physical checks control the integrity of the physical structure of the page. The logical checks control, among other things, whether every row in the base table has a matching row in each nonclustered index, and vice versa, and whether indices are in their correct sort order. Using the PHYSICAL_ONLY option, you can validate only the physical structure of the page. This option causes a much shorter execution time of the command and is therefore recommended for frequent use on production systems.

The DBCC CHECKCATALOG command checks for catalog consistency within the specified database. It performs many cross-referencing checks between tables in the system catalog. After the DBCC CATALOG command finishes, a message is written to the error log. If the DBCC command successfully executes, the message indicates a successful completion and the amount of time that the command ran. If the DBCC command stops because of an error, the message indicates the command was terminated, a state value, and the amount of time the command ran.

If you want to check the allocation and the structural and logical integrity of all the objects in the specified database, use DBCC CHECKDB. (As a matter of fact, this command performs all checks previously described, in the given order.)

NOTE

All DBCC commands that validate the system use the snapshot technology (see Chapter 13) to provide the transactional consistency. In other words, the validation operations do not interfere with the other, ongoing database operations, because they use versions of current rows for validation.

Policy-Based Management

The Database Engine supports Policy-Based Management, a system for managing one or more server instances, databases, or other database objects. Before you learn how this framework works, though, you need to understand some key terms and concepts of it.

Key Terms and Concepts

The following is a list of the key terms regarding Policy-Based Management, which is followed by a description of the concepts related to these terms:

- ▶ Managed target
- ▶ Target set
- ▶ Facet
- ▶ Condition
- ▶ Policy
- ▶ Category

The system manages entities called *managed targets*, which may be server instances, databases, tables, or indices. All managed targets that belong to an instance form a hierarchy. A *target set* is the set of managed targets that results from applying filters to the target hierarchy. For instance, if your managed target is a table, a target set could comprise all indices that belong to that table.

A *facet* is a set of logical properties that models the behavior or characteristics for certain types of managed targets. The number and characteristics of the properties are built into the facet and can be added or removed only by the maker of the facet. Some facets can be applied only to certain types of managed targets.

A *condition* is a Boolean expression that specifies a set of allowed states of a managed target with regard to a facet. Again, some conditions can be applied only to certain types of managed targets.

A *policy* is a condition and its corresponding behavior. A policy can contain only one condition. Policies can be enabled or disabled. They are managed by users through the use of categories.

A policy belongs to one and only one *category*. A category is a group of policies that is introduced to give a user more flexibility in cases where third-party software is hosted. Database owners can subscribe a database to a set of categories. Only policies from the database's subscribed categories can govern that database. All databases implicitly subscribe to the default policy category.

Using Policy-Based Management

This section presents an example that shows how you can use Policy-Based Management. This example will create a policy whose condition is that the index fill factor will be 60 percent for all databases of the instance. (For a description of the FILLFACTOR option, see Chapter 10.)

The following are the three main steps to implement Policy-Based Management:

1. Create a condition based on a facet.
2. Create a policy.
3. Categorize the policy.

Generally, to create a policy, open SQL Server Management Studio, expand the server and then expand Management | Policy Management.

The first step is to create a condition. Right-click Conditions and choose New Condition. In the Create New Condition dialog box (see Figure 15-2), type the condition

Figure 15-2   *The Create New Condition dialog box*

name in the Name field (**SetFillFactor** in this example), and choose Server Configuration in the Facet drop-down list. (Setting a fill factor for all databases of an instance is server-bound and thus belongs to the server configuration.) In the Field column of the Expression area, choose @FillFactor from the drop-down menu and choose = as the operator. Finally, enter **60** in the Value field. Click OK.

The next step is to create a policy based on the condition. In the Policy Management folder, right-click Policies and choose New Policy. In the Name field of the Create New Policy dialog box (see Figure 15-3), type the name for the new policy (**PolicyFillFactor60** in this example). In the Check Condition drop-down list, choose the condition that you have created (SetFillFactor). (This condition can be found under the node called Server Configurations.) Choose On Demand from the Evaluation Mode drop-down list.

Figure 15-3   *The Create New Policy dialog box*

NOTE

Policy administrators can run policies on demand, or enable automated policy execution by using one of the existing execution modes.

After you create a policy, you should categorize it. To categorize a policy, click the Description page in the Create New Policy dialog box (see Figure 15-4). You can place policies in the Default category or in a more specific category. (You can also create your own category by clicking the New button.)

The process described in this section can be applied in the same way to dozens of different policies in relation to servers, databases, and database objects.

Figure 15-4 *Description page of the Create New Policy dialog box*

Summary

This chapter described several features of the system environment of the Database Engine:

▶ System databases

▶ Disk storage

▶ Utilities and commands

▶ Policy-Based Management

The system databases contain system information and high-level information about the whole database system. The most important of them is the **master** database.

The main unit of disk storage is the page. The size of pages is 8KB. The most important page type is the data page. (The form of an index page is almost identical to that of a data page.)

The Database Engine supports many utilities and commands. This chapter discussed three utilities (**sqlcmd, sqlservr,** and **bcp**) and the DBCC validation commands.

Policy-Based Management is a framework supported by the system since SQL Server 2008. It allows you to define and enforce policies for configuring and managing databases and database objects across the enterprise.

The next chapter discusses how you can prevent the loss of data, using backup and recovery.

Exercises

E.15.1

If you create a temporary database, where will its data be stored?

E.15.2

Change the properties of the **model** database so that its size is 4MB.

E.15.3

Name all key terms of Policy-Based Management and discuss their roles and how they relate to one another.

E.15.4

Name all groups for which you can specify a condition.

E.15.5

Generate a policy that disables the use of the Common Language Runtime (CLR).

Chapter 16

Backup, Recovery, and System Availability

In This Chapter

- ▶ Reasons for Data Loss
- ▶ Introduction to Backup Methods
- ▶ Performing Database Backup
- ▶ Performing Database Recovery
- ▶ System Availability
- ▶ Maintenance Plan Wizard

his chapter first covers two of the most important tasks related to system administration: backup and recovery. Backup refers to the process of making copies of the database(s) and/or transaction logs to separate media that can later be used for recovery, if necessary. Recovery is the process of using the backup media to replace uncommitted, inconsistent, or lost data.

System availability refers to keeping the downtime of the database system as low as possible. In this chapter we will describe in detail the following options available for system availability: failover clustering, database mirroring, log shipping and high availability and disaster recovery (HADR). Also, the benefits and disadvantages of each option will be discussed.

At the end of the chapter, Maintenance Plan Wizard is discussed. The wizard provides you with the set of basic tasks needed to maintain a database. Therefore, it can be used, among other things, to backup and restore user databases.

Reasons for Data Loss

Performing backups is a precautionary measure that you have to take to prevent data loss. The reasons for data loss can be divided into the following groups:

- ▶ Program errors
- ▶ Administrator (human) errors
- ▶ Computer failures (system crash)
- ▶ Disk failures
- ▶ Catastrophes (fire, flood, earthquake) or theft

During execution of a program, conditions may arise that abnormally terminate the program. Such program errors affect only the database application and usually have no impact on the entire database system. Because these errors are based on faulty program logic, the database system cannot recover in such situations. The recovery should therefore be done by the programmer, who has to handle such exceptions using the COMMIT and ROLLBACK statements (see Chapter 13).

Another source of data loss is human error. Users with sufficient permissions (DBA, for instance) may accidentally lose or corrupt data (people have been known to drop the wrong table, update or delete data incorrectly, and so on). Of course, ideally, this would never happen, and you can establish practices that make it unlikely that production data will be compromised in this way, but you have to recognize that people make mistakes, and data can be affected. The best that you can do is to try to avoid it, and be prepared to recover when it happens.

A computer failure may occur as a result of various different hardware or software errors. A hardware crash is an example of a system failure. In this case, the contents of the computer's main memory may be lost. A disk failure occurs either when a read/write head of the disk crashes or when the I/O system discovers corrupted disk blocks during I/O operations.

In the case of catastrophes or theft, the system must have enough information available to recover from the failure. This is normally done by means of media that offer the needed recovery information on a piece of hardware that is stored separately and thus has not been damaged or lost by the catastrophe or theft.

For most of the errors just described, backups, discussed next, can provide a recovery solution.

Introduction to Backup Methods

Database backup is the process of dumping data (from a database, a transaction log, or a file) into backup devices that the system creates and maintains. A backup device can be a disk file or a tape. The Database Engine provides both static and dynamic backups. *Static backup* means that during the backup process, the only active session supported by the system is the one that creates the backup. In other words, user processes are not allowed during backup. *Dynamic backup* means that a database backup can be performed without stopping the database server, removing users, or even closing the files. (The users will not even know that the backup process is in progress.)

The Database Engine provides four different backup methods:

▶ Full database backup

▶ Differential backup

▶ Transaction log backup

▶ File (or filegroup) backup

The following sections describe these backup methods.

Full Database Backup

A full database backup captures the state of the database at the time the backup is started. During the full database backup, the system copies the data as well as the schema of all tables of the database and the corresponding file structures. If the full database backup is executed dynamically, the database system records any activity that takes place during the backup. Therefore, even all uncommitted transactions in the transaction log are written to the backup media.

Differential Backup

A differential backup creates a copy of only the parts of the database that have changed since the last full database backup. (As in a full database backup, any activity that takes place during a differential backup is backed up too.) The advantage of a differential backup is speed. It minimizes the time required to back up a database, because the amount of data to be backed up is considerably smaller than in the case of a full database backup. (Remember that a full database backup includes a copy of all database pages.)

Transaction Log Backup

A transaction log backup considers only the changes recorded in the log. This form of backup is therefore not based on physical parts (pages) of the database, but rather on logical operations—that is, changes executed using the DML statements INSERT, UPDATE, and DELETE. Again, because the amount of data is smaller, this process can be performed significantly quicker than a full database backup and quicker than a differential backup.

NOTE

It does not make sense to back up a transaction log unless a full database backup has been performed at least once.

There are two main reasons to perform a transaction log backup: first, to store the data that has changed since the last transaction log backup or full database backup on a secure medium; second (and more importantly), to properly close the transaction log up to the beginning of the active portion of it. (The active portion of the transaction log contains all uncommitted transactions.)

Using a full database backup and a valid chain of all closed transaction logs, it is possible to propagate a database copy on a different computer. This database copy can then be used to replace the original database in case of a failure. (The same scenario can be established using a full database backup and the last differential backup.)

The Database Engine does not allow you to store the transaction log in the same file in which the database is stored. One reason for this is that if the file is damaged, the use of the transaction log to restore all changes since the last backup will not be possible.

Using a transaction log to record changes in the database is a common feature used by nearly all existing relational DBMSs. Nevertheless, situations may arise in which it becomes helpful to switch this feature off. For example, the execution of a heavy load can last for hours. Such a program runs much faster when the logging is switched off. On the other hand, switching off the logging process is dangerous, as it destroys the valid chain of transaction logs. To ensure successful database recovery, it is strongly recommended that you perform a full database backup after the successful end of the load.

One of the most common system failures occurs because the transaction log is filled up. Be aware that such a problem may cause a complete standstill of the system. If the storage used for the transaction log fills up to 100 percent, the system must stop all running transactions until the transaction log storage is freed again. This problem can be avoided only by making frequent backups of the transaction log: each time you close a portion of the actual transaction log and store it to a different storage media, that portion of the log becomes reusable, and the system thus regains disk space.

NOTE

A differential backup and a transaction log backup both minimize the time required to back up the database. But there is one significant difference between them: the transaction log backup contains all changes of a row that has been modified several times since the last backup, whereas a differential backup contains only the last modification of that row.

Some differences between log backups and differential backups are worth noting. The benefit of differential backups is that you save time in the restore process, because to recover a database completely, you need a full database backup and only the *latest* differential backup. If you use log backups for the same scenario, you have to apply a full database backup and *all* existing log backups to bring the database to a consistent state. A disadvantage of differential backups is that you cannot use them to recover data to a specific point in time, because they do not store intermediate changes to the database.

File or Filegroup Backup

File (or filegroup) backup allows you to back up specific database files (or filegroups) instead of the entire database. In this case, the Database Engine backs up only files you specify. Individual files (or filegroups) can be restored from a database backup, allowing recovery from a failure that affects only a small subset of the database files. You can use either a database backup or a filegroup backup to restore individual files or filegroups. This means that you can use database and transaction log backups as your backup procedure and still be able to restore individual files (or filegroups) from the database backup.

NOTE

File backup is also called file-level backup. This type of backup is recommended only when a database that should be backed up is very large and there is not enough time to perform a full database backup.

Performing Database Backup

You can perform backup operations using the following:

▶   Transact-SQL statements
▶   SQL Server Management Studio

Each of these backup methods is described in the following sections.

Backing Up Using Transact-SQL Statements

All types of backup operations can be executed using two Transact-SQL statements:

▶   BACKUP DATABASE
▶   BACKUP LOG

Before these two Transact-SQL statements are described, the existing types of backup devices will be explained.

Types of Backup Devices

The Database Engine allows you to back up databases, transaction logs, and files to the following backup devices:

▶   Disk
▶   Tape

NOTE

There is also another form of backup device called a network share. I will not describe it separately because it is simply a special form of a disk drive that specifies a network drive to use for backups.

Disk files are the most common media used for storing backups. Disk backup devices can be located on a server's local hard disk or on a remote disk on a shared network resource. The Database Engine allows you to append a new backup to a file that already contains backups from the same or different databases. By appending a new backup set to existing media, the previous contents of the media remain intact, and the new backup is written after the end of the last backup on the media. (The *backup set* includes all stored data of the object you chose to back up.) By default, the Database Engine always appends new backups to disk files.

CAUTION

Do not back up to a file on the same physical disk where the database or its transaction log is stored! If the disk with the database crashes, the backup that is stored on the same disk will also be damaged.

Tape backup devices are generally used in the same way as disk devices. However, when you back up to a tape, the tape drive must be attached locally to the system. The advantage of tape devices relative to disk devices is their simple administration and operation.

NOTE

Always verify the backup on a network to ensure that there are no possible network errors.

BACKUP DATABASE Statement

The BACKUP DATABASE statement is used to perform a full database backup or a differential database backup. This statement has the following syntax:

```
BACKUP DATABASE {db_name | @variable}
    TO device_list
    [MIRROR TO device_list2]
    [WITH | option_list]
```

db_name is the name of the database that should be backed up. (The name of the database can also be supplied using a variable, **@variable**.) **device_list** specifies one or more device names, where the database backup will be stored. **device_list** can be a list of names of disk files or tapes. The syntax for a device is

```
{ logical_device_name | @logical_device_name_var }
    | { DISK | TAPE } =  { 'physical_device_name' | @physical_device_
name_var }
```

where the device name can be either a logical name (or a variable) or a physical name beginning with the DISK or TAPE keyword. (The TAPE option will be removed in a future version of SQL Server.)

The MIRROR TO option indicates that the accompanying set of backup devices is a mirror within a mirrored media set. The backup devices must be identical in type and number to the devices specified in the TO clause. In a mirrored media set, all the backup devices must have the same properties. (See also the description of mirrored media in the section "Database Mirroring" later in this chapter.)

option_list comprises several options that can be specified for the different backup types. The most important options are the following:

- ► DIFFERENTIAL
- ► NOSKIP/SKIP
- ► NOINIT/INIT
- ► NOFORMAT/FORMAT
- ► UNLOAD/NOUNLOAD
- ► MEDIANAME and MEDIADESCRIPTION
- ► BLOCKSIZE
- ► COMPRESSION

The first option, DIFFERENTIAL, specifies a differential database backup. All other clauses in the list concern full database backups.

The SKIP option disables the backup set expiration and name checking, which is usually performed by BACKUP DATABASE to prevent overwrites of backup sets. The NOSKIP option, which is the default, instructs the BACKUP statement to check the expiration date and name of all backup sets before allowing them to be overwritten.

The INIT option is used to overwrite any existing data on the backup media. This option does not overwrite the media header, if one exists. If there is a backup that has not yet expired, the backup operation fails. In this case, use the combination of SKIP and INIT options to overwrite the backup device. The NOINIT option, which is the default, appends a backup to existing backups on the media.

The FORMAT option is used to write a header on all of the files (or tape volumes) that are used for a backup. Therefore, use this option to initialize a backup medium. When you use the FORMAT option to back up to a tape device, the INIT option and the SKIP option are implied. Similarly, the INIT option is implied if the FORMAT option is specified for a file device. NOFORMAT, which is the default, specifies that the backup operation processes the existing media header and backup sets on the media volumes.

The UNLOAD and NOUNLOAD options are performed only if the backup medium is a tape device. The UNLOAD option, which is the default, specifies that the tape is automatically rewound and unloaded from the tape device after the backup is completed. Use the NOUNLOAD option if the database system should not rewind (and unload) the tape from the tape device automatically.

MEDIADESCRIPTION and MEDIANAME specify the description and the name of the media set, respectively. The BLOCKSIZE option specifies the physical block size, in bytes. The supported sizes are 512, 1024, 2048, 4096, 8192, 16384, 32768, and 65536 (64KB) bytes. The default is 65536 bytes for tape devices and 512 bytes otherwise.

The Database Engine supports backup compression. To specify backup compression, use the COMPRESSION option of the BACKUP DATABASE statement. Example 16.1 backs up the **sample** database and compresses the backup file.

EXAMPLE 16.1

```
USE master;
BACKUP DATABASE sample
   TO DISK = 'C:\sample.bak'
   WITH INIT, COMPRESSION;
```

NOTE

If you get the "Access Denied" error for the C: \directory, change the storage location of the sample.bak file to another directory (tmp, for instance).

If you want to know whether the particular backup file is compressed, use the output of the RESTORE HEADERONLY statement, which is described later in this chapter.

BACKUP LOG Statement

The BACKUP LOG statement is used to perform a backup of the transaction log. This statement has the following syntax:

```
BACKUP LOG {db_name | @variable}
   TO device_list
     [MIRROR TO device_list2]
   [WITH option_list]
```

db_name, **@variable**, **device_list**, and **device_list2** have the same meanings as the parameters with the same names in the BACKUP DATABASE statement. **option_list** has the same options as the BACKUP DATABASE statement and also supports the specific log options NO_TRUNCATE, NORECOVERY, and STANDBY.

You should use the NO_TRUNCATE option if you want to back up the transaction log without truncating it—that is, this option does not clear the committed transactions in the log. After the execution of this option, the system writes all recent database activities in the transaction log. Therefore, the NO_TRUNCATE option allows you to recover data right up to the point of the database failure.

The NORECOVERY option backs up the tail of the log and leaves the database in the restoring state. NORECOVERY is useful when failing over to a secondary database or when saving the tail of the log before a restore operation. The STANDBY option backs up the tail of the log and leaves the database in a read-only and standby state. (The restore operation and the standby state are explained later in this chapter.)

Backing Up Using Management Studio

Before you can perform a database or transaction log backup, you must specify (or create) backup devices. SQL Server Management Studio allows you to create disk devices and tape devices in a similar manner. In both cases, expand the server, expand Server Objects, right-click Backup Devices, and choose New Backup Device. In the Backup Device dialog box (see Figure 16-1), enter the name of either the disk device

Figure 16-1 *The Backup Device dialog box*

(if you clicked File) or the tape device (if you clicked Tape). In the former case, you can click the ... button on the right side of the field to display existing backup device locations. In the latter case, if Tape cannot be activated, then no tape devices exist on the local computer.

After you specify backup devices, you can do a database backup. Expand the server, expand Databases, right-click the database, and choose Tasks | Back Up. The Back Up Database dialog box appears (see Figure 16-2). On the General page of the dialog box, choose the backup type in the Backup Type drop-down list (Full, Differential, or Transaction Log), enter the backup set name in the Name field, and optionally enter a description of this set in the Description field. In the same dialog box, you can choose an expiration date for the backup.

Figure 16-2 *The Back Up Database dialog box, General page*

In the Destination frame, select an existing device by clicking Add. (The Remove button allows you to remove one or more backup devices from the list of devices to be used.)

On the Options page (see Figure 16-3), to append to an existing backup on the selected device, click the Append to the Existing Backup Set radio button. Choosing the Overwrite All Existing Backup Sets radio button in the same frame overwrites any existing backups on the selected backup device.

For verification of the database backup, click Verify Backup when Finished in the Reliability frame. On the Options page, you can also choose to back up to a new media set by clicking the Back Up to a New Media Set, and Erase All Existing Backup Sets radio button and then entering the media set name and description.

Figure 16-3 *The Back Up Database dialog box, Options page*

For creation and verification of a differential database backup or transaction log backup, follow the same steps, but choose the corresponding backup type in the Backup Type field on the General page.

After you have chosen all your options, click OK. The database or the transaction log is then backed up. You can display the name, physical location, and the type of the backup devices by selecting the server, expanding the Server Objects folder, expanding the Backup Devices folder, and then selecting the particular file.

Scheduling Backups with Management Studio

A well-planned timetable for the scheduling of backup operations will help you avoid system shortages when users are working. SQL Server Management Studio supports this planning by offering an easy-to-use graphical interface for scheduling backups. Scheduling backups using SQL Server Management Studio is explained in detail in the following chapter.

Determining Which Databases to Back Up

The following databases should be backed up regularly:

► The **master** database

► All production databases

Backing Up the master Database

The **master** database is the most important system database because it contains information about all of the databases in the system. Therefore, you should back up the **master** database on a regular basis. Additionally, you should back up the **master** database anytime certain statements and stored procedures are executed, because the Database Engine modifies the **master** database automatically.

> **NOTE**
> You can perform full database backups of the **master** database only. (The system does not support differential, transaction log, and file backups for the **master** database.)

Many activities cause the modification of the **master** database. Some of them are listed here:

► The creation, alteration, and removal of a database

► The alteration of the transaction log

> **NOTE**
>
> *Without a backup of the **master** database, you must completely rebuild all system databases, because if the **master** database is damaged, all references to the existing user-defined databases are lost.*

Backing Up Production Databases

You should back up each production database on a regular basis. Additionally, you should back up any production database when the following activities are executed:

- ► After creating it
- ► After creating indices
- ► After clearing the transaction log
- ► After performing nonlogged operations

Always make a full database backup after it has been created, in case a failure occurs between the creation of the database and the first regular database backup. Remember that backups of the transaction log cannot be applied without a full database backup.

Backing up the database after creation of one or more indices saves time during the restore process, because the index structures are backed up together with the data. Backing up the transaction log after creation of indices does not save time during the restore process at all, because the transaction log records only the fact that an index was created (and does not record the modified index structure).

Backing up the database after clearing the transaction log is necessary because the transaction log no longer contains a record of database activity, which is used to recover the database. All operations that are not recorded to the transaction log are called nonlogged operations. Therefore, all changes made by these operations cannot be restored during the recovery process.

Performing Database Recovery

Whenever a transaction is submitted for execution, the Database Engine is responsible either for executing the transaction completely and recording its changes permanently in the database or for guaranteeing that the transaction has no effect at all on the database. This approach ensures that the database is consistent in case of a failure, because failures do not damage the database itself, but instead affect transactions that are in progress at the time of the failure. The Database Engine supports both automatic and manual recovery, which are discussed next in turn.

Automatic Recovery

Automatic recovery is a fault-tolerant feature that the Database Engine executes every time it is restarted after a failure or shutdown. The automatic recovery process checks to see if the restoration of databases is necessary. If it is, each database is returned to its last consistent state using the transaction log.

During automatic recovery, the Database Engine examines the transaction log from the last checkpoint to the point at which the system failed or was shut down. (A *checkpoint* is the most recent point at which all data changes are written permanently to the database from memory. Therefore, a checkpoint ensures the physical consistency of the data.) The transaction log contains committed transactions (transactions that are successfully executed, but their changes have not yet been written to the database) and uncommitted transactions (transactions that are not successfully executed before a shutdown or failure occurred). The Database Engine rolls forward all committed transactions, thus making permanent changes to the database, and undoes the part of the uncommitted transactions that occurred before the checkpoint.

The Database Engine first performs the automatic recovery of the **master** database, followed by the recovery of all other system databases. Then, all user-defined databases are recovered.

Manual Recovery

A manual recovery of a database specifies the application of the full backup of your database and subsequent application of all transaction logs in the sequence of their creation. (Alternatively, you can use the full database backup together with the last differential backup of the database.) After this, the database is in the same (consistent) state as it was at the point when the transaction log was backed up for the last time.

When you recover a database using a full database backup, the Database Engine first re-creates all database files and places them in the corresponding physical locations. After that, the system re-creates all database objects.

The Database Engine can process certain forms of recovery dynamically (in other words, while an instance of the database system is running). Dynamic recovery improves the availability of the system, because only the data being restored is unavailable. Dynamic recovery allows you to restore either an entire database file or a filegroup. (Microsoft calls dynamic recovery "online restore.")

Is My Backup Set Ready for Recovery?

After executing the BACKUP statement, the selected device (tape or disk) contains all data of the object you chose to back up. The stored data is called a *backup set*. Before you start a recovery process, you should be sure that

▶ The backup set contains the data you want to restore

▶ The backup set is usable

The Database Engine supports a set of Transact-SQL statements that allows you to confirm that the backup set is usable and contains the proper data. The following four statements, among others, belong to it:

▶ RESTORE LABELONLY

▶ RESTORE HEADERONLY

▶ RESTORE FILELISTONLY

▶ RESTORE VERIFYONLY

The following subsection describes these statements.

RESTORE LABELONLY   This statement is used to display the header information of the media (disk or tape) used for a backup process. The output of the RESTORE LABELONLY statement is a single row that contains the summary of the header information (name of the media, description of the backup process, and date of a backup process).

NOTE

RESTORE LABELONLY reads just the header file, so use this statement if you want to get a quick look at what your backup set contains.

RESTORE HEADERONLY   Whereas the RESTORE LABELONLY statement gives you concise information about the header file of your backup device, the RESTORE HEADERONLY statement gives you information about backups that are stored on a backup device. This statement displays a one-line summary for each backup on a backup device. In contrast to RESTORE LABELONLY, using RESTORE HEADERONLY can be time consuming if the device contains several backups.

The output of RESTORE HEADERONLY contains a **Compressed** column, which tells you whether the backup file is compressed (value 1) or not.

RESTORE FILELISTONLY   The RESTORE FILELISTONLY statement returns a result set with a list of the database and log files contained in the backup set. You can display information about only one backup set at a time. For this reason, if the specified backup device contains several backups, you have to specify the position of the backup set to be processed.

You should use RESTORE FILELISTONLY if you don't know exactly either which backup sets exist or where the files of a particular backup set are stored. In both cases, you can check all or part of the devices to make a global picture of existing backups.

RESTORE VERIFYONLY   After you have found your backup, you can do the next step: verify the backup without using it for the restore process. You can do the verification with the RESTORE VERIFYONLY statement, which checks the existence of all backup devices (tapes or files) and whether the existing information can be read.

In contrast to the previous three statements, RESTORE VERIFYONLY supports two specific options:

▶ **LOADHISTORY**   Causes the backup information to be added to the backup history tables

▶ **STATS**   Displays a message each time another percentage of the reading process completes, and is used to gauge progress (the default value is 10)

Restoring Databases and Logs Using Transact-SQL Statements

All restore operations can be executed using two Transact-SQL statements:

▶ RESTORE DATABASE

▶ RESTORE LOG

The RESTORE DATABASE statement is used to perform the restore process for a database. The general syntax of this statement is

```
RESTORE DATABASE {db_name | @variable}
    [FROM device_list]
    [WITH option_list]
```

db_name is the name of the database that will be restored. (The name of the database can be supplied using a variable, **@variable**.) **device_list** specifies one or more names of devices on which the database backup is stored. (If you do not specify the FROM clause, only the process of automatic recovery takes place, not the restore of a backup, and you must specify either the RECOVERY, NORECOVERY, or STANDBY option. This action can take place if you want to switch over to a standby server.) **device_list** can be a list of names of disk files or tapes. **option_list** comprises several options that can be specified for the different backup forms. The most important options are

- ▶ RECOVERY/NORECOVERY/STANDBY
- ▶ CHECKSUM/NO_CHECKSUM
- ▶ REPLACE
- ▶ PARTIAL
- ▶ STOPAT
- ▶ STOPATMARK
- ▶ STOPBEFOREMARK

The RECOVERY option instructs the Database Engine to roll forward any committed transaction and to roll back any uncommitted transaction. After the RECOVERY option is applied, the database is in a consistent state and is ready for use. This option is the default.

NOTE

Use the RECOVERY option either with the last transaction log to be restored or to restore with a full database backup without subsequent transaction log backups.

With the NORECOVERY option, the Database Engine does not roll back uncommitted transactions because you will be applying further backups. After the NORECOVERY option is applied, the database is unavailable for use.

NOTE

Use the NORECOVERY option with all but the last transaction log to be restored.

The STANDBY option is an alternative to the RECOVERY and NORECOVERY options and is used with the standby server. (The standby server is discussed later, in the section "Using a Standby Server.") In order to access data stored on the standby server, you usually recover the database after a transaction log is restored. On the other hand, if you recover the database on the standby server, you cannot apply additional logs from the production server for the restore process. In that case, you use the STANDBY option to allow users read access to the standby server. Additionally, you allow the system to restore additional transaction logs. The STANDBY option implies the existence of the undo file that is used to roll back changes when additional logs are restored.

The CHECKSUM option initiates the verification of both the backup checksums and page checksums, if present. If checksums are absent, RESTORE proceeds without verification. The NO_CHECKSUM option explicitly disables the validation of checksums by the restore operation.

The REPLACE option replaces an existing database with data from a backup of a different database. In this case, the existing database is first destroyed, and the differences regarding the names of the files in the database and the database name are ignored. (If you do not use the REPLACE option, the database system performs a safety check that guarantees an existing database is not replaced if the names of files in the database, or the database name itself, differ from the corresponding names in the backup set.)

The PARTIAL option specifies a partial restore operation. With this option you can restore a portion of a database, consisting of its primary filegroup and one or more secondary filegroups, which are specified in an additional option called FILEGROUP. (The PARTIAL option is not allowed with the RESTORE LOG statement.)

The STOPAT option allows you to restore a database to the state it was in at the exact moment before a failure occurred by specifying a point in time. The Database Engine restores all committed transactions that were recorded in the transaction log before the specified point in time. If you want to restore a database by specifying a point in time, execute the RESTORE DATABASE statement using the NORECOVERY clause. After that, execute the RESTORE LOG statement to apply each transaction log backup, specifying the name of the database, the backup device from which the transaction log backup will be restored, and the STOPAT clause. (If the backup of a log does not contain the requested time, the database will not be recovered.)

The STOPATMARK and STOPBEFOREMARK options specify to recover to a mark. This topic is described a bit later, in the section "Recovering to a Mark."

The RESTORE DATABASE statement is also used to restore a database from a differential backup. The syntax and the options for restoring a differential backup are the same as for restoring from a full database backup. During a restoration from a differential backup, the Database Engine restores only that part of the database that has changed since the last full database backup. Therefore, restore the full database backup *before* you restore a differential backup!

The RESTORE LOG statement is used to perform a restore process for a transaction log. This statement has the same syntax form and the same options as the RESTORE DATABASE statement.

Restoring Databases and Logs Using Management Studio

To restore a database from a full database backup, expand the server, choose Databases, right-click the database, and choose Tasks | Restore | Database. The Restore Database dialog box appears (see Figure 16-4). On the General page, select databases to which and from which you want to restore. Then check the backup set that you want to use for your backup process.

> **NOTE**
>
> *If you restore from the log backup, do not forget the sequence of restoring different types of backups. First restore the full database backup. Then restore all corresponding transaction logs in the sequence of their creation.*

Figure 16-4   *The Restore Database dialog box, General page*

Figure 16-5   *The Restore Database dialog box, Options page*

To select the appropriate restore options, choose the Options page (see Figure 16-5) of the Restore Database dialog box. In the upper part of the window, choose one or more restore types. In the lower part of the window, you can choose one of the three existing options. Choosing the first option, Leave the Database Ready to Use by Rolling Back Uncommitted Transactions, instructs the Database Engine to roll forward any committed transaction and to roll back any uncommitted transaction. After applying this option, the database is in a consistent state and is ready for use. This option is equivalent to the RECOVERY option of the RESTORE DATABASE statement.

NOTE

Use this option only with the last transaction log to be restored or with a full database restore when no subsequent transaction logs need to be applied.

If you click the second option, Leave the Database Non-operational, and Do Not Roll Back Uncommitted Transactions, the Database Engine does not roll back uncommitted transactions because you will be applying further backups. After you apply this option, the database is unavailable for use, and additional transaction logs should be restored. This option is equivalent to the NORECOVERY option of the RESTORE DATABASE statement.

NOTE

Use this option with all but the last transaction log to be restored or with a differential database restore.

Choosing the third option, Leave the Database in Read-only Mode, specifies the file (in the Standby File text box) that is subsequently used to roll back the recovery effects. This option is equivalent to the STANDBY option in the RESTORE DATABASE statement.

The process of a database restoration from a differential database backup is equivalent to the process of a restoration from a full database backup. In this case, you have to check Differential Database Backup as the backup type in the Restore Database dialog box. The only difference to restoration with the full database backup is that only the first option in the lower half of the Options page (Leave the Database Ready to Use by Rolling Back Uncommitted Transactions) can be applied to the restoration from a differential database backup.

NOTE

If you restore from a differential backup, first restore the full database backup before you restore the corresponding differential one. In contrast to transaction log backups, only the latest differential backup is applied, because it includes all changes since the full backup.

To restore a database with a new name, expand Databases, right-click the database, and choose Tasks | Restore | Database. On the General page of the Restore Database dialog box, in the To Database drop-down box enter the name of the database you want to create, and in the From Database drop-down box enter the name of the database whose backup is used.

Recovering to a Mark

The Database Engine allows you to use the transaction log to recover to a specific mark. Log marks correspond to a specific transaction and are inserted only if the transaction commits. This allows the marks to be tied to a particular amount of work and provides the ability to recover to a point that includes or excludes this work.

NOTE

If a marked transaction spans multiple databases on the same database server, the marks are recorded in the logs of all the affected databases.

The BEGIN TRANSACTION statement supports the WITH MARK clause to insert marks into the logs. Because the name of the mark is the same as its transaction, a transaction name is required. (The **description** option specifies a textual description of the mark.)

The transaction log records the mark name, description, database, user, date and time information, and the log sequence number (LSN). To allow their reuse, the transaction names are not required to be unique. The date and time information is used along with the name to uniquely identify the mark.

You can use the RESTORE LOG statement (with either the STOPATMARK clause or the STOPBEFOREMARK clause) to specify recovering to a mark. The STOPATMARK clause causes the recovery process to roll forward to the mark and include the transaction that contains the mark. If you specify the STOPBEFOREMARK clause, the recovery process excludes the transaction that contains the mark.

Both clauses just described support AFTER **datetime**. If this option is omitted, recovery stops at the first mark with the specified name. If the option is specified, recovery stops at the first mark with the specified name exactly at or after **datetime**.

Restoring the master Database

The corruption of the **master** system database can be devastating for the whole system because it comprises all system tables that are necessary to work with the database system. The restore process for the **master** database is quite different from the same process for user-defined databases.

A damaged **master** database makes itself known through different failures. These failures include the following:

▶ Inability to start the MSSQLSERVER process

▶ An input/output error

▶ Execution of the DBCC command points to such a failure

Two different ways exist to restore the **master** database. The easier way, which is available only if you can start your database system, is to restore the **master** database from the full database backup. If you can't start your system, then you must go the more difficult route and use the **sqlservr** command.

To restore your **master** database, start your instance in single-user mode. Of the two ways to do it, my favorite is to use the command window and execute the **sqlservr** command (from the command prompt) with the option **–m**. Although the use of this command is more difficult, this approach allows you to restore the **master** database in the most cases. In the second step, you restore the **master** database together with all other databases using the last full database backup.

NOTE

*If there have been any changes to the **master** database since the last full database backup, you will need to re-create those changes manually.*

Restoring Other System Databases

The restore process for all system databases other than **master** is similar. Therefore, I will explain this process using the **msdb** database. The **msdb** database needs to be restored from a backup when either the **master** database has been rebuilt or the **msdb** database itself has been damaged. If the **msdb** database is damaged, restore it using the existing backups. If there have been any changes after the **msdb** database backup was created, re-create those changes manually. (You can find the description of the **msdb** system database in Chapter 15.)

NOTE

*You cannot restore a database that is being accessed by users. Therefore, when restoring the **msdb** database, the SQL Server Agent service should be stopped. (SQL Server Agent accesses the **msdb** database.)*

Recovery Models

A recovery model allows you to control to what extent you are ready to risk losing committed transactions if a database is damaged. It also determines the speed and size of your transaction log backups. Additionally, the choice of a recovery model has an impact on the size of the transaction log and therefore on the time period needed to back up the log. The Database Engine supports three recovery models:

- ▶ Full
- ▶ Bulk-logged
- ▶ Simple

The following sections describe these recovery models.

Full Recovery Model

During full recovery, all operations are written to the transaction log. Therefore, this model provides complete protection against media failure. This means that you can restore your database up to the last committed transaction that is stored in the log file. Additionally, you can recover data to any point in time (prior to the point of failure). To guarantee this, such operations as SELECT INTO and the execution of the **bcp** utility are fully logged too.

Besides point-in-time recovery, the full recovery model allows you also to recover to a log mark. Log marks correspond to a specific transaction and are inserted only if the transaction commits.

The full recovery model also logs all operations concerning the CREATE INDEX statement, implying that the process of data recovery now includes the restoration of index creations. That way, the re-creation of the indices is faster, because you do not have to rebuild them separately.

The disadvantage of this recovery model is that the corresponding transaction log may be very voluminous and the files on the disk containing the log will be filled up very quickly. Also, for such a voluminous log, you will need significantly more time for backup.

NOTE

If you use the full recovery model, the transaction log must be protected from media failure. For this reason, using RAID 1 to protect transaction logs is strongly recommended. (RAID 1 is explained in the section "Using RAID Technology" later in this chapter.)

Bulk-Logged Recovery Model

Bulk-logged recovery supports log backups by using minimal space in the transaction log for certain large-scale or bulk operations. The logging of the following operations is minimal and cannot be controlled on an operation-by-operation basis:

► SELECT INTO

► CREATE INDEX (including indexed views)

► **bcp** utility and BULK INSERT

Although bulk operations are not fully logged, you do not have to perform a full database backup after the completion of such an operation. During bulk-logged recovery, transaction log backups contain both the log and the results of a bulk operation. This simplifies the transition between full and bulk-logged recovery models.

The bulk-logged recovery model allows you to recover a database to the end of a transaction log backup (that is, up to the last committed transaction). Additionally, you can restore your database to any point in time if you haven't performed any bulk operations. The same is true for the restore operation to a named log mark.

The advantage of the bulk-logged recovery model is that bulk operations are performed much faster than under the full recovery model, because they are not fully logged. On the other side, the Database Engine backs up all the modified extents, together with the log itself. Therefore, the log backup needs a lot more space than in the case of the full recovery. (The time to restore a log backup is significantly increased, too.)

Simple Recovery Model

In the simple recovery model, the transaction log is truncated whenever a checkpoint occurs. Therefore, you can recover a damaged database only by using the full database backup or the differential backup, because they do not require log backups. Backup strategy for this model is very simple: restore the database using existing database backups and, if differential backups exist, apply the most recent one.

NOTE

The simple recovery model doesn't mean that there is no logging at all. The log content won't be used for backup purposes, but it is used at the checkpoint time, where all the transactions in the log are committed or rolled back.

The advantages of the simple recovery model are that the performance of all bulk operations is very high and requirements for the log space are very small. On the other hand, this model requires the most manual work because all changes since the most recent database (or differential) backup must be redone. Point-in-time and page restore are not allowed with this recovery model. Also, file restore is available only for read-only secondary filegroups.

NOTE

Do not use the simple recovery model for production databases.

Changing and Editing a Recovery Model

You can change the recovery model by using the RECOVERY option of the ALTER DATABASE statement. The part of the syntax of the ALTER DATABASE statement concerning recovery models is

```
SET RECOVERY [FULL | BULK_LOGGED | SIMPLE]
```

There are two ways in which you can edit the current recovery model of your database:

▶ Using the **databasepropertyex** property function
▶ Using the **sys.databases** catalog view

If you want to display the current model of your database, use the recovery value for the second parameter of the **databaseproperty** function. Example 16.2 shows the query that displays the recovery model for the **sample** database. (The function displays one of the values FULL, BULK_LOGGED, or SIMPLE.)

EXAMPLE 16.2

```
SELECT databasepropertyex('sample', 'recovery')
```

The **recovery_model_desc** column of the **sys.databases** catalog view displays the same information as the **databasepropertyex** function, as Example 16.3 shows.

EXAMPLE 16.3

```
SELECT name, database_id, recovery_model_desc AS model
       FROM sys.databases
       WHERE name = 'sample'
```

The result is

name	database_id	model
sample	7	FULL

System Availability

Ensuring the availability of your database system and databases is one of the most important issues today. There are several techniques that you can use to ensure their availability, which can be divided in two groups: those that are components of the Database Engine and those that are not implemented in the database server. The following two techniques are not part of the Database Engine:

▶ Using a standby server
▶ Using RAID technology

The following techniques belong to the database system:

- Failover clustering
- Database mirroring
- Log shipping
- High availability and disaster recovery (HADR)
- Replication

The following sections describe these techniques, other than replication, which is discussed in Chapter 18.

Using a Standby Server

A standby server is just what its name implies—another server that is standing by in case something happens to the production server (also called the primary server). The standby server contains files, databases (system and user-defined), and user accounts identical to those on the production server.

A standby server is implemented by initially restoring a full database backup of the database and applying transaction log backups to keep the database on the standby server synchronized with the production server. To set up a standby server, set the **read only** database option to true. This option prevents users from performing any write operations in the database.

The general steps to use a copy of a production database are as follows:

- Restore the production database using the RESTORE DATABASE statement with the STANDBY clause.
- Apply each transaction log to the standby server using the RESTORE LOG statement with the STANDBY clause.
- When applying the final transaction log backup, use the RESTORE LOG statement with the RECOVERY clause. (This final statement recovers the database without creating a file with before images, making the database available for write operations, too.)

After the database and transaction logs are restored, users can work with an exact copy of the production database. Only the noncommitted transactions at the time of failure will be permanently lost.

NOTE

If the production server fails, user processes are not automatically brought to the standby server. Additionally, all user processes need to restart any tasks with the uncommitted transactions due to the failure of the production server.

Using RAID Technology

RAID (redundant array of inexpensive disks) is a special disk configuration in which multiple disk drives build a single logical unit. This process allows files to span multiple disk devices. RAID technology provides improved reliability at the cost of performance decrease. Generally, there are six RAID levels, 0 through 5. Only three of these levels, levels 0, 1, and 5, are significant for database systems.

RAID can be hardware or software based. Hardware-based RAID is more costly (because you have to buy additional disk controllers), but it usually performs better. Software-based RAID can be supported usually by the operating system. Windows operating systems provide RAID levels 0, 1, and 5. RAID technology has impacts on the following features:

▶ Fault tolerance

▶ Performance

The benefits and disadvantages of each RAID level in relation to these two features are explained next.

RAID provides protection from hard disk failure and accompanying data loss with three methods: disk striping, mirroring, and parity. These three methods correspond to RAID levels 0, 1, and 5, respectively.

RAID 0 (Disk Striping)

RAID 0 specifies disk striping without parity. Using RAID 0, the data is written across several disk drives in order to allow data access more readily, and all read and write operations can be speeded up. For this reason, RAID 0 is the fastest RAID configuration. The disadvantage of disk striping is that it does not offer fault tolerance at all. This means that if one disk fails, all the data on that array become inaccessible.

RAID 1 (Mirroring)

Mirroring is the special form of disk striping that uses the space on a disk drive to maintain a duplicate copy of all files. Therefore, RAID 1, which specifies disk mirroring, protects data against media failure by maintaining a copy of the database (or a part of it) on another disk. If there is a drive loss with mirroring in place, the files for the lost drive can be rebuilt by replacing the failed drive and rebuilding the damaged files. The hardware configurations of mirroring are more expensive, but they provide additional speed. (Also, hardware configurations of mirroring implement some caching options that provide better throughput.) The advantage of the Windows solution for mirroring is that it can be configured to mirror disk partitions, while the hardware solutions are usually implemented on the entire disk.

In contrast to RAID 0, RAID 1 is much slower, but the reliability is higher. Also, RAID 1 costs much more than RAID 0 because each mirrored disk drive must be doubled. It can sustain at least one failed drive and may be able to survive failure of up to half the drives in the set of mirrored disks without forcing the system administrator to shut down the server and recover from file backup. (RAID 1 is the best-performing RAID option when fault tolerance is required.)

Mirroring also has performance impacts in relation to read and write operations. When mirroring is used, write operations decrease performance, because each such operation costs two disk I/O operations, one to the original and one to the mirrored disk drive. On the other hand, mirroring increases performance of read operations, because the system will be able to read from either disk drive, depending on which one is least busy at the time.

RAID 5 (Parity)

Parity is implemented by calculating recovery information about data written to disk and writing that parity information on the other drives that form the RAID array. If a drive fails, a new drive is inserted into the RAID array and the data on that failed drive is recovered by taking the recovery information (parity) written on the other drives and using this information to regenerate the data from the failed drive.

The advantage of parity is that you need one additional disk drive to protect any number of existing disk drives. The disadvantages of parity concern performance and fault tolerance. Due to the additional costs associated with calculating and writing parity, additional disk I/O operations are required. (Read I/O operation costs are the same for mirroring and parity.) Also, using parity, you can sustain only one failed drive before the array must be taken offline and recovery from backup media must be performed. Because disk striping with parity requires additional costs associated with calculating and writing parity, RAID 5 requires four disk I/O operations, whereas RAID 0 requires only one operation and RAID 1 two operations.

Database Mirroring

As you already know, mirroring can be supported through hardware or software. The advantage of the software support for mirroring is that it can be configured to mirror disk partitions, while the hardware solutions are usually implemented on the entire disk. This section discusses the Windows solution for database mirroring and how you can set it up.

To set up database mirroring, use two servers with a database that will be mirrored from one server to the other. The former is called the principal server, while the latter is called the mirrored server. (The copy of the database on the mirrored server is called the mirrored database.)

Database mirroring allows continuous streaming of the transaction log from the principal server to the mirrored server. The copy of the transaction log activity is written to the log of the mirrored database, and the transactions are executed on it. If the principal server becomes unavailable, applications can reconnect to the database on the mirrored server without waiting for recovery to finish. Unlike failover clustering, the mirrored server is fully cached and ready to accept workloads because of its synchronized state. It is possible to implement up to four mirrored backup sets. (To implement mirroring, use the MIRROR TO option of either the BACKUP DATABASE statement or the BACKUP LOG statement.)

There is also the third server, called the witness server. It determines which server is the principal server and which is the mirrored server. This server is only needed when automatic failover is required. (To enable automatic failover, you must turn on the synchronous operating mode—that is, set the SAFETY option of the ALTER DATABASE statement to FULL.)

Another performance issue in relation to database mirroring is the possibility to automatically compress the data sent to the mirror. The Database Engine compresses the stream data if at least a 12.5 percent compression ratio can be achieved. That way, the system reduces the consumption of log data that is sent from the principal server to mirrored server(s).

Failover Clustering

Failover clustering is a process in which the operating system and database system work together to provide availability in the event of failures. A failover cluster consists of a group of redundant servers, called nodes, that share an external disk system. When a node within the cluster fails, the instance of the Database Engine on that machine shuts down. Microsoft Cluster Service transfers resources from a failing machine to an equally configured target node automatically. The transfer of resources from one node to the other node in a cluster occurs very quickly.

The advantage of failover clustering is that it protects your system against hardware failures, because it provides a mechanism to automatically restart the database system on another node of the cluster. On the other hand, this technology has a single point of failure in the set of disks, which cluster nodes share and cannot protect from data errors. Another disadvantage of this technology is that it does not increase performance or scalability. In other words, an application cannot scale any further on a cluster than it can on one node.

In summary, failover clustering provides server redundancy, but it doesn't provide data file redundancy. On the other side, database mirroring doesn't provide server redundancy, but provides both database redundancy and data file redundancy.

Log Shipping

Log shipping allows the transaction logs from one database to be constantly sent and used by another database. This allows you to have a warm standby server and also provides a way to offload data from the source machine to read-only destination computers. The target database is an exact copy of the primary database, because the former receives all changes from the latter. You have the ability to make the target database a new primary database if the primary server, which hosts the original database, becomes unavailable. When the primary server becomes available again, you can reverse the server roles again.

Log shipping does not support automatic failover. Therefore, if the source database server fails, you must recover the target database yourself, either manually or through custom code.

In summary, log shipping is similar to database mirroring in that it provides database redundancy. On the other hand, database mirroring significantly extends the capabilities of log shipping because it allows you to update the target database through a direct connection and in real time.

High-Availability and Disaster Recovery (HADR)

Database mirroring as a technique to achieve high availability has several drawbacks:

▶ Read-only queries cannot by executed against the mirror.

▶ The technique can be applied only on two instances of SQL Server.

▶ The technique mirrors only the objects inside the database; objects such as logins cannot be protect using mirroring.

To overcome these drawbacks of database mirroring, SQL Server 2012 introduces a new technique called high availability and disaster recovery (HADR). HADR allows you to maximize availability for your databases. Before I explain how HADR works, I will discuss the concept of availability groups, replicas, and modes.

Availability Groups, Replicas, and Modes

An *availability group* comprises a set of failover servers called *availability replicas*. Each availability replica has a local copy of each of the databases in the availability group. One of these replicas, called the *primary replica*, maintains the primary copy of each database. The primary replica makes these databases, called *primary databases*, available to users for read-write access. For each primary database, another availability replica, known as a *secondary replica*, maintains a failover copy of the database, known as a *secondary database*.

Availability replicas can be hosted only by instances of SQL Server 2012 that reside on Windows Server Failover Clustering (WSFC) nodes. The SQL Server instances can be either failover cluster instances or stand-alone instances. The server instance on which the primary replica is located is known as the *primary location*. An instance on which a secondary replica is located is known as a *secondary location*. The instances that host availability replicas for a given availability group must reside on separate WSFC nodes.

The *availability mode* is a property that is set independently for each availability replica. The availability mode of a secondary replica determines whether the primary replica waits to commit transactions on a database until the secondary replica has written the records in the corresponding transaction logs to disk.

Each replica within an availability group is assigned one of the following roles:

- ▶ Primary role
- ▶ Secondary role
- ▶ Resolving role

The current primary replica has the primary role. (At a given time, only one replica can have this role.) Each secondary replica has the secondary role. The resolving role indicates that the current status of an availability replica is changing.

Within a session, the primary and secondary roles are potentially interchangeable, in a process known as *role switching*. Role switching involves a failover that transfers the primary role to the secondary replica. The process transitions the role of the secondary replica to primary and vice versa. The database of the new primary replica becomes the new primary database. When the former primary replica becomes available, its database becomes a secondary database.

Configuration of HADR

The configuration of HADR is very complex, because, as a prerequisite, you have to create a two-node cluster, the description of which is beyond the scope of this book. For this reason, I will give just a brief description of the necessary steps.

To configure HADR, you have to execute the following steps (in the given order):

1. Install the database instances on both nodes.
2. Enable the HADR feature on both instances. Choose SQL Server Configuration Manager | SQL Server Services, right-click the instance, and choose Properties. On the SQL HADR tab, check Enable SQL HADR Service.
3. Create an availability group in the primary instance. Expand the Management folder in Management Studio, right-click Availability Groups, and choose New Availability Group.
4. Start data synchronization. Click the Start Data Synchronization button on the Results page of the New Availability Group dialog box.
5. Test the availability groups. Create a table on the primary replica, using the ON PRIMARY clause in the CREATE TABLE statement, and insert some rows.
6. Test the failover. Choose Management | Availability Groups | AVG | Availability Replicas, right-click the secondary replica, and choose Force Failover. After that, the roles of the secondary and primary replicas should be interchanged.

NOTE

The detailed description of HADR can be found in Books Online and at the following URLs: www.brentozar .com/archive/2010/11/sql-server-denali-database-mirroring-rocks/ and www.7388.info/index.php/article/ sql/2011-01-17/5235.html.

Maintenance Plan Wizard

The Maintenance Plan Wizard provides you with the set of basic tasks needed to maintain a database. It ensures that your database performs well, is regularly backed up, and is free of inconsistencies.

NOTE

*To create or manage maintenance plans, you have to be a member of the **sysadmin** fixed server role.*

To start the Maintenance Plan Wizard, expand the server in SQL Server Management Studio, expand Management, right-click Maintenance Plans, and choose Maintenance Plan Wizard. As you can see on the starting page of the Maintenance Plan Wizard, you can perform the following administration tasks:

▶ Check database integrity
▶ Perform index maintenance

▶ Update database statistics

▶ Perform database backups

NOTE

I will show you how to use the Maintenance Plan Wizard to perform database backups. All other tasks can be performed in a similar manner.

Click Next on the starting page, and the next wizard page, Select Plan Properties (see Figure 16-6), enables you to select properties for your plan, enter the plan's name, and, optionally, describe the plan. Also, you can choose between separate schedules for each task or a single schedule for the entire plan. This example will perform the backup of the **sample** database, so name the plan **Backup-sample** and choose the Single Schedule for the Entire Plan radio button. The Schedule field allows you to create a schedule for the execution of the plan or to execute it on demand. (Chapter 17 describes in detail how you can create such a schedule. For purposes of this example, leave the Schedule field set to Not Scheduled (On Demand).)

Click Next, and the wizard enables you to choose between full, differential, and transaction log backups. (For the description of these options, see "Introduction to

Figure 16-6 *The Select Plan Properties wizard page*

Backup Methods" at the beginning of this chapter.) Check Back Up Database (Full) and click Next, which opens the Select Maintenance Task Order page. You can then specify the order in which the tasks should be performed. (In this case, there is no order, because there is only one task to be performed.) Click Next, and the Back Up Database Full page appears.

The next page, Define Back Up Database (Full) Task, enables you to specify several different options, as shown in Figure 16-7. First, select the database(s) on which the task

Figure 16-7   *The Define Back Up Database (Full) Task wizard page*

should be performed. Then, select a destination for the backup files. The destination includes the media type and their location. (You can also specify an expiration date for your backup set.)

The next option, Create a Backup File for Every Database, allows you to create a separate file for each database you have specified in the Database(s) drop-down list box. Click this radio button, because this is the preferred way to maintain the backup of several databases. Check the last option, Verify Backup Integrity, so that the Database Engine checks the integrity of the backup files. Click Next to continue.

The Select Report Options wizard page allows you to write a report to a specific file and/or send an e-mail message. An e-mail message can be sent only to an existing operator. (Chapter 17 describes in detail how you can create an operator.)

To complete the wizard, click Finish. The wizard performs the task and creates a corresponding report.

To view the history of an existing maintenance plan, expand Management, expand Maintenance Plans, right-click the name of the plan, and choose View History. The Log File Viewer with the history of the selected plan is shown.

Summary

The system administrator or database owner should periodically make a backup copy of the database and its transaction log. The Database Engine enables you to make two kinds of backup copies of the database: full and differential. A full backup captures the state of the database at the time the statement is issued and copies it to the backup media (file or tape device). A differential backup copies the parts of the database that have changed since the last full database backup. The benefit of the differential backup is that it completes more rapidly than the full database backup for the same database. (There is also a transaction log backup, which copies transaction logs to a backup media.)

The Database Engine performs automatic recovery each time a system failure occurs that does not cause any media failure. (Automatic recovery is also performed when the system is started after each shutdown of the system.) During automatic recovery, any committed transaction found in the transaction log is written to the database, and any uncommitted transaction is rolled back. After any media failure, it may be necessary to manually recover the database from the archived copy of it and its transaction logs. To recover a database, a full database backup and only the latest differential backup must be used. If you use transaction logs to restore a database, use the full database backup first and then apply all existing transaction logs in the sequence of their creation to bring the database to the consistent state that it was in before the last transaction log backup was created.

The Database Engine supports several proprietary techniques that are used to enhance the availability of database systems and databases:

▶ Failover clustering

▶ Database mirroring

▶ Log shipping

▶ High availability and disaster recovery (HADR)

In relation to these techniques, there are three important issues:

▶ Server redundancy

▶ Database redundancy

▶ Data file redundancy

Server redundancy means that an application runs on two or more servers in such a way to provide fault tolerance. (Clustering is one of the most important server redundancy technologies.) Database redundancy means that a fault tolerance is guaranteed for a database with all its applications. (Data file redundancy is defined similarly.)

Failover clustering provides server redundancy, but doesn't provide database and data file redundancy. Log shipping provides database redundancy, but doesn't provide server redundancy. The disadvantage of log shipping is that it doesn't provide automatic failover.

Database mirroring doesn't provide server redundancy, but provides both database redundancy and data file redundancy. Database mirroring significantly extends the capabilities of log shipping, because it allows you to update the target database through a direct connection and in real time.

HADR is similar to database mirroring, but supports clustering, too. Thus, HADR provides server redundancy as well as database and data file redundancy. The primary goal of HADR is to support database availability while also giving you the benefits of disaster recovery.

The Maintenance Plan Wizard is a general tool, which you can use for set of basic tasks needed to maintain a database. It ensures that your database regularly backed up, and therefore free of inconsistencies. (We describe it in this chapter, because the wizard is usually used in relation to backup and restore operations.)

The next chapter describes all the system features that allow you to automate system administration tasks.

Exercises

E.16.1

Discuss the differences between the differential backup and transaction log backup.

E.16.2

When should you back up your production database?

E.16.3

How can you make a differential backup of the **master** database?

E.16.4

Discuss the use of different RAID technologies with regard to fault tolerance of a database and its transaction log.

E.16.5

What are the main differences between manual and automatic recovery?

E.16.6

Which statement should you use to verify your backup, without using it for the restore process?

E.16.7

Discuss the advantages and disadvantages of the three recovery models.

E.16.8

Discuss the similarities and differences between failover clustering, database mirroring, and log shipping.

Chapter 17

Automating System Administration Tasks

In This Chapter

▶ **Starting SQL Server Agent**
▶ **Creating Jobs and Operators**
▶ **Alerts**

One of the most important advantages of the Database Engine in relation to other relational DBMSs is its capability to automate administrative tasks and hence to reduce costs. The following are examples of some important tasks that are performed frequently and therefore could be automated:

▶ Backing up the database and transaction log

▶ Transferring data

▶ Dropping and re-creating indices

▶ Checking data integrity

You can automate all these tasks so that they occur on a regular schedule. For example, you can set the database backup task to occur every Friday at 8:00 p.m. and the transaction log backup task to occur daily at 10:00 p.m.

The components of the Database Engine that are used in automation processes include the following:

▶ SQL Server service (MSSQLSERVER)

▶ Windows Application log

▶ SQL Server Agent service

Why does the Database Engine need these three components to automate processes? In relation to automation of administration tasks, the MSSQLSERVER service is needed to write events to the Windows Application log. Some events are written automatically, and some must be raised by the system administrator (see the detailed explanation later in this chapter).

The Windows Application log is where all application and system messages of Windows operating systems and messages of their components are written. The role of the Windows Application log in the automation process is to notify SQL Server Agent about existing events.

SQL Server Agent is another service that connects to the Windows Application log and the MSSQLSERVER service. The role of SQL Server Agent in the automation process is to take an action after a notification through the Windows Application log. The action can be performed in connection with the MSSQLSERVER service or some other application. Figure 17-1 shows how these three components work together.

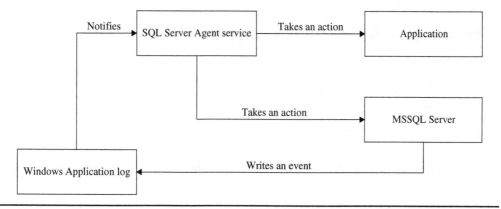

Figure 17-1 *SQL Server automation components*

Starting SQL Server Agent

SQL Server Agent executes jobs and fires alerts. As you will see in the upcoming sections, jobs and alerts are defined separately and can be executed independently. Nevertheless, jobs and alerts may also be complementary processes, because a job can invoke an alert and vice versa.

Consider an example: A job is executed to inform the system administrator about an unexpected filling of the transaction log that exceeds a tolerable limit. When this event occurs, the associated alert is invoked and, as a reaction, the system administrator may be notified by e-mail or pager.

Another critical event is a failure in backing up the transaction log. When this happens, the associated alert may invoke a job that truncates the transaction log. This reaction will be appropriate if the reason for the backup failure is an overflow (filling up) of the transaction log. In other cases (for example, the target device for the backup copy is full), such a truncation will have no effect. This example shows the close connection that may exist between events that have similar symptoms.

SQL Server Agent allows you to automate different administrative tasks. Before you can do this, the process has to be started. To start SQL Server Agent, right-click SQL Server Agent and choose Start.

As already stated, the invocation of an alert can also include the notification of one or more operators by e-mail using Database Mail. Database Mail is an enterprise solution for sending e-mail messages from the Database Engine. Using Database Mail, your applications can send e-mail messages to users. The messages may contain query results, and may also include files from any resource on your network.

Creating Jobs and Operators

Generally, there are three steps to follow if you want to create a job:

1. Create a job and its steps.
2. Create a schedule of the job execution if the job is not to be executed on demand.
3. Notify operators about the status of the job.

The following sections explain these steps using an example.

Creating a Job and Its Steps

A job may contain one or more steps. There are different ways in which a job step can be defined. The following list contains some of them.

▶ **Using Transact-SQL statements**   Many job steps contain Transact-SQL statements. For example, if you want to automate database or transaction log backups, you use the BACKUP DATABASE statement or BACKUP LOG statement, respectively.

▶ **Using the operating system (CmdExec)**   Some jobs may require the execution of a SQL Server utility, which usually will be started with the corresponding command. For example, if you want to automate the data transfer from your database server to a data file, or vice versa, you could use the **bcp** utility.

▶ **Invoking a program**   As another alternative, it may be necessary to execute a program that has been developed using Visual Basic or some other programming language. In this case, you should always include the path drive letter in the Command text box when you start such a program. This is necessary because SQL Server Agent has to find the executable file.

If the job contains several steps, it is important to determine which actions should be taken in case of a failure. Generally, the Database Engine starts the next job step if the previous one was successfully executed. However, if a job step fails, any job steps that follow will not be executed. Therefore, you should always specify how often each step should be retried in the case of failure. And, of course, it will be necessary to eliminate the reason for the abnormal termination of the job step. (Obviously, a repeated job execution will always lead to the same error if the cause is not repaired.)

NOTE

The number of attempts depends on the type and content of the executed job step (batch, command, or application program).

You can create a job using the following:

▶ SQL Server Management Studio

▶ System stored procedures (**sp_add_job** and **sp_add_jobstep**)

SQL Server Management Studio is used in this example, which creates a job that backs up the **sample** database. To create this job, connect to an instance of the Database Engine in Object Explorer and then expand that instance. Expand SQL Server Agent, right-click Jobs, and choose New Job. (SQL Server Agent must be running.) The New Job dialog box appears (see Figure 17-2). On the General page, enter a name for the job in the Name box. (The name of the job for backing up the **sample** database will be **backup_sample**.)

For the Owner field, click the ellipsis (...) button and choose the owner responsible for performing the job. In the Category drop-down list, choose the category to which the job belongs. You can add a description of the job in the Description box, if you wish.

NOTE

If you have to manage several jobs, categorizing them is recommended. This is especially useful if your jobs are executed in a multiserver environment.

Check the Enabled check box to enable the job.

NOTE

All jobs are enabled by default. SQL Server Agent disables jobs if the job schedule is defined either at a specific time that has passed or on a recurring basis with an end date that has also passed. In both cases, you must re-enable the job manually.

Figure 17-2 *The New Job dialog box*

Each job must have one or more steps. Therefore, in addition to defining job properties, you must create at least one step before you can save the job. To define one or more steps, click the Steps page in the New Job dialog box and click New. The New Job Step dialog box appears, as shown in Figure 17-3. Enter a name for the job step. (It is called **backup** in the example.) In the Type drop-down list, choose Transact-SQL script (T-SQL), because the backup of the sample database will be executed using the Transact-SQL statement BACKUP DATABASE.

In the Database drop-down list, choose the **master** database, because this system database must be the current database if you want to back up a database.

Figure 17-3 *The New Job Step dialog box, General page*

You can either enter the Transact-SQL statement directly in the Command box or invoke it from a file. In the former case, enter the following statements, after you change the path for the backup file:

```
EXEC sp_addumpdevice 'disk', 'backup_file1', 'C:\sample_backup'
BACKUP DATABASE sample TO backup_file1
```

As you probably guessed, the **sp_addumpdevice** system procedure adds a backup device to an instance of the Database Engine. To invoke the Transact-SQL statement from a file, click Open and select the file. The syntax of the statement(s) can be checked by clicking Parse.

Creating a Job Schedule

Each created job can be executed on demand (that is, manually by the user) or by using one or more schedules. A scheduled job can occur at a specific time or on a recurring schedule.

NOTE

Each job can have multiple schedules. For example, the backup of the transaction log of a production database can be executed with two different schedules, depending on the time of day. This means that during peak business hours, you can execute the backup more frequently than during non-peak hours.

To create a schedule for an existing job using SQL Server Management Studio, select the Schedules page in the Job Properties dialog box and click New. (The Job Properties dialog box is the same dialog box as shown in Figure 17-2). If the Job Properties dialog box is not active, expand SQL Server Agent, expand Jobs, and click the job you want to process.

NOTE

If you get the warning, "The On Access action of the last step will be changed from Get Next Step to Quit with Success," click Yes.

The New Job Schedule dialog box appears (see Figure 17-4).

Figure 17-4   *The New Job Schedule dialog box*

For the **sample** database, set the schedule for the backup to be executed every Friday at 8:00 P.M. To do this, enter the name in the Name dialog box and choose Recurring in the Schedule Type drop-down list. In the Frequency section, choose Weekly in the Occur drop-down list, and check Friday. In the Daily Frequency section, click the Occurs Once At radio button, and enter the time (**20:00:00**). In the Duration section, choose the start date in the Start Date drop-down list, and then click the End Date radio button and choose the end date in the corresponding drop-down list. (If the job should be scheduled without the end date, click No End Date.)

Notifying Operators About the Job Status

When a job completes, several methods of notification are possible. For example, you can instruct the system to write a corresponding message to the Windows Application log, hoping that the system administrator reads this log from time to time. A better choice is to explicitly notify one or more operators using e-mail, pager, and/or the **net send** command.

Before an operator can be assigned to a job, you have to create an entry for it. To create an operator using SQL Server Management Studio, expand SQL Server Agent, right-click Operators, and choose New Operator. The New Operator dialog box appears (see Figure 17-5). On the General page, enter the name of the operator in the Name box. Specify one or more methods of notifying the operator (via e-mail, pager, or the **net send** address). In the Pager on Duty Schedule section, enter the working hours of the operator.

To notify one or more operators after the job finishes (successfully or unsuccessfully), return to the Job Properties dialog box of the job, select the Notifications page (see Figure 17-6), and check the corresponding boxes. (Besides e-mail, pager, or the **net send** command notification, in this dialog box you also have the option of writing the message to the Windows Application log and/or deleting the job.)

Viewing the Job History Log

The Database Engine stores the information concerning all job activities in the **sysjobhistory** system table of the **msdb** system database. Therefore, this table represents the job history log of your system. You can view the information in this table using SQL Server Management Studio. To do this, expand SQL Server Agent, expand Jobs, right-click the job, and choose View History. The Log File Viewer dialog box shows the history log of the job.

Figure 17-5   *The New Operator dialog box*

Figure 17-6   *The Job Properties dialog box, Notifications page*

Each row of the job history log is displayed in the details pane, which contains, among other information, the following:

▶ Date and time when the job step occurred

▶ Whether the job step completed successfully or unsuccessfully

▶ Operators who were notified

▶ Duration of the job

▶ Errors or messages concerning the job step

By default, the maximum size of the job history log is 1000 rows, while the number of rows for a particular job is limited to 100. (The job history log is automatically cleared when the maximum size of rows is reached.) If you want to store the information about each job, and your system has several jobs, increase the size of the job history log and/or the number of rows per job. Using SQL Server Management Studio, right-click SQL Server Agent and choose Properties. In the SQL Server Agent Properties dialog box, select the History page and enter the new values for the maximum job history log size and maximum job history rows per job. You can also check Automatically Remove Agent History and specify a time interval after which logs should be deleted.

Alerts

The information about execution of jobs and system error messages is stored in the Windows Application log. SQL Server Agent reads this log and compares the stored messages with the alerts defined for the system. If there is a match, SQL Server Agent fires the alert. Therefore, alerts can be used to respond to potential problems (such as filling up the transaction log), different system errors, or user-defined errors. Before explaining how you create alerts, this section discusses system error messages and two logs, the SQL Server Agent error log and the Windows Application log, which are used to capture all system messages (and thus most of the errors).

Error Messages

System errors are grouped in four different groups. The Database Engine provides extensive information about each error. The information is structured and includes the following:

▶ A unique error message number

▶ An additional number between 0 and 25, which represents the error's severity level

▶ A line number, which identifies the line where the error occurred

▶ The error text

NOTE

The error text not only describes the detected error but also may recommend how to resolve the problem, which can be very helpful to the user.

Example 17.1 queries a nonexistent table in the **sample** database.

EXAMPLE 17.1

```
USE sample;
SELECT * FROM authors;
```

The result is

```
Msg 208, Level 16, State 1, Line 2
Invalid object name 'authors'.
```

To view the information concerning error messages, use the **sys.messages** catalog view. The three most important columns of this view are **message_id**, **severity**, and **text**.

Each unique error number has a corresponding error message. (The error message is stored in the **text** column, and the corresponding error number is stored in the **message_id** column of the **sys.messages** catalog view.) In Example 17.1, the message concerning the nonexistent or incorrectly spelled database object corresponds to error number –208.

The severity level of an error (the **severity** column of the **sys.messages** catalog view) is represented in the form of a number between 0 and 25. The levels between 0 and 10 are simply informational messages, where nothing needs to be fixed. All levels from 11 through 16 indicate different program errors and can be resolved by the user. The values 17 and 18 indicate software and hardware errors that generally do not terminate the running process. All errors with a severity level of 19 and greater are fatal system errors. The connection of the program generating such an error is closed, and its process will then be removed.

The messages relating to program errors (that is, the levels between 11 and 16) are shown on the screen only. All system errors (errors with a severity level of 19 or greater) will also be written to the log.

In order to resolve an error, you usually need to read the detailed description of the corresponding error. You can also find detailed error descriptions in Books Online.

System error messages are written to the SQL Server Agent error log and to the Windows Application log. The following two sections describe these two components.

SQL Server Agent Error Log

SQL Server Agent creates an error log that records warnings and errors by default. The following warnings and errors are displayed in the log:

▶ Warning messages that provide information about potential problems

▶ Error messages that usually require intervention by a system administrator

The system maintains up to ten SQL Server Agent error logs. The current log is called **Current**, while all other logs have an extension that indicates the relative age of the log. For example, **Archive #1** indicates the newest archived error log.

The SQL Server Agent error log is an important source of information for the system administrator. With it, he or she can trace the progress of the system and determine which corrective actions to take.

To view the SQL Server Agent error logs from SQL Server Management Studio, expand the instance in Object Explorer, expand SQL Server Agent, and expand Error Logs. Click one of the files to view the desired log. The log details appear in the details pane of the Log File Viewer dialog box.

Windows Application Log

The Database Engine also writes system messages to the Windows Application log. The Windows Application log is the location of all operating system messages for the Windows operating systems, and it is where all application messages are stored. You can view the Windows Application log using the Event Viewer.

Viewing errors in the Windows Application log has some advantages compared to viewing them in the SQL Server Agent error log. The most important is that the Windows Application log provides an additional component for the search for desired strings.

To view information stored in the Windows Application log, choose Start | Control Panel | Administrative Tools | Event Viewer. In the Event Viewer window, you can choose between system, security, and application messages. For SQL Server system messages, click Application. SQL Server events are identified by the entry MSSQLSERVER.

Defining Alerts to Handle Errors

An alert can be defined to raise a response to a particular error number or to the group of errors that belongs to a specific severity code. Furthermore, the definition of an alert for a particular error is different for system errors and user-defined errors. (The creation of alerts on user-defined errors is described later in this chapter.)

The rest of this section shows how you can create alerts using SQL Server Management Studio.

Creating Alerts on System Errors

Example 13.5, in which one transaction was deadlocked by another transaction, will be used to show how to create an alert about a system error number. If a transaction is deadlocked by another transaction, the victim must be executed again. This can be done, among other ways, by using an alert.

To create the deadlock (or any other) alert, expand SQL Server Agent, right-click Alerts, and choose New Alert. In the New Alert dialog box (see Figure 17-7), enter the name of the alert in the Name box, choose SQL Server Event Alert in the Type drop-down list, and choose <all databases> from the Database Name drop-down list. Click the Error Number radio button, and enter **1205**. (This error number indicates a deadlock problem, where the current process was selected as the "victim.")

The second step defines the response for the alert. In the same dialog box, click the Response page (see Figure 17-8). First check Execute Job, and then choose the job to execute when the alert occurs. (The example here defines a new job called **deadlock_all_db** that restarts the victim transaction.) Check Notify Operators, and then, in the Operator List pane, select operators and choose the methods of their notifications (e-mail, pager, and/or the **net send** command).

NOTE

In the preceding example, it is assumed that the victim process will be terminated. Actually, after receiving the deadlock error 1205, the program resubmits the failed transaction on its own.

Creating Alerts on Error Severity Levels

You can also define an alert that will raise a response on error severity levels. As you already know, each system error has a corresponding severity level that is a number between 0 and 25. The higher the severity level is, the more serious the error. Errors with severity levels 20 through 25 are fatal errors. Errors with severity levels 19 through 25 are written to the Windows Application log.

Figure 17-7 *The New Alert dialog box, General page*

NOTE

Always define an operator to be notified when a fatal error occurs.

As an example of how you can create alerts in relation to severity levels, here's how you use SQL Server Management Studio to create the particular alert for severity level 25. First, expand SQL Server Agent, right-click Alerts, and choose New Alert. In the Name box, enter a name for this alert (for example, **Severity 25 errors**). In the Type drop-down

Figure 17-8 *The New Alert dialog box, Response page*

list, choose SQL Server event alert. In the Database Name drop-down list, choose the **sample** database. Click the Severity radio button and choose 025 – Fatal Error.

On the Response page, enter one or more operators to be notified via e-mail, pager, and/or the **net send** command when an error of severity level 25 occurs.

Creating Alerts on User-Defined Errors

In addition to creating alerts on system errors, you can create alerts on customized error messages for individual database applications. Using such messages (and alerts), you can define solutions to problems that might occur in an application.

The following steps are necessary if you want to create an alert on a user-defined message:

1. Create the error message.
2. Raise the error from a database application.
3. Define an alert on the error message.

An example is the best way to illustrate the creation of such an alert: the alert is fired if the shipping date of a product is earlier than the order date. (For the definition of the **sales** table, see Chapter 5.)

NOTE

Only the first two steps are described here, because an alert on a user-defined message is defined similarly to an alert on a system error message.

Creating an Error Message To create a user-defined error message, you can use either SQL Server Management Studio or the **sp_addmessage** stored procedure. Example 17.2 creates the error message for the example using the **sp_addmessage** stored procedure.

EXAMPLE 17.2

```
sp_addmessage @msgnum=50010, @severity=16,
@msgtext='The shipping date of a product is earlier than the order date',
@lang='us_english', @with_log='true'
```

The **sp_addmessage** stored procedure in Example 17.2 creates a user-defined error message with error number 50010 (the **@msgnum** parameter) and severity level 16 (the **@severity** parameter). All user-defined error messages are stored in the **sysmessages** system table of the **master** database and can be viewed by using the **sys.messages** catalog view. The error number Example 17.2 is 50010 because all user-defined errors must be greater than 50000. (All error message numbers less than 50000 are reserved for the system.)

For each user-defined error message, you can optionally use the **@lang** parameter to specify the language in which the message is displayed. This specification may be necessary if multiple languages are installed on your computer. (When the **@lang** parameter is omitted, the session language is the default language.)

By default, user-defined messages are not written to the Windows Application log. On the other hand, you must write the message to this log if you want to raise an alert on it. If you set the **@with_log** parameter of the **sp_addmessage** system procedure to TRUE, the message will be written to the log.

Raising an Error Using Triggers To raise an error from a database application, you invoke the RAISERROR statement. This statement returns a user-defined error message and sets a system flag in the **@@error** global variable. (You can also handle error messages using TRY/CATCH blocks.)

Example 17.3 creates the trigger **t_date_comp**, which returns a user-defined error of 50010 if the shipping date of a product is earlier than the order date.

NOTE

*To execute Example 17.3, the table **sales** must exist (see Example 5.21).*

EXAMPLE 17.3

```
USE sample;
GO
CREATE TRIGGER t_date_comp
   ON sales
   FOR INSERT AS
   DECLARE @order_date DATE
   DECLARE @shipped_date DATE
SELECT @order_date=order_date, @shipped_date=ship_date FROM INSERTED
   IF @order_date > @shipped_date
          RAISERROR (50010, 16, -1)
```

Now, if you insert the following row in the **sales** table, the shipping date of a product is earlier than the order date:

```
INSERT INTO sales VALUES (1, '01.01.2007', '01.01.2006')
```

the system will return the user-defined error message:

```
Msg 50010, Level 16, State 1, Procedure t_date_comp, Line 8
```

Summary

The Database Engine allows you to automate and streamline many administrator tasks, such as database backups, data transfers, and index maintenance. For the execution of such tasks, SQL Server Agent must be running.

To automate a task, you have to execute several steps:

► Create a job

► Create operators

► Create alerts

Job and *task* are synonymous, so when you create a job, you create the particular task that you want to automate. The easiest way to create a job is to use SQL Server Management Studio, which allows you to define one or more job steps and create an execution schedule.

When a job (successfully or unsuccessfully) completes, you can notify one or more persons, using operators. Again, the general way to create an operator is to use SQL Server Management Studio.

Alerts are defined separately and can also be executed independently of jobs. An alert can handle individual system errors, user-defined errors, or groups of errors belonging to one of 25 severity levels.

The next chapter discusses data replication.

Exercises

E.17.1

Name several administrative tasks that could be automated.

E.17.2

You want to back up the transaction log of your database every hour during peak business hours and every four hours during nonpeak hours. What should you do?

E.17.3

You want to test performance of your production database in relation to locks and want to know whether the lock wait time is more than 30 seconds. How could you be notified automatically when this event occurs?

E.17.4

Specify all parts of a SQL Server error message.

E.17.5

Which are the most important columns of the **sys.messages** catalog view concerning errors?

Chapter 18

Data Replication

In This Chapter

Today, market forces require most companies to set up their computers (and the applications running on them) so that they focus on business and on customers. As a result, data used by these applications must be available ad hoc at different locations and at different times. Such a data environment is provided by several distributed databases that include multiple copies of the same information.

The traveling salesperson represents a good example of how a distributed data environment is used. During the day, the salesperson usually uses a laptop to query all necessary information from the database (prices and availability of products, for example) to inform customers on the spot. Afterwards, in the hotel room, the salesperson again uses the laptop—this time to transmit data (about the sold products) to headquarters.

From this scenario, you can see that a distributed data environment has several benefits compared to centralized computing:

▶ It is directly available to the people who need it, when they need it.

▶ It allows local users to operate autonomously.

▶ It reduces network traffic.

▶ It makes nonstop processing cheaper.

On the other hand, a distributed data environment is much more complex than the corresponding centralized model and therefore requires more planning and administration.

The introductory part of this chapter discusses distributed transactions and compares them with data replication, which is the topic of this chapter. After that, the chapter introduces replication elements and explains the existing replication types. The last part of the chapter describes three wizards that are used to manage replication.

Distributed Data and Methods for Distributing

There are two general methods for distributing data on multiple database servers:

▶ Distributed transactions

▶ Data replication

A distributed transaction is a transaction in which all updates to all locations (where the distributed data is stored) are gathered together and executed synchronously. Distributed database systems use a method called *two-phase commit* to implement distributed transactions.

Each database involved in a distributed transaction has its own recovery technique, which is used in case of error. (Remember that all statements inside a transaction are executed in their entirety or are cancelled.) A global recovery manager (called a coordinator) coordinates the two phases of distributed processing.

In the first phase of this process, the coordinator checks whether all participating sites are ready to execute their part of the distributed transaction. The second phase consists of the actual execution of the transaction at all participating sites. During this process, any error at any site causes the coordinator to stop the transaction. In this case, it sends a message to each local recovery manager to undo the part of the transaction that is already executed at that site.

NOTE

The Microsoft Distributed Transaction Coordinator (DTC) supports distributed transactions using two-phase commit.

During the data replication process, copies of the data are distributed from a source database to one or more target databases located on separate computers. Because of this, data replication differs from distributed transactions in two ways: timing and delay in time.

In contrast to the distributed transaction method, in which all data is distributed on all participating sites at the same time, data replication allows sites to have different data at the same time. Additionally, data replication is an asynchronous process. This means that there is a certain delay during which all copies of data are matched on all participating sites. (This delay can last from a couple of seconds to several days or weeks.)

Data replication is, in most cases, a better solution than distributed transactions because it is more reliable and cheaper. Experience with two-phase commit has shown that administration becomes very difficult if the number of participating sites increases. Also, the increased number of participating sites decreases the reliability, because the probability that a local part of a distributed transaction will fail increases with the increased number of nodes. (If one local part fails, the entire distributed transaction will fail, too.)

Another reason to use data replication instead of centralized data is performance: clients at the site where the data is replicated experience improved performance because they can access data locally rather than using a network to connect to a central database server.

SQL Server Replication: An Overview

Generally, replication is based on one of two different concepts:

▶ Using transaction logs

▶ Using triggers

As already stated in Chapter 16, the Database Engine keeps all values of modified rows ("before" as well as "after" values) in system files called transaction logs. If selected rows need to be replicated, the system starts a new process that reads the data from the transaction log and sends it to one or more target databases.

The other method is based on triggers. The modification of a table that contains data to be replicated fires the corresponding trigger, which in turn creates a new table with the data and starts a replication process.

Both concepts have their benefits and disadvantages. The log-based replication is characterized by improved performance, because the process that reads data from the transaction log runs asynchronously and has little effect on the performance of the overall system. On the other hand, the implementation of log-based replication is very complex for companies, because the database system not only has to manage additional processes and buffers but also has to solve the concurrency problems between system and replication processes that access the transaction log.

NOTE

The Database Engine uses both concepts: the transaction log method for transactional replication and triggers for merge replication. (Transactional and merge replications are described in detail later in this chapter.)

Publishers, Distributors, and Subscribers

The Database Engine replication is based on the so-called publisher–subscriber metaphor. This metaphor describes the different roles servers can play in a replication process. One or more servers publish data that other servers can subscribe to. In between there exists a distributor that stores the changes and forwards them further (to the subscribers). Hence, a node can have one (or more) different roles in a replication scenario:

▶ **Publisher (or publishing server)**   Maintains its source databases, makes data available for replication, and sends the modified data to the distributor

▶ **Distributor (or distribution server)**   Receives all changes to the replicated data from the publisher and stores and forwards them to the appropriate subscribers

▶ **Subscriber (or subscription server)**   Receives and maintains published data

A database server can play many roles in a replication process. For example, a server can act as the publisher and the distributor at the same time. This scenario is appropriate for a process with few replications and few subscribers. If there are a lot of subscribers for the publishing information, the distributor can be located on its own server. Figure 18-1 shows a simple scenario in which one instance is both the publishing and distribution server and three other instances are subscription servers. (The section "Replication Models" later in this chapter discusses in detail possible replication scenarios.)

NOTE

You can replicate only user-defined databases.

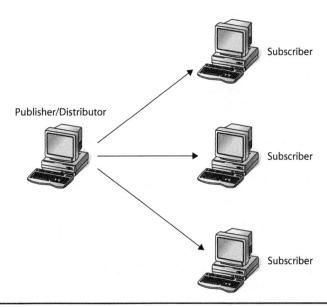

Figure 18-1   *Central publisher with the distributor*

Publications and Articles

The unit of data to be published is called a *publication*. An *article* contains data from a table and/or one or more stored procedures. A table article can be a single table or a subset of data in a table. A stored procedure article can contain one or more stored procedures that exist at the publication time in the database.

A publication contains one or more articles. Each publication can contain data only from one database.

NOTE

A publication is the basis of a subscription. This means that you cannot subscribe directly to an article, because an article is always part of a publication.

A *filter* is the process that restricts information, producing a subset. Therefore, a publication contains one or more of the following items that specify types of table articles:

▶ Table

▶ Vertical filter

▶ Horizontal filter

▶ A combination of vertical and horizontal filters

A vertical filter contains a subset of the columns in a table. A horizontal filter contains a subset of rows in a table.

Publications are tightly connected to subscriptions. A subscription can be initiated in two different ways:

▶ Using a push subscription

▶ Using a pull subscription

With a *push subscription*, all the administration of setting up subscriptions is performed on the publisher during the definition of a publication. (Besides the publisher, the distributor also creates and manages push subscriptions.) Push subscriptions simplify and centralize administration, because the usual replication scenario contains one publisher and many subscribers. The benefit of a push subscription is higher security, because the initialization process is managed at one place. On the other hand, the performance of the distributor can suffer because the overall distribution of subscriptions runs at once.

With a *pull subscription*, the subscriber initiates and manages the subscription. The pull subscription is more selective than the push subscription, because the subscriber can select publications to subscribe to. In contrast to the push subscription, the pull subscription should be used for publications with low security and a high number of subscribers.

NOTE

The downloading of data from the Internet is a typical form of pull subscription.

There is a special type of pull subscription called *anonymous subscription*. Generally, information concerning subscribers is kept on the distribution server. If the workload on this server should be reduced (because of too many subscribers, for instance), it is possible to allow subscribers to initiate their own ("anonymous") subscriptions.

The Distribution Database

The **distribution** database is a system database that is installed on the distribution server when the replication process is initiated. This database holds all replicated transactions from the publisher that need to be forwarded to the subscribers.

In many cases, a single **distribution** database is sufficient. However, if multiple publishing servers communicate with a single distribution server, you can create a **distribution** database for each publishing server. Doing so ensures that the data flowing through each **distribution** database is distinct.

Agents

During the data replication process, the Database Engine uses several agents to manage different tasks. The system supports, among others, the following agents:

▶   Snapshot agent

▶   Log Reader agent

▶   Distribution agent

▶   Merge agent

The following subsections describe these agents.

Snapshot Agent

The Snapshot agent generates the schema and data of the published tables and stores them on the distribution server. The schema of a table and the corresponding data file build the synchronization set that represents the snapshot of the table at a particular time. (A *snapshot* is essentially what it sounds like: a snapshot of the data to be replicated.) The status of the synchronization of that set is recorded in the **distribution** database. Whether the Snapshot agent creates new snapshot files each time it runs depends on the type of replication and options chosen.

Log Reader Agent

If the transaction log of the system is used to replicate data, all transactions that contain the data to be replicated are marked for replication. A component called the Log Reader agent searches for marked transactions and copies them from the transaction log on the publisher to the distribution server. These transactions are stored in the **distribution** database. Each database that uses the transaction log for replication has its own Log Reader agent running on the distribution server.

Distribution Agent

After the transactions and snapshots are stored in the **distribution** database, they have to be moved to the subscribers. This task is handled by the Distribution agent, which moves transactions and snapshots to subscribers, where they are applied to the target tables in the subscription databases.

The task of the Distribution agent is different for pull and push subscriptions. For push subscriptions, the agent pushes out the changes to the subscriber. For pull subscriptions, the agents pulls the transactions from the distribution server. (All actions that change data on the publisher are applied to the subscriber in chronological order.)

Merge Agent

As you already know, the Snapshot agent prepares files containing the table schema and data and stores them at the distributor site. If both the publisher and subscribers can update replicated data, then a synchronization job is necessary that sends all changed data to the other sites. This job is performed by the Merge agent. In other words, the Merge agent can send replicated data to the subscribers and to the publisher. Before the send process is started, the Merge agent also stores the appropriate information that is used to track possible conflicts.

Replication Types

The Database Engine provides the following replication types, which are discussed in the following subsections:

- ▶ Transactional
- ▶ Peer-to-peer
- ▶ Snapshot
- ▶ Merge

Transactional Replication

In transactional replication, the transaction log of the system is used to replicate data. All transactions that contain the data to be replicated are marked for replication. The Log Reader agent searches for marked transactions and copies them from the transaction log on the publisher to the **distribution** database. The Distribution agent moves transactions to subscribers, where they are applied to the target tables in the subscription databases.

NOTE

All tables published using transactional replication must explicitly contain a primary key. The primary key is required to uniquely identify the rows of the published table, because a row is the transfer unit in transactional replication.

Transactional replication can replicate tables (or parts of tables) and one or more stored procedures. The use of stored procedures by transactional replication increases performance, because the amount of data to be sent over a network is usually significantly smaller. Instead of replicated data, only the stored procedure is sent to the subscribers, where it is executed. You can configure the delay of synchronization time between the publisher on one side and subscribers on the other during a transactional replication. (All these changes are propagated by the Log Reader and Distribution agents.)

NOTE

Before transactional replication can begin, a copy of the entire database must be transferred to each subscriber; this is performed by executing a snapshot.

A special form of transactional replication is peer-to-peer transactional replication, which will be discussed next.

Peer-to-Peer Transactional Replication

Peer-to-peer is another form of transactional replication, in which each server is at the same time a publisher, distributor, and subscriber for the same data. In other words, all servers contain the same data, but each server is responsible for the modification of its own partition of data. (Note that data partitions on different servers can intersect.)

Peer-to-peer transactional replication is best explained through an example. Suppose that a company has several branch offices in different cities and that each office server has the same data set as all other servers. On the other hand, the entire data is partitioned in subsets, and each office server can update only its own subset of data. When data is modified on one of the office servers, the changes are replicated to all other servers (subscribers) in the peer-to-peer network. (Users in each office can read data without any restrictions.)

The benefits of this replication form are

▶ The entire system scales well.

▶ The entire system provides high availability.

A system that supports peer-to-peer transactional replication scales well because each server serves only local users. (Users can update only the data partition that belongs to their local server. For read operations, all data is stored locally, too.)

The high availability is based on the fact that if one or more servers go offline, all other servers can continue to operate, because all data they need for read and write operations is stored locally. When an offline server is online again, the replication process restarts and the server receives all data modifications that have happened at the other sites.

Conflict Detection in Peer-to-Peer Replication With peer-to-peer replication, you can change data at any node. Therefore, data changes at different nodes could conflict with each other. (If a row is modified at more than one node, it can cause a conflict.)

The Database Engine supports the option to enable conflict detection across a configured topology. With this option enabled, a conflicting change is treated as a critical error that causes the failure of the Distribution agent. In the event of a conflict, the scenario remains in an inconsistent state until the conflict is resolved and the data is made consistent on all participating servers.

NOTE

*You can enable conflict detection using the system procedures **sp_addpublication** and **sp_configure_ peerconflictdetection**.*

Conflicts in peer-to-peer replication are detected by the stored procedures that apply changes to each node, based on a hidden column in each published table. This hidden column stores an identifier that combines a unique ID that you specify for each node and the version of the row. The procedures are executed by the Distribution agent and they apply insert, update, and delete operations from other peers. If one of the procedures detects a conflict when it reads the hidden column value, it raises an error.

NOTE

The hidden column can be accessed only by a user that is logged in through the dedicated administrator connection (DAC). For the description of DAC, see Chapter 15.

When a conflict occurs in peer-to-peer transactional replication, the "Peer-to-peer conflict detection alert" is raised. You should configure this alert so that you are notified when a conflict occurs. (The previous chapter explains how alerts can be configured and discusses the ways to notify operators.) Books Online describes several approaches for handling the conflicts that occur.

NOTE

You should try to avoid conflicts in a peer-to-peer replication, even if conflict detection is enabled.

Snapshot Replication

The simplest type of replication, snapshot replication, copies the data to be published from the publisher to all subscribers. (The difference between snapshot replication and transactional replication is that the former sends all the published data to the subscribers and the latter sends only the changes of data to the subscribers.)

NOTE

Transactional and snapshot replications are one-way replications, meaning the only changes to the replicated data are made at the publishing server. Therefore, the data at all subscription servers is read-only, except for the changes made by replication processes.

In contrast to transactional replication, snapshot replication requires no primary key for tables. The reason is obvious: the unit of transfer in snapshot replication is a snapshot file and not a row of a table. Another difference between these two replication types concerns a delay in time: snapshot replication is replicated periodically, which means the delay is significant because all published data (changed and unchanged) is transferred from the publisher to the subscribers.

NOTE

*Snapshot replication does not use the **distribution** database directly. However, the **distribution** database contains status information and other details that are used by snapshot replication.*

Merge Replication

In transactional and snapshot replication, the publisher sends the data, and a subscriber receives it. (There is no possibility that a subscriber sends replicated data to the publisher.) Merge replication allows the publisher and subscribers to update data to be replicated. Because of that, conflicts can arise during a replication process.

When you use the merge replication scenario, the system makes three important changes to the schema of the publication database:

▶ It identifies a unique column for each replicated row.

▶ It adds several system tables.

▶ It creates triggers for tables in which data is replicated.

The Database Engine creates or identifies a unique column in the table with the replicated data. If the base table already contains a column with the UNIQUEIDENTIFIER data type and the ROWGUIDCOL property, the system uses that column to identify each replicated row. If there is no such column in the table, the system adds the column **rowguid** of the UNIQUEIDENTIFIER data type with the ROWGUIDCOL property.

NOTE

UNIQUEIDENTIFIER columns may contain multiple occurrences of a value. The ROWGUIDCOL property additionally indicates that the values of the column of the UNIQUEIDENTIFIER data type uniquely identify rows in the table. Therefore, a column of the data type UNIQUEIDENTIFIER with the ROWGUIDCOL property contains unique values for each row across all networked computers in the world and thus guarantees the uniqueness of replicated rows across multiple copies of the table on the publisher and subscribers.

The addition of new system tables provides the way to detect and resolve any update conflict. The Database Engine stores all changes concerning the replicated data in the merge system tables **msmerge_contents** and **msmerge_tombstone** and joins them with the table that contains replicated data to resolve the conflict.

The Database Engine creates triggers on tables that contain replicated data on all sites to track changes to the data in each replicated row. These triggers determine the changes made to the table, and they record them in the **msmerge_contents** and **msmerge_tombstone** system tables.

Conflict detection is done by the Merge agent using the column lineage of the **msmerge_contents** system table when a conflict is detected. The resolution of it can be either priority based or custom based.

Priority-based resolution means that any conflict between new and old values in the replicated row is resolved automatically based on assigned priorities. (The special case of the priority-based method specifies the "first wins" method, where the timely first change of the replicated row is the winner.) The priority-based method is the default. The *custom-based* method uses customized triggers based on business rules defined by the database administrator to resolve conflicts.

Replication Models

The previous section introduced different replication types that the Database Engine uses to distribute data between different nodes. The replication types (transactional, snapshot, peer-to-peer, and merge) provide the functionality for maintaining replicated data. *Replication models* are used by a company to design its own data replication. Each replication model can be implemented using one or more existing replication types. Both the replication type and replication model are usually specified at the same time.

Depending on requirements, several replication models can be used. The basic ones are as follows:

▶ Central publisher with distributor

▶ Central publisher with a remote distributor

▶ Central subscriber with multiple publishers

▶ Multiple publishers with multiple subscribers

The following sections describe these models.

Central Publisher with Distributor

In the central publisher with distributor model, there is one publisher and usually one distributor, which are hosted on one instance of the Database Engine (see Figure 18-1). The publisher creates publications that are distributed by the distributor to several subscribers. The publications designed by this model and received at a subscriber are usually read-only.

The advantage of this model is its simplicity. For this reason, the model is usually used to create a copy of a database, which is then used for interactive queries and simple report generation. (Another situation for using this model is to maintain a remote copy of a database, which could be used by remote systems in the case of communication breakdown.)

On the other hand, if your instance of the Database Engine is tuned such that all system resources are maximized, you should choose another data replication model.

Central Publisher with a Remote Distributor

If the amount of publishing data is not very large, the publisher and distributor can reside on one server. Otherwise, using two separate servers for publishing and distribution is recommended because of performance issues. (If there is a heavy load of data to be published, the distributor is usually the bottleneck.) Figure 18-2 shows the replication model with the central publisher and a separate distributor.

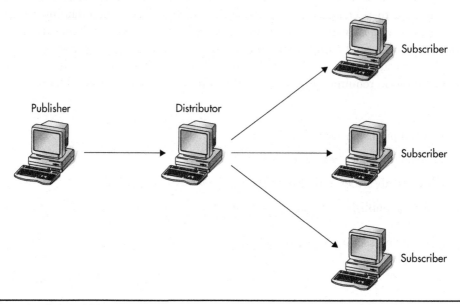

Figure 18-2   *Central publisher with a remote distributor*

NOTE

This scenario can be used as a starting point to increase a number of publishing servers and/or subscribing servers.

Central Subscriber with Multiple Publishers

The scenario described at the beginning of this chapter of the traveling salesperson who transmits data to headquarters is a typical example of the central subscriber with multiple publishers. The data is gathered at a centralized subscriber, and several publishers send their data.

For this model, you can use either the peer-to-peer transactional or merge replication type, depending on the use of replicated data. If publishers publish (and therefore update) the same data to the subscriber, merge replication should be used. If each publisher has its own data to publish, peer-to-peer transactional replication should be used. (In this case, published tables will be filtered horizontally, and each publisher will be the owner of a particular table fragment.)

Multiple Publishers with Multiple Subscribers

The replication model in which some or all of the servers participating in data replication play the role of the publisher and the subscriber is known as multiple publishers with multiple subscribers. In most cases, this model includes several distributors that are usually placed at each publisher (see Figure 18-3).

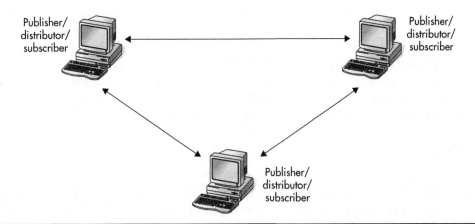

Figure 18-3 *Multiple publishers with multiple subscribers*

This model can be implemented using merge replication only, because publications are modified at each publishing server. (The only other way to implement this model is to use the distributed transactions with two-phase commit.)

Managing Replication

All servers that participate in a replication must be registered. (Server registration is described in Chapter 3.) After registering servers, the distribution server, publishing server(s), and subscription server(s) must be set up. The following sections describe configuration of these processes using the corresponding wizards.

> **NOTE**
>
> *You should create a dedicated account for replication instead of using the administrator account.*

Configuring the Distribution and Publication Servers

Before you install publishing databases, you must install the distribution server and configure the **distribution** database. You can set up a distribution server by using the Configure Distribution Wizard. This wizard allows you to configure the distributor and the **distribution** database and to enable publisher(s). With the wizard you can

- ▶ Configure your server to be a distributor that can be used by other publishers
- ▶ Configure your server to be a publisher that acts as its own distributor
- ▶ Configure your server to be a publisher that uses another server as its distributor

This section shows a scenario for data replication of the **sample** database using the following computers: **NTB00716** and **NTB01101**. The former will be used as a publisher and distributor, while the latter will be the subscriber. The first step is to use the Configure Distribution Wizard to set up the **NTB00716** server to be a publisher that acts as its own distributor. (Additionally, the wizard will create the **distribution** database.)

> **NOTE**
>
> *You can also use the system procedures **sp_adddistributor** and **sp_adddistributiondb** to set up the distribution server and the **distribution** database. **sp_adddistributor** sets up the distribution server by creating a new row in the **sysservers** system table. **sp_adddistributiondb** creates a new **distribution** database and installs the distribution schema.*

To start the wizard, start SQL Server Management Studio, expand the instance, right-click Replication, and select Configure Distribution. The Configure Distribution Wizard appears. On the Distributor page, choose the **NTB00716** server as the distribution server and click Next. After that, select the folder in which snapshots from publisher(s) that use the distribution server will be stored and click Next. On the Distribution Database page, select the name of the **distribution** database and log files and click Next. On the Publishers page, enable the publisher(s) (the **NTB00716** server in this example), choose whether to finish the configuration process immediately or generate the script file to start the distribution configuration later, and then click Next. Figure 18-4 shows the summary of all steps that you have made to configure the **NTB00716** server as the distributor and publisher.

NOTE

The existing publishing and distribution on a server can be disabled using the Disable Publishing and Distribution Wizard. To start the wizard, right-click Replication and choose Disable Publishing and Distribution.

Figure 18-4   *Complete the Wizard page for the distributor and publisher(s)*

After you configure the distribution and publishing servers, you must set up the publishing process. This is done with the New Publication Wizard, explained in the following section.

Setting Up Publications

You can use the New Publication Wizard to

▶   Select the data and database objects you want to replicate

▶   Filter the published data so the subscribers receive only the data they need

Assume that you want to publish the data of the **employee** table from the **NTB00716** server to the **NTB01101** server using the snapshot replication type. In this case, the entire **employee** table is the publication unit.

To create a publication, expand the server node of the publishing server (**NTB00716**), expand the Replication folder, right-click the Local Publications folder, and choose New Publication. The New Publication Wizard appears. On the first two pages, choose the database to publish (**sample**) and the publication type (in this case, the snapshot publication) and click Next. Then select at least one object for publication and click Next (in this example, select the entire **employee** table). The New Publication Wizard also allows you to filter (horizontally or vertically) the data that you want to publish. The snapshot of the selected data can be initialized immediately and/or scheduled to run periodically. (For our example, we will create the snapshot immediately.)

On the Agent Security page, specify the security settings for the Snapshot agent. To do this, click the Security Settings button and type the Windows user account under which the Snapshot agent process will run. (The user account must be entered in the form *domain_name\account_name*.) Click Next. In the Wizard Actions page, you can decide to finish the configuration process immediately or generate the script file to start the publication creation later. Figure 18-5 shows the summary of all steps made to set up the **employee** table as a publication unit.

The last step is to configure the subscription servers, discussed in the following section.

Configuring Subscription Servers

A task that concerns subscribers but has to be performed at the publisher is enabling the publisher to subscribe. Use SQL Server Management Studio to enable a subscriber at the publishing server. First expand the publishing server, expand Replication, right-click Local Subscriptions, and choose New Subscriptions. The New Subscription Wizard appears. You can use the wizard to

Figure 18-5 *Complete the Wizard page for the publication unit*

▶ Create one or more subscriptions to a publication

▶ Specify where and when to run agents that synchronize the subscription

On the Publication page, choose the publication for which you want to create one or more subscriptions and then click Next. (In this example, choose the **replicate_ employee** publication, which was already generated with the New Publication Wizard.)

On the Distribution Agent Location page, you must choose between the push and pull subscriptions. A push subscription means that the synchronization of subscriptions is administered centrally. For this replication, check Run All Agents at the Distributor. To specify the pull subscription, check Run Each Agent at Its Subscriber. Click Next. (Because our subscription is pushed from the central publisher, we choose the first option.)

On the Subscribers page, you must specify all subscription servers. If the subscription servers have not been added, click Add SQL Server Subscriber, select all servers to which data will be replicated, and click Next. Before you finish the process, the wizard shows you the summary of the subscription configuration.

Summary

Data replication is the preferred method for data distribution because it is cheaper than using distributed transactions. The Database Engine allows you to choose one of four possible replication types (snapshot, transactional, merge, and peer-to-peer replication), depending on the physical model you use. Theoretically, any replication model can use any of the replication types, although each (basic) model has a corresponding type that is used in most cases.

A publication is the smallest unit of replication. A single database can have many publications with different replication types. (Otherwise, each publication corresponds to only one database.)

To configure the replication process, you must first set up the distribution server and the distribution system database and configure the publishing server(s). In the next step, you have to define one or more publications. Finally, you have to configure the subscription server(s). The Database Engine supports these steps with three different wizards: the Configure Distribution Wizard, New Publication Wizard, and New Subscription Wizard.

The next two chapters discuss the overall performance of the system. Chapter 19 explains how the query optimizer of the Database Engine works, while Chapter 20 discusses performance tuning. These chapters close the third part of the book.

Exercises

E.18.1

Why do you need a primary key for data replication? Which replication type requires a primary key?

E.18.2

How can you limit network traffic and/or database size?

E.18.3

Update conflicts are not recommended. How can you minimize them?

E.18.4

When does the system use the Log Reader agent, the Merge agent, and the Snapshot agent, respectively?

Chapter 19

Query Optimizer

In This Chapter

- ▶ Phases of Query Processing
- ▶ How Query Optimization Works
- ▶ Tools for Editing the Optimizer Strategy
- ▶ Optimization Hints

The question that generally arises when the Database Engine (or any other relational database system) executes a query is how the data that is necessary for the query can be accessed and processed in the most efficient manner. The component of a database system that is responsible for the processing is called the query optimizer.

The task of the *query optimizer* (or just *optimizer*) is to consider a variety of possible execution strategies for querying the data in relation to a given query and to select the most efficient strategy. The selected strategy is called the *execution plan* of the query. The optimizer makes its decisions using considerations such as how big the tables are that are involved in the query, what indices exist, and what Boolean operator(s) (AND, OR, NOT) are used in the WHERE clause. Generally, these considerations are called *statistics*.

The beginning of the chapter introduces the phases of query processing and then explains in depth how the third phase, query optimization, works. This lays the foundation for the practical examples presented in the subsequent sections. Following that, you are introduced to the different tools that you can use to edit how the query optimizer does its work. The end of the chapter presents optimization hints that you can give to the optimizer in special situations where it cannot find the optimal solution.

Phases of Query Processing

The task of the optimizer is to work out the most efficient execution plan for a given query. This task is done using the following four phases (see Figure 19-1).

Figure 19-1 *Phases in processing a query*

NOTE

This chapter refers to using the query optimizer for queries in SELECT statements. The query optimizer is also used for INSERT, UPDATE, and DELETE statements. The INSERT statement can contain a subquery, while the UPDATE and DELETE statements often have a WHERE clause that has to be processed.

1. **Parsing**   The query's syntax is validated and the query is transformed in a tree. After that, the validation of all database objects referenced by the query is checked. (For instance, the existence of all columns referenced in the query is checked and their IDs are determined.) After the validation process, the final query tree is formed.
2. **Query compilation**   The query tree is compiled by the query optimizer.
3. **Query optimization**   The query optimizer takes as input the compiled query tree generated in the previous step and investigates several access strategies before it decides how to process the given query. To find the most efficient execution plan, the query optimizer first makes the query analysis, during which it searches for search arguments and join operations. The optimizer then selects which indices to use. Finally, if join operations exist, the optimizer selects the join order and chooses one of the join processing techniques. (These optimization phases are discussed in detail in the following section.)
4. **Query execution**   After the execution plan is generated, it is permanently stored and executed.

NOTE

For some statements, parsing and optimization can be avoided if the Database Engine knows that there is only one viable plan. (This process is called trivial plan optimization.*) An example of a statement for which a trivial plan optimization can be used is the simple form of the INSERT statement.*

How Query Optimization Works

As you already know from the previous section, the query optimization phase can be divided into the following phases:

- ▶ Query analysis
- ▶ Index selection
- ▶ Join order selection
- ▶ Join processing techniques

The following sections describe these phases. Also, at the end of this section, plan caching will be introduced.

Query Analysis

During the query analysis, the optimizer examines the query for search arguments, the use of the OR operator, and the existence of join criteria, in that order. Because the use of the OR operator and the existence of join criteria are self-explanatory, only search arguments are discussed.

A search argument is the part of a query that restricts the intermediate result set of the query. The main purpose of search arguments is to allow the use of existing indices in relation to the given expression. The following are examples of search arguments:

▶ emp_fname = 'Moser'

▶ salary >= 50000

▶ emp_fname = 'Moser' AND salary >= 50000

There are several expression forms that cannot be used by the optimizer as search arguments. To the first group belongs all expressions with the NOT (<>) operator. Also, if you use the expression on the left side of the operator, the existing expression cannot be used as a search argument.

The following are examples of expressions that are not search arguments:

▶ NOT IN ('d1', 'd2')

▶ emp_no <> 9031

▶ budget * 0.59 > 55000

The main disadvantage of expressions that cannot be used as search arguments is that the optimizer cannot use existing indices in relation to the expression to speed up the performance of the corresponding query. In other words, the only access the optimizer uses in this case is the table scan.

Index Selection

The identification of search arguments allows the optimizer to decide whether one or more existing indices will be used. In this phase, the optimizer checks each search argument to see if there are indices in relation to the corresponding expression. If an index exists, the optimizer decides whether or not to use it. This decision depends mainly on the selectivity of the corresponding expression. The *selectivity* of an expression is defined as the ratio of the number of rows satisfying the condition to the total number of rows in the table.

The optimizer checks the selectivity of an expression with the indexed column by using statistics that are created in relation to the distribution of values in a column. The query optimizer uses this information to determine the optimal query plan by estimating the cost of using an index to execute the query.

The following sections discuss in detail selectivity of an expression with the indexed column and statistics. (Because statistics exist in relation to both indices and columns, they are discussed separately in two sections.)

NOTE

The Database Engine automatically creates (index and column) statistics if the database option called AUTO_CREATE_STATISTICS is activated. (This option is described later in this chapter.)

Selectivity of an Expression with the Indexed Column

As you already know, the optimizer uses indices to improve query execution time. When you query a table that doesn't have indices, or if the optimizer decides not to use an existing index, the system performs a table scan. During the table scan, the Database Engine sequentially reads the table's data pages to find the rows that belong to the result set. *Index access* is an access method in which the database system reads and writes data pages using an existing index. Because index access significantly reduces the number of I/O read operations, it often outperforms table scan.

The Database Engine uses a nonclustered index to search for data in one of two ways. If you have a heap (a table without a clustered index), the system first traverses the nonclustered index structure and then retrieves a row using the row identifier. If you have a clustered table, however, the traversal of the nonclustered index structure is followed by the traversal of the index structure of the table's clustered index. On the other hand, the use of a clustered index to search for data is always unique: the Database Engine starts from the root of the corresponding B^+-tree and usually after three or four read operations reaches the leaf nodes, where the data is stored. For this reason, the traversing of the index structure of a clustered index is almost always significantly faster than the traversing of the index structure of the corresponding nonclustered index.

From the preceding discussion, you can see that the answer to which access method (index scan or table scan) is faster isn't straightforward and depends on the selectivity and the index type.

Tests that I performed showed that a table scan often starts to perform better than a nonclustered index access when at least 10 percent of the rows are selected. In this case, the optimizer's decision of when to switch from nonclustered index access to a table scan must not be correct. (If you think that the optimizer forces a table scan prematurely, you can use the INDEX query hint to change its decision, as discussed later in this chapter.)

For several reasons, the clustered index usually performs better than the nonclustered index. When the system scans a clustered index, it doesn't need to leave the B$^+$-tree structure to scan data pages, because the pages already exist at the leaf level of the tree. Also, a nonclustered index requires more I/O operations than a corresponding clustered index. Either the nonclustered index needs to read data pages after traversing the B$^+$-tree or, if a clustered index for another table's column(s) exists, the nonclustered index needs to read the clustered index's B$^+$-tree structure.

Therefore, you can expect a clustered index to perform significantly better than a table scan even when selectivity is poor (that is, the percentage of returned rows is high, because the query returns many rows). The tests that I performed showed that when the selectivity of an expression is 75 percent or less, the clustered index access is generally faster than the table scan.

Index Statistics

Index statistics are generally created when an index for the particular column(s) is created. The creation of index statistics for an index means that the Database Engine creates a *histogram* based on up to 200 values of the column. (Therefore, up to 199 intervals are built.) The histogram specifies, among other things, how many rows exactly match each interval, the average number of rows per distinct value inside the interval, and the density of values.

NOTE

Index statistics are always created for one column. If your index is a composite (multicolumn) index, the system generates statistics for the first column in the index.

If you want to create index statistics explicitly, you can use the following tools:

▶ **sp_createstats** system procedure
▶ SQL Server Management Studio

The **sp_createstats** system procedure creates single-column statistics for all columns of all user tables in the current database. The new statistic has the same name as the column where it is created.

To use SQL Server Management Studio for index statistics creation, expand the server, expand the Databases folder, expand the database, expand the Tables folder, expand the table, right-click Statistics, and choose New Statistics. The New Statistics on Table dialog box appears. In the dialog box, specify first the name for the new statistics. After that, click the Add button, select column(s) of the table to which to add the statistics, and click OK. Finally, click OK in the New Statistics on Table dialog box.

As the data in a column changes, index statistics become out of date. The out-of-date statistics can significantly influence the performance of the query. The Database Engine can automatically update index statistics if the database option AUTO_UPDATE_STATISTICS is activated (set to ON). In that case, any out-of-date statistics required by a query for optimization are automatically updated during query optimization.

There is also another database option, AUTO_CREATE_STATISTICS, that builds any missing statistics required by a query for optimization. Both options can be activated (or deactivated) using either the ALTER DATABASE statement or SQL Server Management Studio.

Column Statistics

As you already know from the previous section, the Database Engine creates statistics for every existing index. The system can create statistics for nonindexed columns too. These statistics are called *column statistics*. Together with index statistics, column statistics are used to optimize execution plans. The Database Engine creates statistics for a nonindexed column that is a part of the condition in the WHERE clause.

There are several situations in which the existence of column statistics can help the optimizer to make the right decision. One of them is when you have a composite index on two or more columns. For such an index, the system generates statistics only for the first column in the index. The existence of column statistics for the second column (and all other columns) of the composite index can help the optimizer to choose the optimal execution plan.

The Database Engine supports two catalog views in relation to column statistics (these views can be used to edit the information concerning index statistics, too):

▶   sys.stats

▶   sys.stats_columns

The **sys.stats** view contains a row for each statistic of a table or a view. Besides the **name** column, which specifies the name of the statistics, this catalog view has, among others, two other columns:

▶   **auto_created**   Statistics created by the optimizer

▶   **user_created**   Statistics explicitly created by the user

The **sys.stats_columns** view contains additional information concerning columns that are part of the **sys.stats** view. (To ascertain this additional information, you have to join both views.)

Join Order Selection

Generally, the order in which two or more joined tables are written in the FROM clause of a SELECT statement doesn't influence the decision made by the optimizer in relation to their processing order.

As you will see in the next section, many different factors influence the decision of the optimizer regarding which table will be accessed first. On the other hand, you can influence the join order selection by using the FORCE ORDER hint (discussed in detail later in the chapter).

Join Processing Techniques

The join operation is the most time-consuming operation in query processing. The Database Engine supports the following three different join processing techniques, so the optimizer can choose one of them depending on the statistics for both tables:

▶ Nested loop

▶ Merge join

▶ Hash join

The following subsections describe these techniques.

Nested Loop

Nested loop is the processing technique that works by "brute force." In other words, for each row of the outer table, each row from the inner table is retrieved and compared. The pseudo-code in Algorithm 19.1 demonstrates the nested loop processing technique for two tables.

ALGORITHM 19.1

```
(A and B are two tables.)
for each row in the outer table A do:
     read the row
     for each row in the inner table B do:
        read the row
          if A.join_column = B.join_column then
```

```
                    accept the row and add it to the resulting set
            end if
        end for
end for
```

In Algorithm 19.1, every row selected from the outer table (table A) causes the access of all rows of the inner table (table B). After that, the comparison of the values in the join columns is performed and the row is added to the result set if the values in both columns are equal.

The nested loop technique is very slow if there is no index for the join column of the inner table. Without such an index, the Database Engine would have to scan the outer table once and the inner table *n* times, where *n* is the number of rows of the outer table. Therefore, the query optimizer usually chooses this method if the join column of the *inner* table is indexed, so the inner table does not have to be scanned for each row in the outer table.

Merge Join

The merge join technique provides a cost-effective alternative to constructing an index for nested loop. The rows of the joined tables must be physically sorted using the values of the join column. Both tables are then scanned in order of the join columns, matching the rows with the same value for the join columns. The pseudo-code in Algorithm 19.2 demonstrates the merge join processing technique for two tables.

ALGORITHM 19.2

```
a. Sort the outer table A in ascending order using the join column
b. Sort the inner table B in ascending order using the join column
for each row in the outer table A do:
    read the row
    for each row from the inner table B with a value less than or equal
to the join column do:
        read the row
        if A.join_column = B.join_column then
            accept the row and add it to the resulting set
        end if
    end for
end for
```

The merge join processing technique has a high overhead if the rows from both tables are unsorted. However, this method is preferable when the values of both join columns are sorted in advance. (This is always the case when both join columns are primary keys of corresponding tables, because the Database Engine creates by default the clustered index for the primary key of a table.)

Hash Join

The hash join technique is usually used when there are no indices for join columns. In the case of the hash join technique, both tables that have to be joined are considered as two inputs: the build input and the probe input. (The smaller table usually represents the build input.) The process works as follows:

1. The value of the join column of a row from the build input is stored in a hash bucket depending on the number returned by the hashing algorithm.
2. Once all rows from the build input are processed, the processing of the rows from the probe input starts.
3. Each value of the join column of a row from the probe input is processed using the same hashing algorithm.
4. The corresponding rows in each bucket are retrieved and used to build the result set.

NOTE

The hash join technique requires no index. Therefore, this method is highly applicable for ad hoc queries, where indices cannot be expected. Also, if the optimizer uses this processing technique, it could be a hint that you should create additional indices for one or both join columns.

Plan Caching

The Database Engine uses a set of memory caches as a storage space for data and for execution plans of queries. The first time such a query is executed, the compiled version of the query is stored in the memory. (The part of memory used to store compiled query plans is called the *plan cache*.) When the same query is executed for the second time, the Database Engine checks whether an existing plan is stored in the plan cache. If so, the plan is used, and the recompilation of the query does not take place.

NOTE

The process of plan caching for stored procedures is analogous.

Influencing Execution Plans

There are several ways in which you can influence execution plans. This section describes two of them:

- ▸ The **optimize for ad hoc workloads** option
- ▸ DBCC FREEPROCCACHE

optimize for ad hoc workloads is an advanced configuration option that prevents the system from placing an execution plan in cache on the first execution of the corresponding statement. In other words, the Database Engine places only a stub of the execution plan instead of the entire plan. This stub contains the minimum information, which is necessary for the system to find matches with the future queries. The idea behind this is to reduce the uncontrolled growth of the plan cache. (Keep in mind that the execution plan for the simple query with a couple of indexed columns in the SELECT list needs about 20KB of memory. The plan cache for complicated queries can be significantly larger.)

DBCC FREEPROCCACHE removes all plans from the plan cache. This command can be useful for testing purposes. In other words, if you want to determine which plans are cached (in other words, when particular query plans are reused), you can clear the cache using this command. (You can also use the command to remove a specific plan from the plan cache by specifying the parameter for the plan handle.)

Displaying Information Concerning the Plan Cache

To display information concerning the plan cache, you can use the following dynamic management views:

- ▶ sys.dm_exec_cached_plans
- ▶ sys.dm_exec_query_stats
- ▶ sys.dm_exec_sql_text

All these views will be described in the section "Dynamic Management Views and Query Optimizer" later in the chapter.

Tools for Editing the Optimizer Strategy

The Database Engine supports several tools that enable you to edit what the query optimizer is doing. You can use the following tools, among others:

- ▶ SET statement (to display textual or XML execution plans)
- ▶ Management Studio (to display graphical execution plans)
- ▶ Dynamic management views and functions
- ▶ SQL Server Profiler (discussed in detail in Chapter 20)

The following sections describe the first three tools.

NOTE

*Almost all examples in this chapter use the **AdventureWorks** database. If your system doesn't contain this database, the introductory part of the book describes how you can download it.*

SET Statement

To understand the different options of the SET statement, you have to know that there are three different forms for how the execution plan of a query can be displayed:

▶ Textual form

▶ Using XML

▶ Graphical form

The first two forms use the SET statement, so these two forms are discussed in the following subsections. (The graphical form of execution plans is discussed a bit later, in the section "Management Studio and Graphical Execution Plans.")

Textual Execution Plan

The phrase "textual execution plan" means that the execution plan of a query is displayed in text form. Therefore, the output of a textual execution plan is returned in the form of rows. The Database Engine uses vertical bars to show the dependencies between the operations taking place. Textual execution plans can be displayed using the following options of the SET statement:

▶ SHOWPLAN_TEXT

▶ SHOWPLAN_ALL

Users running a query can display the textual execution plan for the query by activating (setting the option to ON) either SHOWPLAN_TEXT or SHOWPLAN_ALL, before they enter the corresponding SELECT statement. The SHOWPLAN_ALL option displays the same detailed information about the selected execution plan for the query as SHOWPLAN_TEXT with the addition of an estimate of the resource requirements for that statement.

Example 19.1 shows the use of the SET SHOWPLAN_TEXT option.

NOTE

Once you activate the SET SHOWPLAN_TEXT option, all consecutive Transact-SQL statements will not be executed until you deactivate this option with SET SHOWPLAN_TEXT OFF. (The SET SHOWPLAN_XML statement is another statement with the same property.)

EXAMPLE 19.1

```
SET SHOWPLAN_TEXT ON;
GO
USE AdventureWorks;
SELECT * FROM HumanResources.Employee e JOIN Person.Address a
                       ON e.BusinessEntityID = a.AddressID
                        AND e.BusinessEntityID = 10;
GO
SET SHOWPLAN_TEXT OFF;
```

The following textual plan shows the output of Example 19.1:

```
|--Nested Loops(Inner Join)
     |--Clustered Index Seek
(OBJECT:([AdventureWorks].[Person].[Address].[PK_Address_AddressID] AS
[a]), SEEK:([a].[AddressID]=(10)) ORDERED FORWARD)
     |--Compute Scalar
(DEFINE:([e].[OrganizationLevel]=[AdventureWorks].[HumanResources]
.[Employee].[OrganizationLevel] as [e].[OrganizationLevel]))
          |--Compute Scalar
(DEFINE:([e].[OrganizationLevel]=[AdventureWorks].[HumanResources]
.[Employee].[OrganizationNode] as [e].[OrganizationNode].GetLevel()))
               |--Clustered Index Seek
(OBJECT:([AdventureWorks].[HumanResources].[Employee].[PK_Employee_
BusinessEntityID] AS [e]), SEEK:([e].[BusinessEntityID]=(10)) ORDERED
FORWARD)
```

Before we discuss the execution plan of Example 19.1, you need to understand how to read its textual form. The indentation of operators determines the operator execution: the operator that is indented the furthest is executed first. If two or more operators have the same indentation, they are processed from the top downward. Now, if you take a look at the output of Example 19.1, you will see that there are three operators, Nested Loops, Compute Scalar, and Clustered Index Seek. (All operators are preceded by a bar, |.) The Clustered Index Seek operator for the **Employee** table is executed first. After that, the Compute Scalar operator is applied to the **Employee** table and the Clustered Index Seek operator is applied to the **Address** table. At the end, both tables (**Employee** and **Address**) are joined using the nested loop processing techniques.

NOTE

The Compute Scalar operator evaluates an expression to produce a computed scalar value. This may then be referenced elsewhere in the query, as in the case above. Also, each Clustered Index Seek operator seeks for the rows using the corresponding clustered indices of the tables.

NOTE

Index access has two forms: index scan and index seek. Index scan processes the entire leaf level of an index tree, while index seek returns index values (or rows) from one or more ranges of an index.

XML Execution Plan

The phrase "XML execution plan" means that the execution plan of a query is displayed as an XML document. (For more information about XML, see Chapter 26.) The most important advantage of using XML execution plans is that such plans can be ported from one system to another, allowing you to use it in another environment. (How to save execution plans in a file is explained a bit later.)

The SET statement has two options in relation to XML:

▶   SHOWPLAN_XML

▶   STATISTICS XML

The SHOWPLAN_XML option returns information as a set of XML documents. In other words, if you activate this option, the Database Engine returns detailed information about how the statements are going to be executed in the form of a well-formed XML document, without executing them. Each statement is reflected in the output by a single document. Each document contains the text of the statement, followed by the details of the execution steps.

Example 19.2 shows how the SHOWPLAN_XML option can be used.

EXAMPLE 19.2

```
SET SHOWPLAN_XML ON;
GO
USE AdventureWorks;
SELECT * FROM HumanResources.Employee e JOIN      Person.Address a
                        ON e.BusinessEntityID = a.AddressID
                        AND e.BusinessEntityID = 10;
GO
SET SHOWPLAN_XML OFF;
```

The main difference between the SHOWPLAN_XML and STATISTICS XML options is that the output of the latter is generated at run time. For this reason, STATISTICS XML includes the result of the SHOWPLAN_XML option as well as additional run-time information.

To save an XML execution plan in a file, in the Results pane, right-click the SQL Server XML Showplan that contains the query plan and choose Save Results As. In the Save <Grid or Text> Results dialog box, in the Save As Type box, click All Files (*.*). In the File Name box, provide a name with the **.sqlplan** suffix, and then click Save.

To open a saved XML execution plan, choose File | Open in Management Studio and then click File. In the Open File dialog box, set Files of Type to Execution Plan Files (*.sqlplan) to generate a filtered list of saved XML plans. Select the plan and click Open.

NOTE
You can also open the saved execution plan by double-clicking it. After that, the plan will be opened in SQL Server Management Studio and its graphical form will be displayed.

Other Options of the SET Statement

The SET statement has many other options, which are used in relation to locking, transaction, and date/time statements. Concerning statistics, the Database Engine supports the following three options of the SET statement:

- ▶ STATISTICS IO
- ▶ STATISTICS TIME
- ▶ STATISTICS PROFILE

The STATISTICS IO option causes the system to display statistical information concerning the amount of disk activity generated by the query—for example, the number of read and write I/O operations processed with the query. The STATISTICS TIME option causes the system to display the processing, optimization, and execution time of the query.

When the STATISTICS PROFILE option is activated, each executed query returns its regular result set, followed by an additional result set that shows the profile of the query execution.

Example 19.3 shows the use of the STATISTICS PROFILE option of the SET statement.

EXAMPLE 19.3

```
SET STATISTICS PROFILE ON;
GO
USE AdventureWorks;
SELECT * FROM HumanResources.Employee e JOIN   Person.Address a
                        ON e.BusinessEntityID = a.AddressID
                        AND e.BusinessEntityID = 10;
GO
SET STATISTICS PROFILE OFF;
```

The result of Example 19.3, which is not shown because of its length, contains the output of the SET STATISTICS IO and SET SHOWPLAN_ALL statements.

Management Studio and Graphical Execution Plans

A graphical execution plan is the best way to display the execution plan of a query if you are a beginner or want to take a look at different plans in a short time. This form of display uses icons to represent operators in the query plan.

As an example of how graphical execution plans can be initiated and what they look like, Figure 19-2 shows the graphical execution plan for the query in Example 19.1. To display an execution plan in the graphical form, write the query in Query Editor of SQL Server Management Studio and click the Display Estimated Execution Plan button in the toolbar of Management Studio. (The alternative way is to choose Query | Display Estimated Execution Plan.)

If you take a look at Figure 19-2, you will see that there is one icon for each operator of the execution plan. If you move the mouse over one of the icons, its detailed information appears, including the estimated I/O and CPU costs, estimated number of rows and their size, and the cost of the operator. The arrows between the icons represent the data flow. (You can also click an arrow, in which case the related information, such as estimated number of rows and estimated row size, will be displayed.)

To "read" the graphical execution plan of a query, you have to follow the flow of information from right to left and from top to bottom. (It is analogous to the flow of information in a textual execution plan.)

NOTE

The thickness of arrows in the graphical execution plan is related to the number of rows returned by the corresponding operator. The thicker the arrow, the more rows that will be returned.

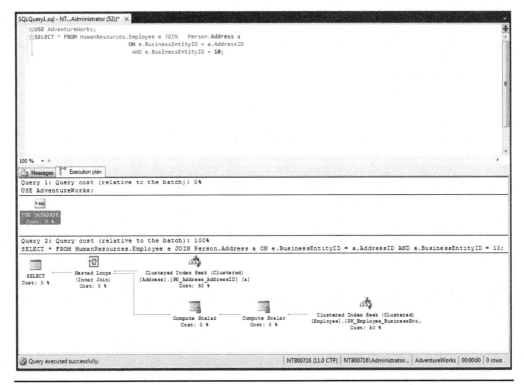

Figure 19-2   *Graphical execution plan for the query in Example 19.1*

As its name suggests, clicking the Display Estimated Execution Plan button displays the estimated plan of the query, without executing it. There is another button, Include Actual Execution Plan, that executes the query and additionally displays its execution plan. The actual execution plan contains additional information in relation to the estimated one, such as the actual number of processed rows and the actual number of executions for each operator.

Examples of Execution Plans

This section presents several queries related to the **AdventureWorks** database, together with their execution plans. These examples demonstrate the topics already discussed, enabling you to see how the query optimizer works in practice.

Example 19.4 introduces a new table (**new_addresses**) in the **sample** database.

EXAMPLE 19.4

```
USE sample;
SELECT * into new_addresses
 FROM AdventureWorks.Person.Address;
GO
CREATE INDEX i_stateprov on new_addresses(StateProvinceID)
```

Example 19.4 copies the content of the **Address** table from the **Person** schema of the **AdventureWorks** database into the **new_addresses** table of the **sample** database. This is necessary because the former table contains several indices, which hinders direct use of the **Address** table of the **AdventureWorks** database to show specific properties of the query optimizer. (Besides that, the example creates an index on the **StateProvinceID** column of that table.)

Example 19.5 shows a query with high selectivity and shows the textual plan that the optimizer chooses in such a case.

EXAMPLE 19.5

```
-- high selectivity
SET SHOWPLAN_TEXT ON;
GO
USE sample;
SELECT * FROM new_addresses a
     WHERE a.StateProvinceID = 32;
GO
SET SHOWPLAN_TEXT OFF;
```

The textual output of Example 19.5 is

```
|--Nested Loops(Inner Join, OUTER REFERENCES:([Bmk1000]))
     |--Index Seek(OBJECT:([sample].[dbo].[new_addresses].[i_stateprov]
AS [a]), SEEK:([a].[StateProvinceID]=(32)) ORDERED FORWARD)
     |--RID Lookup(OBJECT:([sample].[dbo].[new_addresses] AS [a]),
 SEEK:([Bmk1000]=[Bmk1000]) LOOKUP ORDERED FORWARD)
```

NOTE

The Nested Loops operator in the output is displayed even though the query in Example 19.5 accesses only one table. Since SQL Server 2005, this operator is always shown when there are two operators that are "joined" together (like the RID Lookup and Index Seek operators in Example 19.5).

The filter in Example 19.5 selects only one row from the **new_addresses** table. (The total count of rows in this table is 19614.) For this reason, the selectivity of the expression in the WHERE clause is very high (1/19614). In such a case, as you can see from the output of Example 19.5, the existing index on the **StateProvinceID** column is used by the optimizer.

Example 19.6 shows the same query as in Example 19.5, but with another filter.

EXAMPLE 19.6

```
-- low selectivity
SET SHOWPLAN_TEXT ON;
GO
USE sample;
SELECT * FROM new_addresses a
     WHERE a.StateProvinceID = 9;
GO
SET SHOWPLAN_TEXT OFF;
```

The textual plan of Example 19.6 is

```
|--Table Scan(OBJECT:([sample].[dbo].[new_addresses] AS [a]),
WHERE:([sample].[dbo].[new_addresses].[StateProvinceID] as [a].
[StateProvinceID]=(9)))
```

Although the query in Example 19.6 differs from the query in Example 19.5 only by a value on the right side of the condition in the WHERE clause, the execution plan that the optimizer chooses differs significantly. In this case, the existing index won't be used, because the selectivity of the filter is low. (The ratio of the number of rows satisfying the condition to the total number of rows in the table is 4564/19614 = 0.23, or 23 percent.)

Example 19.7 shows the use of the clustered index.

EXAMPLE 19.7

```
SET SHOWPLAN_TEXT ON;
GO
USE AdventureWorks;
SELECT * FROM HumanResources.Employee
     WHERE HumanResources.Employee.BusinessEntityID = 10;
GO
SET SHOWPLAN_TEXT OFF;
```

The textual output of Example 19.7 is

```
|--Compute Scalar
(DEFINE:([AdventureWorks].[HumanResources].[Employee].[OrganizationLevel]
=[AdventureWorks].[HumanResources].[Employee].[OrganizationLevel]))
        |--Compute Scalar
(DEFINE:([AdventureWorks].[HumanResources].[Employee]
.[OrganizationLevel]=[AdventureWorks].[HumanResources].[Employee]
.[OrganizationNode].GetLevel()))
            |--Clustered Index Seek
(OBJECT:([AdventureWorks].[HumanResources].[Employee]
.[PK_Employee_BusinessEntityID]),SEEK:([AdventureWorks].[HumanResources]
.[Employee].[BusinessEntityID]=CONVERT_IMPLICIT(int,[@1],0)) ORDERED
FORWARD)
```

The query in Example 19.7 uses the **PK_Employee_BusinessEntityID** clustered index. This clustered index is created implicitly by the system because the **BusinessEntityID** column is the primary key of the **Employee** table. (For the description of the Compute Scalar operator see Example 19.1.)

Example 19.8 shows the use of the nested loop technique.

EXAMPLE 19.8

```
SET SHOWPLAN_TEXT ON;
GO
USE AdventureWorks;
SELECT * FROM HumanResources.Employee e JOIN
                Person.Address a
                        ON e.BusinessEntityID = a.AddressID
                        AND e.BusinessEntityID = 10;
GO
SET SHOWPLAN_TEXT OFF;
```

The textual output of Example 19.8 is

```
|--Nested Loops(Inner Join)
    |--Clustered Index Seek
(OBJECT:([AdventureWorks].[Person].[Address].[PK_Address_AddressID] AS
[a]), SEEK:([a].[AddressID]=(10)) ORDERED FORWARD)
    |--Compute Scalar
(DEFINE:([e].[OrganizationLevel]=[AdventureWorks].[HumanResources]
.[Employee].[OrganizationLevel] as [e].[OrganizationLevel]))
```

```
          |--Compute Scalar
(DEFINE:([e].[OrganizationLevel]=[AdventureWorks].[HumanResources]
.[Employee].[OrganizationNode] as [e].[OrganizationNode].GetLevel()))
               |--Clustered Index Seek
(OBJECT:([AdventureWorks].[HumanResources].[Employee]
.[PK_Employee_BusinessEntityID] AS [e]),SEEK:([e]
.[BusinessEntityID]=(10)) ORDERED FORWARD)
```

The query in Example 19.8 uses the nested loop technique even though the join columns of the tables are at the same time their primary keys. For this reason, one could expect that the merge join technique would be used. The query optimizer decides to use nested loop because there is an additional filter (e.EmployeeID = 10) that reduces the result set of the query to a single row.

Example 19.9 shows the use of the hash join technique.

EXAMPLE 19.9

```
SET SHOWPLAN_TEXT ON;
GO
USE AdventureWorks;
SELECT * FROM Person.Address a JOIN Person.StateProvince s
   ON a.StateProvinceID = s.StateProvinceID;
GO
SET SHOWPLAN_TEXT OFF;
```

The textual output of the query in Example 19.9 is

```
  |--Hash Match(Inner Join, HASH:([s].[StateProvinceID])=([a].
[StateProvinceID]))
       |--Clustered Index
Scan (OBJECT:([AdventureWorks].[Person].[StateProvince].
[PK_StateProvince_StateProvinceID] AS [s]))
       |--Clustered Index Scan
(OBJECT:([AdventureWorks].[Person].[Address].[PK_Address_AddressID] AS
[a]))
```

Although both join columns in the ON clause are primary keys of the particular tables (**Address** and **StateProvince**), the query optimizer doesn't choose the merge join method. The reason is that *all* (19,614) rows of the **Address** table belong to the result set. In such a case, the use of the hash join method is more beneficial than the other two processing techniques.

Dynamic Management Views and Query Optimizer

There are many dynamic management views (and functions) that are directly related to query optimization. In this section, the following DMVs are discussed:

- ▶ sys.dm_exec_query_optimizer_info
- ▶ sys.dm_exec_query_plan
- ▶ sys.dm_exec_query_stats
- ▶ sys.dm_exec_sql_text
- ▶ sys.dm_exec_text_query_plan
- ▶ sys.dm_exec_procedure_stats
- ▶ sys.dm_exec_cached_plans

sys.dm_exec_query_optimizer_info

The **sys.dm_exec_query_optimizer_info** view is probably the most important DMV in relation to the work of the query optimizer because it returns detailed statistics about its operation. You can use this view when tuning a workload to identify query optimization problems or improvements.

The **sys.dm_exec_query_optimizer_info** view contains three columns: **counter**, **occurrence**, and **value**. The **counter** column specifies the name of the optimizer event, while the **occurrence** column displays the cumulative number of occurrences of these events. The value of the **value** column contains additional information concerning events. (Not all events deliver a **value** value.)

Using this view, you can, for example, display the total number of optimizations, the elapsed time value, and the final cost value to compare the query optimizations of the current workload and any changes observed during the tuning process.

Example 19.10 shows the use of the **sys.dm_exec_query_optimizer_info** view.

EXAMPLE 19.10

```
USE sample;
SELECT counter, occurrence, value
        FROM sys.dm_exec_query_optimizer_info
        WHERE value IS NOT NULL
        AND counter LIKE 'search 1%';
```

The result is

counter	occurrence	value
search 1	117	1
search 1 time	95	0.0120736842105263
search 1 tasks	117	513.982905982906

The **counter** column displays the phases of the optimization process. Therefore, Example 19.11 investigates how many times optimization Phase 1 is executed. (There are three optimization phases, Phase 0, Phase 1, and Phase 2, which are specified by the values **search 0**, **search 1**, and **search 2**, respectively.)

NOTE

Because of its complexity, the optimization process is broken into three phases. The first phase (Phase 0) considers only nonparallel execution plans. If the cost of Phase 0 isn't optimal, Phase 1 will be executed, in which both nonparallel plans and parallel plans are considered. Phase 2 takes into account only parallel plans.

sys.dm_exec_query_plan

As you already know, execution plans for batches and Transact-SQL statements are placed in the cache. That way, they can be used anytime by the optimizer. You can examine the cache using several DMVs. One of these is the **sys.dm_exec_query_plan** view, which returns all execution plans that are stored in the cache of your system. (The execution plans are displayed in XML format.)

NOTE

Books Online contains several useful examples of this DMV.

Each query plan stored in the cache is identified by a unique identifier called a *plan handle*. The **sys.dm_exec_query_plan** view requires a plan handle to retrieve the execution plan for a particular Transact-SQL query or batch. This handle can be displayed using the **sys.dm_exec_query_stats** DMV, which is discussed next.

sys.dm_exec_query_stats

The **sys.dm_exec_query_stats** view returns aggregate performance statistics for cached query plans. The view contains one row per query statement within the cached plan, and the lifetime of the rows is tied to the plan itself.

Example 19.11 shows the use of the **sys.dm_exec_query_stats** view.

EXAMPLE 19.11

```
SELECT ecp.objtype AS  Object_Type ,
(SELECT t. text  FROM sys.dm_exec_sql_text(qs.sql_handle) AS t) AS
 Adhoc_Batch ,qs. execution_count  AS  Counts ,
qs. total_worker_time  AS  Total_Worker_Time ,
(qs. total_worker_time  / qs. execution_count ) AS  Avg_Worker_Time ,
(qs. total_physical_reads  / qs. execution_count ) AS  Avg_Physical_Reads ,
(qs. total_logical_writes  / qs. execution_count ) AS  Avg_Logical_Writes ,
(qs. total_logical_reads  / qs. execution_count ) AS  Avg_Logical_Reads ,
qs. total_clr_time  AS  Total_CLR_Time ,
(qs. total_clr_time  / qs. execution_count ) AS  Avg_CLR_Time ,
qs. total_elapsed_time  AS  Total_Elapsed_Time ,
(qs. total_elapsed_time  / qs. execution_count ) AS  Avg_Elapsed_Time ,
qs. last_execution_time  AS  Last_Exec_Time ,
qs. creation_time  AS  Creation_Time
     FROM sys.dm_exec_query_stats AS qs
   JOIN sys.dm_exec_cached_plans ecp ON qs.plan_handle = ecp.plan_handle
   ORDER BY  Counts  DESC;
```

Example 19.11 joins the **sys.dm_exec_query_stats** and **sys.dm_exec_cached_plans** views to return execution plans for all cached plans, which are ordered by the count of their execution times.

sys.dm_exec_sql_text and sys.dm_exec_text_query_plan

The previous view, **sys.dm_exec_query_stats**, can be used with several other DMVs to display different properties of queries. In other words, each DMV that needs the plan handle to identify the query will be "joined" with the **sys.dm_exec_query_stats** view to display the required information. One such view is **sys.dm_exec_sql_text**. This view returns the text of the SQL batch that is identified by the specified handle. Books Online shows a very useful example that "joins" the **sys.dm_exec_sql_text** and **sys. dm_exec_query_stats** views to return the text of SQL queries that are being executed in batches, and then provides statistical information about them.

In contrast to the **sys.dm_exec_sql_text** view, **sys.dm_exec_text_query_plan** returns the execution plan of the batch in XML format. Similar to the previous views, this one is specified by the plan handle. (The plan specified by the plan handle can either be cached or currently executing.)

sys.dm_exec_procedure_stats

This DMV is similar to the **sys.dm_exec_query_stats** view. It returns aggregate performance statistics for cached stored procedures. The view contains one row per stored procedure, and the lifetime of the row is as long as the stored procedure remains cached. When a stored procedure is removed from the cache, the corresponding row is eliminated from this view.

sys.dm_exec_cached_plans

This view returns a row for each query plan that is cached by the Database Engine for faster query execution. You can use this view to find cached query plans, cached query text, the amount of memory taken by cached plans, and the reuse count of the cached plans.

The most important columns of this view are **cacheobjtype** and **usecount**. The former specifies the type of object in the cache, while the latter determines the number of times this cache object has been used since its inception.

Optimization Hints

In most cases, the query optimizer chooses the fastest execution plan. However, there are some special situations in which the optimizer, for some particular reasons, cannot find the optimal solution. In such cases, you should use optimization hints to force it to use a particular execution plan that could perform better.

Optimization hints are optional parts in a SELECT statement that instruct the query optimizer to execute one specific behavior. In other words, by using optimization hints, you do not allow the query optimizer to search and find the way to execute a query because you tell it exactly what to do.

Why Use Optimization Hints

You should use optimization hints only temporarily and for testing. In other words, avoid using them as a permanent part of a query. There are two reasons for this statement. First, if you force the optimizer to use a particular index and later define an index that results in better performance of the query, the query and the application to which it belongs cannot benefit from the new index. Second, Microsoft continuously strives to make the query optimizer better. If you bind a query to a specific execution plan, the query cannot benefit from new and improved features in the subsequent versions of SQL Server.

There are two reasons why the optimizer sometimes does not choose the fastest execution plan:

▶ The query optimizer is not perfect

▶ The system does not provide the optimizer with the appropriate information

NOTE

Optimization hints can help you only if the execution plan chosen by the optimizer is not optimal. If the system does not provide the optimizer with the appropriate information, use the AUTO_CREATE_STATISTICS and AUTO_UPDATE_STATISTICS database options to create or modify existing statistics.

Types of Optimization Hints

The Database Engine supports the following types of optimization hints:

▶ Table hints

▶ Join hints

▶ Query hints

▶ Plan guides

The following sections describe these hints.

NOTE

The examples that follow demonstrate the use of optimization hints, but they don't give you any recommendations about using them in any particular query. (In most cases shown in these examples, the use of hints would be counterproductive.)

Table Hints

You can apply table hints to a single table. The following table hints are supported:

▶ INDEX

▶ NOEXPAND

▶ FORCESEEK

The INDEX hint is used to specify one or more indices that are then used in a query. This hint is specified in the FROM clause of the query. You can use this hint to force index access if the optimizer for some reason chooses to perform a table scan for a given query. (Also, the INDEX hint can be used to prevent the optimizer from using a particular index.)

Examples 19.12 and 19.13 show the use of the INDEX hint.

EXAMPLE 19.12

```
SET SHOWPLAN_TEXT ON;
GO
USE sample;
SELECT  * FROM new_addresses a WITH ( INDEX(i_stateprov))
   WHERE a.StateProvinceID = 9;
GO
SET SHOWPLAN_TEXT OFF;
```

The textual output of Example 19.12 is

```
|--Nested Loops(Inner Join, OUTER REFERENCES:([Bmk1000],
[Expr1004]) WITH UNORDERED PREFETCH)
      |--Index Seek(OBJECT:([sample].[dbo].[new_addresses].[i_stateprov] AS [a]),
SEEK:([a].[StateProvinceID]=(9)) ORDERED FORWARD)
      |--RID Lookup(OBJECT:([sample].[dbo].[new_addresses] AS [a]),
SEEK:([Bmk1000]=[Bmk1000]) LOOKUP ORDERED FORWARD)
```

Example 19.12 is identical to Example 19.6, but contains the additional INDEX hint. This hint forces the query optimizer to use the **i_stateprov** index. Without this hint, the optimizer chooses the table scan, as you can see from the output of Example 19.6.

The other form of the INDEX query hint, INDEX(0), forces the optimizer to not use any of the existing nonclustered indices. Example 19.13 shows the use of this hint.

EXAMPLE 19.13

```
SET SHOWPLAN_TEXT ON;
GO
USE AdventureWorks;
SELECT * FROM Person.Address a
      WITH(INDEX(0))
      WHERE a.StateProvinceID = 32;
GO
SET SHOWPLAN_TEXT OFF;
```

The textual output of Example 19.13 is

```
|--Clustered Index Scan
(OBJECT:([AdventureWorks].[Person].[Address].[PK_Address_AddressID] AS [a]),
 WHERE:([AdventureWorks].[Person].[Address].[StateProvinceID] as
 [a].[StateProvinceID]=(32)))
```

NOTE

If a clustered index exists, INDEX(0) forces a clustered index scan and INDEX(1) forces a clustered index scan or seek. If no clustered index exists, INDEX(0) forces a table scan and INDEX(1) is interpreted as an error.

The execution plan of the query in Example 19.13 shows that the optimizer uses the clustered index scan, because of the INDEX(0) hint. Without this hint, the query optimizer itself would choose the nonclustered index scan. (You can check this by removing the hint in the query.)

The NOEXPAND hint specifies that any indexed view isn't expanded to access underlying tables when the query optimizer processes the query. The query optimizer treats the view like a table with the clustered index. (For a discussion of indexed views, see Chapter 11.)

The FORCESEEK table hint forces the optimizer to use only an index seek operation as the access path to the data in the table (or view) referenced in the query. You can use this table hint to override the default plan chosen by the query optimizer, to avoid performance issues caused by an inefficient query plan. For example, if a plan contains table or index scan operators, and the corresponding tables cause a high number of reads during the execution of the query, forcing an index seek operation may yield better query performance. This is especially true when inaccurate cardinality or cost estimations cause the optimizer to favor scan operations at plan compilation time.

NOTE

The FORCESEEK hint can be applied to both clustered and nonclustered indices.

Join Hints

Join hints instruct the query optimizer how join operations in a query should be performed. They force the optimizer either to join tables in the order in which they are specified in the FROM clause of the SELECT statement or to use the join processing techniques explicitly specified in the statement. The Database Engine supports several join hints:

▶ FORCE ORDER

▶ LOOP

▶ HASH

▶ MERGE

The FORCE ORDER hint forces the optimizer to join tables in the order in which they are specified in a query. Example 19.14 shows the use of this join hint.

EXAMPLE 19.14

```
SET SHOWPLAN_TEXT ON;
GO
USE AdventureWorks;
SELECT e.BusinessEntityID, e.LoginID, d.DepartmentID
    FROM HumanResources.Employee e, HumanResources.Department d,
        HumanResources.EmployeeDepartmentHistory h
    WHERE d.DepartmentID = h.DepartmentID
    AND h.BusinessEntityID = e.BusinessEntityID
    AND h.EndDate IS NOT NULL
    OPTION(FORCE ORDER);
GO
SET SHOWPLAN_TEXT OFF;
```

The textual output of Example 19.14 is

```
|--Merge Join(Inner Join, MERGE:([d].[DepartmentID],
[e].[BusinessEntityID])=([h].[DepartmentID], [h].[BusinessEntityID]),
RESIDUAL:([AdventureWorks].[HumanResources].[Department].[DepartmentID] as
[d].[DepartmentID]=[AdventureWorks].[HumanResources]
.[EmployeeDepartmentHistory].[DepartmentID] as [h].[DepartmentID] AND
[AdventureWorks].[HumanResources].[EmployeeDepartmentHistory]
.[BusinessEntityID] as [h].[BusinessEntityID]=[AdventureWorks]
.[HumanResources].[Employee].[BusinessEntityID] as [e].[BusinessEntityID]))
        |--Sort(ORDER BY:([d].[DepartmentID] ASC, [e].[BusinessEntityID] ASC))
        |    |--Nested Loops(Inner Join)
        |        |--Index Scan
(OBJECT:([AdventureWorks].[HumanResources].[Employee].[AK_Employee_LoginID]
AS [e]))
        |        |--Clustered Index Scan
(OBJECT:([AdventureWorks].[HumanResources].[Department].[PK_Department_
DepartmentID] AS [d]))
        |--Sort(ORDER BY:([h].[DepartmentID] ASC, [h].[BusinessEntityID] ASC))
            |--Clustered Index Scan
(OBJECT:([AdventureWorks].[HumanResources].[EmployeeDepartmentHistory]
.[PK_EmployeeDepartmentHistory_BusinessEntityID_StartDate_DepartmentID] AS
[h]), WHERE:([AdventureWorks].[HumanResources].[EmployeeDepartmentHistory]
.[EndDate] as [h].[EndDate] IS NOT NULL))
```

As you can see from the textual output of Example 19.14, the optimizer performs the join operation in the order in which the tables appear in the query. This means that the **EmployeeDepartmentHistory** table will be processed first, then the **Department** table, and finally the **Employee** table. (If you execute the query without the FORCE ORDER hint, the query optimizer will process the tables in the opposite order: first **Employee**, then **Department**, and then **EmployeeDepartmentHistory**.)

> **NOTE**
>
> *Keep in mind that this does not necessarily mean that the new execution plan performs better than that chosen by the optimizer.*

The query hints LOOP, MERGE, and HASH force the optimizer to use the nested loop technique, merge join technique, and hash join technique, respectively. These three join hints can be used only when the join operation conforms to the SQL standard— that is, when the join is explicitly indicated with the JOIN keyword in the FROM clause of a SELECT statement.

Example 19.15 shows a query that uses the merge join technique because the hint with the same name is explicitly defined in the SELECT statement. (You can apply the other two hints, HASH and LOOP, in the same way.)

EXAMPLE 19.15

```
SET SHOWPLAN_TEXT ON;
GO
USE AdventureWorks;
SELECT * FROM Person.Address a JOIN Person.StateProvince s
  ON a.StateProvinceID = s.StateProvinceID
    OPTION (MERGE JOIN);
GO
SET SHOWPLAN_TEXT OFF;
```

The textual output of Example 19.15 is

```
|--Merge Join(Inner Join, MERGE:([s].[StateProvinceID])=([a]
.[StateProvinceID]), RESIDUAL:([AdventureWorks].[Person].[StateProvince]
.[StateProvinceID] as [s].[StateProvinceID]=[AdventureWorks].[Person]
.[Address].[StateProvinceID] as [a].[StateProvinceID]))
     |--Clustered Index Scan
(OBJECT:([AdventureWorks].[Person].[StateProvince].[PK_StateProvince_
StateProvinceID] AS [s]), ORDERED FORWARD)
     |--Nested Loops(Inner Join, OUTER REFERENCES:([a].[AddressID],
[Expr1004]) WITH ORDERED PREFETCH)
          |--Index Scan
```

```
(OBJECT:([AdventureWorks].[Person].[Address].[IX_Address_StateProvinceID]
AS [a]), ORDERED FORWARD)
          |--Clustered Index Seek
(OBJECT:([AdventureWorks].[Person].[Address].[PK_Address_AddressID]
AS [a]), SEEK:([a].[AddressID]=[AdventureWorks].[Person].[Address]
.[AddressID] as [a].[AddressID]) LOOKUP ORDERED FORWARD)
```

As you can see from the output of Example 19.15, the query optimizer is forced to use the merge join processing technique. (If the hint is removed, the query optimizer chooses the hash join technique.)

The specific join hint can be written either in the FROM clause of a query or using the OPTION clause at the end of it. The use of the OPTION clause is recommended if you want to write several *different* hints together. Example 19.16 is identical to Example 19.15, but specifies the join hint in the FROM clause of the query. (Note that in this case the INNER keyword is required.)

EXAMPLE 19.16

```
USE AdventureWorks;
SELECT * FROM Person.Address a INNER MERGE JOIN Person.StateProvince s
  ON a.StateProvinceID = s.StateProvinceID;
```

Query Hints

There are several query hints, which are used for different purposes. This section discusses the following query hints:

- ▶ FAST n
- ▶ OPTIMIZE FOR
- ▶ OPTIMIZE FOR UNKNOWN
- ▶ USE PLAN

The FAST n hint specifies that the query is optimized for fast retrieval of the first n rows. After the first n rows are returned, the query continues execution and produces its full result set.

NOTE

This query can be very helpful if you have a very complex query with many result rows, requiring a lot of time for processing. Generally, a query is processed completely and then the system displays the result. This query hint forces the system to display the first n rows immediately after their processing.

The OPTIMIZE FOR hint forces the query optimizer to use a particular value for a local variable when the query is compiled and optimized. The value is used only during query optimization, and not during query execution. This query hint can be used when you create plan guides, which are discussed in the next section.

Example 19.17 shows the use of the OPTIMIZE FOR query hint.

EXAMPLE 19.17

```
DECLARE @city_name nvarchar(30)
SET @city_name = 'Newark'
SELECT * FROM Person.Address
      WHERE City = @city_name
            OPTION ( OPTIMIZE FOR (@city_name = 'Seattle') );
```

Although the value of the **@city_name** variable is set to Newark, the OPTIMIZE FOR hint forces the optimizer to use the value Seattle for the variable when optimizing the query.

The OPTIMIZE FOR UNKNOWN hint instructs the query optimizer to use statistical data instead of the initial values for all local variables when the query is compiled and optimized, including parameters created with forced parameterization. (*Forced parameterization* means that any literal value that appears in a SELECT, INSERT, UPDATE, or DELETE statement, submitted in any form, is converted to a parameter during query compilation. That way, all queries with a different parameter value will be able to reuse the cached query plan instead of having to recompile the statement each time when the parameter value is different.)

The USE PLAN hint takes a plan stored as an XML document as the parameter and advises the Database Engine to use the specified execution plan for the query. (For the storage of an execution plan as an XML document, see the description of the SHOWPLAN_XML option of the SET statement earlier in this chapter, in the section "XML Execution Plan.")

Plan Guides

As you know from the previous section, hints are explicitly specified in the SELECT statement to influence the work of the query optimizer. Sometimes you cannot or do not want to change the text of the SELECT statement directly. In that case, it is still possible to influence the execution of queries by using plan guides. In other words, plan guides allow you to use a particular optimization hint without changing the syntax of the SELECT statement.

NOTE

The main purpose of plan guides is to avoid hard-coding of hints in cases where it is not recommended or not possible (for third-party application code, for instance).

Plan guides are created using the **sp_create_plan_guide** system procedure. This procedure creates a plan guide for associating query hints or actual query plans with queries in a database. Another system procedure, **sp_control_plan_guide**, enables, disables, or drops an existing plan guide.

NOTE

There are no Transact-SQL DDL statements for creation and deletion of plan guides. A subsequent SQL Server version will hopefully support such statements.

The Database Engine supports three types of plan guides:

▶ **SQL**   Matches queries that execute in the context of stand-alone Transact-SQL statements and batches that are not part of a database object

▶ **OBJECT**   Matches queries that execute in the context of routines and DML triggers

▶ **TEMPLATE**   Matches stand-alone queries that are parameterized to a specified form

Example 19.18 shows how you can create the optimization hint from Example 19.15, without the modification of the corresponding SELECT statement.

EXAMPLE 19.18

```
sp_create_plan_guide  @name = N'Example_19_15',
@stmt = N'SELECT * FROM Person.Address a JOIN Person.StateProvince s
  ON a.StateProvinceID = s.StateProvinceID',
@type = N'SQL',
@module_or_batch = NULL,
@params = NULL,
@hints = N'OPTION (HASH JOIN)'
```

As you can see from Example 19.18, the **sp_create_plan_guide** system procedure has several parameters. The **@name** parameter specifies the name of the new plan guide. The **@stmt** parameter comprises the T-SQL statement, while the **@type** parameter specifies the type of the plan guide (SQL, OBJECT, or TEMPLATE). The optimization hint is specified in the **@hints** parameter. (You can also use SQL Server Management Studio to create plan guides.)

To edit information related to plan guides, use the **sys.plan_guides** catalog view. This view contains a row for each plan guide in the current database. The most important columns are **plan_guide_id**, **name**, and **query_text**. The **plan_guide_id** column specifies the unique identifier of the plan guide, while the **name** column defines its name. The **query_text** column specifies the text of the query on which the plan guide is created.

Summary

The query optimizer is the part of the Database Engine that decides how to best perform a query. It generates several query execution plans for the given query and selects the plan with the lowest cost.

The query optimization phase can be divided into the following phases: query analysis, index selection, and join order selection. During the query analysis phase, the optimizer examines the query for search arguments, the use of the OR operator, and the existence of join criteria, in that order. The identification of search arguments allows the optimizer to decide whether one or more existing indices will be used.

The order in which two or more joined tables are written in the FROM clause of a SELECT statement doesn't influence the optimizer's decision regarding their processing order. The Database Engine supports three different join processing techniques that can be used by the optimizer. Which technique the optimizer chooses, depends on existing statistics for joined tables.

The Database Engine supports many tools that can be used to edit execution plans. The most important are textual and graphical display of the plan and dynamic management views.

You can influence the work of the optimizer by using optimization hints. The Database Engine supports many optimization hints, which can be grouped as follows: table hints, join hints, and query hints.

Plan guides allow you to influence the optimization process of queries, without modifying a particular SELECT statement, as in the case of query hints.

The next chapter discusses performance tuning.

Chapter 20

Performance Tuning

In This Chapter

- ▶ Factors That Affect Performance
- ▶ Monitoring Performance
- ▶ Choosing the Right Tool for Monitoring
- ▶ Other Performance Tools of SQL Server

Improving the performance of a database system requires many decisions, such as where to store data and how to access the data. This task is different from other administrative tasks because it comprises several different steps that concern all aspects of software and hardware. If the database system is not performing optimally, the system administrator must check many factors and possibly tune software (operating system, database system, database applications) and hardware.

The performance of the Database Engine (and any other relational DBMS) is measured by two criteria:

▶ Response time

▶ Throughput

Response time measures the performance of an individual transaction or program. Response time is treated as the length of time from the moment a user enters a command or statement until the time the system indicates that the command (statement) has completed. To achieve optimum response time of an overall system, almost all existing commands and statements (90 to 95 percent of them) must not cross the specified response time limit.

Throughput measures the overall performance of the system by counting the number of transactions that can be handled by the Database Engine during the given time period. (The throughput is typically measured in transactions per second.) Therefore, there is a direct relation between response time of the system and its throughput: when the response time of a system degrades (for example, because many users concurrently use the system), the throughput of the system degrades too.

This chapter discusses performance issues and the tools for tuning the database system that are relevant to daily administration of the system. In the first part of the chapter the factors that affect performance are described. After that, some recommendations are given for how to choose the right tool for the administration job. At the end of the chapter, tools for monitoring the database system are presented.

Factors That Affect Performance

Factors affecting performance fall into three general categories:

▶ Database applications

▶ Database system

▶ System resources

These factors in turn can be affected by several other factors, as discussed in the following sections.

Database Applications and Performance

The following factors can affect the performance of database applications:

▶ Application-code efficiency
▶ Physical design

Application-Code Efficiency

Applications introduce their own load on the system software and on the Database Engine. For this reason, they can contribute to performance problems if you make poor use of system resources. Most performance problems in application programs are caused by the improper choice of Transact-SQL statements and their sequence in an application program.

The following list gives some of the ways you can improve overall performance by modifying code in an application:

▶ Use clustered indices
▶ Do not use the NOT IN predicate

Clustered indices generally improve performance. Performance of a range query is the best if you use a clustered index for the column in the filter. When you retrieve only a few rows, there is no significant difference between the use of a nonclustered index and a clustered index.

The NOT IN predicate is not optimizable; in other words, the query optimizer cannot use it as a search argument (the part of a query that restricts the intermediate result set of the query). Therefore, the expression with the NOT IN predicate always results in a table scan.

NOTE

More hints on how code modification can improve overall performance are given in Chapter 19.

Physical Design

During physical database design, you choose the specific storage structures and access paths for the database files. In this design step, it is sometimes recommended that you denormalize some of the tables in the database to achieve good performance for various database applications. *Denormalizing* tables means coupling together two or more normalized tables, resulting in some redundant data.

emp_no	emp_fname	emp_lname	dept_no
25348	Matthew	Smith	d3
10102	Ann	Jones	d3
18316	John	Barrimore	d1
29346	James	James	d2
2581	Elke	Hansel	d2
28559	Sybill	Moser	d1
9031	Elsa	Bertoni	d2

dept_no	dept_name	location
d1	Research	Dallas
d2	Accounting	Seattle
d3	Marketing	Dallas

Table 20-1   *The employee and department Tables*

To demonstrate the process of denormalization, consider this example: Table 20-1 shows two tables from the **sample** database, **department** and **employee**, that are normalized. (For more information on data normalization, see Chapter 1.) Data in those two tables can be specified using just one table, **dept_emp** (see Table 20-2), which shows the denormalized form of data stored in the tables **department** and **employee**. In contrast to the tables **department** and **employee**, which do not contain any data redundancies, the **dept_emp** table contains a lot of redundancies, because two columns of this table (**dept_name** and **location**) are dependent on the **dept_no** column.

emp_no	emp_fname	Emp_lname	dept_no	dept_name	Location
25348	Matthew	Smith	d3	Marketing	Dallas
10102	Ann	Jones	d3	Marketing	Dallas
18316	John	Barrimore	d1	Research	Dallas
29346	James	James	d2	Accounting	Seattle
2581	Elke	Hansel	d2	Accounting	Seattle
28559	Sybill	Moser	d1	Research	Dallas
9031	Elsa	Bertoni	d2	Accounting	Seattle

Table 20-2   *The dept_emp Table*

Data denormalization has two benefits and two disadvantages. First the benefits: If you have a column that is dependent on another column of the table (such as the **dept_ name** column in the **dept_emp** table, which is dependent on the **dept_no** column) for data often required by queries, you can avoid the use of the join operation, which would affect the performance of applications. Second, denormalized data requires fewer tables than normalized data.

On the other hand, a denormalized table requires additional amounts of disk space, and data modification is difficult because of data redundancy.

Another option in the physical database design that contributes to good performance is the creation of indices. Chapter 10 gives several guidelines for the creation of indices, and examples are given later in this chapter.

The Database Engine and Performance

The Database Engine can substantially affect the performance of an entire system. The two most important components of the Database Engine that affect performance are

- ▶ Query optimizer
- ▶ Locks

Query Optimizer

The optimizer formulates several query execution plans for fetching the data rows that are required to process a query and then decides which plan should be used. The decision concerning the selection of the most appropriate execution plan includes which indices should be used, how to access tables, and the order of joining tables. All of these decisions can significantly affect the performance of database applications. The optimizer is discussed in detail in the previous chapter.

Locks

The database system uses locks as the mechanism for protecting one user's work from another's. Therefore, locks are used to control the access of data by all users at the same time and to prevent possible errors that can arise from the concurrent access of the same data.

Locking affects the performance of the system through its granularity—that is, the size of the object that is being locked and the isolation level. Row-level locking provides the best system performance, because it leaves all but one row on the page unlocked and hence allows more concurrency than page- or table-level locking.

Isolation levels affect the duration of the lock for SELECT statements. Using the lower isolation levels, such as READ UNCOMMITTED and READ COMMITTED, the data availability, and hence the concurrency, of the data can be improved. (Locking and isolation levels are explained in detail in Chapter 13.)

System Resources and Performance

The Database Engine runs on the Windows operating system, which itself uses underlying system resources. These resources have a significant impact on the performance of both the operating system and the database system. Performance of any database system depends on four main system resources:

► Central processing unit (CPU)

► Memory

► Disk I/O

► Network

The CPU, together with memory, is the key component for marking the speed of a computer. It is also the key to the performance of a system, because it manages other resources of the system and executes all applications. It executes user processes and interacts with other resources of your system. Performance problems in relation to the CPU can occur when the operating system and user programs are making too many requests on it. Generally, the more CPU power available for your computer, the better the overall system is likely to perform.

The Database Engine dynamically acquires and frees memory as needed. Performance problems concerning memory can occur only if there is not enough of it to do the required work. When this occurs, many memory pages are written to a pagefile. (The notion of a *pagefile* is explained in detail later in this chapter.) If the process of writing to a pagefile happens very often, the performance of the system can degrade. Therefore, similar to the CPU rule, the more memory available for your computer, the better the system is likely to perform.

There are two issues concerning disk I/O: disk speed and disk transfer rate. The disk speed determines how fast read and write operations to disk are executed. The disk transfer rate specifies how much data can be written to disk during a time unit (usually measured in seconds). Obviously, the faster the disk, the larger the amount of data being processed. Also, more disks are generally better than a single disk when many users are using the database system concurrently. (In this case, access to data is usually spread across many disks, thus improving the overall performance of the system.)

For a client/server configuration, a database system sometimes performs poorly if there are many client connections. In that case, the amount of data that needs to be transferred across the network possibly exceeds the network capacity. To avoid such a performance bottleneck, the following general recommendations should be taken into account:

▶ If a database server sends any rows to an application, only the rows needed by the application should be sent.

▶ If a long-lasting user application executes strictly on the client side, move it to the server side (by executing it as a stored procedure, for example).

All four of these system resources are dependent on each other. This means that performance problems in one resource can cause performance problems in the other resources. Similarly, an improvement concerning one resource can significantly increase performance of some other (or even all) resources. For example:

▶ If you increase the number of CPUs, each CPU can share the load evenly and therefore can remedy the disk I/O bottleneck. On the other hand, the inefficient use of the CPU is often the result of a preexisting heavy load on disk I/O and/or memory.

▶ If more memory is available, there is more chance of finding a page needed by the application (rather than reading the page from disk), which results in a performance gain. By contrast, reading from the disk drive instead of drawing from the immensely faster memory slows the system down considerably, especially if there are many concurrent processes.

The following sections describe in detail disk I/O and memory.

Disk I/O

One purpose of a database is to store, retrieve, and modify data. Therefore, the Database Engine, like any other database system, must perform a lot of disk activity. In contrast to other system resources, a disk subsystem has two moving parts: the disk itself and the disk head. The rotation of the disk and the movement of the disk head need a great deal of time; therefore, disk reads and writes are two of the highest-cost operations that a database system performs. (For instance, access to a disk is significantly slower than memory access.)

The Database Engine stores the data in 8KB pages. The buffer cache of RAM is also divided into 8KB pages. The system reads data in units of pages. Reads occur not only for data retrieval, but also for any modification operations such as UPDATE and DELETE because the database system must read the data before it can be modified.

If the needed page is in the buffer cache, it will be read from memory. This I/O operation is called *logical I/O* or *logical read*. If it is not in memory, the page is read from disk and put in the buffer cache. This I/O operation is called *physical I/O* or *physical read*. The buffer cache is shared because the Database Engine uses the architecture with only one memory address space. Therefore, many users can access the same page. A logical write occurs when data is modified in the buffer cache. Similarly, a physical write occurs when the page is written from the buffer cache to disk. Therefore, more logical write operations can be made on one page before it is written to disk.

The Database Engine has a few components that have great impact on performance because they significantly consume the I/O resources:

▶   Read ahead

▶   Checkpoint

Read ahead is described in the following section, while checkpoint is explained in detail in Chapter 16.

Read Ahead   The optimal behavior of a database system would be to read data and never have to wait for a disk read request. The best way to perform this task is to know the next several pages that the user will need and to read them from the disk into the buffer pool *before* they are requested by the user process. This mechanism is called *read ahead*, and it allows the system to optimize performance by processing large amounts of data effectively.

The component of the Database Engine called Read Ahead Manager manages the read-ahead processes completely internally, so a user has no way to influence this process. Instead of using the usual 8KB pages, the Database Engine uses 64KB blocks of data as the unit for read-ahead reads. That way, the throughput for I/O requests is significantly increased. The read-ahead mechanism is used by the database system to perform large table scans and index range scans. Table scans are performed using the information that is stored in index allocation map (IAM) pages to build a serial list of the disk addresses that must be read. (IAM pages are allocation pages containing information about the extents that a table or index uses.) This allows the database system to optimize its I/O as large, sequential reads in disk order. Read Ahead Manager reads up to 2MB of data at a time. Each extent is read with a single operation.

NOTE

The Database Engine provides multiple serial read-ahead operations at once for each file involved in the table scan. This feature can take advantage of striped disk sets.

For index ranges, the Database Engine uses the information in the intermediate level of index pages immediately above the leaf level to determine which pages to read. The system scans all these pages and builds a list of the leaf pages that must be read. During this operation, the contiguous pages are recognized and read in one operation. When there are many pages to be retrieved, the Database Engine schedules a block of reads at a time.

The read-ahead mechanism can also have negative impacts on performance if too many pages for a process are read and the buffer cache is unnecessarily filled up. The only thing you can do in this case is create the indices you will actually need.

There are several performance counters and dynamic management views that are related to read-ahead activity. They are explained in detail later in this chapter.

Memory

Memory is a crucial resource component, not only for the running applications but also for the operating system. When an application is executed, it is loaded into memory and a certain amount of memory is allocated to the application. (In Microsoft terminology, the total amount of memory available for an application is called its *address space*.)

Microsoft Windows supports virtual memory. This means that the total amount of memory available to applications is the amount of physical memory (or RAM) in the computer plus the size of the specific file on the disk drive called pagefile. (The name of the pagefile on Windows is **pagefile.sys**.) Once data is moved out of its location in RAM, it resides in the pagefile. If the system is asked to retrieve data that is not in the proper RAM location, it will load the data from the location where it is stored and produce a so-called page fault.

NOTE

pagefile.sys should be placed on a different drive from the drive on which files used by the Database Engine are placed, because the paging process can have a negative impact on disk I/O activities.

For an entire application, only a portion of it resides in RAM. (Recently referenced pages can usually be found in RAM.) When the information the application needs is not in RAM, the operating system must page (that is, read the page from the pagefile into RAM). This process is called *demand paging*. The more the system has to page, the worse the performance is.

NOTE

When a page in RAM is required, the oldest page of the address space for an application is moved to the pagefile to make room for the new page. The replacement of pages is always limited to the address space of the current application. Therefore, there is no chance that pages in the address space of other running applications will be replaced.

As you already know, a page fault occurs if the application makes a request for information and the data page that contains that information is not in the proper RAM location of the computer. The information may either have been paged out to the pagefile or be located somewhere else in RAM. Therefore, there are two types of page fault:

▶ **Hard page fault** The page has been paged out (to the pagefile) and has to be brought into RAM from the disk drive.

▶ **Soft page fault** The page is found in another location in RAM.

Soft page faults consume only RAM resources. Therefore, they are better for performance than hard page faults, which cause disk reads and writes to occur.

NOTE

Page faults are normal in a Windows operating system environment because the operating system requires pages from the running applications to satisfy the need for memory of the starting applications. However, excessive paging (especially with hard page faults) is a serious performance problem because it can cause disk bottlenecks and start to consume the additional power of the processor.

Monitoring Performance

All the factors that affect performance can be monitored using different components. These components can be grouped in the following categories:

▶ Counters of Performance Monitor

▶ Dynamic management views (DMVs) and catalog views

▶ DBCC commands

▶ System stored procedures

This section first gives an overview of Performance Monitor and then describes all components for monitoring performance in relation to the four factors: CPU, memory, disk access, and network.

Performance Monitor: An Overview

Performance Monitor is a Windows graphical tool that provides the ability to monitor Windows activities and database system activities. The benefit of this tool is that it is tightly integrated with the Windows operating system and therefore displays reliable values concerning different performance issues. Performance Monitor provides a lot of performance objects, and each performance object contains several counters. These counters can be monitored locally or over the network.

Performance Monitor supports three different presentation modes:

▶ **Graphic mode**   Displays the selected counters as colored lines, with the X axis representing time and the Y axis representing the value of the counter. (This is the default display mode.)

▶ **Histogram mode**   Displays the selected counters as colored horizontal bars that represent the data sampling values.

▶ **Report mode**   Displays the values of counters textually.

To start Performance Monitor, choose Start | Administrative Tools | Performance Monitor. The starting window of Performance Monitor, shown in Figure 20-1, contains

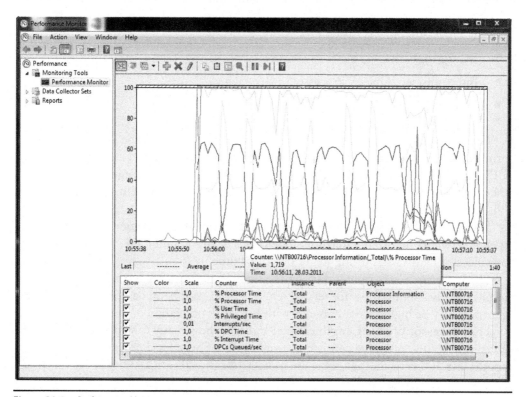

Figure 20-1   *Performance Monitor*

one default counter: **% Processor Time** (Object: Processor). This counter is very important, but you will need to display the values of several other counters.

To add a counter for monitoring, click the plus sign in the toolbar of Performance Monitor, select the performance object to which the counter belongs, choose the counter, and click Add. To remove a counter, highlight the line in the bottom area and click Delete. (The following sections describe, among other things, the most important counters in relation to the CPU, memory, I/O, and network.)

Monitoring the CPU

This section contains two subsections related to monitoring the CPU. The first subsection describes several Performance Monitor counters, while the second discusses catalog views and DMVs that you can use for the same purpose.

Monitoring the CPU Using Counters

The following counters are related to monitoring the CPU:

▶ % Processor Time (Object: Processor)

▶ % Interrupt Time (Object: Processor)

▶ Interrupts/sec (Object: Processor)

▶ Processor Queue Length (Object: System)

The **% Processor Time** counter displays system-wide CPU usage and acts as the primary indicator of processor activity. The lower the value of this counter, the better CPU usage that can be achieved. You should try to reduce CPU usage if the value of the counter is constantly greater than 90. (CPU usage of 100 percent is acceptable only if it happens for short periods of time.)

The **% Interrupt Time** counter shows you the percentage of time that the CPU spends servicing hardware interrupts. The values of this counter are important if at least one piece of hardware is trying to get processor time.

The **Interrupts/sec** counter displays the number of times per second the processor receives hardware interrupts for service requests from peripheral devices. This number generally may be high in environments with high disk utilization or networking demands.

The **Processor Queue Length** counter indicates how many threads are waiting for execution. If this counter is consistently higher than 5 when the processor utilization approaches 100 percent, then there are more active threads available than the machine's processors are able to handle.

Monitoring the CPU Using Views

The following catalog views and DMVs are used, among others, to monitor CPU usage:

- ▶ sys.sysprocesses
- ▶ sys.dm_exec_requests
- ▶ sys.dm_exec_query_stats

The **sys.sysprocesses** catalog view can be useful if you want to identify processes that use the most processor time. Example 20.1 shows the use of this catalog view.

EXAMPLE 20.1

```
USE master;
SELECT spid, dbid, uid, cpu
    FROM master.dbo.sysprocesses
    order by cpu DESC;
```

The view contains information about processes that are running on an instance. These processes can be client processes or system processes. The view belongs to the **master** system database. The most important columns of the view are **spid** (session ID), **dbid** (ID of the current database), **uid** (ID of the user who executes the current command), and **cpu** (cumulative CPU time for the process).

The **sys.dm_exec_requests** dynamic management view provides the same information as the **sys.sysprocesses** catalog view, but the names of the corresponding columns are different. Example 20.2 displays the same information as Example 20.1.

EXAMPLE 20.2

```
SELECT session_id, database_id, user_id, cpu_time, sql_handle
    FROM sys.dm_exec_requests
    order by cpu_time DESC;
```

The **sql_handle** column of the view points to the area in which the entire batch is stored. If you want to reduce the information to only one statement, you have to use the columns **statement_start_offset** and **statement_end_offset** to shorten the result. (All other column names are self-explanatory.)

NOTE

This DMV is especially worthwhile if you want to identify long-running queries.

Another DMV that can be used to display the information of such cached Transact-SQL statements and stored procedures using the most CPU time is **sys.dm_exec_query_stats**. (You can find the description of this DMV in Chapter 19.) Example 20.3 shows the use of this view.

EXAMPLE 20.3

```
SELECT TOP 20 SUM(total_worker_time) AS cpu_total,
        SUM(execution_count) AS exec_ct, COUNT(*) AS all_stmts, plan_handle
      FROM sys.dm_exec_query_stats
     GROUP BY plan_handle
      ORDER BY cpu_total;
```

The **total_worker_time** column of the **sys.dm_exec_query_stats** view displays the total amount of CPU time that was consumed by executions of cached SQL statements and stored procedures since it was compiled. The **execution_count** column displays the number of times that the cached plans have been executed since they were last compiled. (The TOP clause reduces the number of the displayed rows according to the parameter and the ORDER BY clause. This clause is described in detail in Chapter 23.)

Monitoring Memory

This section contains three subsections related to monitoring memory. The first subsection describes several Performance Monitor counters, the second discusses DMVs you can use for the same purpose, and the last is devoted to using the DBCC MEMORYSTATUS command.

Monitoring Memory Using Counters

The following Performance Monitor counters are used to monitor memory:

▶ Buffer Cache Hit Ratio (Object: Memory)

▶ Pages/sec (Object: Memory)

▶ Page Faults/sec (Object: Memory)

The **Buffer Cache Hit Ratio** counter displays the percentage of pages that did not require a read from disk. The higher this ratio, the less often the system has to go to the hard disk to fetch data, and performance overall is boosted. Note that there is no ideal value for this counter because it is application specific.

NOTE

This counter is different from most other counters, because it is not a real-time measurement, but rather an average value of all the days since the last restart of the Database Engine.

The **Pages/sec** counter displays the amount of paging (that is, the number of pages read or written to disk per second). The counter is an important indicator of the types of faults that cause performance problems. If the value of this counter is too high, you should consider adding more physical memory.

The **Page Faults/sec** counter displays the average number of page faults per second. This counter includes both soft page and hard page faults. As you already know, page faults occur when a system process refers to a virtual memory page that is not currently within the working set in the physical memory. If the requested page is on the standby list or a page currently shared with another process, a *soft page fault* is generated and the memory reference is resolved without physical disk access. However, if the referenced page is currently in the paging file, a *hard page fault* is generated and the data must be fetched from the disk.

Monitoring Memory Using Dynamic Management Views

The following DMVs are related to memory:

▶ sys.dm_os_memory_clerks

▶ sys.dm_os_memory_objects

The **sys.dm_os_memory_clerks** view returns the set of all memory clerks that are active in the current instance. You can use this view to find memory allocations by different memory types. Example 20.4 shows the use of this view.

EXAMPLE 20.4

```
SELECT type, SUM(pages_kb)
    FROM sys.dm_os_memory_clerks
    WHERE pages_kb != 0
    GROUP BY type
     ORDER BY 2 DESC;
```

The **type** column of the **sys.dm_os_memory_clerks** view describes the type of memory clerk. The **pages_kb** column specifies the amount of memory allocated by using the single page allocator of a memory node.

> **NOTE**
>
> *The Database Engine memory manager consists of a three-layer hierarchy. At the bottom of the hierarchy are memory nodes. The next level consists of memory clerks, memory caches, and memory pools. The last layer consists of memory objects. These objects are generally used to allocate memory.*

The **sys.dm_os_memory_objects** view returns memory objects that are currently allocated by the database system. This DMV is primarily used to analyze memory usage and to identify possible memory leaks, as shown in Example 20.5.

EXAMPLE 20.5

```
SELECT type , SUM(pages_in_bytes) AS total_memory
    FROM sys.dm_os_memory_objects
    GROUP BY type
    ORDER BY total_memory DESC;
```

Example 20.5 groups all memory objects according to their type and then uses the values of the **pages_in_bytes** column to display the total memory of each group.

Monitoring Memory Using the DBCC MEMORYSTATUS Command

The DBCC MEMORYSTATUS command provides a snapshot of the current memory status of the Database Engine. The command's output is useful in troubleshooting issues that relate to the memory consumption of the Database Engine or to specific out-of-memory errors (many of which automatically print this output in the error log).

The output of this command has several parts, including the "Process/System Counts" part, which delivers important information concerning the total amount of memory (the Working set parameter) and the actual memory used by the Database Engine (the Available Physical Memory parameter).

Monitoring the Disk System

This section contains two subsections that discuss monitoring the disk system. The first subsection describes several Performance Monitor counters, while the second describes the corresponding DMVs that you can use to monitor the disk system.

Monitoring the Disk System Using Counters

The following counters are related to monitoring the disk system:

- ▶ % Disk Time (Object: Physical Disk)
- ▶ Current Disk Queue Length (Object: Physical Disk)
- ▶ Disk Read Bytes/sec (Object: Physical Disk)
- ▶ Disk Write Bytes/sec (Object: Physical Disk)
- ▶ % Disk Time (Object: Logical Disk)
- ▶ Current Disk Queue Length (Object: Logical Disk)
- ▶ Disk Read Bytes/sec (Object: Logical Disk)
- ▶ Disk Write Bytes/sec (Object: Logical Disk)

As you can see from the preceding list, the names of the Performance Monitor counters for the Physical Disk object and the Logical Disk object are the same. (The difference between physical and logical objects is explained in Chapter 5.) These counters have the same purpose for each of the objects as well, so the following descriptions explain the counters only for the Physical Disk object.

The **% Disk Time** counter displays the amount of time that the hard disk actually has to work. It provides a good relative measure of how busy your disk system is, and it should be used over a longer period of time to indicate a potential need for more I/O capacity.

The **Current Disk Queue Length** counter tells you how many I/O operations are waiting for the disk to become available. This number should be as low as possible.

The **Disk Read Bytes/sec** counter shows the rate at which bytes were transferred from the hard disk during read operations, while **Disk Write Bytes/sec** provides the rate at which bytes were transferred to the hard disk during write operations.

Monitoring the Disk System Using DMVs

The following DMVs can be useful to display information concerning the disk system:

- ▶ sys.dm_os_wait_stats
- ▶ sys.dm_io_virtual_file_stats

The **sys.dm_os_wait_stats** view returns information about the waits encountered by threads that are in execution. Use this view to diagnose performance issues with the Database Engine and with specific queries and batches. Example 20.6 shows the use of this view.

EXAMPLE 20.6

```
SELECT wait_type, waiting_tasks_count, wait_time_ms
      FROM sys.dm_os_wait_stats
      ORDER BY wait_type;
```

The most important columns of this view are **wait_type** and **waiting_tasks_count**. The former displays the names of the wait types, while the latter displays the number of waits on the corresponding wait type.

The second view, **sys.dm_io_virtual_file_stats**, displays the file activity within a database allocation. Example 20.7 shows the use of this view.

EXAMPLE 20.7

```
SELECT database_id, file_id, num_of_reads,
      num_of_bytes_read, num_of_bytes_written
      FROM sys.dm_io_virtual_file_stats (NULL, NULL);
```

The columns of the **sys.dm_io_virtual_file_stats** view are self-explanatory. As you can see from Example 20.7, this view has two parameters. The first, **database_id**, specifies the unique ID number of the database, while the second, **file_id**, specifies the ID of the file. (When NULL is specified, all databases, i.e., all files in the instance of the Database Engine are returned.)

Monitoring the Network Interface

This section comprises three subsections related to monitoring the network interface. The first subsection describes several Performance Monitor counters, the second discusses the corresponding DMV, and the last one describes the **sp_monitor** system procedure.

Monitoring the Network Interface Using Counters

The following Performance Monitor counters are related to monitoring the network:

► Bytes Total/sec (Object: Network Interface)

► Bytes Received/sec (Object: Network Interface)

► Bytes Sent/sec (Object: Network Interface)

The **Bytes Total/sec** counter monitors the number of bytes that are sent and received over the network per second. (This includes both the Database Engine and non–Database Engine network traffic.) Assuming your server is a dedicated database server, the vast majority of the traffic measured by this counter should be from the Database Engine. A consistently low value for this counter indicates that network problems may be interfering with your application.

To find out how much data is being sent back and forth from your server to the network, use the **Bytes Received/sec** and **Bytes Sent/sec** counters. The former displays the rate at which network data (in bytes) are received, while the latter checks the outbound rate. These counters will help you to find out how busy your actual server is over the network.

Monitoring the Network Interface Using a DMV

The **sys.dm_exec_connections** view returns information about the connections established to the instance of the Database Engine and the details of each connection. Examples 20.8 and 20.9 show the use of this view.

EXAMPLE 20.8

```
SELECT net_transport, auth_scheme
    FROM sys.dm_exec_connections
    WHERE session_id=@@SPID;
```

Example 20.8 displays the basic information about the current connection: network transport protocol and authentication mechanism. The condition in the WHERE clause reduces the output to the current session. (The @@spid global variable, which is described in Chapter 4, returns the identifier of the current server process.)

EXAMPLE 20.9

```
SELECT num_reads, num_writes
    FROM sys.dm_exec_connections;
```

Two important columns of this DMV, which are used in Example 20.9, are **num_reads** and **num_writes**. The former displays the number of packet reads that have occurred over the current connection, while the latter provides information about the number of packet writes that have occurred over this connection.

Monitoring the Network Interface Using a System Procedure

The **sp_monitor** system procedure can be very useful to monitor data concerning the network interface because it displays the information in relation to packets sent and received as a running total. This system procedure also displays statistics, such as the number of seconds the CPU has been doing system activities, the number of seconds the system has been idle, and the number of logins (or attempted logins) to the system.

Choosing the Right Tool for Monitoring

The choice of an appropriate tool depends on the performance factors to be monitored and the type of monitoring. The type of monitoring can be

- ▶ Real time
- ▶ Delayed (by saving information in the file, for example)

Real-time monitoring means that performance issues are investigated as they are happening. If you want to display the actual values of one or a few performance factors, such as the number of users or number of attempted logins, use dynamic management views because of their simplicity. In fact, dynamic management views can only be used for real-time monitoring. Therefore, if you want to trace performance activities during a specific time period, you have to use a tool such as SQL Server Profiler (see the next section).

Probably the best all-around tool for monitoring is Performance Monitor because of its many options. First, you can choose the performance activities you want to track and then display them simultaneously. Second, Performance Monitor allows you to set thresholds on specific counters (performance factors) to generate alerts that notify operators. This way, you can react promptly to any performance bottlenecks. Third, you can report performance activities and investigate the resulting chart log files later.

The following sections describe SQL Server Profiler and the Database Engine Tuning Advisor.

SQL Server Profiler

SQL Server Profiler is a graphical tool that lets system administrators monitor and record database and server activities, such as login, user, and application information. SQL Server Profiler can display information about several server activities in real time, or it can create filters to focus on particular events of a user, types of commands, or types of Transact-SQL statements. Among others, you can monitor the following events using SQL Server Profiler:

- ▶ Login connections, attempts, failures, and disconnections
- ▶ CPU use of a batch

- ▶ Deadlock problems
- ▶ All DML statements (SELECT, INSERT, UPDATE, and DELETE)
- ▶ The start and/or end of a stored procedure

The most useful feature of SQL Server Profiler is the ability to capture activities in relation to queries. These activities can be used as input for the Database Engine Tuning Advisor, which allows you to select indices and indexed views for one or more queries. For this reason, the following section discusses the features of SQL Server Profiler together with the Database Engine Tuning Advisor.

Database Engine Tuning Advisor

The Database Engine Tuning Advisor is part of the overall system and allows you to automate the physical design of your databases. As mentioned earlier, the Database Engine Tuning Advisor is tightly connected to SQL Server Profiler, which can display information about several server activities in real time, or it can create filters to focus on particular events of a user, types of commands, or Transact-SQL statements.

The specific feature of SQL Server Profiler that is used by the Database Engine Tuning Advisor is its ability to watch and record batches executed by users and to provide performance information, such as CPU use of a batch and corresponding I/O statistics, as explained next.

Providing Information for the Database Engine Tuning Advisor

The Database Engine Tuning Advisor is usually used together with SQL Server Profiler to automate tuning processes. You use SQL Server Profiler to record into a trace file information about the workload being examined. (As an alternative to a workload file, you can use any file that contains a set of Transact-SQL statements. In this case, you do not need SQL Server Profiler.) The Database Engine Tuning Advisor can then read the file and recommend several physical objects, such as indices, indexed views, and partitioning schema, that should be created for the given workload.

Example 20.10 creates two new tables, **orders** and **order_details**. These tables will be used to demonstrate the recommendation of physical objects by the Database Engine Tuning Advisor.

NOTE

If your **sample** database already contains the **orders** table, you have to drop it using the DROP TABLE statement.

EXAMPLE 20.10

```
USE sample;
CREATE TABLE orders
    (orderid INTEGER NOT NULL,
     orderdate DATE,
     shippeddate DATE,
     freight money);
CREATE TABLE order_details
    (productid INTEGER NOT NULL,
     orderid INTEGER NOT NULL,
     unitprice money,
     quantity INTEGER);
```

To demonstrate the use of the Database Engine Tuning Advisor, many more rows are needed in both tables. Examples 20.11 and 20.12 insert 3000 rows in the **orders** table and 30,000 rows in the **order_details** table, respectively.

EXAMPLE 20.11

```
-- This batch inserts 3000 rows in the table orders
USE sample;
declare @i int, @order_id integer
          declare @orderdate datetime
          declare @shipped_date datetime
          declare @freight money
          set @i = 1
          set @orderdate = getdate()
          set @shipped_date = getdate()
          set @freight = 100.00
        while @i < 3001
          begin
          insert into orders (orderid, orderdate, shippeddate, freight)
            values(@i, @orderdate, @shipped_date, @freight)
          set @i = @i+1
          end
```

EXAMPLE 20.12

```
-- This batch inserts 30000 rows in order_details and modifies some of them
USE sample;
declare @i int, @j int
          set @i = 3000
```

```
set @j = 10
while @j > 0
begin
if @i > 0
    begin
    insert into order_details (productid, orderid, quantity)
            values (@i, @j, 5)
    set @i = @i - 1
    end
else begin
    set @j = @j - 1
    set @i = 3000
    end
end
go
update order_details set quantity = 3
        where productid in (1511, 2678)
```

The query in Example 20.13 will be used as an input file for SQL Server Profiler. (Assume that no indices are created for the columns that appear in the SELECT statement.) First start SQL Server Profiler. Choose All Programs | Microsoft SQL Server 2012 | Performance Tools | SQL Server Profiler. On the File menu, choose New Trace. After connecting to the server, the Trace Properties dialog box appears. Type a name for the trace and select an output .trc file for the Profiler information (in the Save to File field). Click Run to start the capture and use SQL Server Management Studio to execute the query in Example 20.13.

EXAMPLE 20.13

```
USE sample;
SELECT orders.orderid, orders.shippeddate
        FROM orders
    WHERE orders.orderid between 806 and 1600
    and not exists (SELECT order_details.orderid
                    FROM order_details
                    WHERE order_details.orderid = orders.orderid);
```

Finally, stop SQL Server Profiler by choosing File | Stop Trace and selecting the corresponding trace.

Working with the Database Engine Tuning Advisor

The Database Engine Tuning Advisor analyzes a workload and recommends the physical design of one or more databases. The analysis will include recommendations to add, remove, or modify the physical database structures, such as indices, indexed views, and partitions. The Database Engine Tuning Advisor will recommend a set of physical database structures that will optimize the tasks included in the workload.

To use the Database Engine Tuning Advisor, shown in Figure 20-2, choose Start | All Programs | Microsoft SQL Server 2012 | Performance Tools | Database Engine Tuning Advisor. (The alternative way is to start SQL Server Profiler and choose Tools | Database Engine Tuning Advisor.)

In the Session Name field, type the name of the session for which the Database Engine Tuning Advisor will create tuning recommendations. In the Workload frame,

Figure 20-2   *Database Engine Tuning Advisor: General tab*

choose either File or Table. If you choose File, enter the name of the trace file. If you choose Table, you must enter the name of the table that is created by SQL Server Profiler. (Using SQL Server Profiler, you can capture and save data about each workload to a file or to a SQL Server table.)

NOTE

Running SQL Server Profiler can place a heavy burden on a busy instance of the Database Engine.

In the Select Databases and Tables to Tune frame, choose one or more databases and/or one or more tables that you want to tune. (The Database Engine Tuning Advisor can tune a workload that involves multiple databases. This means that the tool can recommend indices, indexed views, and partitioning schema on any of the databases in the workload.)

To choose options for tuning, click the Tuning Options tab (see Figure 20-3). Most of the options on this tab are divided into three groups:

▶ **Physical Design Structures (PDS) to use in database**   Allows you to choose which physical structures (indices and/or indexed views) should be recommended by the Database Engine Tuning Advisor, after tuning the existing workload. (The Evaluate Utilization of Existing PDS Only option causes the Database Engine Tuning Advisor to analyze the existing physical structures and recommend which of them should be deleted.)

▶ **Partitioning strategy to employ**   Allows you to choose whether or not partitioning recommendations should be made. If you opt for partitioning recommendations, you can also choose the type of partitioning, full or aligned. (Partitioning is discussed in detail in Chapter 25.)

▶ **Physical Design Structures (PDS) to keep in database**   Enables you to decide which, if any, existing structures should remain intact in the database after the tuning process.

For large databases, tuning physical structures usually requires a significant amount of time and resources. Instead of starting an exhaustive search for possible indexes, the Database Engine Tuning Advisor offers (by default) the restrictive use of resources. This operation mode still gives very accurate results, although the number of resources tuned is significantly reduced.

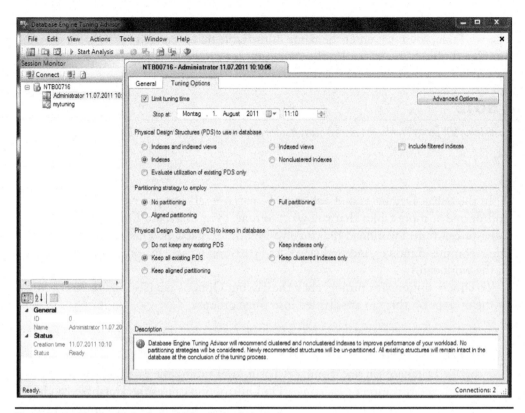

Figure 20-3   *Database Engine Tuning Advisor: Tuning Options tab*

During the specification of tuning options, you can define additional customization options by clicking Advanced Options, which opens the Advanced Tuning Options dialog box (see Figure 20-4). Checking the check box at the top of the dialog box enables you to define the maximum space for recommendations. Increase the maximum space to 20MB if you intend to start an exhaustive search. (For large databases, selection of physical structures usually requires a significant amount of resources. Instead of starting an exhaustive search, the Database Engine Tuning Advisor offers you the option to restrict the space used for tuning.)

Of all index tuning options, one of the most interesting is the second option in this dialog box, which enables you to determine the maximum number of columns per index. A single-column index or a composite index built on two columns can be used several times for a workload with many queries and requires less storage space than a composite index built on four or more columns. (This applies in the case where you use

Figure 20-4 *Advanced Tuning Options dialog box*

a workload file on your own instead of using SQL Server Profiler's trace for the specific workload.) On the other hand, a composite index built on four or more columns may be used as a covering index to enable index-only access for some of the queries in the workload. (For more information on covering indices, see Chapter 10.)

After you select options in the Advanced Tuning Options dialog box, click OK to close it. You can then start the analysis of the workload. To start the tuning process, choose Actions | Start Analysis. After you start the tuning process for the trace file of the query in Example 20.13, the Database Engine Tuning Advisor creates tuning recommendations, which you can view by clicking the Recommendations tab, as shown in Figure 20-5. As you can see, the Database Engine Tuning Advisor recommends the creation of two indices.

The Database Engine Tuning Advisor recommendations concerning physical structures can be viewed using a series of reports that provide information about very interesting options. These reports enable you to see how the Database Engine Tuning Advisor evaluated the workload. To see these reports, click the Reports tab in the Database Engine Tuning Advisor dialog box after the tuning process is finished. You can see the following reports, among others:

- ▶ **Index Usage Report (recommended configuration)** Displays information about the expected usage of the recommended indexes and their estimated sizes

- ▶ **Index Usage Report (current configuration)** Presents the same information about expected usage for the existing configuration

- ▶ **Index Detail Report (recommended configuration)** Displays information about the names of all recommended indices and their types

Figure 20-5   *Database Engine Tuning Advisor: Recommendations tab*

► **Index Detail Report (current configuration)**   Presents the same information for the actual configuration, before the tuning process was started

► **Table Access Report**   Displays information about the costs of all queries in the workload (using tables in the database)

► **Workload Analysis Report**   Provides information about the relative frequencies of all data modification statements (costs are calculated relative to the most expensive statement with the current index configuration)

There are three ways in which you can apply recommendations: immediately, scheduled, or after saving to the file. If you choose Actions | Apply Recommendations, the recommendations will be applied immediately. Similarly, if you choose Actions | Save Recommendations, the recommendations will be saved to the file. (This alternative is useful if you generate the script with one (test) system and intend to use the tuning recommendation with another (production) system.) The third option, Actions | Evaluate Recommendations, is used to evaluate the recommendations produced by the Database Engine Tuning Advisor.

Other Performance Tools of SQL Server

SQL Server supports two additional performance tools:

▶ Performance Data Collector

▶ Resource Governor

The following sections describe these tools.

Performance Data Collector

Generally, it is very hard for DBAs to track down performance problems. The reason for this is that DBAs usually are not there at the exact time a problem occurs, and thus they have to react to an existing problem by first tracking it down.

Microsoft has included an entire infrastructure called Performance Data Collector to solve the problem. Performance Data Collector is a component that is installed as a part of an instance of the Database Engine and can be configured to run either on a defined schedule or nonstop. The tool has three tasks:

▶ To collect different sets of data related to performance

▶ To store this data in the management data warehouse (MDW)

▶ To allow a user to view collected data using predefined reports

To use Performance Data Collector, you have to configure the MDW first. To do this using SQL Server Management Studio, expand the server, expand Management, right-click Data Collection, and click Configure Management Data Warehouse. The Configure Management Data Warehouse Wizard appears. The wizard has two tasks: to create the MDW and to set up data collection. After you complete these tasks, you can run Performance Data Collector and view the reports it generates.

Creating the MDW

After you click Next on the Welcome screen of the wizard, the Select Configuration Task wizard screen appears. Choose the Create or Upgrade a Management Data

Figure 20-6   *Configuring MDW storage by selecting a server and database*

Warehouse option and click Next. On the Configure Data Warehouse Storage
screen (see Figure 20-6), choose a server and database to host your management data
warehouse and click Next. On the Map Login and Users screen, map existing logins
and users to management data warehouse roles (see Figure 20-7). This activity has to
be performed explicitly because no user is a member of a management data warehouse
role by default. Click Next when you are finished. On the Complete the Wizard screen,
verify the configuration and click Finish.

Setting Up Data Collection

After setting up the MDW, you have to start data collection. Restart the Configure
Management Data Warehouse Wizard and this time choose Set Up Data Collection on
the Select Configuration Task screen. Click Next. On the Configure Management Data
Warehouse Storage screen (see Figure 20-8), specify the server name and the name of
the data warehouse that you created in the prior section, and then specify where you
want collected data to be cached locally before it is uploaded to the MDW. Click Next.
On the Complete the Wizard screen, click Finish. The wizard finishes its work, giving
you a summary of the executed tasks.

Figure 20-7 *Mapping logins and users to management data warehouse roles*

Figure 20-8 *Configure Management Data Warehouse Storage*

Viewing Reports

Once Performance Data Collector is configured and active, the system will start collecting performance information and uploading the data to the MDW. Also, three new reports (Server Activity History, Disk Usage Summary, and Query Statistics History) will be created for viewing data collected by Performance Data Collector. To open the reports, right-click Data Collection, click Reports, and choose one of these reports under Management Data Warehouse.

The first report, Server Activity History, displays performance statistics for system resources described in this chapter. The second report, Disk Usage Summary, displays the starting size and average daily growth of data and log files. The last report, Query Statistics History, displays query execution statistics.

Resource Governor

One of the biggest problems in relation to performance tuning is trying to manage resources with the competing workloads on a shared database server. You can solve this problem using either server virtualization or several instances. In both cases, it is not possible for an instance to ascertain whether the other instances (or virtual machines) are using memory and the CPU. Resource Governor manages such a situation by enabling one instance to reserve a portion of a system resource for a particular process.

Generally, Resource Governor enables DBAs to define resource limits and priorities for different workloads. That way, consistent performance for processes can be achieved.

Resource Governor has two main components:

▶ Workload groups
▶ Resource pools

When a process connects to the Database Engine, it is classified and then assigned to a workload group based on that classification. (The classification is done using either a built-in classifier or a user-defined function.) One or more workload groups are then assigned to specific resource pools (see Figure 20-9).

NOTE

Only CPU and memory can be managed by Resource Governor. In other words, the tool doesn't support I/O and network system resources.

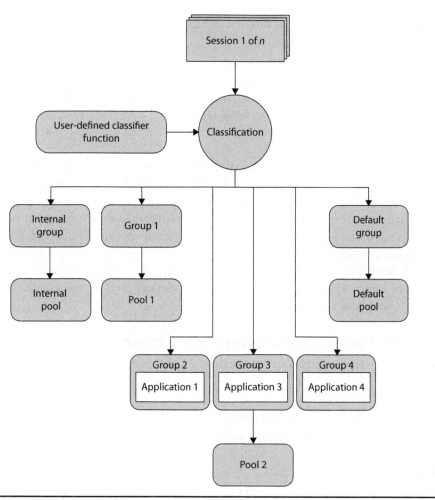

Figure 20-9 *Architecture of Resource Governor*

As you can see in Figure 20-9, there are two different workload groups:

▶ Internal group
▶ Default group

The internal group is used to execute certain system functions, while the default group is used when the process doesn't have a defined classification. (You cannot modify the classification for the internal group. However, monitoring of the workload of the internal group is possible.)

> **NOTE**
>
> *The internal and default groups are predefined workload groups. In addition to them, the tool allows the specification of 18 additional (user-defined) workload groups.*

A resource pool represents the allocation of system resources of the Database Engine. Each resource pool has two different parts, which specify the minimum and maximum resource reservation. While minimum allocations of all pool resources cannot overlap, the sum of them cannot exceed 100 percent of all system resources. On the other hand, the maximum value of a resource pool can be set between its minimal value and 100 percent.

Analogous to workload groups, there are two predefined resource pools: the internal pool and the default pool. The internal pool contains the system resources, which are used by the internal processes of the system. The default pool contains both the default workload group and user-defined groups.

Creation of Workload and Resource Groups

The following steps are necessary to create workload and resource groups:

1. Create resource pools.
2. Create workload groups and assign them to pools.
3. For each workload group, define and register the corresponding classification function.

> **NOTE**
>
> *Resource Governer can be managed using SQL Server Management Studio or Transact-SQL statements. This section describes how the preceding steps can be executed using SSMS. The corresponding T-SQL statements will be mentioned, without any further explanation.*

Before you create new resource pools, you have to check whether Resource Governor is enabled. To do this, start Management Studio, expand the server, expand Management, right-click Resource Governor, and click Enable. (Alternatively, you can use the ALTER RESOURCE GOVERNOR T-SQL statement.)

> **NOTE**
>
> *Resource pools and workload groups can be created in one dialog box, as described next.*

To create a new resource pool, in Management Studio, expand the instance, expand Management, expand Resource Governor, right-click Resource Pools, and click New Resource Pool. The Resource Governor Properties dialog box appears (see Figure 20-10).

Generally, when you create a new resource pool, you have to specify its name and the minimum and maximum boundaries for CPU and memory. Therefore, in the Resource Pools table of the Resource Governor Properties dialog box, click the first column of the first empty row and type the name of the new pool. After that, specify the minimum and maximum values for CPU and memory.

You can specify a corresponding workload group in the same dialog box (see Figure 20-10). In the Workload Groups table, double-click the empty cell in the Name column and type the name of the corresponding group. Optionally, you can specify several different properties for that workload group. Click OK to exit the dialog box.

NOTE

To create a new resource pool using T-SQL, use the CREATE RESOURCE POOL statement. To create a new workload group, use the CREATE WORKLOAD GROUP statement.

Figure 20-10 *Resource Governor Properties dialog box*

After you specify the new pool and its corresponding workload group, you have to create a classification function. This function is a user-defined function that is used to create any association between a workload group and users. (An example of such a function can be found in the description of the ALTER RESOURCE GOVERNOR statement in Books Online.)

Monitoring Configuration of Resource Governor

The following two DMVs can be used to monitor workload groups and resource pools:

▶ sys.dm_resource_governor_workload_groups

▶ sys.dm_resource_governor_resource_pools

The **sys.dm_resource_governor_workload_groups** view displays the information concerning workload groups. The **total_query_optimization_count** column of this view displays the cumulative count of query optimizations in this workload group; if the value is too high, it may indicate memory pressure.

The **sys.dm_resource_governor_resource_pools** view displays the information concerning resource pools. The **total_cpu_usage_ms** and **used_memory_kb** columns specify the total usage of CPU and the used memory, respectively, and indicate how your resource pools consume these two system resources.

Summary

Performance issues can be divided into proactive and reactive response areas. Proactive issues concern all activities that affect performance of the overall system and that will affect future systems of an organization. Proper database design and proper choice of the form of Transact-SQL statements in application programs belong to the proactive response area. Reactive performance issues concern activities that are undertaken after the performance bottleneck occurs. SQL Server offers a variety of tools (graphical components, Transact-SQL statements, and stored procedures) that can be used to view and trace performance problems of a SQL Server system.

Of all components, Performance Monitor and dynamic management views are the best tools for monitoring because you can use them to track, display, report, and trace any performance bottlenecks.

The next chapter starts the Analysis Services part of the book. It introduces general terms and concepts that you need to know about this important topic.

Exercises

E.20.1

Discuss the differences between SQL Server Profiler and the Database Engine Tuning Advisor.

E.20.2

Discuss the differences between Performance Data Collector and Resource Governor.

Part IV

SQL Server and Business Intelligence

Chapter 21

Business Intelligence: An Introduction

In This Chapter

- ▶ Online Transaction Processing vs. Business Intelligence
- ▶ Data Warehouses and Data Marts
- ▶ Data Warehouse Design
- ▶ Cubes and Their Architectures
- ▶ Data Access

The goal of this chapter is to introduce you to an important area of database technology: business intelligence (BI). The first part of the chapter explains the difference between the online transaction processing world on one side and the BI world on the other side. A *data store* for a BI process can be either a data warehouse or a data mart. Both types of data store are discussed, and their differences are listed in the second part of the chapter. The design of data in BI and the need for creation of aggregate tables are explained at the end of the chapter.

Online Transaction Processing vs. Business Intelligence

From the beginning, relational database systems were used almost exclusively to capture primary business data, such as orders and invoices, using processing based on transactions. This focus on business data has its benefits and its disadvantages. One benefit is that the poor performance of early database systems improved dramatically, to the point that today many database systems can execute thousands of transactions per second (using appropriate hardware). On the other hand, the focus on transaction processing prevented people in the database business from seeing another natural application of database systems: using them to filter and analyze needed information out of all the existing data in an enterprise or department.

Online Transaction Processing

As already stated, performance is one of the main issues for systems that are based upon transaction processing. These systems are called online transaction processing (OLTP) systems. A typical example of an operation performed by an OLTP system is to process the withdrawal of money from a bank account using a teller machine. OLTP systems have some important properties, such as:

▶ Short transactions—that is, high throughput of data

▶ Many (possibly hundreds or thousands of) users

▶ Continuous read and write operations based on a small number of rows

▶ Data of medium size that is stored in a database

The performance of a database system will increase if transactions in the database application programs are short. The reason is that transactions use locks (see Chapter 13) to prevent possible negative effects of concurrency issues. If transactions are long lasting, the number of locks and their duration increases, decreasing the data availability for other transactions and thus their performance.

Large OLTP systems usually have many users working on the system simultaneously. A typical example is a reservation system for an airline company which must process thousands of requests for travel arrangements in a single country, or all over the world, almost immediately. In this type of system, most users expect that their response-time requirements will be fulfilled by the system and the system will be available during working hours (or 24 hours a day, seven days a week).

Users of an OLTP system execute their DML statements continuously—that is, they use both read and write operations at the same time and steadily. (Because data of an OLTP system is continuously modified, that data is highly dynamic.) All operations (or results of them) on a database usually include only a small amount of data, although it is possible that the database system must access many rows from one or more tables stored in the database.

In recent years, the amount of data stored in an *operational* database (that is, a database managed by an OLTP system) has increased steadily. Today, there are many databases that store several or even dozens of gigabytes of data. As you will see, this amount of data is still relatively small in relation to data warehouses.

Business Intelligence Systems

Business intelligence is the process of integrating enterprise-wide data into a single data store from which end users can run ad hoc queries and reports to analyze the existing data. In other words, the goal of BI is to keep data that can be accessed by users who make their business decisions on the basis of the analysis. These systems are often called *analytic* or *informative* systems because, by accessing data, users get the necessary information for making better business decisions.

The goals of BI systems are different from the goals of OLTP systems. The following is a query that is typical for a BI system: "What is the best-selling product category for each sales region in the third quarter of the year 2011?" Therefore, a BI system has very different properties from those listed for an OLTP system in the preceding section. The most important properties of a BI system are as follows:

- ▶ Periodic write operations (load) with queries based on a huge number of rows
- ▶ Small number of users
- ▶ Large size of data stored in a database

Other than loading data at regular intervals (usually daily), BI systems are mostly read-only systems. (Therefore, the nature of the data in such a system is static.) As will be explained in detail later in this chapter, data is gathered from different sources, cleaned (made consistent), and loaded into a database called a data warehouse (or data mart). The cleaned data is usually not modified—that is, users query data using SELECT statements to obtain the necessary information (and modification operations are very seldom).

Because BI systems are used to gain information, the number of users that simultaneously use such a system is relatively small in relation to the number of users that simultaneously use an OLTP system. Users of a BI system usually generate reports that display different factors concerning the finances of an enterprise (or department), or they execute complex queries to compare data.

NOTE

Another difference between OLTP and BI systems that actually affects the user's behavior is the daily schedule— that is, when those systems are available for use during a day. An OLTP system can be used nonstop (if it is designed for such a use), whereas a BI system can be used only as soon as data is made consistent and is loaded into the database.

In contrast to databases in OLTP systems that store only current data, BI systems must also track historical data. (Remember that BI systems make comparisons between data gathered in different time periods.) For this reason, the amount of data stored in a data warehouse is very large.

Data Warehouses and Data Marts

A *data warehouse* can be defined as a database that includes all corporate data and that can be uniformly accessed by users. That's the concise definition; explaining the notion of a data warehouse is much more involved. An enterprise usually has a large amount of data stored at different times and in different databases (or data files) that are managed by distinct DBMSs. These DBMSs need not be relational: some enterprises still have databases managed by hierarchical or network database systems. A special team of software specialists examines source databases (and data files) and converts them into a target store: the data warehouse. Additionally, the converted data in a data warehouse must be consolidated, because it holds the information that is the key to the corporation's operational processes. (*Consolidation* of data means that all equivalent queries executed upon a data warehouse at different times provide the same result.) The data consolidation in a data warehouse is provided in several steps:

- ► Data assembly from different sources (also called extraction)
- ► Data cleaning (in other words, transformation process)
- ► Quality assurance of data

Data must be carefully assembled from different sources. In this process, data is extracted from the sources, converted to an intermediate schema, and moved to a temporary work area. For data extraction, you need tools that extract exactly the data that must be stored in the data warehouse.

Data cleaning ensures the integrity of data that has to be stored in the target database. For example, data cleaning must be done on incorrect entries in data fields, such as addresses, or incompatible data types used to define the same date fields in different sources. For this process, the data cleaning team needs special software. An example will help explain the process of data cleaning more clearly. Suppose that there are two data sources that store personal data about employees and that both databases have the attribute **Gender**. In the first database, this attribute is defined as CHAR(6), and the data values are "female" and "male." The same attribute in the second database is declared as CHAR(1), with the values "f" and "m." The values of both data sources are correct, but for the target data source you must clean the data—that is, represent the values of the attribute in a uniform way.

The last part of data consolidation—quality assurance of data—involves a data validation process that specifies the data as the end user should view and access it. Because of this, end users should be closely involved in this process. When the process of data consolidation is finished, the data will be loaded in the data warehouse.

NOTE

The whole process of data consolidation is called ETL (extraction, transformation, loading). Microsoft provides a component called SQL Server Integration Services (SSIS) to support users during the ETL process.

By their nature (as a store for the overall data of an enterprise), data warehouses contain huge amounts of data. (Some data warehouses contain dozens of terabytes or even petabytes of data.) Also, because they must encompass the enterprise, implementation usually takes a lot of time, which depends on the size of the enterprise. Because of these disadvantages, many companies start with a smaller solution called a data mart.

Data marts are data stores that include all data at the department level and therefore allow users to access data concerning only a single part of their organization. For example, the marketing department stores all data relevant to marketing in its own data mart, the research department puts the experimental data in the research data mart, and so on. Because of this, a data mart has several advantages over a data warehouse:

▶ Narrower application area

▶ Shorter development time and lower cost

▶ Easier data maintenance

▶ Bottom-up development

As already stated, a data mart includes only the information needed by one part of an organization, usually a department. Therefore, the data that is intended for use by such a small organizational unit can be more easily prepared for the end user's needs.

The average development time for a data warehouse is two years and the average cost is $5 million. On the other hand, costs for a data mart average $200,000, and such a project takes about three to five months. For these reasons, development of a data mart is preferred, especially if it is the first BI project in your organization.

The fact that a data mart contains significantly smaller amounts of data than a data warehouse helps you to reduce and simplify all tasks, such as data extraction, data cleaning, and quality assurance of data. It is also easier to design a solution for a department than to design one for the entire organization. (For more information on BI design and a dimensional model, see the next section of this chapter.)

If you design and develop several data marts in your organization, it is possible to unite them all in one big data warehouse. This bottom-up process has several advantages over designing a data warehouse at once. First, each data mart may contain identical target tables that can be unified in a corresponding data warehouse. Second, some tasks are logically enterprise-wide, such as the gathering of financial information by the accounting department. If the existing data marts will be linked together to build a data warehouse for an enterprise, a global repository (that is, the data catalog that contains information about all data stored in sources and in the target database) is required.

NOTE

Be aware that building a data warehouse by linking data marts can be very troublesome because of possible significant differences in the structure and design of existing data marts. Different parts of an enterprise may use different data models and have different instructions for data representation. For this reason, at the beginning of this bottom-up process, it is strongly recommended that you make a single view of all data that will be valid at the enterprise level; do not allow departments to design data separately.

Data Warehouse Design

Only a well-planned and well-designed database will allow you to achieve good performance. Relational databases and data warehouses have a lot of differences that require different design methods. Relational databases are designed using the well-known entity-relationship (ER) model, while the dimensional model is used for the design of data warehouses and data marts.

Using relational databases, data redundancy is removed using normal forms (see Chapter 1). The normalization process divides each table of a database that includes redundant data into two separate tables. The process of normalization should be finished when all tables of a database contain only nonredundant data.

The highly normalized tables are advantageous for OLTP because all transactions can be made as simple and short as possible. On the other hand, BI processes are based on queries that operate on a huge amount of data and are neither simple nor short. Therefore, the highly normalized tables do not suit the design of data warehouses, because the goal of BI systems is significantly different: there are few concurrent transactions, and each transaction accesses a very large number of records. (Imagine the huge amount of data belonging to a data warehouse that is stored in hundreds of tables. Most queries will join dozens of large tables to retrieve data. Such queries cannot be performed well, even if you use hardware with parallel processors and a database system with the best query optimizer.)

Data warehouses cannot use the ER model because this model is suited to design databases with nonredundant data. The logical model used to design data warehouses is called a *dimensional model*.

NOTE
There is another important reason why the ER model is not suited to the design of data warehouses: the use of data in a data warehouse is unstructured. This means the queries are partly executed ad hoc, allowing a user to analyze data in totally different ways. (On the other hand, OLTP systems usually have database applications that are hard-coded and therefore contain queries that are not modified often.)

In dimensional modeling, every particular model is composed of one table that stores measures and several other tables that describe dimensions. The former is called the *fact table*, and the latter are called *dimension tables*. Examples of data stored in a fact table include inventory sales and expenditures. Dimension tables usually include time, account, product, and employee data. Figure 21-1 shows an example of the dimensional model.

Figure 21-1   *Example of the dimensional model: star schema*

Each dimension table usually has a single-part primary key and several other attributes that describe this dimension closely. On the other hand, the primary key of the fact table is the combination of the primary keys of all dimension tables (see Figure 21-1). For this reason, the primary key of the fact table is made up of several foreign keys. (The number of dimensions also specifies the number of foreign keys in the fact table.) As you can see in Figure 21-1, the tables in a dimensional model build a star-like structure. Therefore, this model is often called *star schema*.

Another difference in the nature of data in a fact table and the corresponding dimension tables is that most nonkey columns in a fact table are numeric and additive, because such data can be used to execute necessary calculations. (Remember that a typical query on a data warehouse fetches thousands or even millions of rows at a time, and the only useful operation upon such a huge amount of rows is to apply an aggregate function, such as sum, maximum, or average). For example, columns like **Units_of_ product_sold**, **Total_sales**, **Profit**, or **Dollars_cost** are typical columns in the fact table. (Numerical columns of the fact table that do not build the primary key of the table are called *measures*.)

On the other hand, columns of dimension tables are strings that contain textual descriptions of the dimension. For instance, columns such as **Address**, **Location**, and

Name often appear in dimension tables. (These columns are usually used as headers in reports.) Another consequence of the textual nature of columns of dimension tables and their use in queries is that each dimension table contains many more indices than the corresponding fact table. (A fact table usually has only one unique index composed of all columns belonging to the primary key of that table.) Table 21-1 summarizes the differences between fact and dimension tables.

> **NOTE**
>
> *Sometimes it is necessary to have multiple fact tables in a data warehouse. If you have different sets of measures, each set has to be tied to a different fact table.*

Columns of dimension tables are usually highly *denormalized*, which means that a lot of columns depend on each other. The denormalized structure of dimension tables has one important purpose: all columns of such a table are used as column headers in reports. If the denormalization of data in a dimension table is not desirable, a dimension table can be decomposed into several subtables. This is usually necessary when columns of a dimension table build hierarchies. (For example, the **product** dimension could have columns such as **Product_id**, **Category_id**, and **Subcategory_id** that build three hierarchies, with the primary key, **Product_id**, as the root.) This structure, in which each level of a base entity is represented by its own table, is called a *snowflake schema*. Figure 21-2 shows the snowflake schema of the **product** dimension.

The extension of a star schema into a corresponding snowflake schema has some benefits (reduction of used disk space, for example) and one main disadvantage: the snowflake schema requires more join operations to get information from lookup tables, which negatively impacts performance. For this reason, the performance of queries based on the snowflake schema is generally slow. Therefore, the design using the snowflake schema is recommended only in a few very specialized cases.

Fact Table	Dimension Table
Usually one in a dimensional model	Many (12–20)
Contains most rows of a data warehouse	Contains relatively small amount of data
Composite primary key (contains all primary keys of dimension tables)	One column of a table builds the primary key
Non-key columns are numeric and additive	Columns are descriptive and therefore textual

Table 21-1   *The Differences Between Fact and Dimension Tables*

Figure 21-2 *The snowflake schema*

Cubes and Their Architectures

BI systems support different types of data storage. Some of these data storage types are based on a multidimensional database that is also called a cube. A *cube* is a subset of data from the data warehouse that can be organized into multidimensional structures. To define a cube, you first select a fact table from the dimensional schema and identify numerical columns (measures) of interest within it. Then you select dimension tables that provide descriptions for the set of data to be analyzed. To demonstrate this, consider how the cube for car sales analysis might be defined. For example, the fact table may include the measures **Cars_sold, Total_sales,** and **Costs,** while the tables **Models, Quarters,** and **Regions** specify dimension tables. The cube in Figure 21-3 shows all three dimensions: **Models, Regions,** and **Quarters.**

In each dimension there are discrete values called *members.* For instance, the **Regions** dimension may contain the following members: ALL, North America, South America, and Europe. (The ALL member specifies the total of all members in a dimension.)

Additionally, each cube dimension can have a hierarchy of levels that allows users to ask questions at a more detailed level. For example, the **Regions** dimension can include the following level hierarchies: **Country, Province,** and **City.** Similarly, the **Quarters** dimension can include **Month, Week,** and **Day** as level hierarchies.

> **NOTE**
>
> *Cubes and multidimensional databases are managed by special systems called multidimensional database systems (MDBMSs). SQL Server's MDBMS is called Analysis Services.*

Figure 21-3 *Cube with dimensions Models, Quarters, and Regions*

The physical storage of a cube is described after the following discussion of aggregation.

Aggregation

Data is stored in the fact table in its most detailed form so that corresponding reports can make use of it. On the other hand (as stated earlier), a typical query on a fact table fetches thousands or even millions of rows at a time, and the only useful operation upon such a huge amount of rows is to apply an aggregate function (sum, maximum, or average). This different use of data can reduce performance of ad hoc queries if they are executed on low-level (atomic) data, because time- and resource-intensive calculations will be necessary to perform each aggregate function.

For this reason, low-level data from the fact table should be summarized in advance and stored in intermediate tables. Because of their "aggregated" information, such tables are called *aggregate tables*, and the whole process is called *aggregation*.

NOTE

An aggregate row from the fact table is always associated with one or more aggregate dimension table rows. For example, the dimensional model in Figure 21-1 could contain the following aggregate rows: monthly sales aggregates by salespersons by region and region-level aggregates by salespersons by day.

An example will show why low-level data should be aggregated. An end user may want to start an ad hoc query that displays the total sales of the organization for the last month. This would cause the server to sum all sales for each day in the last month. If there are an average of 500 sales transactions per day in each of 500 stores of the organization, and data is stored at the transaction level, this query would have to read 7,500,000 (500 × 500 × 30 days) rows and build the sum to return the result. Now consider what happens if the data is aggregated in a table that is created using monthly sales by store. In this case, the table will have only 500 rows (the monthly total for each of 500 stores), and the performance gain will be dramatic.

How Much to Aggregate?

Concerning aggregation, there are two extreme solutions: no aggregation at all, and exhaustive aggregation for every possible combination of queries that users will need. From the preceding discussion, it should be clear that no aggregation at all is out of the question, because of performance issues. (The data warehouse without any aggregation table probably cannot be used at all as a production data store.) The opposite solution is also not acceptable, for several reasons:

► Enormous amount of disk space needed to store additional data

► Overwhelming maintenance of aggregate tables

► Initial data load too long

Storing additional data that is aggregated at every possible level consumes an additional amount of disk space that increases the initial disk space by a factor of six or more (depending on the amount of the initial disk space and the number of queries that users will need). The creation of tables to hold the aggregates for all existing combinations is an overwhelming task for the system administrator. Finally, building aggregates at initial data load can have devastating results if this load already lasts for a long time and the additional time is not available.

From this discussion you can see that aggregate tables should be carefully planned and created. During the planning phase, keep these two main considerations in mind when determining what aggregates to create:

► Where is the data concentrated?

► Which aggregates would most improve performance?

The planning and creation of aggregate tables is dependent on the concentration of data in the columns of the base fact table. In a data warehouse, where there is no activity on a given day, the corresponding row is not stored at all. So if the system loads a large number of rows, as compared to the number of all rows that can be loaded, aggregating by that column of the base fact table improves performance enormously. In contrast, if the system loads few rows, as compared to the number of all rows that can be loaded, aggregating by that column is not efficient.

Here is another example to demonstrate the preceding discussion. For products in the grocery store, only a few of them (say, 15 percent) are actually sold on a given day. If we have a dimensional model with three dimensions, **Product**, **Store**, and **Time**, only 15 percent of the combination of the three corresponding primary keys for the particular day and for the particular store will be occupied. The daily product sales data will thus be *sparse*. In contrast, if all or many products in the grocery store are sold on a given day (because of a special promotion, for example), the daily product sales data will be *dense*.

To find out which dimensions are sparse and which are dense, you have to build rows from all possible combinations of tables and evaluate them. Usually the **Time** dimension is dense, because there are always entries for each day. Given the dimensions **Product**, **Store**, and **Time**, the combination of the **Store** and **Time** dimensions is dense, because for each day there will certainly be data concerning selling in each store. On the other hand, the combination of the **Store** and **Product** dimensions is sparse (for the reasons previously discussed). In this case, the dimension **Product** is generally sparse, because its appearance in combination with other dimensions is sparse.

The choice of aggregates that would most improve performance depends on end users. Therefore, at the beginning of a BI project, you should interview end users to collect information on how data will be queried, how many rows will be retrieved by these queries, and other criteria.

Physical Storage of a Cube

Online analytical processing (OLAP) systems usually use one of the following three different architectures to store multidimensional data:

- ▶ Relational OLAP (ROLAP)
- ▶ Multidimensional OLAP (MOLAP)
- ▶ Hybrid OLAP (HOLAP)

Generally, these three architectures differ in the way in which they store leaf-level data and precomputed aggregates. (Leaf-level data is the finest grain of data that is defined in the cube's measure group. Therefore, the leaf-level data corresponds to the data of the cube's fact table.)

In ROLAP, the precomputed data isn't stored. Instead, queries access data from the relational database and its tables in order to bring back the data required to answer the question. MOLAP is a type of storage in which the leaf-level data and its aggregations are stored using a multidimensional cube.

Although the logical content of these two storage types is identical for the same data warehouse, and both ROLAP and MOLAP analytic tools are designed to allow analysis of data through the use of the dimensional data model, there are some significant differences between them. The advantages of ROLAP storage type are as follows:

▶ Data is not duplicated

▶ Materialized (that is, indexed) views can be used for aggregation (summaries)

If the data should also be stored in a multidimensional database, a certain amount of data must be duplicated. Therefore, the ROLAP storage type does not need additional storage to copy the leaf-level data. Also, the calculation of aggregation can be executed very quickly with ROLAP if the corresponding summary tables are generated using indexed views.

On the other hand, MOLAP also has several advantages over ROLAP:

▶ Aggregates are stored in a multidimensional form

▶ Query response is generally faster

Using MOLAP, many aggregates are precomputed and stored in a multidimensional cube. That way the system does not have to calculate the result of such an aggregate each time it is needed. In the case of MOLAP, the database engine and the database itself are usually optimized to work together, so the query response may be faster than in ROLAP.

HOLAP storage is a combination of the MOLAP and ROLAP storage types. Precomputed data is stored as in the case of the MOLAP storage, while the leaf-level data is left in the relational database. (Therefore, for queries using aggregation, HOLAP is identical to MOLAP.) The advantage of HOLAP storage is that the leaf-level data is not duplicated.

Data Access

Data in a data warehouse can be accessed using three general techniques:

▶ Reporting

▶ OLAP

▶ Data mining

Reporting is the simplest form of data access. A report is just a presentation of a query result in a tabular form. (Reporting is discussed in detail in Chapter 24.) With OLAP, you analyze data interactively; that is, it allows you to perform comparisons and calculations along any dimension in a data warehouse.

NOTE

Transact-SQL supports all standardized functions and constructs in relation to SQL/OLAP. This topic will be discussed in detail in Chapter 23.

Data mining is used to explore and analyze large quantities of data in order to discover significant patterns. This discovery is not the only task of data mining: using this technique, you must be able to turn the existing data into information and turn the information into action. In other words, it is not enough to analyze data; you have to apply the results of data mining meaningfully and take action upon the given results. (Data mining, as the most complex of the three techniques, will not be covered in this introductory book.)

Summary

At the beginning of a BI project, the main question is what to build: a data warehouse or a data mart. Probably the best answer is to start with one or more data marts that can later be united in a data warehouse. Most of the existing tools in the BI market support this alternative.

In contrast to operational databases that use ER models for their design, the design of data warehouses is best done using a dimensional model. These two models show significant differences. If you are already acquainted with the ER model, the best way to learn and use the dimensional model is to forget everything about the ER model and start modeling from scratch.

After this introductory discussion of general considerations about the BI process, the next chapter discusses the server part of Microsoft Analysis Services.

Exercises

E.21.1

Discuss the differences between operative and analytic systems.

E.21.2

Discuss the differences between the ER and dimensional models.

E.21.3

At the beginning of a project with a data warehouse, there is the so-called ETL (extracting, transforming, loading) process. Explain the three subprocesses.

E.21.4

Discuss the differences between a fact table and corresponding dimension tables.

E.21.5

Discuss the benefits of the three storage types (MOLAP, ROLAP, and HOLAP).

E.21.6

Why is it necessary to aggregate data stored in a fact table?

Chapter 22

SQL Server Analysis Services

In This Chapter

- ▶ SSAS Terminology
- ▶ Developing a Multidimensional Cube Using BIDS
- ▶ Retrieving and Delivering Data
- ▶ Security of SQL Server Analysis Services

S QL Server Analysis Services (SSAS) is a group of services that is used to manage data that is stored in a data warehouse or data mart. SSAS organizes data from a data warehouse into multidimensional cubes (see Chapter 21) with aggregates to allow the execution of sophisticated reports and complex queries. The key features of SSAS are

▶ Ease of use

▶ Support of different architectures

▶ Support of several APIs

SSAS offer wizards for almost every task that is executed during the design and implementation of a data warehouse. For example, the Data Source Wizard allows you to specify one or more data sources, while the Cube Wizard is used to create a multidimensional cube where aggregate data is stored. Additionally, ease of use is guaranteed by Business Intelligence Development Studio (BIDS). You can use this tool to develop databases and other data warehouse objects. This means that BIDS offers one interface for developing SSAS projects as well as SQL Server Integration Services (SSIS) and Reporting Services (SSRS) projects.

In contrast to most other data warehouse systems, SSAS allow you to use the architecture that is most appropriate for your needs. You can choose between the three architectures (MOLAP, ROLAP, and HOLAP) discussed in detail in Chapter 21.

SSAS provides many different APIs that can be used to retrieve and deliver data. One of these is OLE DB for OLAP interface that allows you to access SSAS cubes. Several APIs are described later in this chapter, in the section "Retrieving and Delivering Data."

Security aspects of SSAS are discussed at the end of the chapter.

SSAS Terminology

The following are the most important terms related to SSAS:

▶ Cube

▶ Dimension

▶ Member

▶ Hierarchy

▶ Cell

▶ Level

▶ Measure group

▶ Partition

A *cube* is a multidimensional structure that contains all or part of the data from a data warehouse. Although the term "cube" implies three dimensions, a multidimensional cube generally can have many more dimensions. Each cube contains all other components in the preceding list.

A *dimension* is a set of logically related attributes (stored together in a dimension table) that closely describes measures (stored in the fact table). For instance, **Time**, **Product**, and **Customer** are the typical dimensions that are part of many BI applications. (These three dimensions from the **AdventureWorksDW** database are used in the example in the following section that demonstrates how to create and process a multidimensional cube using BIDS.)

NOTE

One important dimension of a cube is the **Measures** *dimension, which includes all measures defined in the fact table.*

Each discrete value in a dimension is called a *member*. For instance, the members of a **Product** dimension could be **Computers**, **Disks**, and **CPUs**. Each member can be calculated, meaning that its value is calculated at run time using an expression that is specified during the definition of the member. (Because calculated members are not stored on the disk, they allow you to add new members without increasing the size of a corresponding cube.)

Hierarchies specify groupings of multiple members within each dimension. They are used to refine queries concerning data analysis.

Cells are parts of a multidimensional cube that are identified by coordinates (x-, y-, and z-coordinates, if the cube is three-dimensional). This means that a cell is a set containing members from each dimension. For instance, consider the three-dimensional cube in Chapter 21 (see Figure 21-3) that represents car sales for a single region within a quarter. The cells with the following coordinates belong, among others, to the cube:

▶ First quarter, South America, Falcon

▶ Third quarter, Asia, Eagle

When you define hierarchies, you define them in terms of their levels. In other words, *levels* describe the hierarchy from the highest (most summarized) level to the lowest (most detailed) level of data. The following list displays the possible hierarchy levels for the Time dimension:

▶ Quarter (Q1, Q2, Q3, Q4)

▶ Month (January, February, ...)

▶ Day (Day1, Day2, ...)

As you already know from Chapter 21, measures are numerical values, such as price or quantity, that appear in a fact table but do not build its primary key. A *measure group* is a set of measures that together build a logical unit for business purposes. Each measure group is built on the fly, using corresponding metadata information.

A cube can be divided into one or more partitions. *Partitions* are used by SSAS to manage and store data and aggregations for a measure group in a cube. Every measure group has at least one partition, which is created when the measure group is defined. Partitions are a powerful and flexible means of managing large cubes.

Developing a Multidimensional Cube Using BIDS

The main component of SSAS is Business Intelligence Development Studio (BIDS), a management tool that provides one development platform for different BI applications. Built on Visual Studio, BIDS supports an integrated platform for system developers in the business intelligence area.

You can use BIDS not only to create and manage cubes, but also to design capabilities for SQL Server Reporting Services and SQL Server Integration Services. (SSRS is discussed in Chapter 24, while the description of SSIS is beyond the scope of this book.)

NOTE

The user interface of BIDS is similar to the interface of SQL Server Management Studio. However, these two tools differ in their deployment: you should use BIDS to develop BI projects, while the goal of SQL Server Management Studio is mainly to operate and maintain database objects in relation to business intelligence.

The following steps are necessary to create and process a multidimensional cube using Business Intelligence Development Studio:

1. Create a BI project.
2. Identify data sources.

3. Specify data source views.
4. Create a cube.
5. Design storage aggregation.
6. Process the cube.
7. Browse the cube.

The following sections describe in detail these steps.

Create a BI Project

The first step in building an analytic application is to create a new project in BIDS. To start BIDS, choose Start | All Programs | Microsoft SQL Server 2012 | SQL Server Business Intelligence Development Studio. Next, choose File | New | Project. In the New Project dialog box, in the Installed Templates pane (see Figure 22-1), select Analysis Services (under the Business Intelligence folder) and select Analysis Services Multidimensional and Data Mining Project. Type the name of the project

Figure 22-1 *The New Project dialog box*

and its location in the Name and Location text boxes, respectively. For purposes of this example, name the project **BI_Project**, as shown in Figure 22-1. Click OK to create the new project.

The new project is always created in a new solution. A *solution* is the largest management unit in BIDS and always comprises one or more projects. (In this example, the solution has the same name as the project.)

NOTE

If the Solution Explorer pane, which allows you to view and manage objects in a solution or a project, is not visible, choose View | Solution Explorer to view it.

Identify Data Sources

To identify data sources, right-click the Data Sources folder in the Solution Explorer pane and choose New Data Source. The Data Source Wizard appears, which guides you through the process of creating a data source. (This example uses the **AdventureWorksDW** sample database as the data source.)

First, on the Select How to Define the Connection page, make sure that the Create a Data Source Based on an Existing or New Connection radio button is activated and click New. In the Connection Manager dialog box (see Figure 22-2), select Native OLE DB/SQL Server Native Client 11.0 in the Provider drop-down list and select the name of your database server in the Server Name drop-down list. (The choice of Native OLE DB/SQL Server Native Client 11.0 allows you to make a connection to an existing database of an instance of the Database Engine.) In the same dialog box, choose Use Windows Authentication and, from the Select or Enter a Database Name drop-down list, choose the **AdventureWorksDW** database. Before you click OK, click the Test Connection button to test the connection to the database. (The Select How to Define the Connection page appears only when you connect to the data source for the first time.)

The next step of the wizard is the Impersonation Information page. These settings determine which user account SSAS uses when connecting to the underlying source of data using Windows authentication. Which setting is appropriate depends on how this data source is being used. Click the Use a Specific Windows User Name and Password radio button and type your username and password in the corresponding fields. Click Next.

Finally, on the Completing the Wizard page, give the new data source a name (for this example, call it **BI_Source**) and click Finish. The new data source appears in the Solution Explorer pane in the Data Sources folder.

Figure 22-2 *The Connection Manager dialog box*

After identifying data sources in general, you have to determine exactly which data you want to select from the data source. In our example, it means that you have to select tables from the **AdventureWorksDW** database, which will be used to build a cube. This step involves specifying data source views, discussed next.

Specify Data Source Views

To create data source views, right-click the Data Source Views folder in the Solution Explorer pane and choose New Data Source View. The Data Source View Wizard guides you through the steps that are necessary to create a data source view. (This example creates a view called **BI_View**, which is based on the **Customer** and **Project** entities.)

First, on the Select a Data Source page, select an existing relational data source (for this example, select **BI_Source**) and click Next. On the next wizard page, Select Tables and Views, choose tables that belong to your cube either as dimension tables or fact tables. To choose a table, select its name in the Available Objects pane and click the > button to move it to the Included Objects pane. For this example, choose the tables for customers and products (**Dim Customer** and **Dim Product**, respectively) in the **AdventureWorksDW** database. These tables will be used to build cube dimensions. They build the set of dimension tables used for your star schema.

Next, on the same wizard page, you need to specify one or more fact tables that correspond to the preceding dimension tables. (One fact table, together with the corresponding dimension tables, creates a star schema.) To do so, click the Add Related Tables button below the Included Objects pane. This instructs the system to find tables that are related to the **Dim Customer** and **Dim Product** tables. (To find related tables, the system searches all primary key/foreign key relationships that exist in the database.)

The system finds several fact tables and adds them to the Included Objects pane. Of these tables, you need only one, **Fact Internet Sales**, to build the star schema. Besides the corresponding fact tables, the system also searches for and adds other tables that are created separately for a hierarchy level of the corresponding dimension. One such table to keep is **Dim Product Subcategory**, which incarnates a hierarchy level called **Subcategory** of the **Product** dimension. Also keep the **Dim Date** table, because the Time dimension is almost always a part of a cube.

Thus, for your star schema, you need the following five tables (as shown in Figure 22-3):

- ▶ Fact Internet Sales
- ▶ Dim Customer
- ▶ Dim Date
- ▶ Dim Product
- ▶ Dim Product Subcategory

Exclude all other system-chosen tables that appear in the right pane by selecting them and clicking the < button.

After restructuring the tables, click Next. On the Completing the Wizard page, the wizard will be completed by choosing a name for a new source view (**BI_View**).

Figure 22-3   *The Select Tables and Views wizard page*

After you click Finish, the Data Source View Designer displays a graphical representation of the tables in the data schema you have defined, as shown in Figure 22-4. (Data Source View Designer is a tool that is used to show a graphical representation of the data schema you have defined.)

NOTE

*Using drag and drop, I changed the design of the source view in Figure 22-4 so that the tables have the convenient form of the star schema. When you take a look at the figure, you will see that the fact table is in the middle and the corresponding dimension tables build the circle around it. (Figure 22-4 actually has the form of a snowflake schema, because the **Dim Product Subcategory** table presents the hierarchy level of the **Product** dimension.)*

Data Source View Designer offers several useful functions. To inspect the objects you have in your source view, move your mouse pointer to the cross-arrow icon in the

Figure 22-4 *Data Source View Designer with the selected tables*

bottom-right corner. When the pointer changes to a cross-arrow icon, click the icon and hold it. The Navigation window appears. Now you can navigate from one part of the diagram to another part. (This is especially useful when you have a diagram with dozens of entities.) To view the data in a table, right-click the table and choose Explore Data. The content of the table appears in a separate window.

You can also create named queries, which are queries that are persistently stored and therefore can be accessed like any table. To create such a query, click Data Source View in the menu bar and then select the New Named Query icon. The Create Named Query dialog box allows you to create any query in relation to selected tables.

Create a Cube

Before you create a cube, you must specify one or more data sources and create a data source view, as previously described. After that, you can use the Cube Wizard to create a cube.

To create a cube, right-click the Cubes folder of the **BI_Project** project in the Solution Explorer pane and choose New Cube. The welcome page of the Cube Wizard appears. Click Next. On the Select Creation Method page, choose Use Existing Tables, because the data source view exists and can be used to build a cube. Click Next.

On the Select Measure Group Tables page, you select measures from the fact table(s). Therefore, select the only fact table, **Fact Internet Sales**, and click Next. The wizard chooses all possible measures from the selected fact table and presents them on the Select Measures page. Check only the **Total Product Costs** column of the **Fact Internet Sales** table as the single measure (see Figure 22-5). Click Next.

Figure 22-5 *The Select Measures wizard page*

On the Select New Dimensions page, select all three dimensions (**Dim Date**, **Dim Product**, and **Dim Customer**) to be created, based on the available tables. The final page, Completing the Wizard, shows the summary of all selected measures and dimensions. Click Finish to finish creating the cube called BI_Cube.

Design Storage Aggregation

As you already know from Chapter 21, basic data from the fact table can be summarized in advance and stored in persistent tables. This process is called *aggregation*, and it can significantly enhance the response time of queries, because scanning millions of rows to calculate the aggregation on the fly can take a very long time.

There is a tradeoff between storage requirements and the percentage of possible aggregations that are calculated and stored. Creating all possible aggregations in a cube and storing all of them on the disk results in the fastest possible response time for all queries, because the response to each query is almost immediate. The disadvantage of this approach is that the storage and processing time required for the aggregations can be substantial.

On the other hand, if no aggregations are calculated and stored, you do not need any additional disk storage, but response time for queries concerning aggregate functions will be slow because each aggregate has to be calculated on the fly.

SSAS provides the Aggregation Design Wizard to help you design aggregations optimally. To start the wizard, you have first to start the Cube Designer. (The Cube Designer is used to edit various properties of an existing cube, including the measure groups and measures, cube dimensions and dimension relationships.) To start it, right-click the cube in Solution Explorer and select Open or View Designer from the context menu. Now, click the Aggregations tab in the main menu of the Cube Designer. In the table that appears in the Cube Designer (**Fact Internet Sales**), right-click the cell under the Aggregations column and choose Design Aggregations. That starts the Aggregation Design Wizard.

In the first step of the wizard, Review Aggregation Usage, you review aggregation usage settings. In this step, you can include or exclude the attributes that appear on the page. Leave the settings as they are and click Next.

The next step is to specify the number of members in each attribute. You do this on the Specify Object Counts page. For each selected cube object, you have to enter the estimated count value or partition count value, before the wizard starts to create and store the selected aggregations. If you click the Count button, the wizard automatically performs the object counts and displays the obtained counts. (Figure 22-6 shows the Specify Objects Counts page after clicking the Count button.) Click Next.

Figure 22-6 *The Specify Object Counts wizard page*

In the second-to-last step, the Set Aggregation Options page, choose one of the four options to specify up to what point (or not at all) aggregations should be designed:

▶ **Estimated storage reaches __ MB**   Specifies the maximum amount of disk storage that should be used for precomputed aggregations. The larger the amount, the more precomputed aggregations that will be created.

▶ **Performance gain reaches __ %**   Specifies the performance gain that you want to achieve. The higher the percentage of precomputed aggregations, the better the performance.

▶ **I click Stop**   Enables you to decide when to stop the design process.

▶ **Do not design aggregation (0%)**   Specifies that no precomputed aggregations should be created.

NOTE

Generally, you should choose one of the first two alternatives. I prefer the second one, because it is very difficult to estimate the amount of storage for different star schemas and different sets of queries. A value between 80 percent and 90 percent is optimal in most cases.

Figure 22-7   *The Set Aggregation Options wizard page (after clicking Start)*

Figure 22-7 shows the result of choosing the second option with the value set to 80 percent and clicking the Start button. The system created six aggregations and uses 243.4KB for them.

Click the Next button to go to the Completing the Wizard page. On this page, you can choose whether to process aggregations immediately (Deploy and process now) or later (Save the aggregations but do not process them). Choose the second option and click Finish.

Process the Cube

If you chose the Save the Aggregations But Do Not Process Them option as the final step in the preceding section, as recommended, you now have to process the cube. (A cube must be processed when you first create it and each time you modify it. If a cube has a lot of data and precomputed aggregations, processing the cube can be very time consuming.) To process the cube, right-click the name of your cube in the Cubes folder of Solution Explorer and select Process. The system starts processing the cube and displays the progress of this activity (see Figure 22-8).

Figure 22-8   *The Process Progress window*

Browse the Cube

To browse a cube, right-click the cube name (in the Cubes folder of the Solution-Explorer) and choose Browse. The Browse view appears. You can add any dimension to the query by right-clicking the dimension name in the left pane and choosing Add to Query. You can also add a measure from that pane in the same way. (Adding measures first is recommended.) Figure 22-9 shows the tabular representation of the total product costs for Internet sales for different customers and products.

The approach is different if you want to calculate values of measures for particular dimensions and their hierarchies. For example, suppose that you want to deliver for customers with customer IDs 11008 and 11741 total product costs for all products they have ordered in the time period 2006/03/01 through 2006/08/31. In this case, you first drop the measure (**Total Product Cost**) from the left pane into the editing pane, and then you choose values in the pane above it to restrict the conditions for

Figure 22-9 *Total product costs for Internet sales for different customers and products*

each dimension (see Figure 22-10). First, in the Dimension column, choose the **Dim Customer** table, and in the Hierarchy column, choose the primary key of this table (**Customer Key**). In the Operator column, choose Equal, and in the Filter Expression column, choose both values 11008 and 11741 one after the other.

In the same way, choose the conditions for the **Dim Product** dimension table. The only difference is that all product values should be included. For this reason, in the Filter Expression column you should choose the root of the dimension. (The root of each dimension is specified by All.) Finally, the table's column **OrderDate** is chosen for

Figure 22-10 *The total product costs as a crosstab*

the Dim Date dimension table, and with the corresponding key. The Operator column in this case is Range (Inclusive) and the Filter Expression column allows you to type the beginning and end of the time period. As you can see in Figure 22-10, the total product costs for the both customers are 2171.2942.

Retrieving and Delivering Data

Now that you have seen how to build and browse the cube using BIDS, you are ready to learn how to retrieve data from a cube and deliver it to users. The primary goal of Development Studio is to develop BI projects, not to retrieve and deliver data to users. For this task, there are many other interfaces, such as:

▶   PowerPivot for Excel
▶   Multidimensional Expressions (MDX)

- ▶ SQL Server Management Studio
- ▶ OLE DB for OLAP
- ▶ Third-party tools
- ▶ ADOMD.NET

PowerPivot for Excel and MDX are discussed separately in the following two subsections, while the other interfaces in the list are briefly described here. (The reason I give more attention to these two interfaces than the others is that PowerPoint for Excel is the most important interface for end-users, while MDX is a tool that is used by many third-party SSAS solutions.)

To browse a cube in SQL Server Management Studio, start it and connect to the SSAS server on which you deployed your cube. After that, expand the Database folder and expand Cube. You'll see all cubes that you have created for this database. Right-click the cube you want to use and choose Browse. As shown in Figures 22-9 and 22-10, the interface is the same as you saw earlier for SSAS. Thus, you can browse data in the same way as described in the section "Browse the Cube."

NOTE

The most important thing to note when using Management Studio for multidimensional analysis is that you do not connect to the Database Engine. The Database Engine manages relational data, while SSAS stores and manages multidimensional cubes. For this reason, connect to your SSAS server.

OLE DB for OLAP is an industry standard for multidimensional data processing, published by Microsoft. It is a set of entities and interfaces that extends the ability of OLE DB to provide access to multidimensional data stores. OLE DB for OLAP enables users to perform data analysis through interactive access to a variety of possible views of the underlying data. Many independent software vendors use the specification of OLE DB for OLAP to implement different interfaces that allow users to access cubes created by SSAS. Additionally, using OLE DB for OLAP, the vendors can implement OLAP applications that can uniformly access both relational and nonrelational data stored in diverse information sources, regardless of location or type.

ADOMD (ActiveX Data Objects Multidimensional) is a Microsoft .NET Framework data provider that is designed to communicate with SSAS. With this interface, you can access and manipulate objects in a multidimensional cube, enabling web-based OLAP application development. This interface uses the XML for Analysis protocol to communicate with analytical data sources. Commands are usually sent in MDX. By using ADOMD.NET, you can also view and work with metadata.

Querying Data Using PowerPivot for Excel

PowerPivot for Excel is a tool that allows you to analyze data using what is probably the most popular Microsoft tool for such purpose: Microsoft Excel. It is a user-friendly way to perform data analysis using features such as PivotTable, PivotChart views, and slices.

> **NOTE**
>
> To work with PowerPivot, you need Microsoft Office 2010. You can also use SharePoint 2010, but this chapter discusses only PowerPivot for Excel.

Before you learn how to use this tool, take a look at the advantages of PowerPivot:

▶ Familiar Excel tools and features for delivering data are available.

▶ Very large data sets can be loaded from virtually any source.

▶ New analytical capabilities, such as Data Analysis Expressions (DAX), are available.

As you will see in a moment, you can use the same sources that you use for SSAS in almost the same way for PowerPivot. (You will use a cube similar to the one you created in the previous section to learn how to deliver data from a cube. You will use this cube afterward for different exercises.)

Data Analysis Expressions (DAX) is a new PowerPivot language that allows you to define custom calculations in PowerPivot tables and in Excel PivotTables. DAX comprises some of the functions that are used in Excel formulas, and additional operations that are designed to work with relational data.

Working with PowerPivot for Excel

Your first step is to import data from one or more data sources in Excel. Open Excel 2010 and click the PowerPivot tab. In the PowerPivot ribbon, click the PowerPivot Window tab. This opens the PowerPivot for Excel window. Your task is to create a cube similar to the one you already created using SSAS. So, create and process a cube according to the steps described in the previous section and with the table design shown in Figure 22-11.

The following list shows the tables you should choose (see also Figure 22-11):

▶ Fact Internet Sales

▶ Fact Reseller Sales

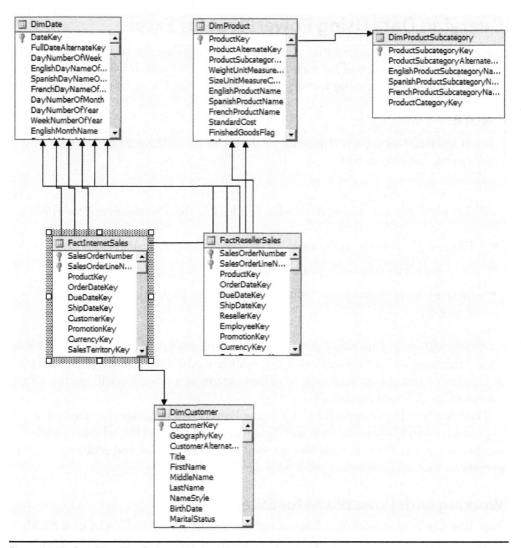

Figure 22-11 *Data Source View Designer with the tables that you have to select*

- ▶ Dim Customer
- ▶ Dim Date
- ▶ Dim Product
- ▶ Dim Product Subcategory

To choose these tables, use the same data source (**BI_Source**) as for the **BI_Cube** cube and create a new source view. After that, use the Cube Wizard to create the new cube (called **BI_Cube2**). In the wizard step called Select Measure Group Tables, choose the following measures from both fact tables (**Fact Internet Sales** and **Fact Reseller Sales**): **Sales Amount, Total Product Costs,** and **Freight**.

The next task after creating the **BI_Cube2** cube is to connect to the cube. To do this, click From Other Sources on the Get External Data tab of the PowerPivot for Excel ribbon and choose SQL Server Analysis Services. This opens the Table Import Wizard with the Connect to a Data Source page displayed, as shown in Figure 22-12. Click Next.

Figure 22-12 *The Connect to a Data Source wizard page*

NOTE

You can choose as a data source Microsoft databases (Access or SQL Server), third-party databases (Oracle, Teradata, etc.), as well as nondatabase data sources.

On the next wizard page, Connect to Microsoft SQL Server Analysis Services, you need to enter the cube information. In the Friendly Connection Name box (see Figure 22-13), type a name for your connection (**PowerPivot_Project**, for instance), enter the server name in the Server or File Name field, and choose how you want to log on to the server. Finally, type the name of an existing cube (BI_Cube2) in the Database Name field. (You can also choose the name of the cube from the list of existing cube names that appears for the particular server.) Click Next.

Table Import Wizard

Connect to Microsoft SQL Server Analysis Services.
Enter the information required to connect to a Microsoft SQL Server Analysis Services database.

Friendly connection name: PowerPivot_Project

Server or File Name: NTB00716

Log on to the server

◉ Use Windows Authentication

○ Use SQL Server Authentication

User name:

Password:

☐ Save my password

Database name: BI_Project

[Advanced] [Test Connection]

[< Back] [Next >] [Finish] [Cancel]

Figure 22-13 *The Connect to Microsoft SQL Server Analysis Services wizard page*

In the next step, you specify an MDX query to select data to import from the data source. You can type (or paste) such a query and click the Validate button, or leave the creation of a query to the Query Designer. (MDX will be described in a moment.)

Click the Design button to graphically create your query. The window of the Table Import Wizard appears (see Figure 22-14). Now you can choose measures from existing fact tables and fields from dimension tables, which you need for your calculations. As shown in Figure 22-14, drag and drop the **Sales Amount** measure from the **Fact Reseller Sales** fact table and the **Date Key** and **Product Key** measures from the **Due Date** and **Dim Product** dimension tables, respectively. Click OK.

The system shows you the corresponding MDX query, which you can now save if you want. Click Finish to end your task. The summary field shows you the success (or failure) of the process.

The PowerPivot for Excel window shows you the selected data (see Figure 22-15). Now you can use one of Excel's presentation forms to present your data. This example explains how you can create cross tabs (pivot tables) from your data to present the data

Figure 22-14 *The Table Import Wizard window*

Figure 22-15 *PowerPivot for Excel showing the selected data*

in Excel. In the PivotTable for Excel ribbon, click PivotTable on the Reports tab. The Create PivotTable dialog box appears. Choose New Worksheet and click OK. The new sheet appears in Excel.

In the right pane, called PowerPivot Field List, you can choose the columns that will be presented in the sheet. (If the Field List doesn't appear, click Field List on the ribbon.) In this example, the measure and the two columns from the dimension tables are checked. Now, you can present data in the sheet by dragging and dropping it into the Row Labels, Column Labels, or Values box. In Figure 22-16, the key column of the Dim Product dimension table is dropped in the Row Labels area, while the key column of the Dim Date dimension table is dropped in the Column Labels area. (The measure is dropped in the Values area.).

Figure 22-16 *Presenting data in an Excel sheet*

NOTE

The data presented in Figure 22-16 shows the calculation using the COUNT aggregate function. If you want to modify the form of calculation (to add the values, for instance), right-click a blank area in the Values box and choose the appropriate function (in this case, SUM).

Querying Data Using Multidimensional Expressions

Multidimensional Expressions (MDX) is a language that you can use to query multidimensional data stored in OLAP cubes. (MDX can also be used to create cubes.) In MDX, the SELECT statement specifies a result set that contains a subset of multidimensional data that has been returned from a cube. To specify a result set, an MDX query must contain the following information:

▶ One or more axes that you use to specify the result set. You can specify up to 128 axes in an MDX query. You use the ON COLUMNS clause to specify the first axis and the ON ROWS clause for the second. If you have more than two axes, the alternative syntax is to use the numbers: ON AXIS(0) for the first axis, ON AXIS(1) for the second one, and so on.

▶ The set of members or tuples to include on each axis of the MDX query. This is written in the SELECT list.

▶ The name of the cube that sets the context of the MDX query, specified in the FROM clause of the query.

▶ The set of members or tuples to include on the "slicer axis," specified in the WHERE clause (see Examples 22.1 and 22.2).

NOTE

The semantic meaning of the WHERE clause in SQL is different from its semantic meaning in MDX. In SQL it means filtering of rows by specified criteria. The WHERE clause in MDX means slicing the multidimensional query. While these concepts are somewhat similar, they are not equivalent.

Example 22.1 will be used to explain the syntax of the language. You can execute your MDX queries directly in SQL Server Management Studio. Use the MDX Query Editor to design and execute statements and scripts written in the MDX language. First, type scripts in the query editor pane. Then, to execute the scripts, press F5 or click Execute on the toolbar.

EXAMPLE 22.1

Display for each customer total product costs that are due on March 1, 2007:

```
SELECT [Measures].MEMBERS ON COLUMNS,
       [Dim Customer].[Customer Key].MEMBERS ON ROWS
FROM BI_Cube
WHERE ([Due Date].[Date Key].[20070301])
```

Example 22.1 queries data from the **BI_Cube** cube. The SELECT list of the first query axis displays all members of the **Measures** dimension. In other words, it displays the values of the **Total Product Costs** column, because the only existing measure in this cube is **Total Product Costs**. The second query axis displays all members of the **Customer Key** column of the **Dim Customer** dimension.

The FROM clause indicates that the data source in this case is the **BI_Cube** cube. The WHERE clause "slices" through the **Due Date** dimension according to the key values using the single date value 2007/03/01.

Example 22.2 shows another MDX query.

EXAMPLE 22.2

Calculate for the customer with the customer key 11741 and for the product with the product key 7 the total product costs that are due in March 2007:

```
SELECT [Measures].MEMBERS ON COLUMNS
                 FROM BI_Cube
WHERE ({[Due Date].[Date Key].[20070301]:[Due Date].[Date key].[20070331]},
                 [Dim Customer].[Customer Key].[11741],
                 [Dim Product].[Product Key].[7])
```

The SELECT list in the query in Example 22.2 contains only the members of the **Measures** dimension. For this reason, the query displays the value of the **Total Product Costs** column. The WHERE clause in Example 22.2 is more complex than in Example 22.1. First, there are three slices, which are separated using commas. Only one member of the **Customer** dimension and one member of the **Product** dimension are used for slicing, while from the **Due Date** dimension, the dates from 2007/03/01 through 2007/03/31 are sliced. (As you can see from the query, the : sign is used to specify a range of dates.)

NOTE

MDX is a very complex language. This section provided only a concise description of the language. Use Books Online to learn more about this language. Also, I highly recommend "MDX for Everyone" by Mosha Pasumansky, one of the founders of the MDX language. You can find this article at www.mosha.com/msolap/articles/ MDXForEveryone.htm.

Security of SQL Server Analysis Services

SQL Server Analysis Services security issues correspond to the security issues of the Database Engine. This means that SSAS supports the same general features— authorization and authentication—that the Database Engine does, but in a restricted form.

Authorization defines which user has legitimate access to SSAS. This issue is tightly connected to the operating system authorization. In other words, SSAS imposes user authorization based on the access rights granted to the user by the Windows operating system.

You can limit the number of users that can perform administrative functions for SSAS. You can also specify which end users can access data and delineate the types of operations they can perform. Additionally, you can control their access at different levels of data, such as the cube, dimension, and cube cell level. This is done using roles.

As you already know, a database role specifies a group of database users that can access the same objects of the database. Each role is defined at the SSAS database level and then assigned to cubes. After that, individual users or other roles are assigned to that role.

To create a role, right-click the Roles folder in the Solution Explorer pane and choose New Role. Change the default name of the role in the Properties window. After that, in the main window, shown in Figure 22-17, you can use the various tabs to specify different controls for the role. On the Membership tab, you can specify all users who should be members of the role. (Figure 22-17 shows several users added to the **BI_Role** role.) The Data Sources and Cubes tabs specify the data sources—that is, cubes that can be used by the role's members. Authorization for the specific cell can be assigned using the Cell Data tab. The Dimensions and Dimensions Data tabs specify which dimensions (dimensional data) can be accessed.

Figure 22-17 *Creation of a new role for SSAS*

Summary

With its SQL Server Analysis Services, Microsoft offers a set of data warehousing components that can be used for entry- and intermediate-level data analysis. The main component of SSAS is Business Intelligence Development Studio (BIDS), which is based on Visual Studio and gives users an easy way to design and develop data warehouses and data marts.

SSAS is wizard oriented, with wizards for almost every task that is executed during the design and implementation of a data warehouse. The Data Source Wizard allows you to specify one or more data sources, while the Cube Wizard is used to create a multidimensional cube where aggregate data is stored. To import tables you can use the Table Import Wizard, and the Aggregation Design Wizard is used to to help you design and create aggregations optimally.

To deliver analytic data to users, you can use any of several different interfaces. The most important are SQL Server Management Studio, MDX, and OLE DB for OLAP.

The next chapter describes SQL/OLAP extensions in Transact-SQL.

Exercises

E.22.1

Using SQL Server Management Studio and the **BI_Cube2** cube, find the amount of sales for all products for a customer with the customer number 11111.

E.22.2

Using SQL Server Management Studio and the **BI_Cube2** cube, find the total product costs for all customers and for the product with the product number 14.

Chapter 23

Business Intelligence and Transact-SQL

In This Chapter

Have you ever tried to write a Transact-SQL query that computes the percentage change in values between the last two quarters? Or one that implements cumulative sums or sliding aggregations? If you have ever tried, you know how difficult these tasks are. Today, you don't have to implement them anymore. The SQL:1999 standard has adopted a set of online analytical processing (OLAP) functions that enable you to easily perform these calculations as well as many others that used to be very complex for implementation. This part of the SQL standard is called SQL/OLAP. Therefore, SQL/OLAP comprises all functions and operators that are used for data analysis.

Using OLAP functions has several advantages for users:

▶ Users with standard knowledge of the SQL language can easily specify the calculations they need.

▶ Database systems, such as the Database Engine, can perform these calculations much more efficiently.

▶ Because there is a standard specification of these functions, they're now much more economical for tool and application vendors to exploit.

▶ Almost all the analytic functions proposed by the SQL:1999 standard are implemented in enterprise database systems in the same way. For this reason, you can port queries in relation to SQL/OLAP from one system to another, without any code changes.

The Database Engine offers many extensions to the SELECT statement that can be used primarily for analytic operations. Some of these extensions are defined according to the SQL:1999 standard and some are not. The following sections describe both standard and nonstandard SQL/OLAP functions and operators.

The most important extension of Transact-SQL concerning data analysis is the window construct, which will be described next.

Window Construct

A window (in relation to SQL/OLAP) defines a partitioned set of rows to which a function is applied. The number of rows that belong to a window is dynamically determined in relation to the user's specifications. The window construct is specified using the OVER clause.

The standardized window construct has three main parts:

▶ Partitioning
▶ Ordering
▶ Aggregation grouping

NOTE

The Database Engine doesn't support aggregation grouping yet, so this feature is not discussed here.

Before you delve into the window construct and its parts, take a look at the table that will be used for the examples. Example 23.1 creates the **project_dept** table, shown in Table 23-1, which is used in this chapter to demonstrate Transact-SQL extensions concerning SQL/OLAP.

dept_name	emp_cnt	budget	date_month
Research	5	50000	01.01.2007
Research	10	70000	02.01.2007
Research	5	65000	07.01.2007
Accounting	5	10000	07.01.2007
Accounting	10	40000	02.01.2007
Accounting	6	30000	01.01.2007
Accounting	6	40000	02.01.2008
Marketing	6	100000	01.01.2008
Marketing	10	180000	02.01.2008
Marketing	3	100000	07.01.2008
Marketing	NULL	120000	01.01.2008

Table 23-1   *Content of the project_dept Table*

EXAMPLE 23.1

```
USE sample;
CREATE TABLE project_dept
     ( dept_name CHAR( 20 ) NOT NULL,
       emp_cnt INT,
       budget FLOAT,
       date_month DATE );
```

The **project_dept** table contains several departments and their employee counts as well as budgets of projects that are controlled by each department. Example 23.2 shows the INSERT statements that are used to insert the rows shown in Table 23-1.

EXAMPLE 23.2

```
USE sample;
INSERT INTO project_dept VALUES
    ('Research', 5, 50000, '01.01.2007');
INSERT INTO project_dept VALUES
    ('Research', 10, 70000, '02.01.2007');
INSERT INTO project_dept VALUES
    ('Research', 5, 65000, '07.01.2007');
INSERT INTO project_dept VALUES
    ('Accounting', 5, 10000, '07.01.2007');
INSERT INTO project_dept VALUES
    ('Accounting', 10, 40000, '02.01.2007');
INSERT INTO project_dept VALUES
    ('Accounting', 6, 30000, '01.01.2007');
INSERT INTO project_dept VALUES
    ('Accounting', 6, 40000, '02.01.2008');
INSERT INTO project_dept VALUES
    ('Marketing', 6, 100000, '01.01.2008');
INSERT INTO project_dept VALUES
    ('Marketing', 10, 180000, '02.01.2008');
INSERT INTO project_dept VALUES
    ('Marketing', 3, 100000, '07.01.2008');
INSERT INTO project_dept VALUES
    ('Marketing', NULL, 120000, '01.01.2008');
```

Partitioning

Partitioning allows you to divide the result set of a query into groups, so that each row from a partition will be displayed separately. If no partitioning is specified, the entire set of rows comprises a single partition. Although the partitioning looks like a grouping using the GROUP BY clause, it is not the same thing. The GROUP BY clause collapses the rows in a partition into a single row, whereas the partitioning within the window construct simply organizes the rows into groups without collapsing them.

The following two examples show the difference between partitioning using the window construct and grouping using the GROUP BY clause. Suppose that you want to calculate several different aggregates concerning employees in each department. Example 23.3 shows how the OVER clause with the PARTITION BY clause can be used to build partitions.

EXAMPLE 23.3

Using the window construct, build partitions according to the values in the **dept_name** column and calculate the sum and the average for the Accounting and Research departments:

```
USE sample;
SELECT dept_name,   budget,
              SUM( emp_cnt ) OVER( PARTITION BY dept_name ) AS emp_cnt_sum,
              AVG( budget ) OVER( PARTITION BY dept_name )  AS budget_avg
                FROM project_dept
                WHERE dept_name IN ('Accounting', 'Research');
```

The result is

dept_name	budget	emp_cnt_sum	budget_avg
Accounting	10000	27	30000
Accounting	40000	27	30000
Accounting	30000	27	30000
Accounting	40000	27	30000
Research	50000	20	61666.6666666667
Research	70000	20	61666.6666666667
Research	65000	20	61666.6666666667

Example 23.3 uses the OVER clause to define the corresponding window construct. Inside it, the PARTITION BY option is used to specify partitions. (Both partitions in Example 23.3 are grouped using the values in the **dept_name** column.) Finally, an aggregate function is applied to the partitions. (Example 23.3 calculates two aggregates, the sum of the values in the **emp_cnt** column and the average value of budgets.) Again, as you can see from the result of the example, the partitioning organizes the rows into groups without collapsing them.

Example 23.4 shows a similar query that uses the GROUP BY clause.

EXAMPLE 23.4

Group the values in the **dept_name** column for the Accounting and Research departments and calculate the sum and the average for these two groups:

```
USE sample;
SELECT dept_name, SUM(emp_cnt) AS cnt, AVG( budget ) AS budget_avg
    FROM project_dept
    WHERE dept_name IN ('Accounting', 'Research')
    GROUP BY dept_name;
```

The result is

dept_name	cnt	budget_avg
Accounting	27	30000
Research	20	61666.6666666667

As already stated, when you use the GROUP BY clause, each group collapses in one row.

NOTE

There is another significant difference between the OVER clause and the GROUP BY clause. As can be seen from Example 23.3, when you use the OVER clause, the corresponding SELECT list can contain any column name from the table. This is obvious, because partitioning organizes the rows into groups without collapsing them. (If you add the budget column in the SELECT list of Example 23.4, you will get an error.)

Ordering and Framing

The ordering within the window construct is like the ordering in a query. First, you use the ORDER BY clause to specify the particular order of the rows in the result set. Second, it includes a list of sort keys and indicates whether they should be sorted in ascending or descending order. The most important difference is that ordering inside a window is applied only *within* each partition.

In contrast to SQL Server 2008, SQL Server 2012 supports ordering inside a window construct for aggregate functions. In other words, the OVER clause for aggregate functions can contain now the ORDER BY clause, too. Example 23.5 shows this.

EXAMPLE 23.5

Using the window construct, partition the rows of the **project_dept** table using the values in the **dept_name** column and sort the rows in each partition using the values in the **budget** column:

```
USE sample;
SELECT dept_name, budget, emp_cnt,
    SUM(budget) OVER(PARTITION BY dept_name ORDER BY budget) AS sum_dept
     FROM project_dept;
```

The query in Example 23.5, which is generally called "cumulative aggregations," or in this case "cumulative sums," uses the ORDER BY clause to specify ordering within the particular partition. This functionality can be extended using framing. Framing means that the result can be further narrowed using two boundary points that restrict the set of rows to a subset (see the following example).

EXAMPLE 23.6

```
USE sample;
SELECT dept_name, budget, emp_cnt,
    SUM(budget) OVER(PARTITION BY dept_name ORDER BY budget
        ROWS BETWEEN UNBOUNDED PRECEDING AND CURRENT ROW)
        AS sum_dept
 FROM project_dept;
```

Example 23.6 uses two clauses: UNBOUNDED PRECEDING and CURRENT ROW to specify the boundary points of the selected rows. For the query in the example this means that based on the order of the budget values the displayed subset of rows is with no low boundary point and until the current row. (The result set contains all together 11 rows.)

The frame bounds used in Example 23.6 are not the only ones you can use. The UNBOUNDED FOLLOWING clause means that the specified frame does not have an upper boundary point. Also, both boundary points can be specified using an offset from the current row. In other words, you can use the **n** PRECEDING or **n** FOLLOWING clauses to specify **n** rows before or **n** rows after the current one, respectively. Therefore, the following frame specifies all together three rows: the current row, the previous one, and the next one:

```
ROWS BETWEEN 1 PRECEDING and 1 FOLLOWING
```

SQL Server 2012 also introduces two new functions related to framing: LEAD and LAG. LEAD has the ability to compute an expression on the next rows (rows that are going to come after the current row). In other words, the LEAD function returns the next **n**th row value in an order. The function has three parameters: The first one specifies the name of the column to compute the leading row, the second one is the index of the leading row relative to the current row, and the last one is the value to return if the offset points to a row outside of the partition range. (The semantics of the LAG function is similar: it returns the previous **n**th row value in an order.)

Example 23.6 uses the ROWS clause to limit the rows within a partition by physically specifying the number of rows preceding or following the current row. Alternatively, SQL Server 2012 supports the RANGE clause, which logically limits the rows within a partition. In other words, when you use the ROWS clause, the exact number of rows will be specified based on the defined frame. On the other hand, the RANGE clause does not define the exact number of rows, because the specified frame can contain duplicates, too.

You can use several columns from a table to build different partitioning schemas in a query, as shown in Example 23.7.

EXAMPLE 23.7

Using the window construct, build two partitions for the Accounting and Research departments: one using the values of the **budget** column and the other using the values of the **dept_name** column. Calculate the sums for the former partition and the averages for the latter partition.

```
USE sample;
SELECT dept_name, CAST( budget AS INT ) AS budget,
 SUM( emp_cnt ) OVER( PARTITION BY budget ) AS emp_cnt_sum,
 AVG( budget ) OVER( PARTITION BY dept_name )  AS budget_avg
 FROM project_dept
WHERE dept_name IN ('Accounting', 'Research');
```

The result is

dept_name	budget	emp_cnt_sum	budget_avg
Accounting	10000	5	30000
Accounting	30000	6	30000
Accounting	40000	16	30000
Accounting	40000	16	30000
Research	50000	5	61666.6666666667
Research	65000	5	61666.6666666667
Research	70000	10	61666.6666666667

The query in Example 23.7 has two different partitioning schemas: one over the values of the **budget** column and one over the values of the **dept_name** column. The former is used to calculate the number of employees in relation to the departments with the same budget. The latter is used to calculate the average value of budgets of departments grouped by their names.

Example 23.8 shows how you can use the NEXT VALUE FOR expression of the CREATE SEQUENCE statement to control the order in which the values are generated using the OVER clause. (For the description of the CREATE SEQUENCE statement, see Chapter 6.)

EXAMPLE 23.8

```
USE sample;
CREATE SEQUENCE Seq START WITH 1 INCREMENT BY 1;
GO
CREATE TABLE T1 (col1 CHAR(10), col2 CHAR(10));
GO
INSERT INTO dbo.T1(col1, col2)
  SELECT NEXT VALUE FOR Seq OVER(ORDER BY dept_name ASC), budget
  FROM (SELECT dept_name, budget
        FROM project_dept
        ORDER BY budget, dept_name DESC
        OFFSET 0 ROWS FETCH FIRST 5 ROWS ONLY) AS D;
```

The content of the T1 table is as follows:

col1	col2
1	10000
2	30000
3	40000
4	40000
5	50000

The first two statements create the **Seq** sequence and the auxiliary table **T1**. The following INSERT statement uses a subquery to filter the five departments with the highest budget, and generates sequence values for them. This is done using OFFSET/ FETCH, which is described in Chapter 6. (You can find several other examples concerning OFFSET/FETCH in the subsection with the same name later in this chapter.)

Extensions of GROUP BY

Transact-SQL extends the GROUP BY clause with the following operators and functions:

▶ CUBE

▶ ROLLUP

▶ Grouping functions

▶ Grouping sets

The following sections describe these operators and functions.

CUBE Operator

This section looks at the differences between grouping using the GROUP BY clause alone and grouping using GROUP BY in combination with the CUBE and ROLLUP operators. The main difference is that the GROUP BY clause defines one or more columns as a group such that all rows within any group have the same values for those columns. CUBE and ROLLUP provide additional summary rows for grouped data. These summary rows are also called multidimensional summaries.

The following two examples demonstrate these differences. Example 23.9 applies the GROUP BY clause to group the rows of the **project_dept** table using two criteria: **dept_name** and **emp_cnt**.

EXAMPLE 23.9

Using GROUP BY, group the rows of the **project_dept** table that belong to the Accounting and Research departments using the **dept_name** and **emp_cnt** columns:

```
USE sample;
SELECT dept_name, emp_cnt, SUM(budget) sum_of_budgets
    FROM project_dept
    WHERE dept_name IN ('Accounting', 'Research')
    GROUP BY dept_name, emp_cnt;
```

The result is

dept_name	emp_cnt	sum_of_budgets
Accounting	5	10000
Research	5	115000
Accounting	6	70000
Accounting	10	40000
Research	10	70000

Example 23.10 and its result set shows the difference when you additionally use the CUBE operator.

EXAMPLE 23.10

Group the rows of the **project_dept** table that belong to the Accounting and Research departments using the **dept_name** and **emp_cnt** columns and additionally display all possible summary rows:

```
USE sample;
SELECT dept_name, emp_cnt, SUM(budget) sum_of_budgets
     FROM project_dept
       WHERE dept_name IN ('Accounting', 'Research')
       GROUP BY CUBE (dept_name, emp_cnt);
```

The result is

dept_name	emp_cnt	sum_of_budgets
Accounting	5	10000
Research	5	115000
NULL	5	125000
Accounting	6	70000
NULL	6	70000
Accounting	10	40000
Research	10	70000
NULL	10	110000
Accounting	NULL	120000
Research	NULL	185000
NULL	NULL	305000

The main difference between the last two examples is that the result set of Example 23.9 displays only the values in relation to the grouping, while the result set of Example 23.10 contains, additionally, all possible summary rows. (Because the CUBE operator displays every possible combination of groups and summary rows, the number of rows is the same, regardless of the order of columns in the GROUP BY clause.) The placeholder for the values in the unneeded columns of summary rows is displayed as NULL. For example, the following row from the result set

```
NULL              NULL        305000
```

shows the grand total (that is, the sum of all budgets of all existing projects in the table), while the row

```
NULL                    5                        125000
```

shows the sum of all budgets for all projects that employ exactly five employees.

NOTE

The syntax of the CUBE operator in Example 23.10 corresponds to the standardized syntax of that operator. Because of its backward compatibility, the Database Engine also supports the old-style syntax:

```
USE sample;
SELECT dept_name, emp_cnt, SUM(budget) sum_of_budgets
     FROM project_dept
       WHERE dept_name IN ('Accounting', 'Research')
     GROUP BY dept_name, emp_cnt
     WITH CUBE;
```

ROLLUP Operator

In contrast to CUBE, which returns every possible combination of groups and summary rows, the group hierarchy using ROLLUP is determined by the order in which the grouping columns are specified. Example 23.11 shows the use of the ROLLUP operator.

EXAMPLE 23.11

Group the rows of the **project_dept** table that belong to the Accounting and Research departments using the **dept_name** and **emp_cnt** columns and additionally display summary rows for the **dept_name** column:

```
USE sample;
SELECT dept_name, emp_cnt, SUM(budget) sum_of_budgets
          FROM project_dept
            WHERE dept_name IN ('Accounting', 'Research')
            GROUP BY ROLLUP (dept_name, emp_cnt);
```

The result is

dept_name	emp_cnt	sum_of_budgets
Accounting	5	10000
Accounting	6	70000

dept_name	emp_cnt	sum_of_budgets
Accounting	10	40000
Accounting	NULL	120000
Research	5	115000
Research	10	70000
Research	NULL	185000
NULL	NULL	305000

As you can see from the result of Example 23.11, the number of retrieved rows in this example is smaller than the number of displayed rows in the example with the CUBE operator. The reason is that the summary rows are displayed only for the first column in the GROUP BY ROLLUP clause.

NOTE

The syntax used in Example 23.11 is the standardized syntax. The old-style syntax for ROLLUP is similar to the syntax for CUBE, which is shown in the second part of Example 23.10.

Grouping Functions

As you already know, NULL is used in combination with CUBE and ROLLUP to specify the placeholder for the values in the unneeded columns. In such a case, it isn't possible to distinguish NULL in relation to CUBE and ROLLUP from the NULL value. Transact-SQL supports the following two standardized grouping functions that allow you to resolve the problem with the ambiguity of NULL:

- ▶ GROUPING
- ▶ GROUPING_ID

The following subsections describe in detail these two functions.

GROUPING Function

The GROUPING function returns 1 if the NULL in the result set is in relation to CUBE or ROLLUP, and 0 if it represents the group of NULL values.

Example 23.12 shows the use of the GROUPING function.

EXAMPLE 23.12

Using the GROUPING function, clarify which NULL values in the result of the following SELECT statement display summary rows:

```
USE sample;
SELECT dept_name, emp_cnt, SUM(budget) sum_b, GROUPING(emp_cnt) gr
          FROM project_dept
            WHERE dept_name IN ('Accounting', 'Marketing')
            GROUP BY ROLLUP (dept_name, emp_cnt);
```

The result is

dept_name	emp_cnt	sum_b	gr
Accounting	5	10000	0
Accounting	6	70000	0
Accounting	10	40000	0
Accounting	NULL	120000	1
Marketing	NULL	120000	0
Marketing	3	100000	0
Marketing	6	100000	0
Marketing	10	180000	0
Marketing	NULL	500000	1
NULL	NULL	620000	1

If you take a look at the grouping column (**gr**), you will see that some values are 0 and some are 1. The value 1 indicates that the corresponding NULL in the **emp_cnt** column specifies a summary value, while the value 0 indicates that NULL stands for itself, i.e., it is the NULL value.

GROUPING_ID Function

The GROUPING_ID function computes the level of grouping. GROUPING_ID can be used only in the SELECT list, HAVING clause, or ORDER BY clause when GROUP BY is specified.

Example 23.13 shows the use of the GROUPING_ID function.

EXAMPLE 23.13

```
USE sample;
SELECT dept_name, YEAR(date_month), SUM(budget),
GROUPING_ID (dept_name,  YEAR(date_month)) AS gr_dept
   FROM project_dept
   GROUP BY ROLLUP (dept_name,  YEAR(date_month));
```

The result is

dept_name	date_month	budget	gr_dept
Accounting	2007	80000	0
Accounting	2008	40000	0
Accounting	NULL	120000	1
Marketing	2008	500000	0
Marketing	NULL	500000	1
Research	2007	185000	0
Research	NULL	185000	1
NULL	NULL	805000	3

The GROUPING_ID function is similar to the GROUPING function, but becomes very useful for determining the summarization of multiple columns, as is the case in Example 23.13. The function returns an integer that, when converted to binary, is a concatenation of the 1s and 0s representing the summarization of each column passed as the parameter of the function. (For example, the value 3 of the **gr_dept** column in the last row of the result means that summarization is done over both the **dept_name** and **date_month** columns. The binary value $(11)_2$ is equivalent to the value 3 in the decimal system.)

Grouping Sets

Grouping sets are an extension to the GROUP BY clause that lets users define several groups in the same query. You use the GROUPING SETS operator to implement grouping sets. Example 23.14 shows the use of this operator.

EXAMPLE 23.14

Calculate the sum of budgets for the Accounting and Research departments using the combination of values of the **dept_name** and **emp_cnt** columns first, and after that using the values of the single column **dept_name**:

```
USE sample;
SELECT dept_name, emp_cnt, SUM(budget) sum_budgets
          FROM project_dept
          WHERE dept_name IN ('Accounting', 'Research')
          GROUP BY GROUPING SETS ((dept_name, emp_cnt),(dept_name));
```

The result is

dept_name	emp_cnt	sum_budgets
Accounting	5	10000
Accounting	6	70000
Accounting	10	40000
Accounting	NULL	120000
Research	5	115000
Research	10	70000
Research	NULL	185000

As you can see from the result set of Example 23.14, the query uses two different groupings to calculate the sum of budgets: first using the combination of values of the **dept_name** and **emp_cnt** columns, and second using the values of the single column **dept_name**. The first three rows of the result set display the sum of budgets for three different groupings of the first two columns (Accounting, 5; Accounting, 6; and Accounting, 10). The fourth row displays the sum of budgets for all Accounting departments. The last three rows displays the similar results for the Research department.

You can use the series of grouping sets to replace the ROLLUP and CUBE operators. For instance, the following series of grouping sets

```
GROUP BY GROUPING SETS ((dept_name, emp_cnt), (dept_name), ())
```

is equivalent to the following ROLLUP clause:

```
GROUP BY ROLLUP (dept_name, emp_cnt)
```

Also,

```
GROUP BY GROUPING SETS ((dept_name, emp_cnt), (emp_cnt, dept_name),
(dept_name), ())
```

is equivalent to the following CUBE clause:

```
GROUP BY CUBE (dept_name, emp_cnt)
```

OLAP Query Functions

Transact-SQL supports two groups of functions that are categorized as OLAP query functions:

▶ Ranking functions

▶ Statistical aggregate functions

The following subsections describe these functions.

NOTE

The GROUPING function, discussed previously, also belongs to the OLAP functions.

Ranking Functions

Ranking functions return a ranking value for each row in a partition group. Transact-SQL supports the following ranking functions:

▶ RANK

▶ DENSE_RANK

▶ ROW_NUMBER

Example 23.15 shows the use of the RANK function.

EXAMPLE 23.15

Find all departments with a budget not greater than 30000, and display the result set in descending order:

```
USE sample;
SELECT RANK() OVER(ORDER BY budget DESC) AS rank_budget,
                    dept_name, emp_cnt, budget
    FROM project_dept
    WHERE budget <= 30000;
```

The result is

rank_budget	dept_name	emp_cnt	budget
1	Accounting	6	30000
2	Accounting	5	10000

Example 23.15 uses the RANK function to return a number (in the first column of the result set) that specifies the rank of the row among all rows. The example uses the

OVER clause to sort the result set by the **budget** column in the descending order. (In this example, the PARTITION BY clause is omitted. For this reason, the whole result set will belong to only one partition.)

NOTE

The RANK function uses logical aggregation. In other words, if two or more rows in a result set are tied (have a same value in the ordering column), they will have the same rank. The row with the subsequent ordering will have a rank that is one plus the number of ranks that precede the row. For this reason, the RANK function displays "gaps" if two or more rows have the same ranking.

Example 23.16 shows the use of the two other ranking functions, DENSE_RANK and ROW_NUMBER.

EXAMPLE 23.16

Find all departments with a budget not greater than 40000, and display the dense rank and the sequential number of each row in the result set:

```
USE sample;
SELECT DENSE_RANK() OVER( ORDER BY budget DESC ) AS dense_rank,
       ROW_NUMBER() OVER( ORDER BY budget DESC ) AS row_number,
       dept_name, emp_cnt, budget
   FROM project_dept
   WHERE budget <= 40000;
```

The result is

dense_rank	row_number	dept_name	emp_cnt	budget
1	1	Accounting	10	40000
1	2	Accounting	6	40000
2	3	Accounting	6	30000
3	4	Accounting	5	10000

The first two columns in the result set of Example 23.16 show the values for the DENSE_RANK and ROW_NUMBER functions, respectively. The output of the DENSE_RANK function is similar to the output of the RANK function (see Example 23.15). The only difference is that the DENSE_RANK function returns no "gaps" if two or more ranking values are equal and thus belong to the same ranking.

The use of the ROW_NUMBER function is obvious: it returns the sequential number of a row within a result set, starting at 1 for the first row.

In the last two examples, the OVER clause is used to determine the ordering of the result set. As you already know, this clause can also be used to divide the result set produced by the FROM clause into groups (partitions), and then to apply an aggregate or ranking function to each partition separately.

Example 23.17 shows how the RANK function can be applied to partitions.

EXAMPLE 23.17

Using the window construct, partition the rows of the **project_dept** table according to the values in the **date_month** column. Sort the rows in each partition and display them in ascending order.

```
USE sample;
SELECT date_month, dept_name, emp_cnt, budget,
     RANK() OVER( PARTITION BY date_month ORDER BY emp_cnt desc ) AS rank
     FROM project_dept;
```

The result is

date_month	dept_name	emp_cnt	budget	rank
2007-01-01	Accounting	6	30000	1
2007-01-01	Research	5	50000	2
2007-02-01	Research	10	70000	1
2007-02-01	Accounting	10	40000	1
2007-07-01	Research	5	65000	1
2007-07-01	Accounting	5	10000	1
2008-01-01	Marketing	6	100000	1
2008-01-01	Marketing	NULL	120000	2
2008-02-01	Marketing	10	180000	1
2008-02-01	Accounting	6	40000	2
2008-07-01	Marketing	3	100000	1

The result set of Example 23.17 is divided (partitioned) into eight groups according to the values in the **date_month** column. After that the RANK function is applied to each partition. If you take a closer look and compare the previous example with Example 23.5, you will see that the last example works, while Example 23.5 displays an error, although both examples use the same window construct. As previously stated, Transact-SQL currently supports the OVER clause for aggregate functions only with the PARTITION BY clause, but in the case of ranking functions, the system supports general SQL standard syntax with the PARTITION BY and ORDER BY clauses.

Statistical Aggregate Functions

Chapter 6 introduced statistical aggregate functions. There are four of them:

▶ **VAR**   Computes the variance of all the values listed in a column or expression.

▶ **VARP**   Computes the variance for the population of all the values listed in a column or expression.

▶ **STDEV**   Computes the standard deviation of all the values listed in a column or expression. (The standard deviation is computed as the square root of the corresponding variance.)

▶ **STDEVP**   Computes the standard deviation for the population of all the values listed in a column or expression.

You can use statistical aggregate functions with or without the window construct. Example 23.18 shows how the functions VAR and STDEV can be used with the window construct.

EXAMPLE 23.18

Using the window construct, calculate the variance and standard deviation of budgets in relation to partitions formed using the values of the **dept_name** column:

```
USE sample;
SELECT dept_name,    budget,
            VAR(budget) OVER(PARTITION BY dept_name) AS budget_var,
            STDEV(budget) OVER(PARTITION BY dept_name)  AS budget_stdev
            FROM project_dept
            WHERE dept_name in ('Accounting', 'Research');
```

The result is

dept_name	budget	budget_var	budget_stdev
Accounting	10000	200000000	14142.135623731
Accounting	40000	200000000	14142.135623731
Accounting	30000	200000000	14142.135623731
Accounting	40000	200000000	14142.135623731
Research	50000	108333333,333333	10408.3299973306
Research	70000	108333333,333333	10408.3299973306
Research	65000	108333333,333333	10408.3299973306

Example 23.18 uses the statistical aggregate functions VAR and STDEV to calculate the variance and standard deviation of budgets in relation to partitions formed using the values of the **dept_name** column.

Standard and Nonstandard Analytic Functions

The Database Engine contains the following standard and nonstandard OLAP functions:

- ▶ TOP
- ▶ OFFSET/FETCH
- ▶ NTILE
- ▶ PIVOT and UNPIVOT

The second function, OFFSET/FETCH, is specified in the SQL standard, while the three others are Transact-SQL extensions. The following sections describe these analytic functions and operators.

TOP Clause

The TOP clause specifies the first n rows of the query result that are to be retrieved. This clause should always be used with the ORDER BY clause, because the result of such a query is always well defined and can be used in table expressions. (A table expression specifies a sample of a grouped result table.) A query with TOP but without the ORDER BY clause is nondeterministic, meaning that multiple executions of the query with the same data must not always display the same result set.

Example 23.19 shows the use of this clause.

EXAMPLE 23.19

Retrieve the four projects with the highest budgets:

```
USE sample;
SELECT TOP (4) dept_name, budget
   FROM project_dept
   ORDER BY budget DESC;
```

The result is

dept_name	budget
Marketing	180000
Marketing	120000
Marketing	100000
Marketing	100000

As you can see from Example 23.19, the TOP clause is part of the SELECT list and is written in front of all column names in the list.

NOTE

You should write the input value of TOP inside parentheses, because the system supports any self-contained expression as input.

The TOP clause is a nonstandard Transact-SQL implementation used to display the ranking of the top *n* rows from a table. A query equivalent to Example 23.19 that uses the window construct and the RANK function is shown in Example 23.20.

EXAMPLE 23.20

Retrieve the four projects with the highest budgets:

```
USE sample;
SELECT dept_name, budget
     FROM (SELECT dept_name, budget,
                    RANK() OVER (ORDER BY budget DESC) AS rank_budget
                       FROM project_dept) part_dept
     WHERE rank_budget <= 4;
```

The TOP clause can also be used with the additional PERCENT option. In that case, the first *n* percent of rows are retrieved from the result set. The additional option WITH TIES specifies that additional rows will be retrieved from the query result if they have the same value in the ORDER BY column(s) as the last row that belongs to the displayed set. Example 23.21 shows the use of the PERCENT and WITH TIES options.

EXAMPLE 23.21

Retrieve the top 25 percent of rows with the smallest number of employees:

```
USE sample;
SELECT TOP (25) PERCENT WITH TIES  emp_cnt, budget
   FROM project_dept
ORDER BY emp_cnt ASC;
```

The result is

emp_cnt	budget
NULL	120000
3	100000
5	50000
5	65000
5	10000

The result of Example 23.21 contains five rows, because there are three projects with five employees.

You can also use the TOP clause with UPDATE, DELETE, and INSERT statements. Example 23.22 shows the use of this clause with the UPDATE statement.

EXAMPLE 23.22

Find the three projects with the highest budget amounts and reduce them by 10 percent:

```
USE sample;
UPDATE TOP (3) project_dept
   SET budget = budget * 0.9
    WHERE budget in (SELECT TOP (3) budget
    FROM project_dept
    ORDER BY budget desc);
```

Example 23.23 shows the use of the TOP clause with the DELETE statement.

EXAMPLE 23.23

Delete the four projects with the smallest budget amounts:

```
USE sample;
DELETE TOP (4)
  FROM project_dept
  WHERE budget IN
                (SELECT TOP (4) budget FROM project_dept
                    ORDER BY budget ASC);
```

In Example 23.23, the TOP clause is used first in the subquery, to find the four projects with the smallest budget amounts, and then in the DELETE statement, to delete these projects.

OFFSET/FETCH

Chapter 6 showed how OFFSET/FETCH can be used for server-side paging. This application of OFFSET/FETCH is only one of many. Generally, OFFSET/FETCH allows you to filter several rows according to the given order. Additionally, you can specify how many rows of the result set should be skipped and how many of them should be returned. For this reason, OFFSET/FETCH is similar to the TOP clause. However, there are certain differences:

► OFFSET/FETCH is a standardized way to filter data, while the TOP clause is an extension of Transact-SQL. For this reason, it is possible that OFFSET/FETCH will replace the TOP clause in the future.

► OFFSET/FETCH is more flexible than TOP insofar as it allows skipping of rows using the OFFSET clause. (The Database Engine doesn't allow you to use the FETCH clause without OFFSET. In other words, even when no rows are skipped, you have to set OFFSET to 0.)

► The TOP clause is more flexible than OFFSET/FETCH insofar as it can be used in DML statements INSERT, UPDATE, and DELETE (see Examples 23.22 and 23.23).

Examples 23.24 and 23.25 show how you can use OFFSET/FETCH with the ROW_NUMBER() ranking function. (Before you execute the following examples, repopulate the **project_dept** table. First delete all the rows, and then execute the INSERT statements from Example 23.2.)

EXAMPLE 23.24

```
USE sample;
 SELECT date_month, budget, ROW_NUMBER()
   OVER (ORDER BY date_month DESC, budget DESC) as row_no
   FROM project_dept
   ORDER BY date_month DESC, budget DESC
   OFFSET 5 ROWS FETCH NEXT 4 ROWS ONLY;
```

The result is

date_month	Budget	row_no
2007-07-01	65000	6
2007-07-01	10000	7
2007-02-01	70000	8
2007-02-01	40000	9

Example 23.24 displays the rows of the **project_dept** table in relation to the **date_month** and **budget** columns. (The first five rows of the result set are skipped and the next four are displayed.) Additionally, the row number of these rows is returned. The row number of the first row in the result set starts with 6 because row numbers are assigned to the result set *before* the filtering. (OFFSET/FETCH is part of the ORDER BY clause and therefore is executed after the SELECT list, which includes the ROW_NUMBER function. In other words, the values of ROW_NUMBER are determined before OFFSET/FETCH is applied.)

If you want to get the row numbers starting with 1, you need to modify the SELECT statement. Example 23.25 shows the necessary modification.

EXAMPLE 23.25

```
 USE sample;
SELECT *, ROW_NUMBER()
 OVER (ORDER BY date_month DESC, budget DESC) as row_no
 FROM (SELECT date_month, budget
   FROM project_dept
   ORDER BY date_month DESC, budget DESC
   OFFSET 5 ROWS FETCH NEXT 4 ROWS ONLY) c;
```

The result of Example 23.25 is identical to the result of Example 23.24 except that row numbers start with 1. The reason is that in Example 23.25 the query with OFFSET/FETCH is written as a table expression inside the outer query with the ROW_NUMBER() function in the SELECT list. That way, the values of ROW_NUMBER() are determined before OFFSET/FETCH is executed.

NTILE Function

The NTILE function belongs to the ranking functions. It distributes the rows in a partition into a specified number of groups. For each row, the NTILE function returns the number of the group to which the row belongs. For this reason, this function is usually used to arrange rows into groups.

NOTE

The NTILE function breaks down the data based only on the count of values.

Example 23.26 shows the use of the NTILE function.

EXAMPLE 23.26

```
USE sample;
SELECT dept_name, budget,
  CASE NTILE(3) OVER (ORDER BY budget ASC)
    WHEN 1 THEN 'Low'
    WHEN 2 THEN 'Medium'
    WHEN 3 THEN 'High'
  END AS groups
FROM project_dept;
```

The result is

dept_name	budget	groups
Accounting	10000	Low
Accounting	30000	Low
Accounting	40000	Low
Accounting	40000	Low
Research	50000	Medium
Research	65000	Medium
Research	70000	Medium
Marketing	100000	Medium
Marketing	100000	High
Marketing	120000	High
Marketing	180000	High

Pivoting Data

Pivoting data is a method that is used to transform data from a state of rows to a state of columns. Additionally, some values from the source table can be aggregated before the target table is created.

There are two operators for pivoting data:

- ► PIVOT
- ► UNPIVOT

The following subsections describe these operators in detail.

PIVOT Operator

PIVOT is a nonstandard relational operator that is supported by Transact-SQL. You can use it to manipulate a table-valued expression into another table. PIVOT transforms such an expression by turning the unique values from one column in the expression into multiple columns in the output, and it performs aggregations on any remaining column values that are desired in the final output.

To demonstrate how the PIVOT operator works, let us use a table called **project_ dept_pivot**, which is derived from the **project_dept** table specified at the beginning of this chapter. The new table contains the **budget** column from the source table and two additional columns: **month** and **year**. The **year** column of the **project_dept_pivot** table contains the years 2007 and 2008, which appear in the **date_month** column of the **project_dept** table. Also, the **month** columns of the **project_dept_pivot** table (**january**, **february**, and **july**) contain the summaries of budgets corresponding to these months in the **project_dept** table.

Example 23.27 creates the **project_dept_pivot** table.

EXAMPLE 23.27

```
USE sample;
SELECT budget, month(date_month) as month, year(date_month) as year
 INTO project_dept_pivot
FROM project_dept;
```

The content of the new table is given in Table 23-2.

Suppose that you get a task to return a row for each year, a column for each month, and the budget value for each year and month intersection. Table 23-3 shows the desired result.

budget	Month	year
50000	1	2007
70000	2	2007
65000	7	2007
10000	7	2007
40000	2	2007
30000	1	2007
40000	2	2008
100000	1	2008
180000	2	2008
100000	7	2008
120000	1	2008

Table 23-2 *Content of the project_dept_pivot Table*

Example 23.28 demonstrates how you can solve this problem using the standard SQL language.

EXAMPLE 23.28

```
USE sample;
SELECT year,
    SUM(CASE WHEN month = 1 THEN budget END ) AS January,
     SUM(CASE WHEN month = 2 THEN budget END ) AS February,
        SUM(CASE WHEN month = 7 THEN budget END ) AS July
        FROM project_dept_pivot
        GROUP BY year;
```

Year	January	February	July
2007	80000	110000	75000
2008	220000	220000	100000

Table 23-3 *Budgets for each year and month*

The process of pivoting data can be divided into three steps:

▶ **Group the data**   Generate one row in the result set for each distinct "on rows" element. In Example 23.28, the "on rows" element is the **year** column and it appears in the GROUP BY clause of the SELECT statement.

▶ **Manipulate the data**   Spread the values that will be aggregated to the columns of the target table. In Example 23.28, the columns of the target table are all distinct values of the **month** column. To implement this step, you have to apply a CASE expression for each of the different values of the **month** column: 1 (January), 2 (February), and 7 (July).

▶ **Aggregate the data**   Aggregate the data values in each column of the target table. Example 23.28 uses the SUM function for this step.

Example 23.29 solves the same problem as Example 23.28 using the PIVOT operator.

EXAMPLE 23.29

```
USE sample;
SELECT year, [1] as January, [2] as February, [7] July FROM
    (SELECT budget, year, month from project_dept_pivot) p2
    PIVOT (SUM(budget)  FOR month IN ([1],[2],[7])) AS P;
```

The SELECT statement in Example 23.29 contains an inner query, which is embedded in the FROM clause of the outer query. The PIVOT clause is part of the inner query. It starts with the specification of the aggregation function: SUM (of budgets). The second part specifies the pivot column (**month**) and the values from that column to be used as column headings—the first, second, and seventh months of the year. The value for a particular column in a row is calculated using the specified aggregate function over the rows that match the column heading.

The most important advantage of using the PIVOT operator in relation to the standard solution is its simplicity in the case in which the target table has many columns. In this case, the standard solution is verbose because you have to write one CASE expression for each column in the target table.

UNPIVOT Operator

The UNPIVOT operator performs the reverse operation of PIVOT, by rotating columns into rows. Example 23.30 shows the use of this operator.

EXAMPLE 23.30

```
USE sample;
CREATE TABLE project_dept_pvt (year int, January float, February float,
July float);
INSERT INTO project_dept_pvt VALUES (2007, 80000, 110000, 75000);
INSERT INTO project_dept_pvt VALUES (2008, 50000, 80000, 30000);
--UNPIVOT the table
SELECT year, month, budget
FROM
    (SELECT year, January, February, July
        FROM project_dept_pvt) p
            UNPIVOT (budget FOR month IN (January, February, July)
          )AS unpvt;
```

The result is

year	month	budget
2007	January	80000
2007	February	110000
2007	July	75000
2008	January	50000
2008	February	80000
2008	July	30000

Example 23.30 uses the **project_dept_pvt** table to demonstrate the UNPIVOT relational operator. UNPIVOT's first input is the column name (**budget**), which holds the normalized values. After that, the FOR option is used to determine the target column name (**month**). Finally, as part of the IN option, the selected values of the target column name are specified.

NOTE

UNPIVOT is not the exact reverse of PIVOT, because any NULL values in the table being transformed cannot be used as column values in the output.

Summary

SQL/OLAP extensions in Transact-SQL support data analysis facilities. There are four main parts of SQL/OLAP that are supported by the Database Engine:

- Window construct
- Extensions of the GROUP BY clause
- OLAP query functions
- Standard and nonstandard analytic functions

The window construct is the most important extension. In combination with ranking and aggregate functions, it allows you to easily calculate analytic functions, such as cumulative and sliding aggregates, as well as rankings. There are several extensions to the GROUP BY clause that are described in the SQL standard and supported by the Database Engine: the CUBE, ROLLUP, and GROUPING SETS operators as well as the grouping functions GROUPING and GROUPING_ID.

The most important analytic query functions are ranking functions: RANK, DENSE_RANK, and ROW_NUMBER. Transact-SQL supports several nonstandard analytic functions and operators, TOP, NTILE, PIVOT, and UNPIVOT, as well as a standard one, OFFSET/FETCH.

The next chapter describes Reporting Services, a business intelligence component of SQL Server.

Exercises

E.23.1

Find the average number of the employees in the Accounting department. Solve this problem:

    a. using the window construct
    b. using the GROUP BY clause

E.23.2

Using the window construct, find the department with the highest budget for the years 2007 and 2008.

E.23.3

Find the sum of employees according to the combination of values in the departments and budget amounts. All possible summary rows should be displayed, too.

E.23.4

Solve E.23.3 using the ROLLUP operator. What is the difference between this result set and the result set of E.23.3?

E.23.5

Using the RANK function, find the three departments with the highest number of employees.

E.23.6

Solve E.23.5 using the TOP clause.

E.23.7

Calculate the ranking of all departments for the year 2008 according to the number of employees. Display the values for the DENSE_RANK and ROW_NUMBER functions, too.

Chapter 24

SQL Server Reporting Services

In This Chapter

- ► **Introduction to Data Reports**
- ► **SQL Server Reporting Services Architecture**
- ► **Configuration of SQL Server Reporting Services**
- ► **Creating Reports**
- ► **Managing Reports**

his chapter describes Microsoft's enterprise reporting tool called SQL Server Reporting Services. After first introducing the general structure of a report, the chapter explains the main components of Reporting Services and describes the configuration of an installed instance of Reporting Services. After that, you'll see how you can create reports using Business Intelligence Development Studio. Two examples are provided, one without parameters and the other with parameters, to explain each step in the creation process. The processing of a report is then explained. Finally, different ways to deliver a designed and deployed report are shown.

Introduction to Data Reports

A report is one of the interfaces through which users can interact with database systems. Using reports, the data is visualized and displayed to users. The data can be displayed in many different formats.

Generally, data reports have the following properties:

▶ *A report can be used only to display data.* In contrast to forms-based interfaces, which can be used both to read and modify data, a report is a read-only user interface. You can use reports to view data statically or dynamically.

▶ *A report generator supports many different layouts and file formats.* A report presents data in a preformatted form. In other words, you use a report layout to compose items that correspond to result values of the report query. (You can generally design your report either in graphical or tabular form.)

▶ *A report is always based on a corresponding SELECT statement.* Because reports can be used only to display data, each report is based on a SELECT statement, which retrieves data. The difference between the result of a retrieval operation and the corresponding report is that the latter uses various styles and formats to display data, while a result set of each SELECT statement has a static form, which is arranged by the system.

▶ *A report can use parameters, which are part of a particular query and whose values are set at run time.* You can use parameters, as a part of your query, to add flexibility to reports. The values of such parameters are passed from a user or an application program to the query.

▶ *There are always one or more sources that provide input data for the report.* Each report contains a query which retrieves data. This data is stored in one or more sources that are usually relational databases, but can be files, too.

Concerning its structure, each report has the following two instruction sets, which together specify the content of the report:

▶ **Data definition**   Specifies data sources and a dataset. (For the detailed description of data sources and datasets, see the section "Planning Data Sources and Datasets" later in the chapter.) The content of the dataset can be defined using Query Designer. (Query Designer is a graphical tool that allows you to build a query used in your report. This tool is especially helpful for users who do not know the syntax of the SELECT statement and need help to create a report's query.)

▶ **Report layout**   Enables you to present selected data to users. You can specify which column values correspond to which fields and the form and location of headings and page numbers.

Now that you've had this general introduction to reports, you are ready to look at the architecture of SQL Server Reporting Services.

SQL Server Reporting Services Architecture

SQL Server Reporting Services (SSRS) is a Microsoft software system that you can use to generate reports. You can use this system to develop and maintain reports of any kind.

SSRS includes three main components, which represent a server layer, a metadata layer, and an application layer, respectively:

▶ Reporting Services Windows service

▶ Report catalog

▶ Report Manager

These components are described in the following sections, after a brief introduction to the Report Definition Language.

When the information concerning data definition and report layout is gathered, SSRS stores it using the Report Definition Language (RDL). RDL is an XML-based language that is used exclusively for storing report definitions and layouts. RDL is an open schema language, meaning that developers can extend the language with additional XML attributes and elements. (For descriptions of XML in general and XML elements and attributes in particular, see Chapter 26.) RDL is usually generated under Visual Studio, although it may also be used programmatically.

A typical RDL file contains three main sections. The first concerns page style, the second section specifies field definitions, and the last section defines parameters.

NOTE

It is not necessary for you to use RDL to develop reports. The language is important only when you want to create your own RDL files.

Reporting Services Windows Service

As its name implies, Reporting Services Windows service is implemented as a Windows component that comprises two important services in relation to the report server. The first one, Reporting Services Web service, is the application used for the implementation of the Report Manager web site, while the second one, Reporting Services Windows service, allows you to use it as a programmatic interface for reports. (Report Manager will be explained later in this chapter.)

NOTE

Both services, Reporting Services Windows service and Reporting Services Web service, work together and constitute a single report server instance.

As you can see from Figure 24-1, Reporting Services Windows service includes the following components:

▶ Report processor

▶ Data providers

▶ Renderers

▶ Request handler

The report processor manages the execution of a report. It retrieves the definition of the report, which is done in RDL, and determines what is needed for the report. Also, it manages the work of other components that are used to produce a report. The report processor also retrieves data from data sources. After that, it selects a data provider that knows how to extract information from the data source. The task of the data provider is to connect to the data source, get the information for the report, and return it to the processor in the form of corresponding datasets.

When data providers deliver the data for the report, the report processor can begin to process the report's layout. To generate the layout, the processor has to know the

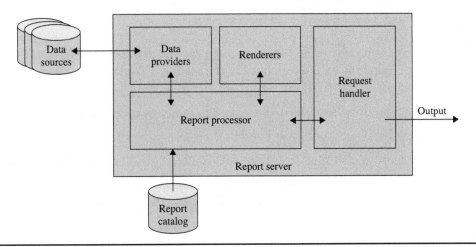

Figure 24-1   *Components of Reporting Services Windows service*

format of the report (HTML or PDF, for instance). The renderers are used to build the corresponding format.

The request handler receives requests for reports and sends them to the report processor. It also delivers the completed report. (The different forms of report delivery will be discussed later in the chapter.)

The Report Catalog

The report catalog contains two databases that are used to store the definitions of all existing reports that belong to a particular service. The stored information includes report names, descriptions, data source connection information, credential information, parameters, and execution properties. The report catalog also stores security settings and information concerning scheduling and delivering data.

SQL Server Reporting Services uses two databases, the Report Server database and the Report Server temporary database, to separate persistent data storage from temporary storage requirements. The databases are created together and bound by name. By default, the database names are **reportserver** and **reportservertempdb**, respectively. The former is used to store the report catalog, while the latter is used as temporary storage for cached reports, and work tables that are generated by the report.

Report Manager

Report Manager is a web-based report access and management tool that runs using a browser. This section only lists tasks that you can accomplish using this tool. Subsequent sections of the chapter will describe how you can use the tool for specific tasks.

Report Manager can be used to do the following:

▶ View, print, subscribe to, and search for reports. The use of Report Manager to create subscriptions will be explained in the section "Standard Subscriptions" later in this chapter.

▶ Determine security issues related to access to items and operations.

▶ Configure parameters of a report and its execution properties.

▶ Create report models that connect to data sources.

▶ Create shared data sources to make data source connections more manageable. (For a description of shared data sources, see the section "Planning Data Sources and Datasets" later in this chapter.)

▶ Create data-driven subscriptions that roll out reports to a large recipient list. (Data-driven subscriptions are described in the section with the same name later in this chapter.)

▶ Launch Report Builder to create reports that you can save and run on the report server.

The next section explains how you can configure an installed instance of SSRS.

Configuration of SQL Server Reporting Services

You use Reporting Services Configuration Manager (RSCM) to configure an already installed instance of Reporting Services. As you already know from Chapter 2, which explained how to install SSRS, during the installation phase you had the option to install and configure the report server or to install it without configuring it at that time.

If you chose the Install, But Do Not Configure the Report Server option during the installation phase (see Figure 2-9), you must use RSCM to configure the report server before you can use it. If you installed the report server by using the default configuration installation option, you can use RSCM to verify or modify the settings that were specified during the installation process.

NOTE

RSCM is installed automatically when you install SSRS, and you can use it to configure local and remote report servers.

To start Reporting Services Configuration Manager, choose Start | All Programs | Microsoft SQL Server 2012 | Configuration Tools | Reporting Services Configuration

Manager. In the Reporting Services Configuration Connection dialog box, you can select the report server instance you want to configure. In the Server Name field, specify the name of the computer on which the report server instance is installed. (If your instance is installed on a remote computer, click Find to find the instance and to connect to it.) In the Report Server Instance drop-down list box, choose from the drop-down list the SQL Server Reporting Services instance that you want to configure. Click Connect.

Now you can perform the following tasks:

▶ **Configure the Report Server service account** The initially configured account can be modified using RSCM.

▶ **Create and configure URLs** Reporting Services and Report Manager are ASP.NET applications accessed through URLs. You can configure a single URL or multiple URLs for both applications.

▶ **Create and configure the report server database** Use this page to create or change the report server database or update database connection credentials.

▶ **Specify e-mail settings** Specify a Simple Mail Transfer Protocol (SMTP) server and an e-mail account to use report server e-mail.

▶ **Configure the unattended execution account** This account is used for remote connections during scheduled operations or when user credentials are not available.

▶ **Backup encryption keys** This process is necessary if you move the report server installation to another computer.

Now that you are familiar with the components of SQL Server Reporting Services as well as its configuration, you will learn how to create, deploy, and deliver reports.

Creating Reports

SQL Server Reporting Services gives you two tools to use to create reports:

▶ **Business Intelligence Development Studio (BIDS)** A development tool that you use during the development phase. It is tightly integrated with Visual Studio and allows you to develop and test reports before their deployment.

▶ **Report Builder** A stand-alone tool that enables you to do ad hoc reporting without knowing anything about the structure of a particular database or how to create queries using SQL.

NOTE

This book discusses the first option only, creating reports using BIDS. The reason is that Report Builder generally is used not to create new reports but to modify existing ones. For the description of Report Builder, see Books Online.

To start Development Studio, choose Start | All Programs | Microsoft SQL Server 2012 | SQL Server Business Intelligence Development Studio. The first step in building a report is to create a new project to which the report belongs. To build a project, choose File | New | Project. In the New Project dialog box, select the Business Intelligence folder. Type the name of the project and its location in the Name and Location text boxes, respectively. The project in this example is called Project1, as you can see in Figure 24-2.

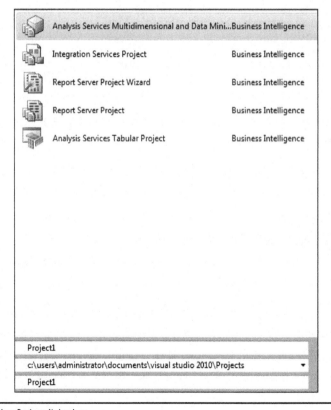

Figure 24-2 *The New Project dialog box*

In the middle pane of the New Project dialog box, you will see two project templates related to reports. The Report Server Project template creates an empty report and leaves you alone to do the rest of the work. The Report Server Project Wizard guides you during the creation phase of a new report.

> **NOTE**
>
> *Generally, SQL Server Reporting Services reports are built using Report Designer, a collection of graphical query and design tools. It provides the Report Data pane, which you can use to organize data used in your report, and tabbed views for Design and Preview so that you can design a report interactively. Report Designer also comprises Query Designer, mentioned earlier in the chapter, to help you specify data for retrieval, and the Expression dialog box, to specify report data to use in the report layout. Report Designer is hosted in BIDS.*

In the following section, you will use the Report Server Project Wizard to create a report. Therefore, select the Report Server Project Wizard icon and click OK. This leads you to the welcome page of the wizard.

Creating Reports with the Report Server Project Wizard

The Report Server Project Wizard welcome page introduces the major steps that it takes you through to create a report:

1. Select a data source from which to retrieve data.
2. Design a query to execute against the data source.
3. Choose the report type.
4. Specify the report layout.
5. Choose the report style.

These steps (and others not listed on the welcome page) are described in the upcoming subsections, followed by a quick summary of how to preview the result set and deploy the report. First, though, you will learn how to plan your data sources and datasets.

Planning Data Sources and Datasets

Before you create a report, you should prepare your data sources for use. You use these sources to create the corresponding tables and/or views, which will be used to retrieve the particular result set. For this reason, the environment in which you prepare data sources is SQL Server Management Studio, with its Transact-SQL capabilities, rather than SSRS.

During the planning phase, you have to work with both data sources and datasets. The differences between these two concepts are described next, followed by a description of how you can use both of them.

Data Sources vs. Datasets   The most important difference between data sources and datasets is that data sources are not included in your report. A data source just delivers information for your report. This information can be stored either in a file or in a database. The task of SSRS is to generate datasets from the given data sources using the set of instructions. This set includes, among other things, the information concerning the type of the source, the name of the database (if the data source is stored in a database) or the file path, and optionally the connection information to the source.

During the execution of a report, SSRS uses this information to generate a new format, called a *dataset*. Therefore, a dataset is just an abstraction of underlying data sources and is used as a direct input for the corresponding report.

Using Data Sources   To include data in a report, you must first create data connections (a synonym for data sources). A data connection includes the data source type, connection information, and the login for connecting. (Creation of data connections is described in the upcoming section "Selecting a Data Source.")

There are two types of data sources: embedded and shared. An embedded data source is defined in the report and used only by that report. In other words, when you want to modify an embedded data source, you have to change the properties of that data source using Report Manager. A shared data source is defined independently from a report and can be used by multiple reports. Shared data sources are useful when you have data sources that are often used.

NOTE

It is recommended that you use shared data sources as much as possible. They make reports easier to manage and report access more secure.

Using Datasets   As you already know, each dataset is an abstraction of corresponding data sources and therefore specifies the fields from the data source that you plan to use in the report. All datasets that you create for a report definition appear in the Datasets window.

Since SQL Server 2008 R2, SSRS has supported shared datasets. Simply put, a shared dataset is a dataset that allows several reports to share a query to provide a consistent set of data for multiple reports. Shared datasets are tightly connected to shared data sources. In other words, you use shared data sources to generate shared datasets.

The query of a shared dataset can include parameters. You can configure a shared dataset to cache query results for specific parameter combinations on first use or by specifying a schedule.

You can use either Business Intelligence Development Studio or Report Builder to create a shared dataset. To create a shared dataset using BIDS, open the Solution Explorer window, right-click the Shared Datasets folder, and click Add New Dataset. In the Dataset Properties window, select a corresponding data source and use the text window to type (or paste) your SELECT statement.

Selecting a Data Source

The data source contains information about the connection to the source database. Click Next on the welcome page of the Report Server Project Wizard to select the data source. On the Select the Data Source page, type the name of the new data source in the Name field. (In this example, call the data source **Source1**.)

The Type drop-down list on the Select Data Source page allows you to choose one of the different data source types. SSRS can create reports from different relational databases (SQL Server, Teradata, and Oracle, among others) or multidimensional databases (Analysis Services). OLE DB, ODBC, and XML data sources can be used, too. After you choose a type, click Edit. The Connection Properties dialog box appears, as shown in Figure 24-3.

Type either **localhost** or the name of your database server as the server name. Below that, choose either Use Windows Authentication or Use SQL Server Authentication. Click the Select or Enter a Database Name radio button and choose from the drop-down list one of the databases as the data source. Before you click OK, click the Test Connection button to test the connection to the database. Clicking Next takes you back to the Select the Data Source page. Click Next to continue the wizard.

Designing a Query

The next step is to design a query that should be executed against the selected data source. On the Design the Query page, you can either type (or paste) an existing query or use the Query Builder component to create a query from scratch.

NOTE

Query Builder corresponds to the similar Access component that you can use to design queries even if you have no knowledge of the SQL language. This component is generally known as QBE (query by example).

For this first report, use the query given in Example 24.1.

Figure 24-3 *The Connection Properties dialog box*

EXAMPLE 24.1

```
SELECT dept_name, emp_lname, emp_fname, job, enter_date
   FROM department d JOIN employee e ON d.dept_no = e.dept_no
                 JOIN works_on w ON w.emp_no = e.emp_no
   WHERE YEAR(enter_date) = 2007
   ORDER BY dept_name;
```

The query in Example 24.1 selects data for employees who entered their job in 2007. The result set of the query is then sorted by department names. After that, click Next.

NOTE

SSRS checks the names of the tables and columns listed in the query. If the system finds any syntax errors, it displays the corresponding message in the new window.

Choosing the Report Type

The next step in creating a report is to select the report type. You can choose between two report types:

▶ **Tabular**   Creates a report in tabular form. Columns of the table correspond to the columns from the SELECT list, while the number of rows in the table depends on the result set of the query.

▶ **Matrix**   Creates a report in matrix form, which is similar to table form but provides functionality of crosstabs. Unlike the tabular report type, which has a static set of columns, the matrix report type can be dynamic.

NOTE

You should use the matrix report type whenever you want to create queries that contain aggregate functions, such as AVG or SUM.

The query in Example 24.1 does not contain any aggregate functions. Therefore, choose the tabular report type and click Next.

Designing the Data in the Table

The Design the Table page (see Figure 24-4) allows you to decide where selected columns will be placed in your report. The Design the Table page contains two groups of fields:

▶ Available fields

▶ Displayed fields

The page also has three views:

▶ Page

▶ Group

▶ Details

Available fields are the columns from the SELECT list of your query. Each column can be moved to one of the views. To move a field to the Page, Group, or Details view, select the field and then click the Page, Group, or Details button, respectively. A *displayed field* is an available field that is assigned to one of the existing views.

Page view lists all columns that appear at the page level, and Group view lists columns that are used to group the resulting set of the query. Details view is used to

Figure 24-4 *The Design the Table page*

display columns that appear in the detail section of the table. Figure 24-4 shows the
Design the Table page with the design of the tabular representation for the resulting set
of Example 24.1. In this example, the **dept_name** column will appear at the page level,
while the **job** column will be used to group the selected rows. When you have chosen
how to group the data in the table, click Next.

NOTE

*The order of the columns can be important, especially for the Group view. To change the order of the columns,
select a column and click the up or down button to the right.*

Specifying the Report Layout

The next step is to specify the layout of your report. The Choose the Table Layout page
has several options:

▶ Stepped

▶ Block

▶ Include subtotals

▶ Enable drilldown

If you choose Stepped, the report will contain one column for each field, with grouping fields appearing in headers to the left of columns from the detail field. In this case, the group footer will not be created. If you include subtotals with this layout type, the subtotal is placed in the group header rows.

The Block option creates a report that contains one column for each field, with group fields appearing in the first detail row for each group. This layout type has group footers only if the Include Subtotals option is activated.

The Enable Drilldown option hides the inner groups of the report and enables a visibility toggle. (You can choose Enable drilldown only if you select the Stepped option.)

To continue, choose Stepped and Include Subtotals and click Next.

Choosing the Report Style

The next step is to choose a style for your report. The Choose the Table Style page allows you to select a template to apply styles such as font, color, and border style to the report. There are several different style templates, such as Forest, Corporate, and Bold. Chose Bold and click Next.

Choosing the Deployment Location and Completing the Wizard

After choosing a report style, there is still one intermediate step if you are creating a report for the first time. In this step, called Choose the Deployment Location, you must choose the URL of the virtual directory of the report server and the deployment folder for your reports. For a report server running in native mode, use the path to the report server where the project is deployed (for example, http://localhost/ReportServer). For a report server running in SharePoint integrated mode, use the URL of the SharePoint site to which the project is deployed (for example, http://localhost). Click Next.

NOTE

SSRS supports two modes of deployment for report server instances: native mode and SharePoint integrated mode. In native mode, which is the default, a report server is a stand-alone application server that provides all viewing, management, processing, and delivery of reports. In SharePoint integrated mode, a report server becomes part of a SharePoint web application deployment. Users of SharePoint Server can store reports in SharePoint libraries and access them from the same SharePoint sites they use to access other business documents.

Finally, you complete the wizard's work by providing a name for the report. Also, you can take a look at the report summary, where all your previous steps during the creation of the report are documented. Click Finish to finish the wizard.

Previewing the Result Set

When you finish the creation of your report using the wizard, there are two tabs in the Report Designer pane that you can use to view the created report in different forms. (If the Report Designer pane isn't visible, click View | Designer.) The tabs correspond to the following views:

▶ Design

▶ Preview

The Design tab allows you to view and modify the layout of your report. The Design mode consists of the following sections: body, page, header, and page footer. You can use the Toolbox and Properties windows to manipulate items in the report. To view these windows, select Toolbox or Properties Window in the View menu. Use the Toolbox window to select items to place them in one of the sections. Each item on the report design surface contains properties that can be managed using the Properties window. Figure 24-5 shows the layout of the report.

To preview the report, click the Preview tab. The report runs automatically, using already specified properties. Figure 24-6 shows the preview for the report that was defined in the previous steps.

Figure 24-5 *The layout of the report*

Figure 24-6 *The preview of the report*

Deploying the Report

Before you can use or distribute a report, you have to deploy it. To do so, right-click the
created report and choose Deploy. The deployment process contains several steps, which
are shown in the Output pane:

```
------ Build started: Project: Project1, Configuration: Debug ------
Build complete -- 0 errors, 0 warnings
------ Deploy started: Project: Project1, Configuration: Debug ------
Deploying to http://localhost/ReportServer
Deploying data source '/Project1/sample'.
Deploying report '/Project1/Report1'.
Deploy complete -- 0 errors, 0 warnings
========== Build: 1 succeeded or up-to-date, 0 failed, 0 skipped ==========
========== Deploy: 1 succeeded, 0 failed, 0 skipped ==========
```

Creating Parameterized Reports

A parameterized report is one that uses input parameters to complete report processing.
The parameters are then used to execute a query that selects specific data for the report.
If you design or deploy a parameterized report, you need to understand how parameter
selections affect the report.

Parameters in SQL Server Reporting Services are used to filter data. They are
specified using the known syntax for variables (**@year**, for instance). If a parameter is

specified in a query, a value must be provided to complete the SELECT statement or stored procedure that retrieves data for a report.

You can define a default value for a parameter. If all parameters have default values, the report will immediately display data when the report is executed. If at least one parameter does not have a default value, the report will display data after the user enters all parameter values.

When the report is run in a browser, the parameter is displayed in a box at the top of the report. When the report is run in the Preview mode, the value of the parameter is displayed in the corresponding box.

An example will be used to show you how to create a parameterized report. This example describes only those steps that are different from the steps already discussed in relation to Example 24.1. The query used in this example, shown in Example 24.2, selects data from the **AdventureWorksDW** database. For this reason, you have to select and define a new data source. The specification of the new source is identical to the specification of the source called **Source1**, except that you choose the **AdventureWorksDW** database instead of the **sample** database.

EXAMPLE 24.2

```
SELECT  t.MonthNumberOfYear AS month,    t.CalendarYear  AS year,
      p.ProductKey AS product_id,   SUM(f.UnitPrice)  AS sum_of_sales,
      COUNT(f.UnitPrice)  AS total_sales
      FROM DimDate t, DimProduct p, FactInternetSales f
      WHERE t.DateKey    = f.OrderDateKey AND   p.ProductKey = f.ProductKey
         AND CalendarYear = @year
      GROUP BY t.CalendarYear, t.MonthNumberOfYear,  p.ProductKey
      ORDER BY 1;
```

The query in Example 24.2 calculates the number and the sum of unit product prices. It also groups the rows according to the list of column names in the GROUP BY clause. The expression

```
CalendarYear = @year
```

in the WHERE clause of the example specifies that the input parameter **@year** in this query is related to the calendar year for which you want to query data.

This report is a typical example of a matrix type report. Values of the **year** column will be assigned to the Page view, values of the **month** column to the Columns view, and values of the **product_id** column to the Rows view. The Details view displays the aggregate values SUM and COUNT.

To start the report in the Preview mode, type the value of the **CalendarYear** parameter (2008, for instance) and click the View Report tab. Figure 24-7 shows a part of this report.

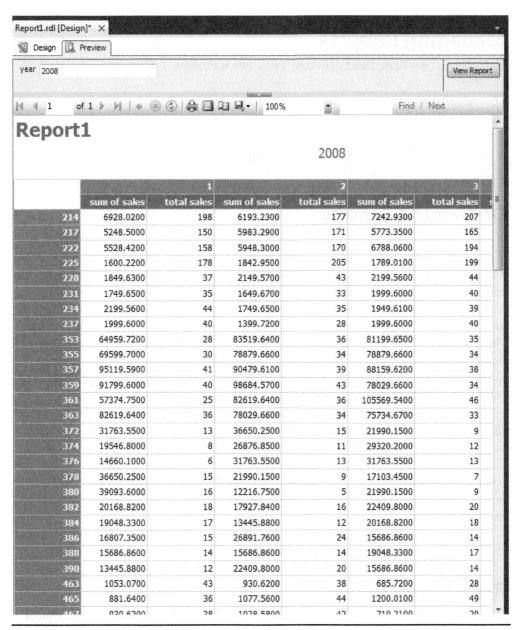

Figure 24-7   *A preview of part of the report*

Managing Reports

Reports can be accessed and delivered using two methods:

- ▶ On demand
- ▶ Subscription based

These two methods are described next, followed by a discussion of your report delivery options.

On-Demand Reports

As you already know, before you can use or distribute a report, you have to deploy it. This can be done on demand. On-demand access allows users to select the reports from a report-viewing tool. You can use Report Manager or a browser to view a report. This section explains how you can view on-demand reports using a browser.

Reporting Services Web service allows you to access reports on demand. All reports are organized in a hierarchical namespace and accessed through virtual directories. If you used the default values to configure URLs, you should be able to access the Report Server Web service using URLs that specify the computer name or localhost as the host name: http://localhost/ReportServer. The default virtual directory for Report Manager is http://localhost/Reports/. (Both default values can be modified.)

To view a report on demand, select the report from the corresponding folder hierarchy. In this case, the report server creates a temporary snapshot for the purpose of delivering the report. The snapshot is discarded after delivery.

There are several possibilities for running reports on demand. The first one is to specify that a report queries the corresponding data source each time a user runs the report. In this case, a new instance of the report is generated each time a new user executes the report.

If you want to enhance performance, cached reports should be your choice. (Cached reports will be discussed in detail in a moment.)

Report Subscription

On-demand reporting requires report selection each time you want to view a report's result. By contrast, subscription-based access automatically generates and delivers reports to a destination.

SQL Server Reporting Services supports two kinds of subscriptions:

- ► Standard subscriptions
- ► Data-driven subscriptions

The following subsections describe these subscription forms.

Standard Subscriptions

A standard subscription usually consists of specific parameters for parameterized reports as well as report presentation options and delivery options. You can use different tools to manage standard subscriptions. Usually, Report Manager is used for this task.

To create a new subscription, open Report Manager and locate the report for which you want to add a subscription. Hover over the report, and click the drop-down arrow. In the drop-down menu, click Subscribe. This opens the New Subscription page for the report.

The first step is to choose a delivery mode. You can choose between e-mail or the file share method. When you choose file share as the delivery method, you have to provide the file name, path, render format, and security information.

The next step is to configure a schedule. You can specify a schedule for a particular report only or use a shared schedule for several subscriptions. (If your report has parameters, you have to determine which values are assigned to parameters when the subscription is started.)

Data-Driven Subscriptions

A data-driven subscription delivers reports to a list of recipients determined at run time. This type of subscription differs from a standard subscription in the way it gets subscription information: some settings from a data source are provided at run time, and other settings are static (that is, they are provided from the subscription definition). Static aspects of a data-driven subscription include the report that is delivered, the delivery extension, connection information to an external data source that contains subscriber data, and a query. Dynamic settings of the subscription are obtained from the row set produced by the query, including a subscriber list and user-specific delivery extension preferences or parameter values.

NOTE

SQL Server Enterprise Edition is required if you want to use data-driven subscriptions.

The next section discusses how you can process reports.

Report Delivery Options

Report processing begins with a published report definition, which includes a query, layout information, and code. Report and data processing together create a dataset with layout information, which is stored as an intermediate format. After processing is complete, reports are compiled as a CLR assembly and delivered to the report server.

When a report is deployed on the report server, it is configured by default to be run on demand. The subsection "On-Demand Reports" in the previous section describes how reports are used on demand. This section describes additional options that you can use to execute a report:

▶   Cached reports

▶   Execution snapshots

Cached Reports

Caching means that a report is generated only for the first user who opens it, and thereafter is retrieved from the cache for all subsequent users who work with the same report. A report server can cache a copy of a processed report and return that copy when a user opens the report. To a user, the only evidence available to indicate the report is a cached copy is the date and time that the report ran. If the date or time is not current and the report is not a snapshot, the report was retrieved from cache.

As you probably guessed, caching shortens the time to retrieve frequently accessed reports. Also, this technique is recommended for large reports. If the server is rebooted, all cached instances are reinstated when the Report Server Web service is restarted.

The contents of the cache are volatile and can change as new reports are added or existing ones dropped. If you require a more predictable caching strategy, you should create an execution snapshot, which is described next.

Execution Snapshots

The main disadvantage of cached reports is that the first user who wants to use the particular report has to wait until the system creates it. A more user-friendly method would be for the system to create the report automatically, so even the first user doesn't have to wait. This is supported by execution snapshots.

An execution snapshot is a way to create cached reports that contain data captured at a specific point in time. The benefit of an execution snapshot is that no user has to wait, because the data has already been accessed from the report's data source(s) and stored in the Report Server temporary database. That way, the report will be rendered very quickly. The disadvantage of execution snapshots is that data can become stale, if the time difference between the creation of the report snapshot and access of the report is too long.

The main difference between execution snapshots and cached reports is that cached reports are created as a result of a user action, while execution snapshots are created automatically by the system.

Summary

SQL Server Reporting Services is the SQL Server–based enterprise reporting tool. To create a report, you can use the Report Server Project Wizard or Report Builder. The definition of a report, which comprises the corresponding query, layout information, and code, is stored using the XML-based Report Definition Language (RDL). SSRS processes the report definition into one of the standard formats, such as HTML or PDF.

Reports can be accessed on demand or delivered based on a subscription. When you execute a report on demand, a new instance of the report will usually be generated each time you run the report. Subscription-based reports can be either standard or data driven. Reports based on a standard subscription usually consist of specific parameters as well as report presentation options and delivery options. A data-driven subscription delivers reports to a list of recipients determined at run time.

To shorten the time of report execution, thereby increasing performance, you can either cache your reports or use execution snapshots. The main difference between execution snapshots and cached reports is that cached reports are created as a result of a user action, while execution snapshots are created automatically by the system.

The next chapter describes optimization techniques for business intelligence.

Exercises

E.24.1

Get the employee numbers and names for all clerks. Create a report in the matrix report type using this query. Use Report Manager to view a report.

E.24.2

Use the **sample** database and get the budgets and project names of projects being worked on by employees in the Research department who have an employee number < 25000. Create a report in the table report type using this query. Use a browser to view the report.

Chapter 25

Optimizing Techniques for Relational Online Analytical Processing

In This Chapter

- ▶ **Data Partitioning**
- ▶ **Star Join Optimization**
- ▶ **Columnstore Index**

Threshold this chapter describes several optimizing techniques pertaining to relational online analytical processing (ROLAP). In other words, these techniques can be applied only to *relational storage* of multidimensional data. The first part of this chapter discusses when it is reasonable to store all entity instances in a single table and when it is better, for performance reasons, to partition the table's data. After a general introduction to data partitioning and the type of partitioning supported by the Database Engine, the steps that you have to follow to partition your table(s) are discussed in detail. You will then be given some partitioning techniques that can help increase system performance, followed by a list of important suggestions for how to partition your data and indices.

The second part of this chapter explains the technique called star join optimization. Two examples are presented to show you in which cases the query optimizer uses this technique instead of usual join processing techniques. The role of bitmap filters will be explained, too.

The final part of the chapter explains the use of the columnstore index. You will see how to create such an index and use it to increase the performance of a group of data warehouse queries. The limitations of the implementation of this data warehouse technique in SQL Server 2012 will be discussed too.

Data Partitioning

The easiest and most natural way to design an entity is to use a single table. Also, if all instances of an entity belong to a table, you don't need to decide where to store its rows physically, because the database system does this for you. For this reason there is no need for you to do any administrative tasks concerning storage of table data, if you don't want to.

On the other hand, one of the most frequent causes of poor performance in relational database systems is contention for data that resides on a single I/O device. This is especially true if you have one or more very large tables with millions of rows. In that case, on a system with multiple CPUs, partitioning the table can lead to better performance through parallel operations.

By using data partitioning, you can divide very large tables (and indices too) into smaller parts that are easier to manage. This allow many operations to be performed in parallel, such as loading data and query processing.

Partitioning also improves the availability of the entire table. By placing each partition on its own disk, you can still access one part of the entire data even if one or more disks are unavailable. In that case, all data in the available partitions can be used for read and write operations. The same is true for maintenance operations.

If a table is partitioned, the query optimizer can recognize when the search condition in a query references only rows in certain partitions and therefore can limit its search to those partitions. That way, you can achieve significant performance gains, because the query optimizer has to analyze only a fraction of data from the partitioned table.

NOTE

Data partitioning brings performance benefits only for huge tables. For this reason, partition only tables with at least several hundred thousand rows.

How the Database Engine Partitions Data

A table can be partitioned using any column of the table. Such a column is called the *partition key*. (It is also possible to use a group of columns for the particular partition key.) The values of the partition key are used to partition table rows to different filegroups.

Two other important notions in relation to partitioning are the partition scheme and partition function. The *partition scheme* maps the table rows to one or more filegroups. The *partition function* defines how this mapping is done. In other words, the partition function defines the algorithm that is used to direct the rows to their physical location.

The Database Engine supports only one form of partitioning, called range partitioning. *Range partitioning* divides table rows into different partitions based on the value of the partition key. Hence, by applying range partitioning you will always know in which partition a particular row will be stored.

NOTE

Besides range partitioning, there are several other forms of partitioning. One of them is called hash partitioning. In contrast to range partitioning, hash partitioning places rows one after another in partitions by applying a hashing function to the partition key. Hash partitioning is not supported by the Database Engine.

The steps for creating partitioned tables using range partitioning are described next.

Steps for Creating Partitioned Tables

Before you start to partition database tables, you have to complete the following steps:

1. Set partition goals.
2. Determine the partition key and number of partitions.
3. Create a filegroup for each partition.
4. Create the partition function and partition scheme.
5. Create partitioned indices (optionally).

All of these steps will be explained in the following sections.

Set Partition Goals

Partition goals depend on the type of applications that access the table that should be partitioned. There are several different partition goals, each of which could be a single reason to partition a table:

▶ Improved performance for individual queries

▶ Reduced contention

▶ Improved data availability

If your primary goal of table partitioning is to improve performance for individual queries, then distribute all table rows evenly. That way, the database system doesn't have to wait for data retrieval from a partition that has more rows than other partitions. Also, if such queries access data by performing a table scan against significant portions of a table, then you should partition the table rows only. (Partitioning the corresponding index will just add overhead in such a case.)

Data partitioning can reduce contention when many simultaneous queries perform an index scan to return just a few rows from a table. In this case, you should partition the table and index with a partition scheme that allows each query to eliminate unneeded partitions from its scan. To reach this goal, start by investigating which queries access which parts of the table. Then partition table rows so that different queries access different partitions.

Partitioning improves the availability of the database. By placing each partition on its own filegroup and locating each filegroup on its own disk, you can increase the data availability, because if one disk fails and is no longer accessible, only the data in that partition is unavailable. While the system administrator services the corrupted disk, limited access still exists to other partitions of the table.

Determine the Partition Key and Number of Partitions

A table can be partitioned using any table column. The values of the partition key are used to partition table rows to different filegroups. For the best performance, each partition should be stored in a separate filegroup, and each filegroup should be stored on one separate disk device. By spreading the data across several disk devices, you can balance the I/O and improve query performance, availability, and maintenance.

You should partition the data of a table using a column that does not frequently change. If you use a column that is often modified, any update operation of that column can force the system to move the modified rows from one partition to the other, and this could be time consuming.

Create a Filegroup for Each Partition

To achieve better performance, higher data availability, and easier maintenance, you will use different filegroups to separate table data. The number of filegroups depends mostly on the hardware you have. When you have multiple CPUs, partition your data so that each CPU can access data on one disk device. If the Database Engine can process multiple partitions in parallel, the processing time of your application will be significantly reduced.

Each data partition must map to a filegroup. To create a filegroup, you use either the CREATE DATABASE or ALTER DATABASE statement. Example 25.1 shows the creation of a database called **test_partitioned** with one primary filegroup and two other filegroups.

NOTE

*Before you create the **test_partitioned** database, you have to change the physical addresses of all .mdf and .ndf files in Example 25.1 according to the file system you have on your computer.*

EXAMPLE 25.1

```
USE master;
CREATE DATABASE test_partitioned
ON PRIMARY
  ( NAME='MyDB_Primary',
    FILENAME=
        'd:\mssql\PT_Test_Partitioned_Range_df.mdf',
    SIZE=2000,
    MAXSIZE=5000,
    FILEGROWTH=1 ),
FILEGROUP MyDB_FG1
  ( NAME = 'FirstFileGroup',
    FILENAME =
        'd:\mssql\MyDB_FG1.ndf',
    SIZE = 1000MB,
    MAXSIZE=2500,
    FILEGROWTH=1 ),
FILEGROUP MyDB_FG2
  ( NAME = 'SecondFileGroup',
    FILENAME =
        'f:\mssql\MyDB_FG2.ndf',
    SIZE = 1000MB,
    MAXSIZE=2500,
    FILEGROWTH=1 );
```

Example 25.1 creates a database called **test_partitioned**, which contains a primary filegroup, **MyDB_Primary**, and two other filegroups, **MyDB_FG1** and **MyDB_FG2**. The **MyDB_FG1** filegroup is stored on the D: drive, while the **MyDB_FG2** filegroup is stored on the F: drive.

If you want to add filegroups to an existing database, use the ALTER DATABASE statement. Example 25.2 shows how to create another filegroup for the **test_partitioned** database.

EXAMPLE 25.2

```
USE master;
ALTER DATABASE test_partitioned
   ADD FILEGROUP MyDB_FG3
GO
ALTER DATABASE test_partitioned
ADD FILE
  ( NAME = 'ThirdFileGroup',
    FILENAME =
        'G:\mssql\MyDB_FG3.ndf',
    SIZE = 1000MB,
    MAXSIZE=2500,
    FILEGROWTH=1)
TO FILEGROUP MyDB_FG3;
```

Example 25.2 uses the ALTER DATABASE statement to create an additional filegroup called **MyDB_FG3**. The second ALTER DATABASE statement adds a new file to the created filegroup. Notice that the TO FILEGROUP option specifies the name of the filegroup to which the new file will be added.

Create the Partition Function and Partition Scheme

The next step after creating filegroups is to create the partition function, using the CREATE PARTITION FUNCTION statement. The syntax of the CREATE PARTITION FUNCTION is as follows:

```
CREATE PARTITION FUNCTION function_name(param_type)
    AS RANGE [ LEFT | RIGHT ]
      FOR VALUES ( [ boundary_value [ ,...n ] ] )
```

function_name defines the name of the partition function, while **param_type** specifies the data type of the partition key. **boundary_value** specifies one or more boundary values for each partition of a partitioned table or index that uses the partition function.

The CREATE PARTITION FUNCTION statement supports two forms of the RANGE option: RANGE LEFT and RANGE RIGHT. RANGE LEFT determines that the boundary condition is the upper boundary in the first partition. According to this, RANGE RIGHT specifies that the boundary condition is the lower boundary in the last partition. If not specified, RANGE LEFT is the default.

Before the partition function can be defined, you have to specify the table that will be used for partitioning. In this chapter's examples, the **orders** table will be used. Example 25.3 creates the table. (Check first whether your **sample** database already contains the **orders** table. If so, drop it.)

EXAMPLE 25.3

```
USE sample;
CREATE TABLE orders
    (orderid INTEGER NOT NULL,
     orderdate DATE,
     shippeddate DATE,
     freight money);
GO
declare @i int , @order_id integer
           declare @orderdate datetime
           declare @shipped_date datetime
           declare @freight money
           set @i = 1
           set @orderdate = getdate()
           set @shipped_date = getdate()
           set @freight = 100.00
         while @i < 1000001
         begin
         insert into orders (orderid, orderdate, shippeddate, freight)
           values( @i, @orderdate, @shipped_date, @freight)
         set @i = @i+1
         end
```

The CREATE TABLE statement in Example 25.3 creates the **orders** table, while the subsequent batch loads one million rows in that table.

Example 25.4 shows the definition of the partition function for the **orders** table with 1,000,000 rows.

EXAMPLE 25.4

```
USE test_partitioned;
CREATE PARTITION FUNCTION myRangePF1 (int)
    AS RANGE LEFT FOR VALUES (500000);
```

The **myRangePF1** partition function specifies that there will be two partitions and that the boundary value is 500,000. This means that all values of the partition key that are smaller than or equal to 500,000 will be placed in the first partition, while all values greater than 500,000 will be stored in the second partition. (Note that the boundary value is related to the values in the partition key, which in this example is the column **orderid** of the **orders** table. As you will see, you specify the name of the partition key in the corresponding CREATE TABLE statement.)

The created partition function is useless if you don't associate it with specific filegroups. As mentioned earlier in the chapter, you make this association via a partition scheme, and you use the CREATE PARTITION SCHEME statement to specify the association between a partition function and the corresponding filegroups. Example 25.5 shows the creation of the partition scheme for the partition function in Example 25.4.

EXAMPLE 25.5

```
USE test_partitioned;
CREATE PARTITION SCHEME myRangePS1
    AS PARTITION myRangePF1
    TO (MyDB_FG1, MyDB_FG2);
```

Example 25.5 creates the partition scheme called **myRangePS1**. According to this scheme, all values to the left of the boundary value (i.e., all values < 500,000) will be stored in the **MyDB_FG1** filegroup. Also, all values to the right of the boundary value will be stored in the **MyDB_FG2** filegroup.

NOTE

When you define a partition scheme, you must be sure to specify a filegroup for each partition, even if multiple partitions will be stored on the same filegroup.

The creation of a partitioned table is slightly different from the creation of a nonpartitioned one. As you might guess, the CREATE TABLE statement must contain the name of the partition scheme and the name of the table column that will be used as the partition key. Example 25.6 shows the enhanced form of the CREATE TABLE statement that is used to define partitioning of the **orders** table.

EXAMPLE 25.6

```
USE test_partitioned;
CREATE TABLE orders
   (orderid INTEGER NOT NULL,
    orderdate DATETIME,
    shippeddate DATETIME,
    freight money)
ON myRangePS1 (orderid);
```

The ON clause at the end of the CREATE TABLE statement is used to specify the already-defined partition scheme (see Example 25.5). Using this scheme, the specified partition scheme ties together the column of the table (**orderid**) with the partition function where the data type (INT) of the partition key is specified (see Example 25.4).

Create Partitioned Indices

When you partition table data, you can partition the indices that are associated with that table, too. You can partition table indices using the existing partition scheme for that table or a different one. When both the indices and the table use the same partition function and the same partitioning columns (in the same order), the table and index are said to be aligned. When a table and its indices are aligned, the database system can move partitions in and out of partitioned tables very effectively, because the partitioning of both database objects is done with the same algorithm. For this reason, in the most practical cases it is recommended that you use aligned indices.

Example 25.7 shows the creation of a clustered index for the **orders** table. This index is aligned because it is partitioned using the partition scheme of the **orders** table.

EXAMPLE 25.7

```
USE test_partitioned;
CREATE UNIQUE CLUSTERED INDEX CI_orders
 ON orders(orderid)
  ON myRangePS1(orderid);
```

As you can see from Example 25.7, the creation of the partitioned index for the **orders** table is done using the enhanced form of the CREATE INDEX statement. This form of the CREATE INDEX statement contains an additional ON clause that specifies the partition scheme. If you want to align the index with the table, specify the same partition scheme as for the corresponding table. (The first ON clause is part of the standard syntax of the CREATE INDEX statement and specifies the column for indexing.)

Partitioning Techniques for Increasing System Performance

The following partitioning techniques can significantly increase performance of your system:

▶ Table collocation

▶ Partition-aware seek operation

▶ Parallel execution of queries

Table Collocation

Besides partitioning a table together with the corresponding indices, the Database Engine also supports the partitioning of two tables using the same partition function. This partition form means that rows of both tables that have the same value for the partition key are stored together at a specific location on the disk. This concept of data partitioning is called *collocation*.

Suppose that, besides the **orders** table (see Example 25.3), there is also an **order_details** table, which contains zero, one, or more rows for each unique order ID in the **orders** table. If you partition both tables using the same partition function on the join columns **orders.orderid** and **order_details.orderid**, the rows of both tables with the same value for the **orderid** columns will be stored together on the disk. Suppose that there is a unique order with the identification number 49031 in the **orders** table and five corresponding rows in the **order_details** table. In the case of collocation, all six rows will be stored side by side on the disk. (The same procedure will be applied to all rows of these tables with the same value for the **orderid** columns.)

This technique has significant performance benefits when, accessing more than one table, the data to be joined is located at the same partition. In that case the system doesn't have to move data between different data partitions.

Partition-Aware Seek Operation

The internal representation of a partitioned table appears to the query processor as a composite (multicolumn) index with an internal column as the leading column. (This column, called **partitionedID**, is a hidden computed column used internally by the system to represent the ID of the partition containing a specific row.)

For example, suppose there is a **tab** table with three columns, **col1**, **col2**, and **col3**. (**col1** is used to partition the table, while **col2** has a clustered index.) The Database Engine treats internally such a table as a nonpartitioned table with the schema **tab (partitionID, col1, col2, col3)** and with a clustered index on the composite key **(partitionedID, col2)**. This allows the query optimizer to perform seek operations based on the computed column **partitionID** on any partitioned table or index. That way, the performance of a significant number of queries on partitioned tables can be improved because the partition elimination is done earlier.

Parallel Execution of Queries

In SQL Server versions prior to 2008, one thread is allocated per partition when multiple partitions are queried. In other words, one partition is not shared between multiple threads and therefore the work on one partition cannot be parallelized. (For the description of parallel queries, see Chapter 15.) This can cause performance problems on systems with many CPUs if the table has fewer partitions than CPUs. In that case, not all the CPUs will be used to process the query.

Since SQL Server 2008, the Database Engine provides two query execution strategies for parallel query plans on partitioned objects:

▶ **Single-thread-per-partition strategy**   The query optimizer assigns one thread per partition to execute a parallel query plan that accesses multiple partitions. One partition is not shared between multiple threads, but multiple partitions can be processed in parallel.

▶ **Multiple-threads-per-partition strategy**   The query optimizer assigns multiple threads per partition regardless of the number of partitions to be accessed. In other words, all available threads start at the first partition to be accessed and scan forward. As each thread reaches the end of the partition, it moves to the next partition and begins scanning forward. The thread does not wait for the other threads to finish before moving to the next partition.

Which strategy the query optimizer chooses depends on your environment. It chooses the single-thread-per-partition strategy if queries are I/O-bound and include more partitions than the degree of parallelism. It chooses the multiple-threads-per-partition strategy in the following cases:

▶ Partitions are striped evenly across many disks

▶ Your queries use fewer partitions than the number of available threads

▶ Partition sizes differ significantly within a single table

Guidelines for Partitioning Tables and Indices

The following suggestions are guidelines for partitioning tables and indices:

▶ Do not partition every table. Partition only those tables that are accessed most frequently.

▶ Consider partitioning a table if it is a huge one, meaning it contains at least several hundred thousand rows.

▶ For best performance, use partitioned indices to reduce contention between sessions.

▶ Balance the number of partitions with the number of processors on your system. If it is not possible for you to establish a 1:1 relationship between the number of partitions and the number of processors, specify the number of partitions as a multiple factor of the number of processors. (For instance, if your computer has four processors, the number of partitions should be divisible by four.)

▶ Do not partition the data of a table using a column that changes frequently. If you use a column that changes often, any update operation of that column can force the system to move the modified rows from one partition to another, and this could be very time consuming.

▶ For optimal performance, partition the tables to increase parallelism, but do not partition their indices. Place the indices in a separate filegroup.

Star Join Optimization

As you already know from Chapter 21, the star schema is a general form for structuring data in a data warehouse. A star schema usually has one fact table, which is connected to several dimension tables. The fact table can have 100 million rows or more, while dimension tables are fairly small relative to the size of the corresponding fact table. Generally, in decision support queries, several dimension tables are joined with the corresponding fact table. The convenient way for the query optimizer to execute such queries is to join each of the dimension tables used in the query with the fact table, using the primary/foreign key relationship. Although this technique is the best one for numerous queries, significant performance gains can be achieved if the query optimizer uses special techniques for particular groups of queries. One such specific technique is called star join optimization.

Before you start to explore this new technique, take a look at how the query optimizer executes a query in the convenient way, as shown in Example 25.8.

EXAMPLE 25.8

```
USE AdventureWorksDW;
SELECT ProductAlternateKey
    FROM FactInternetSales f JOIN DimDate t ON f.OrderDateKey = t.DateKey
   JOIN DimProduct d ON d.ProductKey = f.ProductKey
   WHERE CalendarYear BETWEEN 2003 AND 2004
   AND ProductAlternateKey LIKE 'BK%'
   GROUP BY ProductAlternateKey, CalendarYear;
```

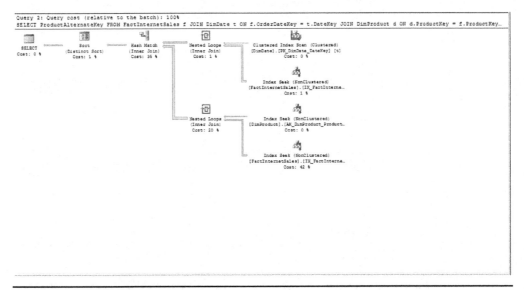

Figure 25-1 *Execution plan of Example 25.8*

The execution plan of Example 25.8 is shown in Figure 25-1.

As you can see from the execution plan in Figure 25-1, the query joins first the **FactInternetSales** fact table with the **DimDate** dimension table using the relationship between the primary key in the dimension table (**DateKey**) and the foreign key in the fact table (**DateKey**). After that, the second dimension table, **DimProduct**, is joined with the fact table in the similar way. At the end, both temporal results are joined together using the hash join method.

The use of the star join optimization technique will be explained using Example 25.9.

EXAMPLE 25.9

```
USE AdventureWorksDWMod;
GO
SELECT F.ProductKey, F.CurrencyKey, D1.CurrencyName, D2.EndDate
FROM dbo.FactInternetSales AS F
JOIN dbo.DimCurrency AS D1 ON F.CurrencyKey = D1.CurrencyKey
JOIN dbo.DimProduct D2 ON F.ProductKey = D2.ProductKey
WHERE D1.CurrencyKey <= 12 AND D2.ListPrice > 50
OPTION (MAXDOP 32);
```

The query optimizer uses the star join optimization technique only when the fact table is very large in relation to the corresponding dimension tables. To ensure that the query optimizer would apply the star join optimization technique, I significantly

Figure 25-2   *Execution plan of Example 25.9*

enhanced the **FactInternetSales** fact table from the **AdventureWorksDW** database. The original size of this table is approximately 64,000 rows, but for this example I created an additional 500,000 rows by generating random values for the **ProductKey**, **SalesOrderNumber**, and **SalesOrderLineNo** columns. Figure 25-2 shows the execution plan of Example 25.9.

The query optimizer detects that the star join optimization technique can be applied and evaluates the use of bitmap filters. (A bitmap filter is a small to midsize set of values that is used to filter data. Bitmap filters are always stored in memory.)

As you can see from the execution plan in Figure 25-2, the fact table is first scanned using the corresponding clustered index. After that the bitmap filters for both dimension tables are applied. (Their task is to filter out the rows from the fact table.) This has been done using the hash join technique. At the end, the significantly reduced sets of rows from both streams are joined together.

NOTE

Do not confuse bitmap filters with bitmap indices! Bitmap indices are persistent structures used in BI as an alternative to B⁺*-tree structures. The Database Engine doesn't support bitmap indices.*

Columnstore Index

As you already know from Chapter 10, index access means that indices are used to access entire rows that fulfill a condition of the given query. This is a general approach and doesn't depend on the number of columns being returned. In other words, the values of all columns of a particular row will be fetched, even if values of only one or two columns are needed. The reason for this is that the Database Engine and all other relational database systems store a table's rows on data pages. (This traditional approach of storing data is called *row store*.)

A new approach to storing data promises to improve performance in cases where the values of only a few columns of a table need to be fetched. Such an approach is called *column store*, and SQL Server 2012 introduces this technique using the index called columnstore. In column store, data is grouped and stored *one column at a time*. The query processor of a database system that supports column store can take advantage of the new data layout and significantly improve query execution time of such queries that retrieve just a few of a table's rows.

Managing Columnstore Index

You can create columnstore indices using either of the following:

▶ Transact-SQL statements

▶ SQL Server Management Studio

The following subsections discuss both methods.

Creating a Columnstore Index Using Transact-SQL

You use the well-known CREATE INDEX statement (with slight extensions) to create a columnstore index in Transact-SQL. Example 25.10 shows the creation of such an index for the **FactInternetSales** table of the **AdventureWorksDW** sample database.

EXAMPLE 25.10

```
USE AdventureWorksDW;
GO
CREATE NONCLUSTERED COLUMNSTORE INDEX cs_index1
  ON FactInternetSales (OrderDateKey, ShipDateKey, UnitPrice);
```

As you can see from the preceding SQL statement, to create a columnstore index, you extend the syntax of the convenient CREATE INDEX statement with the COLUMNSTORE phrase. Note, however, that among the many existing options available for traditional indices, only two are supported for columnstore indices: MAXDOP and DROP_EXISTING. (The MAXDOP option specifies the maximum degree of parallelism, while the DROP_EXISTING option can be used to rebuild the index.)

The CREATE INDEX statement in Example 25.10 creates a columnstore index for three columns of the **FactInternetSales** table: **OrderDateKey**, **ShipDateKey**, and **UnitPrice**. This means that all values of each of the three columns will be grouped and stored separately.

Example 25.11 shows the simple analytical query in relation to the **UnitPrice** column of the **FactInternetSales** table.

EXAMPLE 25.11

```
USE AdventureWorksDW;
GO
SET STATISTICS TIME ON;
GO
SELECT AVG (UnitPrice)
       FROM FactInternetSales;
```

In the case that the **cs_index1** index isn't created, the output of the STATISTICS TIME option of the SET statement is as follows:

```
Table 'FactInternetSales'. Scan count 5, logical reads 25411,
physical reads 2, read-ahead reads 23230, lob logical reads 0,
 lob physical reads 0, lob read-ahead reads 0.
SQL Server Execution Times: CPU time = 280 ms, elapsed time = 9181 ms.
```

When you create the index using Example 25.10 and execute the query in Example 25.11 again, the performance gains (in relation to both elapsed time and the number of logical reads) are dramatic:

```
Table 'FactInternetSales'. Scan count 1, logical reads 779, physical
reads 1, read-ahead reads 2882, lob logical reads 0, lob physical reads
0, lob read-ahead reads 0.
SQL Server Execution Times: CPU time = 109 ms, elapsed time = 155 ms.
```

Creating a Columnstore Index Using SSMS

To create a columnstore index in Object Explorer of SQL Server Management Studio, expand the tree structure of the table for which the index should be created, right-click the Indexes icon, and choose New Index | Nonclustered Columnstore Index. Click Add in the wizard, check the boxes of those columns that will be used for column store, and click OK.

Advantages and Limitations of Columnstore Indices

As a performance-tuning technique, columnstore indices offer significant performance benefits only for a group of queries. The following subsections discuss the advantages and limitations of this technique.

Benefits of Columnstore Indices

The following are the benefits of columnstore indices:

▶ *The system fetches only needed columns.* The smaller the number of fetched columns, the smaller the number of I/O operations required. For instance, if only 10 percent of the length of each data row is retrieved, the use of column store can reduce I/O significantly because only a small part of the data has to be transferred from disk into memory. (This is especially true for data warehouses, where fact tables usually have million of rows.)

▶ *Compression of values is optimal.* Storing data by rows is suboptimal for compressing the data. The reason is that values of columns of a table have many different forms: some of them are numeric and some are strings or dates. Most compression algorithms are based on similarities of a group of values. When data is stored by rows, the possibility to exploit similarity among values is thus limited. By contrast, a column store organizes data in column-wise fashion. Data items from a single column are stored contiguously. Usually, there is repetition and similarity among values within a column. The column store organization allows compression algorithms to exploit that similarity.

▶ *Execution time for queries with special characteristics is significantly faster.* As Example 25.11 demonstrated, if your query retrieves values from a few columns that are indexed with the columnstore index, the query will be executed significantly faster. (Obviously, performance gains decrease as the number of columns in the SELECT list of a query increases.)

▶ *No limitation exists on the number of key columns.* The concept of key columns exists only for row store. Therefore, the limitation on the number of key columns for an index does not apply to columnstore indices. (Also, if a base table has a clustered index, all columns in the clustering key must be present in the nonclustered columnstore index. Otherwise, it will be added to the columnstore index automatically.)

▶ *Columnstore indices work with table partitioning.* No change to the table partitioning syntax is required. A columnstore index on a partitioned table must be partition-aligned with the base table. Therefore, a nonclustered columnstore index can be created on a partitioned table only if the partitioning column is one of the columns in the columnstore index.

Limitations of Columnstore Index

Columnstore indices have been implemented for the first time in SQL Server 2012. For this reason, you cannot expect the implementation to be optimal. The following are some of the restrictions in relation to columnstore indices:

▶ *A table with a columnstore index is read-only.* A table with a columnstore index cannot be updated. (This is not a significant issue for data warehouse systems, because update operations are not executed often.) Books Online describes several ways in which you can circumvent this limitation.

▶ *A columnstore index doesn't support all data types.* SQL Server 2012 allows you to create columnstore indices for common business data types, such as CHAR, VARCHAR, INT, DECIMAL, and FLOAT. The following data types, among others, cannot be included in a columnstore index: BINARY, VARBINARY, VARCHAR(max), and SQL_VARIANT.

▶ *There are several restrictions on clustered and nonclustered columnstore indices.* At the moment, it is not possible to create more than one nonclustered columnstore index per table, and clustered columnstore indices are not available in SQL Server 2012. (You can expect that both limitations will be eliminated in a future version of SQL Server.)

Summary

The Database Engine supports range partitioning of data and indices that is entirely transparent to the application. Range partitioning partitions rows based on the value of the partition key. In other words, the data is divided using the values of the partition key.

If you want to partition your data, you must complete the following steps:

1. Set partition goals.
2. Determine the partition key and number of partitions.
3. Create a filegroup for each partition.
4. Create the partition function and partition scheme.
5. Create partitioned indices (if necessary).

By using different filegroups to separate table data, you achieve better performance, higher data availability, and easier maintenance.

The partition function is used to map the rows of a table or index into partitions based on the values of a specified column. To create a partition function, use the CREATE PARTITION FUNCTION statement. To associate a partition function with specific filegroups, use a partition scheme. When you partition table data, you can partition the indices associated with that table, too. You can partition table indices using the existing partition schema for that table or a different one.

Star join optimization is an index-based optimization technique that supports the optimal use of indices on huge fact tables. The main advantages of this technique are the following:

▶ Significant performance improvements in case of moderately and highly selective star join queries.

▶ No additional storage cost. (The system does not create any new indices, but uses bitmap filters instead.)

SQL Server 2012 supports columnstore indices, which gives you a new way to store values of a table's columns. Because of many restrictions in the current version, the use of this very promising technique should be restricted. In other words, if you intend to use the technique for production databases, test carefully the possible use of columnstore indices first on a nonproduction database.

This chapter is the last chapter of the book's part concerning business intelligence. The next chapter starts the last part of the book and gives you an introduction to XML.

Part V

Beyond Relational Data

Chapter 26

SQL Server and XML

In This Chapter

- ▶ XML: Basic Concepts
- ▶ Schema Languages
- ▶ Storing XML Documents in SQL Server
- ▶ Presenting Data
- ▶ Querying Data

This chapter has four main parts. The first part introduces the Extensible Markup Language (XML), which has become more and more important as a data storage format. This part describes requirements of a well-formed document. It also explains the basic concepts of XML. The second part introduces two schema languages: the Document Type Definition (DTD) language and the XML Schema language.

The third part of the chapter discusses XML in relation to database systems, generally, and in relation to the Database Engine, particularly. The most important storage form, using the XML data type, is introduced after that. The retrieval of stored XML documents using system stored procedures is described in the fourth part of the chapter, followed by a discussion of the presentation of relational data in XML. The end of this part briefly explains the XQuery language and the existing SQL Server XQuery methods.

XML: Basic Concepts

XML is an HTML-like language that is used for data exchange and the digital representation of data. Both HTML and XML are markup languages, meaning that they use tags to represent the logical structure of data, and both are important to the functioning of the World Wide Web. However, unlike HTML, which has a fixed number of tags, each with its own meaning, the repertoire of tags in XML is not set in advance and semantic meaning is not set for any XML tag. (The concise description of HTML is given in the section "XML-Related Languages".)

This section begins by looking at the requirements of a well-formed XML document, after which the three main components of XML are presented: elements, attributes, and namespaces. Next, the World Wide Web is briefly introduced, followed by a discussion of XML-related languages.

Requirements of a Well-Formed XML Document

The following are the requirements of a well-formed XML document, an example of which is shown in Example 26.1:

▶ It has a root element (**PersonList**, in Example 26.1).

▶ Every opening tag is followed by a matching closing tag.

▶ The elements of the document are properly nested.

▶ An attribute must have a value, which is quoted.

EXAMPLE 26.1

```
<?xml version="1.0" encoding="UTF-8"?>
<PersonList Type="Employee">
    <Title> Value="Employee List"></Title>
    <Contents>
        <Employee>
            <Name>Ann Jones</Name>
            <No>10102</No>
             <Deptno>d3</Deptno>
             <Address>
                    <City>Dallas</City>
                    <Street>Main St</Street>
             </Address>
        </Employee>
        <Employee>
            <Name>John Barrimore</Name>
            <No>18316</No>
             <Deptno>d1</Deptno>
             <Address>
                    <City>Seattle</City>
                    <Street>Abbey Rd</Street>
             </Address>
        </Employee>
    </Contents>
</PersonList>
```

An XML document, as shown in Example 26.1, generally contains three parts:

▶ An optional first line that tells the program that receives the document which version of XML it is dealing with (version 1.0 in Example 26.1)

▶ An optional external schema (usually written using DTD or the XML Schema language; see the section "Schema Languages" later in this chapter)

▶ A root element—the element that contains all other elements

The most important component of XML documents is the element, described next.

NOTE

Besides XML elements, attributes, and namespaces, which are described in detail in the following sections, there are also other components of XML documents, such as comments and processing instructions (PIs). These components will not be discussed because they are beyond the scope of this book.

XML Elements

You use XML to digitally represent documents. To represent a document, you have to know its structure. For instance, if you consider a book as a document, it can first be broken into chapters (with titles). Each chapter comprises several sections (with their titles and corresponding figures), and each section has one or more paragraphs.

All parts of an XML document that belong to its logical structure (such as chapters, sections, and paragraphs in the case of a book) are called *elements*. Therefore, in XML, each element represents a component of a document. In Example 26.1, **PersonList**, **Title**, and **Employee** are examples of XML elements. Also, each element can contain other elements. (The parts of an element that do not belong to the logical structure of a document are called character data. For instance, words or sentences in a book can be treated as character data.)

All elements of a document build a hierarchy of elements that is called the tree structure of the document. Each structure has an element on the top level that contains all other elements. This element is called the root element. All elements that do not contain any subelements are called leaves.

NOTE

In contrast to HTML, where valid tags are determined by the language specification, tag names in XML are chosen by the programmer.

The XML elements directly nested within other elements are called children. For instance, in Example 26.1, **Name**, **No**, and **Address** are children of **Employee**, which is a child of **Contents**, which is again a child of the root element **PersonList**.

Each element can have extra information that is attached to it. Such information is called an *attribute*, and it describes the element's properties. Attributes are used together with elements to represent objects. The general syntax of an element together with an attribute and their values is

```
<el_name attr_name="attr_value">el_value</el_name>
```

In the following line from Example 26.1,

```
<PersonList Type="Employee">,
```

Type is the name of an attribute that belongs to the element **PersonList**, and **Employee** is the attribute value.

The following section describes attributes in detail.

XML Attributes

Attributes are used to represent data. Elements can be used for the same purpose, which prompts the question of whether attributes are needed at all, because almost everything you can do using attributes is possible to do with elements (and subelements). However, the following tasks can be accomplished only with attributes:

▶ Define a unique value

▶ Enforce a limited kind of referential constraint

NOTE

There is no general rule for how you should define data. The best rule of thumb is to use an attribute when a property of an element is general, and to use subelements for a specific property of an element.

An attribute can be specified to be an ID type attribute. The value of the ID attribute must be unique within the XML document. Therefore, you can use the ID attribute to define a unique value.

An attribute of type IDREF must refer to a valid ID declared in the same document. In other words, the value of the IDREF attribute must occur in the document as a value of the corresponding ID attribute.

An attribute of type IDREFS specifies a list of strings, separated by blanks, that are referenced by the values of the ID attribute. For instance, the following line shows the XML fragment of an IDREFS attribute:

```
<Department Members="10102 18316"/>
```

(This example assumes that the attribute **No** of the **Employee** element is the ID attribute, while the attribute **Members** of the **Department** element is of the type IDREFS.)

The pairs ID/IDREF and ID/IDREFS correspond to primary key/foreign key relationships in the relational model, with a few differences. In the XML document, the values of different ID type attributes must be distinct. For instance, if you have **CustomerID** and **SalesOrderID** attributes in an XML document, these values must be distinct.

NOTE

ID, IDREF, and IDREFS are data types of the Document Type Definition (DTD), discussed later in this chapter.

XML Namespaces

When using XML, you build a vocabulary of terms that is appropriate for the domain in which you model your data. In this situation, different vocabularies for different domains can cause naming conflicts when you want to mix the domains together in an XML document. (This is usually the case when you want to integrate information obtained from different domains.) For instance, the article element in one domain can reference scientific articles, while the element with the same name in another domain could be related to a sales article. This problem can be solved using XML namespaces.

Generally, the name of every XML tag must be written in the form **namespace:name**, where **namespace** specifies an XML namespace and **name** is an XML tag.

A namespace is always represented by a worldwide unique URI (*uniform resource identifier*), which is usually a URL but can be an abstract identifier, too.

Example 26.2 shows the use of two namespaces.

EXAMPLE 26.2

```
<Faculty xmlns="http://www.fh-rosenheim.de/informatik"
          xmlns:lib="http:// www.fh-rosenheim.de/library">
         <Name>Book</Name>
         <Feature>
         <lib:Title>Introduction to Database Systems</lib:Title>
         <lib:Author>A. Finkelstein</lib:Author>
         </Feature>
</Faculty>
```

Namespaces are defined using the **xmlns** attribute. Example 26.2 specifies two namespaces. The first one is the *default namespace*, because it is specified only with the **xmlns** keyword. Therefore, it is the shorthand for the namespace http://www .fh-rosenheim.de/informatik. The second namespace is specified in the form **xmlns:lib**. The prefix **lib** serves as the shorthand for http://www.fh-rosenheim.de/library.

Tags belonging to the latter namespace should be prefixed with **lib:**. Tags without any prefix belong to the default namespace. (In Example 26.2, two tags belong to the second namespace: **Title** and **Author**.)

NOTE

One of the frequently used prefixes is "xsd". As you can see from Example 26.8, this prefix serves as the shorthand for http://www.w3.org/2001/XMLSchema, the link to the XML Schema specification.

XML and World Wide Web

The Web has become a dominant communications medium because it is used by billions of people for a variety of activities, including business, social, political, governmental, and educational activities. Generally, the Web has four parts:

▶ Web server

▶ Web browser

▶ HTML (Hypertext Markup Language)

▶ HTTP (Hypertext Transfer Protocol)

The web server sends pages (usually HTML pages) to the Web. A web browser receives the pages and displays them on the computer screen. (Microsoft Internet Explorer is an example of a web browser.)

You use HTML to create documents for the Web. This language allows you to format data that is shown using a web browser. The simplicity of HTML is one of the reasons that the Web has gained such importance. However, HTML has one main disadvantage: it can tell you only how the data should look. In other words, the language is used only to describe the layout of data.

HTTP is a protocol that "connects" a web browser with a web server and sends the available pages in both directions. If the pages contain another hyperlink, the protocol is used to connect to that web server, using the given address.

XML-Related Languages

XML is related to two other languages:

▶ SGML

▶ HTML

Standard General Markup Language (SGML) is a very powerful markup language that is used for the interchange of large and complex documents. SGML is used in many areas where there is a necessity for complex documents, such as airplane maintenance. As you will read in just a moment, XML is SGML lite—that is, it is a simplified subset of SGML that is primarily used for the Web.

HTML is the most important markup language used for the Web. Each HTML document is an SGML document with a fixed document type definition. (Fixed document types are described in the next section.) Therefore, HTML is just an instance of SGML.

HTML documents are text files that contain tags, and each tag is written in angle brackets. The most important tags are hyperlinks. You use hyperlinks to reference documents that are managed by a web server. Those references build the network that spans the whole Internet.

HTML has two important features:

▶ It is used only to format a document.

▶ It is not an extensible language.

HTML is a markup language that you can use to describe how the data should look. (On the other hand, this language offers more than a simple formatted language such as LaTeX, because its elements are generalized and descriptive.)

HTML only uses a fixed number of elements. For this reason, you cannot use HTML suitably for particular document types.

Schema Languages

In contrast to HTML, which contains a set of fixed rules that you must follow when you create an HTML document, XML does not have such rules, because this language is intended for many different application areas. Hence, XML includes languages that are used to specify the document structure. The most important schema languages for XML documents are

▶ Document Type Definition (DTD)

▶ XML Schema

The following sections describe these languages.

Document Type Definition

A set of rules for structuring an XML document is called a document type definition (DTD). A DTD can be specified as a part of the XML document, or the XML document can contain a uniform resource locator (URL) indicating where the DTD is stored. A document that conforms to the associated DTD is called a valid document.

NOTE
XML does not require that documents have corresponding DTDs, but it requires that documents be well formed (as described earlier in this chapter).

Example 26.3 shows the DTD for the XML document in Example 26.1.

EXAMPLE 26.3

```
<?xml version="1.0" encoding="UTF-8"?>
<!DOCTYPE PersonList SYSTEM "C:\tmp\Unbenannt4.dtd">
<!ELEMENT EmployeeList (Title, Contents)>
<!ELEMENT Title EMPTY>
<!ELEMENT Contents (Employee*)>
<!ELEMENT Employee (Name, No, Deptno, Address)>
<!ELEMENT Name (Fname, Lname)>
<!ELEMENT Fname (#PCDATA)>
<!ELEMENT Lname (#PCDATA)>
<!ELEMENT No (#PCDATA)>
<!ELEMENT Deptno (#PCDATA)>
<!ELEMENT Address (City, Street) >
<!ELEMENT City (#PCDATA)>
<!ELEMENT Street (#PCDATA)>
<!ATTLIST EmployeeList  Type CDATA #IMPLIED
                        Date CDATA #IMPLIED>
   <!ATTLIST Title Value CDATA  #REQUIRED>
```

NOTE

Both documents (the XML document from Example 26.1 and the DTD in Example 26.3) must be linked together. This link can be generated by an XML editor or manually. In the latter case you have to extend the XML document with the appropriate information.

There are several common DTD components: a name (**EmployeeList** in Example 26.3) and a set of ELEMENT and ATTLIST statements. The name of a DTD must conform to the tag name of the root element of the XML document (see Example 26.1) that uses the DTD for validation. Also, you have to link the XML document with the corresponding DTD file.

Element type declarations must start with the ELEMENT statement, followed by the name of the element type being defined. (Every element in a valid XML document must conform to an element type declared in the DTD.) Also, the order of elements in the DTD must be preserved in the corresponding XML document. In Example 26.3, the first ELEMENT statement specifies that the element **EmployeeList** consists of **Title** and **Contents** elements, in that order. The elements that do not contain any subelements must be declared to be alphanumerical—that is, of type #PCDATA. (The **Title** element is such an element.)

The * sign in the definition of the **Contents** element indicates that there are zero or more elements of the **Employee** type. (Besides *, there are two other signs, ? and +. The ? sign specifies that there is at most one element, while the + sign indicates that there is at least one element.)

Attributes are declared for specific element types using the ATTLIST statement. This means that each attribute declaration starts with the string <!ATTLIST. Immediately after that comes the attribute's name and its data type. In Example 26.3, the **EmployeeList** element is allowed to have the attributes **Type** and **Date**, while the **Title** element can only have the **Value** attribute. (All other elements do not have attributes.)

The #IMPLIED keyword specifies that the corresponding attribute is optional, while the #REQUIRED keyword determines the mandatory form of the attribute.

NOTE

Besides the #PCDATA data type, DTD supports several other data types, such as ID, IDREF, and IDREFS. These data types are explained earlier in this chapter.

Besides the definition of a document's structure, formatting a document can be an important issue. For this task, XML supports another language called Extensible Stylesheet Language (XSL), which allows you to describe how the data of your document should be formatted or displayed.

NOTE

The style of a document is described as a separate unit. For this reason, each document without this additional unit will use the default formatting of the web browser.

XML Schema

XML Schema is a standardized data definition language for XML documents. It defines a set of base types that are supported as types in XML. The XML Schema language contains many advanced features and is therefore significantly more complex than DTD.

NOTE

The XML Schema language is discussed only briefly in this book because of its complexity. An example of the XML Schema language is given later in this chapter (see Example 26.8).

The main features of the XML Schema language are the following:

▶ It uses the same syntax as that used for XML documents. (For this reason, schemas are themselves well-formed XML documents.)

▶ It is integrated with the namespace mechanism. (Although there can be more than one schema definition document for a namespace, a schema definition document defines type in only one namespace.)

▶ It provides a set of base types, the same way SQL provides CHAR, INTEGER, and other standard data types.

▶ It supports primary/foreign key integrity constraints.

Storing XML Documents in SQL Server

As you already know from Chapter 1, the relational data model is the best model to use if you have structured data with the corresponding schema. On the other hand, if the data you use is semistructured, you have to know how to model the data. In that case, XML is a good choice because it is a platform-independent model, which ensures portability of semistructured data.

The goal of all modern database systems, including the Database Engine is to store any kind of data. Therefore, a tight relationship exists between relational databases and XML documents. We'll take a brief look at the general methods for storing XML documents in relational databases before we focus specifically on how XML documents are stored in the Database Engine. There are three general techniques for storing XML documents in relational databases:

▶ As "raw" documents

▶ Decomposed into relational columns

▶ Using native storage

If you store an XML document as a large object (LOB), an exact copy of the data is stored. In this case, XML documents are stored "raw"—that is, in their character string form. The raw form allows you to insert documents very easily. The retrieval of such a document is very efficient if you retrieve the entire document. To retrieve parts of the documents, you need to create special types of indices.

To decompose an XML document into separate columns of one or more tables, you can use its schema. In this case, the hierarchical structure of the document is preserved, while order among elements is ignored. (As you already know, the relational model does not support ordering of columns in a table, whereas elements of an XML document are ordered.) Storing XML documents in decomposed form makes it much easier to index an element if it is placed in its own column.

NOTE

The decomposition process of an XML document into separate columns is also known as "shredding."

Native storage means that XML documents are stored in their parsed form. In other words, the document is stored in an internal representation (Infoset, for instance) that preserves the XML content of the data. (Infoset, or *XML Information Set*, is a standardized specification that provides a set for use in other specifications that need to refer to the information in an XML document.)

Using native storage makes it easy to query information based on the structure of the XML document. On the other hand, reconstructing the original form of the XML document is difficult, because the created content may not be an exact copy of the document. (The detailed information about the significant white spaces, order of attributes, and namespace prefixes in XML documents is generally not retained.)

NOTE

In the rest of this chapter, "XML" has two meanings. First, this term specifies the language, Extended Markup Language. Second, the same term is used to specify the XML data type in the Database Engine. To keep the distinction clear, the term "XML" is used to specify the language, and the phrase "XML data type" is used to specify the data type. (Also, "XML column" means a column of the XML data type.)

SQL Server supports all three general techniques for storing XML documents discussed earlier in this section:

▶ **Raw documents** The Database Engine uses the VARCHAR(MAX) and VARBINARY(MAX) data types to store XML documents as raw documents. (This approach won't be discussed further in this book because of its complexity.)

▶ **Decomposition** The Database Engine can decompose XML documents into separate columns of tables by using the **sp_xml_preparedocument** system procedure. This procedure parses the given document and represents its nodes as a tree. (For further discussion of this system procedure, see the section "Storing XML Documents Using Decomposition" later in this chapter.)

▶ **Native storage**   The XML data type enables you to store XML documents in the native way in a database managed by the Database Engine. (Database systems, such as the Database Engine, that store XML documents in a completely parsed form are called native XML database systems.)

The following sections discuss in detail the last two techniques. Because the use of the XML data type is the most important storage form, native storage is discussed first.

Storing XML Documents Using the XML Data Type

The XML data type is the base data type in Transact-SQL, meaning you can use this data type in the same way you use the standard data types, such as INTEGER or CHARACTER. On the other hand, the XML data type has some limitations, because an XML column cannot be declared using the UNIQUE, PRIMARY KEY, or FOREIGN KEY clauses.

Generally, you can use the XML data type to declare the following:

▶ Table columns

▶ Variables

▶ Input or output parameters (in stored procedures or user-defined functions)

NOTE

The following text describes the use of the XML data type to declare a table column. The use of this type to declare variables or parameters is similar.

Example 26.4 shows the use of the XML data type to declare a column of a table.

EXAMPLE 26.4

```
USE sample;
CREATE TABLE xmltab (id INTEGER NOT NULL PRIMARY KEY,
                            xml_column XML);
```

The CREATE TABLE statement in Example 26.4 creates a table with two columns: **id** and **xml_column**. The **id** column is used to uniquely identify each row of the table. **xml_column** is an XML column that will be used in the following examples to show how XML documents can be stored, indexed, and retrieved.

As previously stated, XML documents can be stored in a native way in a column of the XML data type. Example 26.5 shows the use of the INSERT statement to store such a document.

EXAMPLE 26.5

```
USE sample;
INSERT INTO xmltab VALUES (1,
'<?xml version="1.0"?>
<PersonList Type="Employee">
    <Title> Value="Employee List"></Title>
    <Contents>
        <Employee>
            <Name>Ann Jones</Name>
            <No>10102</No>
            <Deptno>d3</Deptno>
            <Address>
                <City>Dallas</City>
                <Street>Main St</Street>
            </Address>
        </Employee>
        <Employee>
            <Name>John Barrimore</Name>
            <No>18316</No>
            <Deptno>d1</Deptno>
            <Address>
                <City>Seattle</City>
                <Street>Abbey Rd</Street>
            </Address>
        </Employee>
    </Contents>
</PersonList>');
```

The INSERT statement in Example 26.5 inserts two values: the value of the identifier and an XML document. (The inserted XML document is the same document used at the beginning of this chapter; see Example 26.1.) Before the XML document is stored, it will be parsed using the XML parser, which checks its syntax. Actually, the parser checks whether or not the particular XML document is well formed. For instance, if you omit the last row of the XML document (</PersonList>), the XML parser displays the following error message:

```
Msg 9400, Level 16, State 1, Line 3
XML parsing: line 24, character 0, unexpected end of input
```

If you use the SELECT statement to see the content of the **xmltab** table, SQL Server Management Studio uses the XML editor to display XML documents. (To display the entire document in the editor, click the corresponding value in the result set.)

Indexing an XML Column

The Database Engine stores XML values internally as binary large objects. Without an index, these objects are decomposed at run time to evaluate a query, which can be time-consuming. Therefore, the reason for indexing XML columns is to improve query performance.

NOTE

If you want to create any kind of XML indices, the corresponding table must include the explicit definition of the primary key (see Example 26.4).

The system supports a primary XML index and three types of secondary XML indices. The primary XML index indexes all tags, values, and paths within the XML instances of an XML column. Queries use the primary XML index to return scalar values or XML subtrees.

Example 26.6 creates a primary XML index.

EXAMPLE 26.6

```
USE sample;
GO
CREATE PRIMARY XML INDEX i_xmlcolumn ON xmltab(xml_column);
```

As you can see from Example 26.6, the creation of a primary XML index is similar to the creation of an index as described in Chapter 10. A primary XML index uses an XML instance to generate the corresponding relational internal form out of it. That way, the repeated run-time generation of the internal form for queries and updates is omitted.

To further improve search performance, you can create secondary XML indices. A primary XML index must exist before secondary indices can be built. You can create three types of XML secondary indices using different keywords:

▶ **FOR PATH**   Creates a secondary XML index over the document structure

▶ **FOR VALUE**   Creates a secondary XML index over the element and attribute values of the XML column

▶ **FOR PROPERTY**   Creates a secondary XML index that searches for a property

The following list gives you some guidelines for creating secondary XML indices:

▶ If your queries use path expressions on XML columns, the PATH index is likely to speed them up. The most common case is the use of the exist() method on XML columns in the WHERE clause of the Transact-SQL language. (The exist() method is discussed later in this chapter.)

▶ If your queries retrieve multiple values from individual XML instances by using path expressions, the use of the PROPERTY index may be helpful.

▶ If your queries involve retrieval of values within XML instances without knowing the element or attribute names that contain those values, you may want to create the VALUE index.

Example 26.7 shows the creation of a PATH index. (The syntax for creating all other secondary XML indices is analogous.)

EXAMPLE 26.7

```
USE sample;
GO
CREATE  XML INDEX i_xmlcolumn_path ON xmltab(xml_column)
    USING XML INDEX i_xmlcolumn FOR PATH;
```

In Example 26.7 you use the FOR PATH keyword to create the corresponding secondary index. You must specify the USING clause if you want to define any secondary XML index.

XML indices have some limitations in relation to convenient indices:

▶ XML indices cannot be composite indices.

▶ There are no clustered XML indices.

NOTE

The reason for creating XML indices is different from the reason for creating convenient indices. XML indices enhance the performance of queries concerning XML documents, while convenient indices enhance the performance of SQL queries.

SQL Server also supports the corresponding ALTER INDEX and DROP INDEX statements. The ALTER INDEX statement allows you to change the structure of an existing XML index, while the DROP INDEX statement deletes such an index.

There is also a catalog view for XML indices, called **sys.xml_indexes**. This view returns one row per each existing XML index. The most important columns of the view are **using_xml_index_id** and **secondary_type**. The former specifies whether the index is primary or secondary, while the latter determines the type of the secondary index ("P" for PATH, "V" for VALUE, and "R" for PROPERTY secondary index). This view also inherits columns from the **sys.indexes** catalog view.

Typed vs. Untyped XML

As you already know, an XML document can be well formed and valid. (Only a well-formed document can be validated.) An XML document that conforms to one or more given schemas is said to be *schema valid* and is called an *instance document* of the schemas. The XML schemas are used to perform more precise type checking during compilation of queries.

XML data type columns, variables, and parameters may be typed (conform to one or more schemas) or untyped. In other words, whenever a typed XML instance is assigned to an XML column data type, variable, or parameter, the system validates the instance.

The following section explains the use of XML schemas, after which typed XML instances are discussed in more detail.

XML Schemas and SQL Server   An XML schema specifies a set of data types that exist in a particular namespace. You use the XML Schema language to implement a particular XML schema. (Transact-SQL doesn't support the use of DTD to specify an XML schema.) The Database Engine uses the CREATE XML SCHEMA COLLECTION statement to import the schema components into the database. Example 26.8 shows the use of this statement.

EXAMPLE 26.8

```
USE sample;
CREATE XML SCHEMA COLLECTION EmployeeSchema AS
    N'<?xml version="1.0" encoding="UTF-16"?>
    <xsd:schema elementFormDefault="unqualified"
        attributeFormDefault="unqualified"
        xmlns:xsd="http://www.w3.org/2001/XMLSchema" >
        <xsd:element name="employees">
            <xsd:complexType mixed="false">
              <xsd:sequence>
                <xsd:element name="fname" type="xsd:string"/>
                <xsd:element name="lname" type="xsd:string"/>
                <xsd:element name="department" type="xsd:string"/>
                <xsd:element name="salary" type="xsd:integer"/>
```

```
            <xsd:element name="comments" type="xsd:string"/>
        </xsd:sequence>
      </xsd:complexType>
    </xsd:element>
  </xsd:schema>';
```

Example 26.8 shows how the CREATE XML SCHEMA COLLECTION statement can be used to catalog the **EmployeeSchema** schema as a database object. The XML schema for Example 26.8 includes attributes (elements) for employees, such as family name, last name, and salary. (A detailed discussion of the XML Schema language is outside the scope of this introductory book.)

Generally, an XML schema collection has a name, which can be qualified using the relational schema name (**dbo.EmployeeSchema**, for instance). The schema collection consists of one or more schemas that define the types in one or more XML namespaces. If the **targetNamespace** attribute is omitted from an XML schema, that schema does not have an associated namespace. (There is a maximum of one such schema inside an XML schema collection.)

The Database Engine also supports the ALTER XML SCHEMA COLLECTION and DROP XML SCHEMA COLLECTION statements. The former allows you to add new schemas to an existing XML schema collection, while the latter deletes an entire schema collection.

Typed XML Columns, Variables, and Parameters

Each typed XML column, variable, or parameter must be specified with associated schemas. To do this, the name of the schema collection, which is created using the CREATE XML SCHEMA COLLECTION statement, must be written inside the pair of parentheses, after the instance name, as shown in Example 26.9.

EXAMPLE 26.9

```
USE sample;
CREATE TABLE xml_persontab (id INTEGER,
  xml_person XML(EmployeeSchema));
```

The **xml_person** column in Example 26.9 is associated with the XML schema collection **EmployeeSchema** (see Example 26.8). This means that all specifications from defined schemas are used to check whether the content of the **xml_person** column is valid. In other words, when you insert a new value in the typed XML column (or modify an existing value), all constraints specified in the schemas are checked.

The specification of an XML schema collection for the typed XML instance can be extended with two keywords:

► DOCUMENT

► CONTENT

The DOCUMENT keyword specifies that the XML column can contain only XML documents, while the CONTENT keyword, the default value, specifies that the XML column can contain either documents or fragments. (Remember, an XML document must have a single root element, while an XML fragment is an XML construct without a root element.)

Example 26.10 shows the use of the DOCUMENT keyword.

EXAMPLE 26.10

```
USE sample;
CREATE TABLE xml_persontab_doc (id INTEGER,
                        xml_person XML(DOCUMENT EmployeeSchema));
```

The Database Engine supports several catalog views in relation to XML Schema, the most important of which are the following:

► **sys.xml_schema_attributes**   Returns a row per XML schema component that is an attribute

► **sys.xml_schema_elements**   Returns a row per XML schema component that is an element

► **sys.xml_schema_components**   Returns a row per component of an XML schema

Storing XML Documents Using Decomposition

The **sp_xml_preparedocument** system procedure reads the XML text provided as input, parses the text, and represents the parsed document as a tree with the various nodes: elements, attributes, text, and comments.

Example 26.11 shows the use of the **sp_xml_preparedocument** system procedure.

EXAMPLE 26.11

```
USE sample;
DECLARE @hdoc INT
DECLARE @doc VARCHAR(1000)
SET @doc ='<ROOT>
```

```
            <Employee>
                 <Name>Ann Jones</Name>
                 <No>10102</No>
                  <Deptno>d3</Deptno>
                  <Address>Dallas</Address>
            </Employee>
            <Employee>
                  <Name>John Barrimore</Name>
                  <No>18316</No>
                   <Deptno>d1</Deptno>
                   <Address>Seattle</Address>
             </Employee>
</ROOT>'
EXEC sp_xml_preparedocument @hdoc OUTPUT, @doc
```

The XML document in Example 26.11 is stored as a string in the **@doc** variable. This string is decomposed (shredded) by the **sp_xml_preparedocument** system procedure. The procedure returns a handle (**@hdoc**) that can then be used to access the newly created tree representation of the XML document.

NOTE

*The **@hdoc** handle will be used in the first example of the next section to extract data from the XML document.*

The **sp_xml_removedocument** system procedure removes the internal representation of the XML document specified by the document handle and invalidates the document handle.

The next section shows how you can present the stored XML data in the relational form.

Presenting Data

Using the Database Engine, you can present data in the following ways:

▶ Present XML documents and fragments as relational data
▶ Present relational data as XML documents

The following sections discuss these two methods.

Presenting XML Documents as Relational Data

You can generate a set of rows from XML documents and fragments and query it using the Transact-SQL language. You do so by using OpenXML, which lets you use Transact-SQL statements to extract data from an XML document. Using OpenXML, you can retrieve the data from an XML document as if it were in a relational table. (OpenXML is an international standard for documents that can be implemented by multiple applications on multiple platforms.)

Example 26.12 shows how you can query the XML document from Example 26.11 using OpenXML.

NOTE

The code in Example 26.12 must be appended to the code in Example 26.11 and executed together.

EXAMPLE 26.12

```
SELECT * FROM OPENXML (@hdoc, '/ROOT/Employee', 1)
      WITH (name VARCHAR(20)  'Name',
            no INT 'No',
            deptno VARCHAR(6) 'Deptno',
            address VARCHAR(50) 'Address');
```

The result is

name	no	deptno	address
Ann Jones	10102	d3	Dallas
John Barrimore	18316	d1	Seattle

Presenting Relational Data as XML Documents

As you already know from Chapter 6, a SELECT statement queries one or more tables and displays the corresponding result set. The result set is displayed by default as a table. If you want to display the result set of a query as an XML document or fragment, you can use the FOR XML clause in your SELECT statement. With this clause, you can specify one of the four following modes:

► RAW
► AUTO

► EXPLICIT

► PATH

NOTE

The FOR XML clause must be specified at the end of the SELECT statement.

The following sections describe each of these modes. Also, the last section describes directives.

RAW Mode

The FOR XML RAW option transforms each row of the result set into an XML element with the identifier <row>. Each column value is mapped to an attribute of the XML element in which the attribute name is the same as the column name. (This is true only for the non-null columns.)

Example 26.13 shows the use of the FOR XML RAW option specified for the join of the **employee** and **works_on** tables from the **sample** database.

EXAMPLE 26.13

```
USE sample;
SELECT  employee.emp_no, emp_lname, works_on.job
FROM employee, works_on
WHERE employee.emp_no <= 10000
AND employee.emp_no = works_on.emp_no
FOR XML RAW;
```

Example 26.13 displays the following XML document fragment:

```
<row emp_no="2581" emp_lname="Hansel          " job="Analyst       " />
<row emp_no="9031" emp_lname="Bertoni         " job="Manager       " />
<row emp_no="9031" emp_lname="Bertoni         " job="Clerk         " />
```

Without the FOR XML RAW option, the SELECT statement in Example 26.13 would retrieve the following rows:

emp_no	emp_lname	job
2581	Hansel	Analyst
9031	Bertoni	Manager
9031	Bertoni	Clerk

As you can see from both results, the first output produces one XML element for each row in the result set.

AUTO Mode

AUTO mode returns the result set of a query as a simple, nested XML tree. Each table in the FROM clause from which at least one column appears in the SELECT list is represented as an XML element. The columns in the SELECT list are mapped to the appropriate elements' attributes.

Example 26.14 shows the use of AUTO mode.

EXAMPLE 26.14

```
USE sample;
SELECT  employee.emp_no, emp_lname, works_on.job
FROM employee, works_on
WHERE employee.emp_no <= 10000
AND employee.emp_no = works_on.emp_no
FOR XML AUTO;
```

The result is

```
<employee emp_no="9031" emp_lname="Bertoni            ">
  <works_on job="Manager        " />
  <works_on job="Clerk          " />
</employee>
<employee emp_no="2581" emp_lname="Hansel             ">
  <works_on job="Analyst        " />
</employee>
```

NOTE
The result of Example 26.14 is not a valid XML document. As you already know, a valid XML document must have a root element.

The result in Example 26.14 is significantly different from the result in the previous example, although the SELECT statement for both examples is equivalent (except for the specification of the AUTO mode instead of the RAW mode). As you can see from Example 26.14, the result set is displayed as the hierarchy of the **employee** and **works_on** tables. This hierarchy is based on the primary key/foreign key relationship of both tables. For this reason, the data from the **employee** table is displayed first, and the corresponding data from the **works_on** table is displayed after that, at the lower hierarchy level.

The nesting of the elements in the resulting XML document or fragment is based on the order of tables identified by the columns specified in the SELECT clause; therefore, the order in which column names are specified in the SELECT clause is significant. For this reason, in Example 26.14 the values of the **emp_no** column of the **employee** table form the top element in the resulting XML fragment. The values of the **job** column of the **works_on** table form a subelement within the top element.

EXPLICIT Mode

As you can see from Example 26.14, the result set in the AUTO mode is displayed as a simple, nested XML tree. The queries in AUTO mode are good if you want to generate simple hierarchies, because this mode provides little control over the shape of the XML document generated from a query result.

If you want to specify the extended form of the result set, you can use the FOR XML EXPLICIT option. With this option, the result set is displayed as a universal table that has all the information about the resulting XML tree. The data in the table is vertically partitioned into groups. Each group then becomes an XML element in the result set.

Example 26.15 shows the use of the EXPLICIT mode.

EXAMPLE 26.15

```
USE sample;
SELECT 1 AS tag, NULL as parent,
emp_lname AS [employee!1!emp_lname],
NULL AS [works_on!2!job]
FROM employee
UNION
SELECT  2, 1, emp_lname, works_on.job
FROM employee, works_on
WHERE employee.emp_no <= 10000
AND employee.emp_no = works_on.emp_no
ORDER BY [employee!1!emp_lname]
FOR XML EXPLICIT;
```

The result is

```
<employee emp_lname="Barrimore              " />
<employee emp_lname="Bertoni                ">
  <works_on job="Clerk         " />
  <works_on job="Manager       " />
</employee>
<employee emp_lname="Hansel                ">
```

```
    <works_on job="Analyst        " />
</employee>
<employee emp_lname="James            " />
<employee emp_lname="Jones            " />
<employee emp_lname="Moser            " />
<employee emp_lname="Smith            " />
```

As you can see from the SELECT statement in Example 26.15, the FOR XML EXPLICIT option requires two additional metadata columns: **tag** and **parent**. (These two columns are used to determine the primary key/foreign key relationship in the XML tree.) The **tag** column stores the tag number of the current element, while the **parent** column stores the tag number of the parent element. (The parent table is the table with the primary key.) If the parent tag is NULL, the row is placed directly under the root element.

NOTE

Do not use EXPLICIT mode because of its complexity. Use the PATH mode instead (discussed next).

PATH Mode

All three of the FOR XML options previously described have different disadvantages and restrictions. The FOR XML RAW option supports only one level of nesting, while the FOR XML AUTO option requires that all columns selected from the same table occur at the same level. Also, both options do not allow mixing of elements and attributes in the same XML document. On the other hand, the FOR XML EXPLICIT option allows mixing of elements and attributes, but the syntax of this option is cumbersome, as you can see from the previous example.

The FOR XML PATH option allows you to implement in a very easy way almost all queries that require the EXPLICIT mode. In the PATH mode, column names or column aliases are treated as XPath expressions, which indicate how the values are being mapped to XML. (An XPath expression consists of a sequence of nodes, separated by /. For each slash, the system creates another level of hierarchy in the resulting document.)

Example 26.16 shows the use of the PATH mode.

EXAMPLE 26.16

```
USE sample;
SELECT d.dept_name "@Department",
       emp_fname   "EmpName/First",
       emp_lname   "EmpName/Last"
```

```
FROM    Employee e, department d
WHERE   e.dept_no = d.dept_no
AND     d.dept_no = 'd1'
FOR XML PATH;
```

The result is

```
<row Department="Research                      ">
  <EmpName>
    <First>John                 </First>
    <Last>Barrimore             </Last>
  </EmpName>
</row>
<row Department="Research                      ">
  <EmpName>
    <First>Sybill               </First>
    <Last>Moser                 </Last>
  </EmpName>
</row>
```

In the PATH mode, the column names are used as the path in constructing an XML document. The column containing department names starts with @. This means that the **Department** attribute is added to the <row> element. All other columns include a slash in the column name, indicating hierarchy. For this reason, the resulting XML document will have the <EmpName> child under the <row> element and <First> and <Last> elements at the next sublevel.

Directives

The Database Engine supports several different directives that allow you to produce different results when you want to display XML documents and fragments. The following list shows several of these directives:

- ► TYPE
- ► ELEMENTS (with XSINIL)
- ► ROOT

The following subsections describe these directives.

TYPE Directive   The Database Engine allows you to store the result of a relational query as an XML document or fragment in the XML data type by using the TYPE directive. When the TYPE directive is specified, a query with the FOR XML option returns a one-row, one-column result set. (This directive is a common directive, meaning you can use it in all four modes.) Example 26.17 shows the use of the TYPE directive with the AUTO mode.

EXAMPLE 26.17

```
USE sample;
DECLARE @x xml;
SET @x = (SELECT * FROM department
                        FOR XML AUTO, TYPE);
SELECT @x;
```

The result is

```
<department dept_no="d1 " dept_name="Research    " location="Dallas  " />
<department dept_no="d2 " dept_name="Accounting  " location="Seattle " />
<department dept_no="d3 " dept_name="Marketing   " location="Dallas  " />
```

Example 26.17 first declares the variable **@x** as a local variable of the XML data type and assigns the result of the SELECT statement to it. The last SELECT statement in the batch displays the content of the variable.

ELEMENTS Directive   As you already know from Chapter 3, the Database Engine supports NULL values to specify unknown (or missing) values. In contrast to the relational model, XML does not support NULL values, and those values are omitted in the result sets of queries with the FOR XML option.

The Database Engine allows you to display the missing values in an XML document by using the ELEMENTS directive with the XSINIL option. Generally, the ELEMENTS directive constructs the corresponding XML document so that each column value maps to an element. If the column value is NULL, no element is added by default. By specifying the additional XSINIL option, you can request that an element be created for the NULL value as well. In this case, an element with the XSINIL attribute set to TRUE is returned for each NULL value in the column.

ROOT Directive   Generally, queries with the FOR XML option produce XML fragments—XML without a corresponding root element. This can be a problem if an API accepts only XML documents as input. The Database Engine allows you to add the root element using the ROOT directive. By specifying the ROOT directive in the FOR XML query, you can request a single, top-level element for the resulting XML. (The argument specified for the directive provides the name of the root element.)

Example 26.18 shows the use of the ROOT directive.

EXAMPLE 26.18

```
USE sample;
SELECT * FROM department
FOR XML AUTO, ROOT ('AllDepartments');
```

The result is

```
<AllDepartments>
  <department dept_no="d1 " dept_name="Research   " location="Dallas  " />
  <department dept_no="d2 " dept_name="Accounting " location="Seattle " />
  <department dept_no="d3 " dept_name="Marketing  " location="Dallas  " />
</AllDepartments>
```

The query in Example 26.18 displays the XML fragment with all rows from the **department** table. The ROOT directive adds the root specification in the result set with the **AllDepartments** parameter as the root name.

Querying Data

There are two standardized languages that can be used to query XML documents:

▶ XPath

▶ XQuery

XPath a simple query language that is used to navigate through elements and attributes in an XML document. XQuery is a complex query language that uses XPath as its sublanguage. XQuery supports the so-called FLWOR (pronounced "flower") expressions, referring to the FOR, LET, WHERE, ORDER BY, and RETURN clauses. (A detailed discussion of these query languages is beyond the scope of this book. This section provides only a brief introduction.)

The Database Engine supports five methods that can be used to query XML documents with XQuery:

▶ **query()**   Accepts an XQuery statement as input and returns an instance of the XML data type.

▶ **exist()**   Accepts an XQuery statement as input and returns 0, 1, or NULL, depending on the query result.

- ► **value()**   Accepts an XQuery statement as input and returns a single scalar value.

- ► **nodes()**   This method is useful when you want to shred an instance of the **xml** data type into relational data. It allows you to identify nodes that will be mapped into a new row.

- ► **modify()**   You can use this method to insert, modify, and delete XML documents.

Example 26.19 shows the use of the **query()** method.

EXAMPLE 26.19

```
USE sample;
SELECT xml_column.query('/PersonList/Title')
   FROM xmltab
   FOR XML AUTO, TYPE;
```

The result is

```
<xmltab>
      <Title> Value="Employee List"&gt;</Title>
</xmltab>
```

The SELECT list of the query in Example 26.19 contains the **query()** method, which is applied to an instance of the **xml_column** column. The parameter of the method is an XPath expression. (Note that the methods are applied using the dot notation.) The expression '/PersonList/Title' is an absolute expression, where the values of the **Title** element are retrieved. (Remember that XPath expressions are valid XQuery statements because XPath is a sublanguage of XQuery.)

Example 26.20 shows the use of the **exist()** method.

EXAMPLE 26.20

```
SELECT xml_column.exist('/PersonList/Title/@Value=EmployeeList') AS a
   FROM xmltab
   FOR XML AUTO, TYPE;
```

The result is

```
<xmltab a="1" />
```

As you already know, the **exist()** method accepts an XQuery statement as input and returns 0, 1, or NULL, depending on the query result. If the query result is an empty sequence, the return value is 0. A sequence with at least one item returns 1, and NULL is returned if the value of the column is NULL.

The SELECT list of the query in Example 26.20 contains the **exist()** method with an XPath expression that tests whether the **Value** attribute of the XML document has the value **EmployeeList**. (In XPath, the @ sign is used to specify an XML attribute.) The test is evaluated to TRUE, and therefore the return value of the query is 1.

Summary

XML is a format for interchanging and archiving of data. An XML document contains several tags that are chosen by the person who implements the document. All parts of an XML document that belong to its logical structure are called elements. Elements together with their subelements build a hierarchical structure. Each element can have extra information that is attached to it. Such information is called an attribute. Besides elements and attributes, an XML document can also contain namespaces, processing instructions, and comments.

The XML Schema language is a standardized schema language that is used to specify a schema for a given XML document. An XML document that conforms to the associated schema is called a valid document. (There is also another simple schema language called Document Type Definition, which is not standardized.) The XML Schema language comprises data definition statements for XML, in much the same way that DDL contains data definition statements for SQL.

The Database Engine has full support for storing, presenting, and querying XML documents. The most important feature is the existence of the XML data type, which allows the database system to store XML documents as first class objects.

The values of the XML data type can be schema validated if one or more schemas are associated with this type. You can determine the exact data types of elements and attributes only if the corresponding XML document contains types specified by XML schemas. Schema definitions are specified using the CREATE XML SCHEMA COLLECTION statement.

XML also supports several methods, which can be used to query XML documents. These methods contain XPath or XQuery expressions as their parameters.

The next chapter describes spatial data.

Chapter 27

Spatial Data

In This Chapter

- ▶ Introduction
- ▶ Working with Spatial Data Types
- ▶ Displaying Information Concerning Spatial Data
- ▶ New Spatial Data Features in SQL Server 2012

his chapter comprises four parts. The introductory part describes the most important general issues about spatial data that you to need understand before you begin to work with spatial data. Besides different spatial models and formats, this part introduces both of the data types supported by SQL Server: GEOMETRY and GEOGRAPHY. Also, several subtypes of these two root types are described in detail.

The second part of the chapter presents several examples to show how spatial data can be used. In these examples, different methods of the GEOMETRY and GEOGRAPHY data types are applied. Additionally, this part also describes the creation and use of a spatial index.

The third part of the chapter is dedicated to using SQL Server Management Studio to display or plot spatial data in a graphical form. Examples are provided for both spatial data types, and you will see how you can display their results.

The final part discusses new features implemented in SQL Server 2012. It introduces the new subtypes of the GEOMETRY and GEOGRAPHY data types as well as new spatial indices and system stored procedures.

Introduction

In the past few years, the need of businesses to incorporate spatial data into their databases and to manage it using a database system has grown significantly. The most important factor leading to this growth is the proliferation of geographical services and devices, such as Microsoft Virtual Earth and low-priced GPS devices.

Generally, the support of spatial data by a database vendor helps users to make better decisions in several scenarios, such as:

▶ Real-estate analysis ("Find a suitable property within 500m of an elementary school.")

▶ Consumer-based information ("Find the nearest shopping malls to a given ZIP code.")

▶ Market analysis ("Define geographic sales regions and ascertain whether there is a necessity for a new branch office.")

As you already know from Chapter 5, you can use the CREATE TYPE statement to create user-defined data types. The implementation of such types is done using Common Language Runtime (CLR), which is described in Chapter 8. Developers of SQL Server used CLR to implement two new data types in relation to spatial data:

GEOMETRY and GEOGRAPHY. These two data types are discussed after the following brief look at the different models for representing spatial data.

Models for Representing Spatial Data

Generally, there are two different groups of models for representing spatial data:

▶ Geodetic spatial models

▶ Flat spatial models

Planets are complex objects that can be represented using a flattened sphere (called a *spheroid*). A good approximation for the representation of Earth (and other planets) is a globe, where locations on the surface are described using latitude and longitude. (Latitude gives the location of a place on Earth north or south of the equator, while longitude specifies the location in relation to a chosen meridian.) Models that use these measures are called *geodetic models*. Because these models provide a good approximation of spheroids, they provide the most accurate way to represent spatial data.

Flat spatial models (or planar models) use two-dimensional maps to represent Earth. In this case, the spheroid is flattened and projected in a plane. The flattening process results in some deformation of shape and size of the projected (geographic) objects. Flat spatial models work best for small surface areas, because the larger the surface area being represented, the more deformation that occurs.

As you will see in the following two sections, the GEOMETRY data type is based on a flat spatial model, while the GEOGRAPHY data type is based on a geodetic spatial model.

GEOMETRY Data Type

The Open Geospatial Consortium (OGC) introduced the term "geometry" to represent spatial features, such as point locations and lines. Therefore, "geometry" represents data in a two-dimensional plane as points, lines, and polygons using one of the existing flat spatial models.

You can think of "geometry" as a data type with several subtypes, as shown in Figure 27-1. The subclasses are divided into two categories: the base geometry subclasses and the homogeneous collection subclasses. The base geometries include, among others, Point, LineString, and Polygon, while the homogeneous collections include MultiPoint, MultiLineString, and MultiPolygon. As the names imply, the homogeneous collections are collections of base geometries. In addition to sharing base geometry properties, homogeneous collections have their own properties.

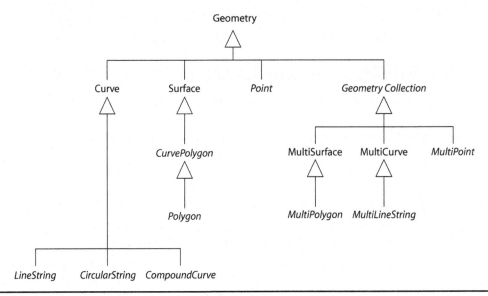

Figure 27-1 *The type hierarchy with the GEOMETRY type as a root*

The types in Figure 27-1 that appear in italic font are instantiable, which means they have instances. All instantiable types are implemented as user-defined data types in SQL Server. The following are the instantiable types:

▶ **Point** A point is a zero-dimensional geometry with single X and Y coordinate values. Therefore, it has a NULL boundary. Optionally, a point can have two additional coordinates: evaluation (Z coordinate) and measure (M coordinate). Points are usually used to build complex spatial types.

▶ **MultiPoint** A multipoint is a collection of zero or more points. The points in a multipoint do not have to be distinct.

▶ **LineString** A line string is a one-dimensional geometry object that has a length and is stored as a sequence of points defining a linear path. Therefore, a line string is defined by a set of points, which define the reference points of it. Linear interpolation between the reference points specifies the resulting line string. A line string is called *simple* if it does not intersect its interior. The endpoints (the boundary) of a *closed* line string occupy the same point in space. A line is called a *ring* if it is both closed and simple.

▶ **MultiLineString** A multiline string is a collection of zero or more line strings.

▶ **Polygon**   A polygon is a two-dimensional geometry object with surface. It is stored as a sequence of points defining its exterior bounding ring and zero or more interior rings. The exterior and any interior rings specify the boundary of a polygon, and the space enclosed between the rings specifies the polygon's interior.

▶ **MultiPolygon**   A multipolygon is a collection of zero or more polygons.

▶ **GeometryCollection**   A geometry collection is a collection of zero or more geometry objects. In other words, this geometry object can contain instances of any subtype of the GEOMETRY data type.

NOTE

As you can see from Figure 27-1, there are three other subtypes that can have instances: CircularString, CompoundCurve, and CurvePolygon. These three subtypes will be discussed in detail in the "New Spatial Data Features in SQL Server 2012" section later in this chapter.

GEOGRAPHY Data Type

While the GEOMETRY data type stores data using X and Y coordinates, the GEOGRAPHY data type stores data as GPS latitude and longitude coordinates. (Longitude represents the horizontal angle and ranges from −180 degrees to +180 degrees, while latitude represents the vertical angle and ranges from −90 degrees to +90 degrees.)

The GEOGRAPHY data type, unlike the GEOMETRY data type, requires the specification of a Spatial Reference System. A Spatial Reference System is a system used to identify a particular coordinate system and is specified by an integer. Information on available integer values in SQL Server 2012 can be found in the **sys.spatial_reference_systems** catalog view. (This view will be discussed later in this chapter.)

NOTE

All instantiable types (see Figure 27-1) that are implemented for the GEOMETRY data type are implemented for the GEOGRAPHY data type, too.

GEOMETRY vs. GEOGRAPHY

As you already know, the GEOMETRY data type is used in flat spatial models, while the GEOGRAPHY data type is used in geodetic models. The main difference between these two groups of models is that with the GEOMETRY data type, distances and areas are given in the same unit of measurement as the coordinates of the instances. (Therefore, the distance between the points (0,0) and (3,4) will always be 5 units.)

This is not the case with the GEOGRAPHY data type, which works with ellipsoidal coordinates that are expressed in degrees of latitude and longitude.

There are also some restrictions placed on the GEOGRAPHY data type. For example, each instance of the GEOGRAPHY data type must fit inside a single hemisphere.

External Data Formats

SQL Server supports three external data formats that can be used to represent spatial data in an implementation-independent form:

▶ **Well-known text (WKT)**   A text markup language for representing spatial reference systems of spatial objects and transformations between spatial reference systems.

▶ **Well-known binary (WKB)**   The binary equivalent of WKT.

▶ **Geography Markup Language (GML)**   The XML grammar defined by OGC to express geographical features. GML is an open interchange format for geographic transactions on the Internet.

These three external data formats are also standardized by the SQL/MM standard, as discussed later in the section "New Subtypes of Circular Arcs."

NOTE

All examples shown in this chapter reference the WKT format, because this format is the easiest to read.

The following examples show the syntax of WKT for the selected types:

▶ **POINT(3,4)**   The values 3 and 4 specify the X coordinate and Y coordinate, respectively.

▶ **LINESTRING(0 0, 3 4)**   The first two values represent the X and Y coordinates of the starting point, while the last two values represent the X and Y coordinates of the end point of the line.

▶ **POLYGON(300 0, 150 0, 150 150, 300 150, 300 0)**   Each pair of numbers represents a point on the edge of the polygon. (The end point of the specified polygon is the same as the starting point.)

Working with Spatial Data Types

As you already know, SQL Server supports two different data types in relation to spatial data: GEOMETRY and GEOGRAPHY. These types are user-defined types implemented by SQL Server developers using CLR. Both data types have several subtypes, which are either instantiable or noninstantiable. For each instantiable subtype, you can create instances and work with them. These instances can be used as values of a table's columns, as well as variables or parameters. As you already guessed, noninstantiable types do not contain instances. In a hierarchy of classes, the root class is usually noninstantiable, while the classes that build the leaves of the hierarchy tree are almost always instantiable. (A root class that is noninstantiable is called an *abstract class.*)

The following two sections describe how you can use these two data types to create and query spatial data. After that, the spatial indices will be introduced.

Working with the GEOMETRY Data Type

An example will help to explain the use of the GEOMETRY data type. Example 27.1 creates a table for nonalcoholic beverage markets in a given city (or state).

EXAMPLE 27.1

```
USE sample;
CREATE TABLE beverage_markets
     (id INTEGER IDENTITY(1,1),
      name VARCHAR(25),
      shape GEOMETRY);
INSERT INTO beverage_markets
            VALUES ('Coke', GEOMETRY::STGeomFromText
            ('POLYGON ((0 0, 150 0, 150 150, 0 150, 0 0))', 0));
INSERT INTO beverage_markets
            VALUES ('Pepsi', GEOMETRY::STGeomFromText
            ('POLYGON ((300 0, 150 0, 150 150, 300 150, 300 0))', 0));
INSERT INTO beverage_markets
            VALUES ('7UP', GEOMETRY::STGeomFromText
            ('POLYGON ((300 0, 150 0, 150 150, 300 150, 300 0))', 0));
INSERT INTO beverage_markets
            VALUES ('Almdudler', GEOMETRY::STGeomFromText
            ('POINT (50 0)', 0));
```

The **beverage_markets** table has three columns. The first is the **id** column, the values of which are generated by the system because this column is specified with the IDENTITY property. The second column, **name**, contains the beverage name. The third column, **shape**, specifies the shape of the market area in which the particular beverage is the most preferred one. The first three INSERT statements create three areas in which a particular beverage is most preferred. All three areas happen to be a polygon. The fourth INSERT statement inserts a point because there is just one place where the particular beverage (Almdudler) can be bought.

NOTE

If you take a look at the specification of the POINT (or POLYGON) data type in Example 27.1, you will see that this specification has an additional parameter as the last parameter, the spatial reference ID (SRID) parameter. This parameter is required, and for the GEOMETRY data type the default value is 0.

Example 27.1 introduces the first method in relation to the GEOMETRY data type: **STGeomFromText()**. This static method is used to insert the coordinates of geometric figures, such as polygons and points. In other words, it returns an instance of the GEOMETRY data type in the WKT format.

NOTE

Generally, a type can have two different groups of methods: static methods and instance methods. Static methods are always applied on the whole type (i.e., class), while instance methods are applied on particular instances of the class. The invocation of methods from both groups is different. Static methods use the sign "::" between the type and the method (for instance, GEOMETRY::STGeomFromText; see Example 27.1), while instance methods use dot notation (for instance, @g.STContains; see Example 27.2).

Besides the **STGeomFromText()** method, SQL Server supports three other similar static methods:

- ▶ **STPointFromText()**   Returns the WKT representation of an instance of the POINT data type
- ▶ **STLineFromText()**   Returns the WKT representation of an instance of the LINESTRING data type augmented with the corresponding elevation and measure values
- ▶ **STPolyFromText()**   Returns the WKT representation of an instance of the MULTIPOLYGON data type augmented with the corresponding elevation and measure values

Spatial data can be queried the same way as relational data. The following examples show a sample of the information that can be found from the content of the **shape** column of the **beverage_markets** table.

NOTE

SQL Server supports a lot of methods that can be applied to instances of the GEOMETRY data type. The following examples describe only some of the most important methods. For more information on other instance methods, refer to Books Online.

Example 27.2 shows the use of the **STContains()** method.

EXAMPLE 27.2

Determine whether the shop that sells Almdudler lies within the area where Coke is the preferred beverage:

```
DECLARE @g geometry;
DECLARE @h geometry;
SELECT @h = shape FROM beverage_markets WHERE name ='Almdudler';
SELECT @g = shape FROM beverage_markets WHERE name = 'Coke';
SELECT @g.STContains(@h);
```

The result is 0.

The **STContains()** method returns 1 if an instance of the GEOMETRY data type completely contains another instance of the same type, which is specified as a parameter of the method. The result of Example 27.2 means that the shop that sells Almdudler does not lie within the area where the preferred beverage is Coke.

Example 27.3 shows the use of the **STLength()** method.

EXAMPLE 27.3

Find the length and the WKT representation of the **shape** column for the Almdudler shop:

```
SELECT id, shape.ToString() AS wkt, shape.STLength() AS length
      FROM beverage_markets
      WHERE name = 'Almdudler' ;
```

The result is

id	wkt	length
4	POINT (50 0)	0

The **STLength()** method in Example 27.3 returns the total length of the elements of the GEOMETRY data type. (The result is 0 because the displayed value is a point.) The **ToString()** method returns a string with the logical representation of the current instance. As you can see from the result of Example 27.3, this method is used to load all properties of the given point and to display it using the WKT format.

Example 27.4 shows the use of the **STIntersects()** method.

EXAMPLE 27.4

Determine whether the region that sells Coke intersects with the region that sells Pepsi:

```
USE sample;
DECLARE @g geometry;
DECLARE @h geometry;
SELECT @h = shape FROM beverage_markets WHERE name = 'Coke';
SELECT @g = shape FROM beverage_markets WHERE name = 'Pepsi';
SELECT @g.STIntersects(@h);
```

The result of Example 27.4 is 1 (TRUE), meaning that the two geometries intersect.

In contrast to Example 27.3, where the column of a table is declared to be of the GEOMETRY data type, Example 27.4 declares the variables **@g** and **@h** using this data type. (As you already know, table columns, variables, and parameters of stored procedures can be declared to be of the GEOMETRY data type.) The **STIntersects()** method returns 1 if a geometry instance intersects another geometry instance. In Example 27.4, the method is applied to both regions, declared by variables, to find out whether the regions intersect.

Example 27.5 shows the use of the **STIntersection()** method.

EXAMPLE 27.5

```
USE sample;
DECLARE @poly1 GEOMETRY = 'POLYGON ((1 1, 1 4, 4 4, 4 1, 1 1))';
DECLARE @poly2 GEOMETRY = 'POLYGON ((2 2, 2 6, 6 6, 6 2, 2 2))';
DECLARE @result GEOMETRY;
SELECT @result = @poly1.STIntersection(@poly2);
SELECT @result.STAsText();
```

The result is (the values are rounded):

```
POLYGON ((2 2, 4 2, 4 4, 2 4, 2 2))
```

The **STIntersection()** method returns an object representing the points where an instance of the GEOMETRY data type intersects another instance of the same type. Therefore, Example 27.5 returns the rectangle where the polygon declared by the **@poly1** variable and the polygon declared by the **@poly2** variable intersect. The **STAsText()** method returns the WKT representation of a GEOMETRY instance, which is the result of the example.

NOTE

*The difference between the **STIntersects()** and **STIntersection()** methods is that the former method tests whether two geometry objects intersect, while the latter displays the intersection object.*

Working with the GEOGRAPHY Data Type

The GEOGRAPHY data type is handled in the same way as the GEOMETRY data type. This means that the same (static and instance) methods that you can apply to the GEOMETRY data type are applicable to the GEOGRAPHY data type, too. For this reason, only Example 27.6 is used to describe this data type.

EXAMPLE 27.6

```
USE AdventureWorks;
SELECT SpatialLocation, City
      FROM Person.Address
      WHERE City = 'Dallas';
```

The result is

SpatialLocation	City
0xE6100000010C4DD260393369404026C0A31BF73458C0	Dallas
0xE6100000010C10A810D1886240403A0F0653663158C0	Dallas
0xE6100000010C4346160AA26440406340F0E64F3B58C0	Dallas
0xE6100000010C107E16DAAD6540403DA892EAD52C58C0	Dallas
0xE6100000010C8044A1422D5F4040F66D784F983758C0	Dallas
0xE6100000010C8E345943826A4040839B00B8E03358C0	Dallas
0xE6100000010CAA5BBD5FAB69404087866D198D3C58C0	Dallas

The **Address** table of the **AdventureWorks** database contains a column called **SpatialLocation**, which is of the GEOGRAPHY data type. Example 27.6 displays the geographic location of all persons living in Dallas. As you can see from the result of this example, the value in the **SpatialLocation** column is the hexadecimal representation of the longitude and latitude of the location where each person lives. (Example 27.10, later in the chapter, uses SQL Server Management Studio to display the result of this query.)

Working with Spatial Indices

As you already know from Chapter 10, indexing is generally used to provide fast access to data. Therefore, spatial indices are necessary to speed up retrieval operations on spatial data.

A spatial index is defined on a table column of the GEOMETRY or GEOGRAPHY data type. In SQL Server, these indices are built using B-trees, which means that the indices represent two dimensions in the linear order of B-trees.

Therefore, before reading data into a spatial index, the system implements a hierarchical uniform decomposition of space. The index-creation process decomposes the space into a four-level grid hierarchy.

The CREATE SPATIAL INDEX statement is used to create a spatial index. The general form of this statement is similar to the convenient CREATE INDEX statement, but contains additional options and clauses, some of which are introduced here:

▶ **GEOMETRY_GRID clause**   Specifies the geometry grid tessellation scheme that you are using. (Tessellation is a process that is performed after reading the data for a spatial object. During this process, the object is fitted into the grid hierarchy by associating it with a set of grid cells that it touches.) Note that GEOMETRY_GRID can be specified only on a column of the GEOMETRY data type.

▶ **BOUNDING_BOX option**   Specifies a numeric four-tuple that defines the four coordinates of the bounding box: the X-min and Y-min coordinates of the lower-left corner, and the X-max and Y-max coordinates of the upper-right corner. This option applies only within the GEOMETRY_GRID clause.

▶ **GEOGRAPHY_GRID clause**   Specifies the geography grid tessellation scheme. This clause can be specified only on a column of the GEOGRAPHY data type.

Example 27.7 shows the creation of a spatial index for the **shape** column of the **beverage_markets** table.

EXAMPLE 27.7

```
USE sample;
GO
ALTER TABLE beverage_markets
 ADD CONSTRAINT prim_key PRIMARY KEY(id);
GO
CREATE SPATIAL INDEX i_spatial_shape
   ON beverage_markets(shape)
   USING GEOMETRY_GRID
   WITH (BOUNDING_BOX = ( xmin=0, ymin=0, xmax=500, ymax=200 ),
    GRIDS = (LOW, LOW, MEDIUM, HIGH),
    PAD_INDEX  = ON );
```

A spatial index can be created only if the primary key for the table with a spatial data column is explicitly defined. For this reason, the first statement in Example 27.7 is the ALTER TABLE statement which defines this constraint.

The subsequent CREATE SPATIAL INDEX statement creates the index using the GEOMETRY_GRID clause. The BOUNDING_BOX option specifies the boundaries inside which the instance of the **shape** column will be placed. The GRIDS option specifies the density of the grid at each level of a tessellation scheme. (The PAD_INDEX option is described in Chapter 10.)

NOTE

SQL Server 2012 introduces additional spatial indices, which are described in the section "New Spatial Data Features in SQL Server 2012" later in this chapter.

SQL Server supports, among others, three catalog views related to spatial data:

▶ sys.spatial_indexes

▶ sys.spatial_index_tessellations

▶ sys_spatial_reference_systems

The **sys.spatial indexes** view represents the main index information of the spatial indices (see Example 27.8). Using the **sys.spatial_index_tessellations** view, you can display the information about the tessellation scheme and parameters of each of the existing spatial indices. The **sys.spatial_reference_systems** view lists all the spatial reference systems supported by SQL Server. (Spatial reference systems are used to identify a particular coordinate system.) The main columns of the view are **spatial_reference_id** and **well_known_text**. The former is the unique identifier of the corresponding reference system, while the latter describes that system.

Example 27.8 shows the use of the **sys_spatial_indexes** catalog view.

EXAMPLE 27.8

```
USE sample;
SELECT object_id, name, type_desc
   FROM sys.spatial_indexes;
```

The result is

object_id	name	type_desc
914102297	i_spatial_shape	SPATIAL

The catalog view in Example 27.8 displays the information about the existing spatial index (created in Example 27.7).

Displaying Information Concerning Spatial Data

Microsoft extended the functionality of SQL Server Management Studio to display spatial data in a graphical form. Two examples will be presented to show this functionality. Example 27.9 uses the GEOMETRY data type, while Example 27.10 is based on the GEOGRAPHY data type.

EXAMPLE 27.9

```
USE sample;
DECLARE @rectangle1 GEOMETRY = 'POLYGON((1 1,  1 4,  4 4, 4 1, 1 1))';
DECLARE @line GEOMETRY = 'LINESTRING (0 2, 4 4)';
SELECT @rectangle1
UNION ALL
SELECT @line
```

To display the result of spatial data in SQL Server Management Studio, click the Spatial Results tab, which is next to the Results tab. In the case of Example 27.9, Management Studio displays a rectangle, showing the content of the **@rectangle1** variable, and the line from the **@line** variable. Figure 27-2 shows the result of Example 27.9.

Example 27.10 shows how you can display the resulting instances of the GEOGRAPHY data type.

EXAMPLE 27.10

```
USE AdventureWorks;
SELECT SpatialLocation, City
     FROM Person.Address
     WHERE City = 'Dallas';
```

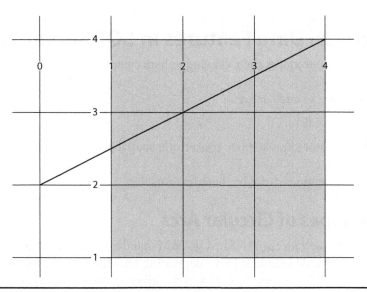

Figure 27-2   *Displaying the result of Example 27.9 in Management Studio*

Example 27.10 is the same as Example 27.6. To plot the result of this example using Management Studio, click again the Spatial Results tab. Figure 27-3 shows the result of Example 27.10.

NOTE

If you move your mouse to one of the points plotted in Figure 27-3, Management Studio displays the associated location addresses.

Figure 27-3   *Displaying the result of Example 27.10 in Management Studio*

New Spatial Data Features in SQL Server 2012

SQL Server 2012 introduces the following enhancements to spatial types:

- ▶ New subtypes of circular arcs
- ▶ New spatial indices
- ▶ New system stored procedures concerning spatial data

The following sections describe these features.

New Subtypes of Circular Arcs

Circular arcs are based on the ANSI SQL/MM standard. (All ANSI standards concerning SQL are divided into parts, depending on which area in relation to SQL is described. SQL/MM specifies Part III and describes spatial data.) Generally, an arc is a closed segment of a curve in the two-dimensional plane. Therefore, a circular arc is a segment of the circumference of a circle. Circular arcs can be specified by themselves or combined with line segments. Also, they can be used as a basis for a new polygon type that contains one or more curve components.

Circular arcs are supported by the GEOMETRY and GEOGRAPHY data types and can be defined using WKT, WKB, and GML data formats.

There are three new types for the following circular arcs:

- ▶ Circular string
- ▶ Compound curve
- ▶ Curve polygon

The following subsections describe these three forms of circular arcs..

Circular String

If you take a look at Figure 27-1, which appears early in the chapter, you will see that a circular string is a direct subtype of the curve type. For this reason, circular strings are the basic curve subtype.

You need at least three points to define a circular string. The first point specifies the start, the second specifies the end of the circular string, and the third must be somewhere along the arc. Circular strings can be linked together, where the last point of the previous curve becomes the first point of the next one. (As you probably guessed, the corresponding subtype is called CIRCULARSTRING.)

Example 27.11 shows how a circular string can be defined using a variable.

EXAMPLE 27.11

```
DECLARE @g GEOMETRY;
SET @g =
GEOMETRY::STGeomFromText ('CIRCULARSTRING(0 -12.5, 0 0, 0 12.5)',0);
```

Compound Curve

Compound curve, as its name suggests, allows you to specify new curves that are composed of either circular strings only or circular and linear strings. The end point of each component is linked together with the starting point of the next one. (The corresponding subtype is called COMPOUNDCURVE.)

Example 27.12 shows how a compound curve can be built using different components.

EXAMPLE 27.12

```
DECLARE @g GEOGRAPHY;
SET @g = GEOGRAPHY::STGeomFromText('
  COMPOUNDCURVE(CIRCULARSTRING(0 -23.43778, 0 0, 0 23.43778),
  CIRCULARSTRING(0 23.43778, -45 23.43778, -90 23.43778),
    CIRCULARSTRING(-90 23.43778, -90 0, -90 -23.43778),
    CIRCULARSTRING(-90 -23.43778, -45 -23.43778, 0 -23.43778) )' ,4326);
```

Example 27.12 constructs an instance of the GEOGRAPHY data type and assigns it to a variable. The variable is made up of a curve polygon, which itself is made up of compound curves, which themselves are made up of circular strings and linear strings. Note that the last parameter of the **STGeomFromText()** method is the value 4326. This is the default SRID value for the GEOGRAPHY data type and corresponds to the WGS 82 spatial reference system. (The SRID value is explained earlier in this chapter.)

Curve Polygons

Curve polygons are composed of linear and circular strings as well as compound curves. As you can see from Figure 27-1, this CURVEPOLYGON type is a direct subtype of the SURFACE type, and the supertype of the POLYGON type. Within a given ring, the first point in a component of a curve polygon must be identical to the last point of the next component.

New Spatial Indices

A new auto grid spatial index has been introduced in SQL Server 2012 for the GEOMETRY and GEOGRAPHY data types. (The functionality of both indices is similar, so I will describe only the auto grid index for the GEOMETRY data type.)

The Geometry Auto Grid Index

The strategy that the new geometry auto grid index uses to pick the right trade-off between performance and efficiency is different from the strategy described earlier in this chapter. It uses eight levels of tessellation for better approximation of objects of various sizes. (The already described "manual grid" spatial index uses only four user-specified levels of tessellation.)

Example 27.13 shows the creation of a geometry auto grid index.

EXAMPLE 27.13

```
CREATE SPATIAL INDEX auto_grid_index
    ON beverage_markets(shape)
    USING GEOMETRY_AUTO_GRID
        WITH (BOUNDING_BOX = (xmin=0, ymin=0, xmax=500, ymax=200 ),
    CELLS_PER_OBJECT = 32, DATA_COMPRESSION = page);
```

The GEOMETRY_AUTO_GRID clause describes the created index as an auto grid index. The CELLS_PER_OBJECT clause specifies the maximum number of cells that tessellation can count per object. The DATA_COMPRESSION clause specifies whether the compression is enabled for the particular spatial index. (All other clauses of the CREATE SPATIAL INDEX statement are described immediately following Example 27.7.)

New System Stored Procedures Concerning Spatial Data

The following system stored procedures are new in SQL Server 2012:

▶ sp_help_spatial_geometry_histogram

▶ sp_help_spatial_geography_histogram

NOTE

The syntax and functionality of both system procedures is similar, so I will discuss only the first one.

The **sp_help_spatial_geometry_histogram** system procedure returns the names and values for a specified set of properties about a geometry spatial index. The result is returned in a table format. You can choose to return a core set of properties or all properties of the index. Example 27.14 shows the use of this system procedure.

EXAMPLE 27.14

```
DECLARE @query geometry
      ='POLYGON((-90.0 -180.0, -90.0 180.0, 90.0 180.0, 90.0 -180.0, -90.0
-180.0))';
EXEC sp_help_spatial_geometry_index 'beverage_markets', 'auto_grid_index', 0,
 @query;
```

The **sp_help_spatial_geometry_index** system procedure in Example 27.14 displays the properties of the spatial index called **auto_grid_index**, created in Example 27.13.

Summary

SQL Server supports two spatial data types: GEOGRAPHY and GEOMETRY. The GEOGRAPHY data type is used to represent spatial data in geodetic models, while the GEOMETRY data type is used with flat spatial models. To work with these data types, you need a set of corresponding operations (methods). For both data types, Microsoft implemented methods specified by OGC that can be used to retrieve spatial data from a table's columns.

SQL Server Management Studio has good support for the GEOMETRY and GEOGRAPHY data types. SSMS uses the Spatial Results tab to display graphically the content of columns with such data types.

SQL Server 2012 introduces the following enhancements to spatial types:

▶ The subtypes of circular arcs: CIRCULARSTRING, COMPOUNDCURVE and CURVEPOLYGON

▶ The auto grid spatial index

▶ The **sp_help_spatial_geometry_histogram** and **sp_help_spatial_geography_histogram** system procedures

The next, final chapter of the book describes SQL Server Full-Text Search.

Chapter 28

SQL Server Full-Text Search

In This Chapter

- Introduction
- Indexing Full-Text Data
- Querying Full-Text Data
- Troubleshooting Full-Text Data
- New Features in SQL Server 2012 FTS

Throughout this chapter is divided into five parts. The introductory part describes general concepts related to full-text data that you need to be aware of before you begin working with it. This part introduces tokens, word breakers, and stop lists and describes their roles in full-text search. It also introduces the different operations that can be performed on tokens and explains how SQL Server Full-Text Search works.

The second part describes the general steps that are required to create a full-text index and then demonstrates how to apply those steps first using Transact-SQL and then using SQL Server Management Studio.

The third part is dedicated to full-text queries. It describes two different predicates and two row functions that can be used for full-text search. For these predicates and functions, several examples are provided to show you how you can solve specific problems in relation to extended operations on words.

Three dynamic management views (DMVs) that can be used to troubleshoot full-text indexing are discussed in the fourth part of the chapter. Two of the DMVs can be used during the indexing phase and the other can be used during the search phase.

The final part of the chapter discusses new features implemented in SQL Server 2012, which include the capability to search extended properties and enhanced functionality of the NEAR clause in the CONTAINS predicate and CONTAINSTABLE row function.

Introduction

A component of SQL Server called Full-Text Search (FTS) allows you to search through data stored in text documents. Such data is usually unstructured, which means that it contains irregularities and ambiguities that make it difficult to understand using traditional computer programs. For this reason, unstructured data does not have a predefined data model.

FTS stores data from text documents in the same way as alphanumerical data is stored in the relational model. This means that such data is stored in table columns of the CHAR, VARCHAR, NCHAR, NVARCHAR, XML, VARBINARY, and VARBINARY(max) data types. (The VARBINARY(max) data type can be used either with or without the FILESTREAM property.)

NOTE

*When a column of a binary data type (such as VARBINARY(max), for instance) contains a document with a supported document-file extension, SQL Server Full-Text Search uses a filter to interpret the binary data. The filter, which implements the **IFilter** interface, extracts the textual information from the document and submits it for indexing. (The following section describes IFilters.)*

Before we discuss how data stored in text documents can be retrieved, let us see how such data must be prepared for the query process. The following subsections introduce general concepts related to full-text data that are useful to know before you begin indexing data stored in text documents in preparation for the query process.

Tokens, Word Breakers, and Stop Lists

A full-text query allows you to search for words within text documents. The basic unit of such a query is called a *token*. In Western languages, this term usually has the same meaning as *word*. In non-Western languages, however, no clear concept of a *word* exists because such languages do not use a white space to separate meaningful strings. In such a case, a full-text component has to make decisions concerning boundaries between two tokens. (This chapter uses the terms *token* and *word* interchangeably.)

Word Breakers and IFilters

As you will see a bit later in the chapter, a full-text component has to index data in documents before the query process can be started. Before indexing, the full-text component locates token boundaries by applying language-specific components called *word breakers* to the text document. Therefore, the main task of word breakers is to break content into tokens and decide how those tokens are stored in the full-text index. (The word breaker for the English language breaks words at white-space boundaries and at punctuation.)

Word breakers for non-English languages index composite words and extract all constituent words. For example, consider the word breaker for the German language, in which a word can be composed of several other words. The German word *Wortzusammensetzung* means "word composition" and is composed of three different words. The task of the German-language word breaker is, among other things, to analyze such words and extract constituent words or characters.

Indexing documents in a VARBINARY, VARBINARY(max), or XML data type column requires extra processing. This processing must be performed by a filter. The filter extracts the textual information from the document and sends the text to the word-breaker component for the language associated with the table column. SQL Server FTS calls such filters *IFilters*.

The choice of a particular IFilter depends on the data type of the table column where the data is stored. This means that for columns of the CHAR, NCHAR, VARCHAR, and NVARCHAR data types, the SQL Server FTS applies the **text** IFilter. Similarly, for the columns of the XML data type, SQL Server FTS applies the **XML** IFilter. (Neither choice can be overridden.)

For the columns of the VARBINARY data type, SQL Server FTS uses the IFilter that corresponds to the file extension of the document. In other words, for a Word document, this extension will be docx, and for a PowerPoint presentation, it will be pptx.

Stop Lists

After the word breakers have done their work, the stop lists are applied. *Stop lists* are lists of selected stop words. *Stop words* (or *noise words*) are words that are ignored during full-text search because their relevance to the content of the text is low. (For instance, English stop words are, among others, *a*, *and*, and *the*.) The practical effect of ignoring these words is that the text becomes shorter, requiring less storage memory for the corresponding full-text index.

NOTE

Since SQL Server 2008, stop lists are stored in the database to which they belong. You can store several stop lists in your database.

You can create your own stop list by using SQL Server Management Studio. After you create your own stop list, you can add new stop words to it, delete one or more existing stop words, delete all stop words, or drop the entire stop list.

Operations on Tokens

Because full-text search works on unstructured data, some special operations are needed. These operations can be divided in three groups:

- ▶ Extended operations on words
- ▶ Matching options
- ▶ Proximity operations

The following subsections discuss these operations.

NOTE

The preceding full-text operations can be combined using logical operators such as AND, OR, and NOT.

Extended Operations on Words

In Chapter 6 you learned how to retrieve information from relational tables by using the LIKE operator, which compares column values with a specified pattern. This operation is very limited because it can only match the given pattern exactly. FTS searches not only for a particular word exactly, but also searches for words related to it. For example, when you query for the word *person*, you might expect to find related words such as *persons* and *personal*. A full-text component should also search for more specific words, such as *man* and *woman*, and synonyms, such as *individual*.

Another form of extended search corrects errors in the given query term and in the text on which the search is done. Spelling errors in search terms are common, so a full-text component should correct common typing errors such as *heirarchy* instead of *hierarchy*.

Matching Options

Matching options identify which factors are significant when deciding whether a term matches a word in the text being searched. A common matching option is to specify that the search is case sensitive. For example, if you want to search for a particular word only when it begins with an uppercase letter, and ignore matches of the same word written in all lowercase letters, you can type the search term with an initial uppercase letter and indicate the search is case sensitive. The use of wildcards is another matching option. For example, an asterisk (*) might be used in a search term to represent any character located at that position in the term. Thus, *lim** would return matches of *limb*, *lime*, *limo*, and *limp*. Yet another matching option is to specify whether or not to ignore diacritics. A diacritic is an additional glyph added to a letter. Examples from English are *naïve* and *café*.

Proximity Operations

If you want to search for several words but receive results only for instances where those words appear close together in the particular text you are searching, you can use a proximity operation. For example, if you want to know whether the words *Microsoft* and *management* are associated in a given text, you can instruct SQL Server FTS to search only for occurrences in which the words appear near each other (the proximity of which you can specify). SQL Server FTS uses the NEAR clause to specify such proximity operations (as shown in Example 28.10, later in the chapter).

NOTE

As you will see in the section "Querying Full-Text Data" later in the chapter, SQL Server FTS supports all three forms of full-text search operations just described.

Relevance Score

When you use a relational query, you always get an exact answer. This is not true in the case of full-text search. The result set of a full-text query can be subjective, and the ordering of the result set depends on the system you use for querying.

SQL Server FTS assigns a *relevance score* to each term that is indexed. The score is based on a calculation of how important the concept behind the term is. (The importance is measured by the number of times the term occurs in the document.) Almost all existing full-text search components use different algorithms to determine a relevance score for each query.

How SQL Server FTS Works

Before you can query a text document, you have to index it. The reason is that only indexed tokens of a text document can be found with good performance. The SQL Server FTS builds a full-text index during a process called *population*, which fills the index with words and the locations in which they occur in documents. The full-text indices are stored in catalogs. You can specify one or more catalogs per database, but one catalog belongs always to a particular database.

Full-text indices are activated on a catalog-by-catalog basis. A catalog can be populated in either of two ways:

▶ **Full population** Clears all data stored in a full-text catalog and repopulates it by building index entries for all rows in all tables covered by the catalog. A full population typically occurs when a catalog is first populated.

▶ **Incremental population** Adjusts only index entries for rows that have been modified since the last population. The benefit of incremental population is speed: it minimizes the time required to populate data, because the number of index entries to be stored is considerably smaller than in the case of the full population.

NOTE

The system always performs the full population if the structure of the table is modified. This includes altering any column, index, or full-text index definition.

SQL Server FTS repopulates full-text indices dynamically. This means that, like regular SQL Server indices, full-text indices can be automatically updated when data is modified (added, updated, or deleted) in the associated table(s). Additionally, you can repopulate a full-text catalog either immediately or using a schedule. With both methods, you can choose a full population or an incremental population.

Because full-text indices can consume a significant amount of disk space, it is important to plan their placement in full-text catalogs. Consider the following guidelines when you assign a table to a catalog:

▶ Keep the full-text index as small as possible. (You can do so by selecting the shortest column as a key.)

▶ If you are indexing a large table, assign the table to its own full-text catalog.

This closes the discussion of full-text basics. Now we can turn our attention to how SQL Server FTS creates full-text indices.

Indexing Full-Text Data

To index text documents stored in a table's column, you have to execute the following steps:

▶ Ensure that the table has a non-null column and that this column has a UNIQUE index.

▶ Enable for full-text indexing a database to which the table belongs.

▶ Create a full-text catalog in which to store full-text indices.

▶ Create a full-text index on the column that will be used for full-text indexing.

You can perform all these tasks using either Transact-SQL or SQL Server Management Studio, as described next, in turn.

Indexing Full-Text Data Using Transact-SQL

To examine in detail how to perform the tasks in the preceding list using Transact-SQL, first create a table called **product**, as shown in Example 28.1. (If your **sample** database already contains a table with the same name, drop the table using the DROP TABLE statement before you execute Example 28.1.) The **product** table will be used to demonstrate full-text querying in the next section.

EXAMPLE 28.1

```
USE sample;
CREATE TABLE product
            (product_id CHAR(5) NOT NULL,
             product_name VARCHAR (30) NOT NULL,
             description VARCHAR(900) NOT NULL);
```

The **product** table in Example 28.1 fulfills all requirements for building a full-text index. First, it has a non-null column (**product_id**). Second, the **description** column of the table is character based (that is, specified using the VARCHAR data type) and can therefore be used for full-text search.

Create a Unique Index

Example 28.2 creates a unique index on the **product_id** column and inserts two rows into the **product** table. These rows will be used to show how full-text data can be queried.

EXAMPLE 28.2

```
USE sample;
CREATE UNIQUE INDEX ind_description
    ON dbo.product(product_id);
GO
INSERT INTO product VALUES (1, 'MS Application Center ', 'This Microsoft
product simplifies the deployment and management of Windows DNA solutions
within farms of servers.  Application Center makes it easy to configure
and manage high-availability server arrays ');
INSERT INTO product VALUES (2, 'MS Commerce Server ', 'Commerce Server
is the fastest way to build an effective Microsoft online business.
It provides all of the personalization, user and product management,
marketing, closed loop analysis, and electronic ordering infrastructure
necessary for both business-to-business and business-to-consumer
e-commerce. ');
```

Enable a Database for Full-Text Indexing

You can use the **sp_fulltext_database** system stored procedure to enable (or disable) full-text indexing for a database. This stored procedure has the following syntax:

```
[EXEC] sp_full_text_database [@action=] 'enable' | 'disable'
```

The **enable** parameter enables full-text indexing for the current database, while the **disable** parameter removes all full-text catalogs in the file system for the current database. Example 28.3 shows how you can enable the **sample** database for full-text indexing.

EXAMPLE 28.3

```
USE sample;
EXEC sp_fulltext_database 'enable';
```

The alternative way to enable your database for full-text indexing is to right-click the database in Object Explorer, choose Properties, and click the Files tab. Check Use Full-Text Indexing and then click OK.

Create a Full-Text Catalog

To create a full-text catalog, you can use either the CREATE FULLTEXT CATALOG statement or the **sp_fulltext_catalog** system procedure.

NOTE

*The **sp_fulltext_catalog** system procedure will be removed in a future version of SQL Server. For this reason, I will discuss only the use of the CREATE FULLTEXT CATALOG statement.*

The CREATE FULLTEXT CATALOG statement creates a full-text catalog for a database. One full-text catalog can have several full-text indices, but a full-text index can be part of only one full-text catalog. Each database can contain zero or more full-text catalogs.

NOTE

Since SQL Server 2008, full-text catalogs are part of the database to which they belong. That allows all indices in a catalog to be rebuilt at once.

Example 28.4 shows how you can create a full-text catalog for the **sample** database.

EXAMPLE 28.4

```
USE sample;
CREATE FULLTEXT CATALOG sample_catalog
   WITH ACCENT_SENSITIVITY = OFF
   AS DEFAULT;
```

The CREATE FULLTEXT CATALOG statement in Example 28.4 creates the catalog called **sample_catalog** for the **sample** database. Using the AS DEFAULT clause, the catalog is specified as the default catalog for this database. This means that each full-text index that is created without the explicit specification of the corresponding catalog will be stored in the default catalog.

NOTE

Do not use the default catalog to store full-text indices of a large table! For performance reasons, such a table should have its own full-text catalog.

The ACCENT_SENSITIVITY clause in Example 28.4 specifies whether the catalog is accent sensitive (ON) or not (OFF). The default value is ON.

NOTE

In addition to the two clauses just described, the CREATE FULLTEXT CATALOG statement supports other clauses, such as ON FILEGROUP, IN PATH, and AUTHORIZATION. You can find the description of these clauses in Books Online.

Transact-SQL also supports the ALTER FULLTEXT CATALOG and DROP FULLTEXT CATALOG statements. The former allows you to change properties of an existing catalog. The most important clause of this statement is REBUILD, which tells the system to rebuild the entire catalog. (When a catalog is rebuilt, the existing catalog is deleted and a new catalog is created in its place.) The DROP FULLTEXT CATALOG statement drops the entire catalog. (You must drop all full-text indices associated with the catalog before you can drop the catalog.)

Create a Full-Text Index

The CREATE FULLTEXT INDEX statement creates a full-text index on a table. Only one full-text index is allowed per table. Example 28.5 shows the use of this statement.

EXAMPLE 28.5

```
USE sample;
CREATE FULLTEXT INDEX
   ON dbo.product(description)
   KEY INDEX ind_description
   ON sample_catalog;
```

The statement in Example 28.5 creates the full-text index for the **description** column of the **product** table. As you can see from this example, the syntax of the statement is similar to the syntax of the convenient CREATE INDEX statement. The additional KEY INDEX clause specifies the name of the unique, non-null index that is necessary to create the full-text index (see Example 28.2). The second ON clause specifies the name of the catalog in which to store the full-text index. (In this example, the specification of the ON clause can be omitted because **sample_catalog** is the default catalog for the **sample** database.)

Two important clauses of this statement are LANGUAGE and TYPE COLUMN. The LANGUAGE clause contains the parameter that can be specified as a string, integer, or hexadecimal value corresponding to the locale identifier (LCID) of a language. If no value is specified, the default language of the instance of the Database Engine is used. (To retrieve the name of the language that corresponds to the given LCID, use the **sys.fulltext_language** catalog view.)

NOTE

*SQL Server FTS supports full-text operations on many different languages. Information about all the supported languages is stored in the **sys.syslanguages** catalog view.*

The TYPE COLUMN clause is necessary when the column with the full-text index stores binary data (VARBINARY(max), for instance). The TYPE COLUMN clause specifies the name of a different column in the table that stores the file extension for the binary data. For example, the binary data might be a .docx file. SQL Server uses the column specified in the TYPE COLUMN clause to associate the binary data with the corresponding software system.

Transact-SQL also supports the ALTER FULLTEXT INDEX and DROP FULLTEXT INDEX statements. The former statement allows you to change the properties of an existing full-text index. The most important clauses of this statement are ADD and DROP. These clauses, respectively, tell the system to add or delete the specified column(s) to or from the index. (Use the DROP clause only on columns that have been enabled previously for full-text indexing.) The DROP FULLTEXT INDEX statement removes the specified index.

Index Full-Text Data Using SQL Server Management Studio

As previously mentioned, the steps necessary to index text documents stored in a table's column can be performed using SQL Server Management Studio, too. To build full-text indices using Management Studio, expand the server, expand the Databases folder, expand the database, and expand the Tables folder. Right-click the table for which you want to create a full-text index, choose Full-Text Index, and click Define Full-Text Index. This starts the Full-Text Indexing Wizard. On the initial screen, click Next. The Select an Index page appears (see Figure 28-1).

Figure 28-1   *The Select an Index page*

Create a unique, non-null index, which you will use as the starting point for the full-text indexing (see also Example 28.2). Click Next.

NOTE

If the table doesn't contain a column with such properties, you will get the message "A unique column must be defined on this table/view." In that case, modify the structure of the table to fulfill these conditions.

In the next step, the wizard selects all character- and image-based columns from the table and shows them on the Select Table Columns page (see Figure 28-2). Check any columns that you want to be eligible for full-text queries and click Next. (Note that if you select several columns, SQL Server FTS creates one composite full-text index for all selected columns.)

The next wizard step is the Select Change Tracking page. This step allows you to choose one of the two population types or to specify that changes should not be tracked (see Figure 28-3). When you define automatic or manual change tracking, a full population of the index occurs. To avoid a population at the end of this wizard, select the Do Not Track Changes option and clear the Start Full Population When Index Is Created check box. Click Next.

Figure 28-2 *The Select Table Columns wizard page*

Figure 28-3 *The Select Change Tracking wizard page*

Figure 28-4 *The Select Catalog, Index Filegroup, and Stoplist page*

The next wizard page, Select Catalog, Index Filegroup, and Stoplist (see Figure 28-4), allows you to choose an existing catalog or create a new one. Click Next.

The next step, Define Population Schedules, is an optional step, which you should skip by clicking Next. Finally, the Summary description appears. Click Finish to end the whole process.

Querying Full-Text Data

SQL Server FTS supports two predicates and two functions that you can use to query text using a full-text index:

- ► FREETEXT predicate
- ► CONTAINS predicate
- ► FREETEXTTABLE function
- ► CONTAINSTABLE function

The following sections describe each of these predicates and functions.

FREETEXT Predicate

The FREETEXT predicate is used to search values in full-text indexed columns that match the meaning in the search condition. Additionally, you can use this predicate if you want to find all words related to the word(s) in the search query.

Example 28.6 shows the use of the FREETEXT predicate for the given string.

EXAMPLE 28.6

```
USE sample;
SELECT product_id, product_name FROM product
    WHERE FREETEXT(description, 'manage');
```

The result is

product_id	product_name
1	MS Application Center

As you can see from Example 28.6, the FREETEXT predicate has two arguments. The first argument specifies the column that is full-text indexed. The second argument specifies the string that is searched in the documents stored in the specified column(s).

Example 28.7 shows the search for the related strings.

EXAMPLE 28.7

```
USE sample;
SELECT product_id, product_name
    FROM product
    WHERE FREETEXT(description, 'fast solution');
```

The result is

product_id	product_name
1	MS Application Center

Example 28.7 shows two things: the implicit use of the Boolean operator OR and the search for words that are similar to but do not exactly match the search terms. (This operation belongs in the extended operations on words category.) Although the second parameter in the FREETEXT predicate in Example 28.7 looks like the search on the

string *fast solution*, it actually searches on one (or both) of two different strings, *fast* and *solution*. (The existence of multiple words in a search string implies the use of the Boolean operator OR.) Also, neither the word *fast* nor the word *solution* appears in one of the rows. As you already know, the FREETEXT predicate searches for related words, too. SQL Server FTS finds the word *solutions* in the first document and the word *fastest* in the second document and considers them to be related to the words *solution* and *fast*, respectively.

CONTAINS Predicate

The CONTAINS predicate is used to search columns containing character-based data types for exact and fuzzy matches. It also allows you to search for particular words and phrases, search for words within close proximity of each another, and search using weighted search. (Weighted search is a search based on frequencies of the search terms in the documents being searched. Weighted search is often used by search engines. It produces a numerical score for each possible document.)

NOTE

The CONTAINS predicate provides significantly more functionality in full-text search than the FREETEXT predicate.

Example 28.8 shows the use of the CONTAINS predicate to search with a wildcard. This operation belongs in the search with matching options category.

EXAMPLE 28.8

```
USE sample;
SELECT product_id, product_name FROM product
    WHERE CONTAINS(description, '  "config*"  ');
```

The result is

product_id	product_name
1	MS Application Center

The CONTAINS predicate in Example 28.8 searches the documents of the **description** column for any word beginning with *config*. The * sign is the wildcard of the CONTAINS predicate and specifies any sequence of zero or more characters.

Therefore, this sign has the same meaning as the percent sign (%) for the LIKE predicate. (As you can see from Example 28.8, you need to use an additional pair of double quotes for the pattern with the wildcard.)

The CONTAINS predicate allows you to combine several operations using the Boolean operators AND, OR, and NOT. Example 28.9 shows the use of the AND operator.

EXAMPLE 28.9

```
USE sample;
SELECT product_id, product_name
   FROM product
     WHERE CONTAINS(description, '  "manage*" AND "market*"  ');
```

The result is

product_id	product_name
2	MS Commerce Server

The query in Example 28.9 retrieves all rows that contain a word beginning with *manage* and a word beginning with *market*.

Example 28.10 shows the use of the NEAR option to match words in close proximity to one another. This operation belongs to a group of proximity operations.

EXAMPLE 28.10

```
USE sample;
SELECT product_id, product_name FROM product
    WHERE CONTAINS(description, 'Microsoft NEAR management');
```

The result is

product_id	product_name
1	MS Application Center
2	MS Commerce Server

As you can see from the result of Example 28.10, SQL Server FTS retrieves both rows, because the words *Microsoft* and *management* appear relatively close to one another in both documents (see also Example 28.17).

NOTE

SQL Server FTS always returns the identity of the rows plus their relevance score. The system uses the latter value to order the result set. (The results set of Example 28.10 shows that the relevance score of the second row is higher than the relevance score of the first row. This is obvious, because both Microsoft and management are closer to each other in the second row than in the first row.)

Example 28.11 shows the use of the FORMSOF clause with the INFLECTIONAL specification.

EXAMPLE 28.11

```
USE sample;
SELECT product_id, product_name FROM product
    WHERE CONTAINS(description,'FORMSOF (INFLECTIONAL, provide)');
```

The result is

product_id	product_name
2	MS Commerce Server

INFLECTIONAL specifies that different forms of the string (plural and singular forms of nouns, comparative forms of adjectives, and various tenses of verbs) are to be matched. Therefore, the SELECT statement in Example 28.11 finds the word *provides* as the form of the verb *provide*.

FREETEXTTABLE Function

As its name indicates, FREETEXTTABLE is a table that contains one or more rows for those columns that contain values matching the word(s) in the specified string. Analogous to the FREETEXT predicate, FREETEXTTABLE also contains rows where values of the full-text indexed column(s) do not exactly match the word(s) in the search condition. FREETEXTTABLE uses the same search conditions as the FREETEXT predicate, but has additional functionality: queries using FREETEXTTABLE specify a relevance score for each row and can therefore display the top **n** matches. (The FREETEXT predicate also calculates a relevance score for all rows of the result set, but it does not use that score when displaying the result set.)

NOTE

FREETEXTTABLE can be referenced in the FROM clause of a SELECT statement like any other table.

Example 28.12 shows the use of the FREETEXTTABLE function.

EXAMPLE 28.12

```
USE sample;
SELECT pr.product_id, pr.product_name
   FROM product pr, FREETEXTTABLE(product,description, 'fast solution',1) ftt
   WHERE pr.product_id = ftt.[key];
```

The result is

product_id	product_name
1	MS Application Center

The query in Example 28.12 joins two tables: the **product** table and FREETEXTTABLE. As you can see from the example, FREETEXTTABLE contains four parameters. The first parameter specifies the name of the table (**product** in this example), the second specifies the name of the column on which full-text search is applied (**description**), the third specifies the search string, and the last parameter specifies an integer that limits the result set to the top **n** matches, ordered by the value of the column called **rank**. (FREETEXTTABLE has two implicit columns named **key** and **rank**, which can be referenced within the query to obtain the appropriate rows and the relevant score values, respectively.)

NOTE

Example 28.12 is similar to Example 28.7, but their results are different because of the last parameter of FREETEXTTABLE.

CONTAINSTABLE Function

Like FREETEXTTABLE, CONTAINSTABLE is a table that returns zero or more rows. CONTAINSTABLE is used to search columns containing character-based data types for exact and fuzzy matches. Additionally, it allows you to search for specific words and phrases, search for words within close proximity of each another and weighted search, too. (CONTAINSTABLE uses the same search conditions as the CONTAINS predicate.)

NOTE

*The syntax of CONTAINSTABLE is analogous to that of FREETEXTTABLE. CONTAINSTABLE has the same four parameters previously described for FREETEXTTABLE. Additionally, CONTAINSTABLE has two implicit columns, **key** and **rank**, with the same meaning.*

Example 28.13 shows the use of CONTAINSTABLE.

EXAMPLE 28.13

```
USE sample;
SELECT pr.product_id, pr.product_name
    FROM product pr INNER JOIN
    CONTAINSTABLE(product, description, 'Microsoft NEAR management',1) ct
    ON pr.product_id = ct.[key]
    ORDER BY ct.rank DESC;
```

The result is

product_id	product_name
1	MS Application Center

The query in Example 28.13 joins two tables: CONTAINSTABLE and the **product** table. This example is similar to Example 28.10, but their results are different: the specification of CONTAINSTABLE contains as the last parameter the number **n** (in Example 28.13, the value 1) that limits the result set to only the top **n** matches, ordered by the value of the relevant score. Also, the ORDER BY clause contains the DESC option and therefore causes the display of the last ranked row.

CONTAINSTABLE can also be used to calculate weighted matches, as shown in Example 28.14.

EXAMPLE 28.14

```
SELECT pr.product_id, pr.product_name
    FROM product pr,
    CONTAINSTABLE ( product, description,
        'ISABOUT (Microsoft WEIGHT(.4), management WEIGHT(.2))') ct
    WHERE pr.product_id = ct.[key]
    ORDER BY ct.rank DESC;
```

The result is

product_id	product_name
2	MS Commerce Server
1	MS Application Center

The ISABOUT clause of the CONTAINSTABLE function matches a full-text column against a group of one or more weighted search terms. Therefore, Example 28.14 searches for all names containing the token *Microsoft* or *management* and assigns a different weighting to each token using the WEIGHT clause with a parameter that specifies the weight. (The value of a weight must be between 0 and 1.)

Troubleshooting Full-Text Data

Problems concerning full-text data can have two sources. The first group of problems occurs during full-text indexing, while the second group of problems happens during the querying phase. You can use the following DMVs to troubleshoot problems concerning full-text data:

▶ sys.dm_fts_index_keywords

▶ sys.dm_fts_index_keywords_by_document

▶ sys.dm_fts_parser

NOTE

The first two DMVs support troubleshooting of problems concerning full-text indexing, while the last one can be used to diagnose problems during the querying phase.

The **sys.dm_fts_index_keywords** DMV returns information about the content of a full-text index for the specified table. Example 28.15 shows the use of this DMV.

EXAMPLE 28.15

```
USE sample;
SELECT keyword, display_term, document_count
                FROM sys.dm_fts_index_keywords (db_id('sample'),
object_id('product'));
```

Example 28.15 displays information related to a full-text index for the **product** table. The **keyword** column shows the hexadecimal representation of the keyword stored in the full-text index. The **display_term** column displays the human-readable format of the keyword, while the **document_count** column specifies the number of documents or rows containing the current term.

The second DMV, **sys.dm_fts_index_keywords_by_document**, has similar functionality to that of the first one, but breaks down the keywords by document. Therefore, this DMV helps you to troubleshoot problems deeper in the document. It contains the same columns as the previous DMV, but additionally supports the following two columns:

▶ **document_id**   ID of the document or row from which the current term was full-text indexed

▶ **occurrence_count**   Number of times the current keyword occurs in the document or row that is indicated by **document_id**

The **sys.dm_fts_parser** DMV displays internal information during the search phase. In other words, the interpretation of a search phrase for the given query is displayed by the system. Example 28.16 shows the use of the **sys.dm_fts_parser** view.

EXAMPLE 28.16

```
USE sample;
SELECT keyword, occurrence, special_term, display_term
        FROM sys.dm_fts_parser (' "The Microsoft business analysis" ',
1033, 0, 0);
```

The result of Example 28.16 is

keyword	occurrence	special_term	display_term
0x007400680065	1	Noise Word	the
0x006D006900630072006F0073006F00660074	2	Exact Match	Microsoft
0x0062007500730069006E006500730073	3	Exact Match	business
0x0061006E0061006C0079007300690073	4	Exact Match	analysis

The **keyword** column shows the hexadecimal representation of the keyword stored in the full-text index. The **occurrence** column indicates the order of each term in the parsing result. The **special_term** column contains information about the characteristics of the term displayed in the **display_term** column being issued by the word breaker.

New Features in SQL Server 2012 FTS

SQL Server 2012 supports two enhancements to full-text search:

► Customizing a proximity search

► Searching extended properties

The following subsections describe these new features.

Customizing a Proximity Search

As you already know from Example 28.10, SQL Server FTS uses the NEAR clause to find tokens that appear relatively close to each other in the corresponding document. In previous versions of SQL Server, the NEAR clause doesn't allow you to specify the distance between the tokens.

In SQL Server 2012 you can customize a proximity search by using the extended NEAR clause of the CONTAINS predicate or CONTAINSTABLE row function. This optional feature allows you to specify the maximum number of nonsearch terms that separate the first and last search terms in a match. Customizing a proximity search with the NEAR clause also enables you to specify that words and phrases are matched only if they occur in the order in which you specify them.

Example 28.17 shows how the proximity search can be applied using the CONTAINSTABLE function.

EXAMPLE 28.17

```
USE sample;
SELECT pr.product_id, pr.product_name
    FROM product pr INNER JOIN
    CONTAINSTABLE ( product, description,
        '(user NEAR analysis)') AS ct
    ON pr.product_id = ct.[key]
    ORDER BY ct.rank DESC;

SELECT pr.product_id, pr.product_name
    FROM product pr INNER JOIN
    CONTAINSTABLE (product, description,
        'NEAR((user, analysis), 3)') AS ct
    ON pr.product_id = ct.[key]
    ORDER BY ct.rank DESC;
```

The first SELECT statement in Example 28.17 shows the functionality of the NEAR clause in earlier versions of SQL Server. The clause specifies to select documents in which both words exist, but does not specify that the words must be within a particular distance of each other. (The clause calculates the distance between the words, but only to determine the rank of each document in the result set.)

The second SELECT statement shows the extended functionality of the NEAR clause. Now, you can use a parameter (in this case, 3) to specify the distance between both words. (The distance of 3 means that no more than three nonsearch terms separate the two search terms.) For this reason, the result of the SELECT statements is different: the result of the first one displays information about the second document, and the result of the second one is empty. (Both words exist in the second document, but their distance is greater than three.)

Searching Extended Properties

SQL Server 2012 allows you to search data stored in a full-text column based not only on content, but on extended properties too. Searching for extended properties is possible only if the particular IFilter exists. (The detailed descriptions of IFilters is given at the beginning of this chapter.)

The first step in searching for extended properties is to create the corresponding property list. You create this list using the CREATE SEARCH PROPERTY LIST statement. Example 28.18 creates the property list for the **description** column of the **product** table.

EXAMPLE 28.18

```
USE sample;
CREATE SEARCH PROPERTY LIST Sample_Properties;
GO
ALTER SEARCH PROPERTY LIST Sample_Properties
   ADD 'MS Tools'
   WITH ( PROPERTY_SET_GUID = 'F29F85E0-4FF9-1068-AB91-08002B27B3D9',
    PROPERTY_INT_ID = 1);
```

The first statement in Example 28.18 creates an empty search property list called **Sample_Properties**. This search property list is used to specify one or more extended properties that you want to include in a full-text index. Using the ADD clause, you can add an extended search property (in this case, MS Tools) to the specified property list. (Adding a property means that it is registered for the search property list.)

The PROPERTY_SET_GUID parameter specifies the globally unique identifier (GUID) of the property set to which the property belongs. The PROPERTY_INT_ID parameter specifies the integer that uniquely identifies the property within its property set.

The created search property list can be assigned to an existing full-text index using the ALTER FULLTEXT INDEX statement, as shown in Example 28.19.

EXAMPLE 28.19

```
USE sample;
ALTER FULLTEXT INDEX ON dbo.product
    SET SEARCH PROPERTY LIST Sample_Properties
    WITH NO POPULATION;
GO
  ALTER FULLTEXT INDEX ON dbo.product
  START FULL POPULATION;
```

NOTE

When you execute Example 28.19, you will get a warning, which you should ignore. (This warning concerns the first statement in the example. The second statement brings the full-text index into a consistent state.)

The first statement in Example 28.19 adds the **Sample_Properties** list to the existing full-text index. (This is done without populating the index.) The second statement populates the index using the full population. (Full and incremental population are described earlier in this chapter.)

You can view the names of the existing property lists using the catalog view called **sys.registered_search_property_lists**, as shown in Example 28.20.

EXAMPLE 28.20

```
USE sample;
SELECT name FROM
     sys.registered_search_property_lists;
```

Summary

Using SQL Server FTS, you can apply a full-text search to documents that are stored in alphanumerical column(s) of a relational table. Before starting a query search, you have to create a full-text index for the column(s) and populate it.

The following types of queries are supported by SQL Server FTS:

▶ Searching for words or phrases

▶ Searching for words in close proximity to each other

▶ Searching for inflectional forms of verbs and nouns

▶ Searching for a word that has a higher designated weighting than another word

SQL Server FTS supports two predicates: FREETEXT and CONTAINS. You should use the CONTAINS predicate because it provides significantly more functionality in full-text search than the FREETEXT predicate. Also, you can use two row functions: FREETEXTTABLE and CONTAINSTABLE. The functionality of FREETEXTTABLE corresponds to the functionality of FREETEXT, and the functionality of CONTAINSTABLE corresponds to the functionality of CONTAINS.

Index

Master Microsoft® SQL Server® 2012 and Microsoft's Powerful Business Intelligence Tools

CPSIA information can be obtained
at www.ICGtesting.com
Printed in the USA
BVOW07s0000271017
498418BV00004B/2/P